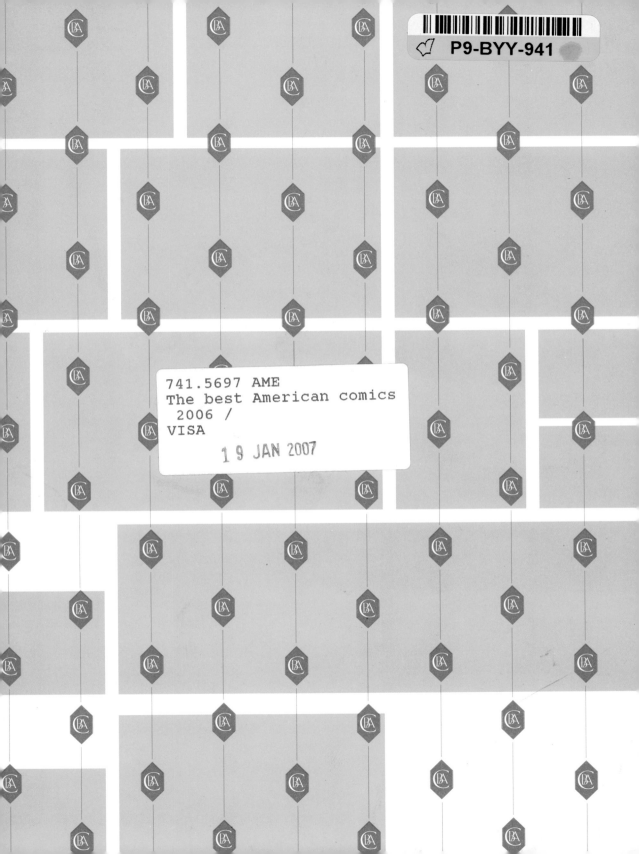

THE BEST AMERICAN
Comics 2006

THE BEST AMERICAN

Comics

2006

EDITED *and with an*
INTRODUCTION *by* HARVEY PEKAR

ANNE ELIZABETH MOORE,
series editor

HOUGHTON MIFFLIN COMPANY
BOSTON · NEW YORK   2006

ISBN-13: 978-0-618-71874-0   ISBN-10: 0-618-71874-5

Book design by Robert Overholtzer

PRINTED IN CHINA   C&C 10 9 8 7 6 5 4 3 2 1

Contents

Preface

CARTOONING has always been popularly characterized, somewhat dismissively (although not entirely inaccurately), as the irrepressible urge to create silly little drawings. Yet when Dan O'Neill and the rest of the cartoonists known collectively as the Air Pirates were taken to court in the 1970s by a target of their silly little drawings, it became clear that contemporary American cartooning is much more than that: it is an act of defiance.

The 1972 case foretold current artistic struggles over intellectual property rights in which musicians, visual artists, filmmakers, and more cartoonists than I care to recount are informed by powerful corporations where the limits to creativity lie — in other words, what is and is not funny. True, the Air Pirates pushed the joke further than most might. They had drawn a Famous Mouse and his Famous Mouse Girlfriend as swear-mouthed, lusty, dope-dealing *animals* and then self-published and -distributed the comics, even sending them to a board meeting of the company they'd targeted.

Legally speaking, this was apparently *not* funny. The Air Pirates were found guilty of copyright infringement, ordered to remit all copies of *Air Pirates Funnies* #1 and #2, restricted from drawing further mice, and fined a combined total of $219,300.58 in attorneys' fees, costs, and damages. The group eventually disbanded, struggling for well-paying work in a field in which, let's face it, their former foe in court still acts as a standard-bearer. A few years ago I became acquainted with O'Neill, now best known for his underground strip *Odd Bodkins*. He was living a modest life in his parents' home, publishing comics irregularly (and not always accepting payment for them), and proclaiming frequently his devotion to the dish franks 'n' beans. Yet to O'Neill, it was a worthwhile battle. Of course, in flagrant disrespect of the court's ruling, he felt he hadn't lost anything. He never adhered to the no-mouse-drawing rule nor paid the fine, which totaled around 48.5 times his annual income in those days. "I'd do it all again," he told me once.

The collection of work you now hold in your hands is a small army of similar examples of insolence. Many of the works are political in nature, disdainful of war, corporate culture, the death penalty, labor rights, and rampant right-wing politics.

Perhaps more significantly, the collection is a new addition to the esteemed line of distinguished titles in the Best American series that's been helping to define literature since 1915. That such an honor would be bestowed upon the traditionally low-brow medium of comics is a direct violation of the laws of both comics history and literature.

I just hope we can get it done before Houghton Mifflin figures this out.

The exact definition of comics is frequently debated, but for the purposes of this series, we've settled on the following, taken in part from Scott McCloud's *Understanding Comics:* comics combine pictures and symbols (including both written language and medium-specific conventions such as speech bubbles) in a sequence meant to communicate with and inspire an emotional response in the reader. Additionally, comics are a published medium—created to be mechanically reproduced, either in print or on the Web. Thus a blue-line Bristol board original, as interesting as it may be as a work of art or to the avid fan, is not (yet) a comic. Photocopy it at least once, however, make sure you've got some panel borders or narration boxes in there, and as far as I'm concerned, you're a published comics creator.

Working within this definition, it was easy to narrow down all the comics produced in North America between January 1, 2004, and August 15, 2005, to a mere bazillion. I looked at stories published in any form: graphic novels, art periodicals, alternative newspapers, anthologies, black-and-white quarter-size minis, standard pamphlets, Sunday funnies, hand-bound screen-printed self-published tales—whatever I could find. My reading list comprised sources as exalted as *The New Yorker* and as humble as *Mad* (although in many comics circles, those descriptors would have to be reversed), and those in between, such as *Moo-Cow Fan Club*, the *New York Times Magazine*, *The Believer*, *World War 3 Illustrated*, *Arthur*, *Nickelodeon*, *The Stranger*, *Kitchen Sink*, and the *Chicago Reader*. I also read graphic novels from mainstream book publishers, including Pantheon, Scholastic, and HarperCollins, as well as Web comics on the Internet. Not to mention, of course, everything I could get my hands on from the comic book publishers Drawn & Quarterly, Oni Press, NBM, Alternative Comics, Image, DC Comics, Top Shelf, Slave Labor Graphics, Fantagraphics Books, Marvel Comics, and Dark Horse Books, as well as pamphlets from smaller houses and minicomics from self-publishers throughout North America.

Choosing thirty from this bazillion to reprint and present here as the "best" involved a grueling combination of mathematical equations, chemical tests, magical spells, and interns, as well as the enthusiasm of the wonderful Harvey Pekar, who thankfully agreed to select final pieces for this inaugural edition. We divided the work cleanly: I sent him one hundred and fifty of my favorite pieces; he chose his favorite thirty. That these ended up a particularly charged group of stories is no random coincidence: Harvey and I share a devotion to inventive yet accessible graphic storytelling.

This has led to the inclusion of several extremely short stories of only one or two pages in length. There are two reasons for the brevity of these strips, as well as most others you will come across. The first is that the medium of comics is still maligned enough that the small percentage of editors who *do* allow comics into their publications prefer they not take up too much space that could otherwise be devoted to *content*. Although this appears now to be changing, comics' reputation as a deviant and childish medium has instilled in publishers a reluctance to view it as intellectually valuable. As comics emerge from their banishment as a niche medium, this series will continue to evolve.

The other reason for the brevity of certain strips is congruent with the first. Artists who work in the comics form are simply adept at concision. There are some who might shorthand this argument to the adage "a picture is worth a thousand words," but they would be wrong. No ratio can describe the literary value of a well-placed sweat droplet, an odorous pair of waft indicators, an overly thick eye-ray, a stupendously emotive motion indicator.

This concision is the natural result of working in a form in which practitioners are granted all tools to re-create language, as well as a reaction to the near inability of editors and publishers to devote space to allow comics to do what they are good at: tell stories. With few established outlets for their work, creators have made new ones, allowing literary comics to flourish under the fluorescent lights of late-night copy centers. Unfortunately for anyone who's ever tried it, it takes a great deal of effort to make a living by self-publishing booklets. I wouldn't be terribly surprised if the $219,300.58 the Air Pirates were ordered to pay was about the same amount all self-publishers earned from all sales of their hand-created work in all the years since 1970, combined. Little fiscal reward and a handful of outlets mean only the rare creator will stick with comics long enough to reach creative maturity. Still, the giddy spirit of the Air Pirates' Dan O'Neill pervades each and every story in this collection. Of course it does: they are the creators of the Best American Comics! Who brought the franks 'n' beans?

A full 17 percent of the little acts of insolence reprinted here come directly from the artists' hands (specifically those of Lilli Carré, Justin Hall, David Heatley, Jesse Reklaw, and Esther Pearl Watson). Another 13 percent appeared originally in alternative papers or Web sites (those by Alison Bechdel, Ivan Brunetti, Lloyd Dangle, and David Lasky). Only two pieces — by Joe Sacco and Ben Katchor — come from so-called established magazines or Web publishers: *The Guardian Online* and *Metropolis* (respectively). The remaining 63 percent come from small or comics publishing houses. And these are a diverse and significant group, including Anders Nilsen's artful offering from Drawn & Quarterly's *Dogs and Water;* Kim Deitch's difficult death-row portrait from *McSweeney's* #13; Olivia Schanzer's rabble-rousing and nonsensical two-pager from Alternative Comics' *Hi-Horse Omnibus;* and Gilbert Shelton's underground classic Wonder Wart-Hog story, brought back to life in Last Gasp's recently revived title *Zap*.

We live in an age of increasing corporate consolidation, one in which big media has only gotten bigger and attempted to exert vast amounts of cultural control — to the degree that big media occasionally steps in to tell even a single small group of goofballs that their silly little naked mouse drawings are not funny. That such a breadth of work as showcased in this collection can still be produced in the independent sector is astounding: the comics field continues to defy the commodification of culture.

Fortunately for those of you who are new to the medium, the entire history of comics is contained in this volume. Or rather, Chris Ware's "Comics: A History" is contained in this volume, a strip that traces the evolution of the medium from cavemen to Rodolphe Töpffer and from Siegel and Shuster to, one assumes, some of the artists Ware's strip stands alongside. Too, evidence of all the things that comics can uniquely achieve is most notably presented in Kurt Wolfgang's complex and profound "Passing Before Life's Very Eyes," which is an exploration both of the sorrow at the end of one man's life and the joyful, playful medium of comics. From Lilli Carré's revisionist mythology of Paul Bunyan to Esther Pearl Watson's smarmy, fictional, high-school perv Wayne, and from Joel Priddy's heartwrenching story of a life wasted in pursuance of the elimination of evil to Robert Crumb's unusually candid autobiographical tale, this book offers up an array of new narrative possibilities that aren't film, aren't museum art, aren't radio, and aren't — if we accept the dictionary definition or common usage of the term — literature. They are comics.

It may bewilder you to read in what is clearly intended to be a literary collection yet the standard definition of literature begins, and often ends, with the terms "written work" or "writings." Neither apply to many comics: most certainly they do not apply to mute comics, those completely without words, such as Rebecca Dart's "RabbitHead" or Ivan Brunetti's untitled piece. In fact, comics defy literature: they openly refuse to obey its rules, entirely re-creating what we know of language.

Yet the sheer range of storytelling forms explored and presented in this volume defiantly mimic what we accept as literature anyway. Autobiography, history, journalism, science fiction, mythology, persuasive and personal essays, poetry, and pure, distilled fiction: stories epic in scope, meditative in tone, and intended to convey information and bring pleasure to the reader. And if that is what we can agree is meant by "written work" — that it can be *read* — then this collection's merit as literature will stand on its own.

Because more than it is meant to prove anything, this collection is meant to be read. Savored, consumed, devoured. Any meaning to be gleaned from these works, any final pronouncements on the literary value of the form, any backlash against the inclusion of lowbrow diversions in a respected literary line will only occur after readers have ingested and been nourished by these stories.

Although a lifelong reader, I only became aware of the profound effect the printed page could have while finishing Toni Morrison's *Song of Solomon* in college. I read the last few pages of the book sobbing, heaving in great, dark gasps, hoping to god my neighbors wouldn't disturb me to offer help. I had heard tell of the potentially devastating consequences of literature: this was the first time I had undergone it.

I have duplicated this experience on only two occasions: during the entirety of Chris Ware's stunning graphic novel *Jimmy Corrigan — The Smartest Kid on Earth* and another time when I came across a particularly moving strip by Lynda Barry in a local alternative newspaper. (This was more embarrassing than I would like to admit, as I was in a café looking at the paper and sobbing as if the want ads, hometown hero cover story, and funnies were my own, long obituary. I have approached *Ernie Pook's Comeek* with great respect and some trepidation ever since.) Usually, I have the opposite loss of control when reading comics: a giggling fit, an out-and-out guffaw, one high-pitched *ha!*

Yet between these two reactions is another, potentially more significant response. It is the gradual sense while reading that something in your chest is rearranging itself, that you are being changed. That you might carry a phrase or an image or a story arc with you and choose, because of it, a different path for your future.

This can be a slight, artistic shift: to stop questioning my work and create with a sense of play, which I underwent while reading Lynda Barry's "Two Questions." It can be political: to appreciate my body as a combative military force, capable of producing great change, as Ruth Wangari inspires us to do in "Nakedness and Power." Or it can be monumental: to value more highly my desire to live my life pleasurably, to forgo the chance to save the world every time it arises, as the titular character does in "The Amazing Life of Onion Jack."

It is this emotional response to reading that I carry in my mind as I ponder the emergence of comics as literature. And I can come up with only one remaining concern. Does the acceptance of comics as a literary form mean I have to stop making jokes about them being best read on the toilet?

Because then I'm against it.

The basic guidelines for inclusion in the Best American Comics are consistent with the ninety-two-year history of the Best American series, although to accommodate the unique aspects of the comics medium we have occasionally modified them. Works must be published in North America — working southward, that's Greenland, Canada, the United States, and Mexico, as well as the entirety of the Internet. (This last not being a place, obviously, rather an acknowledgment of the receptive reading audience to be found at North American computer screens. Greenland and Mexico, you will also notice, are unrepresented in this volume, although I heartily welcome works from these areas that meet our other guidelines.) Works must appear originally in English or have been translated by the author, who her- or himself must be a North American creator or a creator who chooses to make his or her home in North America. In very rare exceptions we look at stories that previously appeared in print in an earlier version but that were significantly altered and published in a new context during the current book's period. All rules are firm in all instances except extenuating ones.

The Best American Comics will appear annually, considering work published between September 1 and August 31 the following year. If you publish, create, or simply enjoy comics, please direct publications our way. If you're a creator or fan, please ask your publisher to add the Best American Comics to their subscription list. And, publishers, please add us! All mail will be forwarded if addressed: Anne Elizabeth Moore, Best American Comics, Houghton Mifflin Company, 215 Park Avenue South, New York, New York 10003. We must receive work by early September for consideration in the next year's volume.

In the pages that follow, Harvey Pekar offers an overview of the economic history of comics, and few would be able to tell it better than he. A staunch defender of the storytelling form and demanding instigator of new directions in the medium, Harvey has worked in literary comics since their '70s renaissance, his devotion never lessening. I first met Harvey while he was on tour with *Our Cancer Year* in 1994 or '95. I was young, intimidated, and knew that what he had been trying to do with comics for decades — prove they were a literary medium worth the attention of the whole world — would become my pet project. I did not know it would also become my job, and to be able to work with him on the first Best American Comics edition was habitually inspiring.

In addition to Harvey, I would be remiss to overlook the contributions of my business partner, Daniel Sinker, my brother, John Alexander Moore, and my editor, Meg Lemke. I cannot express my gratitude to the Air Pirates I work with at *Punk Planet* — reviewers, dogs, subscribers, babies, and all — who proved the single force most vital to actually getting this book done.

Except, of course, for the artists who created these little acts of insolence. Would you, too, do it all again? I bet you would.

ANNE ELIZABETH MOORE

Introduction

W HILE I'M USUALLY not into "best of" collections and awards because of the wide variation in aesthetic taste, I am happy to be working on this Best American Comics collection because it lends legitimacy to the cause of comics, my medium, and their creators. The first *Best American Short Stories* was published by Houghton Mifflin in 1915, and they've been coming out annually ever since then. Recently they've been printing more offbeat titles, e.g., *The Best American Nonrequired Reading,* which contained comic book stories, but this is the first Houghton Mifflin volume devoted solely to best American comics, and it couldn't happen at a better time.

In case you haven't noticed, dime stores and drugstores don't sell comics anymore. Their very existence is being threatened. Kids, traditionally the main supporters of comics, are spending their money on video games now. Comics get less and less space in newspaper funny pages, and the number of comic book shops is shrinking. Alternative comic book creators are having an increasingly difficult time getting their works distributed. Once there were several wholesalers that specialized in handling alternative comics; now there are none of any size. At the 2005 Small Press Expo in Bethesda, Maryland, a number of young cartoon artists gave me samples of their work, and, happily, some were quite good, even original. But I'd never heard of many of the people who produced them. How to get stuff like this to a general audience?

Graphic novels may offer a way out. The ones that are issued by large publishers have a chance to be sold in *"book* book" stores, in addition to the vanishing comic book shops. With comic book stores closing and no viable distribution system in place for smal-press comics, it would seem that graphic novels (relatively thick, square-spined comic books that don't have to be fiction) may be the only way for comics to survive. It's been difficult for them to gain acceptability and respect from the general public throughout their history. However, graphic novels are getting more attention in the press these days. The book departments of large-circulation newspapers and slick magazines review graphic novels, while ignoring conventional, pamphlet-sized comics, which they consider too small and inexpensive to publicize no matter how good their content. And *"book* book" publishers are more willing to produce nonsuperhero comics, which are often aimed at adult readers, than are comics publishers.

Where have modern comics come from? Comics began to make an impact in American newspapers during the 1890s, when one feature, *The Yellow Kid,* became so popular that its ownership was contested by two papers. Some of the early newspaper comics were quite arty, like *Little Nemo,* which forecast the surrealist art movement, and *The Kin-der-Kids* by modernist painter Lyonel Feininger. For decades comics grew like weeds, becoming among the most popular of newspaper features. Their content was far more varied than the matter dealt with in what became known as mainstream comics. Newspaper comics ranged from the crazy exploits of spinach-fueled strong-man Popeye to strips that emphasized the mundane, such as *Gasoline Alley* and J. R. Williams's *Out Our Way.* There were sci-fi comics (*Flash Gordon*) and soap opera comics (*Mary Worth*). In the mid 1930s, enterprising publishers began reprinting newspaper strips in pamphlet or magazine-sized forms called comic books. But the content of these books changed considerably as original features such as *Superman* were introduced in them. Superman, a costumed superhero with a host of extraordinary (super) powers, became extremely popular and gave rise to a raft of other costumed heroes: Captain Marvel, Wonder Woman, and the like. Although there were some fine types of other comics available in the 1940s, such as *Little Lulu* and Carl Barks's *Walt Disney Comics,* superheroes were and remain the matinee idols of comic fans. I remember being crazy about them myself as a first-grader, but after a few years I tired of their predictability — they were formulaic — and turned to novels for enjoyment.

In 1954 a crusade against violence and sexuality in comics led to their near annihilation. There was one very positive movement going on then, however, led by writer, illustrator, and editor Harvey Kurtzman at EC Comics. He began with some relatively realistic war titles, *Two-fisted Tales* and *Frontline Combat,* then inaugurated the revolutionary humor comic, *Mad. Mad* contained in abundance a quality previously rare in comic books — satire.

In 1962 a fellow named Robert Crumb moved into my Cleveland, Ohio, neighborhood. Like me, he was a jazz record collector, and we soon got to be good friends. However, Crumb was also a cartoonist. I remembered my days as a comic book fanatic and took a look at his work, curious as to what he was up to. What I saw astounded me. Crumb had been influenced by *Mad,* but, unlike Kurtzman, he didn't just parody TV shows, movies, other comics, and print advertisements; he satirized real life. The first day I met him, he showed me a book he was working on, his *Big Yum Yum Book.* Its protagonist was a frog named Ogden, who was attending a university and trying to "get in with the in crowd," i.e., the beatniks.

Wow! It occurred to me that if material like this could appear in comics, there was no limit to what you could do with them. They could be like novels and films. The only thing limiting the growth of comics was the people who produced them, from the artists and writers to the publishers, who couldn't see comics as anything but a medium for kids. But help was on the way. People like Crumb, Frank Stack, and Gilbert Shelton began producing "underground" comic book stories. A lot of them focused on sex, drugs, and the new counterculture; there was much uncharted territory still to cover, but at least there were no superheroes.

These men and others such as Spain Rodriguez and S. Clay Wilson coalesced into an alternative comic book movement, which got a lot of support from the emerging hippie counterculture. Thus, a new type of comic was created, though it has not to this day received the amount of attention and financial support it has deserved.

Alternative comics went through a sales slump in the 1970s, due to the end of the Vietnam War. It turned out that when the draft ended, a lot of people in the counterculture became yuppies and the market for underground comics shrank markedly. Undergrounds made a comeback in the 1980s, but then slumped again financially. Head shops are virtually extinct right now, and few retail comic book stores carry underground titles; consequently they are difficult to locate even for people with an interest in them.

From the 1960s to the present, superhero comics like *Spider Man*, *The Fantastic Four*, and *X-Men* remained the most popular. This was absurd. Without dealing with the merits of current superhero comics, they still form a division of the science fiction genre, which should not dominate comics any more than they do prose books, films, or television, all versatile forms of expression. While there is no realistic movement in straight comics, there is one in alternative comics. Realism has been so important in the novel, theater, film, and visual arts. How can mainstream comics ignore it and other movements that flourish in other art forms? Mainstream comics greatly ignore the medium's potential.

In any event, there is a nice variety of comics represented here, although you notice no superhero stuff is included. I looked at superhero stories but just didn't run across any that (I thought) were particularly good. If you're a superhero fan and you're angry because they aren't present here, I guess you'll just have to vent your anger on me.

The length of these stories ranges from one to over forty pages. I dig the one-pagers in here. Man, I know what Rick Geary's "Recollection of Seduction" is about. Like you're the kind of guy who has a tough time keeping a relationship or a marriage going. Then, out of a clear blue sky, a nice-looking, intelligent woman makes a pass at you, but you're so dumbfounded you don't follow through. Years later things are still rough, and one day you think of how you messed up with this girl — didn't even give it a chance — and you want to bash your head against the wall.

Ivan Brunetti's poetic piece tells a story wordlessly. The mouse protagonist is obsessed by a female who doesn't return his affection. He tries painting her, to get her off his mind. When that doesn't work, he paints other things, such as a single dot on a canvas. But he still can't remove her from his system. Note how cleverly Brunetti structures this piece, using just a few colors but engaging the attention of his readers throughout.

In "Goner Pillow Company," Ben Katchor follows the ups and downs in the career of Brooklyn pillow manufacturer Aaron Goner, exhibiting a wonderfully subtle sense of humor.

Hob's "The Supervisor" deals with a nasty supervisor who tries to hassle his employees but in the end is humbled. Let that be a lesson to us all. Then there's David Lasky's one-pager "Diary of a Bread Delivery Guy," which contains his wry and perceptive observations about Econoline vehicles and has a really clever layout.

Some of the stars of the 1960s underground comic movement are still producing top-notch stuff today. *Zap* comics was perhaps the leading underground anthology at one time, and it's still occasionally published. Crumb's "Walkin' the Streets" represents one of his better autobiographical stories. It deals with his late teen years and relationship with his brother Charles, who had a profound influence on him. Perhaps the most striking portion of the narration has to do with the Crumb brothers visiting an African American Holy Roller church and the attempts of the congregation to save their souls.

There's also a *Zap* Wonder Wart-Hog story here by Shelton ("The Wart-Hog That Came In from the Cold"), who is best known for his Freak Brothers syndicated strips. Shelton began publishing Wonder Wart-Hog in the early 1960s for the University of Texas humor magazine, *The Texas Ranger*. It is a sort of funky parody of Superman, with Wonder Wart-Hog having a civilian identity, the mild-mannered reporter Philbert Desanex. It's good to see that Shelton hasn't abandoned this amusing strip after all these years.

Another veteran of the early underground comics movement, Kim Deitch, is represented by "Ready to Die," his eyewitness account of the execution by lethal injection of murderer Ronald Fitzgerald at a Virginia penal institution. Fitzgerald snapped and went on a horrible murdering, raping, robbing spree. Deitch found that he liked Fitzgerald, and that Fitzgerald felt he deserved the punishment he received for his crimes. Deitch's understated text works well in this context.

The 1980s and 1990s saw the rise of some alternative comic book artists who managed to attain at least some national recognition. Beginning in the early 1980s, there was an upswing in interest for underground comics. Among the most well known were those done by the Hernandez brothers, Gilberto and Jaime. Jaime is represented here by "Day by Day with Hopey," which is a day-in-the-life-type story. Cute Chicana Hopey does some glasses shopping and becomes intrigued by the saleswoman, who has a knack for immediately picking out the right frames for her customers. Hopey goes home and discusses the saleswoman with her roommate, Rosie, who doesn't seem too jealous. However, Rosie ends the story by asking Hopey, "Can we have a kid someday?"

Lesbian life is viewed from a female point of view in Alison Bechdel's superb syndicated strip, *Dykes to Watch Out For,* from which "Only Disconnect" is taken. Here one half of a lesbian couple is sternly lecturing the other about the enormous bills she's running up on her charge card. The latter interrupts to propose marriage to the former and is met with the response, "Is this a proposal or some kind of postmodern intimacy avoidance strategy?" Many of Bechdel's strips have been collected in paperback editions. Note the counterpoint of some inane George Bush TV remarks in the background. Bechdel is very sharp politically.

Lynda Barry, one of the most popular of the alternative syndicated cartoonists, in "Two Questions" writes about how she got into overintellectualizing instead of letting lines and pictures and ideas just flow from her. I don't know if everybody does their best work the way she does, but, in any event, she writes an amusing and insightful strip about creativity.

Joe Sacco, a topnotch journalist as well as cartoonist, gained attention with his superb book *Palestine,* which he wrote after living with Palestinian Arabs, and he followed it up with notable books dealing with the Bosnian civil war. In "Complacency Kills," Sacco reports intelligently and economically about being on patrol with American troops in Iraq.

One of today's most talked-about cartoonists, Chris Ware, demonstrates his cleverness in "Comics: A History." Here Ware deals with comics from the Neanderthal era to the present, with stops in Sumer, Egypt, ancient Rome, the Middle Ages, you name it.

"A Street-Level View of the Republican National Convention" is done by another syndicated artist, Lloyd Dangle. Dangle deserves praise for his directness in pointing out what a bunch of dangerous morons George Bush and his supporters are.

David Heatley's "Portrait of My Dad" consists of four pages of vignette strips about the seemingly tragicomic life of Heatley's father, who has a knack for saying things that don't come off the way he wants them to. His kind of clumsy, off-the-wall comments provide a lot of laughs, but Heatley shows respect for him and presents him as a troubled but sympathetic parent. His layouts, which feature tiny panels, are fresh.

"Thirty-three" by Alex Robinson is an affecting tale of a long-lost daughter being reunited with her father. It's a moving but not corny story and features Robinson's strong, direct illustration.

I really like Jonathan Bennett's complex shaggy-dog piece "Dance with the Ventures" a lot, and, being a long-time record collector, can strongly identify with it. From his apartment the protagonist spots a stack of LPs sitting on the street waiting to be picked up with other trash and garbage. Instead of bolting right to them, he takes his time, and when he arrives finds that someone else has beaten him to the junk pile. He tries to be cool about it and walks away, as does the other guy, only to bolt back and find the other cat has returned too, about a second ahead of him. The fear he feels hoping the competitor won't pick up something desirable while he stands there helplessly is palpable.

"The Executive Hour" by Tom Hart has a first-person narrative by a business executive who parodies himself. Going to work at six A.M., he thinks, "This is the twilight time before the labor din and mediocrity morass drown everything out. Rockefeller, Mellon, Forbes, and Father all did their work in this hour — in the twilight time that belongs to us survivors. To us men who choose."

In Anders Nilsen's sparsely worded, enigmatic "The Gift" we encounter a young man with a bundle of his belongings standing next to a large pipeline. Lying next to him near a crashed helicopter and apparently badly wounded is a somewhat older fellow. The older man begs the younger man to shoot him and put him out of his misery, but the latter can't bring himself to do that. Then the young man climbs on top of the pipeline, staring into space and saying, "We were never going anywhere, were we?" Later he returns to the older man to find him challenging a teenager. Both have weapons, but they relent. Finally the younger man shoots the older one. The teenager comes back and the younger guy gives him some of his possessions, including a teddy bear. The teenager mounts his horse and rides away and finally the young man leaves too. The whole drama plays out on a wasteland and leaves me with a feeling of desolation.

Joel Priddy does a clever send-up of superheroes in "The Amazing Life of Onion Jack," following Jack's life from cradle to grave, by which time he has also managed to become "the world's greatest chef."

"Chemical Plant/Another World," taken from John Porcellino's *Diary of a Mosquito Abatement Man* series, finds the mosquito man driving his truck into a chemical plant full of towers, catwalks, wires, and pipes. He explores this mass of machinery as it hisses and steams, wondering if he's dreaming or not. The piece has an eerie, surreal quality.

The longest story in the book, "La Rubia Loca," very well crafted by Justin Hall, is told by Sarah, a woman in her mid-thirties and down on her luck, who tries to get away from it all by taking a bus tour of northern Mexico. Another passenger is a mentally ill Swiss woman whose native language is German. Sarah and the two bus drivers quickly see that the woman needs medical attention, and fast, but do not want to turn her in to a Mexican hospital, because inmates of Mexican mental hospitals sometimes never get out. It's a tale of Sarah and the two drivers trying to get the Swiss woman onto a plane to San Francisco, where help awaits, without attracting the attention of the Mexican authorities. Hall's storytelling is sensitive and has fine continuity.

Rebecca Dart tells "RabbitHead" wordlessly, the protagonist being a human female with a rabbit's head. Although there is no text, Dart's drawing alone makes this a top story. Its characters look like they came out of a book of fantasy, or even a nightmare; they resemble mythological beasts. The panels in "RabbitHead" are often quite small. Perhaps this is Dart's way of making viewers concentrate more on the actions of the characters. It's a fine, abstract piece of work.

"Nakedness and Power," a collaboration by Seth Tobocman, Terisa Turner, and Leigh Brownhill, has to do with the abuses suffered by poor Africans at the hands of corporations and national governments in Kenya and Nigeria. In particular, the courage and ingenuity of women in leading protests against these corrupt institutions is highlighted. The authors show that even poor and working-class people can make a significant difference when combating the forces of capitalist greed.

Lilli Carré displays a subtle sense of humor in "Adventures of Paul Bunyan & His Ox, Babe." Paul and Babe are out in the woods knocking down trees and stop for lunch to have a serious conversation. Paul speaks from the depths of his soul. Babe asks him about hanging out with "me and a few of the boys at a local tavern," and Paul nixes the idea, saying he'd rather curl up with a good book. Turns out he's reading Proust. Then Paul expounds on his troubles with the ladies. They make lewd remarks about his size, and when he kisses them he gets them all wet. He says he feels like the guy in *Of Mice and Men*. Paul and Babe go back and forth about the idea of him finding a place where he'd be looked upon as normal. Their conversation is cut short by the whistle calling them back to work, but if you think you know what Paul Bunyan was really about, better check out this story.

"Thirteen Cats of My Childhood" gives Jesse Reklaw a chance to talk about the large number of cats he's had in his family, and, while he's at it, to write an autobiographical story about growing up in various California locations. His family appears to be close knit when he's little, but as he grows older, differences develop. By the time he's in his late teens, his parents have divorced and his mother has remarried. It's a moving, bittersweet tale.

Kurt Wolfgang's "Passing Before Life's Very Eyes" concerns the last hours of a man who's dying in the hospital. He has a hallucination and revisits his past experiences. In it, a guy turns up to tell him that this dream contains his last moments before he dies. He's outraged that he's not going to heaven but tries to come to terms with the situation as the story ends.

Jessica Abel writes about Carla, a young woman who's teaching in Mexico and staying there over the Christmas/New Year holiday. She's bored. Her drug-dealing boyfriend comes in and she tries to get something going with him, but he blows her off.

Following this, a girlfriend comes in and Carla, still stung by the way her roommate has treated her, gets into an argument with her female acquaintance, who abruptly leaves, despite Carla's attempts to mend the misunderstanding.

"Busted!", Esther Pearl Watson's story about a nutty African American kid talking to his reflection in the school trophy case, is funny and admirable for the accuracy of her dialogue. She's subtitled it "Wayne Is Insane," which seems to be on the money. Another very amusing story, Olivia Schanzer's "Solidarity Forever," opens, "The chain known as Super Food Mart has employed the bums of one West Texas town to tamp down their dumpsters. The repercussions have been felt by a group of bikers who have been dealing speed behind that same dumpster for the last thirty years." Shades of Gilbert Shelton.

Now listen, I'm not claiming these are the absolute best comics issued in a given twelve-month period. I haven't seen all the comics published in that time and neither have the hard-working, painstaking people I'm working with. But there's good, often original stuff in this collection that I hope will open readers' eyes to the breadth of subject matter that comics can deal with effectively. I hope you can understand, even if you don't like every choice in this collection, that they don't have to be about costumed superheroes, cute little kids, and talking animals. "Nakedness and Power," for example, is a dead serious essay about some significant political problems. Though he relies more on humor, Lloyd Dangle makes valid, important political observations in his piece. Political cartoons shouldn't have to be limited to the one-panel drawings you see on editorial pages. They can be long narratives.

Then, too, comics can be about quotidian life, like "Thirteen Cats of My Childhood," "Diary of a Bread Delivery Man," and "Busted!" I have always maintained that there were more gripping dramas and hilarious occurrences in everyday life than you see coming from high-budget films and sitcoms. Check out Esther Pearl Watson's "Busted!" She might've written down exactly what Wayne was saying, then made a slice-of-life comic about it from her notes. Fine. If you see funny things like that happening in your everyday lives, write them down and let us all benefit from your observations. Quotidian life is too often ignored by prose as well as comics writers. If you're into avant-garde work, read "RabbitHead" or "The Gift," both thought-provoking selections. Think about the variety exhibited in this collection. Stories range from fantasies ("RabbitHead") to hard-hitting political nonfiction. There's some fine satire, as in "The Amazing Life of Onion Jack," and subtle realism, such as "Dance with the Ventures." Rick Geary's drawing is technically brilliant, John Porcellino's deceptively simple. Justin Hall's "La Rubia Loca" is highly dramatic, David Heatley's "Portrait of My Dad" understated. The point is, so much territory has been covered, and covered at least competently. If this variety of stories can be done in comics, they can be done brilliantly. That's what doubters-about-comics have to keep in mind. Right now comics are understaffed. Too many excellent writers and illustrators don't even consider the medium when looking for an outlet for their work. The comics-is-for-kids attitude remains difficult to overcome. This collection should have some influence in combating it, though. Give it a shot, you may be pleasantly surprised.

HARVEY PEKAR

THE BEST AMERICAN
Comics 2006

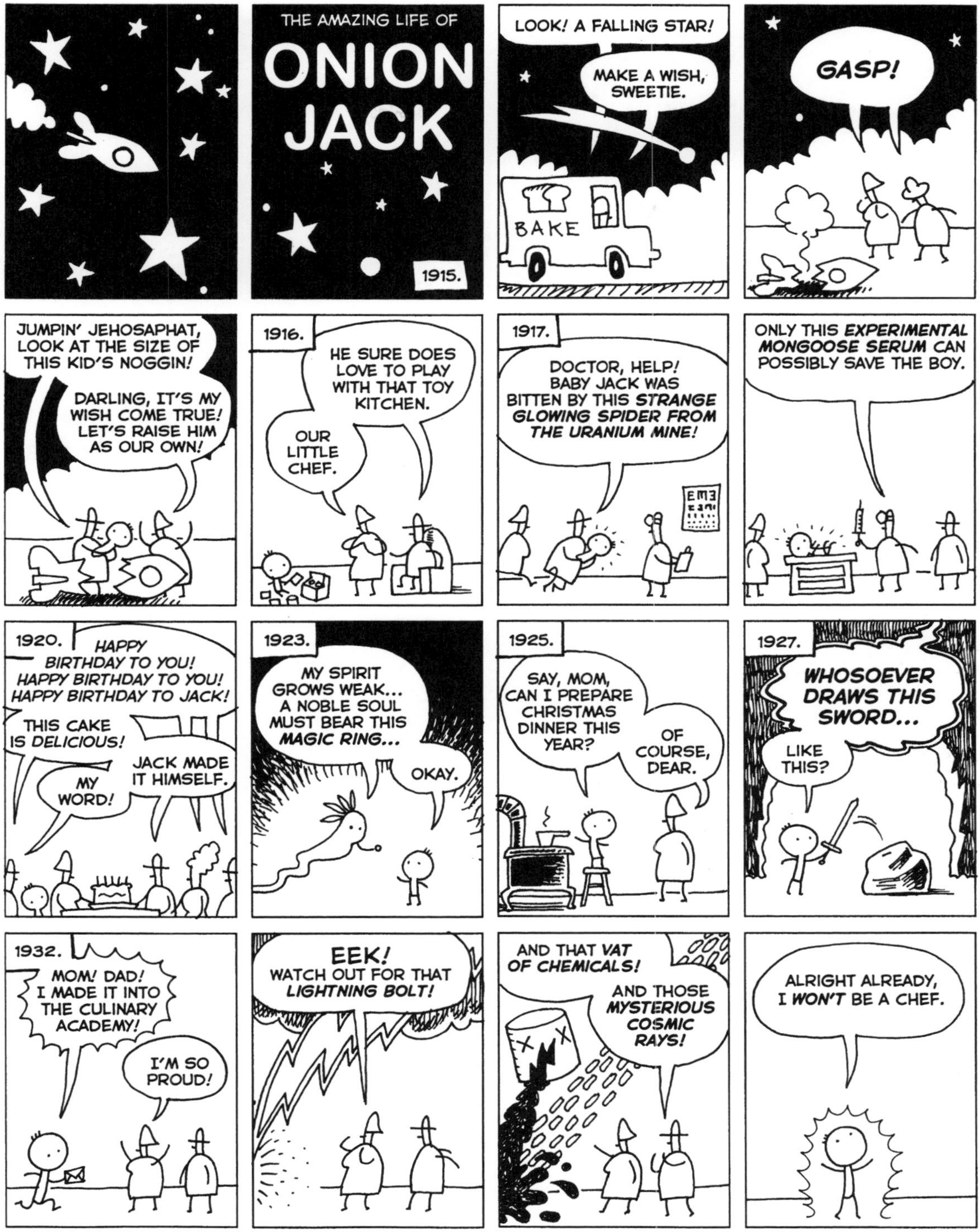

THE AMAZING LIFE OF
ONION JACK
1915.
LOOK! A FALLING STAR!
MAKE A WISH, SWEETIE.
BAKE
GASP!
JUMPIN' JEHOSAPHAT, LOOK AT THE SIZE OF THIS KID'S NOGGIN!
DARLING, IT'S MY WISH COME TRUE! LET'S RAISE HIM AS OUR OWN!
1916.
HE SURE DOES LOVE TO PLAY WITH THAT TOY KITCHEN.
OUR LITTLE CHEF.
1917.
DOCTOR, HELP! BABY JACK WAS BITTEN BY THIS *STRANGE GLOWING SPIDER FROM THE URANIUM MINE!*
ONLY THIS *EXPERIMENTAL MONGOOSE SERUM* CAN POSSIBLY SAVE THE BOY.
1920.
HAPPY BIRTHDAY TO YOU! HAPPY BIRTHDAY TO YOU! HAPPY BIRTHDAY TO JACK!
THIS CAKE IS *DELICIOUS!*
JACK MADE IT HIMSELF.
MY WORD!
1923.
MY SPIRIT GROWS WEAK... A NOBLE SOUL MUST BEAR THIS *MAGIC RING...*
OKAY.
1925.
SAY, MOM, CAN I PREPARE CHRISTMAS DINNER THIS YEAR?
OF COURSE, DEAR.
1927.
WHOSOEVER DRAWS THIS SWORD...
LIKE THIS?
1932.
MOM! DAD! I MADE IT INTO THE CULINARY ACADEMY!
I'M SO PROUD!
EEK! WATCH OUT FOR THAT *LIGHTNING BOLT!*
AND THAT *VAT OF CHEMICALS!*
AND THOSE *MYSTERIOUS COSMIC RAYS!*
ALRIGHT ALREADY, I *WON'T* BE A CHEF.

FROM *Superior Showcase*

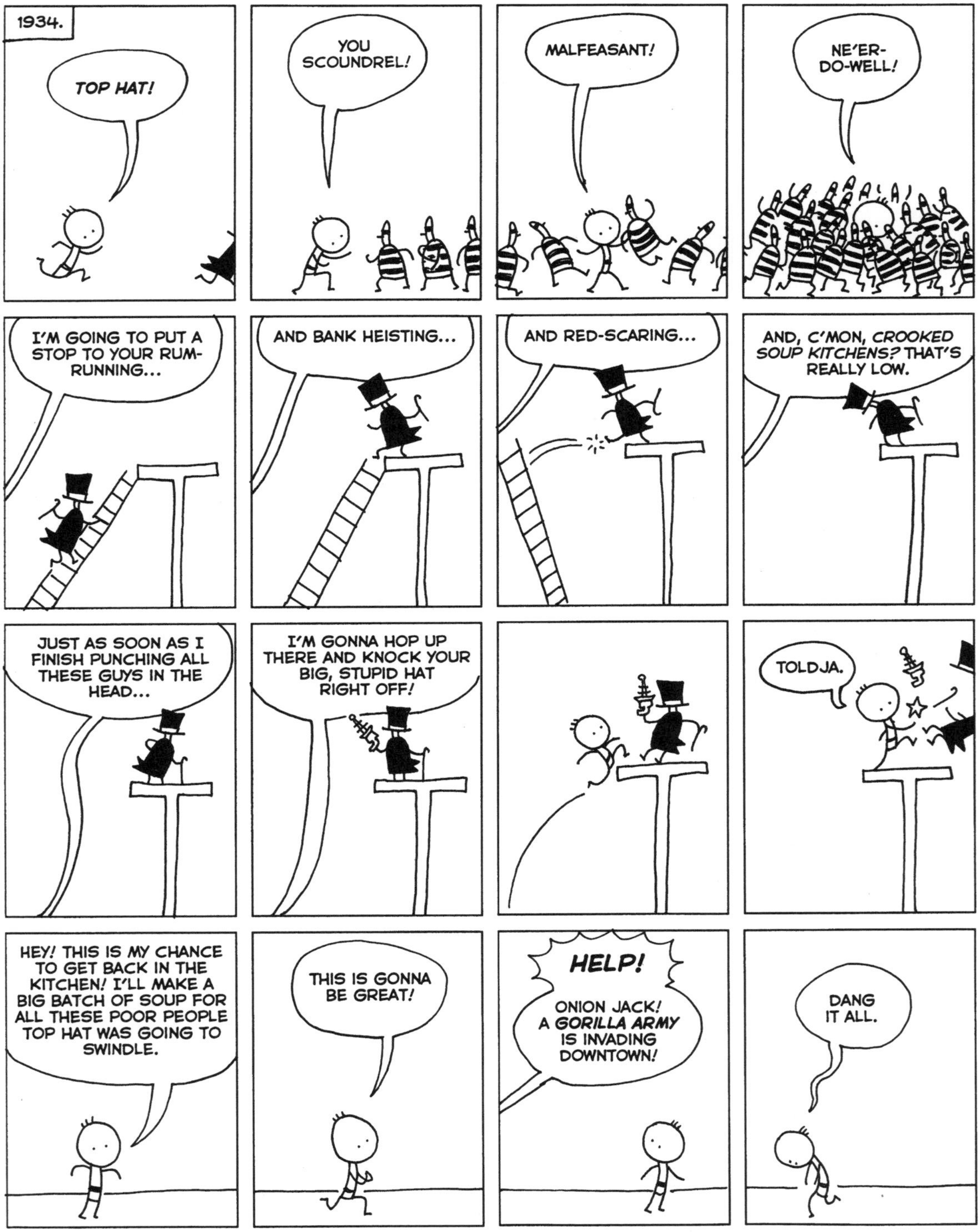

1934.
TOP HAT!
YOU SCOUNDREL!
MALFEASANT!
NE'ER-DO-WELL!
I'M GOING TO PUT A STOP TO YOUR RUM-RUNNING...
AND BANK HEISTING...
AND RED-SCARING...
AND, C'MON, *CROOKED SOUP KITCHENS?* THAT'S REALLY LOW.
JUST AS SOON AS I FINISH PUNCHING ALL THESE GUYS IN THE HEAD...
I'M GONNA HOP UP THERE AND KNOCK YOUR BIG, STUPID HAT RIGHT OFF!
TOLDJA.
HEY! THIS IS MY CHANCE TO GET BACK IN THE KITCHEN! I'LL MAKE A BIG BATCH OF SOUP FOR ALL THESE POOR PEOPLE TOP HAT WAS GOING TO SWINDLE.
THIS IS GONNA BE GREAT!
HELP!
ONION JACK! A *GORILLA ARMY* IS INVADING DOWNTOWN!
DANG IT ALL.

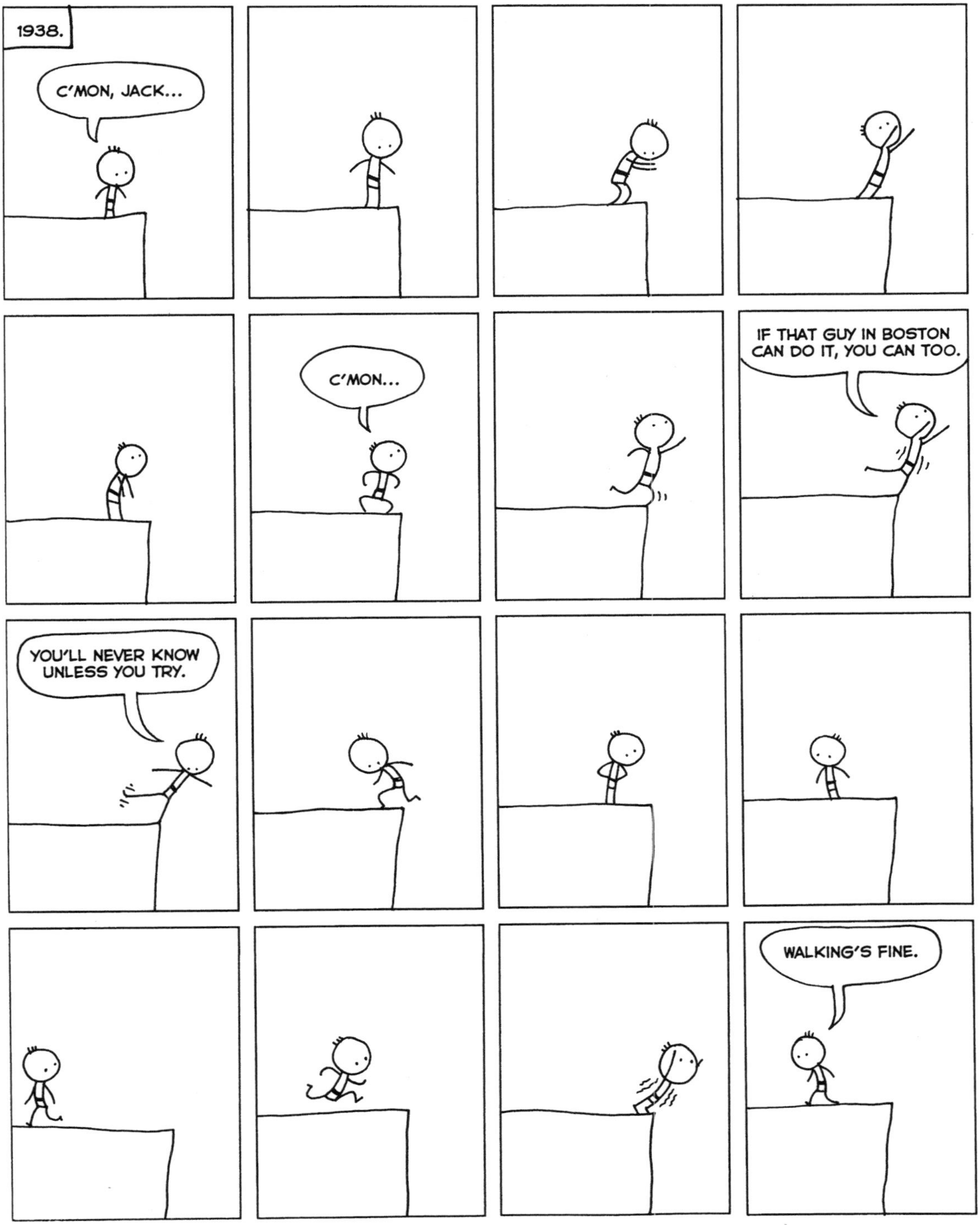
1938.
C'MON, JACK...
C'MON...
IF THAT GUY IN BOSTON CAN DO IT, YOU CAN TOO.
YOU'LL NEVER KNOW UNLESS YOU TRY.
WALKING'S FINE.

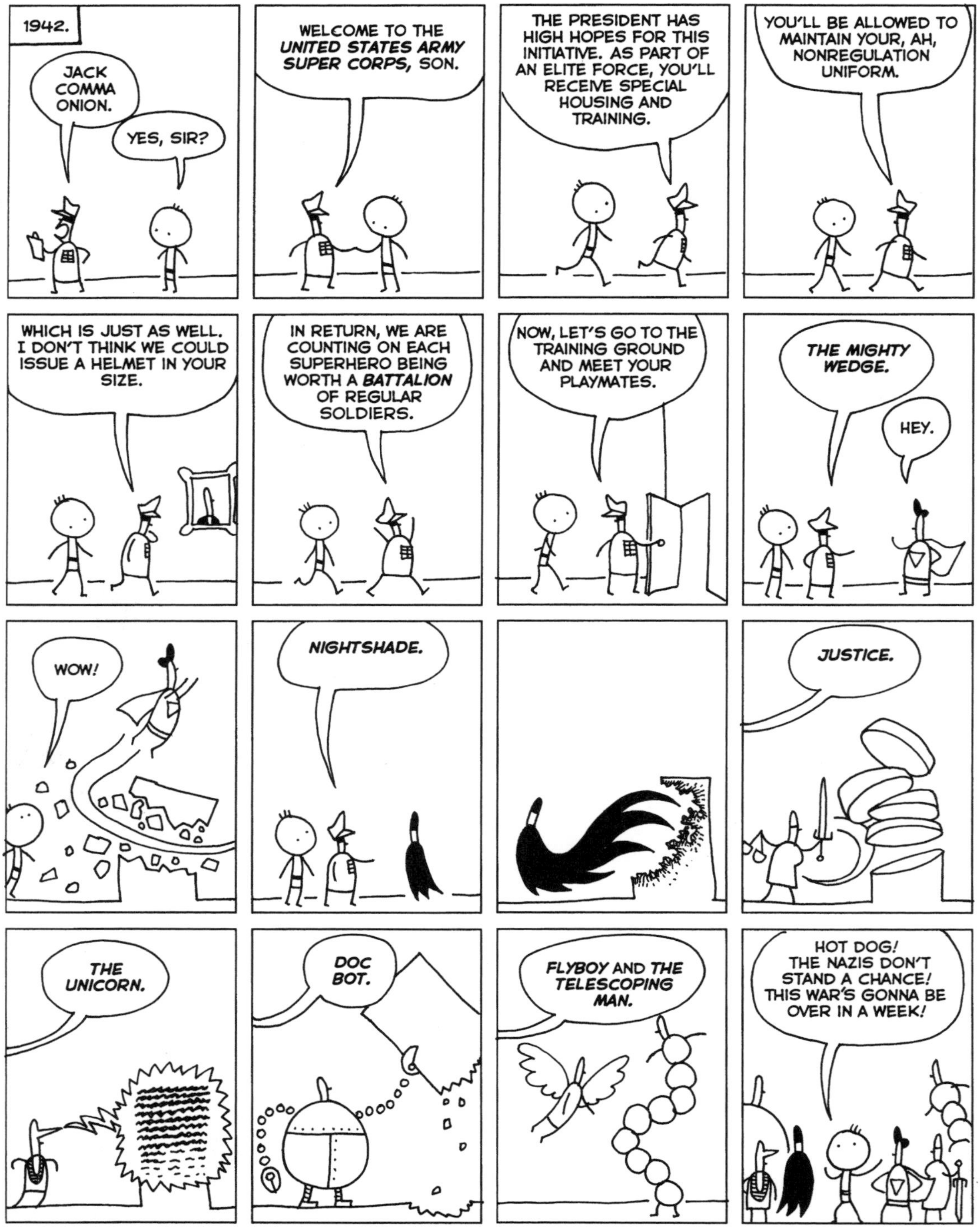
1942.
JACK COMMA ONION.
YES, SIR?
WELCOME TO THE *UNITED STATES ARMY SUPER CORPS,* SON.
THE PRESIDENT HAS HIGH HOPES FOR THIS INITIATIVE. AS PART OF AN ELITE FORCE, YOU'LL RECEIVE SPECIAL HOUSING AND TRAINING.
YOU'LL BE ALLOWED TO MAINTAIN YOUR, AH, NONREGULATION UNIFORM.
WHICH IS JUST AS WELL. I DON'T THINK WE COULD ISSUE A HELMET IN YOUR SIZE.
IN RETURN, WE ARE COUNTING ON EACH SUPERHERO BEING WORTH A *BATTALION* OF REGULAR SOLDIERS.
NOW, LET'S GO TO THE TRAINING GROUND AND MEET YOUR PLAYMATES.
THE MIGHTY WEDGE.
HEY.
WOW!
NIGHTSHADE.
JUSTICE.
THE UNICORN.
DOC BOT.
FLYBOY AND *THE TELESCOPING MAN.*
HOT DOG! THE NAZIS DON'T STAND A CHANCE! THIS WAR'S GONNA BE OVER IN A WEEK!

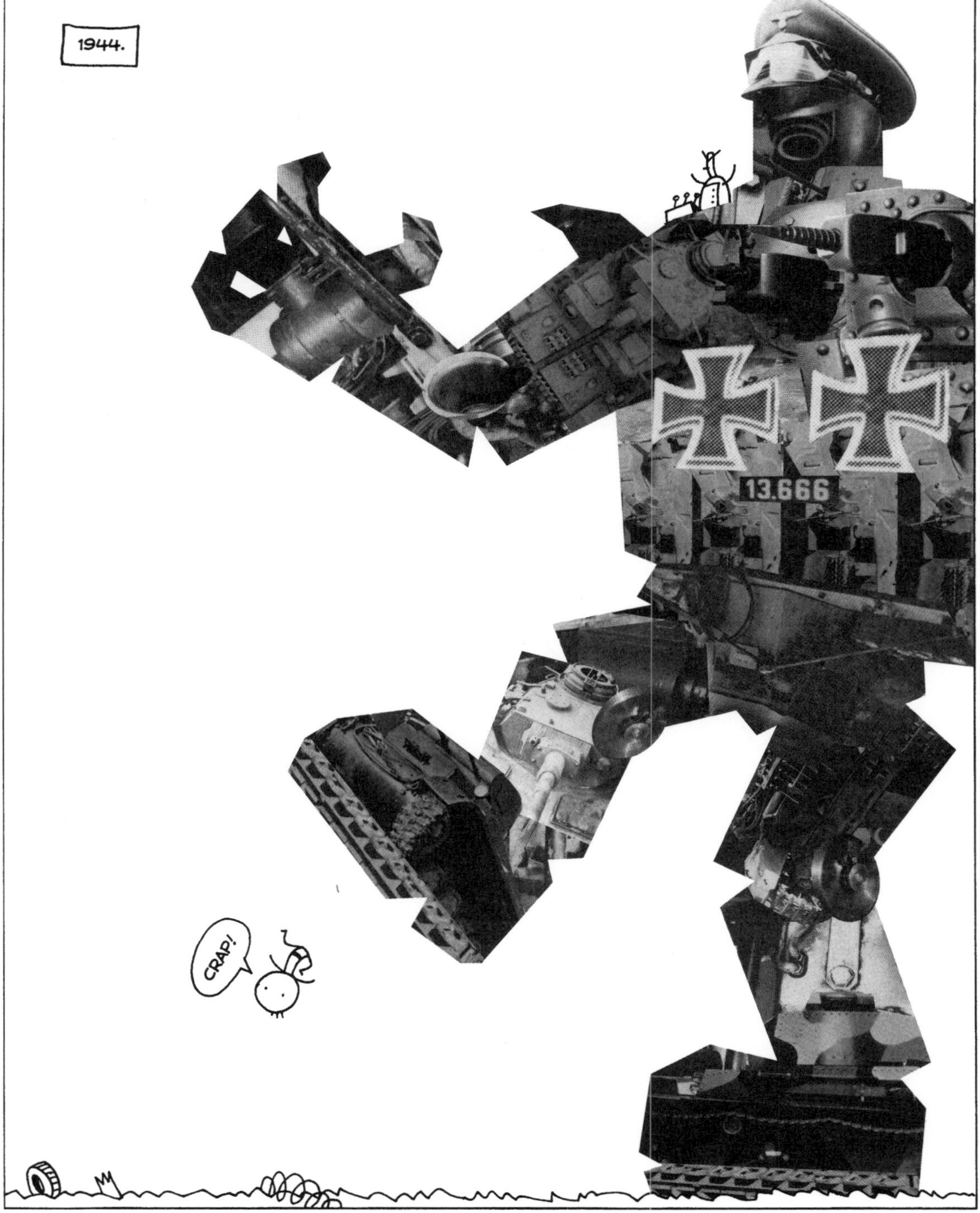
1944.
13.666
CRAP!

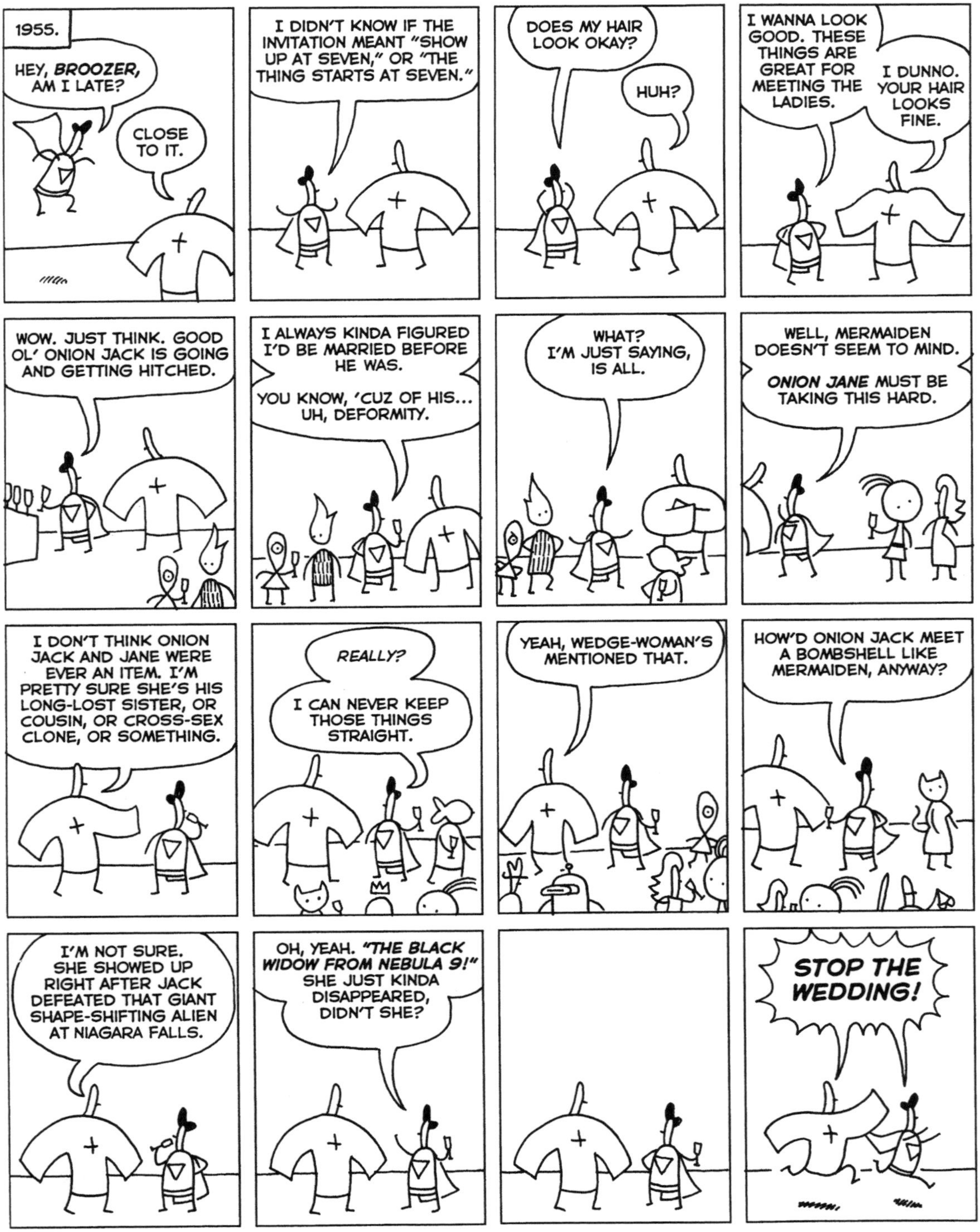
1955.
HEY, ***BROOZER,*** AM I LATE?
CLOSE TO IT.
I DIDN'T KNOW IF THE INVITATION MEANT "SHOW UP AT SEVEN," OR "THE THING STARTS AT SEVEN."
DOES MY HAIR LOOK OKAY?
HUH?
I WANNA LOOK GOOD. THESE THINGS ARE GREAT FOR MEETING THE LADIES.
I DUNNO. YOUR HAIR LOOKS FINE.
WOW. JUST THINK. GOOD OL' ONION JACK IS GOING AND GETTING HITCHED.
I ALWAYS KINDA FIGURED I'D BE MARRIED BEFORE HE WAS.
YOU KNOW, 'CUZ OF HIS... UH, DEFORMITY.
WHAT? I'M JUST SAYING, IS ALL.
WELL, MERMAIDEN DOESN'T SEEM TO MIND.
ONION JANE MUST BE TAKING THIS HARD.
I DON'T THINK ONION JACK AND JANE WERE EVER AN ITEM. I'M PRETTY SURE SHE'S HIS LONG-LOST SISTER, OR COUSIN, OR CROSS-SEX CLONE, OR SOMETHING.
REALLY?
I CAN NEVER KEEP THOSE THINGS STRAIGHT.
YEAH, WEDGE-WOMAN'S MENTIONED THAT.
HOW'D ONION JACK MEET A BOMBSHELL LIKE MERMAIDEN, ANYWAY?
I'M NOT SURE. SHE SHOWED UP RIGHT AFTER JACK DEFEATED THAT GIANT SHAPE-SHIFTING ALIEN AT NIAGARA FALLS.
OH, YEAH. ***"THE BLACK WIDOW FROM NEBULA 9!"*** SHE JUST KINDA DISAPPEARED, DIDN'T SHE?
STOP THE WEDDING!

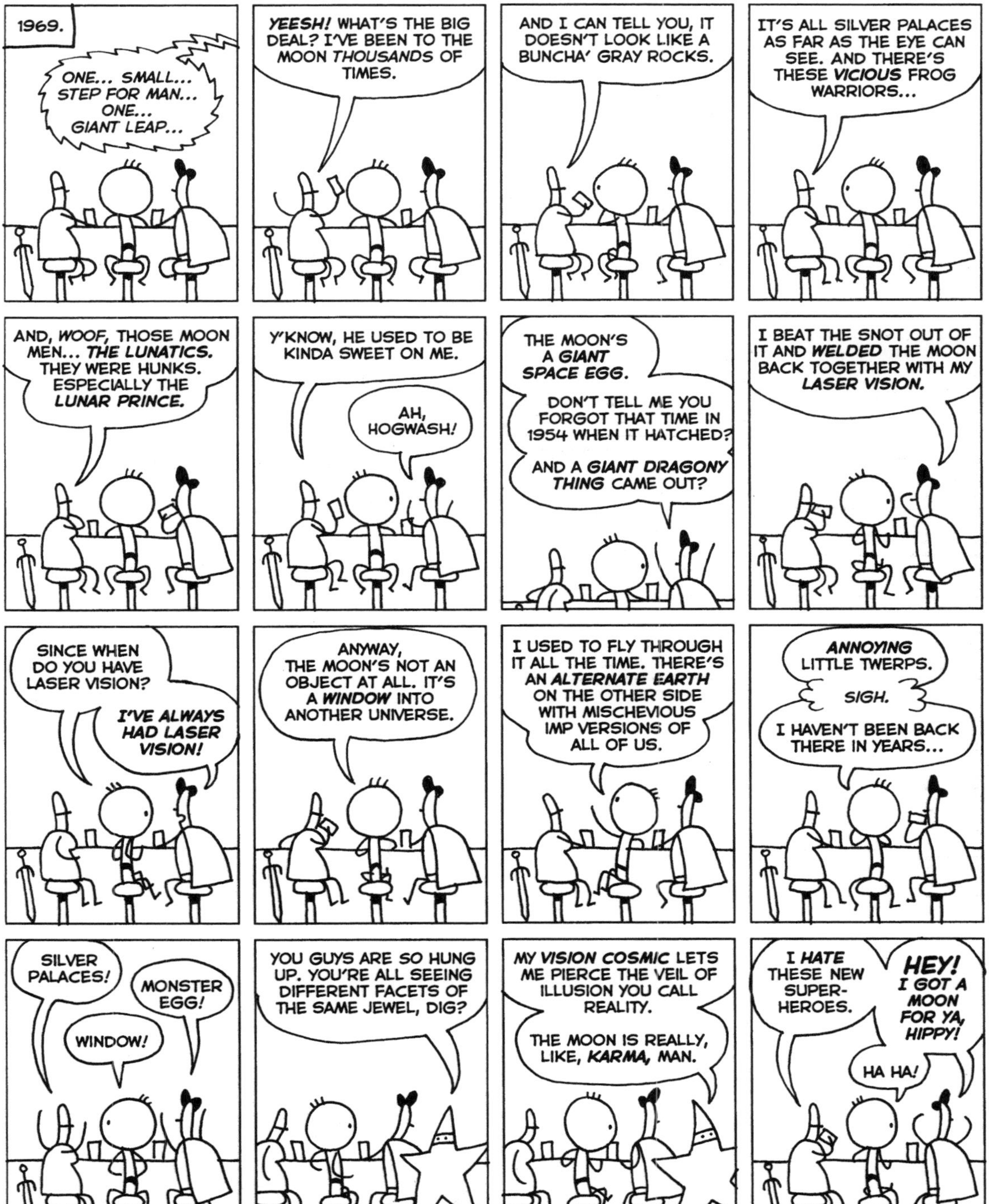
1969.
ONE... SMALL... STEP FOR MAN... ONE... GIANT LEAP...
YEESH! WHAT'S THE BIG DEAL? I'VE BEEN TO THE MOON THOUSANDS OF TIMES.
AND I CAN TELL YOU, IT DOESN'T LOOK LIKE A BUNCHA' GRAY ROCKS.
IT'S ALL SILVER PALACES AS FAR AS THE EYE CAN SEE. AND THERE'S THESE VICIOUS FROG WARRIORS...
AND, WOOF, THOSE MOON MEN... THE LUNATICS. THEY WERE HUNKS. ESPECIALLY THE LUNAR PRINCE.
Y'KNOW, HE USED TO BE KINDA SWEET ON ME.
AH, HOGWASH!
THE MOON'S A GIANT SPACE EGG.
DON'T TELL ME YOU FORGOT THAT TIME IN 1954 WHEN IT HATCHED?
AND A GIANT DRAGONY THING CAME OUT?
I BEAT THE SNOT OUT OF IT AND WELDED THE MOON BACK TOGETHER WITH MY LASER VISION.
SINCE WHEN DO YOU HAVE LASER VISION?
I'VE ALWAYS HAD LASER VISION!
ANYWAY, THE MOON'S NOT AN OBJECT AT ALL. IT'S A WINDOW INTO ANOTHER UNIVERSE.
I USED TO FLY THROUGH IT ALL THE TIME. THERE'S AN ALTERNATE EARTH ON THE OTHER SIDE WITH MISCHEVIOUS IMP VERSIONS OF ALL OF US.
ANNOYING LITTLE TWERPS.
SIGH.
I HAVEN'T BEEN BACK THERE IN YEARS...
SILVER PALACES!
MONSTER EGG!
WINDOW!
YOU GUYS ARE SO HUNG UP. YOU'RE ALL SEEING DIFFERENT FACETS OF THE SAME JEWEL, DIG?
MY VISION COSMIC LETS ME PIERCE THE VEIL OF ILLUSION YOU CALL REALITY.
THE MOON IS REALLY, LIKE, KARMA, MAN.
I HATE THESE NEW SUPER-HEROES.
HEY! I GOT A MOON FOR YA, HIPPY!
HA HA!

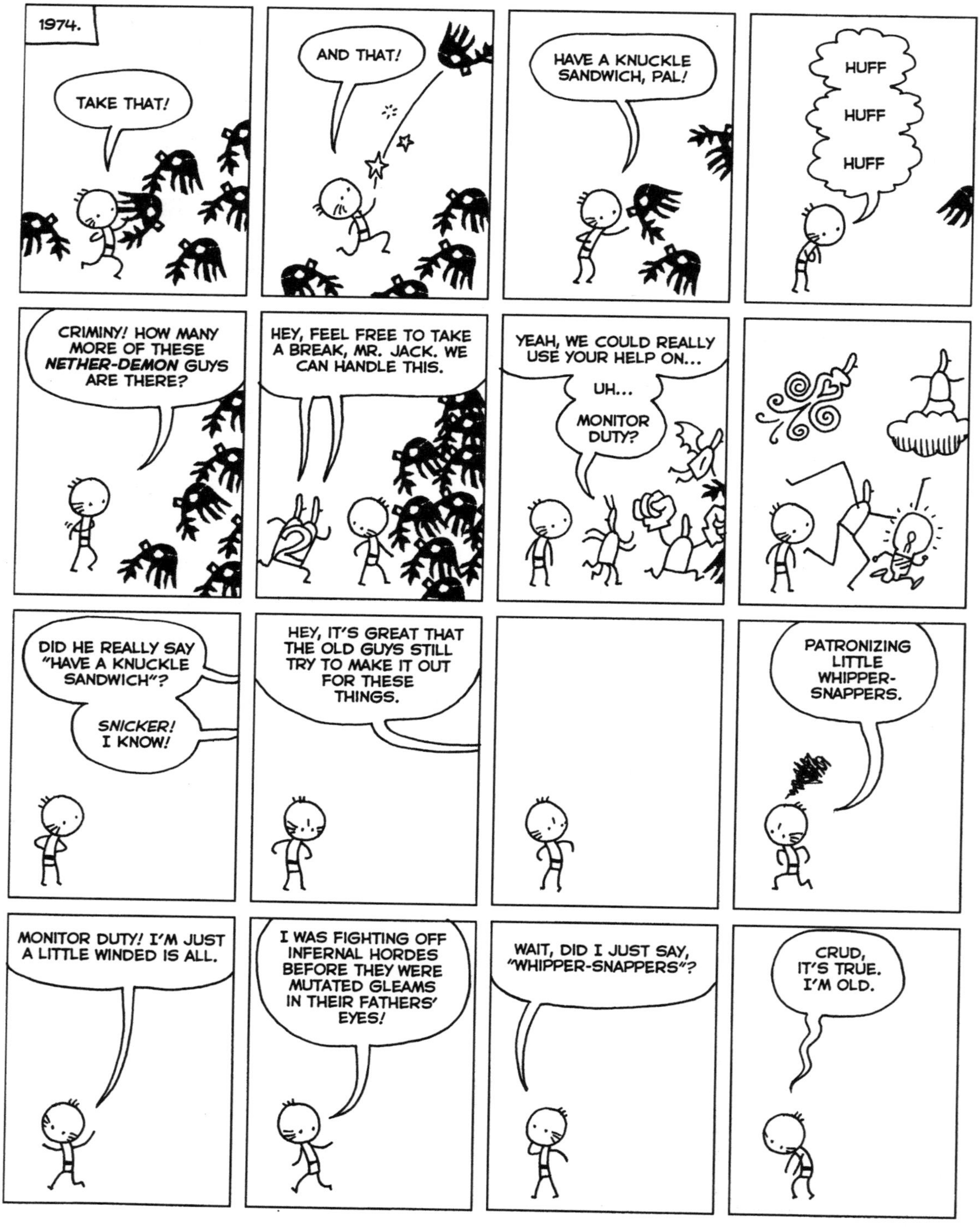
1974.
TAKE THAT!
AND THAT!
HAVE A KNUCKLE SANDWICH, PAL!
HUFF
HUFF
HUFF
CRIMINY! HOW MANY MORE OF THESE NETHER-DEMON GUYS ARE THERE?
HEY, FEEL FREE TO TAKE A BREAK, MR. JACK. WE CAN HANDLE THIS.
YEAH, WE COULD REALLY USE YOUR HELP ON...
UH...
MONITOR DUTY?
DID HE REALLY SAY "HAVE A KNUCKLE SANDWICH"?
SNICKER! I KNOW!
HEY, IT'S GREAT THAT THE OLD GUYS STILL TRY TO MAKE IT OUT FOR THESE THINGS.
PATRONIZING LITTLE WHIPPER-SNAPPERS.
MONITOR DUTY! I'M JUST A LITTLE WINDED IS ALL.
I WAS FIGHTING OFF INFERNAL HORDES BEFORE THEY WERE MUTATED GLEAMS IN THEIR FATHERS' EYES!
WAIT, DID I JUST SAY, "WHIPPER-SNAPPERS"?
CRUD, IT'S TRUE. I'M OLD.

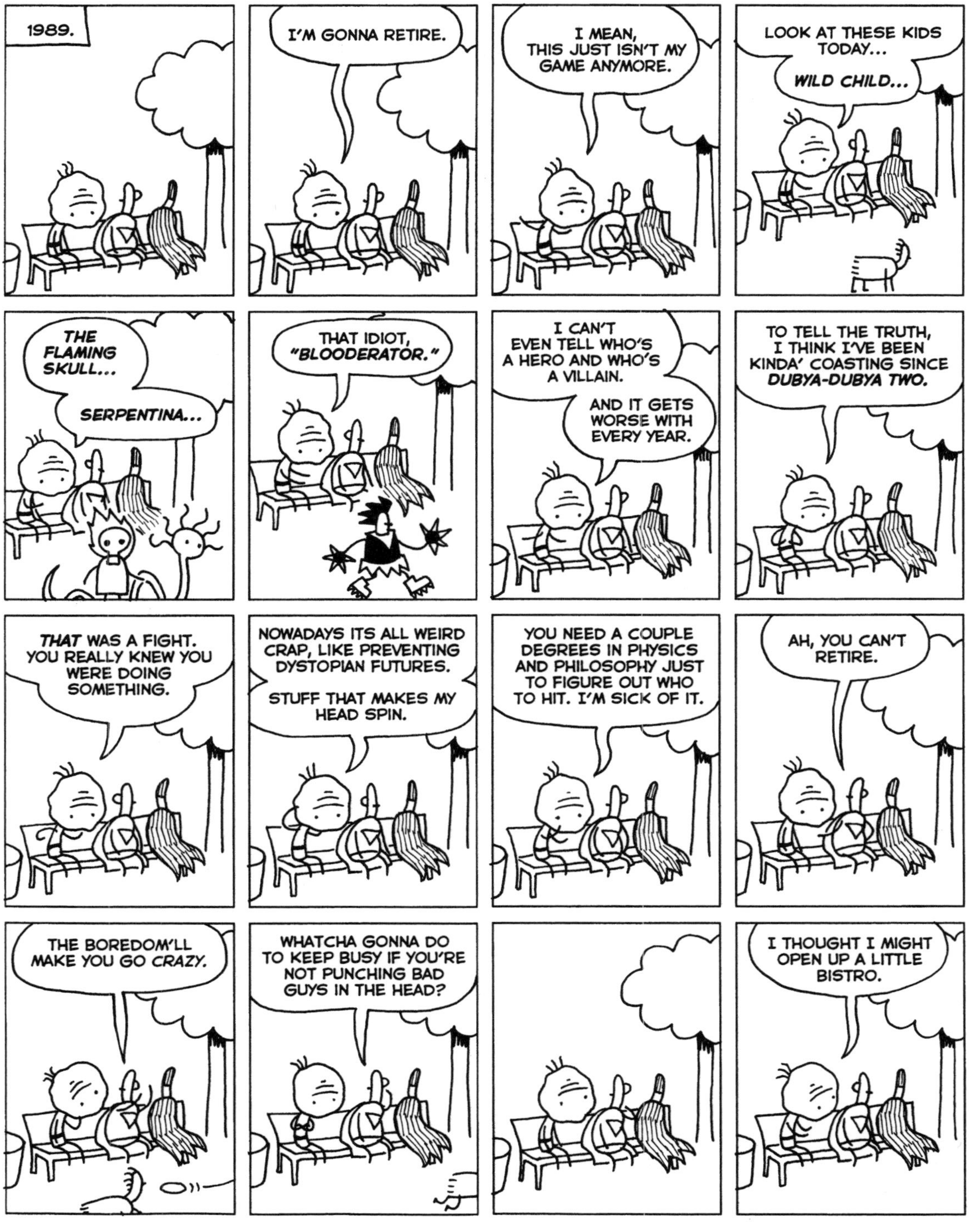
1989.
I'M GONNA RETIRE.
I MEAN, THIS JUST ISN'T MY GAME ANYMORE.
LOOK AT THESE KIDS TODAY...
WILD CHILD...
THE FLAMING SKULL...
SERPENTINA...
THAT IDIOT, "BLOODERATOR."
I CAN'T EVEN TELL WHO'S A HERO AND WHO'S A VILLAIN.
AND IT GETS WORSE WITH EVERY YEAR.
TO TELL THE TRUTH, I THINK I'VE BEEN KINDA' COASTING SINCE DUBYA-DUBYA TWO.
THAT WAS A FIGHT. YOU REALLY KNEW YOU WERE DOING SOMETHING.
NOWADAYS ITS ALL WEIRD CRAP, LIKE PREVENTING DYSTOPIAN FUTURES.
STUFF THAT MAKES MY HEAD SPIN.
YOU NEED A COUPLE DEGREES IN PHYSICS AND PHILOSOPHY JUST TO FIGURE OUT WHO TO HIT. I'M SICK OF IT.
AH, YOU CAN'T RETIRE.
THE BOREDOM'LL MAKE YOU GO CRAZY.
WHATCHA GONNA DO TO KEEP BUSY IF YOU'RE NOT PUNCHING BAD GUYS IN THE HEAD?
I THOUGHT I MIGHT OPEN UP A LITTLE BISTRO.

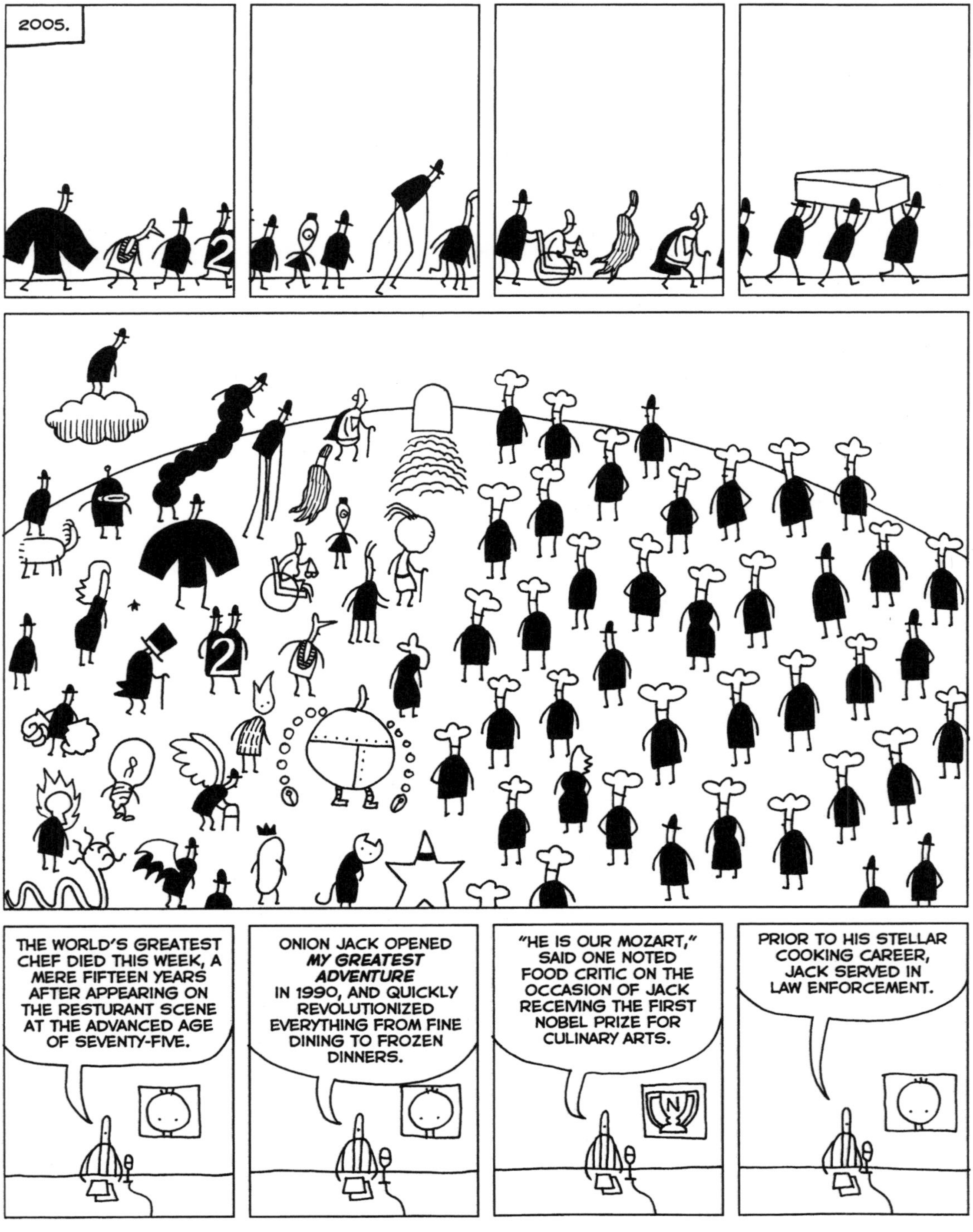
2005.
THE WORLD'S GREATEST CHEF DIED THIS WEEK, A MERE FIFTEEN YEARS AFTER APPEARING ON THE RESTURANT SCENE AT THE ADVANCED AGE OF SEVENTY-FIVE.
ONION JACK OPENED *MY GREATEST ADVENTURE* IN 1990, AND QUICKLY REVOLUTIONIZED EVERYTHING FROM FINE DINING TO FROZEN DINNERS.
"HE IS OUR MOZART," SAID ONE NOTED FOOD CRITIC ON THE OCCASION OF JACK RECEIVING THE FIRST NOBEL PRIZE FOR CULINARY ARTS.
N
PRIOR TO HIS STELLAR COOKING CAREER, JACK SERVED IN LAW ENFORCEMENT.

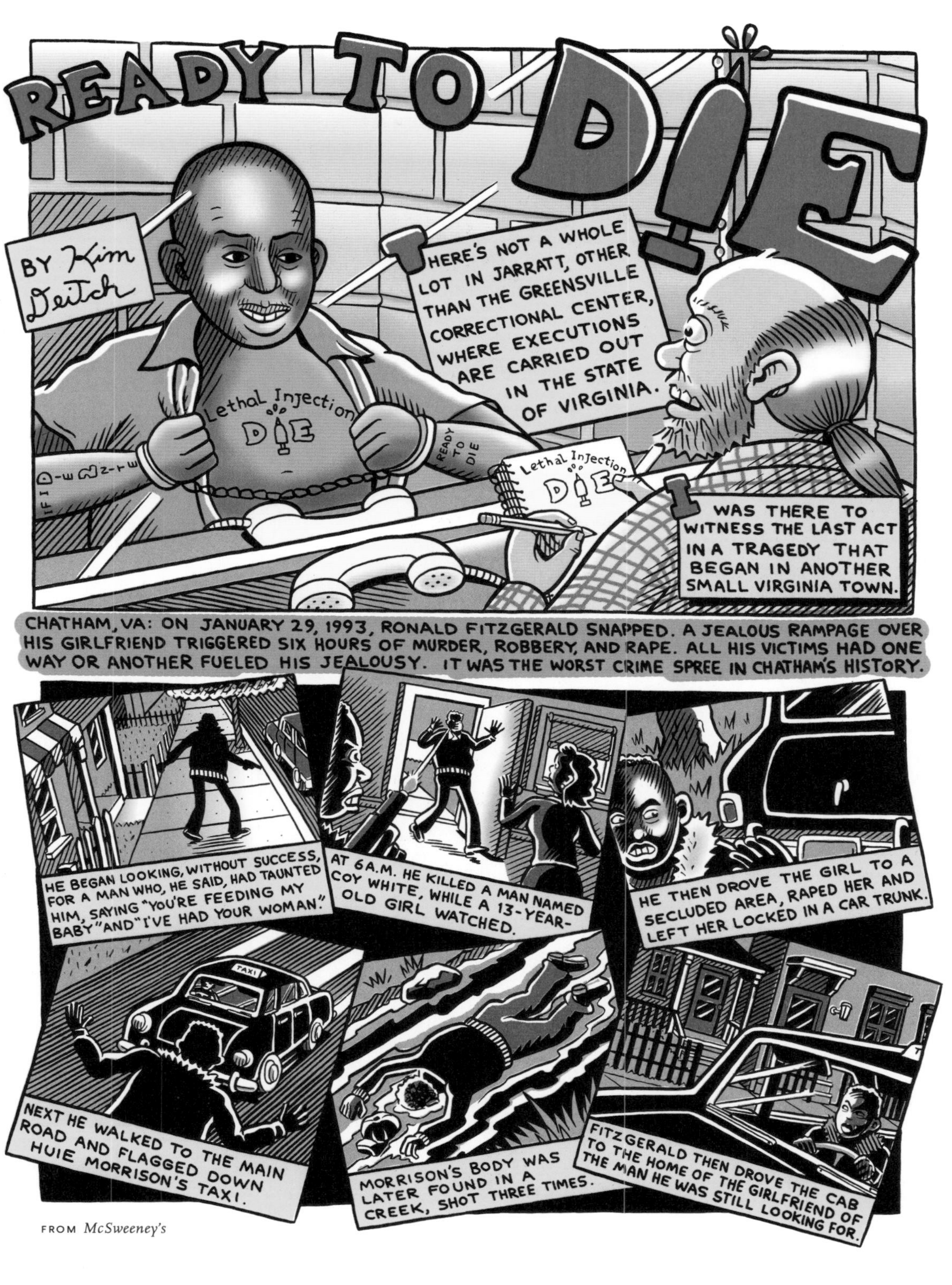
READY TO DIE
BY Kim Deitch
THERE'S NOT A WHOLE LOT IN JARRATT, OTHER THAN THE GREENSVILLE CORRECTIONAL CENTER, WHERE EXECUTIONS ARE CARRIED OUT IN THE STATE OF VIRGINIA.
Lethal Injection DIE
READY TO DIE
Lethal Injection DIE
I WAS THERE TO WITNESS THE LAST ACT IN A TRAGEDY THAT BEGAN IN ANOTHER SMALL VIRGINIA TOWN.
CHATHAM, VA: ON JANUARY 29, 1993, RONALD FITZGERALD SNAPPED. A JEALOUS RAMPAGE OVER HIS GIRLFRIEND TRIGGERED SIX HOURS OF MURDER, ROBBERY, AND RAPE. ALL HIS VICTIMS HAD ONE WAY OR ANOTHER FUELED HIS JEALOUSY. IT WAS THE WORST CRIME SPREE IN CHATHAM'S HISTORY.
HE BEGAN LOOKING, WITHOUT SUCCESS, FOR A MAN WHO, HE SAID, HAD TAUNTED HIM, SAYING "YOU'RE FEEDING MY BABY" AND "I'VE HAD YOUR WOMAN."
AT 6 A.M. HE KILLED A MAN NAMED COY WHITE, WHILE A 13-YEAR-OLD GIRL WATCHED.
HE THEN DROVE THE GIRL TO A SECLUDED AREA, RAPED HER AND LEFT HER LOCKED IN A CAR TRUNK.
TAXI
NEXT HE WALKED TO THE MAIN ROAD AND FLAGGED DOWN HUIE MORRISON'S TAXI.
MORRISON'S BODY WAS LATER FOUND IN A CREEK, SHOT THREE TIMES.
FITZGERALD THEN DROVE THE CAB TO THE HOME OF THE GIRLFRIEND OF THE MAN HE WAS STILL LOOKING FOR.

FROM *McSweeney's*

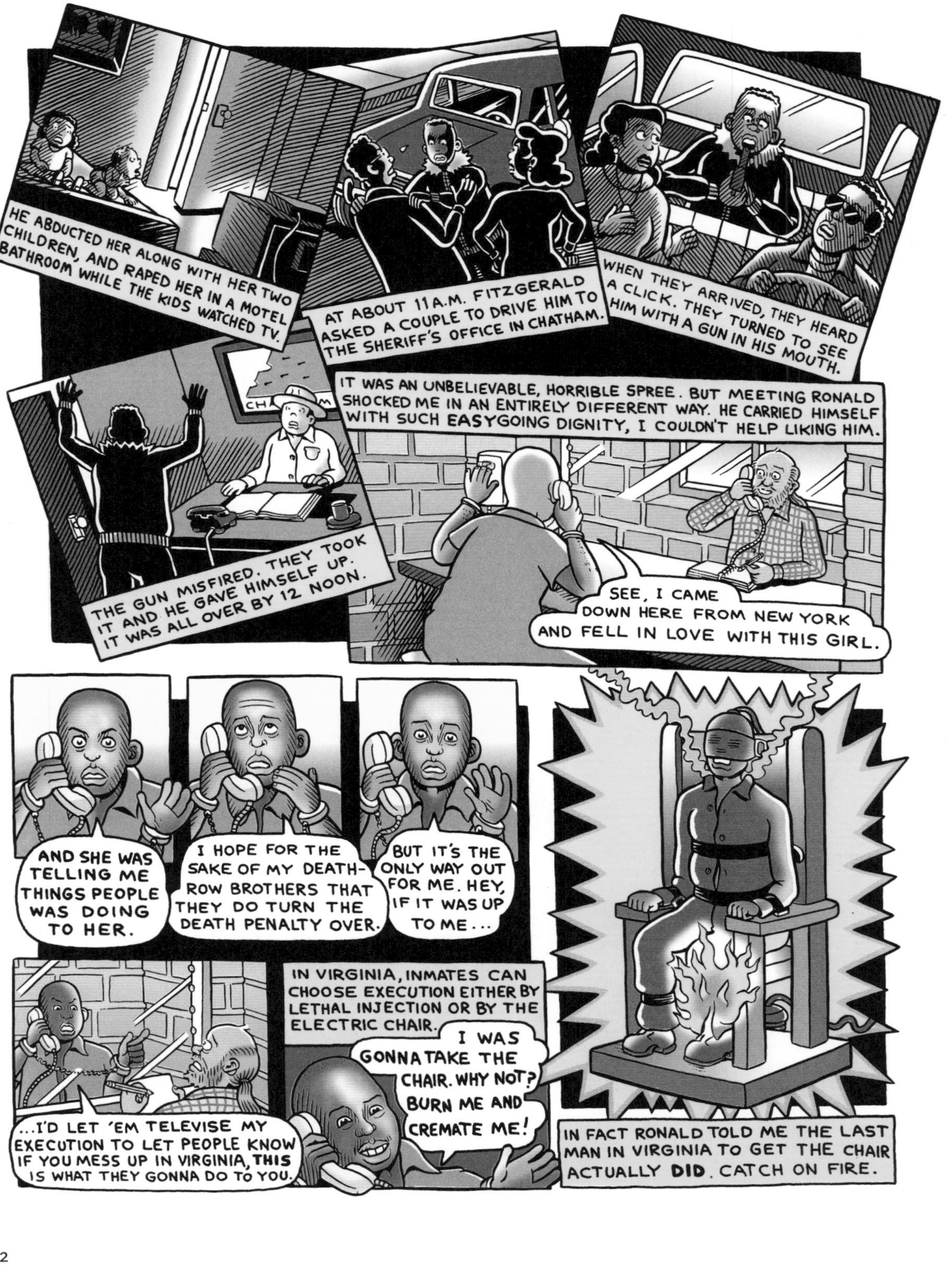
HE ABDUCTED HER ALONG WITH HER TWO CHILDREN, AND RAPED HER IN A MOTEL BATHROOM WHILE THE KIDS WATCHED TV.
AT ABOUT 11 A.M. FITZGERALD ASKED A COUPLE TO DRIVE HIM TO THE SHERIFF'S OFFICE IN CHATHAM.
WHEN THEY ARRIVED, THEY HEARD A CLICK. THEY TURNED TO SEE HIM WITH A GUN IN HIS MOUTH.
THE GUN MISFIRED. THEY TOOK IT AND HE GAVE HIMSELF UP. IT WAS ALL OVER BY 12 NOON.
IT WAS AN UNBELIEVABLE, HORRIBLE SPREE. BUT MEETING RONALD SHOCKED ME IN AN ENTIRELY DIFFERENT WAY. HE CARRIED HIMSELF WITH SUCH EASYGOING DIGNITY, I COULDN'T HELP LIKING HIM.
SEE, I CAME DOWN HERE FROM NEW YORK AND FELL IN LOVE WITH THIS GIRL.
AND SHE WAS TELLING ME THINGS PEOPLE WAS DOING TO HER.
I HOPE FOR THE SAKE OF MY DEATH-ROW BROTHERS THAT THEY DO TURN THE DEATH PENALTY OVER.
BUT IT'S THE ONLY WAY OUT FOR ME. HEY, IF IT WAS UP TO ME...
...I'D LET 'EM TELEVISE MY EXECUTION TO LET PEOPLE KNOW IF YOU MESS UP IN VIRGINIA, THIS IS WHAT THEY GONNA DO TO YOU.
IN VIRGINIA, INMATES CAN CHOOSE EXECUTION EITHER BY LETHAL INJECTION OR BY THE ELECTRIC CHAIR.
I WAS GONNA TAKE THE CHAIR. WHY NOT? BURN ME AND CREMATE ME!
IN FACT RONALD TOLD ME THE LAST MAN IN VIRGINIA TO GET THE CHAIR ACTUALLY DID. CATCH ON FIRE.

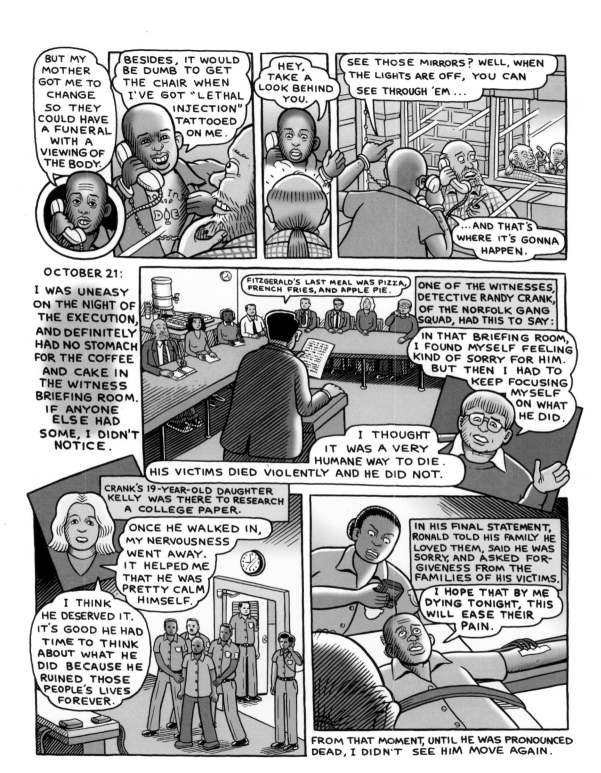

BUT MY MOTHER GOT ME TO CHANGE SO THEY COULD HAVE A FUNERAL WITH A VIEWING OF THE BODY.

BESIDES, IT WOULD BE DUMB TO GET THE CHAIR WHEN I'VE GOT "LETHAL INJECTION" TATTOOED ON ME.

HEY, TAKE A LOOK BEHIND YOU.

SEE THOSE MIRRORS? WELL, WHEN THE LIGHTS ARE OFF, YOU CAN SEE THROUGH 'EM ...

...AND THAT'S WHERE IT'S GONNA HAPPEN.

OCTOBER 21:

I WAS UNEASY ON THE NIGHT OF THE EXECUTION, AND DEFINITELY HAD NO STOMACH FOR THE COFFEE AND CAKE IN THE WITNESS BRIEFING ROOM. IF ANYONE ELSE HAD SOME, I DIDN'T NOTICE.

FITZGERALD'S LAST MEAL WAS PIZZA, FRENCH FRIES, AND APPLE PIE.

ONE OF THE WITNESSES, DETECTIVE RANDY CRANK, OF THE NORFOLK GANG SQUAD, HAD THIS TO SAY:

IN THAT BRIEFING ROOM, I FOUND MYSELF FEELING KIND OF SORRY FOR HIM. BUT THEN I HAD TO KEEP FOCUSING MYSELF ON WHAT HE DID.

I THOUGHT IT WAS A VERY HUMANE WAY TO DIE. HIS VICTIMS DIED VIOLENTLY AND HE DID NOT.

CRANK'S 19-YEAR-OLD DAUGHTER KELLY WAS THERE TO RESEARCH A COLLEGE PAPER.

ONCE HE WALKED IN, MY NERVOUSNESS WENT AWAY. IT HELPED ME THAT HE WAS PRETTY CALM HIMSELF.

I THINK HE DESERVED IT. IT'S GOOD HE HAD TIME TO THINK ABOUT WHAT HE DID BECAUSE HE RUINED THOSE PEOPLE'S LIVES FOREVER.

IN HIS FINAL STATEMENT, RONALD TOLD HIS FAMILY HE LOVED THEM, SAID HE WAS SORRY, AND ASKED FORGIVENESS FROM THE FAMILIES OF HIS VICTIMS.

I HOPE THAT BY ME DYING TONIGHT, THIS WILL EASE THEIR PAIN.

FROM THAT MOMENT, UNTIL HE WAS PRONOUNCED DEAD, I DIDN'T SEE HIM MOVE AGAIN.

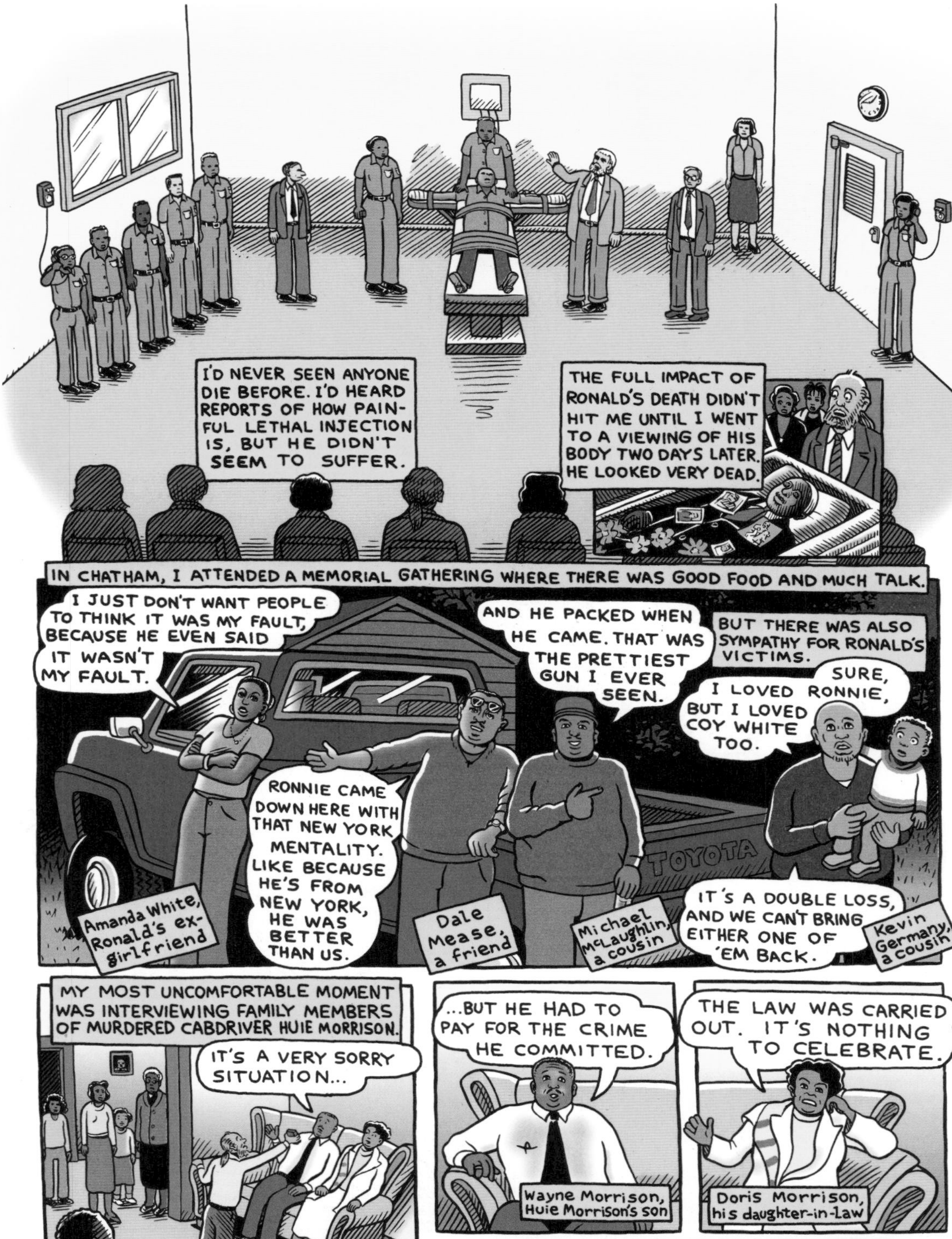

I'D NEVER SEEN ANYONE DIE BEFORE. I'D HEARD REPORTS OF HOW PAINFUL LETHAL INJECTION IS, BUT HE DIDN'T SEEM TO SUFFER.
THE FULL IMPACT OF RONALD'S DEATH DIDN'T HIT ME UNTIL I WENT TO A VIEWING OF HIS BODY TWO DAYS LATER. HE LOOKED VERY DEAD.
IN CHATHAM, I ATTENDED A MEMORIAL GATHERING WHERE THERE WAS GOOD FOOD AND MUCH TALK.
I JUST DON'T WANT PEOPLE TO THINK IT WAS MY FAULT, BECAUSE HE EVEN SAID IT WASN'T MY FAULT.
Amanda White, Ronald's ex-girlfriend
RONNIE CAME DOWN HERE WITH THAT NEW YORK MENTALITY. LIKE BECAUSE HE'S FROM NEW YORK, HE WAS BETTER THAN US.
Dale Mease, a friend
AND HE PACKED WHEN HE CAME. THAT WAS THE PRETTIEST GUN I EVER SEEN.
Michael McLaughlin, a cousin
TOYOTA
BUT THERE WAS ALSO SYMPATHY FOR RONALD'S VICTIMS.
SURE, I LOVED RONNIE, BUT I LOVED COY WHITE TOO.
IT'S A DOUBLE LOSS, AND WE CAN'T BRING EITHER ONE OF 'EM BACK.
Kevin Germany, a cousin
MY MOST UNCOMFORTABLE MOMENT WAS INTERVIEWING FAMILY MEMBERS OF MURDERED CABDRIVER HUIE MORRISON.
IT'S A VERY SORRY SITUATION...
...BUT HE HAD TO PAY FOR THE CRIME HE COMMITTED.
Wayne Morrison, Huie Morrison's son
THE LAW WAS CARRIED OUT. IT'S NOTHING TO CELEBRATE.
Doris Morrison, his daughter-in-law
HUIE MORRISON'S FUNERAL WAS ATTENDED BY NEARLY ONE THOUSAND MOURNERS.

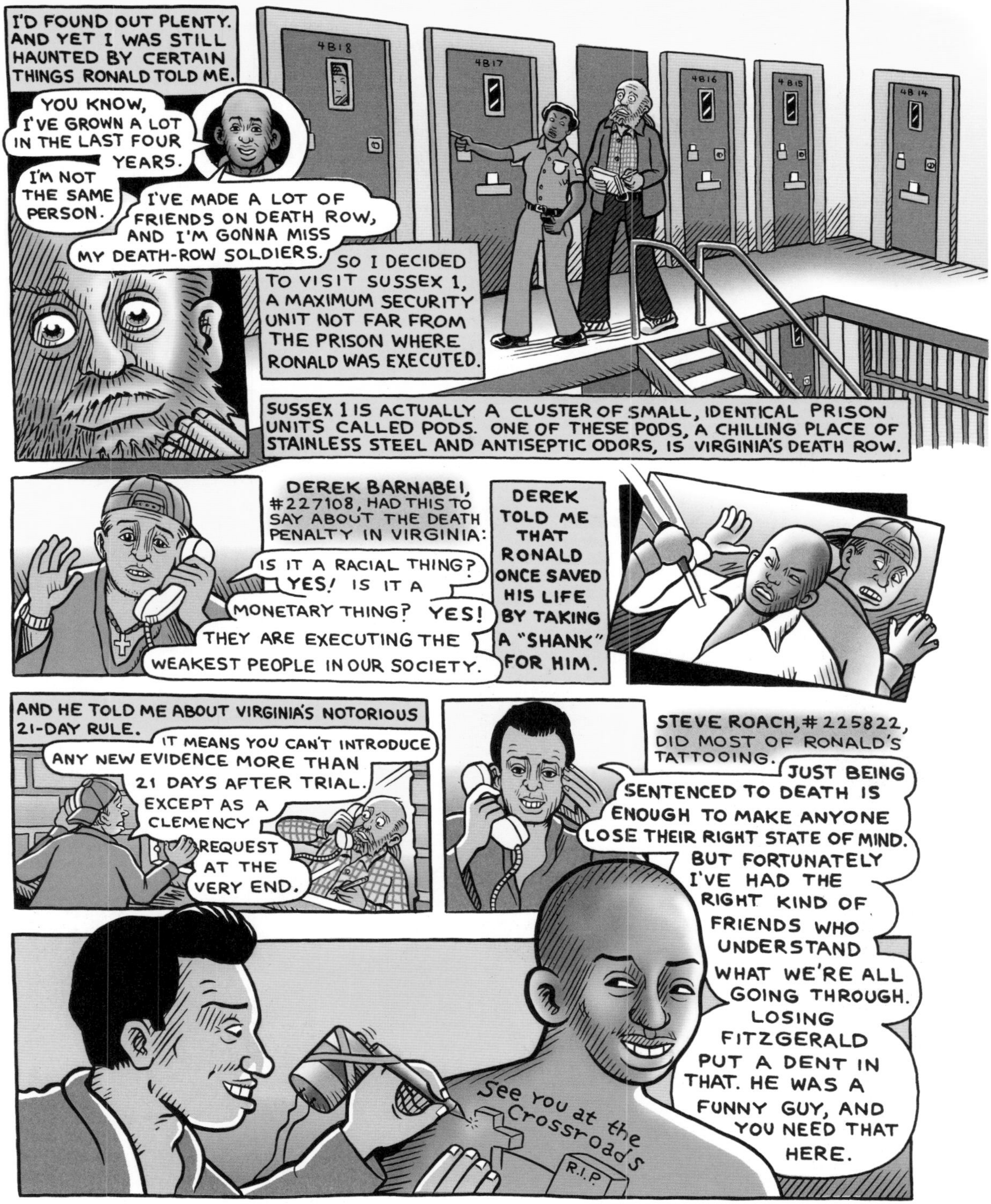

I'D FOUND OUT PLENTY. AND YET I WAS STILL HAUNTED BY CERTAIN THINGS RONALD TOLD ME.
YOU KNOW, I'VE GROWN A LOT IN THE LAST FOUR YEARS.
I'M NOT THE SAME PERSON.
I'VE MADE A LOT OF FRIENDS ON DEATH ROW, AND I'M GONNA MISS MY DEATH-ROW SOLDIERS.
4B18
4B17
4B16
4B15
4B14
SO I DECIDED TO VISIT SUSSEX 1, A MAXIMUM SECURITY UNIT NOT FAR FROM THE PRISON WHERE RONALD WAS EXECUTED.
SUSSEX 1 IS ACTUALLY A CLUSTER OF SMALL, IDENTICAL PRISON UNITS CALLED PODS. ONE OF THESE PODS, A CHILLING PLACE OF STAINLESS STEEL AND ANTISEPTIC ODORS, IS VIRGINIA'S DEATH ROW.
DEREK BARNABEI, #227108, HAD THIS TO SAY ABOUT THE DEATH PENALTY IN VIRGINIA:
IS IT A RACIAL THING? YES! IS IT A MONETARY THING? YES!
THEY ARE EXECUTING THE WEAKEST PEOPLE IN OUR SOCIETY.
DEREK TOLD ME THAT RONALD ONCE SAVED HIS LIFE BY TAKING A "SHANK" FOR HIM.
AND HE TOLD ME ABOUT VIRGINIA'S NOTORIOUS 21-DAY RULE.
IT MEANS YOU CAN'T INTRODUCE ANY NEW EVIDENCE MORE THAN 21 DAYS AFTER TRIAL.
EXCEPT AS A CLEMENCY REQUEST AT THE VERY END.
STEVE ROACH, #225822, DID MOST OF RONALD'S TATTOOING.
JUST BEING SENTENCED TO DEATH IS ENOUGH TO MAKE ANYONE LOSE THEIR RIGHT STATE OF MIND.
BUT FORTUNATELY I'VE HAD THE RIGHT KIND OF FRIENDS WHO UNDERSTAND WHAT WE'RE ALL GOING THROUGH. LOSING FITZGERALD PUT A DENT IN THAT. HE WAS A FUNNY GUY, AND YOU NEED THAT HERE.
See you at the Crossroads
R.I.P.

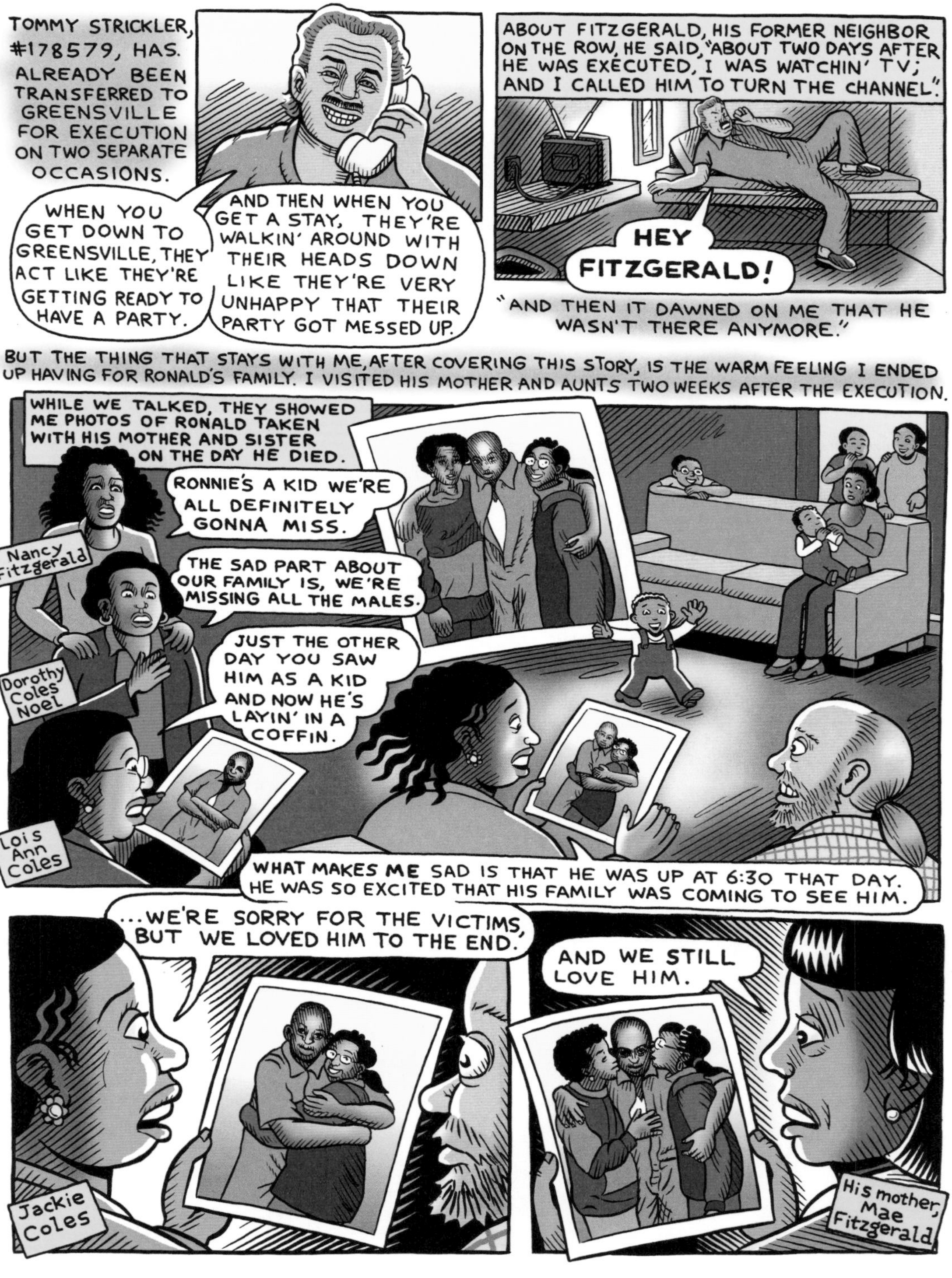
TOMMY STRICKLER, #178579, HAS ALREADY BEEN TRANSFERRED TO GREENSVILLE FOR EXECUTION ON TWO SEPARATE OCCASIONS.
WHEN YOU GET DOWN TO GREENSVILLE, THEY ACT LIKE THEY'RE GETTING READY TO HAVE A PARTY.
AND THEN WHEN YOU GET A STAY, THEY'RE WALKIN' AROUND WITH THEIR HEADS DOWN LIKE THEY'RE VERY UNHAPPY THAT THEIR PARTY GOT MESSED UP.
ABOUT FITZGERALD, HIS FORMER NEIGHBOR ON THE ROW, HE SAID, "ABOUT TWO DAYS AFTER HE WAS EXECUTED, I WAS WATCHIN' TV; AND I CALLED HIM TO TURN THE CHANNEL".
HEY FITZGERALD!
"AND THEN IT DAWNED ON ME THAT HE WASN'T THERE ANYMORE."
BUT THE THING THAT STAYS WITH ME, AFTER COVERING THIS STORY, IS THE WARM FEELING I ENDED UP HAVING FOR RONALD'S FAMILY. I VISITED HIS MOTHER AND AUNTS TWO WEEKS AFTER THE EXECUTION.
WHILE WE TALKED, THEY SHOWED ME PHOTOS OF RONALD TAKEN WITH HIS MOTHER AND SISTER ON THE DAY HE DIED.
RONNIE'S A KID WE'RE ALL DEFINITELY GONNA MISS.
Nancy Fitzgerald
THE SAD PART ABOUT OUR FAMILY IS, WE'RE MISSING ALL THE MALES.
Dorothy Coles Noel
JUST THE OTHER DAY YOU SAW HIM AS A KID AND NOW HE'S LAYIN' IN A COFFIN.
Lois Ann Coles
WHAT MAKES ME SAD IS THAT HE WAS UP AT 6:30 THAT DAY. HE WAS SO EXCITED THAT HIS FAMILY WAS COMING TO SEE HIM.
...WE'RE SORRY FOR THE VICTIMS, BUT WE LOVED HIM TO THE END.
Jackie Coles
AND WE STILL LOVE HIM.
His mother, Mae Fitzgerald

THE GIFT

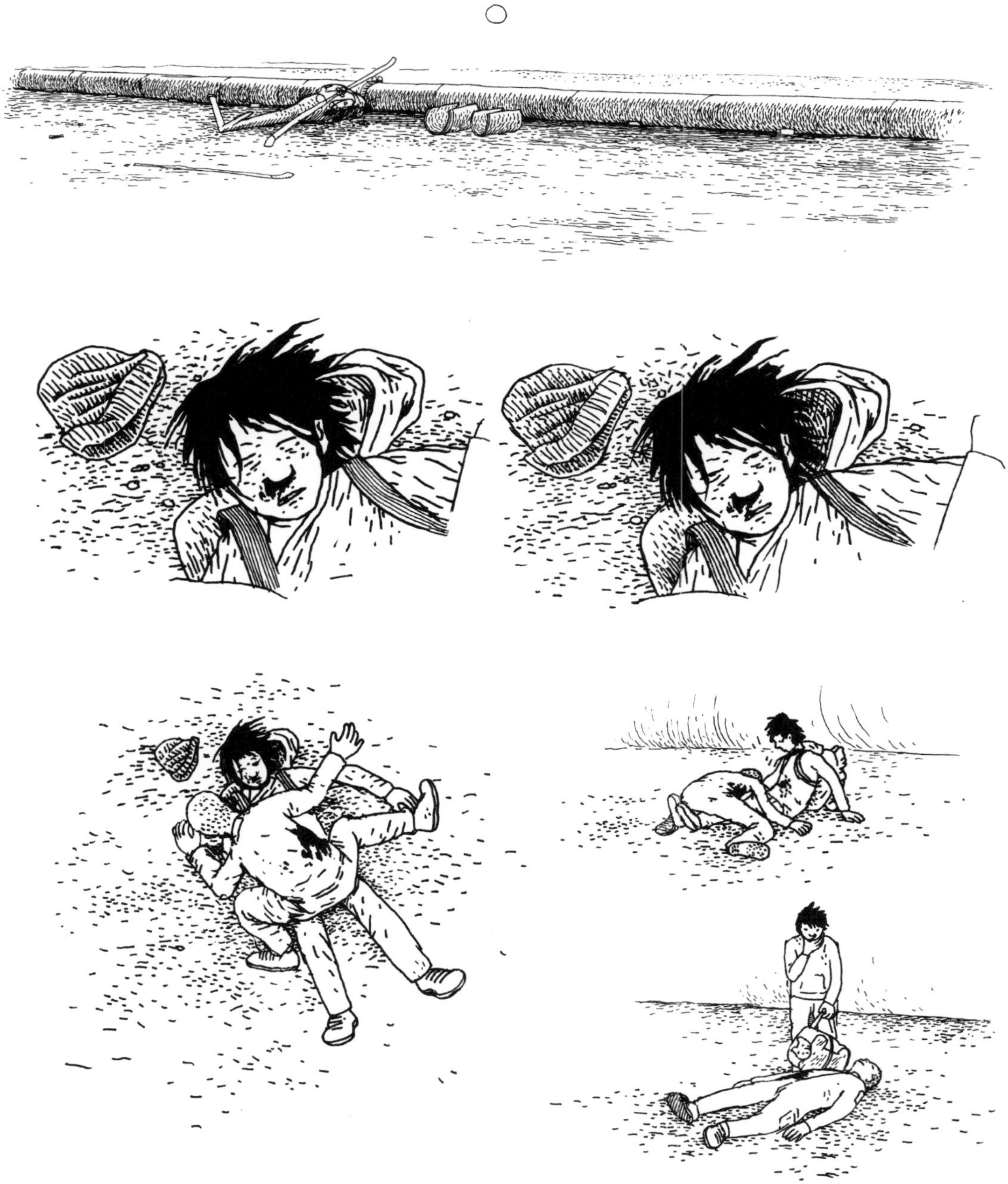

FROM *Dogs and Water*

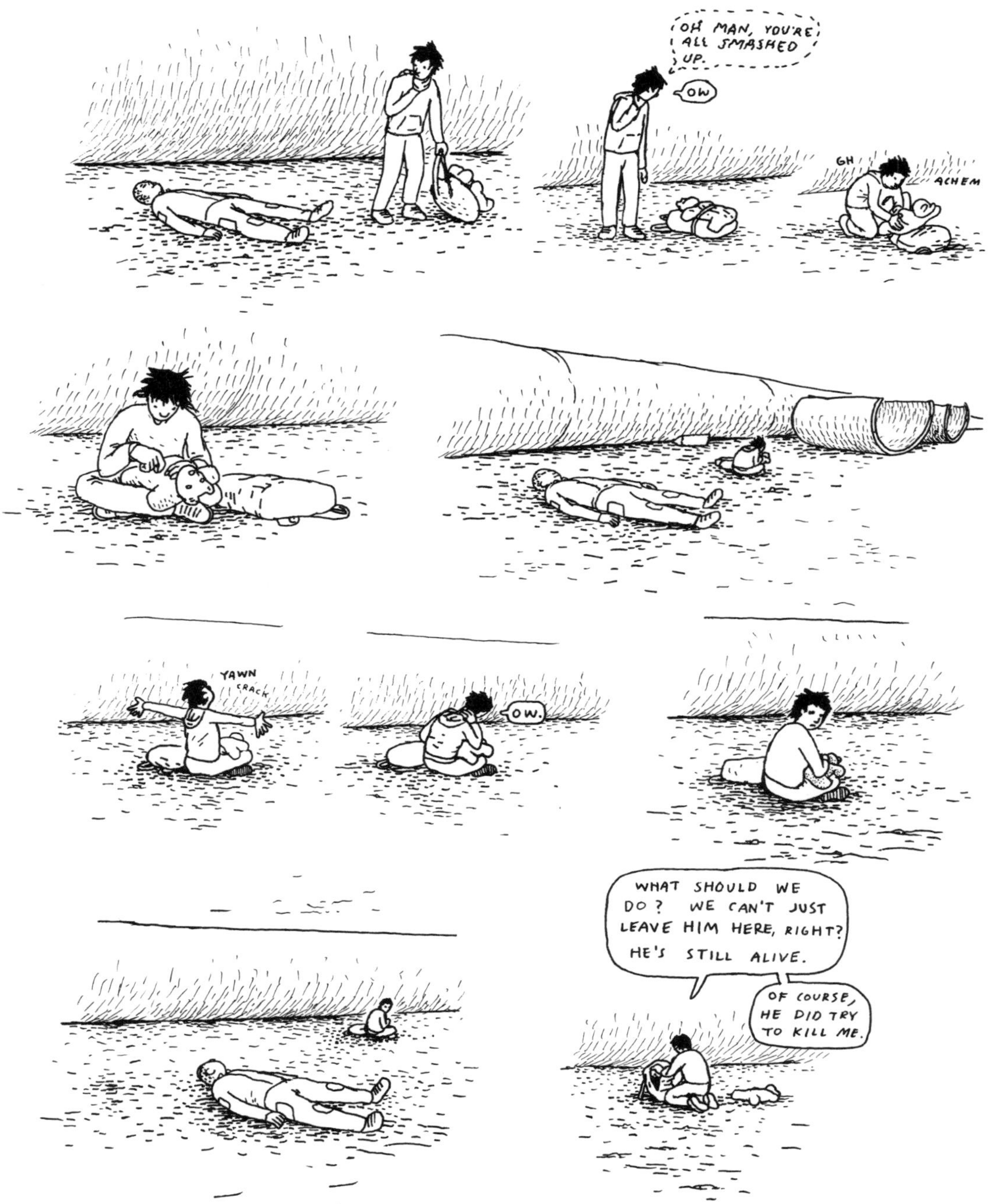
OH MAN, YOU'RE ALL SMASHED UP.
OW
GH
ACHEM
YAWN
CRACK
OW.
WHAT SHOULD WE DO? WE CAN'T JUST LEAVE HIM HERE, RIGHT? HE'S STILL ALIVE.
OF COURSE, HE DID TRY TO KILL ME.

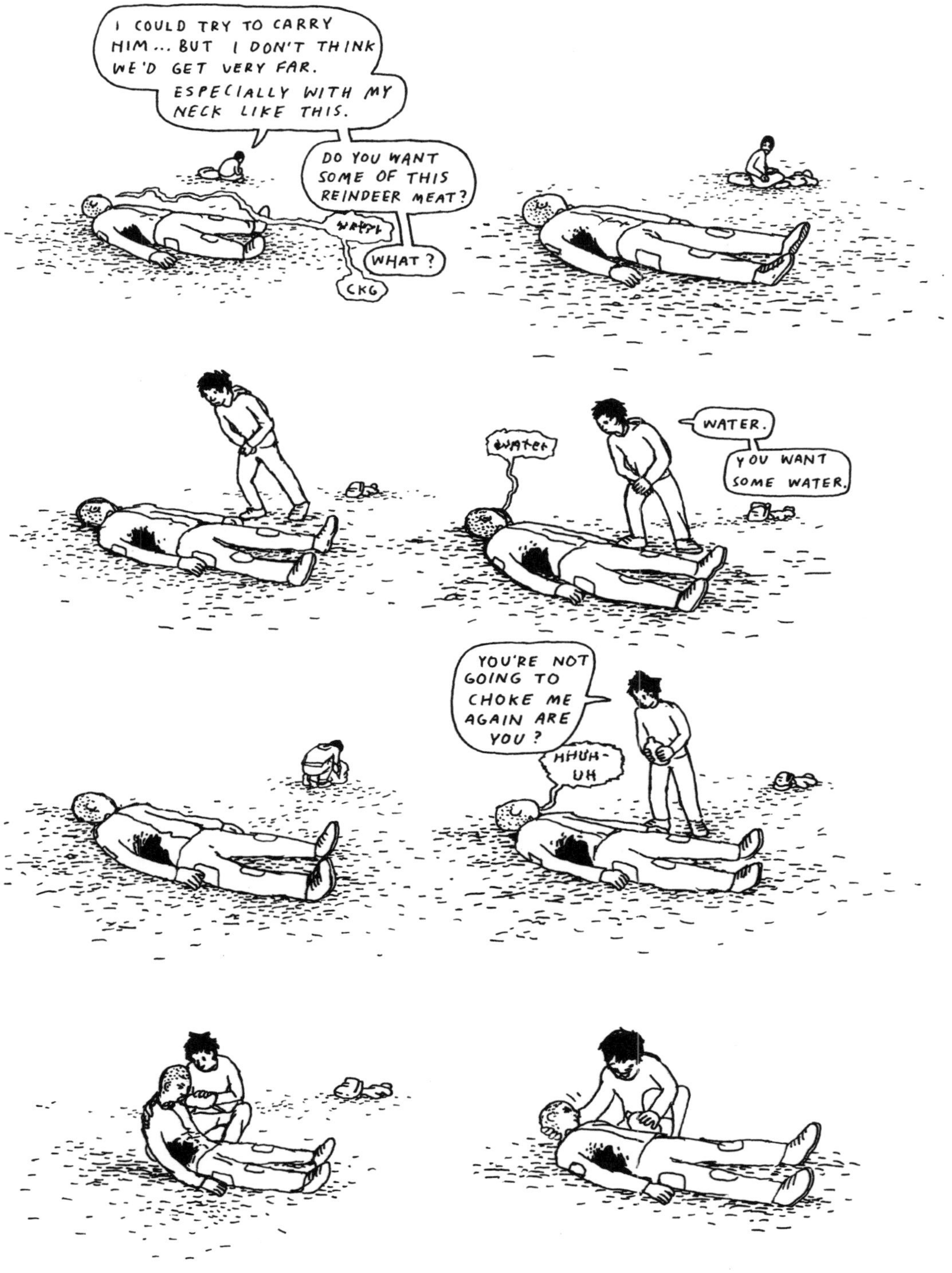

I COULD TRY TO CARRY HIM... BUT I DON'T THINK WE'D GET VERY FAR.
ESPECIALLY WITH MY NECK LIKE THIS.
DO YOU WANT SOME OF THIS REINDEER MEAT?
WHAT?
CKG
water
WATER.
YOU WANT SOME WATER.
YOU'RE NOT GOING TO CHOKE ME AGAIN ARE YOU?
HHUH-UH

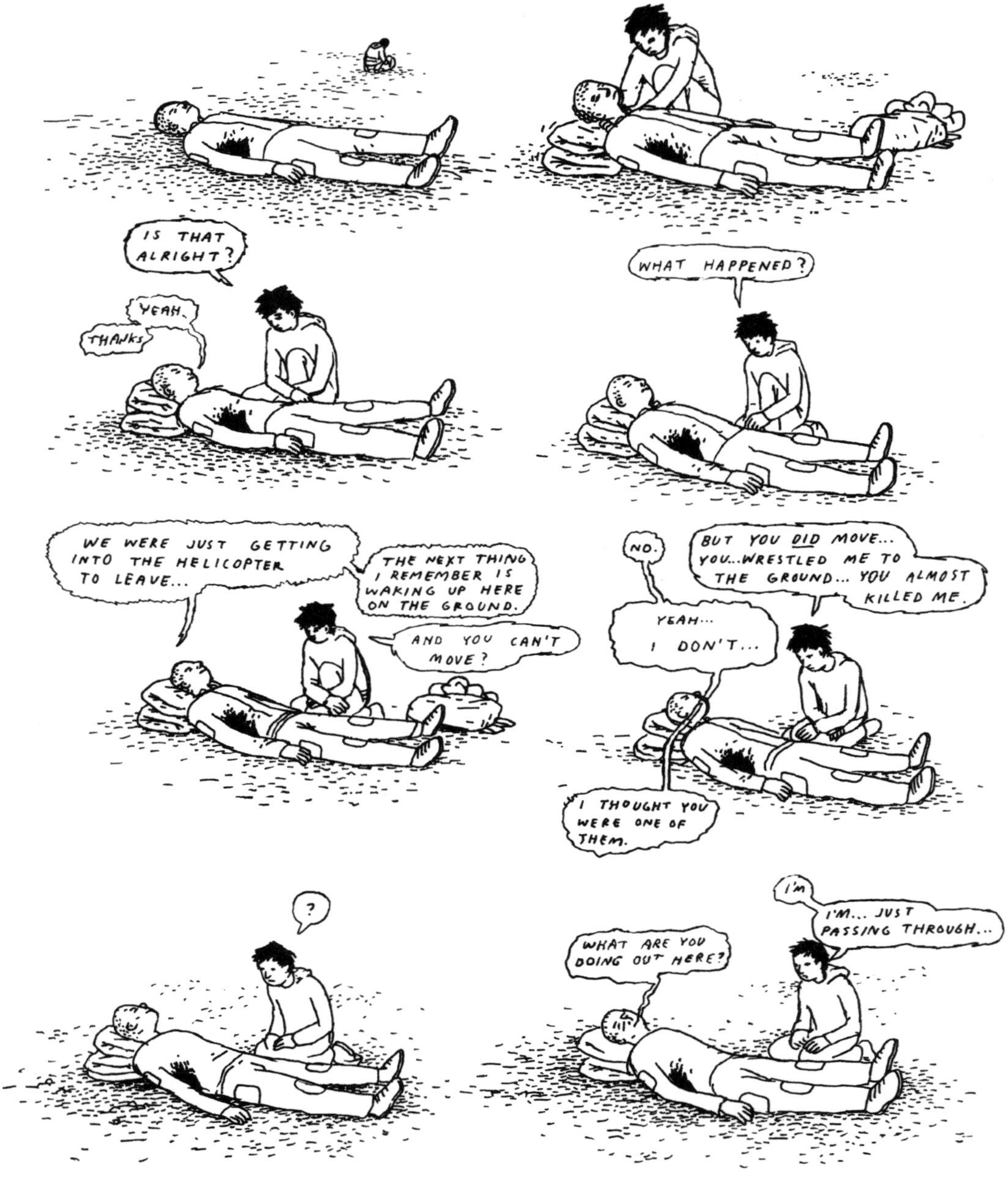
IS THAT ALRIGHT?
YEAH.
THANKS
WHAT HAPPENED?
WE WERE JUST GETTING INTO THE HELICOPTER TO LEAVE...
THE NEXT THING I REMEMBER IS WAKING UP HERE ON THE GROUND.
AND YOU CAN'T MOVE?
NO.
BUT YOU DID MOVE... YOU...WRESTLED ME TO THE GROUND... YOU ALMOST KILLED ME.
YEAH... I DON'T...
I THOUGHT YOU WERE ONE OF THEM.
?
WHAT ARE YOU DOING OUT HERE?
I'M
I'M... JUST PASSING THROUGH...

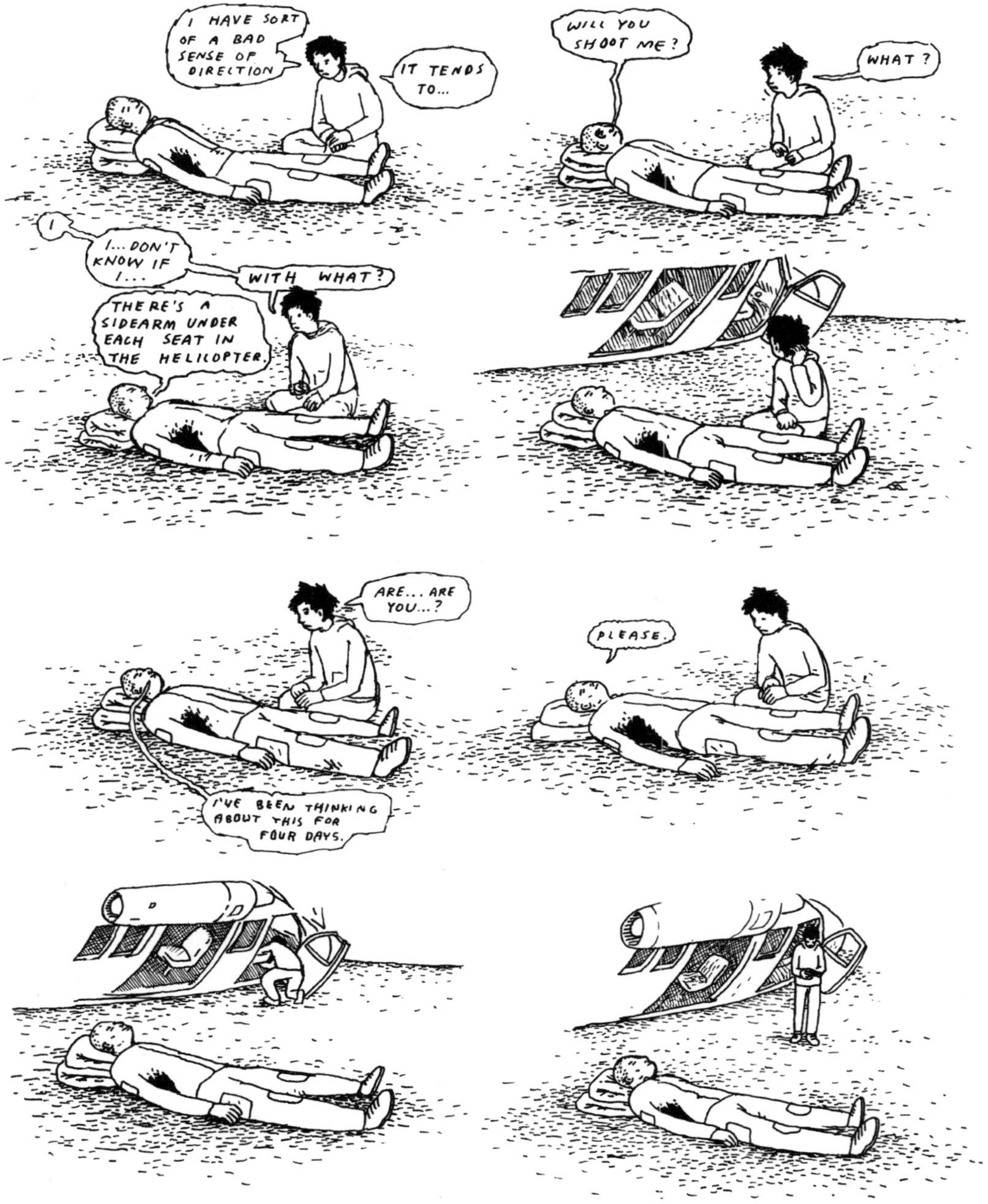
I HAVE SORT OF A BAD SENSE OF DIRECTION
IT TENDS TO...
WILL YOU SHOOT ME?
WHAT?
I
I... DON'T KNOW IF I...
WITH WHAT?
THERE'S A SIDEARM UNDER EACH SEAT IN THE HELICOPTER.
ARE... ARE YOU...?
I'VE BEEN THINKING ABOUT THIS FOR FOUR DAYS.
PLEASE.

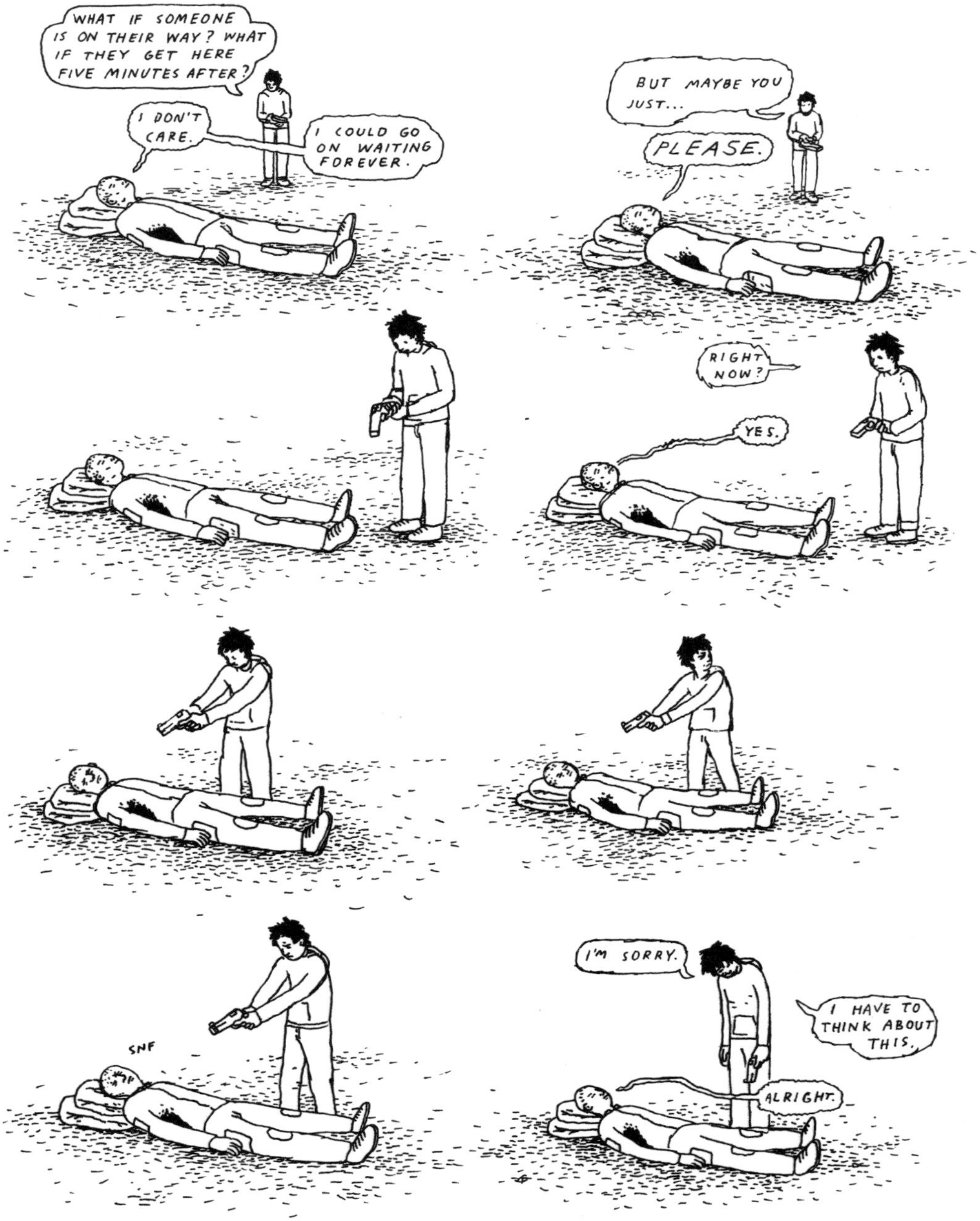
WHAT IF SOMEONE IS ON THEIR WAY? WHAT IF THEY GET HERE FIVE MINUTES AFTER?
I DON'T CARE.
I COULD GO ON WAITING FOREVER.
BUT MAYBE YOU JUST...
PLEASE.
RIGHT NOW?
YES.
SNF
I'M SORRY.
I HAVE TO THINK ABOUT THIS.
ALRIGHT.

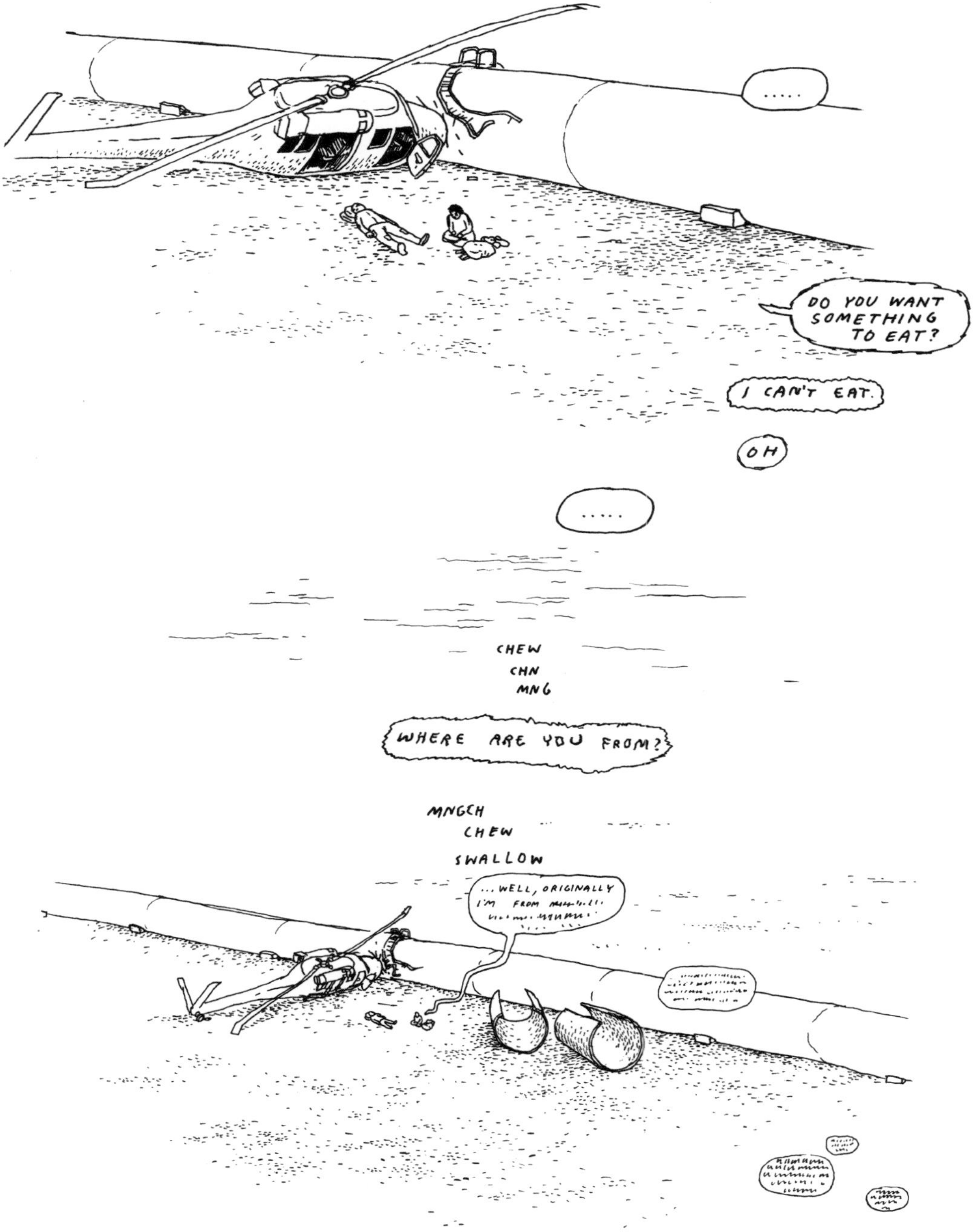
.....
DO YOU WANT SOMETHING TO EAT?
I CAN'T EAT.
OH
.....
CHEW
CHN
MNG
WHERE ARE YOU FROM?
MNGCH
CHEW
SWALLOW
...WELL, ORIGINALLY I'M FROM

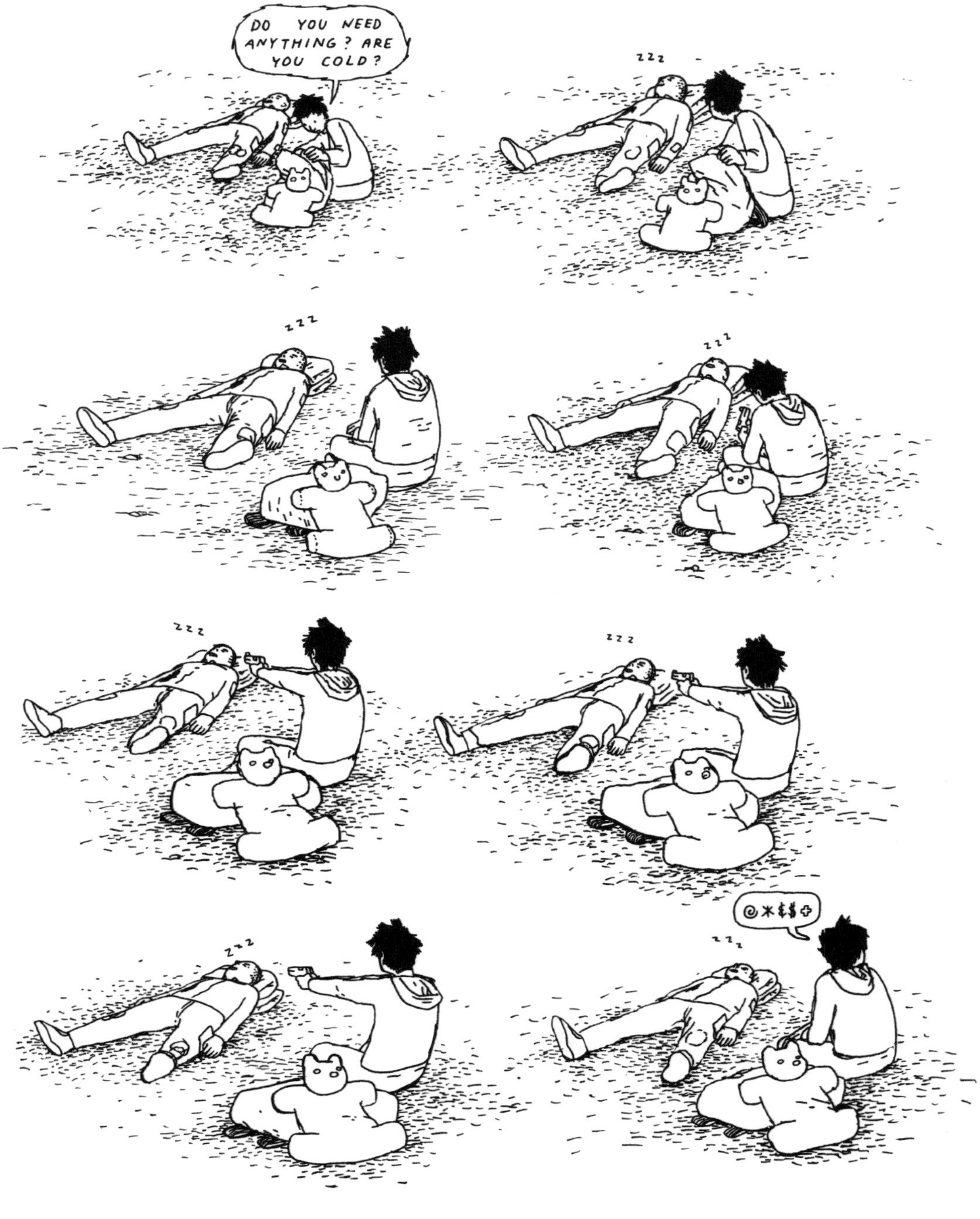
DO YOU NEED ANYTHING? ARE YOU COLD?
zzz
zzz
zzz
zzz
zzz
zzz
@*$$✤
zzz

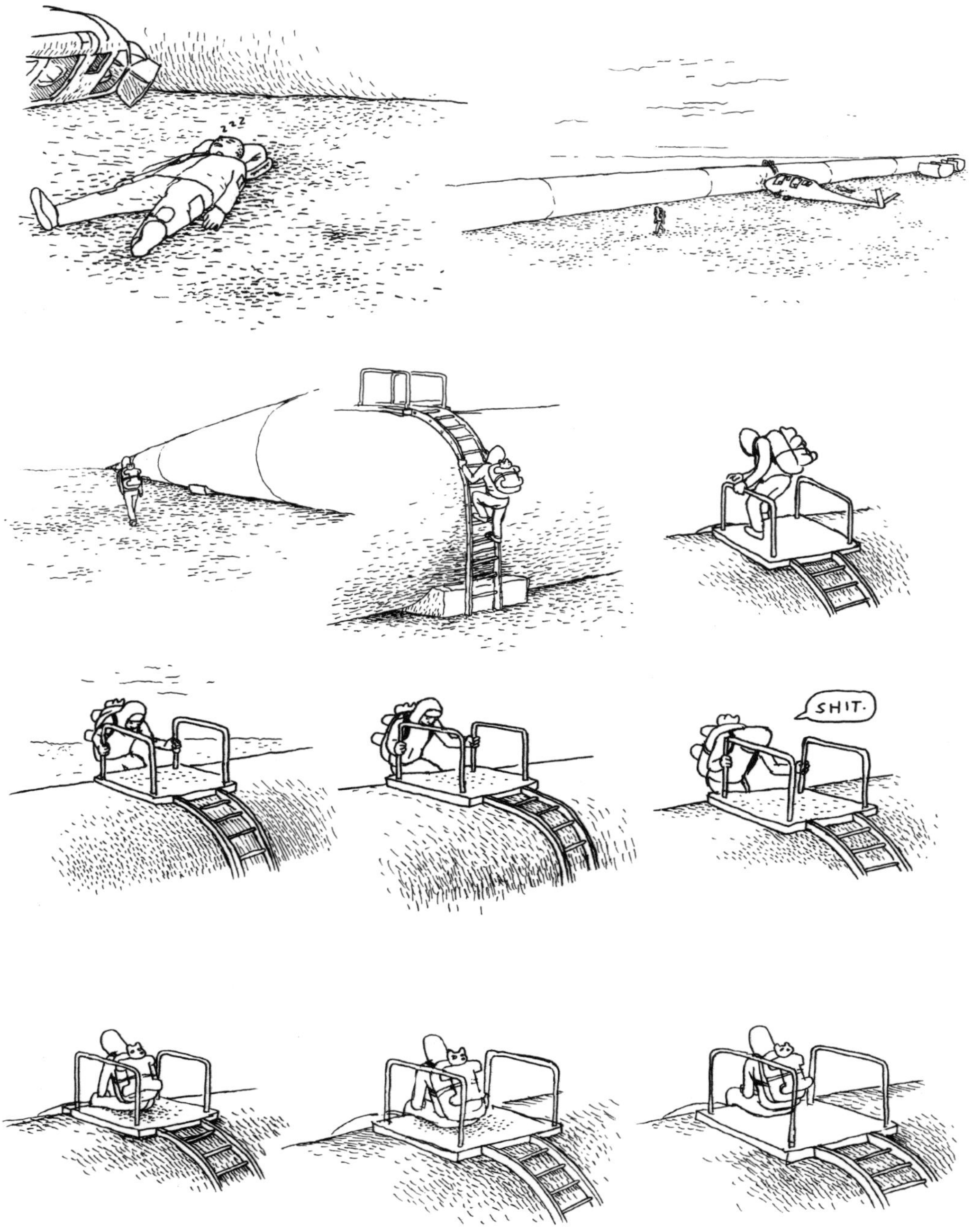
zzz
SHIT.

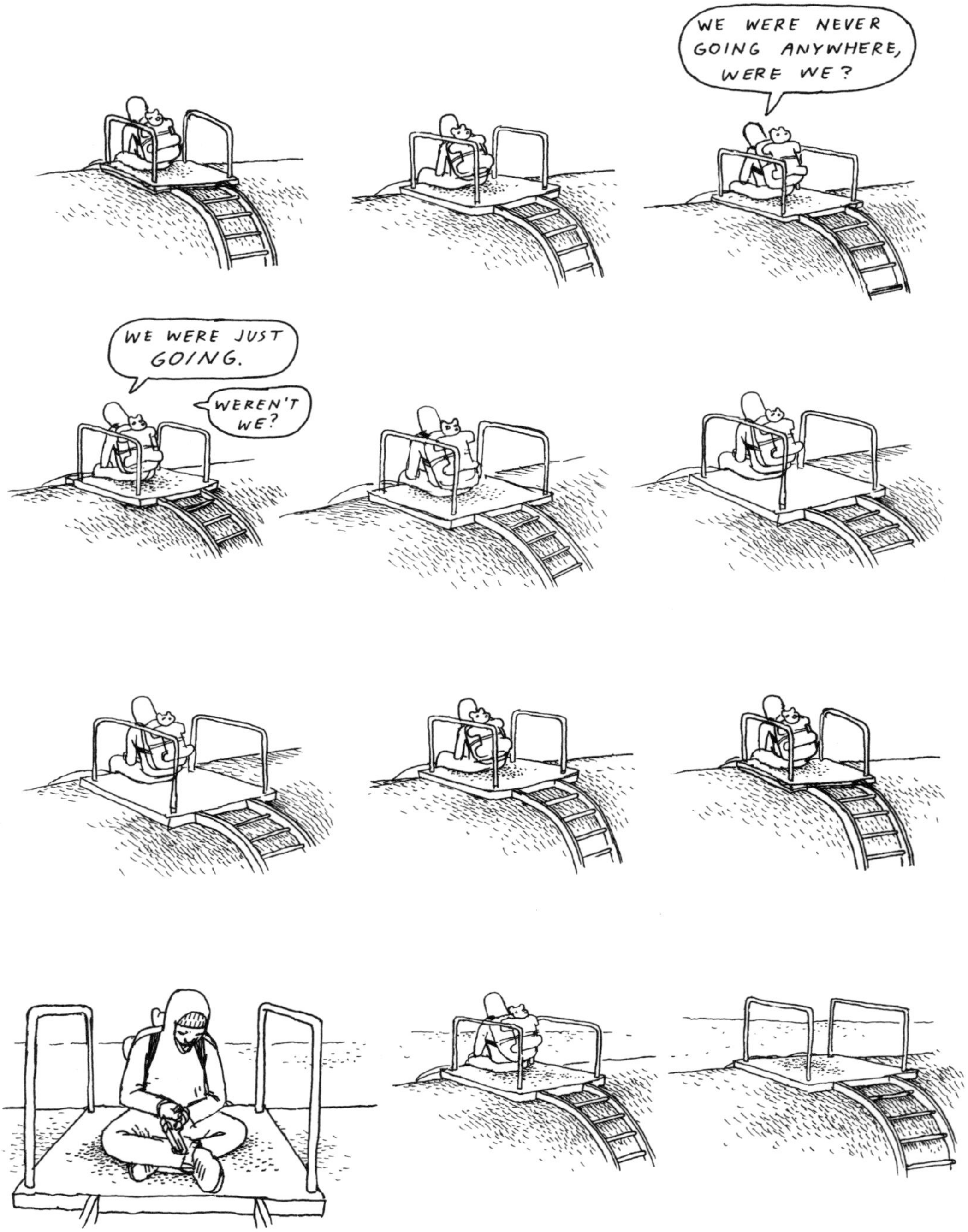
WE WERE NEVER GOING ANYWHERE, WERE WE?
WE WERE JUST GOING.
WEREN'T WE?

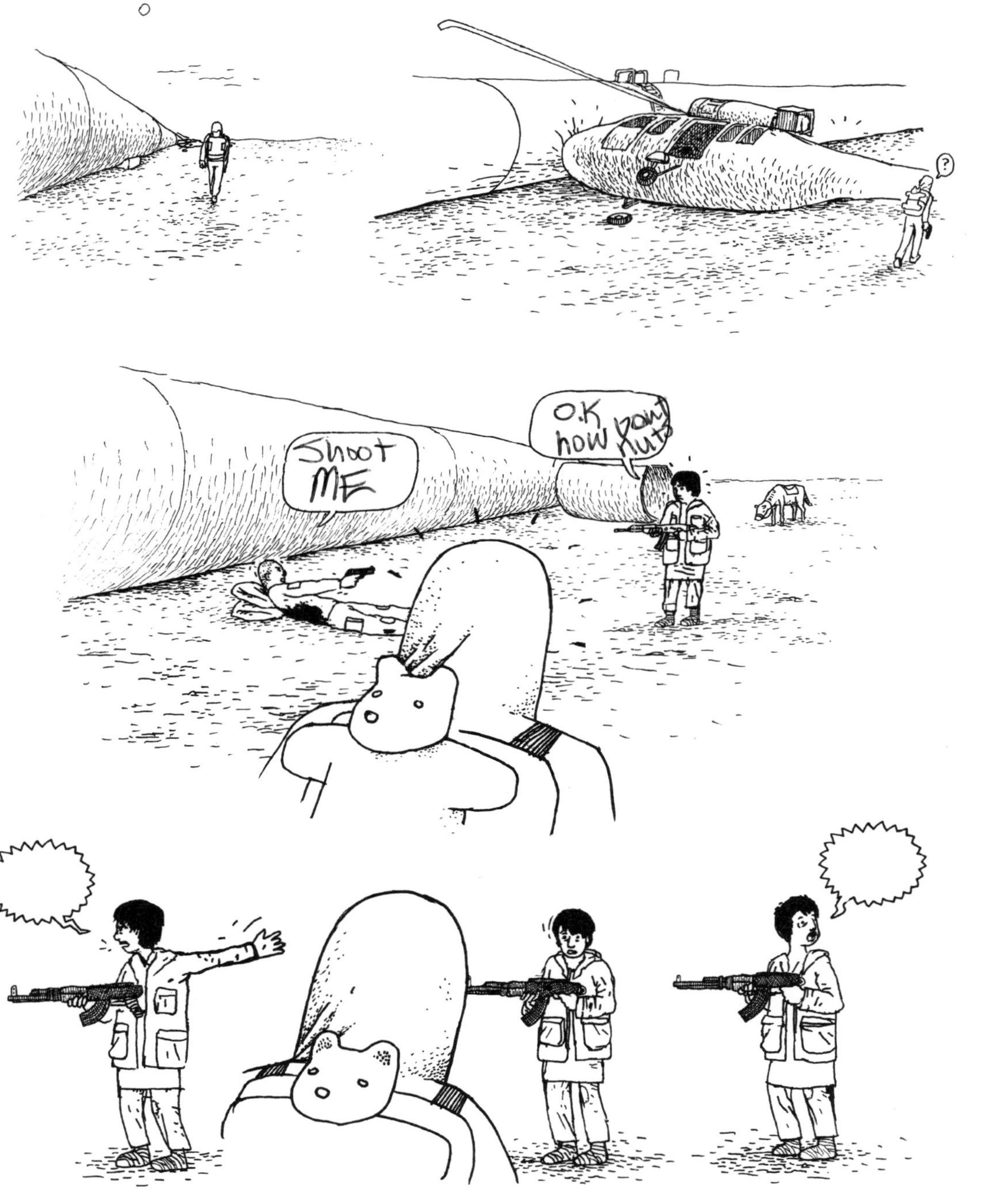
Shoot ME
O.K how
Dont Nuts

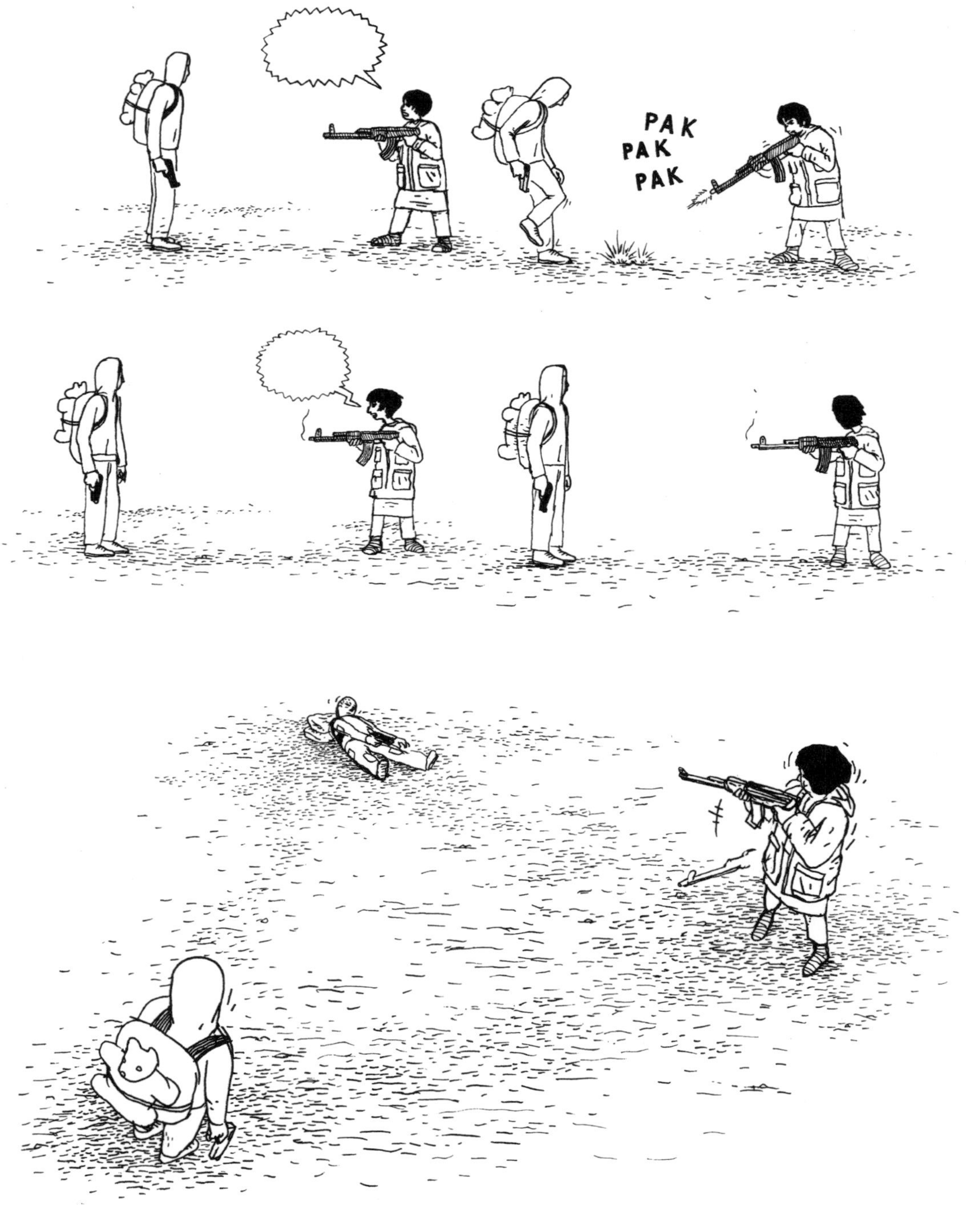
PAK
PAK
PAK

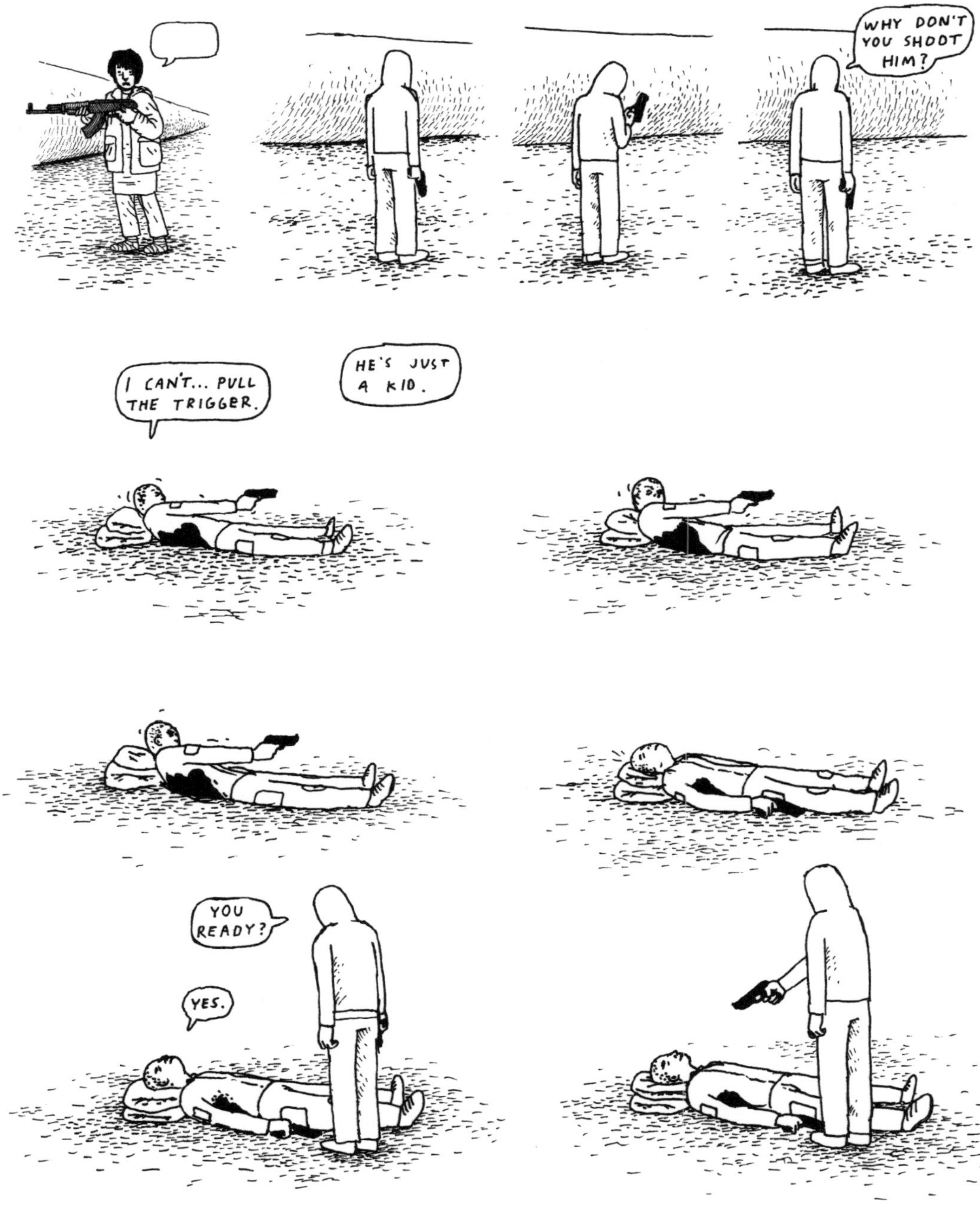

WHY DON'T YOU SHOOT HIM?
I CAN'T... PULL THE TRIGGER.
HE'S JUST A KID.
YOU READY?
YES.

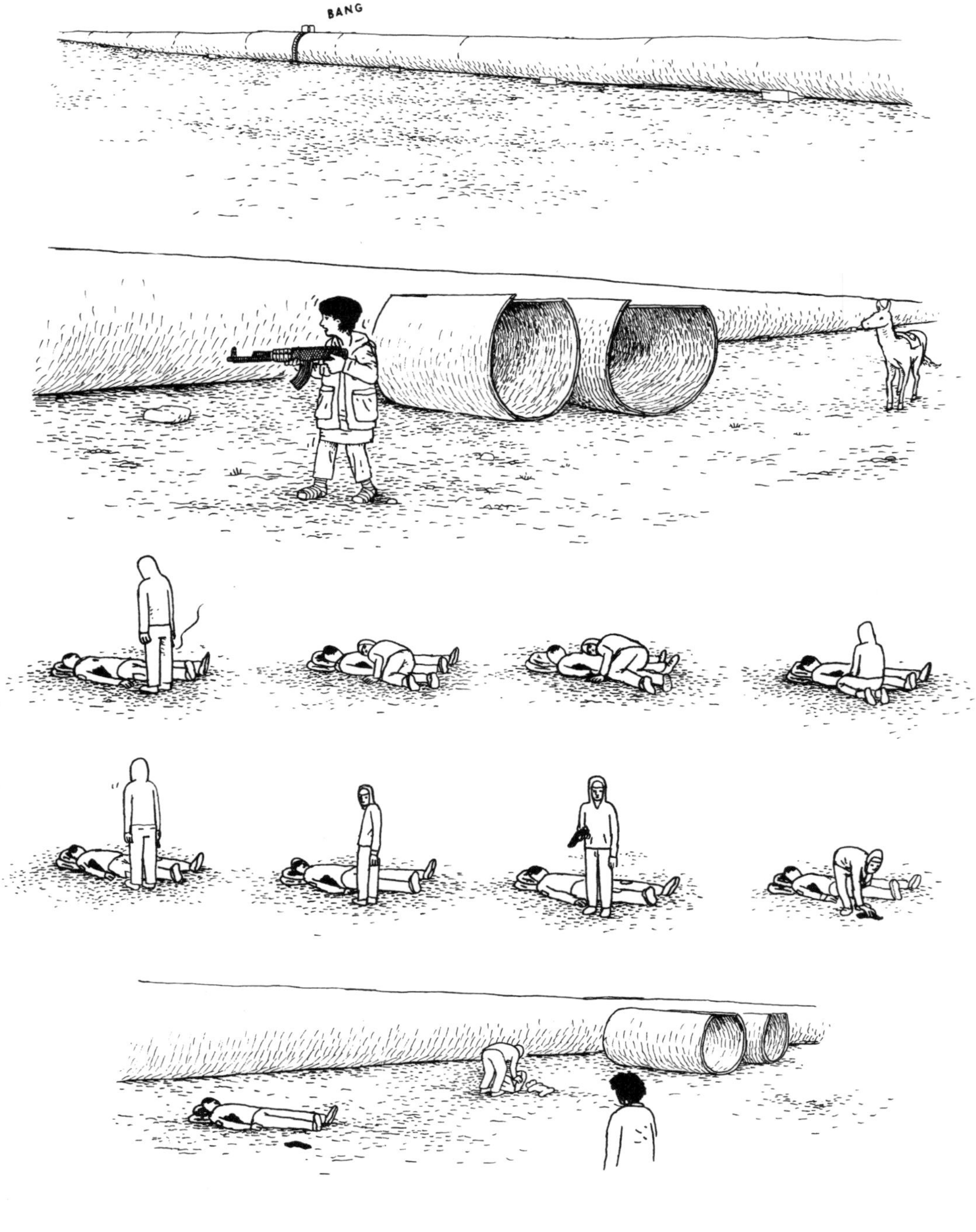
BANG

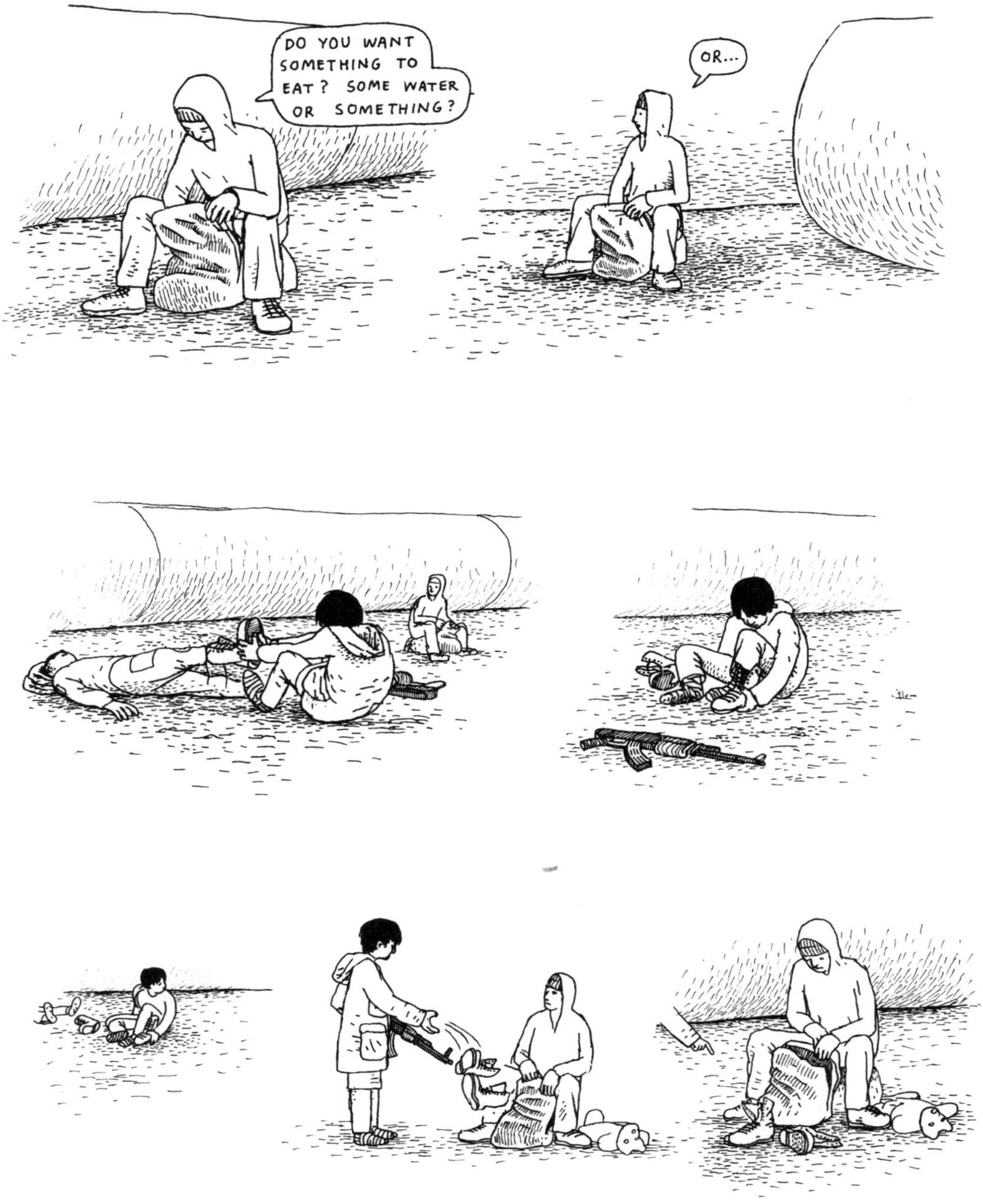
DO YOU WANT SOMETHING TO EAT? SOME WATER OR SOMETHING?
OR...

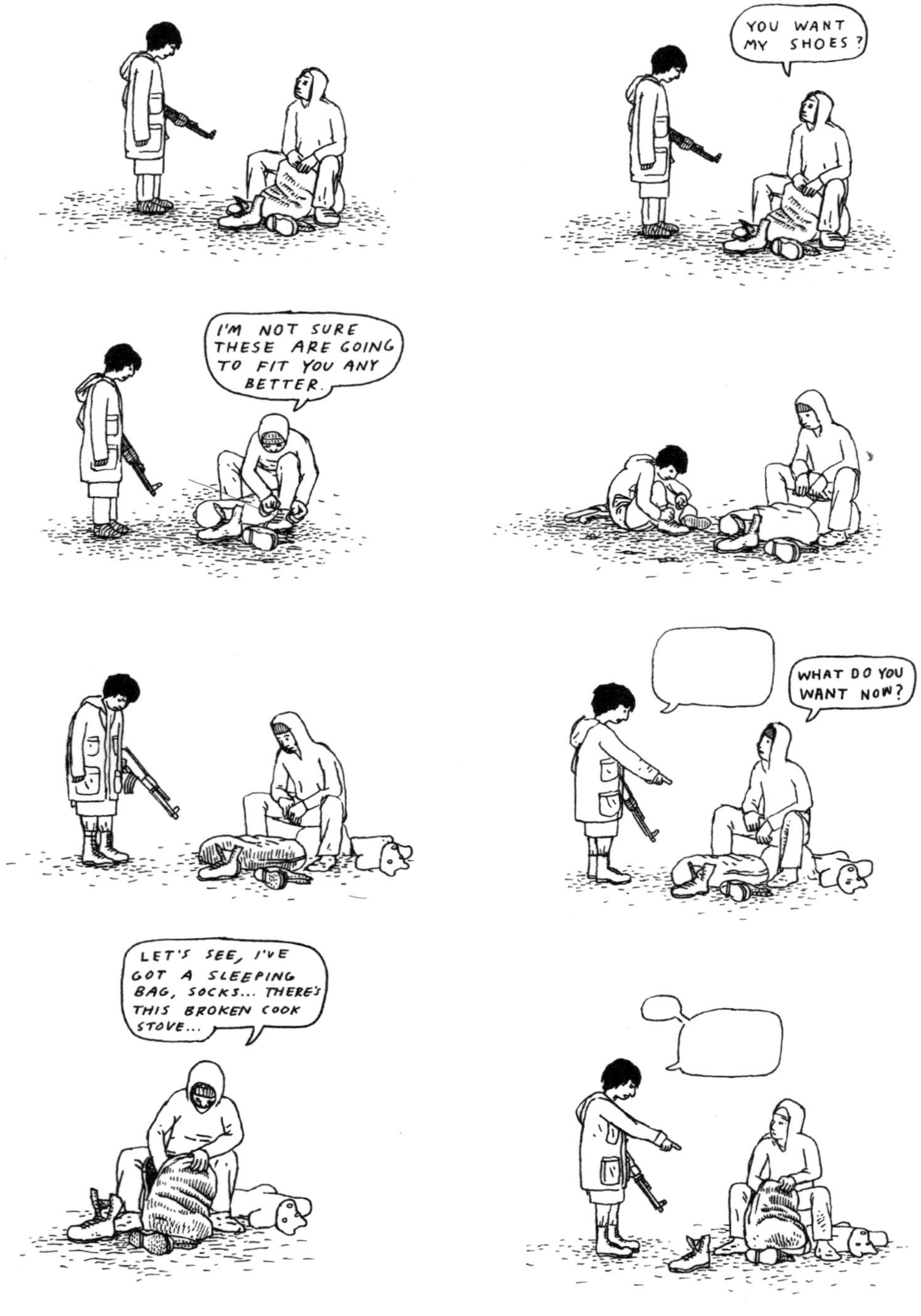
YOU WANT MY SHOES?
I'M NOT SURE THESE ARE GOING TO FIT YOU ANY BETTER.
WHAT DO YOU WANT NOW?
LET'S SEE, I'VE GOT A SLEEPING BAG, SOCKS... THERE'S THIS BROKEN COOK STOVE...

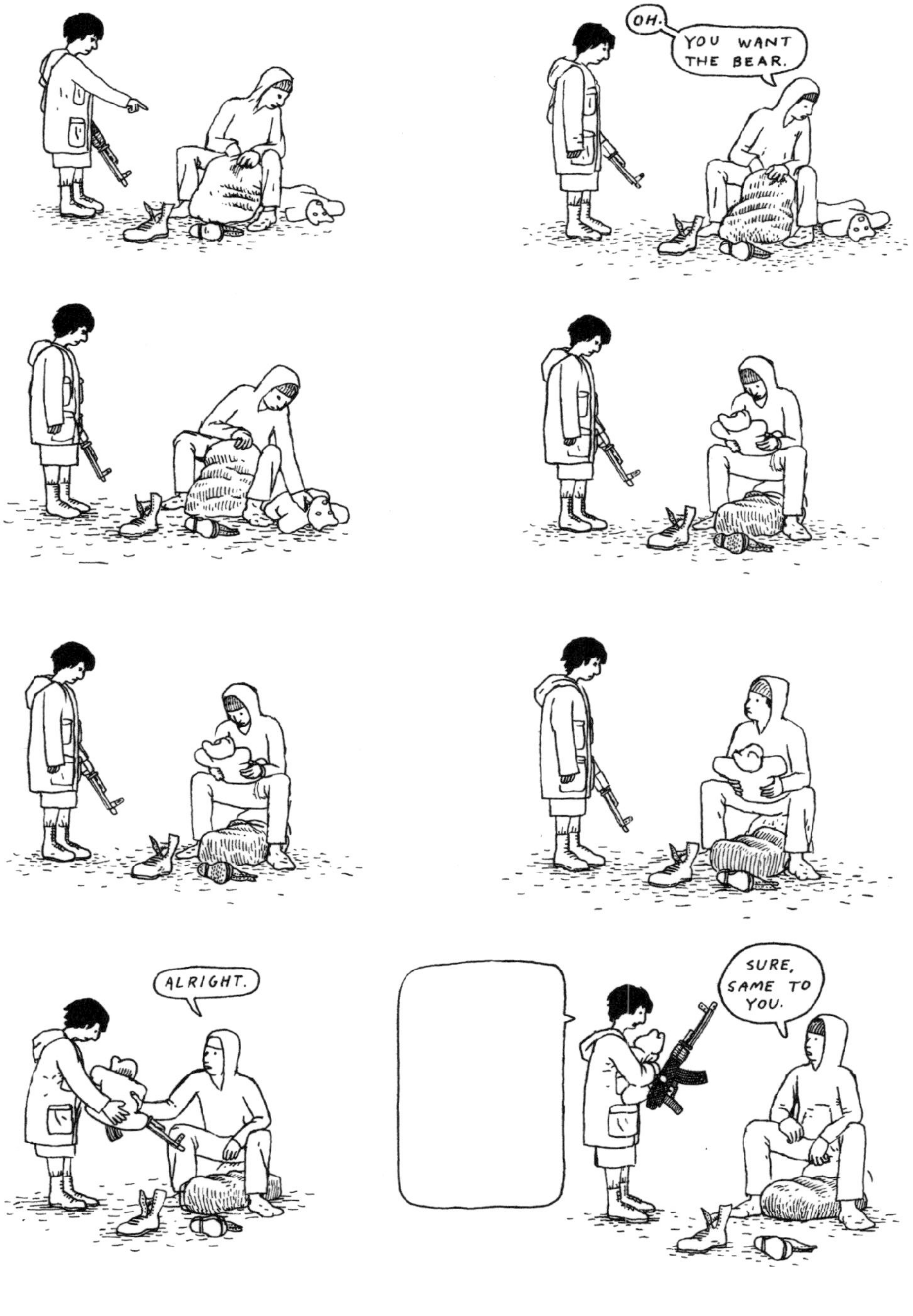
OH.
YOU WANT THE BEAR.
ALRIGHT.
SURE, SAME TO YOU.

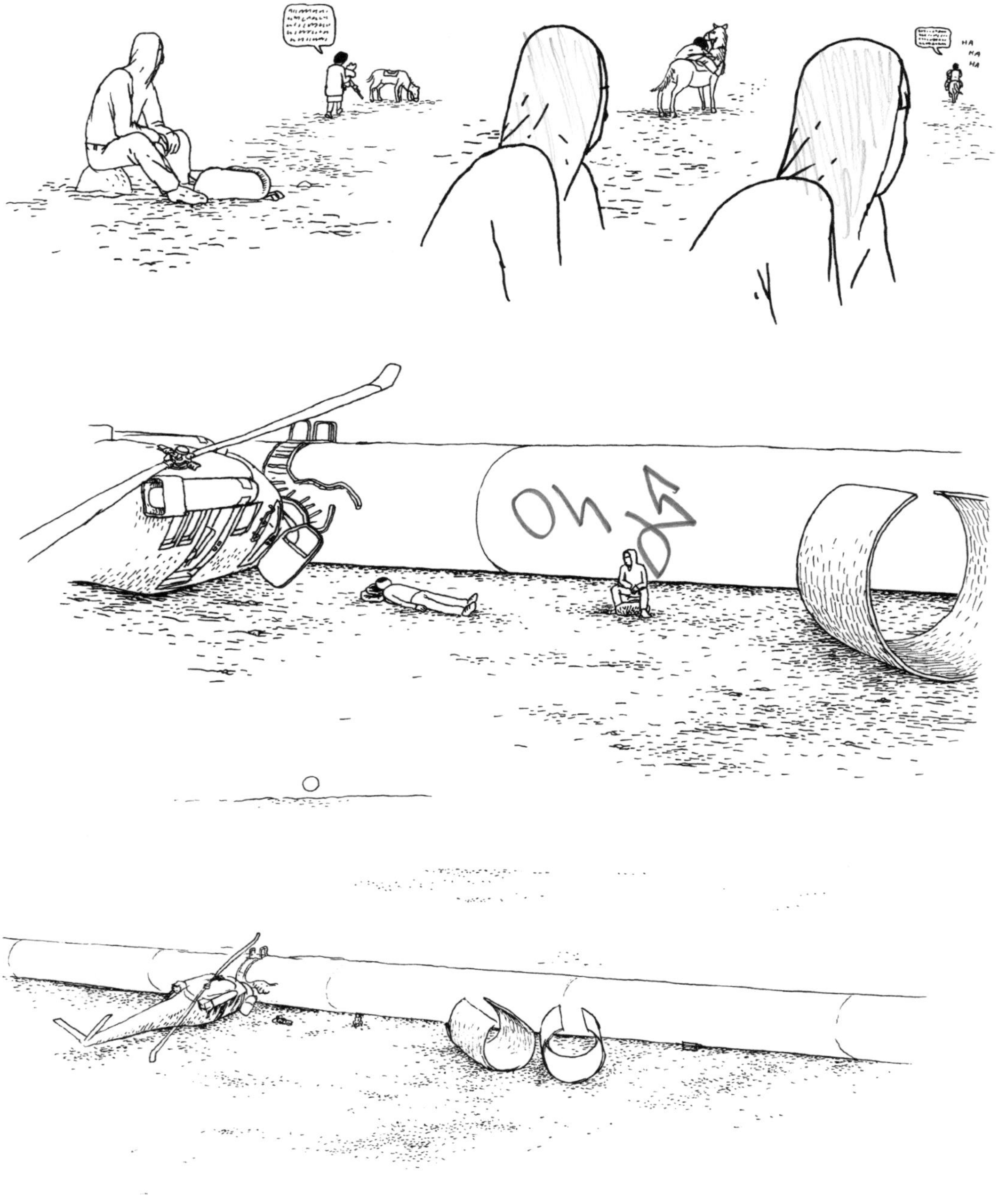
HA HA HA

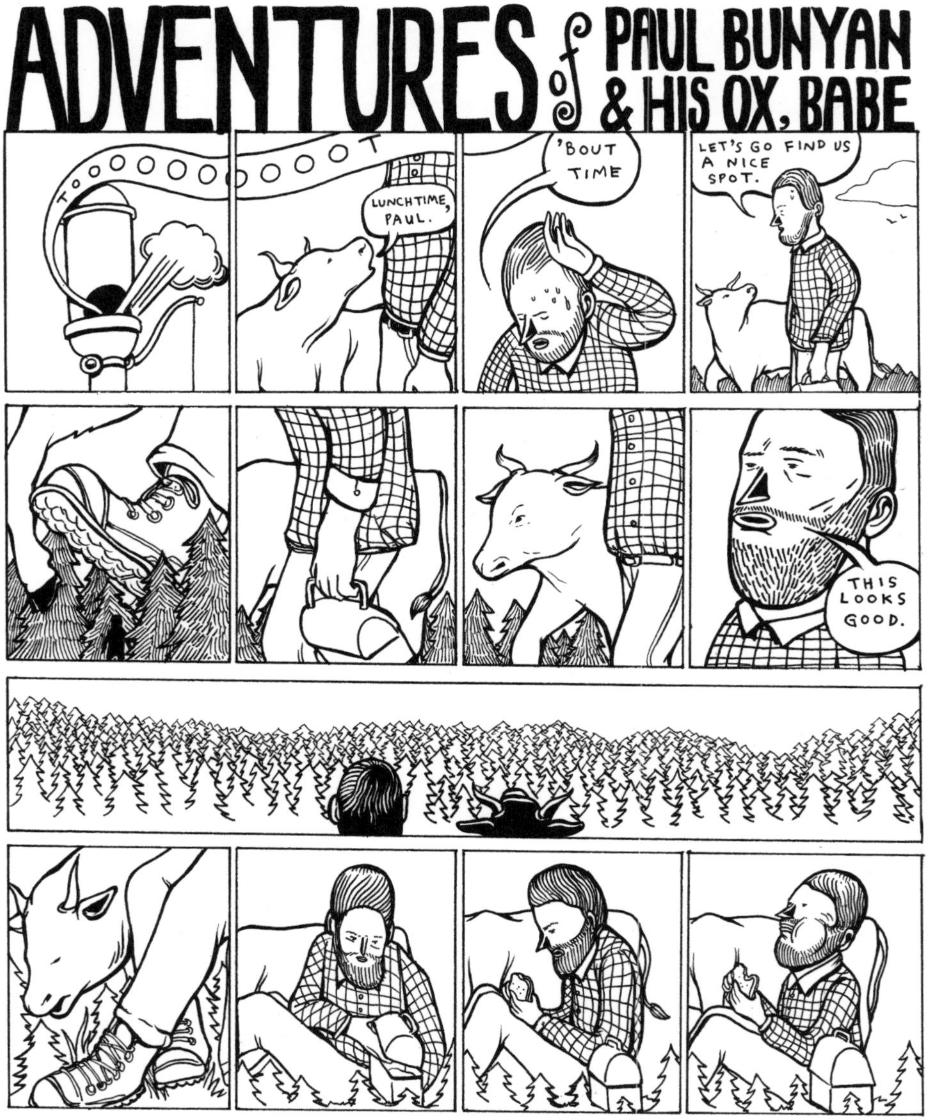
ADVENTURES of PAUL BUNYAN & HIS OX, BABE
TOOOOOOOOOOOT
LUNCHTIME, PAUL.
'BOUT TIME
LET'S GO FIND US A NICE SPOT.
THIS LOOKS GOOD.

FROM *Tales of Woodsman Pete*

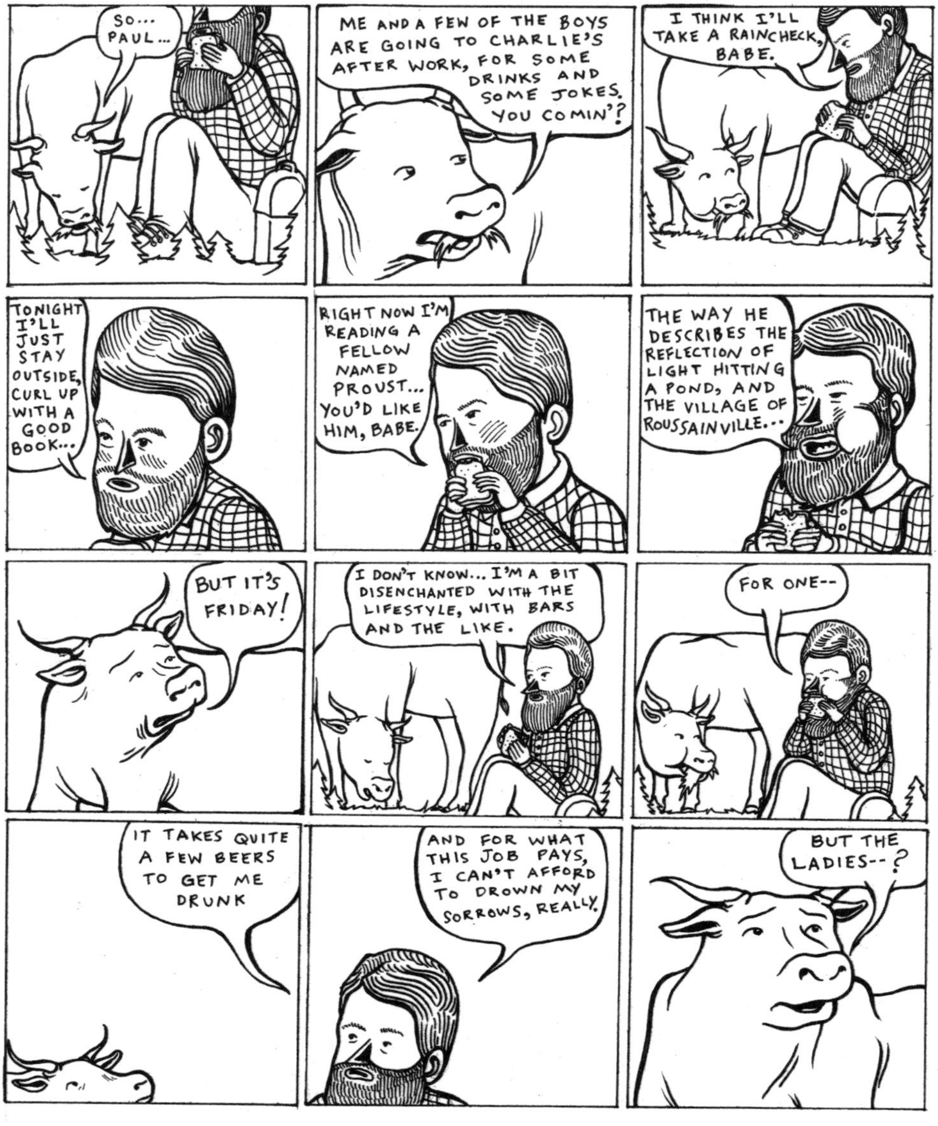
SO... PAUL...
ME AND A FEW OF THE BOYS ARE GOING TO CHARLIE'S AFTER WORK, FOR SOME DRINKS AND SOME JOKES. YOU COMIN'?
I THINK I'LL TAKE A RAINCHECK, BABE.
TONIGHT I'LL JUST STAY OUTSIDE, CURL UP WITH A GOOD BOOK...
RIGHT NOW I'M READING A FELLOW NAMED PROUST... YOU'D LIKE HIM, BABE.
THE WAY HE DESCRIBES THE REFLECTION OF LIGHT HITTING A POND, AND THE VILLAGE OF ROUSSAINVILLE...
BUT IT'S FRIDAY!
I DON'T KNOW... I'M A BIT DISENCHANTED WITH THE LIFESTYLE, WITH BARS AND THE LIKE.
FOR ONE--
IT TAKES QUITE A FEW BEERS TO GET ME DRUNK
AND FOR WHAT THIS JOB PAYS, I CAN'T AFFORD TO DROWN MY SORROWS, REALLY.
BUT THE LADIES--?

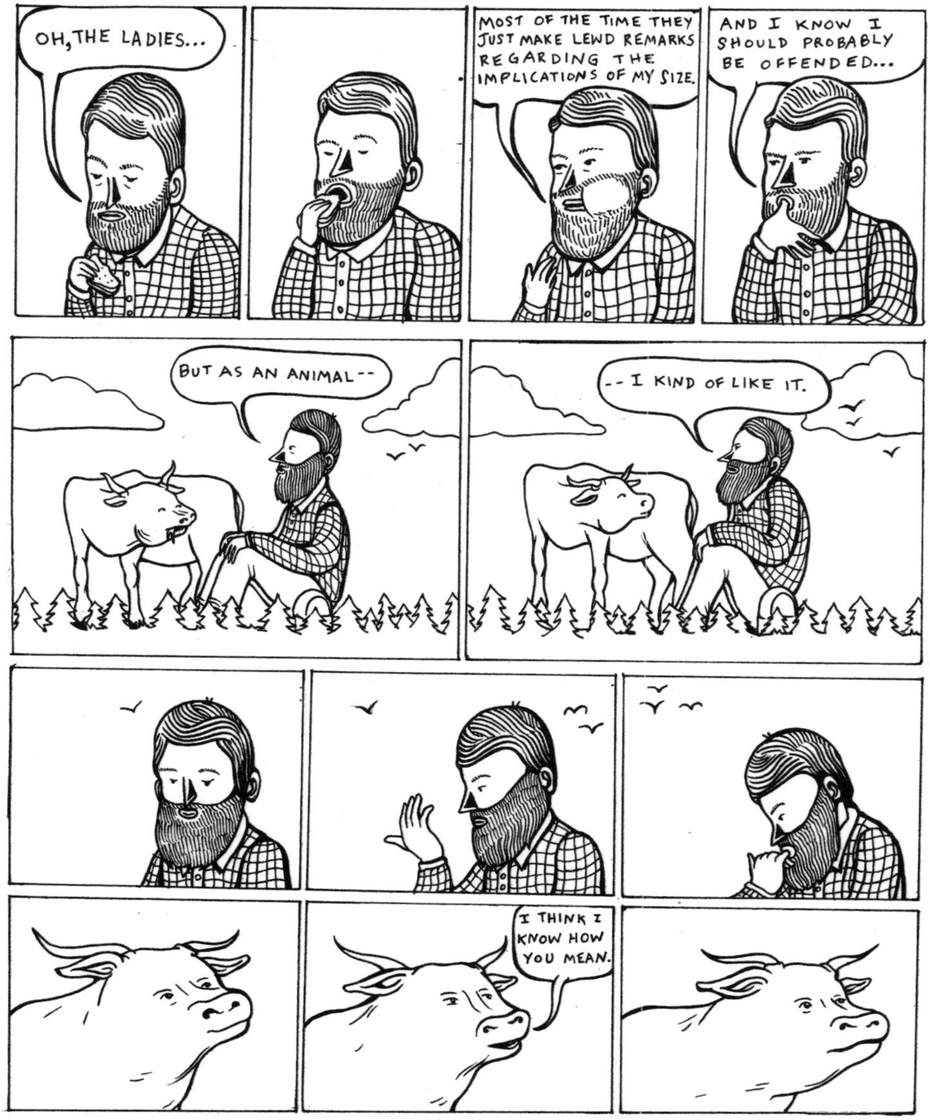
OH, THE LADIES...
MOST OF THE TIME THEY JUST MAKE LEWD REMARKS REGARDING THE IMPLICATIONS OF MY SIZE.
AND I KNOW I SHOULD PROBABLY BE OFFENDED...
BUT AS AN ANIMAL--
-- I KIND OF LIKE IT.
I THINK I KNOW HOW YOU MEAN.

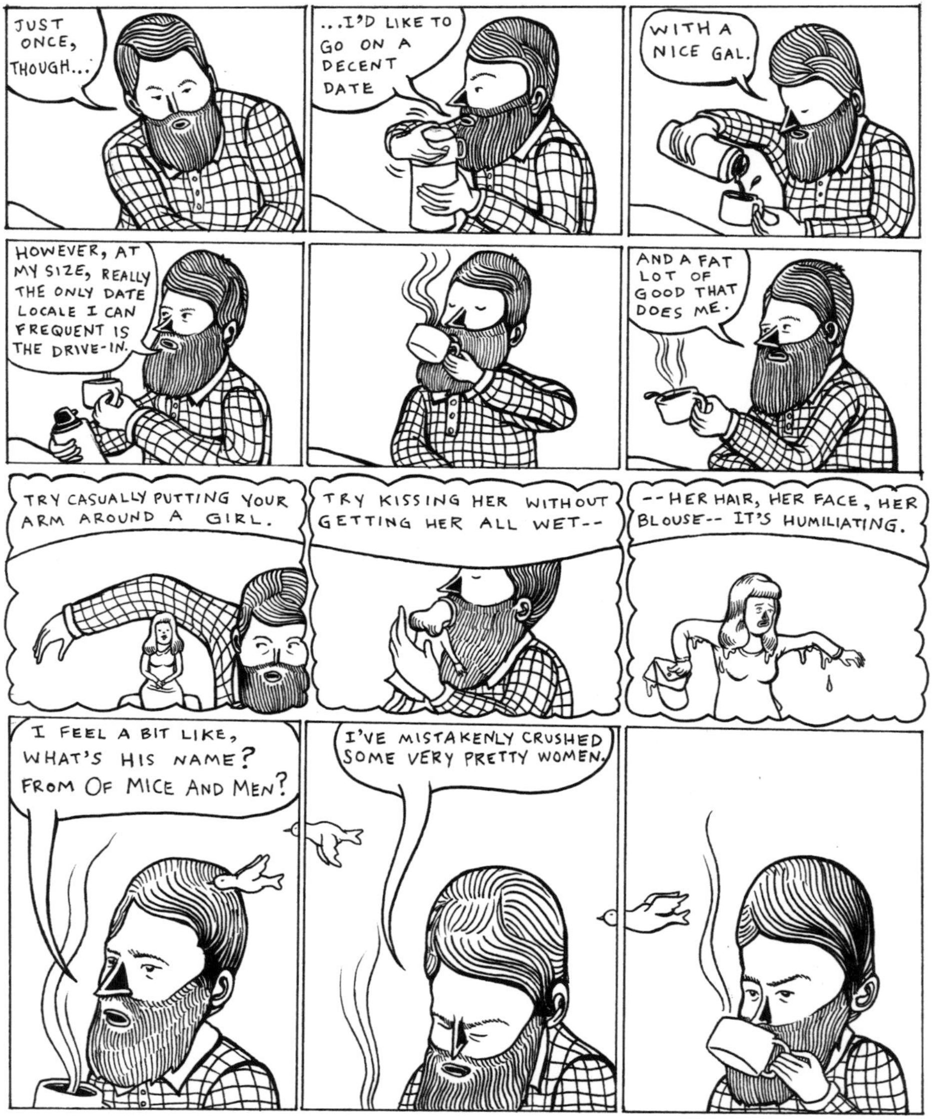
JUST ONCE, THOUGH...
...I'D LIKE TO GO ON A DECENT DATE
WITH A NICE GAL.
HOWEVER, AT MY SIZE, REALLY THE ONLY DATE LOCALE I CAN FREQUENT IS THE DRIVE-IN.
AND A FAT LOT OF GOOD THAT DOES ME.
TRY CASUALLY PUTTING YOUR ARM AROUND A GIRL.
TRY KISSING HER WITHOUT GETTING HER ALL WET--
--HER HAIR, HER FACE, HER BLOUSE-- IT'S HUMILIATING.
I FEEL A BIT LIKE, WHAT'S HIS NAME? FROM OF MICE AND MEN?
I'VE MISTAKENLY CRUSHED SOME VERY PRETTY WOMEN.

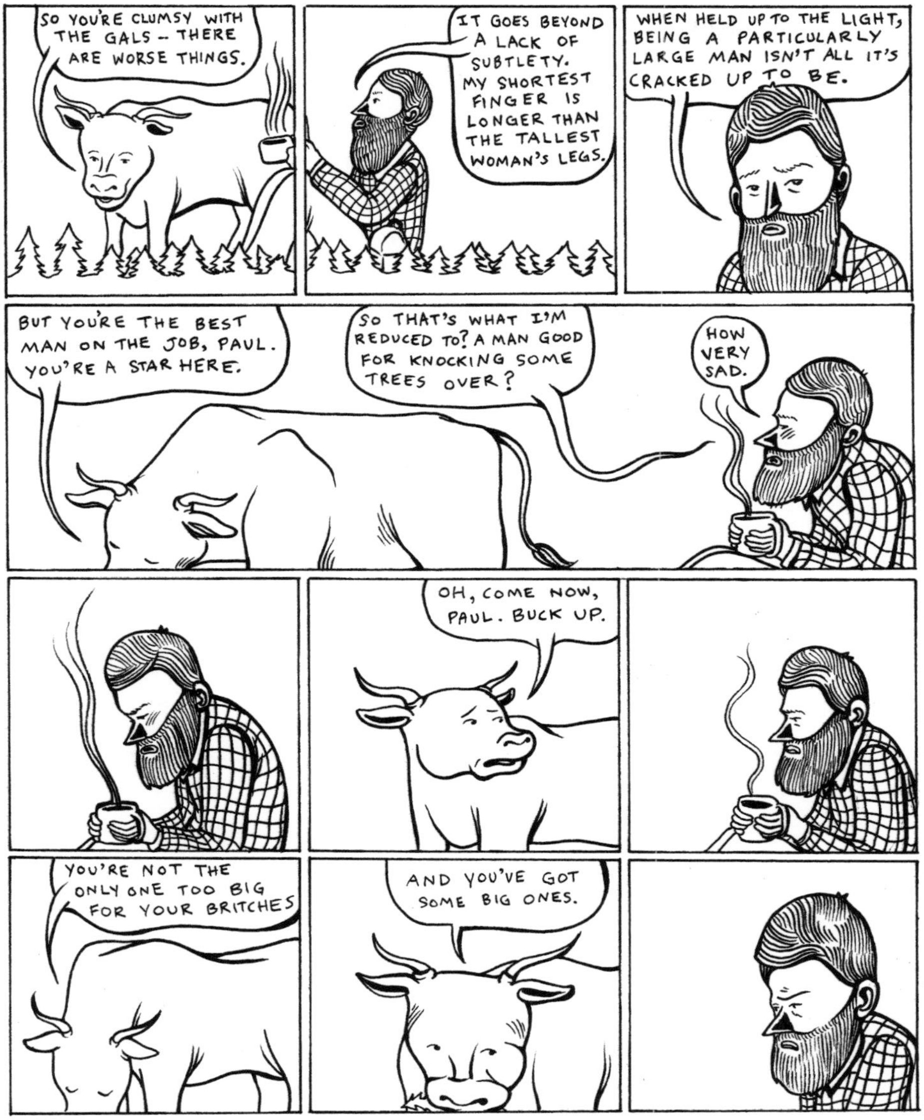
SO YOU'RE CLUMSY WITH THE GALS – THERE ARE WORSE THINGS.
IT GOES BEYOND A LACK OF SUBTLETY. MY SHORTEST FINGER IS LONGER THAN THE TALLEST WOMAN'S LEGS.
WHEN HELD UP TO THE LIGHT, BEING A PARTICULARLY LARGE MAN ISN'T ALL IT'S CRACKED UP TO BE.
BUT YOU'RE THE BEST MAN ON THE JOB, PAUL. YOU'RE A STAR HERE.
SO THAT'S WHAT I'M REDUCED TO? A MAN GOOD FOR KNOCKING SOME TREES OVER?
HOW VERY SAD.
OH, COME NOW, PAUL. BUCK UP.
YOU'RE NOT THE ONLY ONE TOO BIG FOR YOUR BRITCHES
AND YOU'VE GOT SOME BIG ONES.

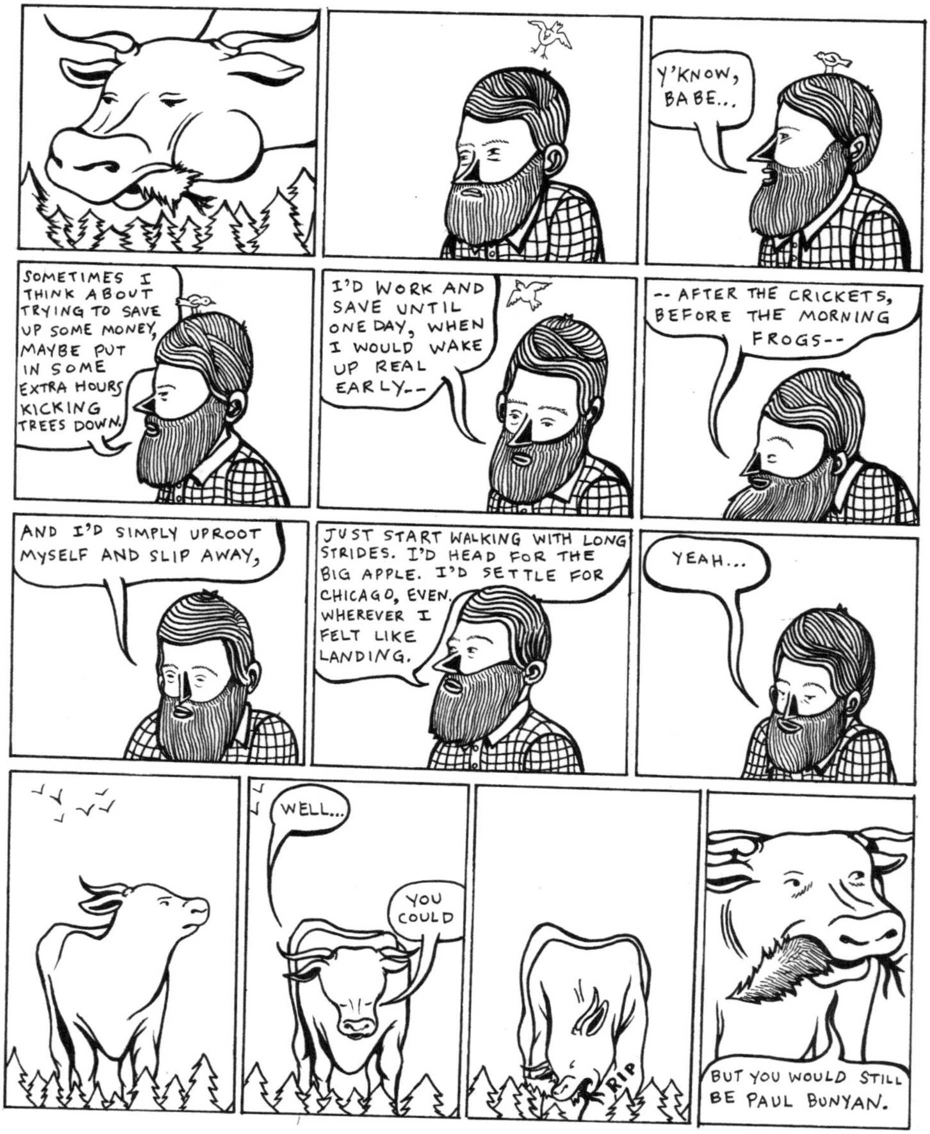
Y'KNOW, BABE...
SOMETIMES I THINK ABOUT TRYING TO SAVE UP SOME MONEY, MAYBE PUT IN SOME EXTRA HOURS KICKING TREES DOWN.
I'D WORK AND SAVE UNTIL ONE DAY, WHEN I WOULD WAKE UP REAL EARLY--
-- AFTER THE CRICKETS, BEFORE THE MORNING FROGS--
AND I'D SIMPLY UPROOT MYSELF AND SLIP AWAY,
JUST START WALKING WITH LONG STRIDES. I'D HEAD FOR THE BIG APPLE. I'D SETTLE FOR CHICAGO, EVEN. WHEREVER I FELT LIKE LANDING.
YEAH...
WELL...
YOU COULD
RIP
BUT YOU WOULD STILL BE PAUL BUNYAN.

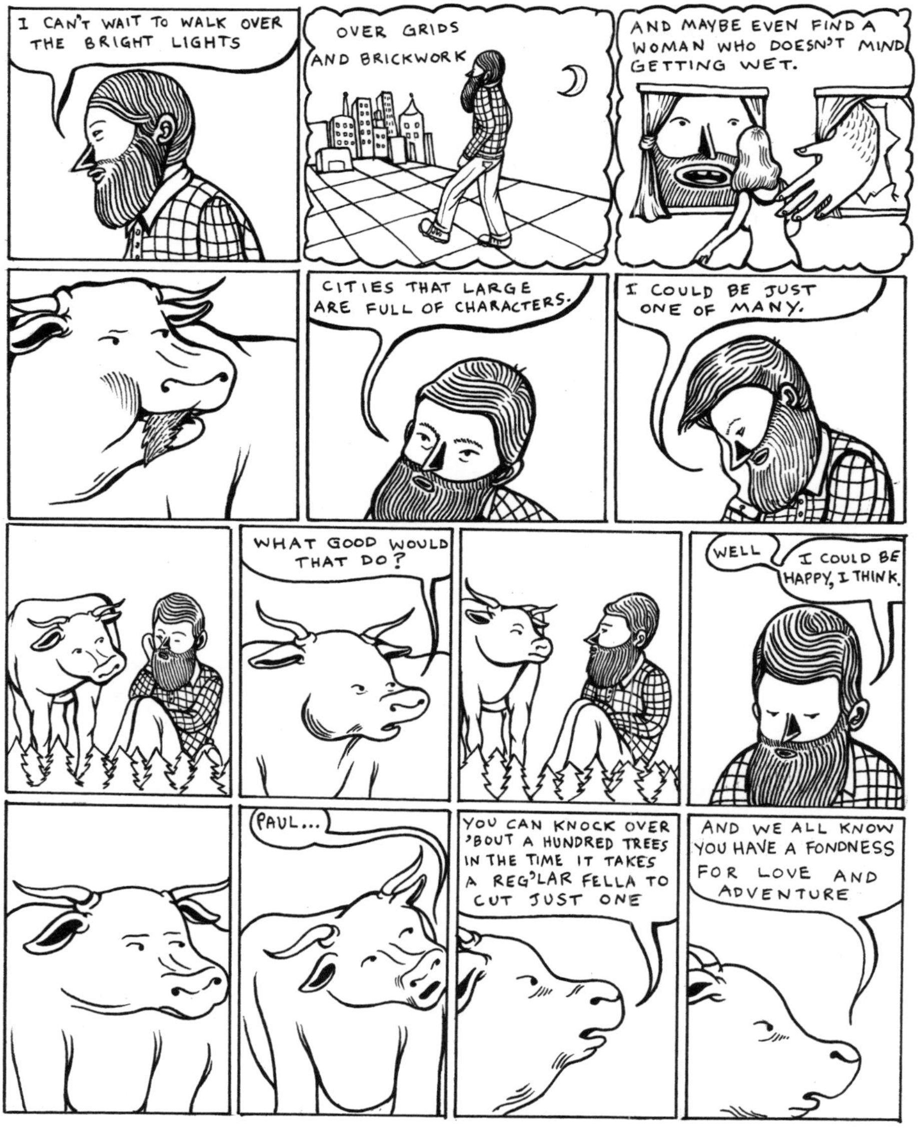
I CAN'T WAIT TO WALK OVER THE BRIGHT LIGHTS
OVER GRIDS
AND BRICKWORK
AND MAYBE EVEN FIND A WOMAN WHO DOESN'T MIND GETTING WET.
CITIES THAT LARGE ARE FULL OF CHARACTERS.
I COULD BE JUST ONE OF MANY.
WHAT GOOD WOULD THAT DO?
WELL
I COULD BE HAPPY, I THINK.
PAUL...
YOU CAN KNOCK OVER 'BOUT A HUNDRED TREES IN THE TIME IT TAKES A REG'LAR FELLA TO CUT JUST ONE
AND WE ALL KNOW YOU HAVE A FONDNESS FOR LOVE AND ADVENTURE

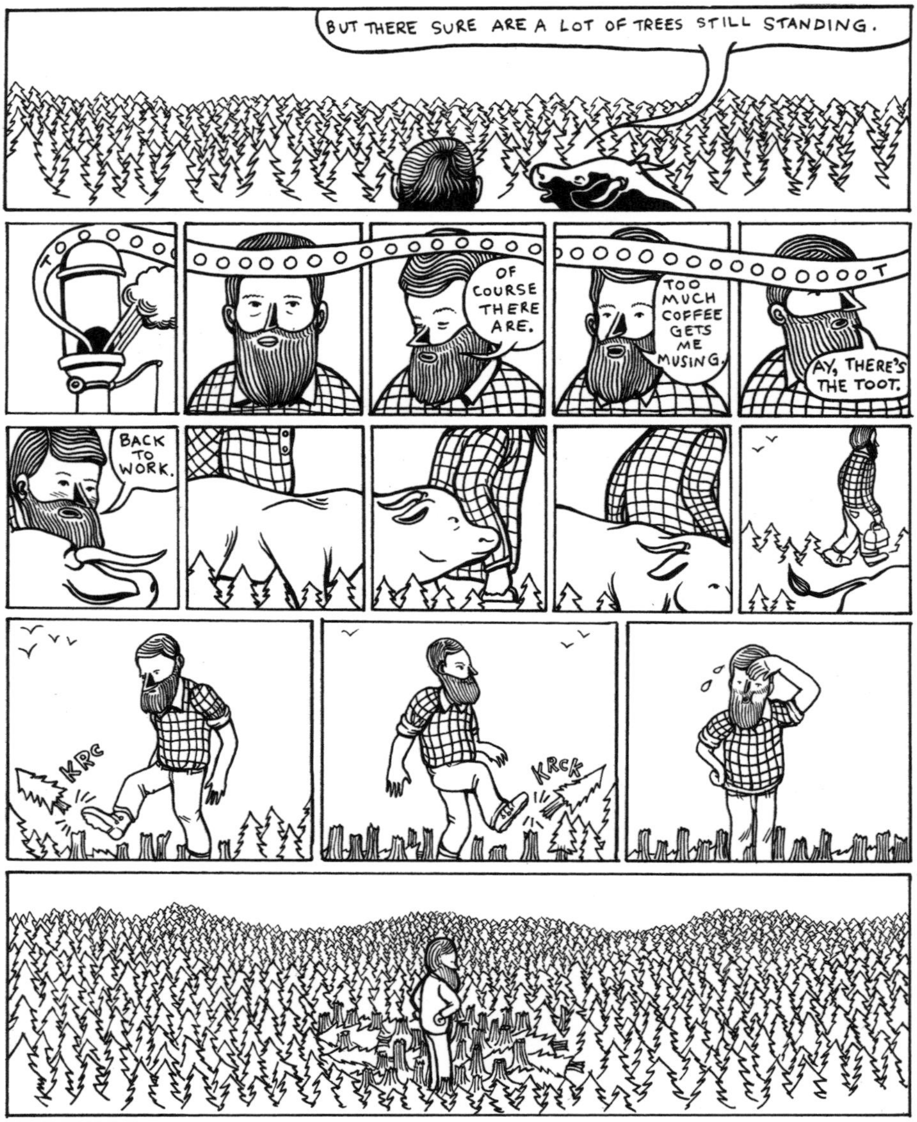
BUT THERE SURE ARE A LOT OF TREES STILL STANDING.
TOOOOOOOOOOOOOOOOOOOOOOOOOOOOOOOOOT
OF COURSE THERE ARE.
TOO MUCH COFFEE GETS ME MUSING.
AY, THERE'S THE TOOT.
BACK TO WORK.
KRC
KRCK

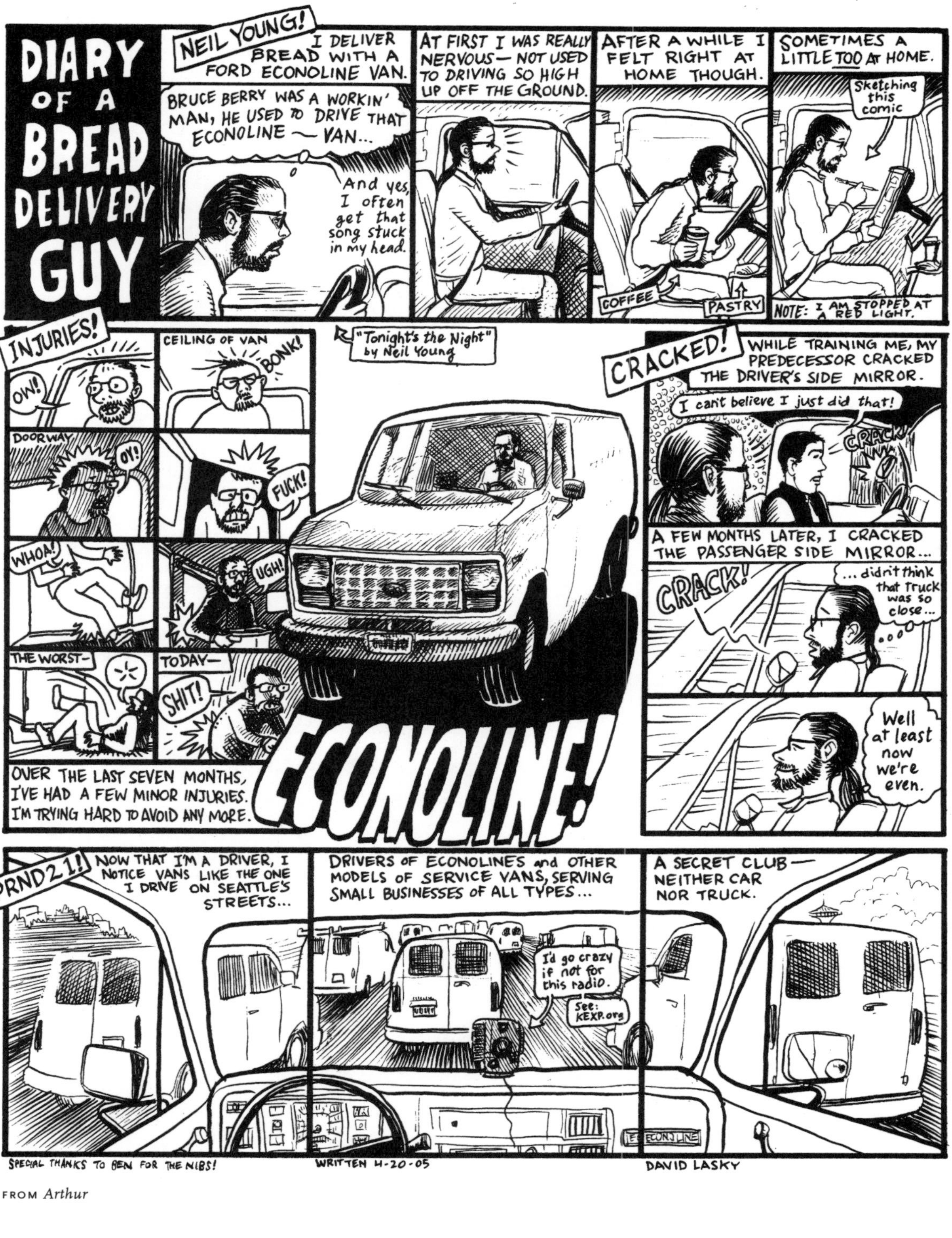
DIARY OF A BREAD DELIVERY GUY
NEIL YOUNG!
I DELIVER BREAD WITH A FORD ECONOLINE VAN.
BRUCE BERRY WAS A WORKIN' MAN, HE USED TO DRIVE THAT ECONOLINE ~ VAN...
And yes, I often get that song stuck in my head.
"Tonight's the Night" by Neil Young
AT FIRST I WAS REALLY NERVOUS— NOT USED TO DRIVING SO HIGH UP OFF THE GROUND.
AFTER A WHILE I FELT RIGHT AT HOME THOUGH.
COFFEE
PASTRY
SOMETIMES A LITTLE TOO AT HOME.
Sketching this comic
NOTE: I AM STOPPED AT A RED LIGHT.
INJURIES!
OW!
CEILING OF VAN
BONK!
DOORWAY
OY!
FUCK!
WHOA!
UGH!
THE WORST-
TODAY—
SHIT!
OVER THE LAST SEVEN MONTHS, I'VE HAD A FEW MINOR INJURIES. I'M TRYING HARD TO AVOID ANY MORE.
ECONOLINE!
CRACKED!
WHILE TRAINING ME, MY PREDECESSOR CRACKED THE DRIVER'S SIDE MIRROR.
I can't believe I just did that!
CRACK!
A FEW MONTHS LATER, I CRACKED THE PASSENGER SIDE MIRROR...
CRACK!
... didn't think that truck was so close...
Well at least now we're even.
PRND21!
NOW THAT I'M A DRIVER, I NOTICE VANS LIKE THE ONE I DRIVE ON SEATTLE'S STREETS...
DRIVERS OF ECONOLINES and OTHER MODELS OF SERVICE VANS, SERVING SMALL BUSINESSES OF ALL TYPES...
I'd go crazy if not for this radio.
See: KEXP.org
A SECRET CLUB— NEITHER CAR NOR TRUCK.
ECONOLINE
SPECIAL THANKS TO BEN FOR THE NIBS!
WRITTEN 4-20-05
DAVID LASKY

FROM *Arthur*

Goner Pillow Company

Without a pillow, one can stand or lean for only a few minutes.

LOOKS LIKE RAIN.

Do they grow tired of the same view?

IT'S UNRECOGNIZABLE FROM LAST YEAR.

Aaron Goner, a Brooklyn-based pillow-manufacturer, has revolutionized the home entertainment industry.

THE WINDOWS ARE ALREADY THERE—ALL THAT'S MISSING ARE THE PILLOWS...

NARROW, PILLOWS FEATHER, DESIGNED SPECIALLY FOR USE ON WINDOW SILLS.

Do they miss cohesive narratives?

HE WAS A DELIVERY BOY; NOW HE OWNS THE PLACE.

Viewers are slowly drawn away from the television and internet.

I GOT THE IDEA FROM MY GRANDMOTHER.

For long-term window-watching, a pillow is a physical necessity.

DO THEY MISS SEEING CELEBRITIES?
ISN'T THAT RANDOLPH ROULAY?
OVER TIME, THE MOST PROSAIC VIEW YIELDS A FORM OF POETRY.
A MALLOW-PINK MAN HAILS A MARIGOLD CAB.
LIQUORS
LIQUORS
TOY
TELEVISION AND DVD SALES DECLINE PRECIPITOUSLY.
VOXS-MOR
TV - APPLIANCES - BRAND
98
50% OFF ALL MAKES
SALE DVD TVS
MR. GONER SUDDENLY DIES OF A MYSTERIOUS ILLNESS.
AN AVIAN FLU?
CONGRESS PLACES A HIGH TARIFF ON THE IMPORTATION OF FEATHERS.
THE SURGEON GENERAL WARNS AGAINST EXCESSIVE ELBOW USE.
UNDER THE DIRECTION OF MR. GONER'S SON, THE FACTORY TURNS EXCLUSIVELY TO THE PRODUCTION OF FOAM RUBBER PILLOWS FOR THE SOFA AND COUCH.
©2005 BEN KATCHOR

FROM *Metropolis*

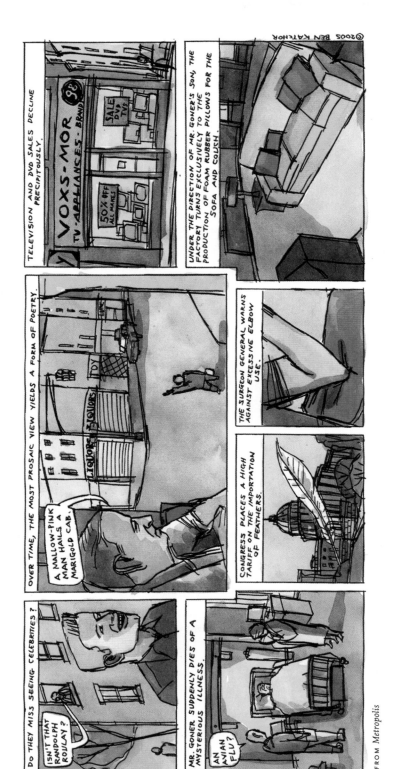

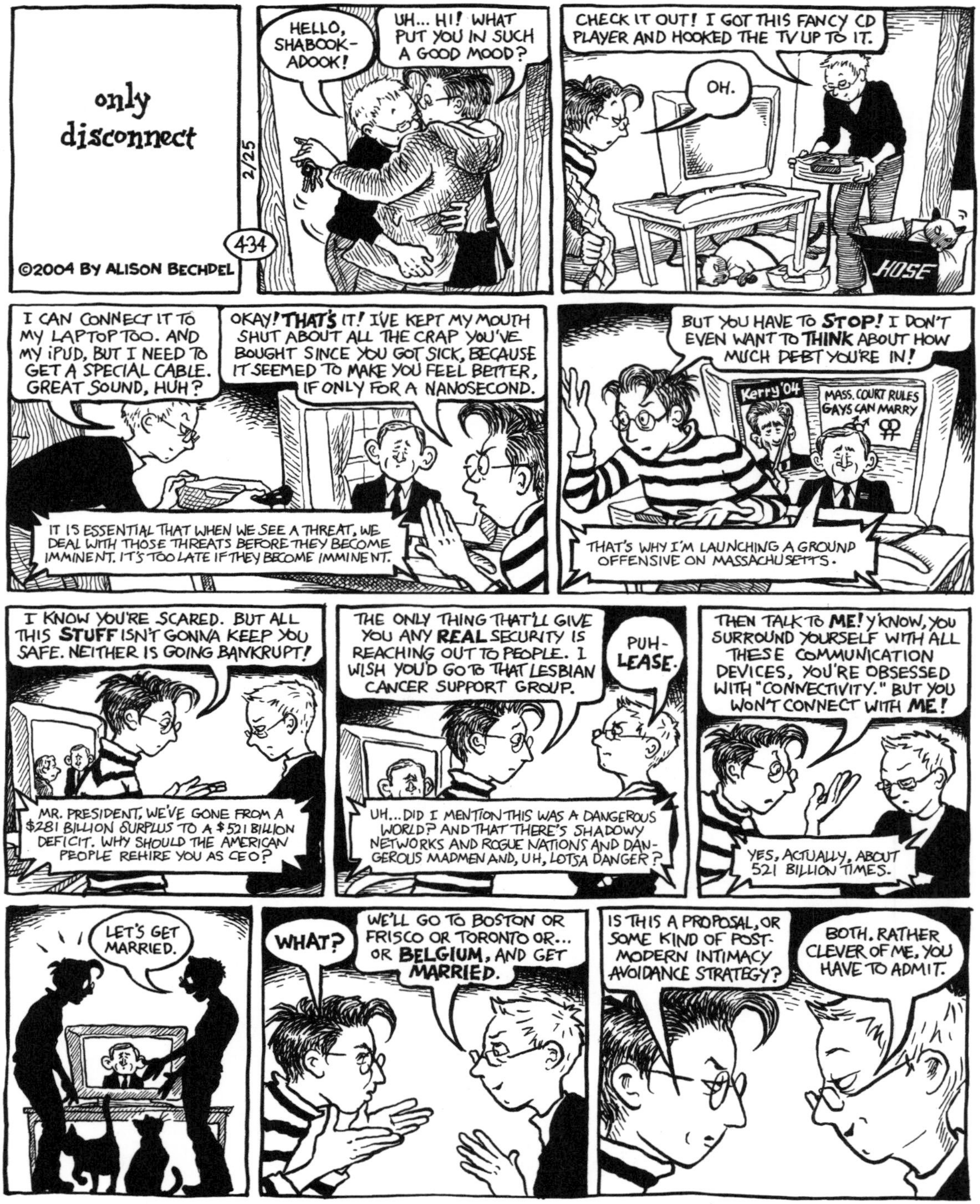
only disconnect
2/25
434
©2004 BY ALISON BECHDEL
HELLO, SHABOOK-ADOOK!
UH... HI! WHAT PUT YOU IN SUCH A GOOD MOOD?
CHECK IT OUT! I GOT THIS FANCY CD PLAYER AND HOOKED THE TV UP TO IT.
OH.
HOSE
I CAN CONNECT IT TO MY LAPTOP TOO. AND MY iPOD, BUT I NEED TO GET A SPECIAL CABLE. GREAT SOUND, HUH?
OKAY! THAT'S IT! I'VE KEPT MY MOUTH SHUT ABOUT ALL THE CRAP YOU'VE BOUGHT SINCE YOU GOT SICK, BECAUSE IT SEEMED TO MAKE YOU FEEL BETTER, IF ONLY FOR A NANOSECOND.
IT IS ESSENTIAL THAT WHEN WE SEE A THREAT, WE DEAL WITH THOSE THREATS BEFORE THEY BECOME IMMINENT. IT'S TOO LATE IF THEY BECOME IMMINENT.
BUT YOU HAVE TO STOP! I DON'T EVEN WANT TO THINK ABOUT HOW MUCH DEBT YOU'RE IN!
Kerry '04
MASS. COURT RULES GAYS CAN MARRY
THAT'S WHY I'M LAUNCHING A GROUND OFFENSIVE ON MASSACHUSETTS.
I KNOW YOU'RE SCARED. BUT ALL THIS STUFF ISN'T GONNA KEEP YOU SAFE. NEITHER IS GOING BANKRUPT!
MR. PRESIDENT, WE'VE GONE FROM A $281 BILLION SURPLUS TO A $521 BILLION DEFICIT. WHY SHOULD THE AMERICAN PEOPLE REHIRE YOU AS CEO?
THE ONLY THING THAT'LL GIVE YOU ANY REAL SECURITY IS REACHING OUT TO PEOPLE. I WISH YOU'D GO TO THAT LESBIAN CANCER SUPPORT GROUP.
PUH-LEASE.
UH...DID I MENTION THIS WAS A DANGEROUS WORLD? AND THAT THERE'S SHADOWY NETWORKS AND ROGUE NATIONS AND DANGEROUS MADMEN AND, UH, LOTSA DANGER?
THEN TALK TO ME! Y'KNOW, YOU SURROUND YOURSELF WITH ALL THESE COMMUNICATION DEVICES, YOU'RE OBSESSED WITH "CONNECTIVITY." BUT YOU WON'T CONNECT WITH ME!
YES, ACTUALLY, ABOUT 521 BILLION TIMES.
LET'S GET MARRIED.
WHAT?
WE'LL GO TO BOSTON OR FRISCO OR TORONTO OR... OR BELGIUM, AND GET MARRIED.
IS THIS A PROPOSAL, OR SOME KIND OF POST-MODERN INTIMACY AVOIDANCE STRATEGY?
BOTH. RATHER CLEVER OF ME, YOU HAVE TO ADMIT.

FROM *Dykes to Watch Out For*

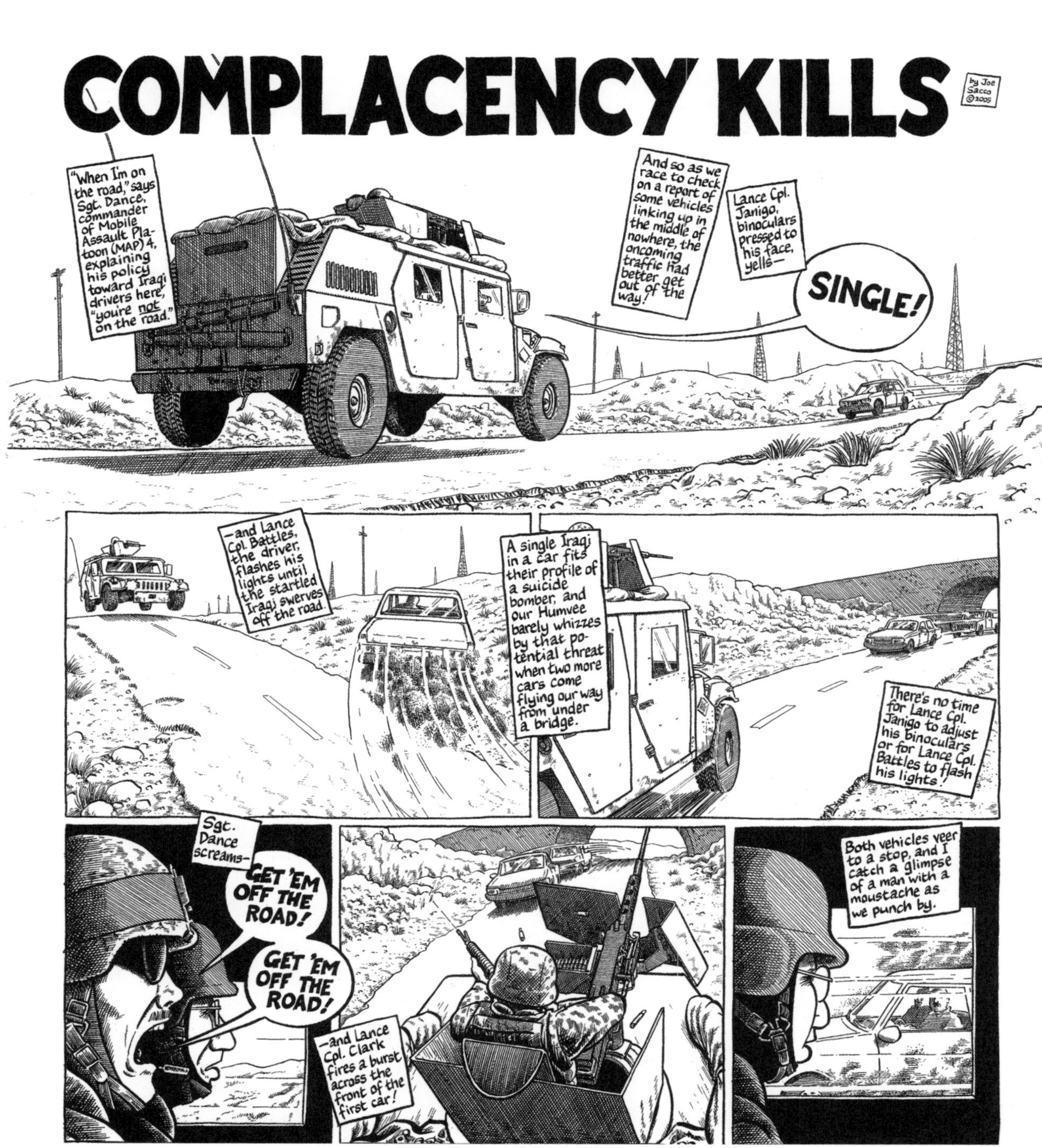
COMPLACENCY KILLS
by Joe Sacco ©2005
"When I'm on the road," says Sgt. Dance, commander of Mobile Assault Platoon (MAP) 4, explaining his policy toward Iraqi drivers here, "you're not on the road."
And so as we race to check on a report of some vehicles linking up in the middle of nowhere, the oncoming traffic had better get out of the way!
Lance Cpl. Janigo, binoculars pressed to his face, yells—
SINGLE!
—and Lance Cpl. Battles, the driver, flashes his lights until the startled Iraqi swerves off the road.
A single Iraqi in a car fits their profile of a suicide bomber, and our Humvee barely whizzes by that potential threat when two more cars come flying our way from under a bridge.
There's no time for Lance Cpl. Janigo to adjust his binoculars or for Lance Cpl. Battles to flash his lights!
Sgt. Dance screams—
GET 'EM OFF THE ROAD!
GET 'EM OFF THE ROAD!
—and Lance Cpl. Clark fires a burst across the front of the first car!
Both vehicles veer to a stop, and I catch a glimpse of a man with a moustache as we punch by.

FROM *The Guardian Online*

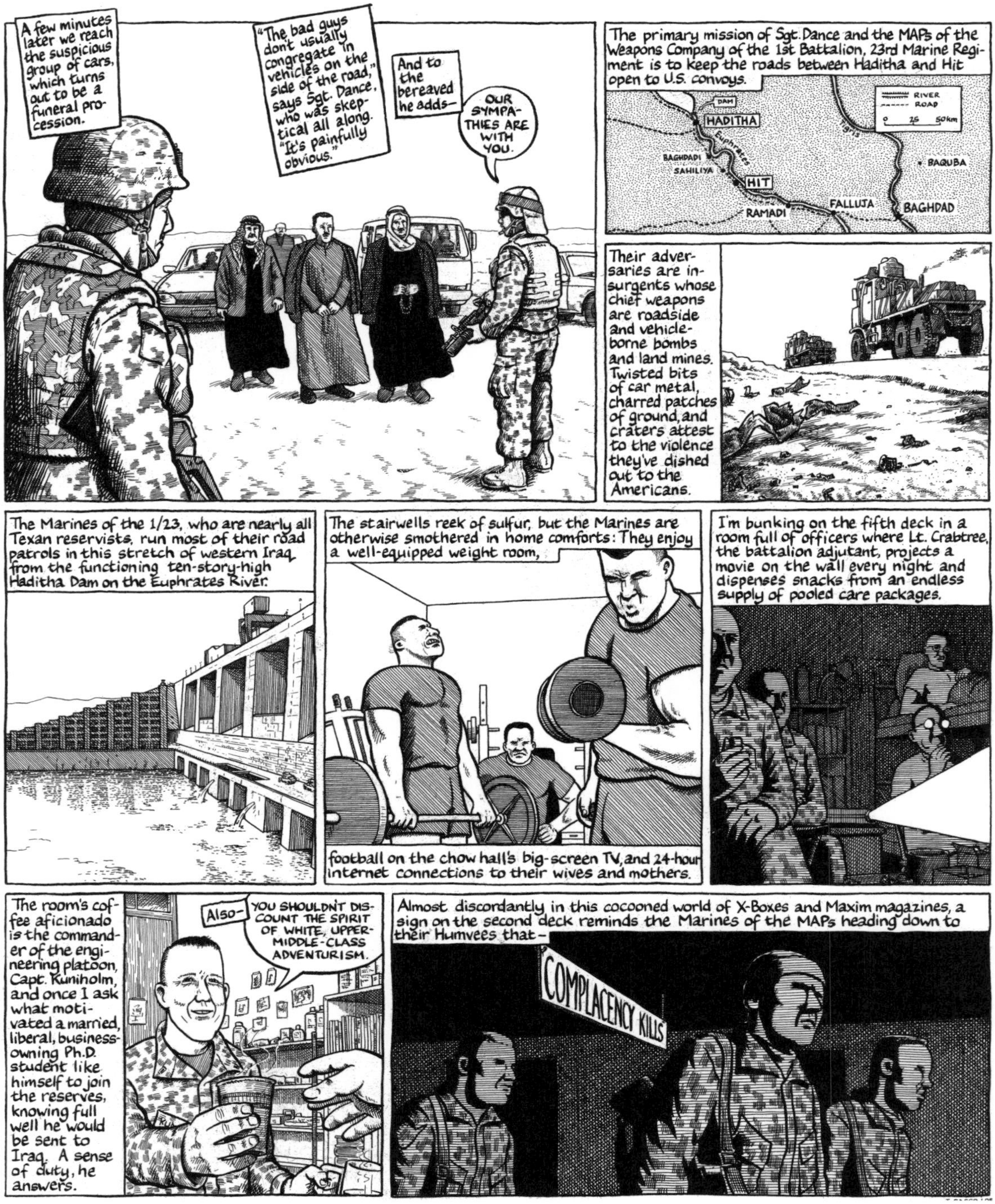
A few minutes later we reach the suspicious group of cars, which turns out to be a funeral procession.
"The bad guys don't usually congregate in vehicles on the side of the road," says Sgt. Dance, who was skeptical all along. "It's painfully obvious."
And to the bereaved he adds–
OUR SYMPATHIES ARE WITH YOU.
The primary mission of Sgt. Dance and the MAPs of the Weapons Company of the 1st Battalion, 23rd Marine Regiment is to keep the roads between Haditha and Hit open to U.S. convoys.
DAM
HADITHA
RIVER
ROAD
0 25 50km
Tigris
Euphrates
BAGHDADI
SAHILIYA
HIT
BAQUBA
RAMADI
FALLUJA
BAGHDAD
Their adversaries are insurgents whose chief weapons are roadside and vehicle-borne bombs and land mines. Twisted bits of car metal, charred patches of ground, and craters attest to the violence they've dished out to the Americans.
The Marines of the 1/23, who are nearly all Texan reservists, run most of their road patrols in this stretch of western Iraq from the functioning ten-story-high Haditha Dam on the Euphrates River.
The stairwells reek of sulfur, but the Marines are otherwise smothered in home comforts: They enjoy a well-equipped weight room,
football on the chow hall's big-screen TV, and 24-hour internet connections to their wives and mothers.
I'm bunking on the fifth deck in a room full of officers where Lt. Crabtree, the battalion adjutant, projects a movie on the wall every night and dispenses snacks from an endless supply of pooled care packages.
The room's coffee aficionado is the commander of the engineering platoon, Capt. Kuniholm, and once I ask what motivated a married, liberal, business-owning Ph.D. student like himself to join the reserves, knowing full well he would be sent to Iraq. A sense of duty, he answers.
Also–
YOU SHOULDN'T DISCOUNT THE SPIRIT OF WHITE, UPPER-MIDDLE-CLASS ADVENTURISM.
Almost discordantly in this cocooned world of X-Boxes and Maxim magazines, a sign on the second deck reminds the Marines of the MAPs heading down to their Humvees that–
COMPLACENCY KILLS

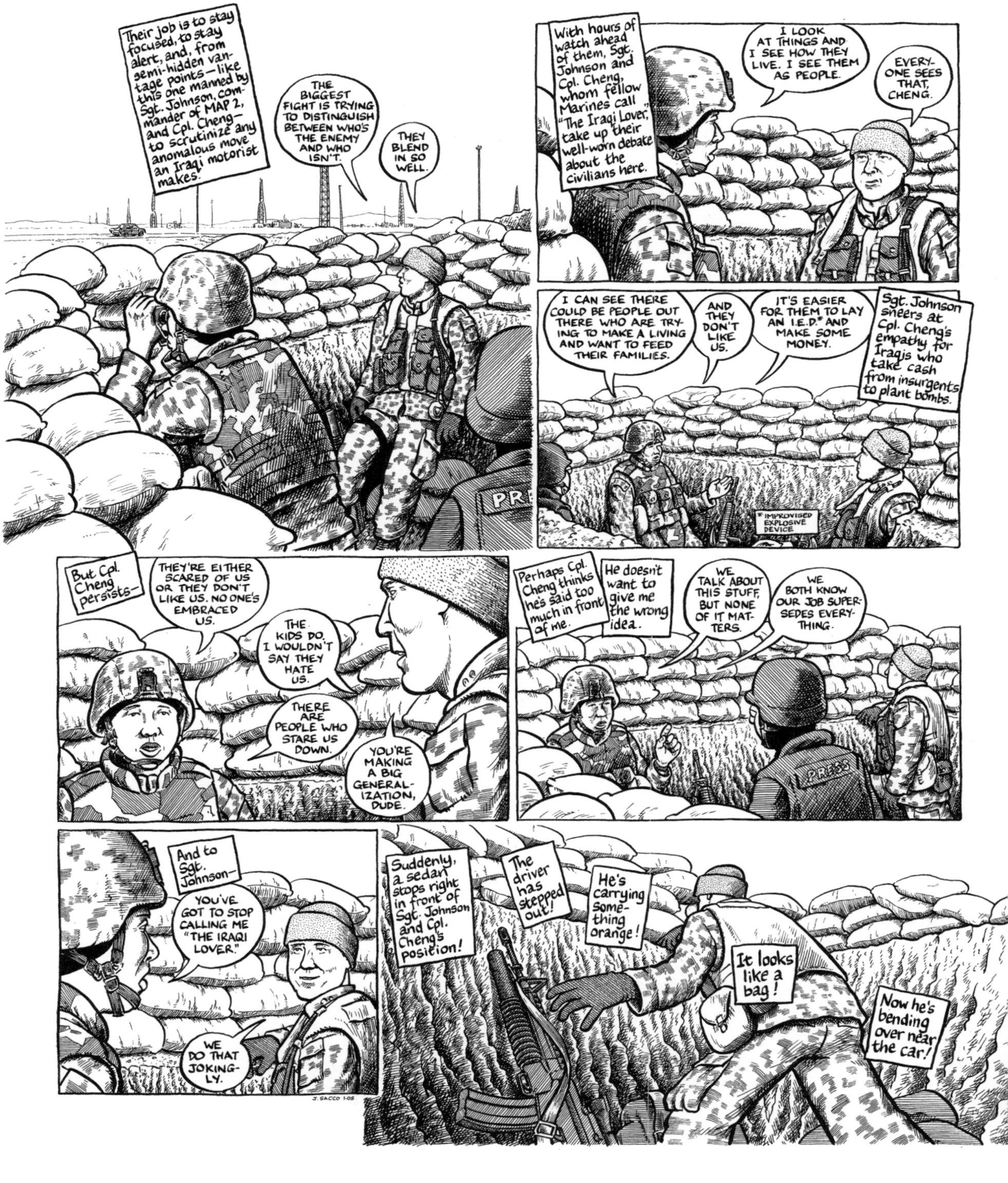

Their job is to stay focused, to stay alert, and, from semi-hidden vantage points—like this one manned by Sgt. Johnson, commander of MAP 2, and Cpl. Cheng—to scrutinize any anomalous move an Iraqi motorist makes.
THE BIGGEST FIGHT IS TRYING TO DISTINGUISH BETWEEN WHO'S THE ENEMY AND WHO ISN'T.
THEY BLEND IN SO WELL.
PRESS
With hours of watch ahead of them, Sgt. Johnson and Cpl. Cheng, whom fellow Marines call "The Iraqi Lover," take up their well-worn debate about the civilians here.
I LOOK AT THINGS AND I SEE HOW THEY LIVE. I SEE THEM AS PEOPLE.
EVERYONE SEES THAT, CHENG.
I CAN SEE THERE COULD BE PEOPLE OUT THERE WHO ARE TRYING TO MAKE A LIVING AND WANT TO FEED THEIR FAMILIES.
AND THEY DON'T LIKE US.
IT'S EASIER FOR THEM TO LAY AN I.E.D.* AND MAKE SOME MONEY.
Sgt. Johnson sneers at Cpl. Cheng's empathy for Iraqis who take cash from insurgents to plant bombs.
*IMPROVISED EXPLOSIVE DEVICE
But Cpl. Cheng persists—
THEY'RE EITHER SCARED OF US OR THEY DON'T LIKE US. NO ONE'S EMBRACED US.
THE KIDS DO. I WOULDN'T SAY THEY HATE US.
THERE ARE PEOPLE WHO STARE US DOWN.
YOU'RE MAKING A BIG GENERALIZATION, DUDE.
Perhaps Cpl. Cheng thinks he's said too much in front of me.
He doesn't want to give me the wrong idea.
WE TALK ABOUT THIS STUFF, BUT NONE OF IT MATTERS.
WE BOTH KNOW OUR JOB SUPERSEDES EVERYTHING.
PRESS
And to Sgt. Johnson—
YOU'VE GOT TO STOP CALLING ME "THE IRAQI LOVER."
WE DO THAT JOKINGLY.
J. SACCO 1-05
Suddenly, a sedan stops right in front of Sgt. Johnson and Cpl. Cheng's position!
The driver has stepped out!
He's carrying something orange!
It looks like a bag!
Now he's bending over near the car!

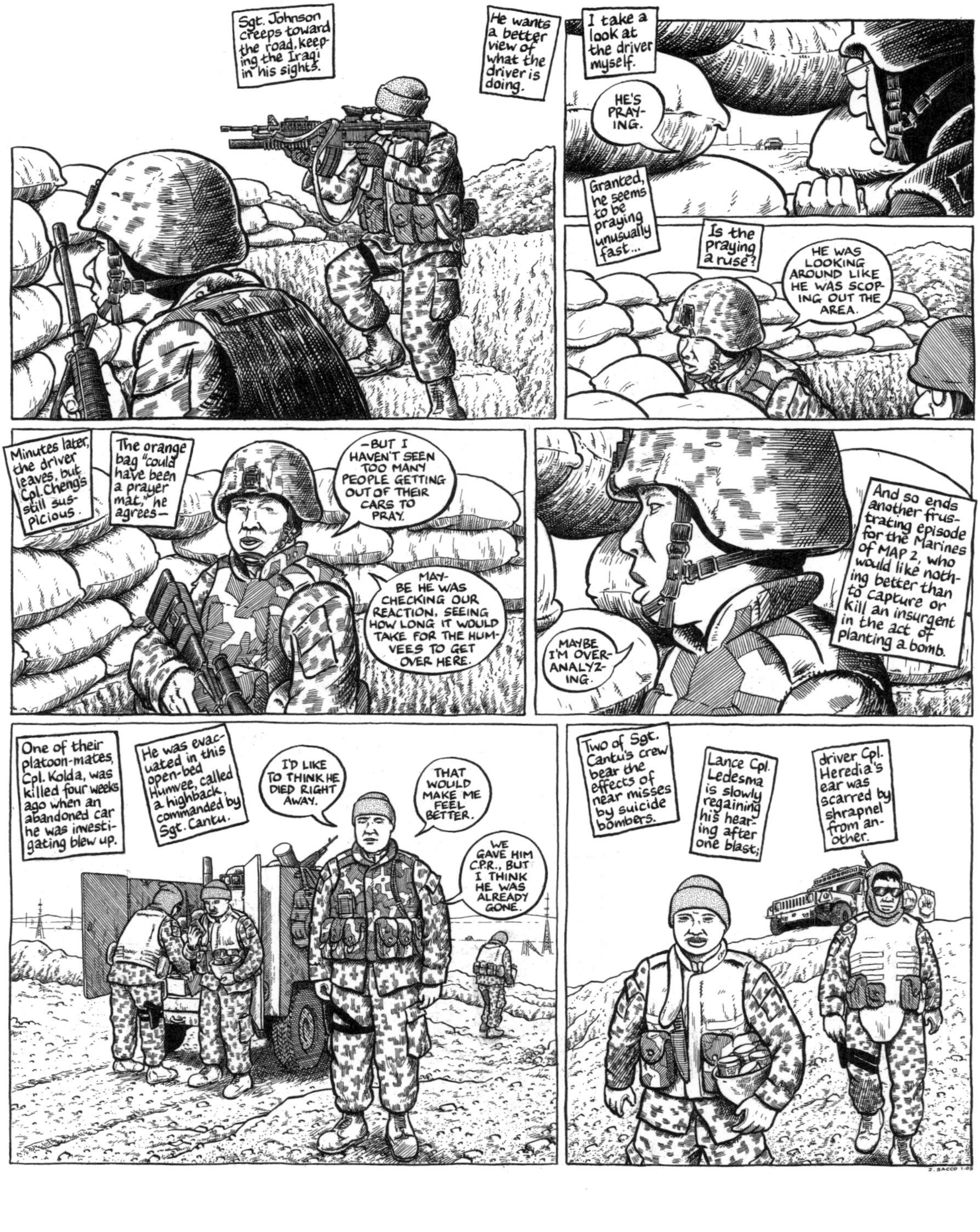
Sgt. Johnson creeps toward the road, keeping the Iraqi in his sights.
He wants a better view of what the driver is doing.
I take a look at the driver myself.
HE'S PRAYING.
Granted, he seems to be praying unusually fast...
Is the praying a ruse?
HE WAS LOOKING AROUND LIKE HE WAS SCOPING OUT THE AREA.
Minutes later, the driver leaves, but Cpl. Cheng's still suspicious.
The orange bag "could have been a prayer mat," he agrees—
—BUT I HAVEN'T SEEN TOO MANY PEOPLE GETTING OUT OF THEIR CARS TO PRAY.
MAYBE HE WAS CHECKING OUR REACTION, SEEING HOW LONG IT WOULD TAKE FOR THE HUMVEES TO GET OVER HERE.
MAYBE I'M OVERANALYZING.
And so ends another frustrating episode for the Marines of MAP 2, who would like nothing better than to capture or kill an insurgent in the act of planting a bomb.
One of their platoon-mates, Cpl. Kolda, was killed four weeks ago when an abandoned car he was investigating blew up.
He was evacuated in this open-bed Humvee, called a highback, commanded by Sgt. Cantu.
I'D LIKE TO THINK HE DIED RIGHT AWAY.
THAT WOULD MAKE ME FEEL BETTER.
WE GAVE HIM C.P.R., BUT I THINK HE WAS ALREADY GONE.
Two of Sgt. Cantu's crew bear the effects of near misses by suicide bombers.
Lance Cpl. Ledesma is slowly regaining his hearing after one blast;
driver Cpl. Heredia's ear was scarred by shrapnel from another.
J. SACCO 1.05

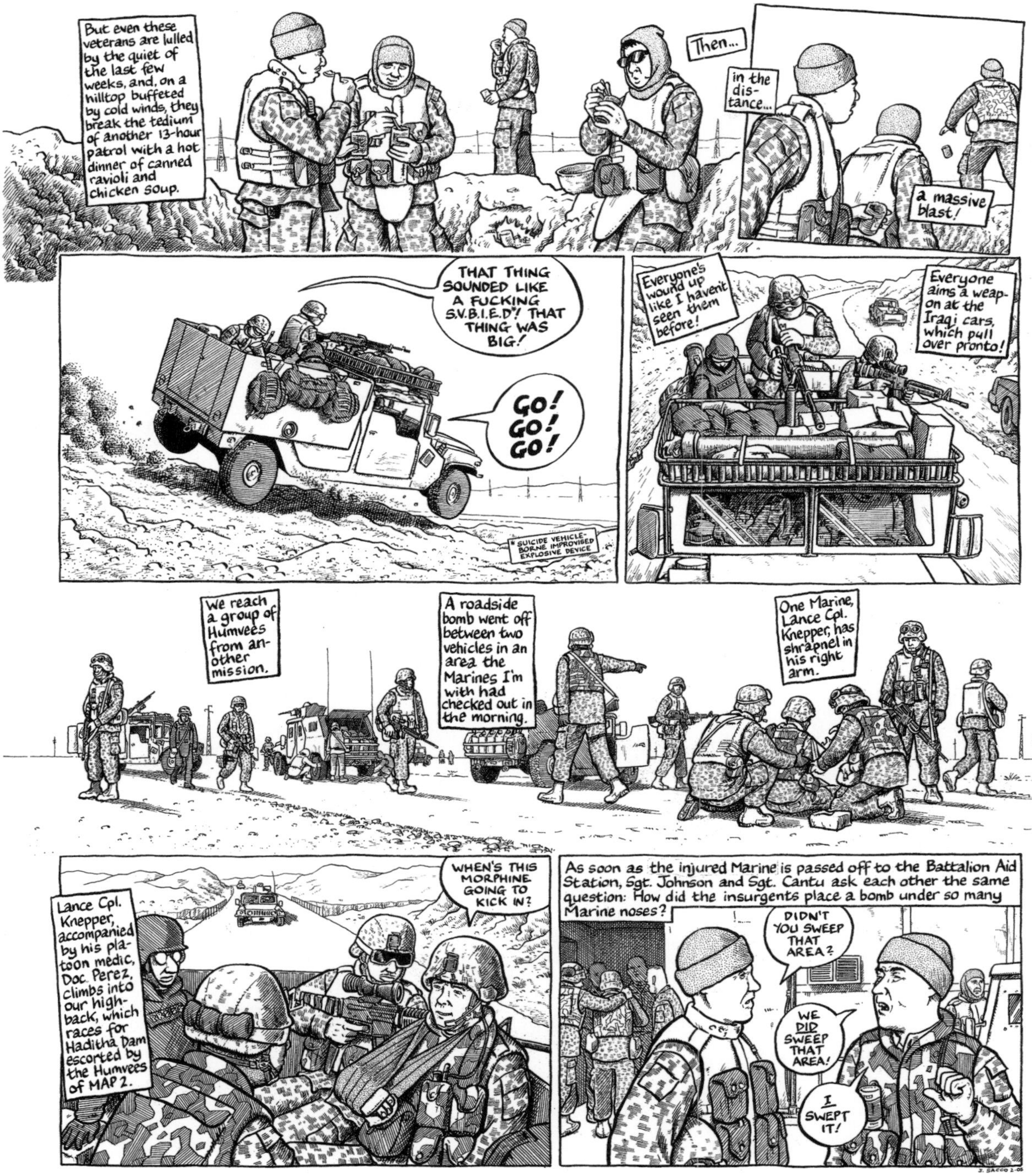
But even these veterans are lulled by the quiet of the last few weeks, and, on a hilltop buffeted by cold winds, they break the tedium of another 13-hour patrol with a hot dinner of canned ravioli and chicken soup.
Then...
in the distance...
a massive blast!
THAT THING SOUNDED LIKE A FUCKING S.V.B.I.E.D*! THAT THING WAS BIG!
GO! GO! GO!
* SUICIDE VEHICLE-BORNE IMPROVISED EXPLOSIVE DEVICE
Everyone's wound up like I haven't seen them before!
Everyone aims a weapon at the Iraqi cars, which pull over pronto!
We reach a group of Humvees from another mission.
A roadside bomb went off between two vehicles in an area the Marines I'm with had checked out in the morning.
One Marine, Lance Cpl. Knepper, has shrapnel in his right arm.
Lance Cpl. Knepper, accompanied by his platoon medic, Doc. Perez, climbs into our highback, which races for Haditha Dam escorted by the Humvees of MAP 2.
WHEN'S THIS MORPHINE GOING TO KICK IN?
As soon as the injured Marine is passed off to the Battalion Aid Station, Sgt. Johnson and Sgt. Cantu ask each other the same question: How did the insurgents place a bomb under so many Marine noses?
DIDN'T YOU SWEEP THAT AREA?
WE DID SWEEP THAT AREA!
I SWEPT IT!
J. SACCO 2-05

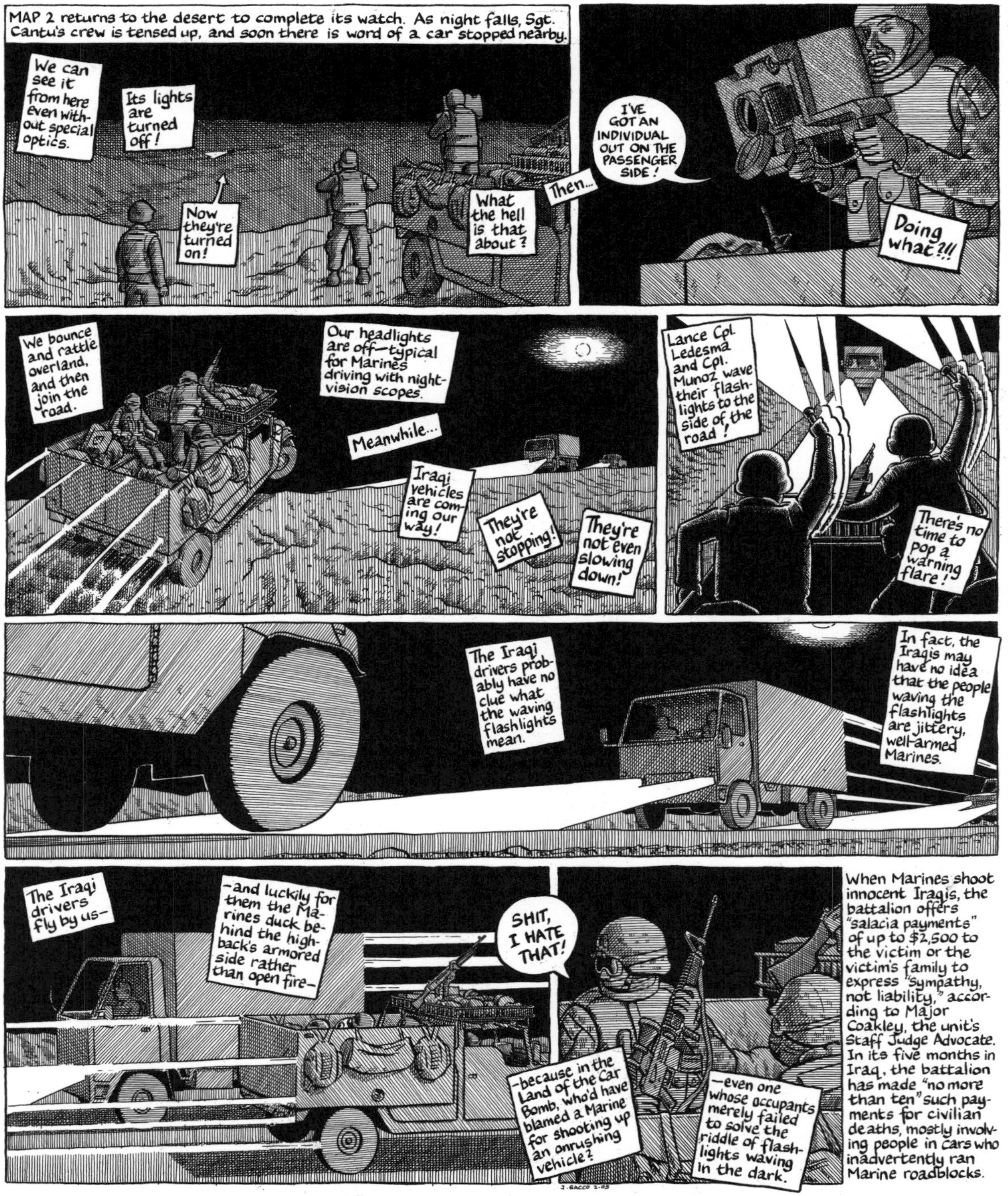
MAP 2 returns to the desert to complete its watch. As night falls, Sgt. Cantu's crew is tensed up, and soon there is word of a car stopped nearby.
We can see it from here even without special optics.
Its lights are turned off!
Now they're turned on!
What the hell is that about?
Then...
I'VE GOT AN INDIVIDUAL OUT ON THE PASSENGER SIDE!
Doing whac?!!
We bounce and rattle overland, and then join the road.
Our headlights are off—typical for Marines driving with night-vision scopes.
Meanwhile...
Iraqi vehicles are coming our way!
They're not stopping!
They're not even slowing down!
Lance Cpl. Ledesma and Cpl. Munoz wave their flashlights to the side of the road!
There's no time to pop a warning flare!
The Iraqi drivers probably have no clue what the waving flashlights mean.
In fact, the Iraqis may have no idea that the people waving the flashlights are jittery, well-armed Marines.
The Iraqi drivers fly by us-
-and luckily for them the Marines duck behind the highback's armored side rather than open fire-
SHIT, I HATE THAT!
-because in the Land of the Car Bomb, who'd have blamed a Marine for shooting up an onrushing vehicle?
-even one whose occupants merely failed to solve the riddle of flashlights waving in the dark.
J. SACCO 2-05
When Marines shoot innocent Iraqis, the battalion offers "salacia payments" of up to $2,500 to the victim or the victim's family to express "sympathy, not liability," according to Major Coakley, the unit's Staff Judge Advocate. In its five months in Iraq, the battalion has made "no more than ten" such payments for civilian deaths, mostly involving people in cars who inadvertently ran Marine roadblocks.

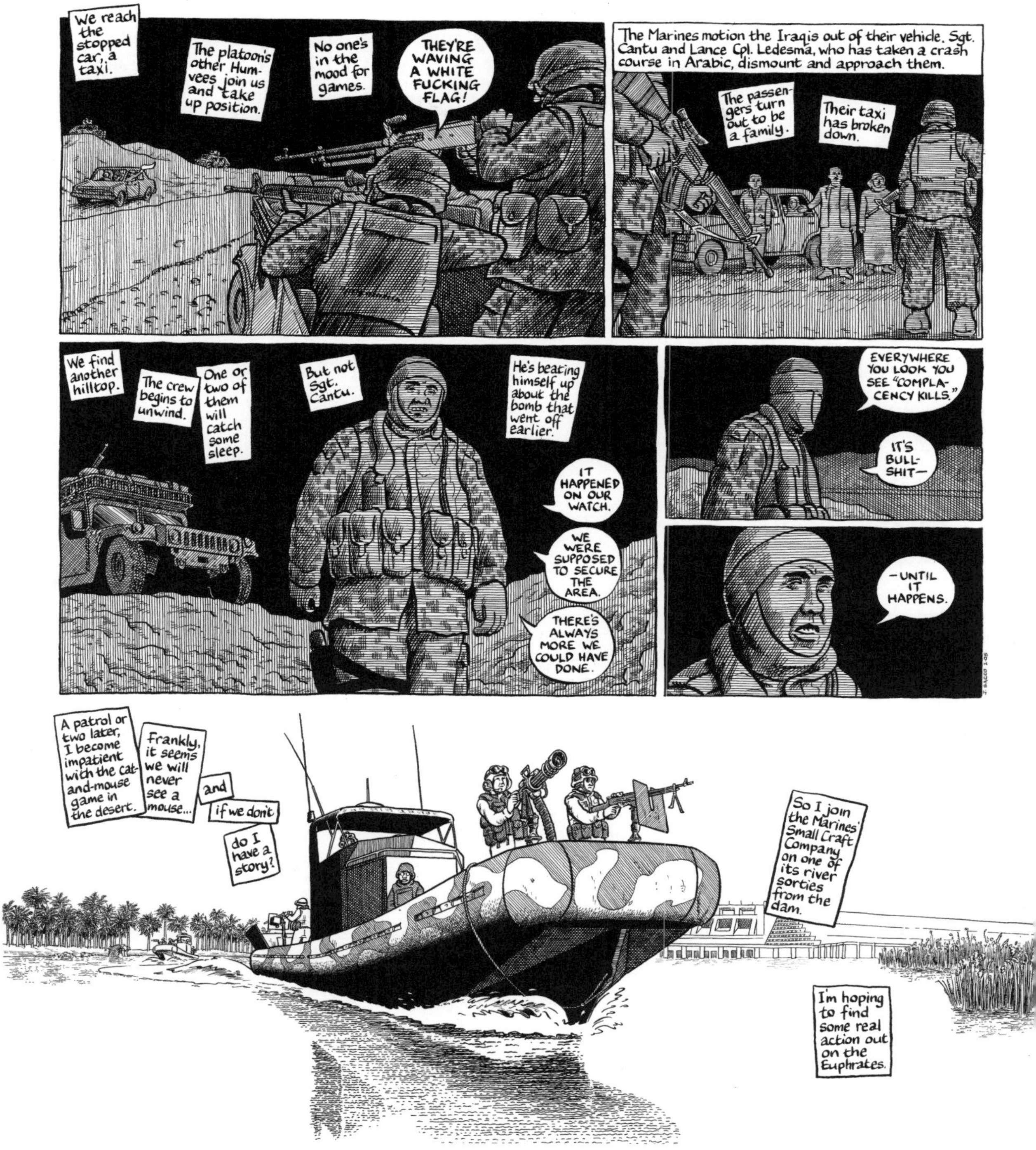

We reach the stopped car, a taxi.
The platoon's other Humvees join us and take up position.
No one's in the mood for games.
THEY'RE WAVING A WHITE FUCKING FLAG!
The Marines motion the Iraqis out of their vehicle. Sgt. Cantu and Lance Cpl. Ledesma, who has taken a crash course in Arabic, dismount and approach them.
The passengers turn out to be a family.
Their taxi has broken down.
We find another hilltop.
The crew begins to unwind.
One or two of them will catch some sleep.
But not Sgt. Cantu.
He's beating himself up about the bomb that went off earlier.
IT HAPPENED ON OUR WATCH.
WE WERE SUPPOSED TO SECURE THE AREA.
THERE'S ALWAYS MORE WE COULD HAVE DONE.
EVERYWHERE YOU LOOK YOU SEE "COMPLACENCY KILLS."
IT'S BULLSHIT—
—UNTIL IT HAPPENS.
A patrol or two later, I become impatient with the cat-and-mouse game in the desert.
Frankly, it seems we will never see a mouse...
and
if we don't
do I have a story?
So I join the Marines' Small Craft Company on one of its river sorties from the dam.
I'm hoping to find some real action out on the Euphrates.

But no such luck.

All we do is intercept a pair of Iraqis who've come too close to the dam.

GET OUT OF HERE!

GET THE FUCK OUT!

Afterwards, section leader Sgt. Czerwinski tells me that the river company has just come off months of hard patrolling and fighting in the Falluja and Ramadi areas. This new assignment at Haditha Dam should be—

—A GOOD BREAK FOR US.

The next day, his unit is ambushed after landing on the river bank to investigate some small arms fire. Lance Cpl. Parrello, who piloted the boat I'd ridden on the day before, is killed. Three others are wounded, including Capt. Kuniholm, my coffee-drinking roommate at the dam, who had jumped on one of the boats on the spur of the moment.

He and the others are medevac'd out.

Within hours, Capt. Kuniholm's 21 pairs of black socks, his four-year-old's drawings, and all his other items are packed up for shipment to his family in North Carolina.

He will not be coming back. His right arm has been severed below the elbow.

A short time later, I leave Haditha Dam on a convoy bound for the Al Asad air base.

The Marines I'm with keep "eyes" on the Iraqi cars that pull over to let us through.

ANY ONE OF THESE VEHICLES COULD BE LOADED WITH BOMBS.

SEE THAT VEHICLE? HE'S GOT HIS HOOD UP.

WATCH THAT FUCKER!

And I catch a glimpse of a man with a moustache as we punch by.

WITHIN A MONTH OF MY LEAVING, THE MARINES OF 1/23 AND THEIR ATTACHED UNITS SUFFERED SEVEN MORE FATALITIES

J. SACCO 1-08

54

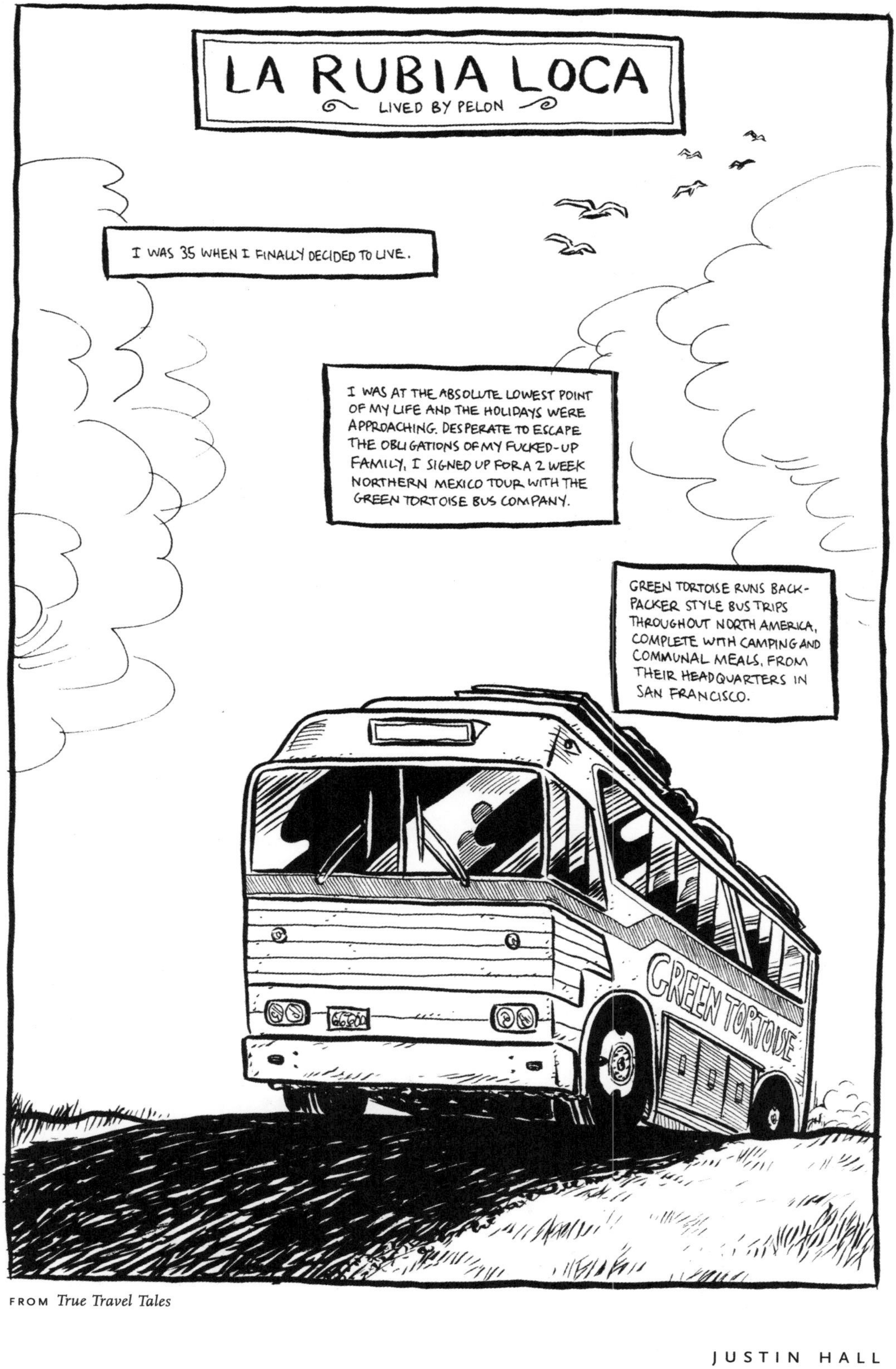
LA RUBIA LOCA
LIVED BY PELON
I WAS 35 WHEN I FINALLY DECIDED TO LIVE.
I WAS AT THE ABSOLUTE LOWEST POINT OF MY LIFE AND THE HOLIDAYS WERE APPROACHING. DESPERATE TO ESCAPE THE OBLIGATIONS OF MY FUCKED-UP FAMILY, I SIGNED UP FOR A 2 WEEK NORTHERN MEXICO TOUR WITH THE GREEN TORTOISE BUS COMPANY.
GREEN TORTOISE RUNS BACK-PACKER STYLE BUS TRIPS THROUGHOUT NORTH AMERICA, COMPLETE WITH CAMPING AND COMMUNAL MEALS, FROM THEIR HEADQUARTERS IN SAN FRANCISCO.
GREEN TORTOISE

FROM *True Travel Tales*

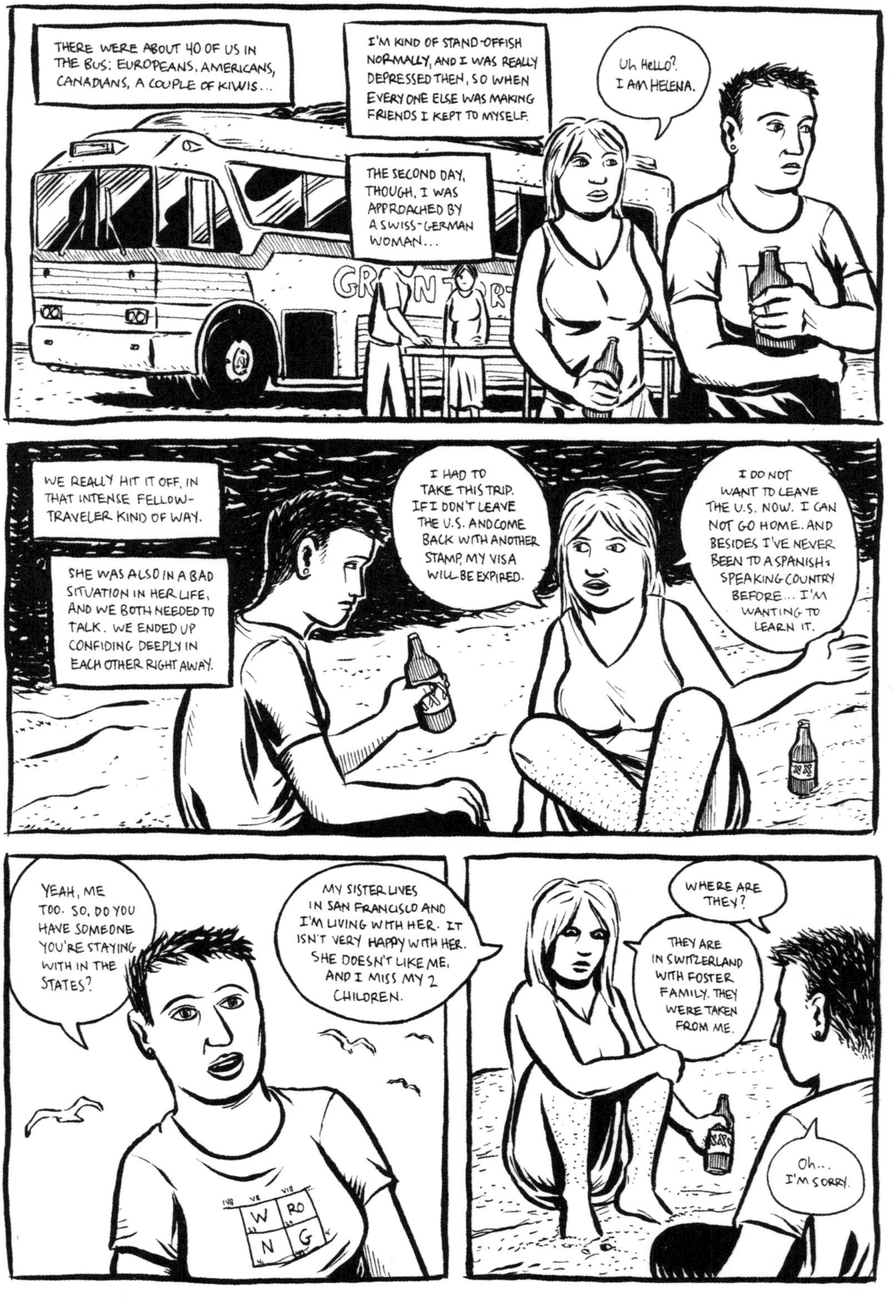
THERE WERE ABOUT 40 OF US IN THE BUS: EUROPEANS, AMERICANS, CANADIANS, A COUPLE OF KIWIS...
I'M KIND OF STAND-OFFISH NORMALLY, AND I WAS REALLY DEPRESSED THEN, SO WHEN EVERYONE ELSE WAS MAKING FRIENDS I KEPT TO MYSELF.
THE SECOND DAY, THOUGH, I WAS APPROACHED BY A SWISS-GERMAN WOMAN...
Uh Hello? I AM HELENA.
WE REALLY HIT IT OFF, IN THAT INTENSE FELLOW-TRAVELER KIND OF WAY.
SHE WAS ALSO IN A BAD SITUATION IN HER LIFE, AND WE BOTH NEEDED TO TALK. WE ENDED UP CONFIDING DEEPLY IN EACH OTHER RIGHT AWAY.
I HAD TO TAKE THIS TRIP. IF I DON'T LEAVE THE U.S. AND COME BACK WITH ANOTHER STAMP, MY VISA WILL BE EXPIRED.
I DO NOT WANT TO LEAVE THE U.S. NOW. I CAN NOT GO HOME. AND BESIDES I'VE NEVER BEEN TO A SPANISH-SPEAKING COUNTRY BEFORE... I'M WANTING TO LEARN IT.
YEAH, ME TOO. SO, DO YOU HAVE SOMEONE YOU'RE STAYING WITH IN THE STATES?
MY SISTER LIVES IN SAN FRANCISCO AND I'M LIVING WITH HER. IT ISN'T VERY HAPPY WITH HER. SHE DOESN'T LIKE ME, AND I MISS MY 2 CHILDREN.
W RO N G
WHERE ARE THEY?
THEY ARE IN SWITZERLAND WITH FOSTER FAMILY. THEY WERE TAKEN FROM ME.
Oh... I'M SORRY.

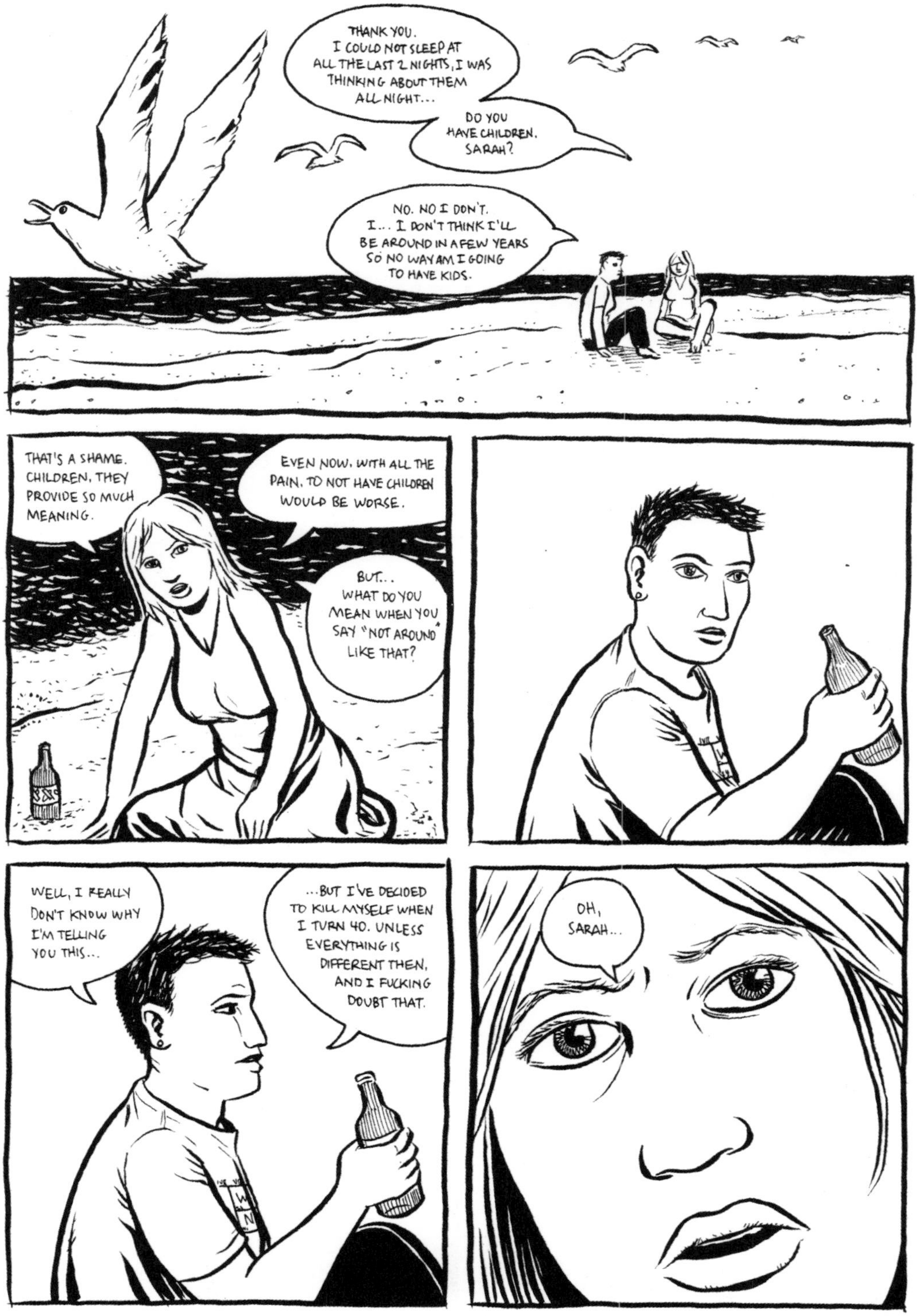
THANK YOU. I COULD NOT SLEEP AT ALL THE LAST 2 NIGHTS, I WAS THINKING ABOUT THEM ALL NIGHT...
DO YOU HAVE CHILDREN, SARAH?
NO. NO I DON'T. I... I DON'T THINK I'LL BE AROUND IN A FEW YEARS SO NO WAY AM I GOING TO HAVE KIDS.
THAT'S A SHAME. CHILDREN, THEY PROVIDE SO MUCH MEANING.
EVEN NOW, WITH ALL THE PAIN, TO NOT HAVE CHILDREN WOULD BE WORSE.
BUT... WHAT DO YOU MEAN WHEN YOU SAY "NOT AROUND" LIKE THAT?
WELL, I REALLY DON'T KNOW WHY I'M TELLING YOU THIS...
...BUT I'VE DECIDED TO KILL MYSELF WHEN I TURN 40. UNLESS EVERYTHING IS DIFFERENT THEN, AND I FUCKING DOUBT THAT.
OH, SARAH...

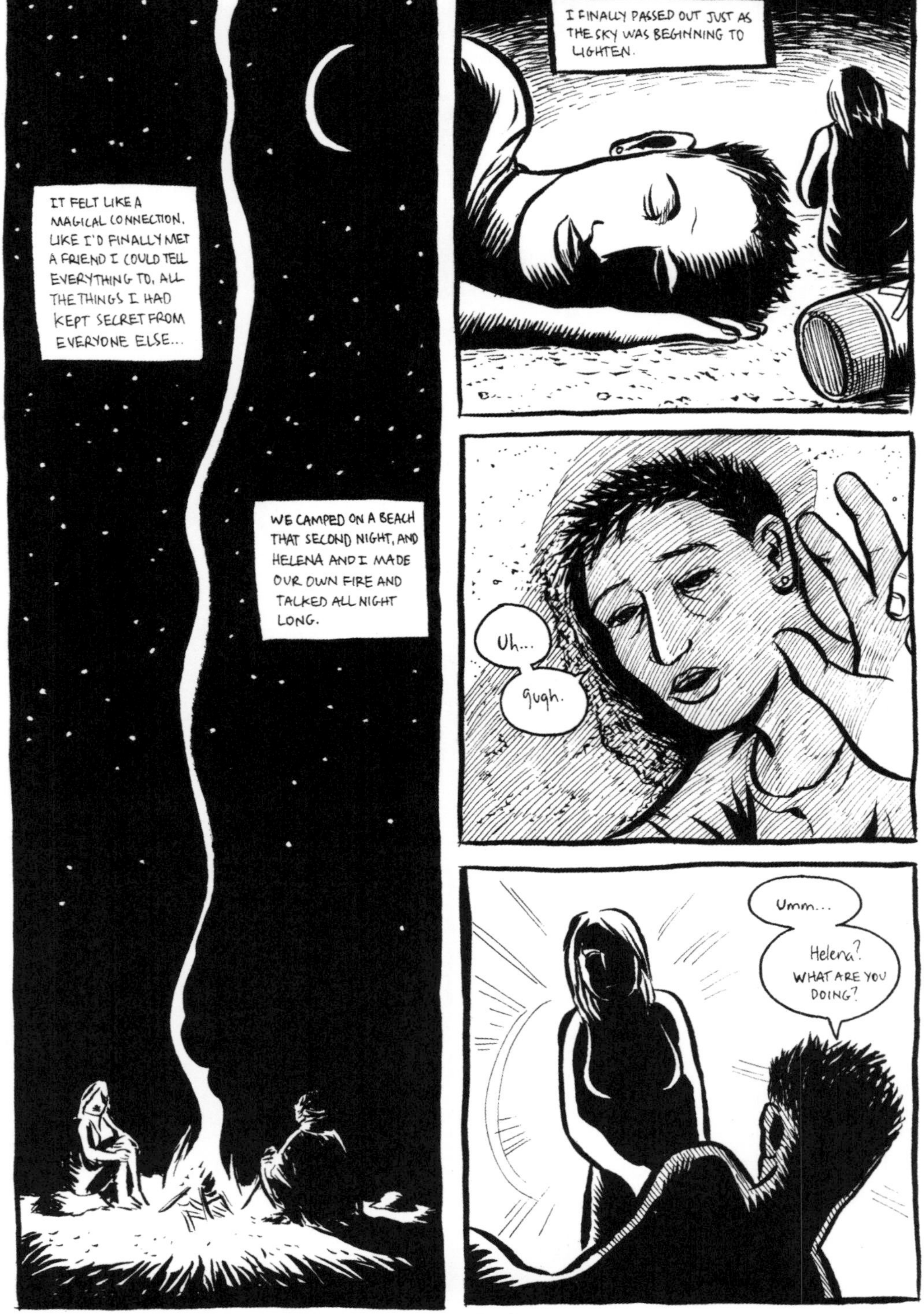
IT FELT LIKE A MAGICAL CONNECTION. LIKE I'D FINALLY MET A FRIEND I COULD TELL EVERYTHING TO, ALL THE THINGS I HAD KEPT SECRET FROM EVERYONE ELSE...
WE CAMPED ON A BEACH THAT SECOND NIGHT, AND HELENA AND I MADE OUR OWN FIRE AND TALKED ALL NIGHT LONG.
I FINALLY PASSED OUT JUST AS THE SKY WAS BEGINNING TO LIGHTEN.
Uh...
Gugh.
Umm...
Helena? WHAT ARE YOU DOING?

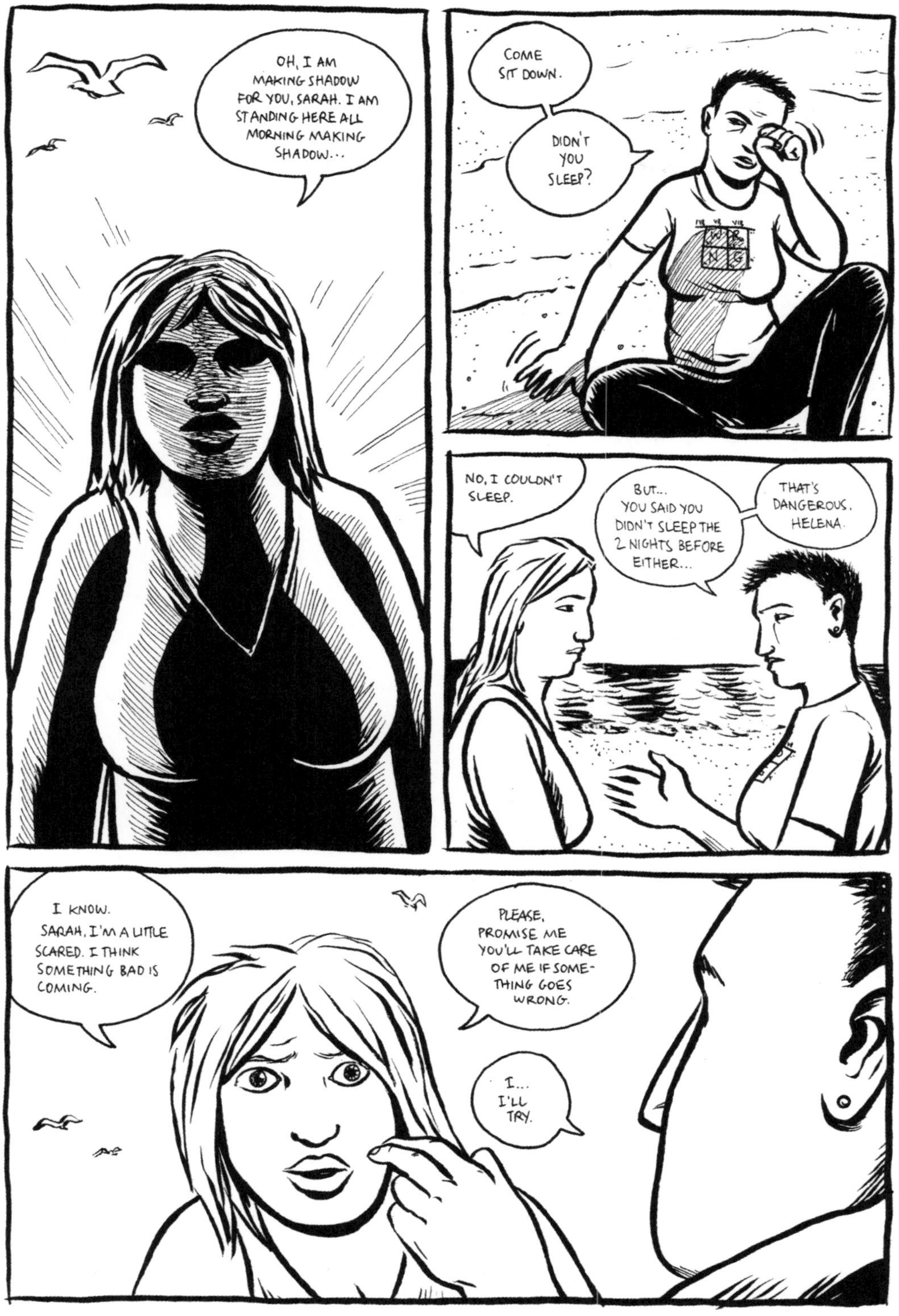
OH, I AM MAKING SHADOW FOR YOU, SARAH. I AM STANDING HERE ALL MORNING MAKING SHADOW...
COME SIT DOWN.
DIDN'T YOU SLEEP?
NO, I COULDN'T SLEEP.
BUT... YOU SAID YOU DIDN'T SLEEP THE 2 NIGHTS BEFORE EITHER...
THAT'S DANGEROUS, HELENA.
I KNOW. SARAH, I'M A LITTLE SCARED. I THINK SOMETHING BAD IS COMING.
PLEASE, PROMISE ME YOU'LL TAKE CARE OF ME IF SOMETHING GOES WRONG.
I... I'LL TRY.

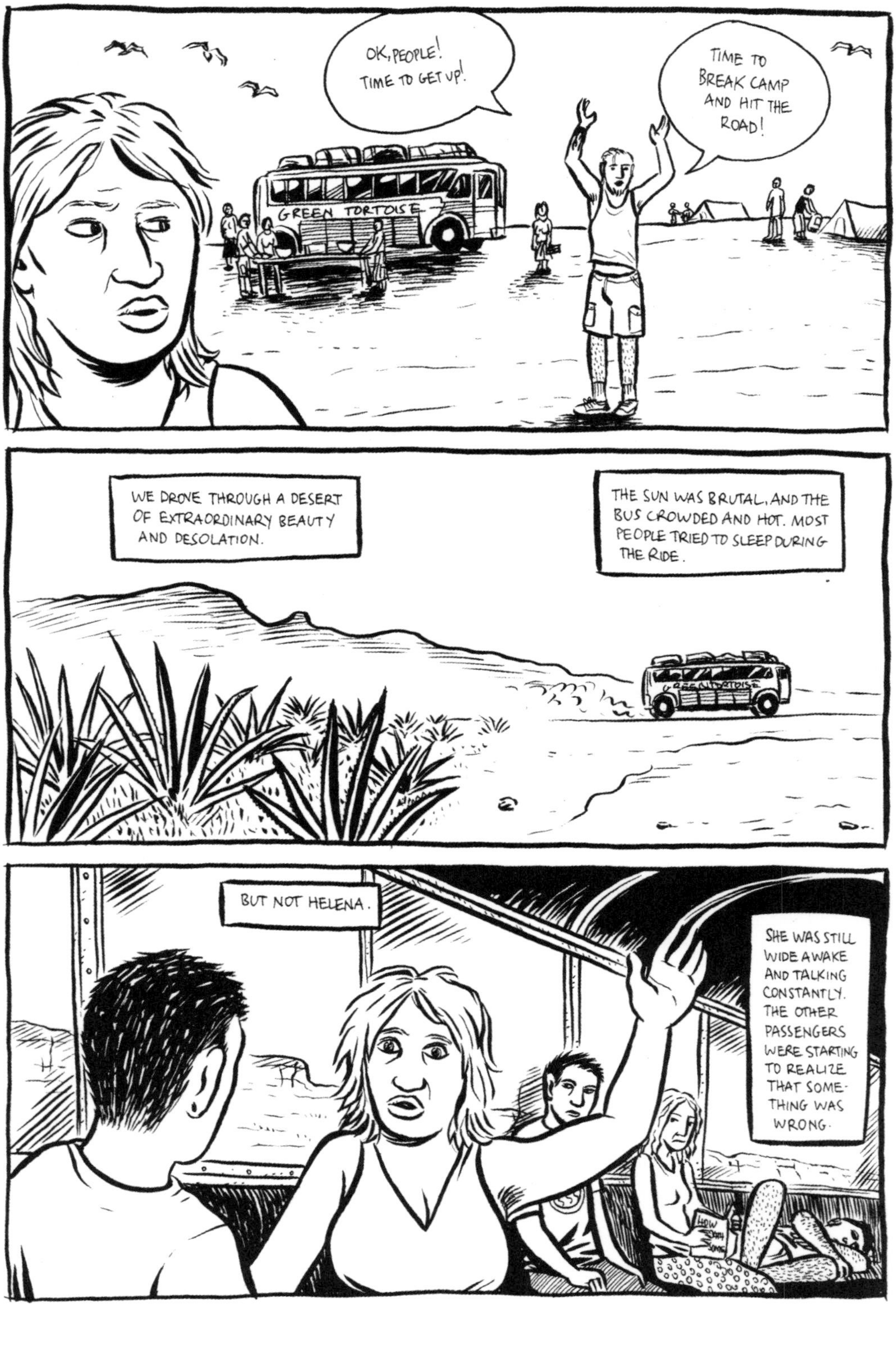
OK, PEOPLE! TIME TO GET UP!
TIME TO BREAK CAMP AND HIT THE ROAD!
GREEN TORTOISE
WE DROVE THROUGH A DESERT OF EXTRAORDINARY BEAUTY AND DESOLATION.
THE SUN WAS BRUTAL, AND THE BUS CROWDED AND HOT. MOST PEOPLE TRIED TO SLEEP DURING THE RIDE.
BUT NOT HELENA.
SHE WAS STILL WIDE AWAKE AND TALKING CONSTANTLY. THE OTHER PASSENGERS WERE STARTING TO REALIZE THAT SOMETHING WAS WRONG.

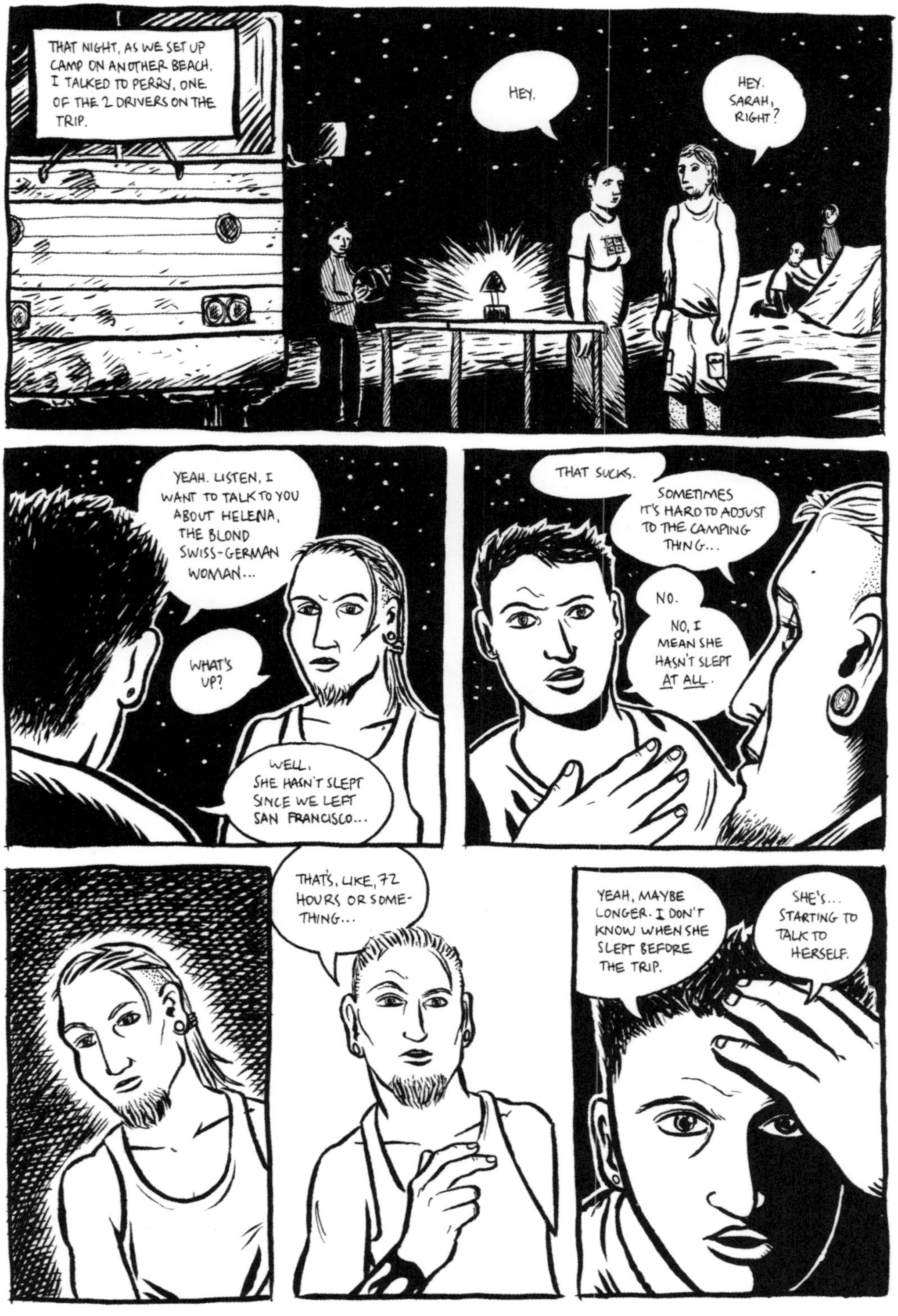
THAT NIGHT, AS WE SET UP CAMP ON ANOTHER BEACH, I TALKED TO PERRY, ONE OF THE 2 DRIVERS ON THE TRIP.
HEY.
HEY. SARAH, RIGHT?
YEAH. LISTEN, I WANT TO TALK TO YOU ABOUT HELENA, THE BLOND SWISS-GERMAN WOMAN...
WHAT'S UP?
WELL, SHE HASN'T SLEPT SINCE WE LEFT SAN FRANCISCO...
THAT SUCKS.
SOMETIMES IT'S HARD TO ADJUST TO THE CAMPING THING...
NO.
NO, I MEAN SHE HASN'T SLEPT AT ALL.
THAT'S, LIKE, 72 HOURS OR SOMETHING...
YEAH, MAYBE LONGER. I DON'T KNOW WHEN SHE SLEPT BEFORE THE TRIP.
SHE'S... STARTING TO TALK TO HERSELF.

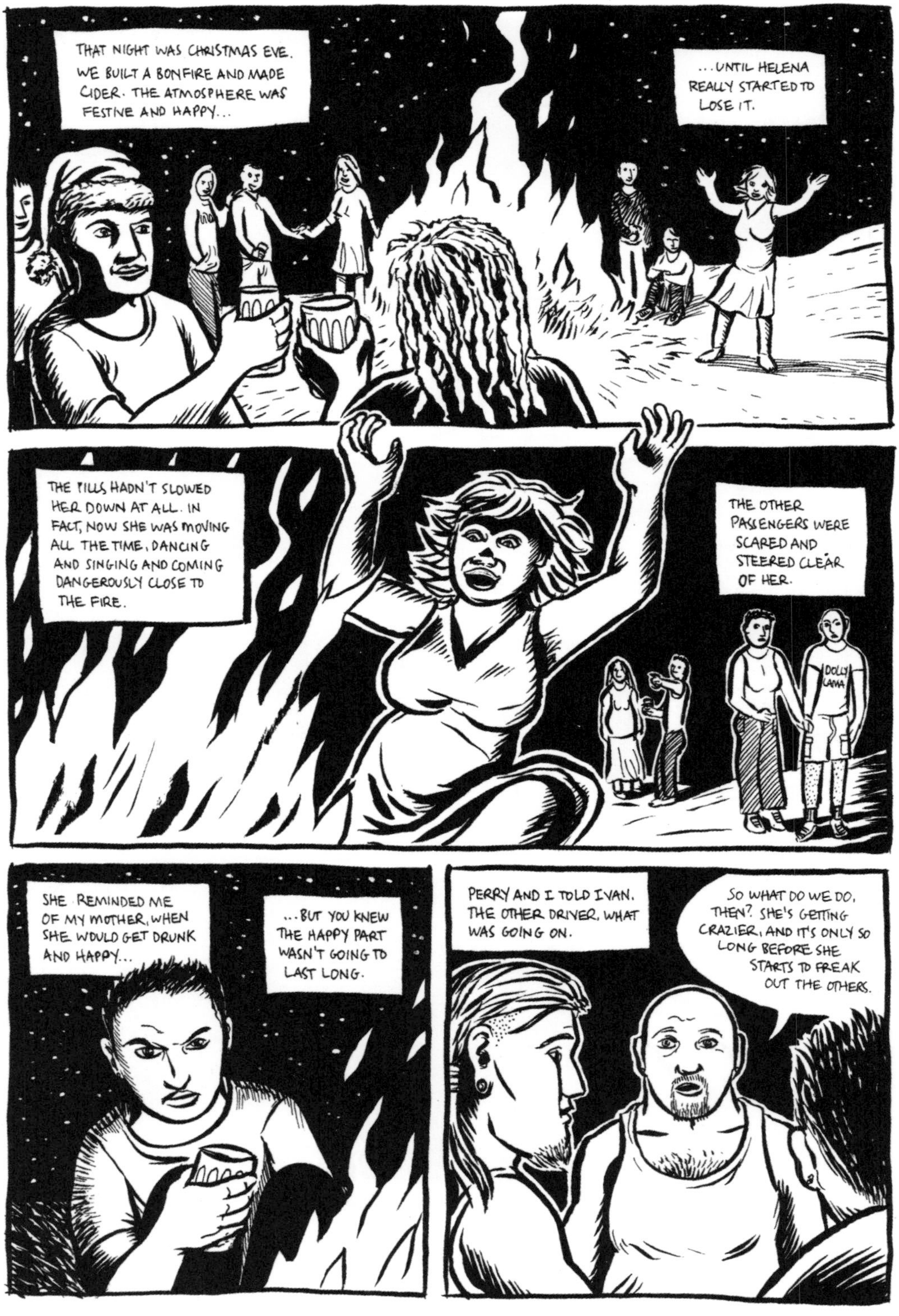
THAT NIGHT WAS CHRISTMAS EVE. WE BUILT A BONFIRE AND MADE CIDER. THE ATMOSPHERE WAS FESTIVE AND HAPPY...
...UNTIL HELENA REALLY STARTED TO LOSE IT.
THE PILLS HADN'T SLOWED HER DOWN AT ALL. IN FACT, NOW SHE WAS MOVING ALL THE TIME, DANCING AND SINGING AND COMING DANGEROUSLY CLOSE TO THE FIRE.
THE OTHER PASSENGERS WERE SCARED AND STEERED CLEAR OF HER.
DOLLY LAMA
SHE REMINDED ME OF MY MOTHER, WHEN SHE WOULD GET DRUNK AND HAPPY...
...BUT YOU KNEW THE HAPPY PART WASN'T GOING TO LAST LONG.
PERRY AND I TOLD IVAN, THE OTHER DRIVER, WHAT WAS GOING ON.
SO WHAT DO WE DO, THEN? SHE'S GETTING CRAZIER, AND IT'S ONLY SO LONG BEFORE SHE STARTS TO FREAK OUT THE OTHERS.

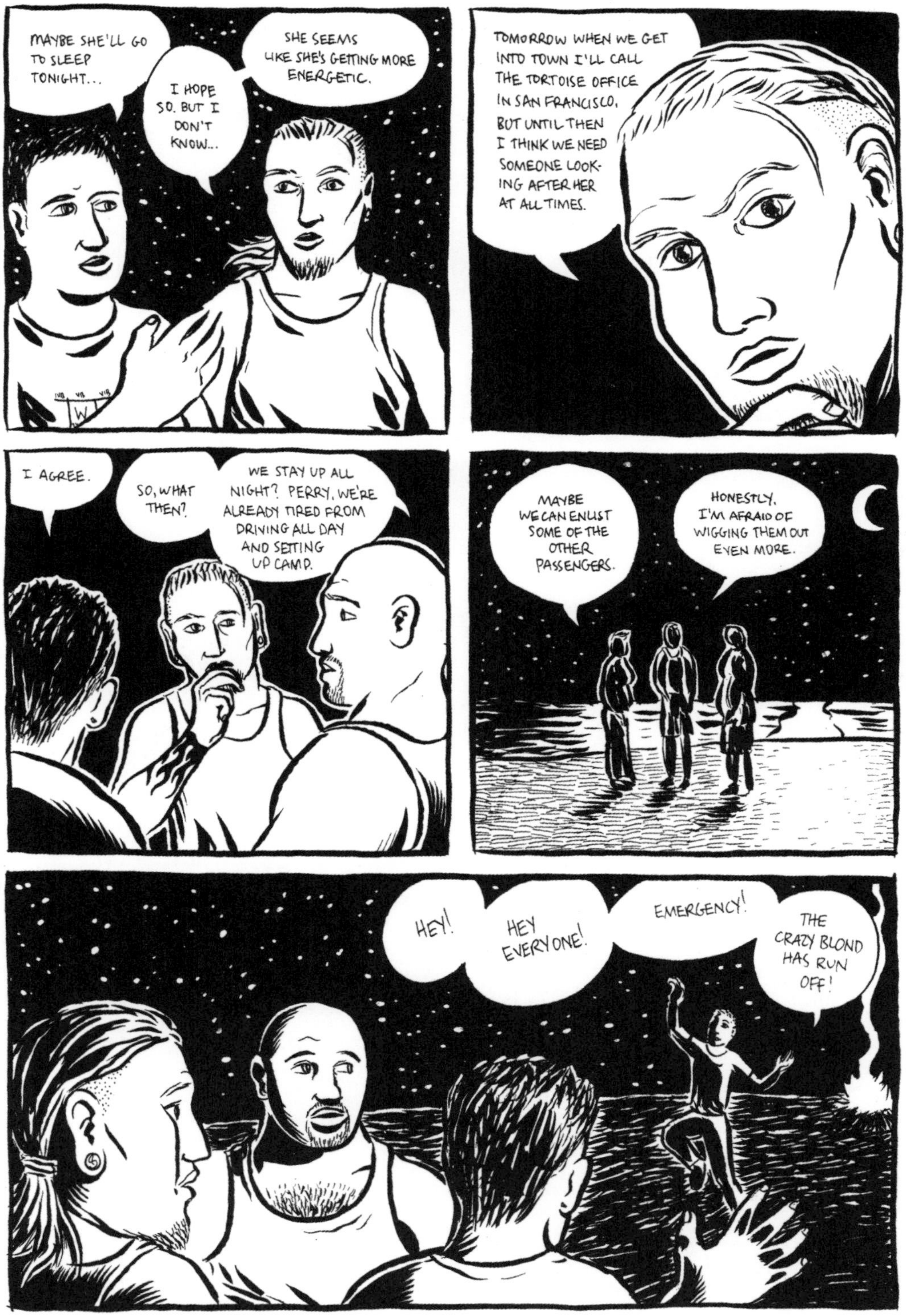
MAYBE SHE'LL GO TO SLEEP TONIGHT...
I HOPE SO. BUT I DON'T KNOW...
SHE SEEMS LIKE SHE'S GETTING MORE ENERGETIC.
TOMORROW WHEN WE GET INTO TOWN I'LL CALL THE TORTOISE OFFICE IN SAN FRANCISCO. BUT UNTIL THEN I THINK WE NEED SOMEONE LOOKING AFTER HER AT ALL TIMES.
I AGREE.
SO, WHAT THEN?
WE STAY UP ALL NIGHT? PERRY, WE'RE ALREADY TIRED FROM DRIVING ALL DAY AND SETTING UP CAMP.
MAYBE WE CAN ENLIST SOME OF THE OTHER PASSENGERS.
HONESTLY, I'M AFRAID OF WIGGING THEM OUT EVEN MORE.
HEY!
HEY EVERYONE!
EMERGENCY!
THE CRAZY BLOND HAS RUN OFF!

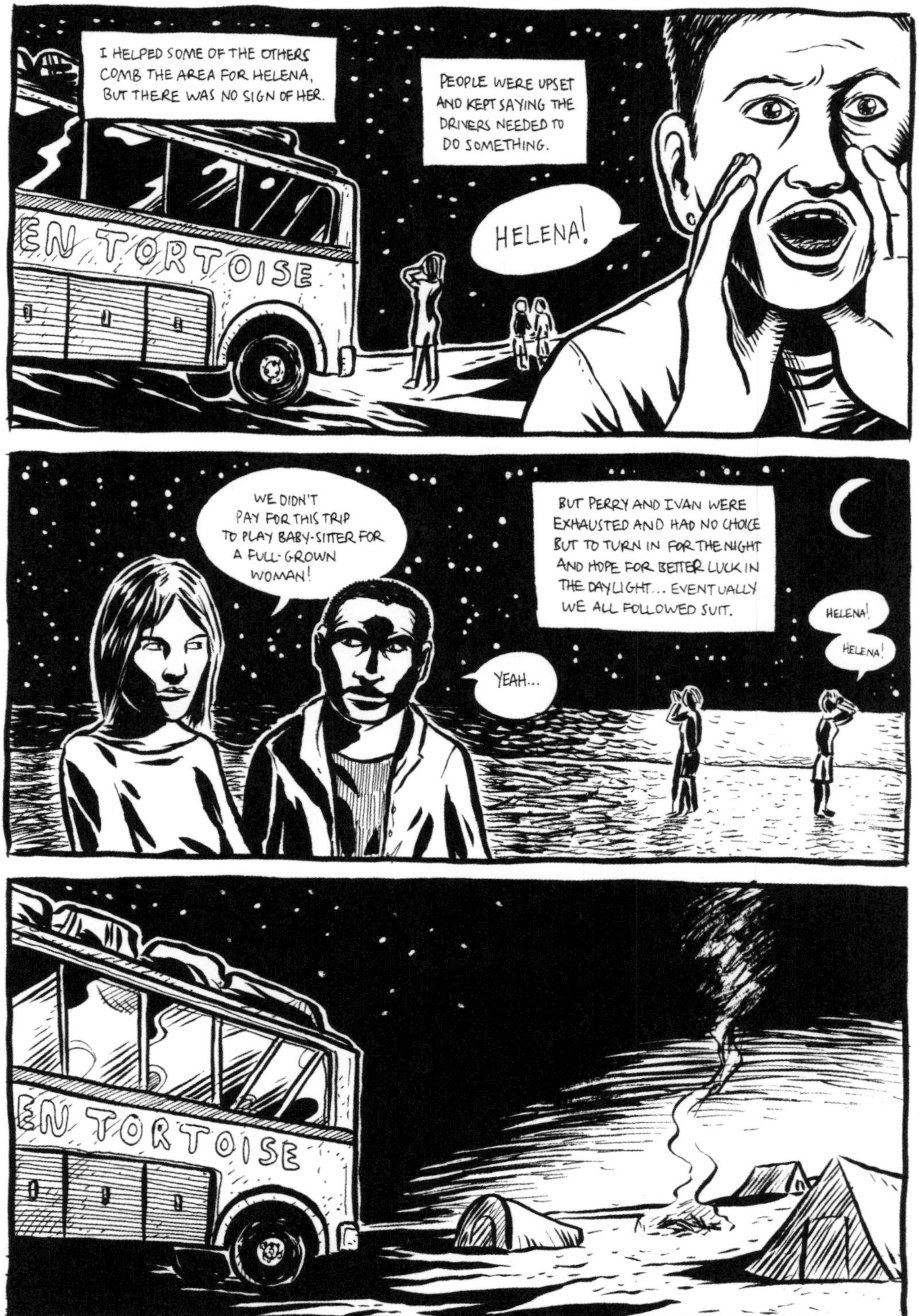
I HELPED SOME OF THE OTHERS COMB THE AREA FOR HELENA, BUT THERE WAS NO SIGN OF HER.
PEOPLE WERE UPSET AND KEPT SAYING THE DRIVERS NEEDED TO DO SOMETHING.
EN TORTOISE
HELENA!
WE DIDN'T PAY FOR THIS TRIP TO PLAY BABY-SITTER FOR A FULL-GROWN WOMAN!
YEAH...
BUT PERRY AND IVAN WERE EXHAUSTED AND HAD NO CHOICE BUT TO TURN IN FOR THE NIGHT AND HOPE FOR BETTER LUCK IN THE DAYLIGHT... EVENTUALLY WE ALL FOLLOWED SUIT.
HELENA!
HELENA!
EN TORTOISE

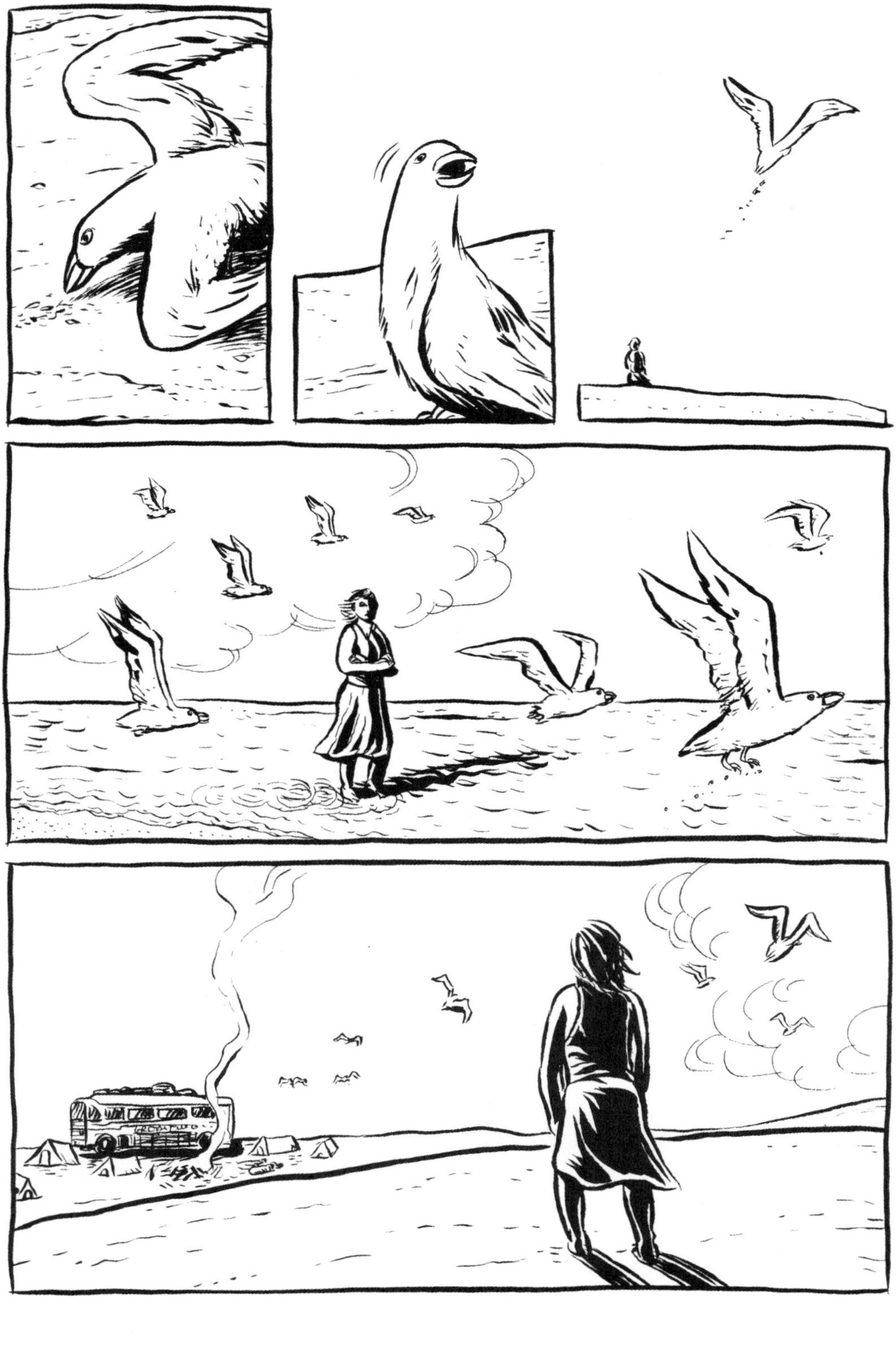

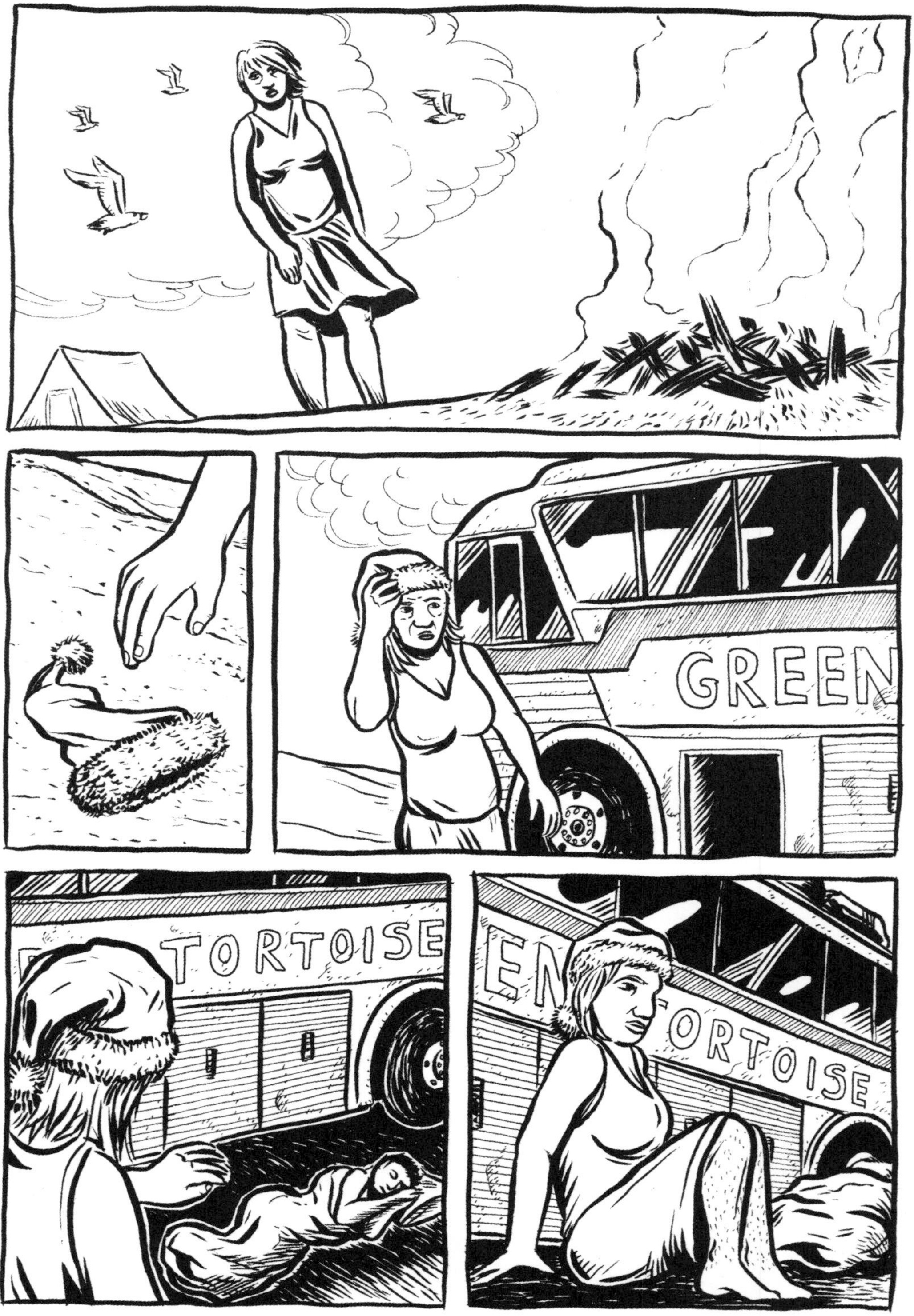
GREEN
TORTOISE
EN
ORTOISE

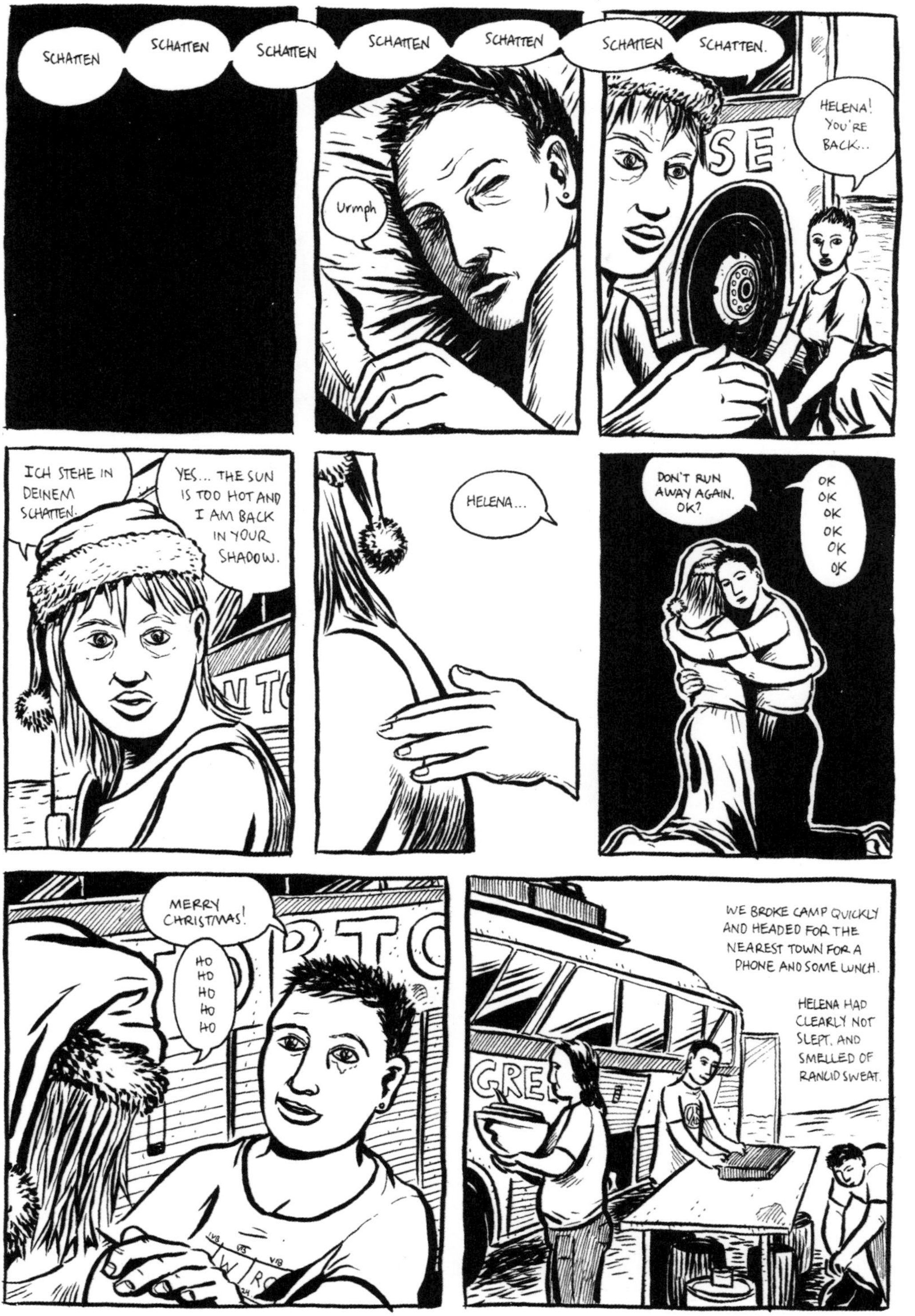
SCHATTEN
SCHATTEN
SCHATTEN
SCHATTEN
SCHATTEN
SCHATTEN
SCHATTEN.
Urmph
HELENA! YOU'RE BACK..
ICH STEHE IN DEINEM SCHATTEN.
YES... THE SUN IS TOO HOT AND I AM BACK IN YOUR SHADOW.
HELENA...
DON'T RUN AWAY AGAIN. OK?
OK OK OK OK OK OK
MERRY CHRISTMAS!
HO HO HO HO HO
WE BROKE CAMP QUICKLY AND HEADED FOR THE NEAREST TOWN FOR A PHONE AND SOME LUNCH.
HELENA HAD CLEARLY NOT SLEPT, AND SMELLED OF RANCID SWEAT.

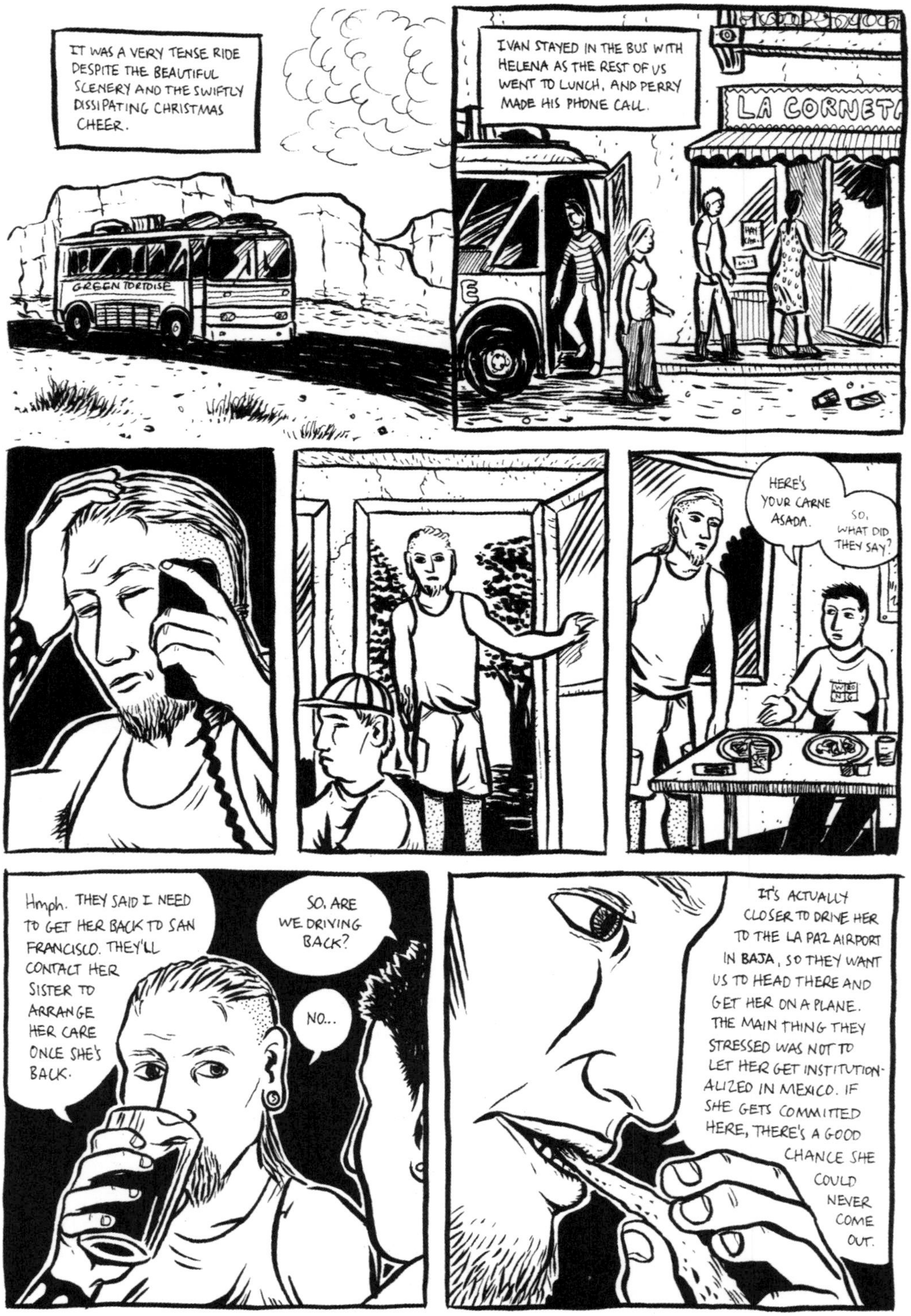

IT WAS A VERY TENSE RIDE DESPITE THE BEAUTIFUL SCENERY AND THE SWIFTLY DISSIPATING CHRISTMAS CHEER.
GREEN TORTOISE
IVAN STAYED IN THE BUS WITH HELENA AS THE REST OF US WENT TO LUNCH, AND PERRY MADE HIS PHONE CALL.
LA CORNETA
HERE'S YOUR CARNE ASADA.
SO, WHAT DID THEY SAY?
Hmph. THEY SAID I NEED TO GET HER BACK TO SAN FRANCISCO. THEY'LL CONTACT HER SISTER TO ARRANGE HER CARE ONCE SHE'S BACK.
SO, ARE WE DRIVING BACK?
NO...
IT'S ACTUALLY CLOSER TO DRIVE HER TO THE LA PAZ AIRPORT IN BAJA, SO THEY WANT US TO HEAD THERE AND GET HER ON A PLANE. THE MAIN THING THEY STRESSED WAS NOT TO LET HER GET INSTITUTIONALIZED IN MEXICO. IF SHE GETS COMMITTED HERE, THERE'S A GOOD CHANCE SHE COULD NEVER COME OUT.

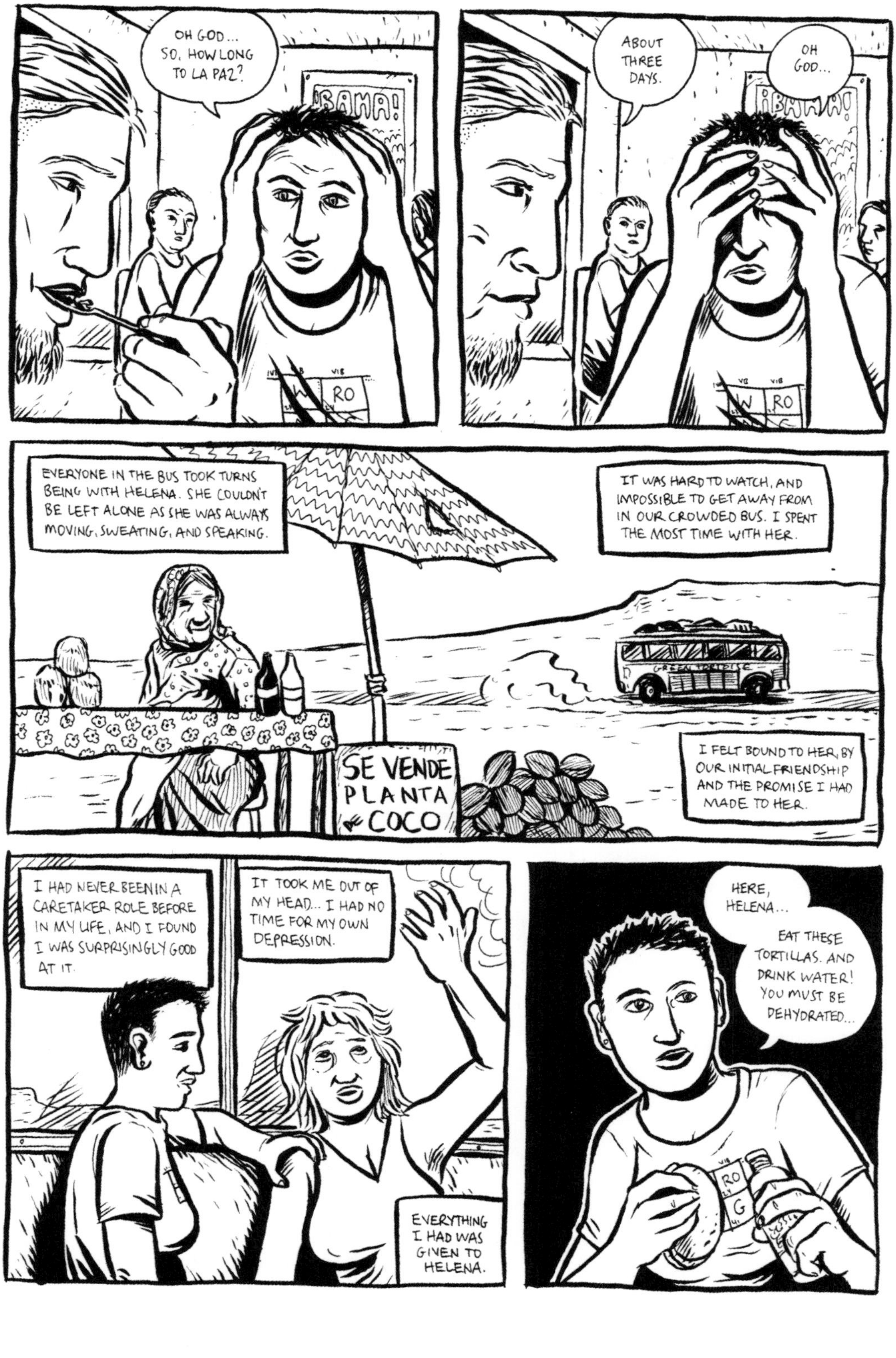
OH GOD... SO, HOW LONG TO LA PAZ?
ABOUT THREE DAYS.
OH GOD...
EVERYONE IN THE BUS TOOK TURNS BEING WITH HELENA. SHE COULDN'T BE LEFT ALONE AS SHE WAS ALWAYS MOVING, SWEATING, AND SPEAKING.
IT WAS HARD TO WATCH, AND IMPOSSIBLE TO GET AWAY FROM IN OUR CROWDED BUS. I SPENT THE MOST TIME WITH HER.
SE VENDE PLANTA COCO
I FELT BOUND TO HER, BY OUR INITIAL FRIENDSHIP AND THE PROMISE I HAD MADE TO HER.
I HAD NEVER BEEN IN A CARETAKER ROLE BEFORE IN MY LIFE, AND I FOUND I WAS SURPRISINGLY GOOD AT IT.
IT TOOK ME OUT OF MY HEAD... I HAD NO TIME FOR MY OWN DEPRESSION.
EVERYTHING I HAD WAS GIVEN TO HELENA.
HERE, HELENA...
EAT THESE TORTILLAS. AND DRINK WATER! YOU MUST BE DEHYDRATED...

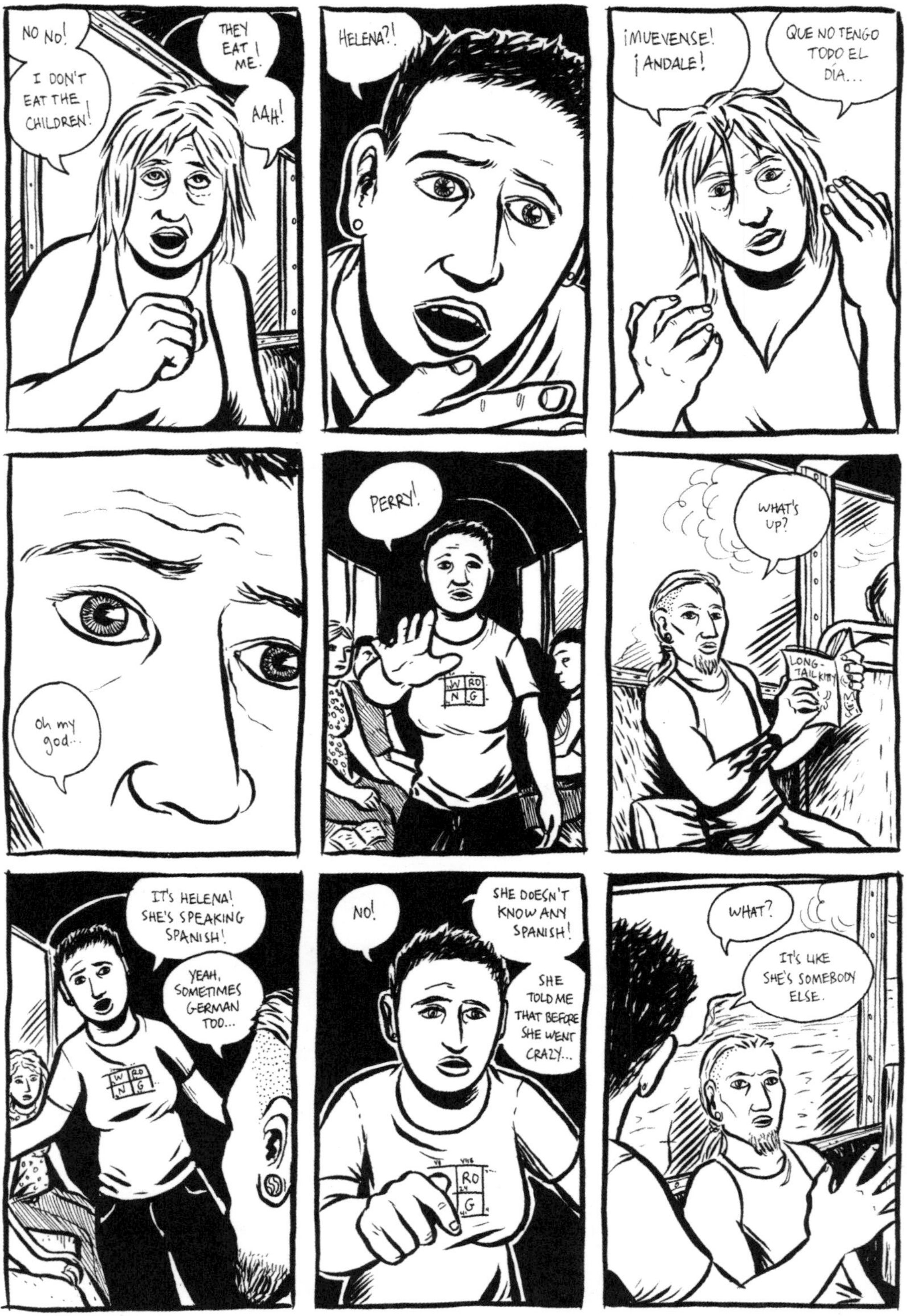
NO NO!
I DON'T EAT THE CHILDREN!
THEY EAT ME.
AAH!
HELENA?!
¡MUEVENSE! ¡ANDALE!
QUE NO TENGO TODO EL DÍA...
Oh my god...
PERRY!
WHAT'S UP?
LONG-TAIL KITTY
IT'S HELENA! SHE'S SPEAKING SPANISH!
YEAH, SOMETIMES GERMAN TOO...
NO!
SHE DOESN'T KNOW ANY SPANISH!
SHE TOLD ME THAT BEFORE SHE WENT CRAZY...
WHAT?
IT'S LIKE SHE'S SOMEBODY ELSE.

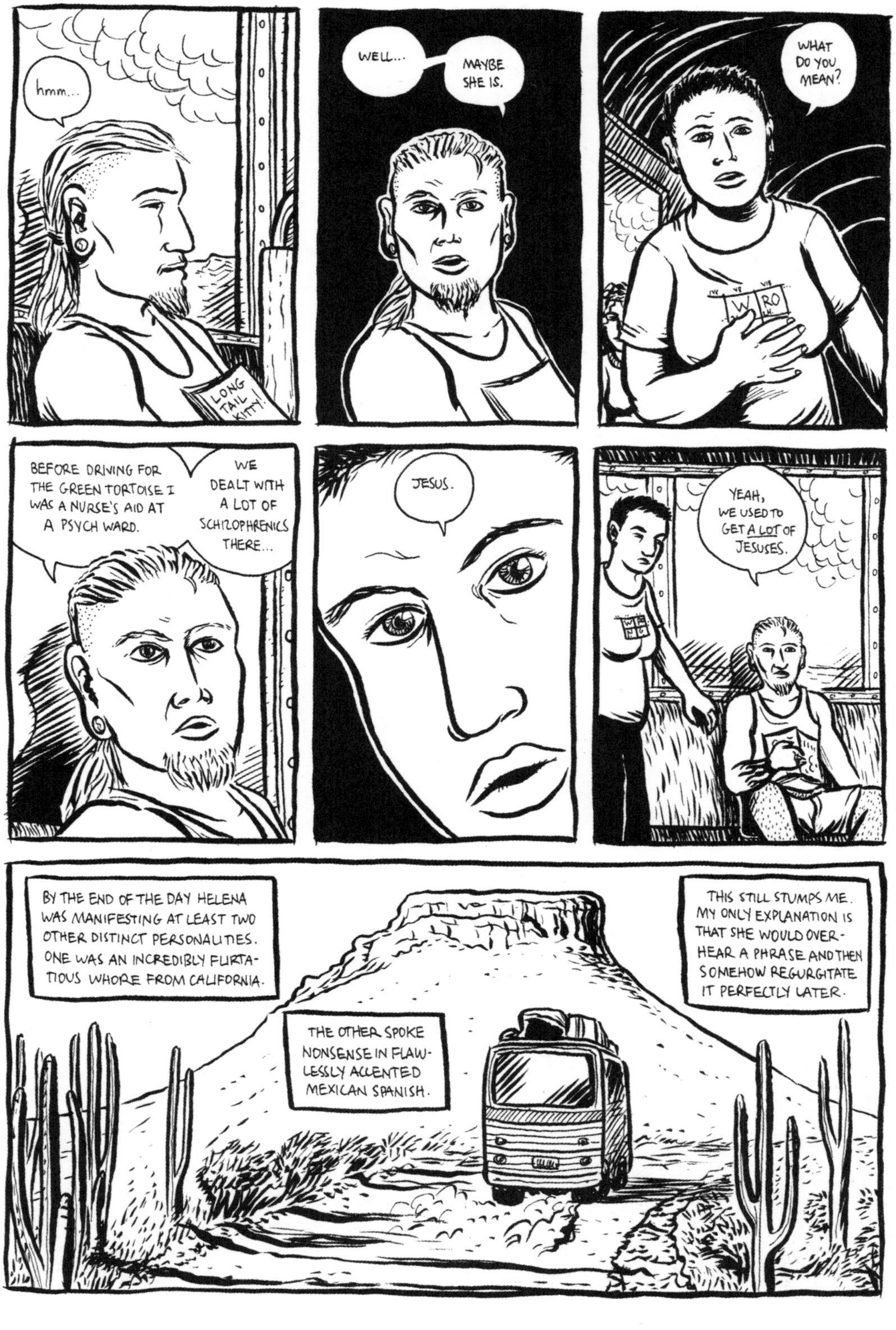
hmm...
LONG TAIL KITTY!
WELL...
MAYBE SHE IS.
WHAT DO YOU MEAN?
BEFORE DRIVING FOR THE GREEN TORTOISE I WAS A NURSE'S AID AT A PSYCH WARD.
WE DEALT WITH A LOT OF SCHIZOPHRENICS THERE...
JESUS.
YEAH, WE USED TO GET A LOT OF JESUSES.
BY THE END OF THE DAY HELENA WAS MANIFESTING AT LEAST TWO OTHER DISTINCT PERSONALITIES. ONE WAS AN INCREDIBLY FLIRTATIOUS WHORE FROM CALIFORNIA.
THE OTHER SPOKE NONSENSE IN FLAWLESSLY ACCENTED MEXICAN SPANISH.
THIS STILL STUMPS ME. MY ONLY EXPLANATION IS THAT SHE WOULD OVERHEAR A PHRASE AND THEN SOMEHOW REGURGITATE IT PERFECTLY LATER.

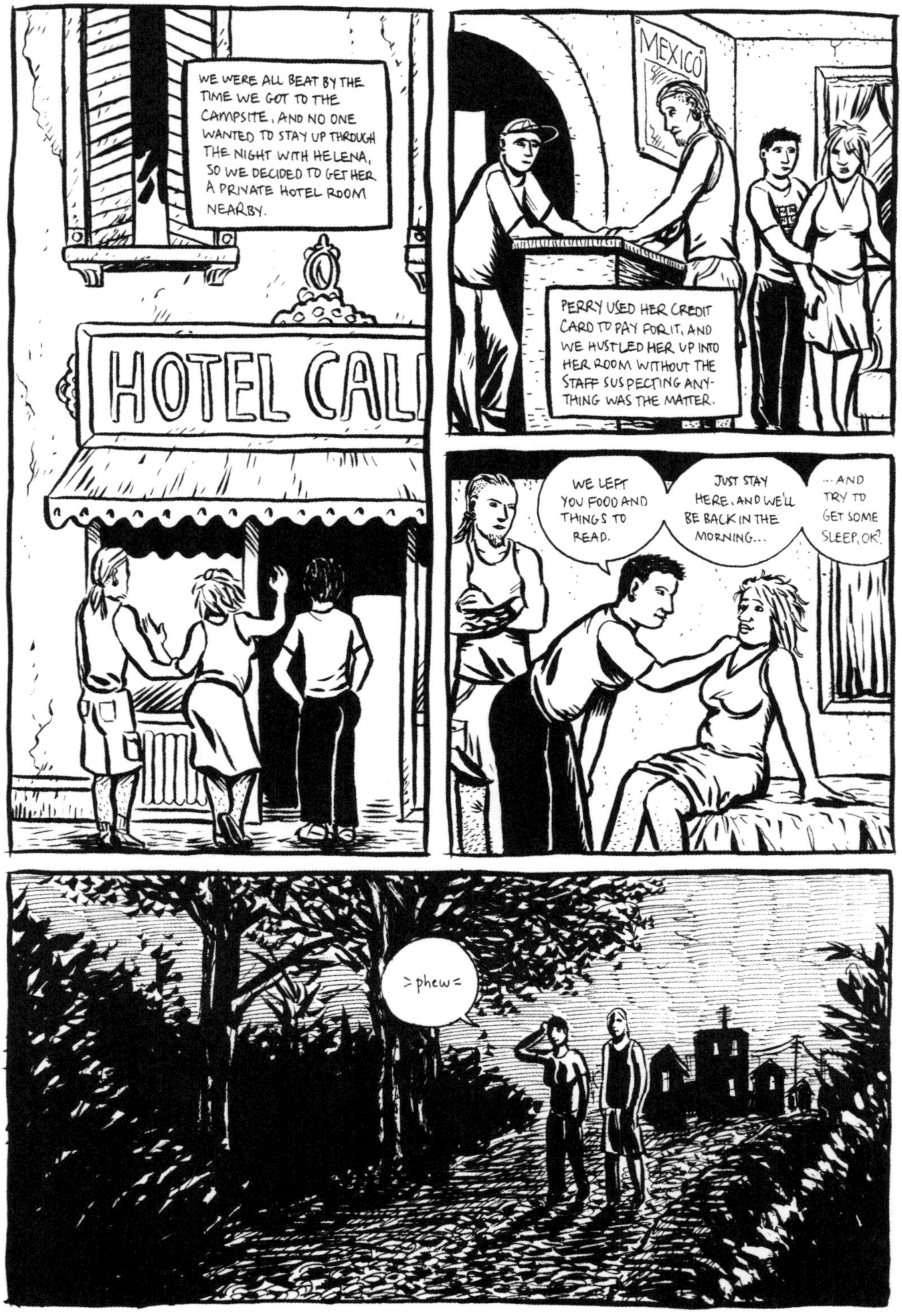
WE WERE ALL BEAT BY THE TIME WE GOT TO THE CAMPSITE, AND NO ONE WANTED TO STAY UP THROUGH THE NIGHT WITH HELENA, SO WE DECIDED TO GET HER A PRIVATE HOTEL ROOM NEARBY.
HOTEL CAL
MEXICO
PERRY USED HER CREDIT CARD TO PAY FOR IT, AND WE HUSTLED HER UP INTO HER ROOM WITHOUT THE STAFF SUSPECTING ANYTHING WAS THE MATTER.
WE LEFT YOU FOOD AND THINGS TO READ.
JUST STAY HERE, AND WE'LL BE BACK IN THE MORNING...
...AND TRY TO GET SOME SLEEP, OK?
=phew=

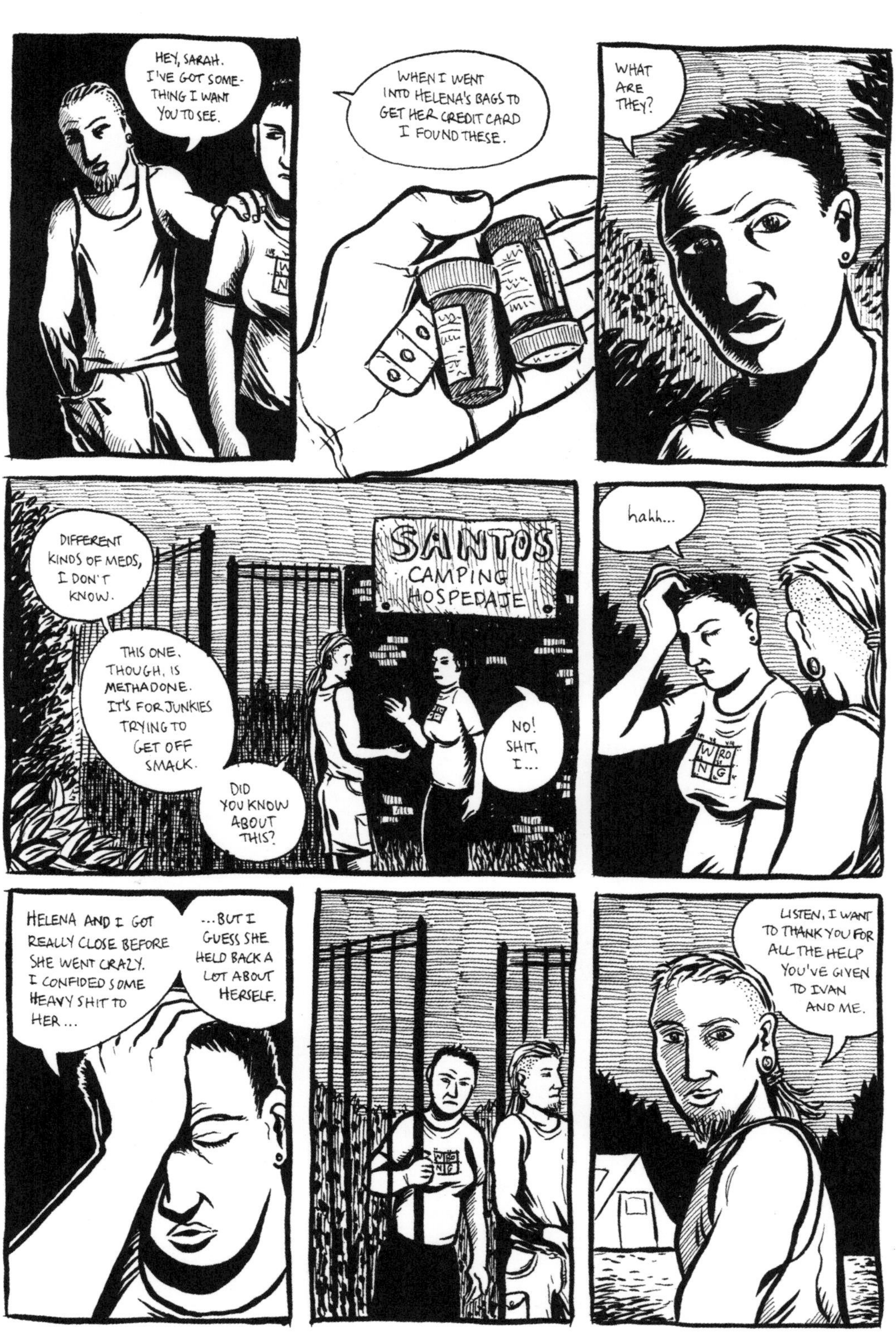
HEY, SARAH. I'VE GOT SOMETHING I WANT YOU TO SEE.
WHEN I WENT INTO HELENA'S BAGS TO GET HER CREDIT CARD I FOUND THESE.
WHAT ARE THEY?
DIFFERENT KINDS OF MEDS, I DON'T KNOW.
SANTOS CAMPING HOSPEDAJE
THIS ONE, THOUGH, IS METHADONE. IT'S FOR JUNKIES TRYING TO GET OFF SMACK.
DID YOU KNOW ABOUT THIS?
NO! SHIT, I...
hahh...
HELENA AND I GOT REALLY CLOSE BEFORE SHE WENT CRAZY. I CONFIDED SOME HEAVY SHIT TO HER...
...BUT I GUESS SHE HELD BACK A LOT ABOUT HERSELF.
LISTEN, I WANT TO THANK YOU FOR ALL THE HELP YOU'VE GIVEN TO IVAN AND ME.

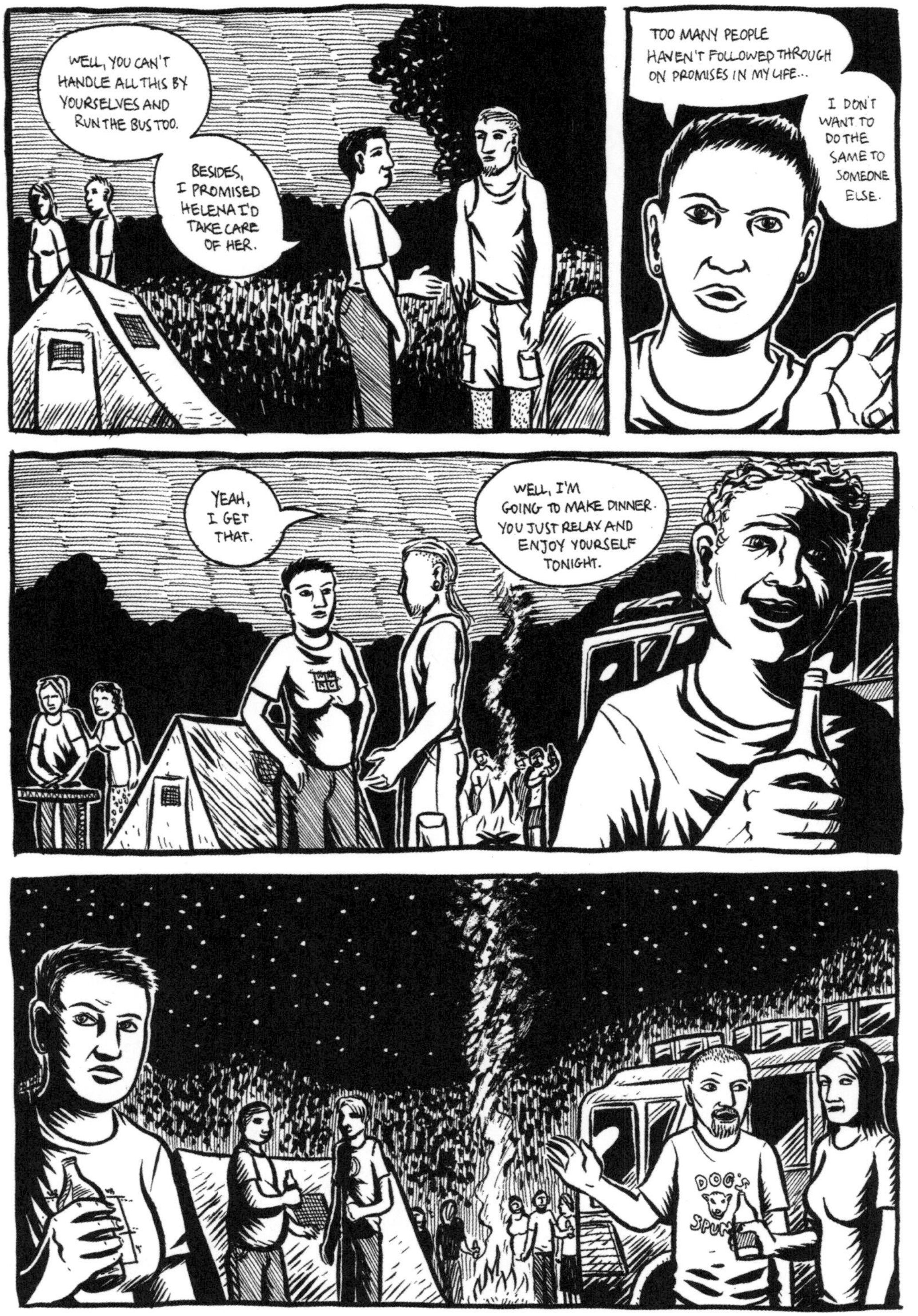
WELL, YOU CAN'T HANDLE ALL THIS BY YOURSELVES AND RUN THE BUS TOO.
BESIDES, I PROMISED HELENA I'D TAKE CARE OF HER.
TOO MANY PEOPLE HAVEN'T FOLLOWED THROUGH ON PROMISES IN MY LIFE...
I DON'T WANT TO DO THE SAME TO SOMEONE ELSE.
YEAH, I GET THAT.
WELL, I'M GOING TO MAKE DINNER. YOU JUST RELAX AND ENJOY YOURSELF TONIGHT.
DOG'S SPUNK

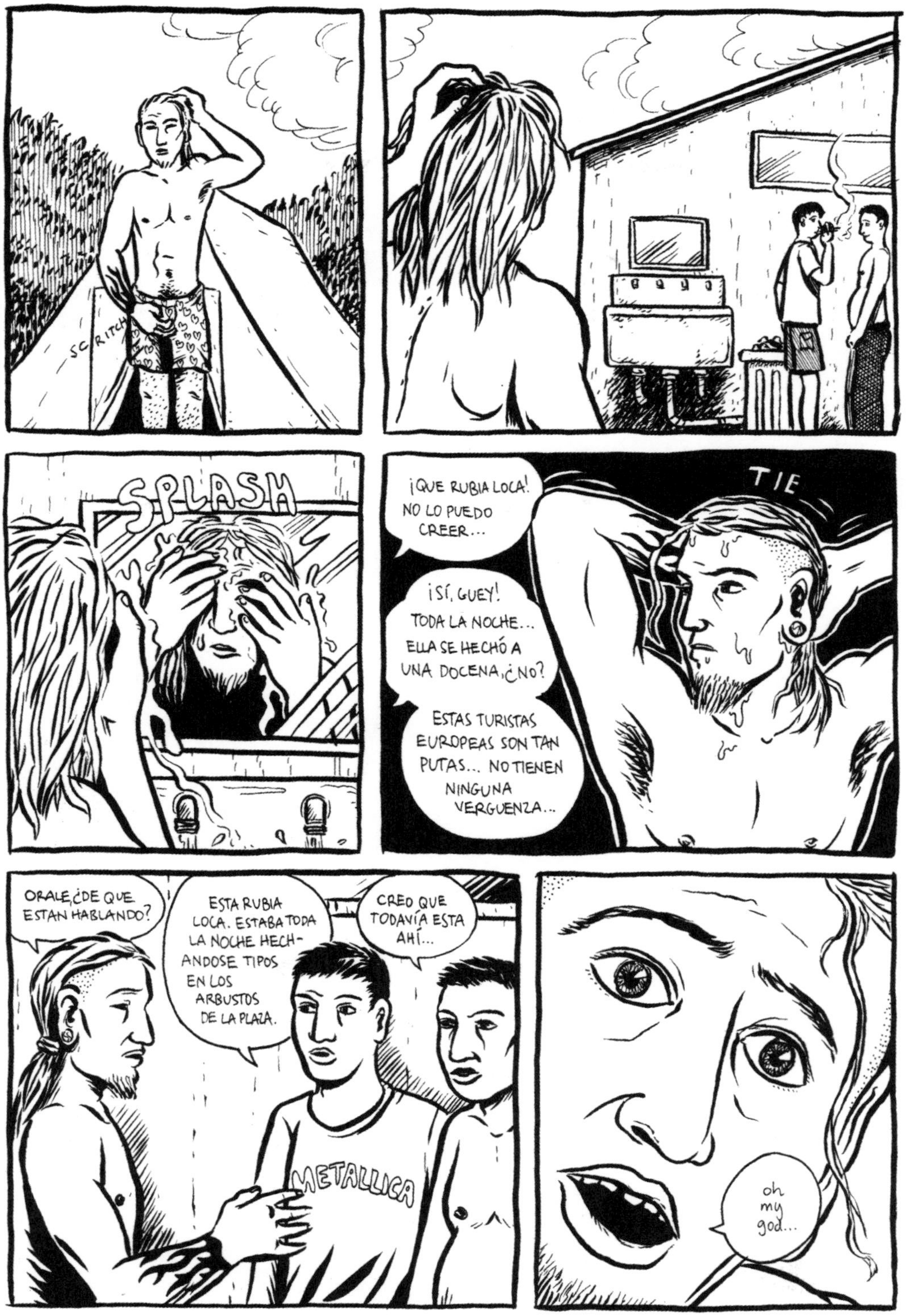
SCRITCH
SPLASH
¡QUE RUBIA LOCA! NO LO PUEDO CREER...
TIE
¡SÍ, GUEY! TODA LA NOCHE... ELLA SE HECHÓ A UNA DOCENA, ¿NO?
ESTAS TURISTAS EUROPEAS SON TAN PUTAS... NO TIENEN NINGUNA VERGUENZA...
ORALE, ¿DE QUE ESTAN HABLANDO?
ESTA RUBIA LOCA. ESTABA TODA LA NOCHE HECH-ANDOSE TIPOS EN LOS ARBUSTOS DE LA PLAZA.
CREO QUE TODAVÍA ESTA AHÍ...
METALLICA
oh my god...

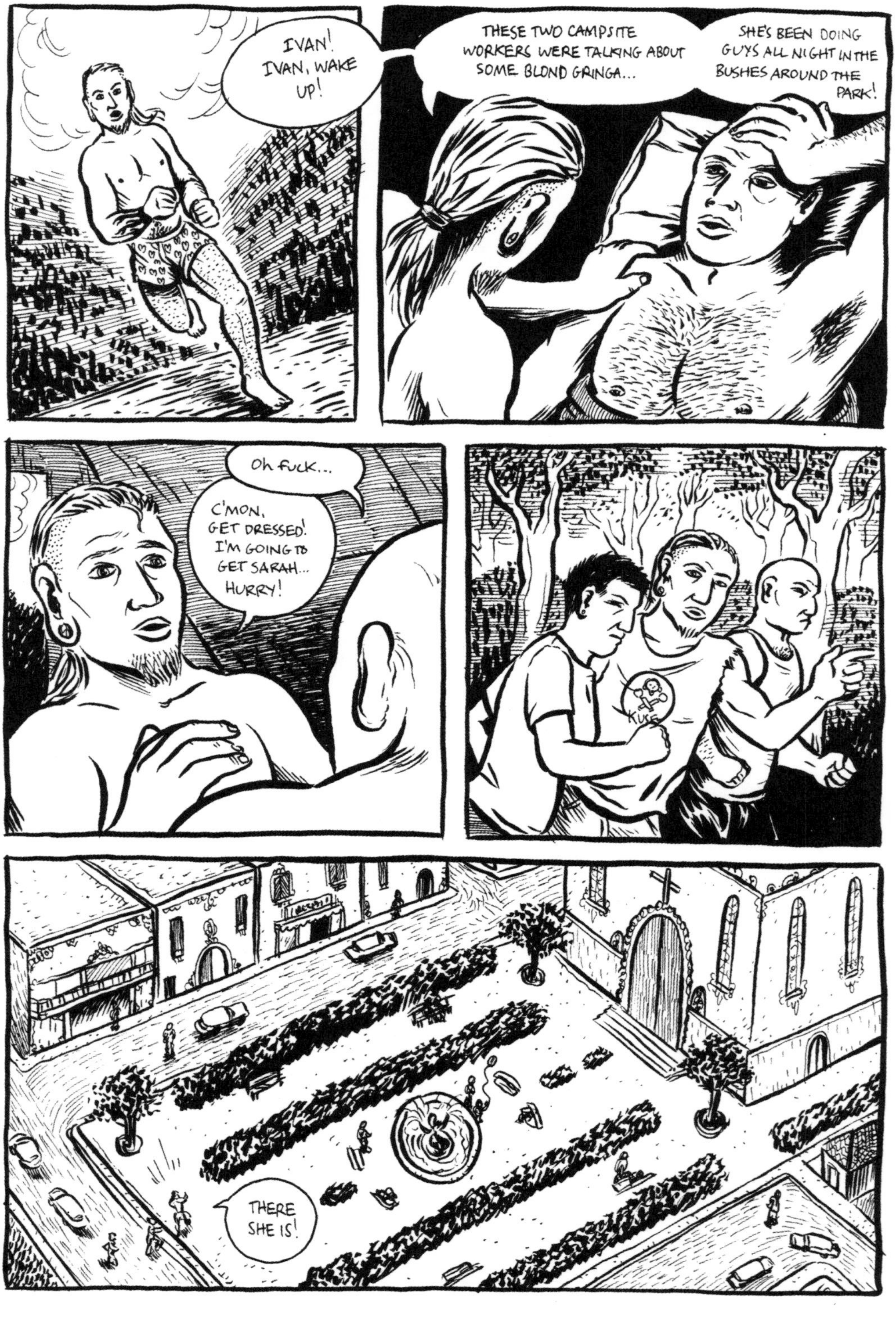
IVAN! IVAN, WAKE UP!
THESE TWO CAMPSITE WORKERS WERE TALKING ABOUT SOME BLOND GRINGA...
SHE'S BEEN DOING GUYS ALL NIGHT IN THE BUSHES AROUND THE PARK!
Oh fuck...
C'MON, GET DRESSED! I'M GOING TO GET SARAH... HURRY!
THERE SHE IS!

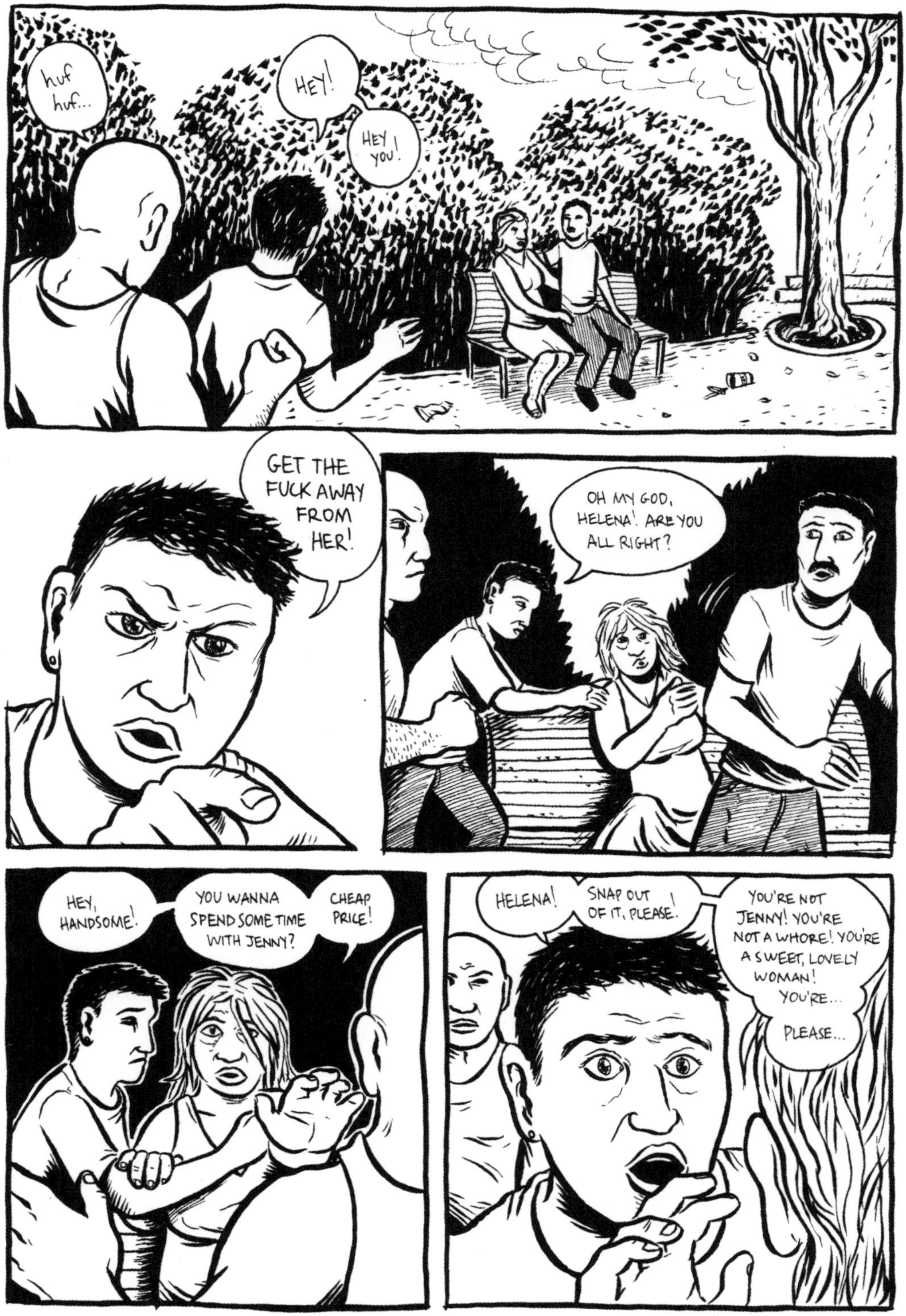
huf huf...
HEY!
HEY YOU!
GET THE FUCK AWAY FROM HER!
OH MY GOD, HELENA! ARE YOU ALL RIGHT?
HEY, HANDSOME!
YOU WANNA SPEND SOME TIME WITH JENNY?
CHEAP PRICE!
HELENA!
SNAP OUT OF IT, PLEASE!
YOU'RE NOT JENNY! YOU'RE NOT A WHORE! YOU'RE A SWEET, LOVELY WOMAN! YOU'RE...
PLEASE...

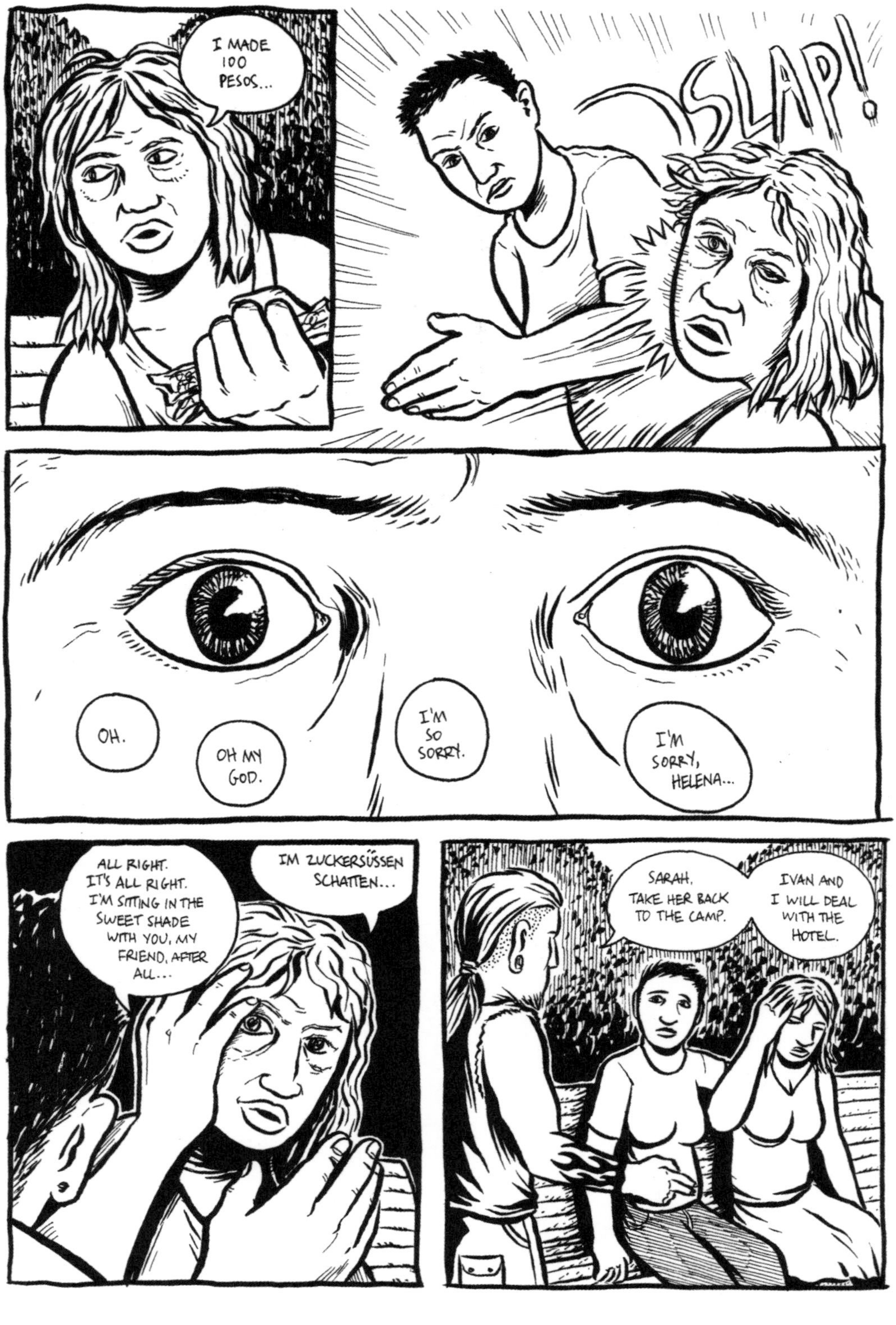
I MADE 100 PESOS...
SLAP!
OH.
OH MY GOD.
I'M SO SORRY.
I'M SORRY, HELENA...
ALL RIGHT. IT'S ALL RIGHT. I'M SITTING IN THE SWEET SHADE WITH YOU, MY FRIEND, AFTER ALL...
IM ZUCKERSÜSSEN SCHATTEN...
SARAH, TAKE HER BACK TO THE CAMP.
IVAN AND I WILL DEAL WITH THE HOTEL.

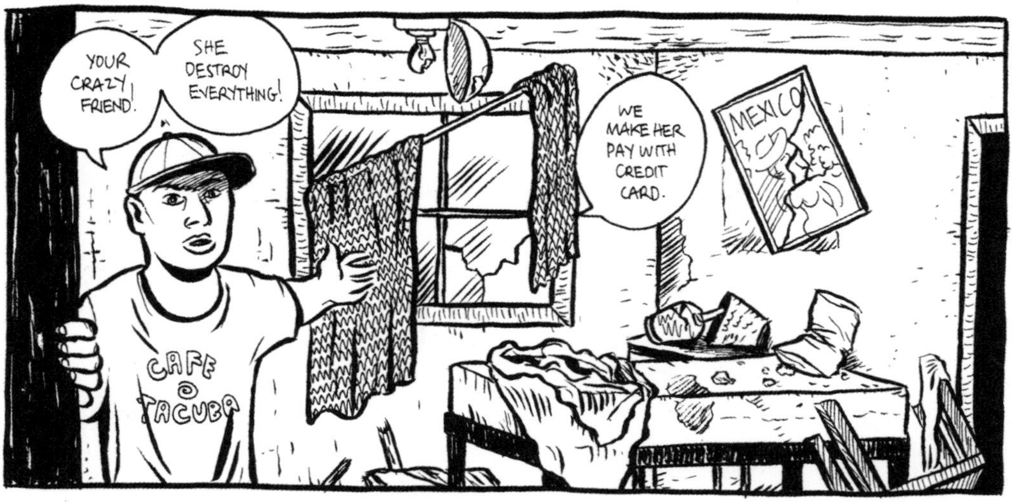
YOUR CRAZY FRIEND!
SHE DESTROY EVERYTHING!
WE MAKE HER PAY WITH CREDIT CARD.
MEXICO
CAFE TACUBA

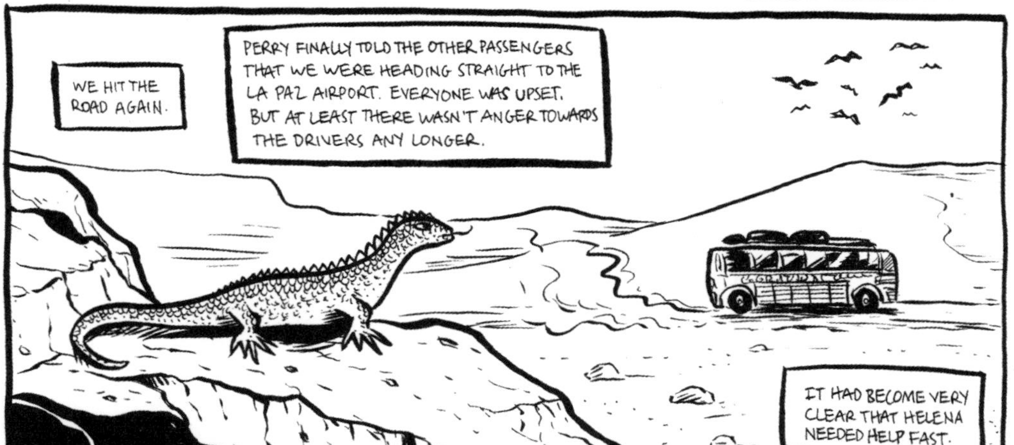
WE HIT THE ROAD AGAIN.
PERRY FINALLY TOLD THE OTHER PASSENGERS THAT WE WERE HEADING STRAIGHT TO THE LA PAZ AIRPORT. EVERYONE WAS UPSET. BUT AT LEAST THERE WASN'T ANGER TOWARDS THE DRIVERS ANY LONGER.
IT HAD BECOME VERY CLEAR THAT HELENA NEEDED HELP FAST.

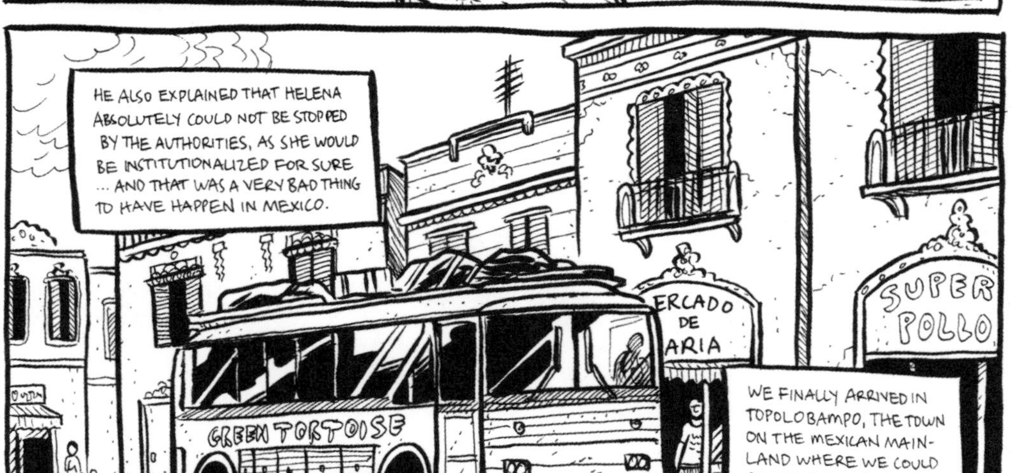
HE ALSO EXPLAINED THAT HELENA ABSOLUTELY COULD NOT BE STOPPED BY THE AUTHORITIES, AS SHE WOULD BE INSTITUTIONALIZED FOR SURE ... AND THAT WAS A VERY BAD THING TO HAVE HAPPEN IN MEXICO.
ERCADO DE ARIA
SUPER POLLO
GREEN TORTOISE
WE FINALLY ARRIVED IN TOPOLOBAMPO, THE TOWN ON THE MEXICAN MAIN-LAND WHERE WE COULD CATCH THE FERRY TO BAJA.

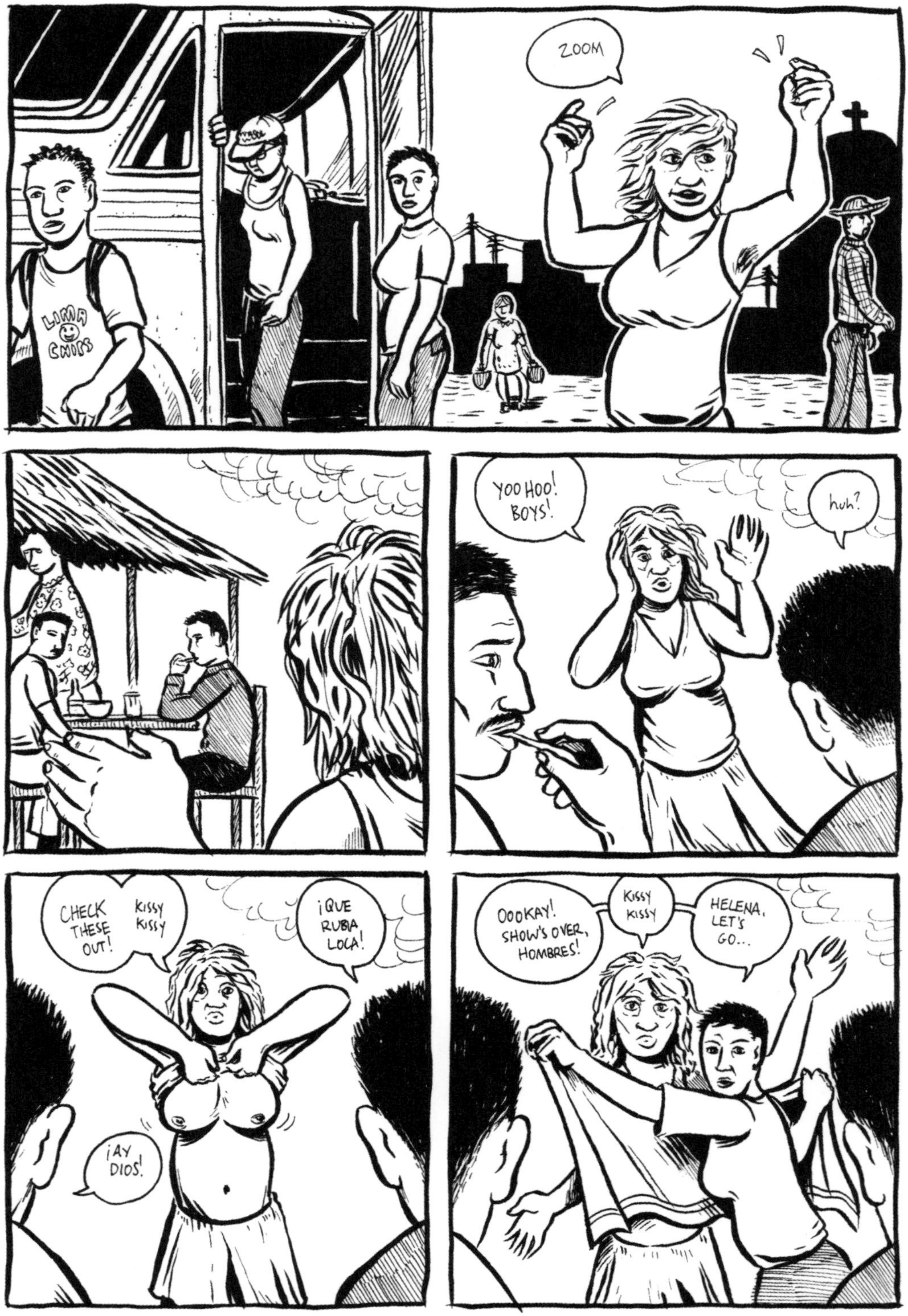
ZOOM
YOO HOO! BOYS!
huh?
CHECK THESE OUT!
KISSY KISSY
¡QUE RUBIA LOCA!
¡AY DIOS!
OOOKAY! SHOW'S OVER, HOMBRES!
KISSY KISSY
HELENA, LET'S GO...

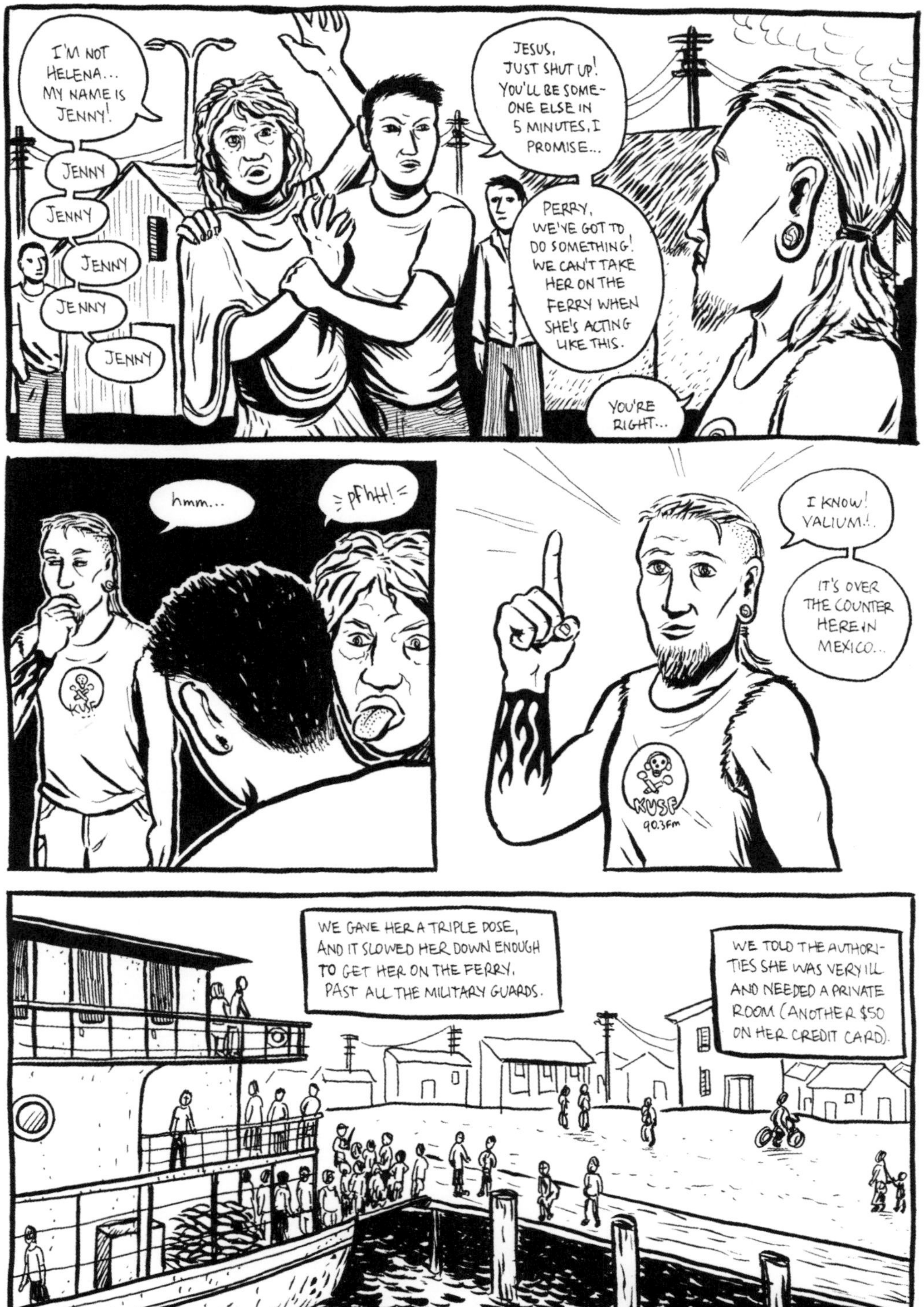
I'M NOT HELENA... MY NAME IS JENNY!
JENNY
JENNY
JENNY
JENNY
JENNY
JESUS, JUST SHUT UP! YOU'LL BE SOME-ONE ELSE IN 5 MINUTES, I PROMISE...
PERRY, WE'VE GOT TO DO SOMETHING! WE CAN'T TAKE HER ON THE FERRY WHEN SHE'S ACTING LIKE THIS.
YOU'RE RIGHT...
hmm...
pfhtt!
KUSF
I KNOW! VALIUM!.
IT'S OVER THE COUNTER HERE IN MEXICO...
KUSF 90.3FM
WE GAVE HER A TRIPLE DOSE, AND IT SLOWED HER DOWN ENOUGH TO GET HER ON THE FERRY, PAST ALL THE MILITARY GUARDS.
WE TOLD THE AUTHORI-TIES SHE WAS VERY ILL AND NEEDED A PRIVATE ROOM (ANOTHER $50 ON HER CREDIT CARD).

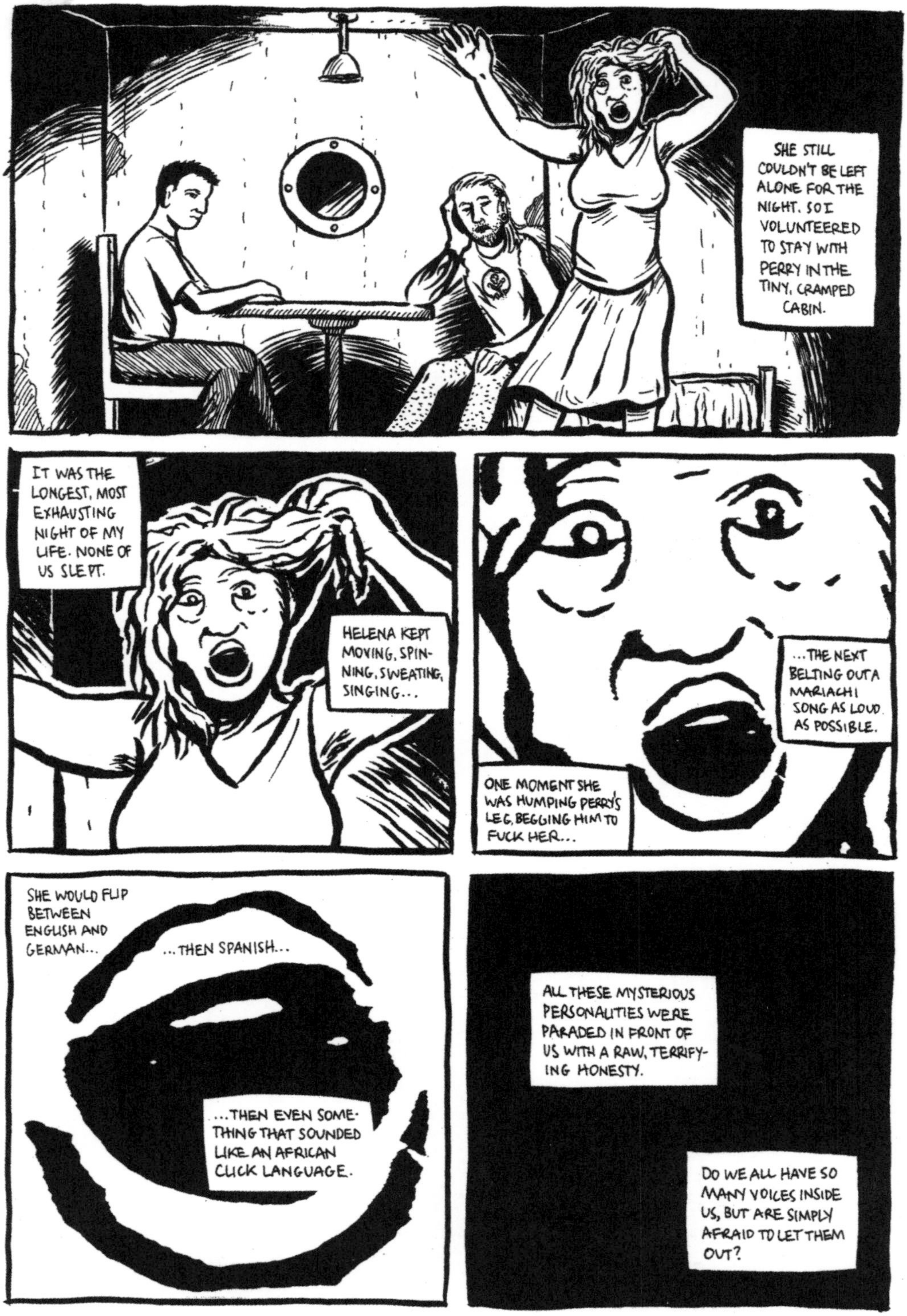
SHE STILL COULDN'T BE LEFT ALONE FOR THE NIGHT. SO I VOLUNTEERED TO STAY WITH PERRY IN THE TINY, CRAMPED CABIN.
IT WAS THE LONGEST, MOST EXHAUSTING NIGHT OF MY LIFE. NONE OF US SLEPT.
HELENA KEPT MOVING, SPINNING, SWEATING, SINGING...
ONE MOMENT SHE WAS HUMPING PERRY'S LEG, BEGGING HIM TO FUCK HER...
...THE NEXT BELTING OUT A MARIACHI SONG AS LOUD AS POSSIBLE.
SHE WOULD FLIP BETWEEN ENGLISH AND GERMAN...
...THEN SPANISH...
...THEN EVEN SOMETHING THAT SOUNDED LIKE AN AFRICAN CLICK LANGUAGE.
ALL THESE MYSTERIOUS PERSONALITIES WERE PARADED IN FRONT OF US WITH A RAW, TERRIFYING HONESTY.
DO WE ALL HAVE SO MANY VOICES INSIDE US, BUT ARE SIMPLY AFRAID TO LET THEM OUT?

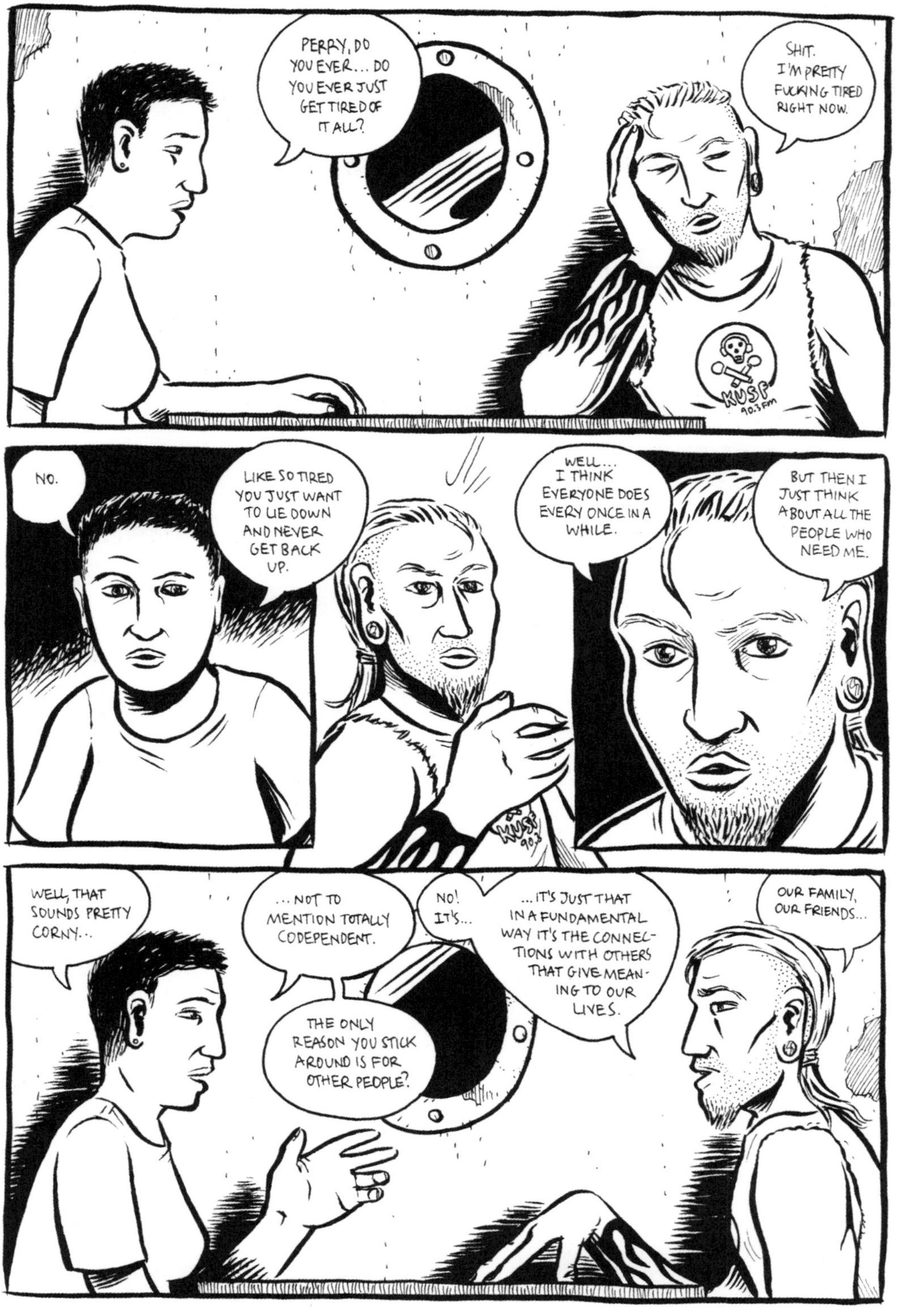
PERRY, DO YOU EVER... DO YOU EVER JUST GET TIRED OF IT ALL?
SHIT. I'M PRETTY FUCKING TIRED RIGHT NOW.
KUSF 90.3 FM
NO.
LIKE SO TIRED YOU JUST WANT TO LIE DOWN AND NEVER GET BACK UP.
WELL... I THINK EVERYONE DOES EVERY ONCE IN A WHILE.
BUT THEN I JUST THINK ABOUT ALL THE PEOPLE WHO NEED ME.
WELL, THAT SOUNDS PRETTY CORNY...
...NOT TO MENTION TOTALLY CODEPENDENT.
THE ONLY REASON YOU STICK AROUND IS FOR OTHER PEOPLE?
NO! IT'S...
...IT'S JUST THAT IN A FUNDAMENTAL WAY IT'S THE CONNECTIONS WITH OTHERS THAT GIVE MEANING TO OUR LIVES.
OUR FAMILY, OUR FRIENDS...

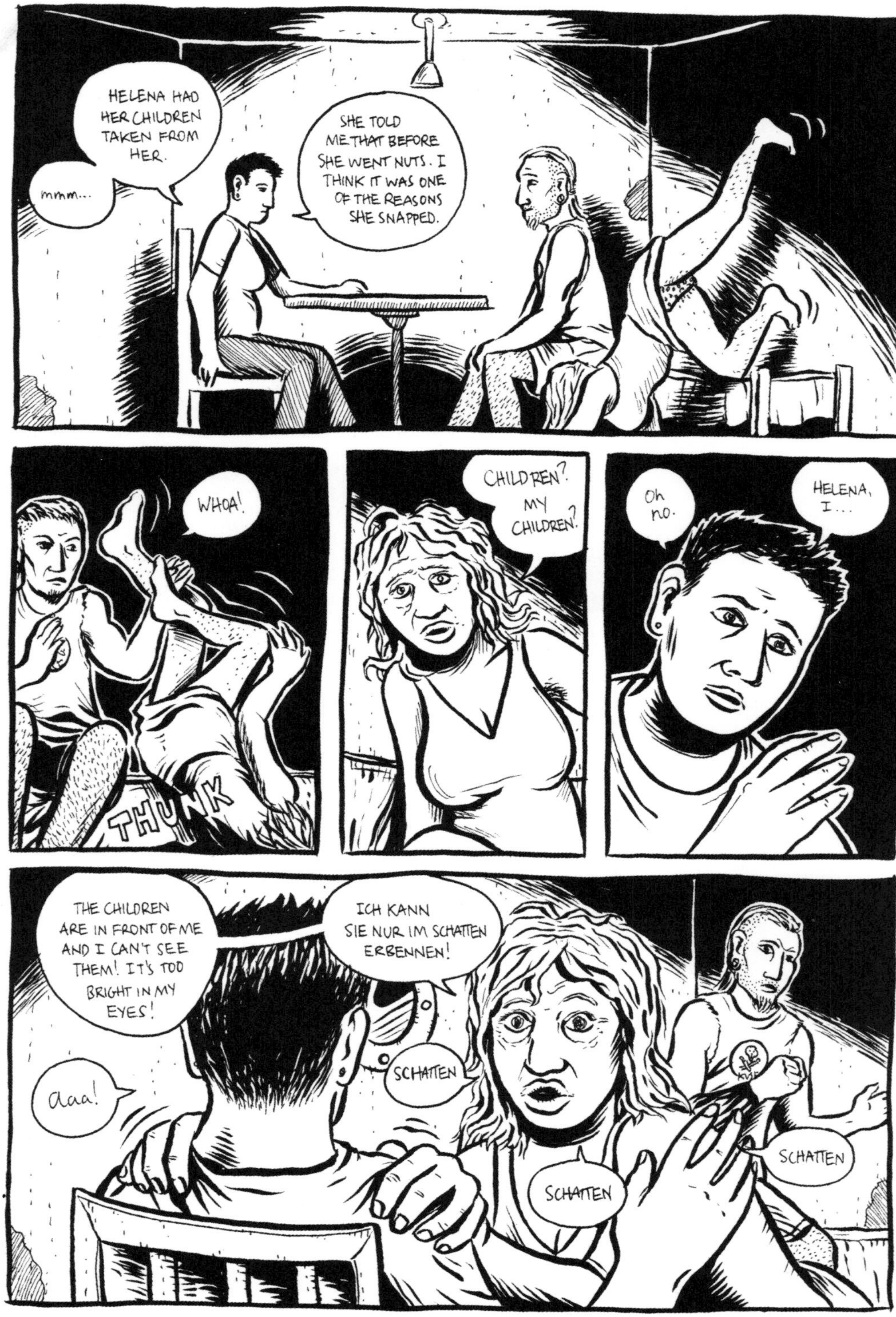
HELENA HAD HER CHILDREN TAKEN FROM HER.
mmm...
SHE TOLD ME THAT BEFORE SHE WENT NUTS. I THINK IT WAS ONE OF THE REASONS SHE SNAPPED.
WHOA!
THUNK
CHILDREN? MY CHILDREN?
Oh no.
HELENA, I...
THE CHILDREN ARE IN FRONT OF ME AND I CAN'T SEE THEM! IT'S TOO BRIGHT IN MY EYES!
ICH KANN SIE NUR IM SCHATTEN ERBENNEN!
aaa!
SCHATTEN
SCHATTEN
SCHATTEN

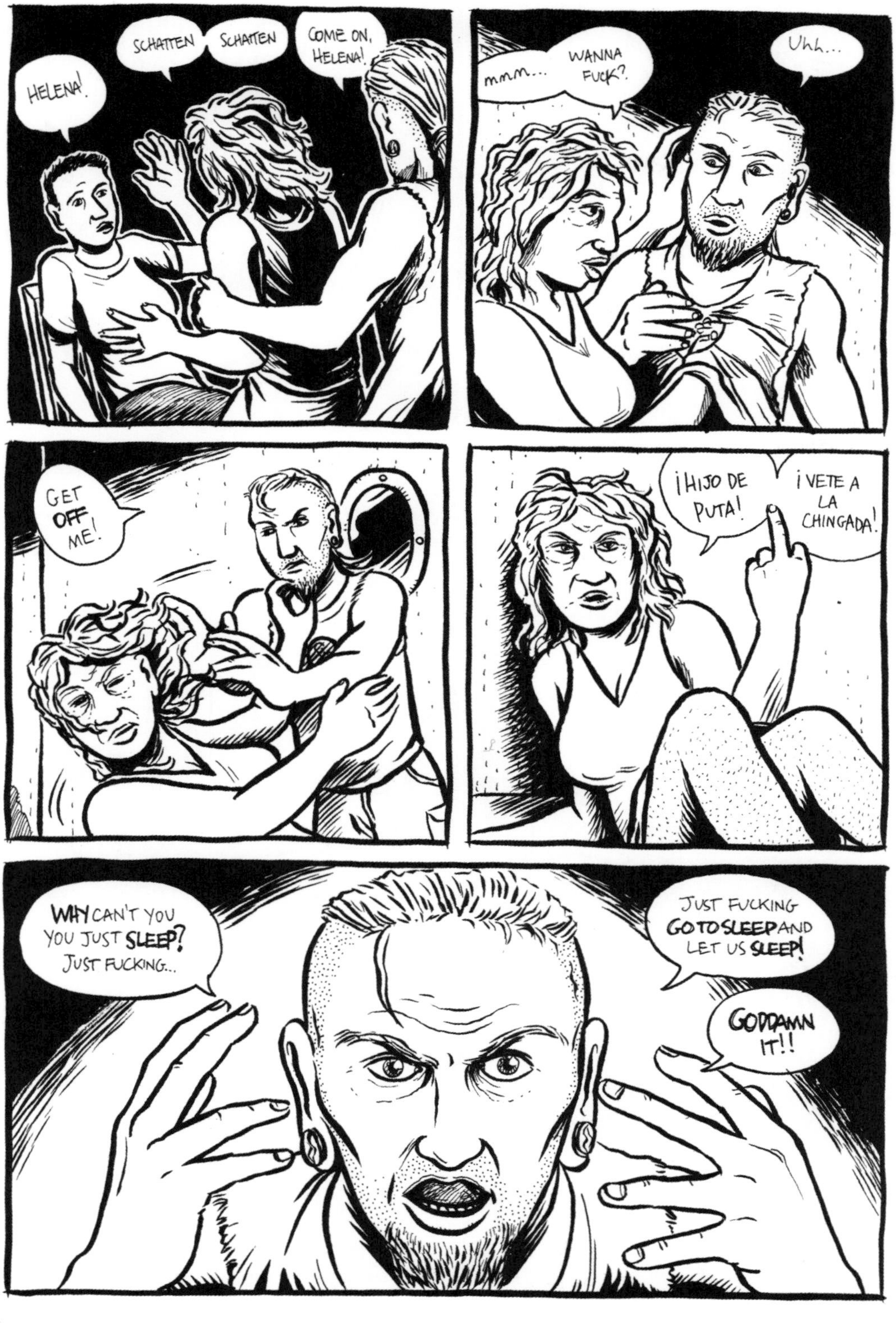
HELENA!
SCHATTEN
SCHATTEN
COME ON, HELENA!
mmm...
WANNA FUCK?
Uhh...
GET OFF ME!
¡HIJO DE PUTA!
¡VETE A LA CHINGADA!
WHY CAN'T YOU YOU JUST SLEEP? JUST FUCKING...
JUST FUCKING GO TO SLEEP AND LET US SLEEP!
GODDAMN IT!!

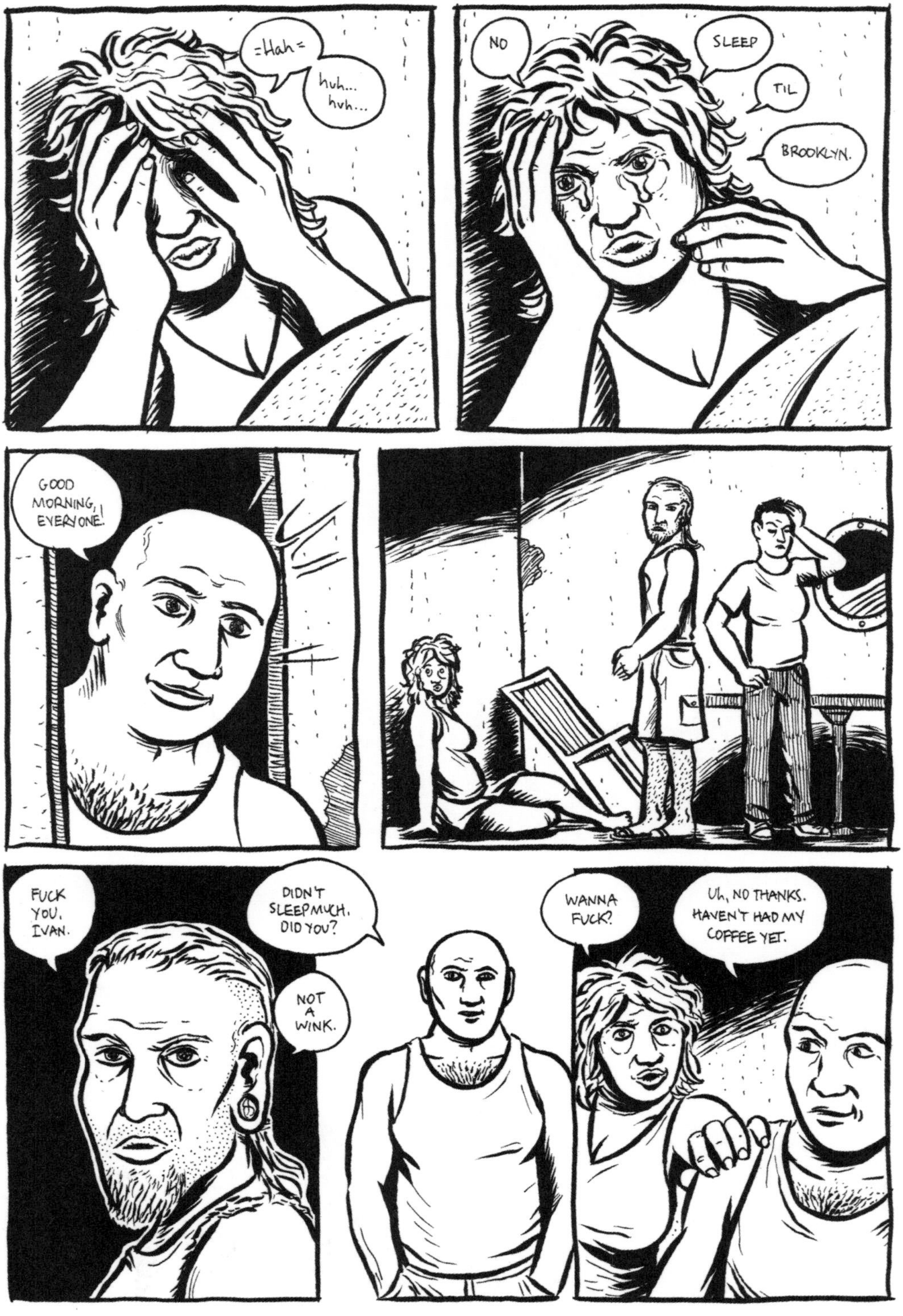
=Hah=
huh... huh...
NO
SLEEP
TIL
BROOKLYN.
GOOD MORNING, EVERYONE!
FUCK YOU, IVAN.
DIDN'T SLEEP MUCH, DID YOU?
NOT A WINK.
WANNA FUCK?
Uh, NO THANKS. HAVEN'T HAD MY COFFEE YET.

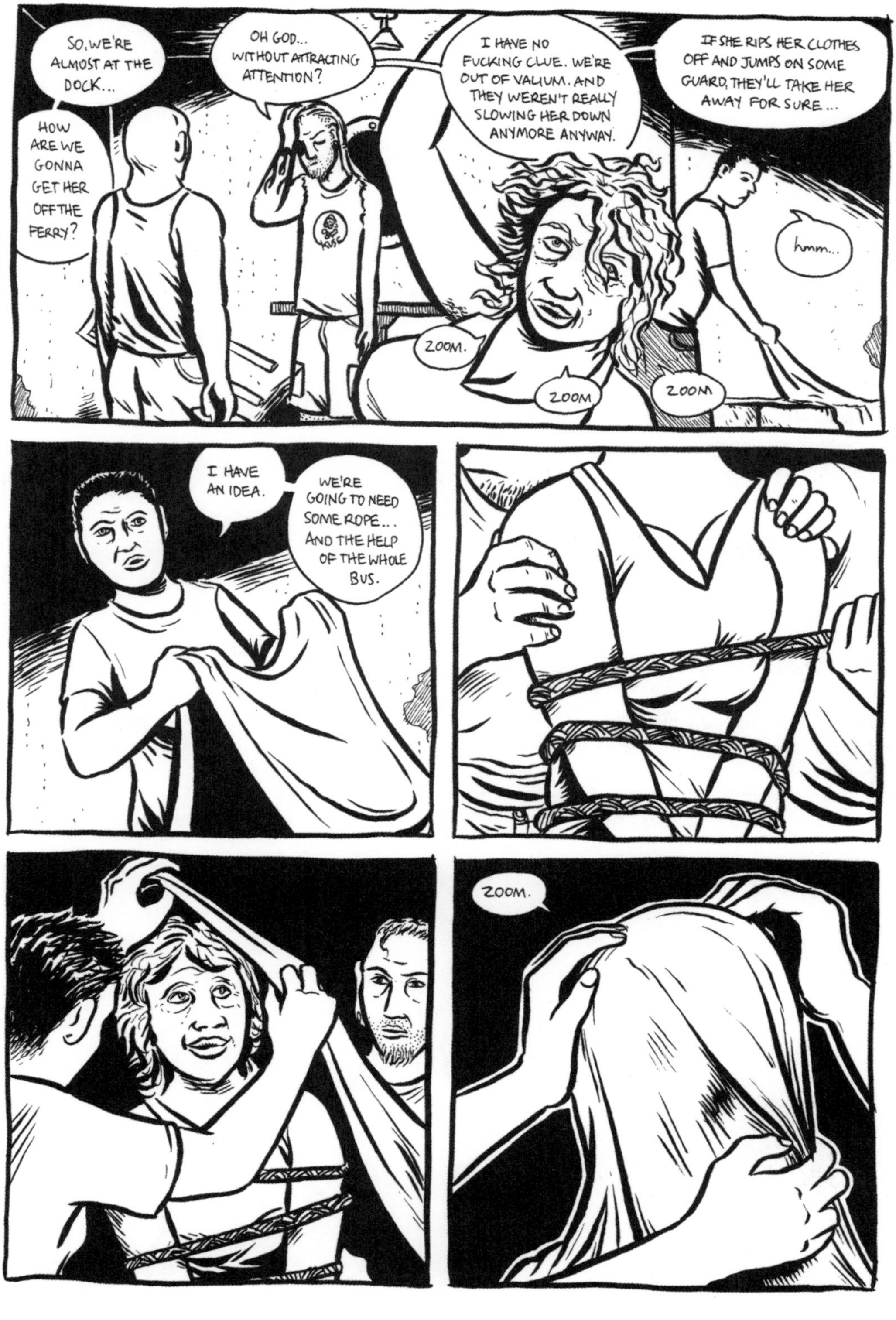

SO, WE'RE ALMOST AT THE DOCK...
HOW ARE WE GONNA GET HER OFF THE FERRY?
OH GOD... WITHOUT ATTRACTING ATTENTION?
I HAVE NO FUCKING CLUE. WE'RE OUT OF VALIUM. AND THEY WEREN'T REALLY SLOWING HER DOWN ANYMORE ANYWAY.
IF SHE RIPS HER CLOTHES OFF AND JUMPS ON SOME GUARD, THEY'LL TAKE HER AWAY FOR SURE...
hmm...
ZOOM.
ZOOM
ZOOM
I HAVE AN IDEA.
WE'RE GOING TO NEED SOME ROPE... AND THE HELP OF THE WHOLE BUS.
ZOOM.

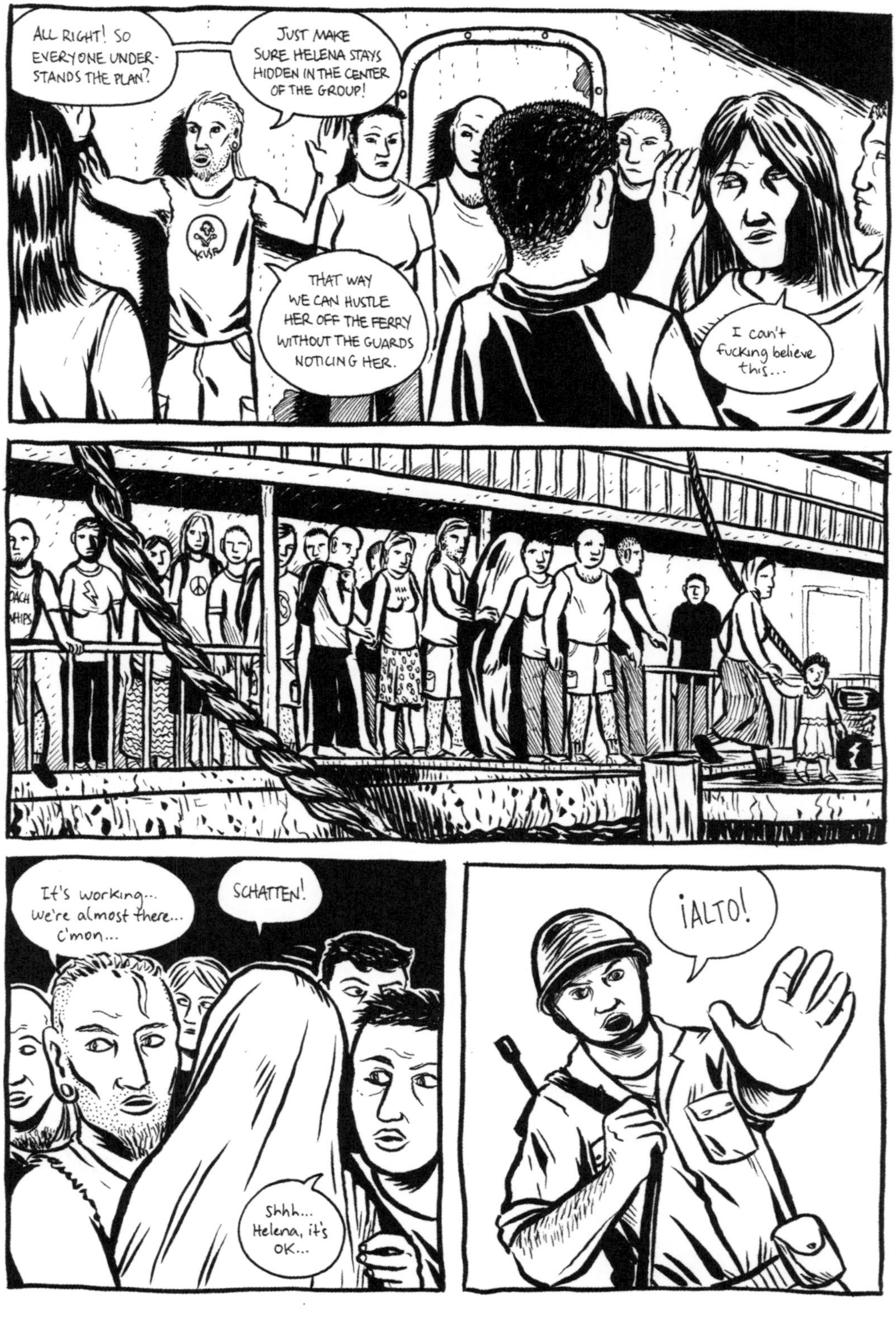

ALL RIGHT! SO EVERYONE UNDERSTANDS THE PLAN?
JUST MAKE SURE HELENA STAYS HIDDEN IN THE CENTER OF THE GROUP!
THAT WAY WE CAN HUSTLE HER OFF THE FERRY WITHOUT THE GUARDS NOTICING HER.
I can't fucking believe this...
It's working... we're almost there... c'mon...
SCHATTEN!
Shhh... Helena, it's OK...
¡ALTO!

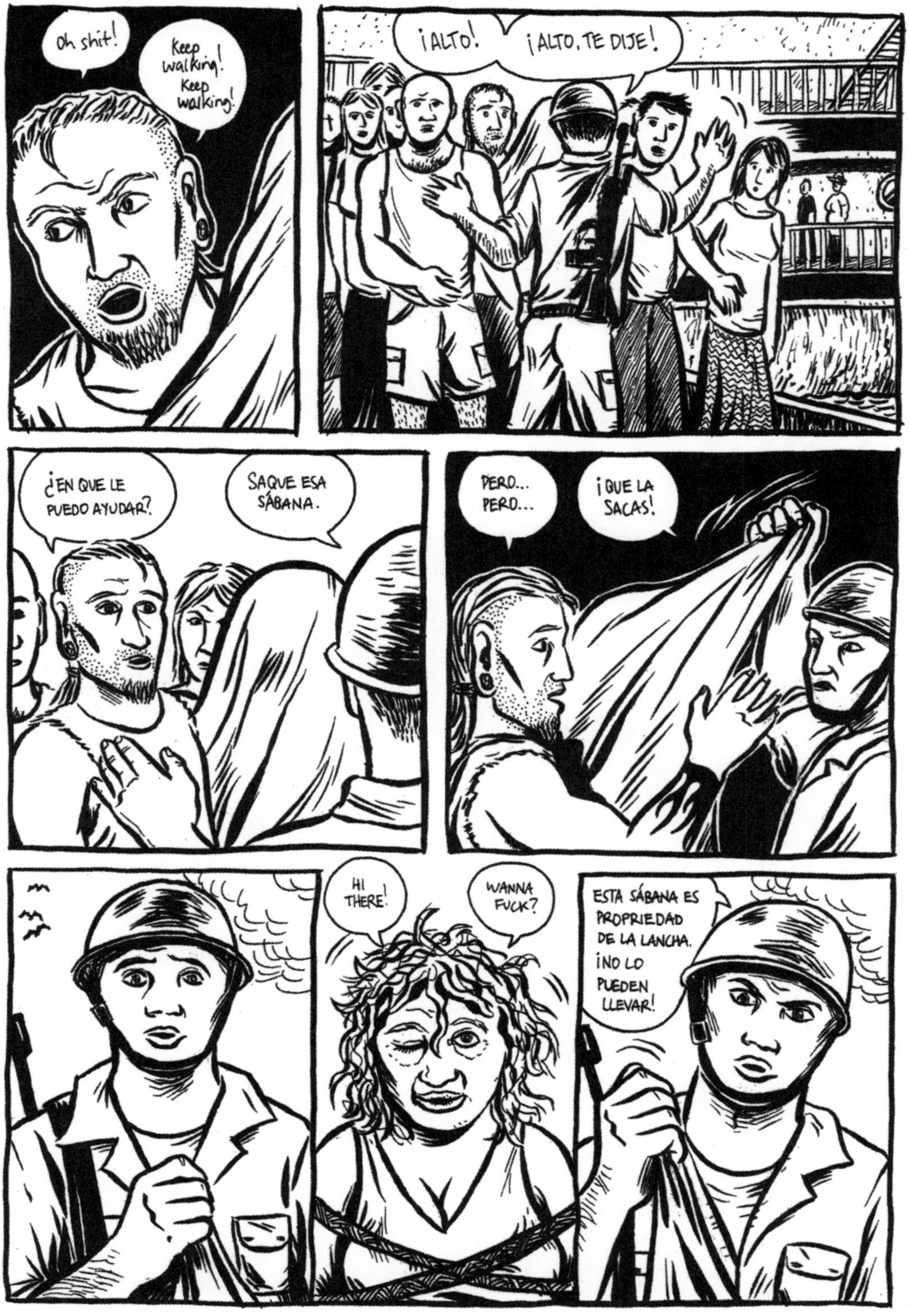
Oh shit!
Keep walking! Keep walking!
¡ALTO!
¡ALTO, TE DIJE!
¿EN QUE LE PUEDO AYUDAR?
SAQUE ESA SÁBANA.
PERO... PERO...
¡QUE LA SACAS!
HI THERE!
WANNA FUCK?
ESTA SÁBANA ES PROPRIEDAD DE LA LANCHA. ¡NO LO PUEDEN LLEVAR!

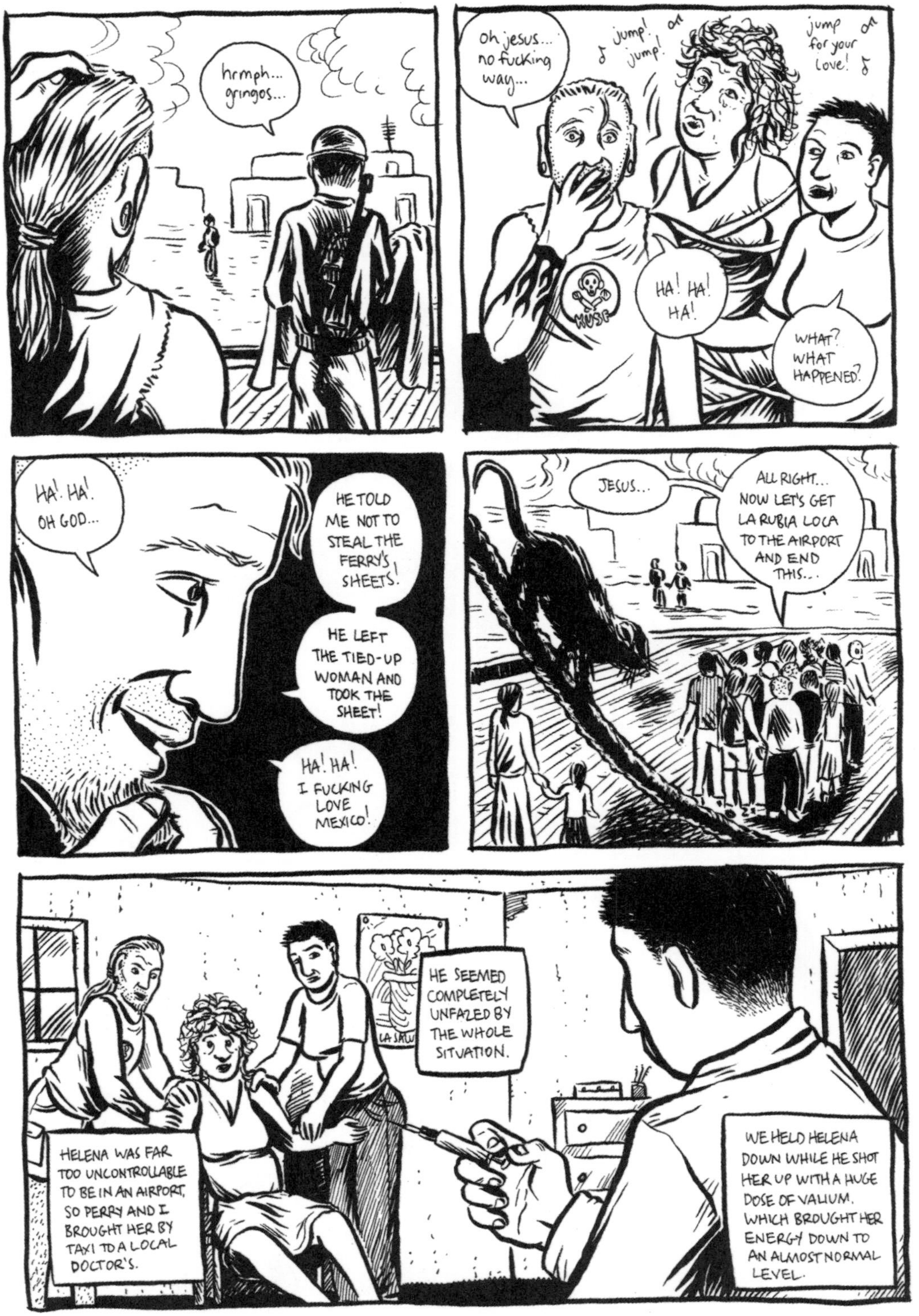
hrmph... gringos...
oh jesus... no fucking way...
jump! jump!
jump for your love!
HA! HA! HA!
WHAT? WHAT HAPPENED?
HA! HA! OH GOD...
HE TOLD ME NOT TO STEAL THE FERRY'S SHEETS!
HE LEFT THE TIED-UP WOMAN AND TOOK THE SHEET!
HA! HA! I FUCKING LOVE MEXICO!
JESUS...
ALL RIGHT... NOW LET'S GET LA RUBIA LOCA TO THE AIRPORT AND END THIS...
HE SEEMED COMPLETELY UNFAZED BY THE WHOLE SITUATION.
HELENA WAS FAR TOO UNCONTROLLABLE TO BE IN AN AIRPORT, SO PERRY AND I BROUGHT HER BY TAXI TO A LOCAL DOCTOR'S.
WE HELD HELENA DOWN WHILE HE SHOT HER UP WITH A HUGE DOSE OF VALIUM, WHICH BROUGHT HER ENERGY DOWN TO AN ALMOST NORMAL LEVEL.

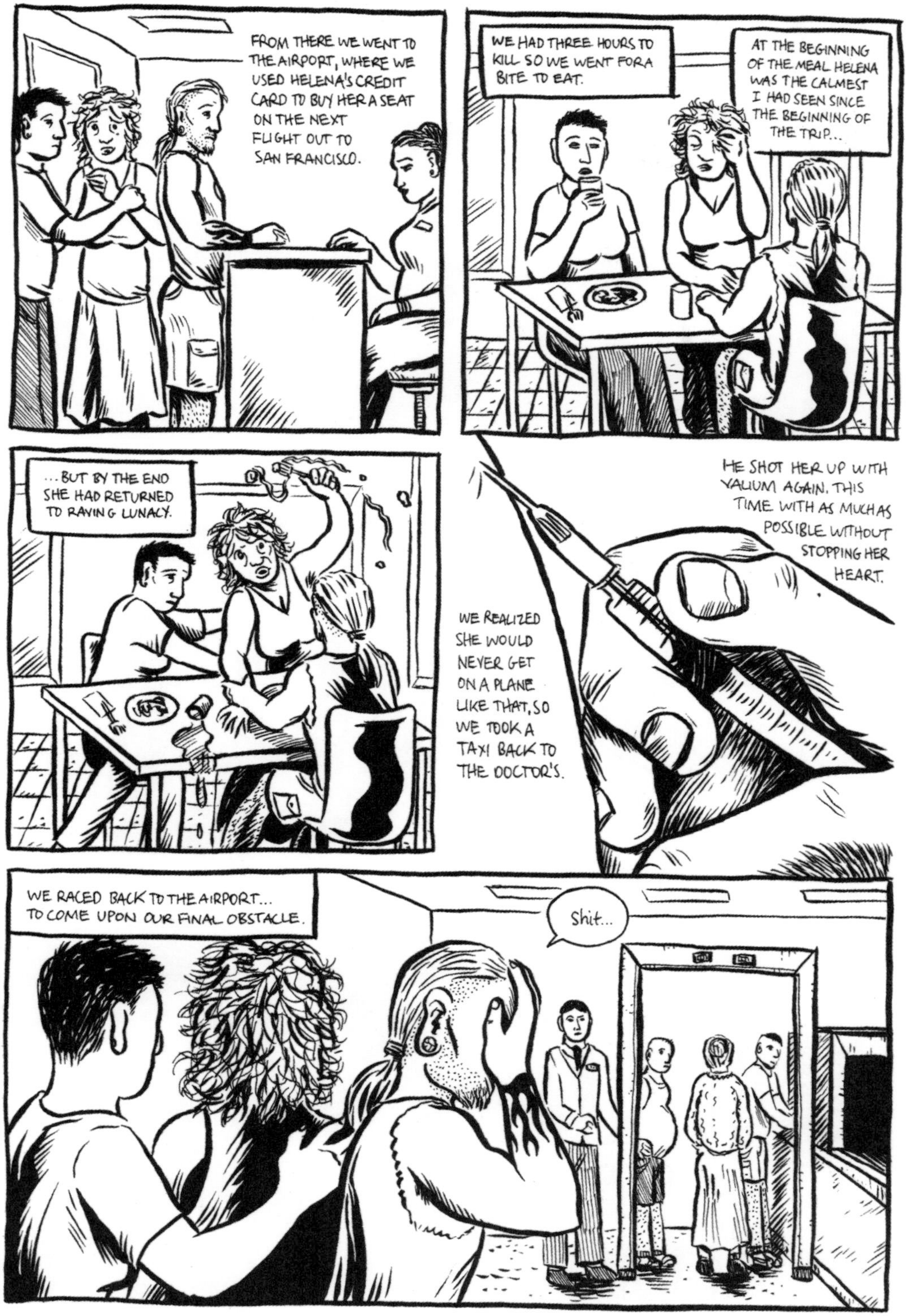
FROM THERE WE WENT TO THE AIRPORT, WHERE WE USED HELENA'S CREDIT CARD TO BUY HER A SEAT ON THE NEXT FLIGHT OUT TO SAN FRANCISCO.
WE HAD THREE HOURS TO KILL SO WE WENT FOR A BITE TO EAT.
AT THE BEGINNING OF THE MEAL HELENA WAS THE CALMEST I HAD SEEN SINCE THE BEGINNING OF THE TRIP...
...BUT BY THE END SHE HAD RETURNED TO RAVING LUNACY.
WE REALIZED SHE WOULD NEVER GET ON A PLANE LIKE THAT, SO WE TOOK A TAXI BACK TO THE DOCTOR'S.
HE SHOT HER UP WITH VALIUM AGAIN. THIS TIME WITH AS MUCH AS POSSIBLE WITHOUT STOPPING HER HEART.
WE RACED BACK TO THE AIRPORT... TO COME UPON OUR FINAL OBSTACLE.
Shit...

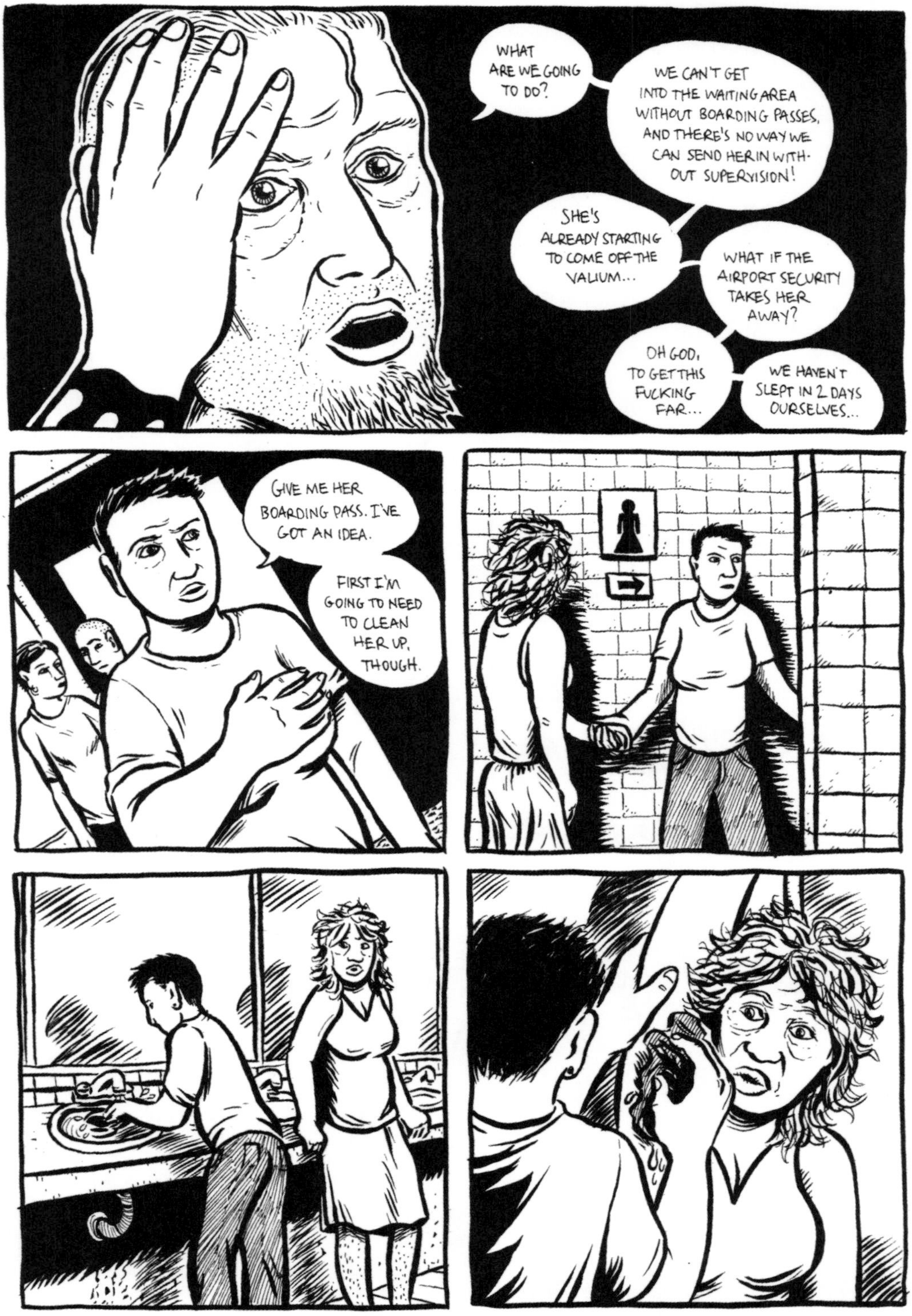

WHAT ARE WE GOING TO DO?
WE CAN'T GET INTO THE WAITING AREA WITHOUT BOARDING PASSES, AND THERE'S NO WAY WE CAN SEND HER IN WITHOUT SUPERVISION!
SHE'S ALREADY STARTING TO COME OFF THE VALIUM...
WHAT IF THE AIRPORT SECURITY TAKES HER AWAY?
OH GOD, TO GET THIS FUCKING FAR...
WE HAVEN'T SLEPT IN 2 DAYS OURSELVES...
GIVE ME HER BOARDING PASS. I'VE GOT AN IDEA.
FIRST I'M GOING TO NEED TO CLEAN HER UP, THOUGH.

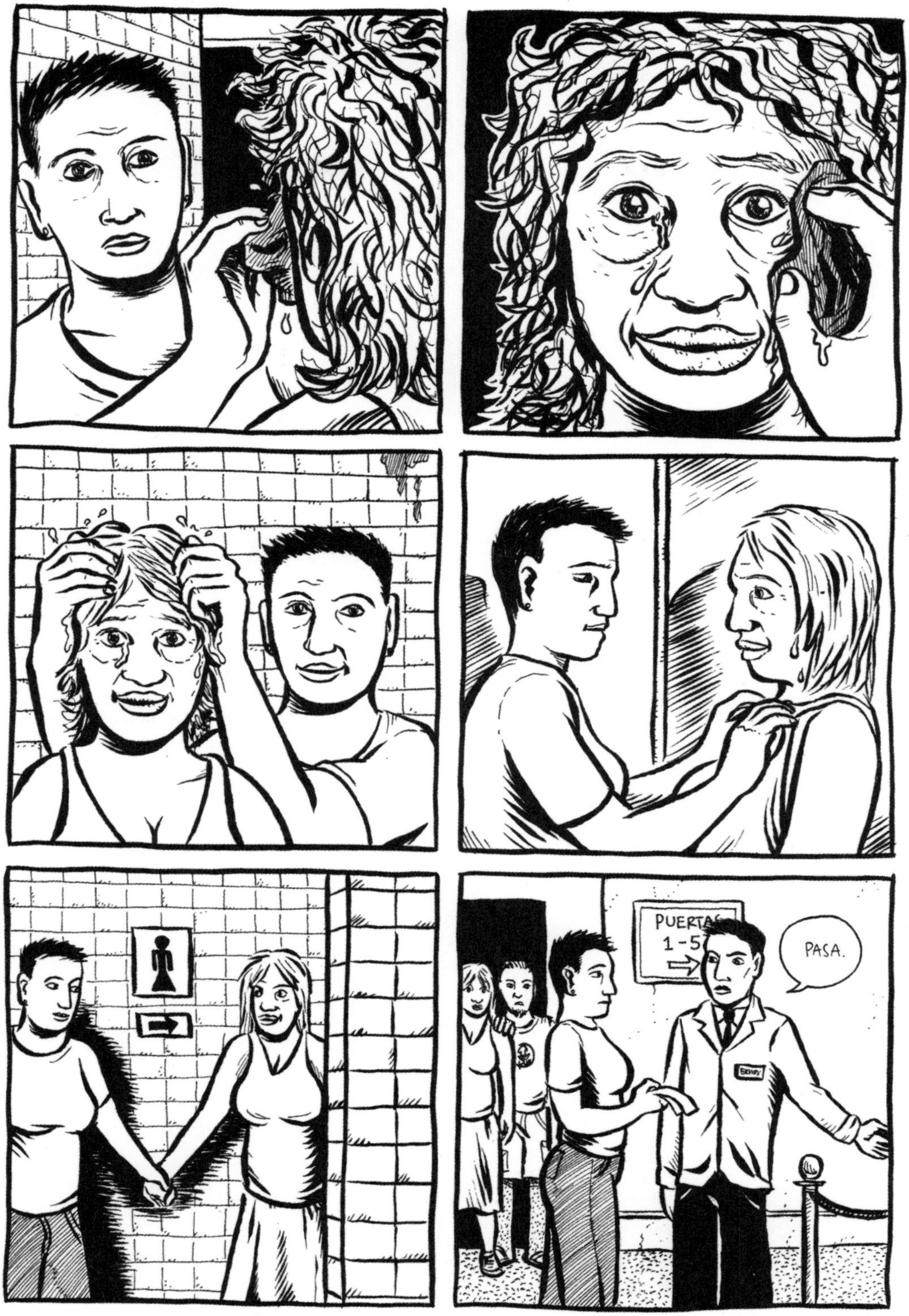
PUERTAS
1-5
PASA.

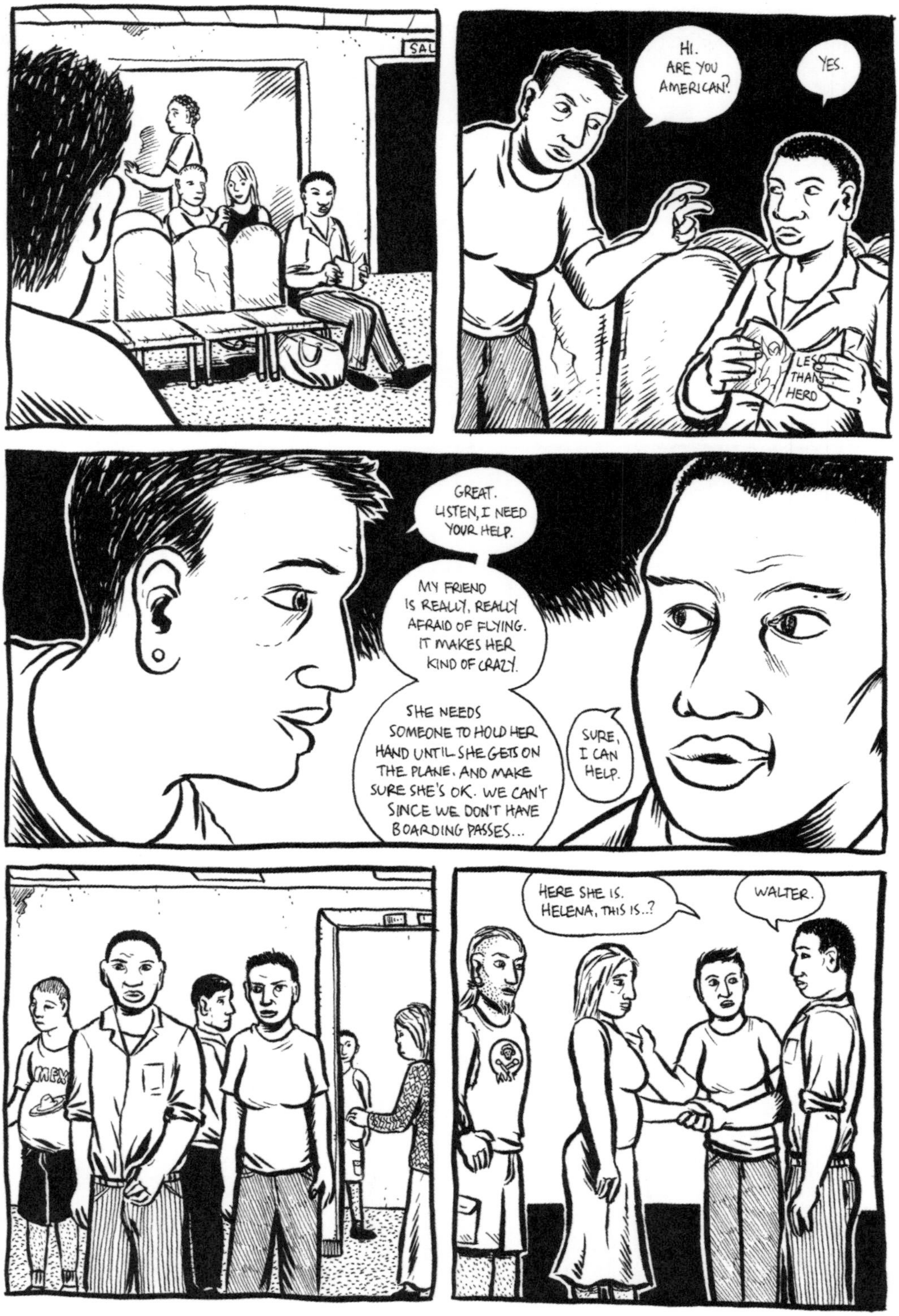
SAL
HI. ARE YOU AMERICAN?
YES.
LESS THAN HERO
GREAT. LISTEN, I NEED YOUR HELP.
MY FRIEND IS REALLY, REALLY AFRAID OF FLYING. IT MAKES HER KIND OF CRAZY.
SHE NEEDS SOMEONE TO HOLD HER HAND UNTIL SHE GETS ON THE PLANE. AND MAKE SURE SHE'S OK. WE CAN'T SINCE WE DON'T HAVE BOARDING PASSES...
SURE, I CAN HELP.
HERE SHE IS. HELENA, THIS IS..?
WALTER.

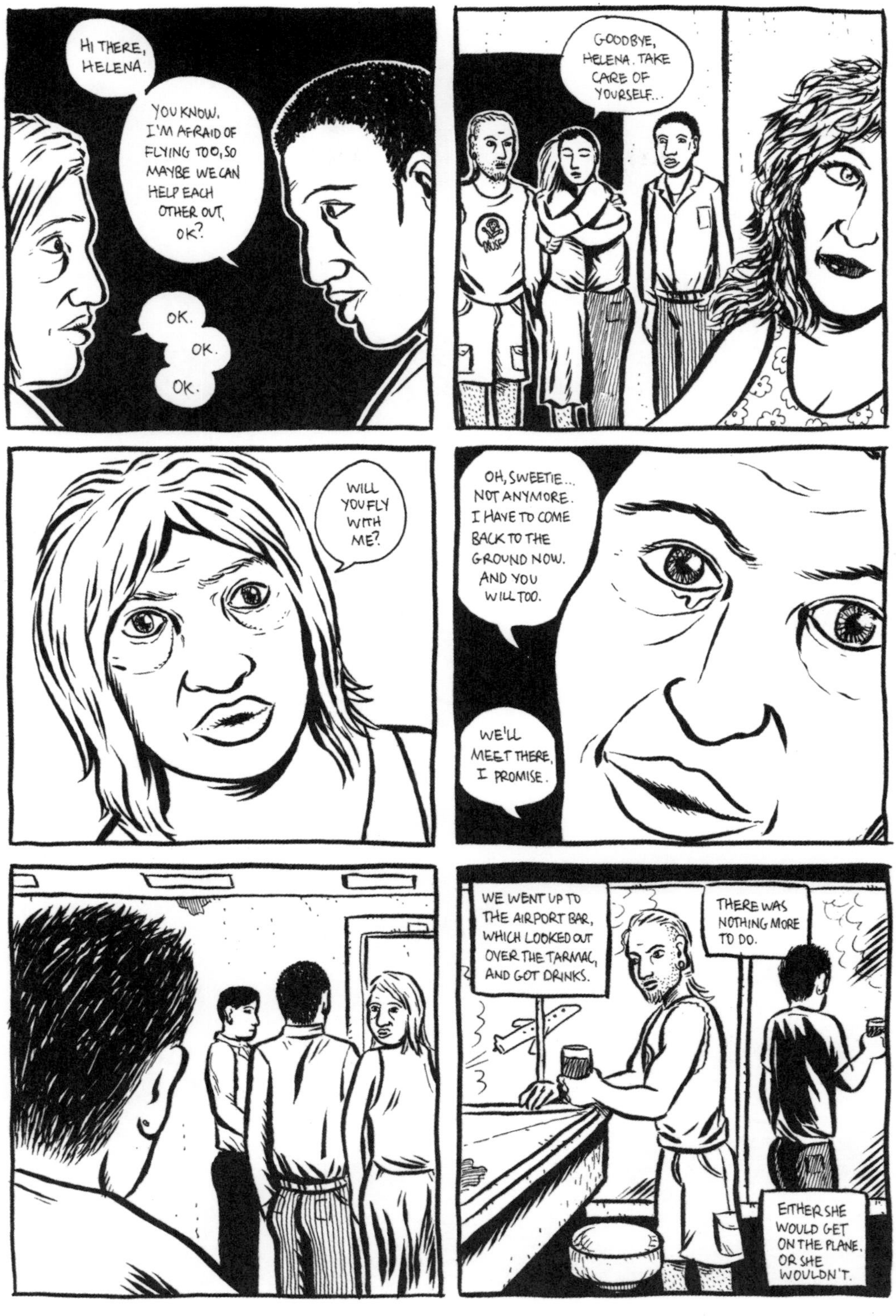

HI THERE, HELENA.
YOU KNOW, I'M AFRAID OF FLYING TOO, SO MAYBE WE CAN HELP EACH OTHER OUT, OK?
OK.
OK.
OK.
GOODBYE, HELENA. TAKE CARE OF YOURSELF...
WILL YOU FLY WITH ME?
OH, SWEETIE... NOT ANYMORE. I HAVE TO COME BACK TO THE GROUND NOW. AND YOU WILL TOO.
WE'LL MEET THERE, I PROMISE.
WE WENT UP TO THE AIRPORT BAR, WHICH LOOKED OUT OVER THE TARMAC, AND GOT DRINKS.
THERE WAS NOTHING MORE TO DO.
EITHER SHE WOULD GET ON THE PLANE. OR SHE WOULDN'T.

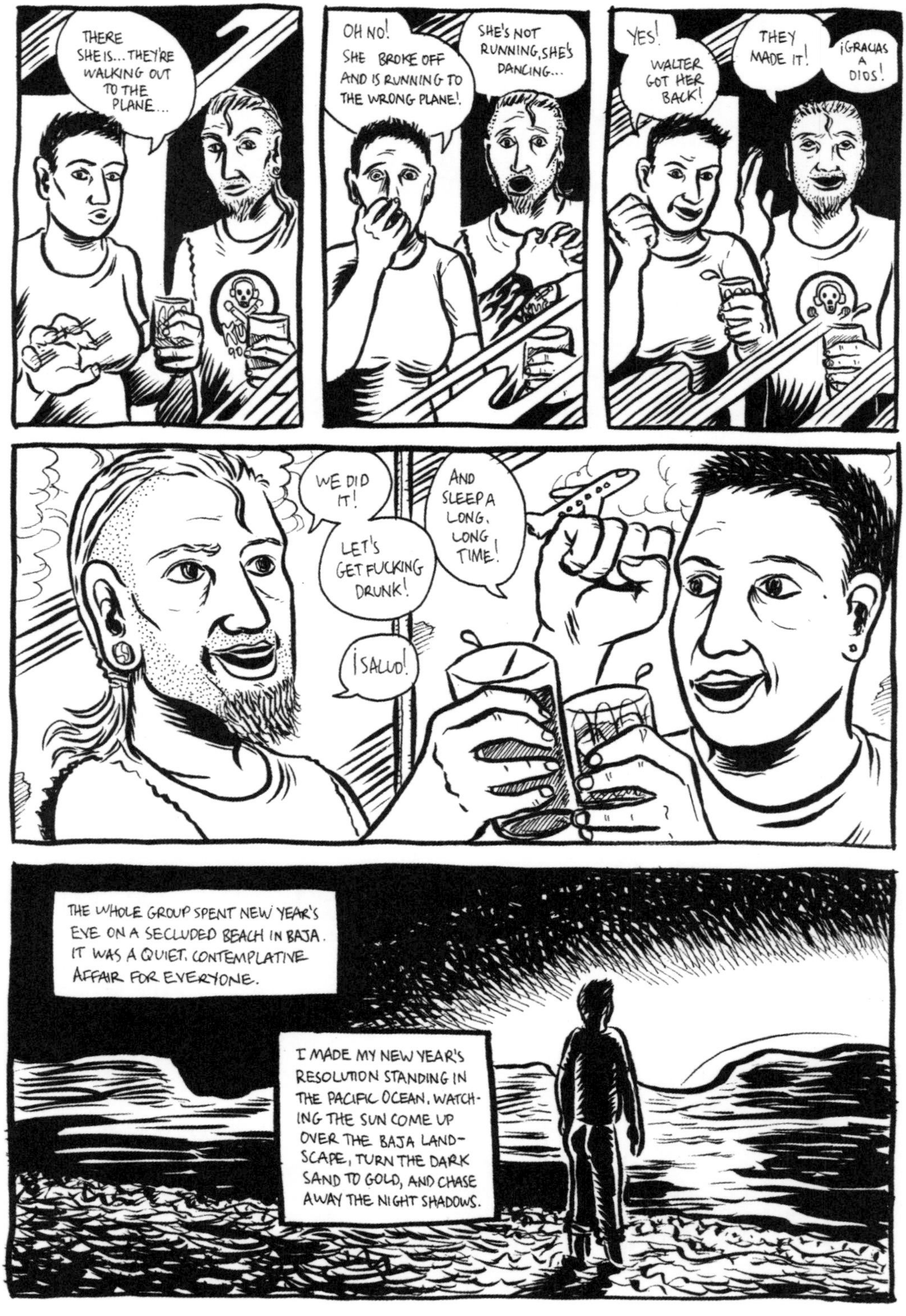
THERE SHE IS... THEY'RE WALKING OUT TO THE PLANE...
OH NO! SHE BROKE OFF AND IS RUNNING TO THE WRONG PLANE!
SHE'S NOT RUNNING, SHE'S DANCING...
YES! WALTER GOT HER BACK!
THEY MADE IT!
¡GRACIAS A DIOS!
WE DID IT!
LET'S GET FUCKING DRUNK!
AND SLEEP A LONG, LONG TIME!
¡SALUD!
THE WHOLE GROUP SPENT NEW YEAR'S EVE ON A SECLUDED BEACH IN BAJA. IT WAS A QUIET, CONTEMPLATIVE AFFAIR FOR EVERYONE.
I MADE MY NEW YEAR'S RESOLUTION STANDING IN THE PACIFIC OCEAN, WATCHING THE SUN COME UP OVER THE BAJA LANDSCAPE, TURN THE DARK SAND TO GOLD, AND CHASE AWAY THE NIGHT SHADOWS.

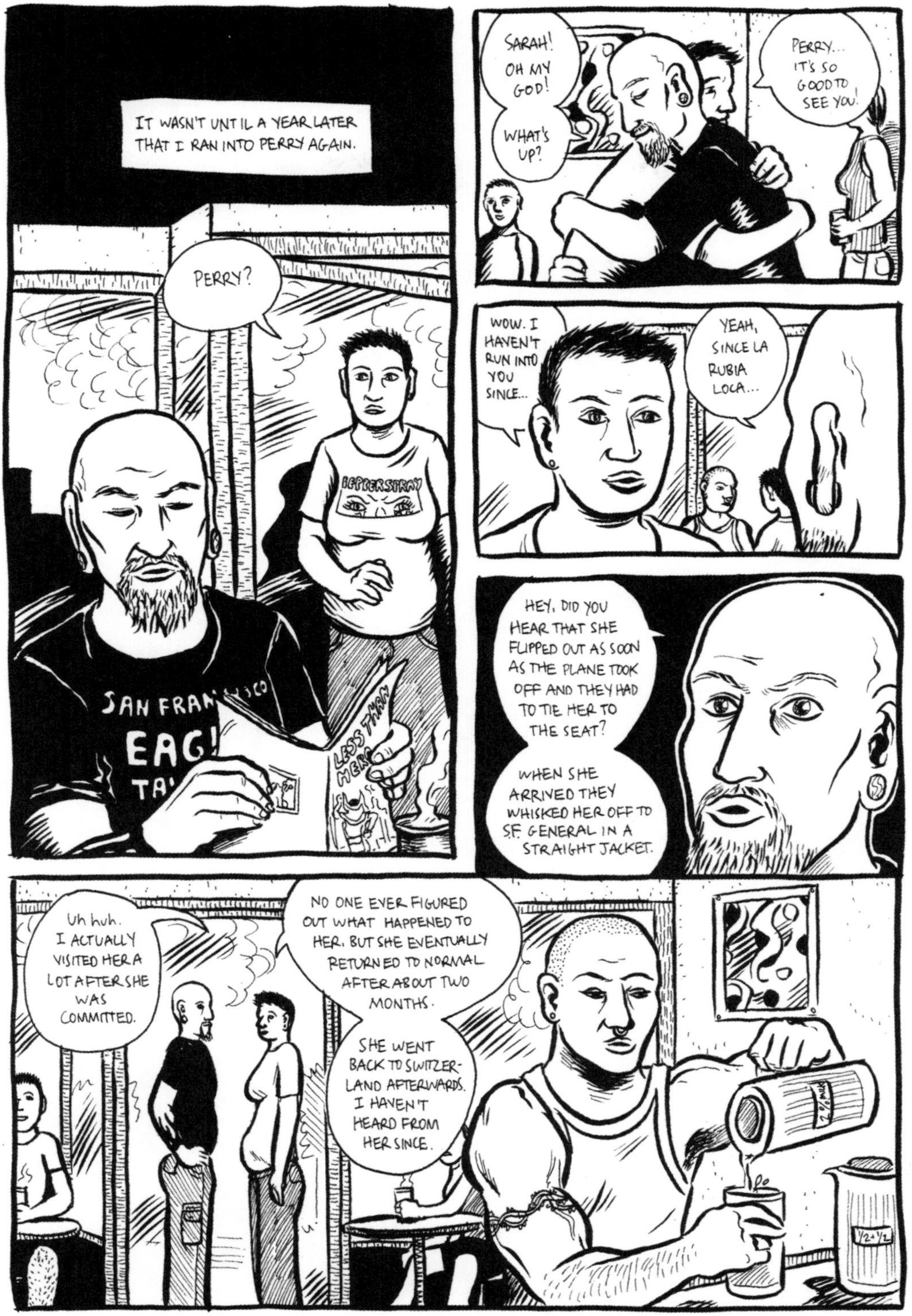
IT WASN'T UNTIL A YEAR LATER THAT I RAN INTO PERRY AGAIN.
PERRY?
PEPPERSPRAY
SAN FRANCISCO EAG TA
LESS THAN HERO
SARAH! OH MY GOD!
WHAT'S UP?
PERRY... IT'S SO GOOD TO SEE YOU!
WOW. I HAVEN'T RUN INTO YOU SINCE...
YEAH, SINCE LA RUBIA LOCA...
HEY, DID YOU HEAR THAT SHE FLIPPED OUT AS SOON AS THE PLANE TOOK OFF AND THEY HAD TO TIE HER TO THE SEAT?
WHEN SHE ARRIVED THEY WHISKED HER OFF TO S.F. GENERAL IN A STRAIGHT JACKET.
Uh huh. I ACTUALLY VISITED HER A LOT AFTER SHE WAS COMMITTED.
NO ONE EVER FIGURED OUT WHAT HAPPENED TO HER, BUT SHE EVENTUALLY RETURNED TO NORMAL AFTER ABOUT TWO MONTHS.
SHE WENT BACK TO SWITZERLAND AFTERWARDS. I HAVEN'T HEARD FROM HER SINCE.

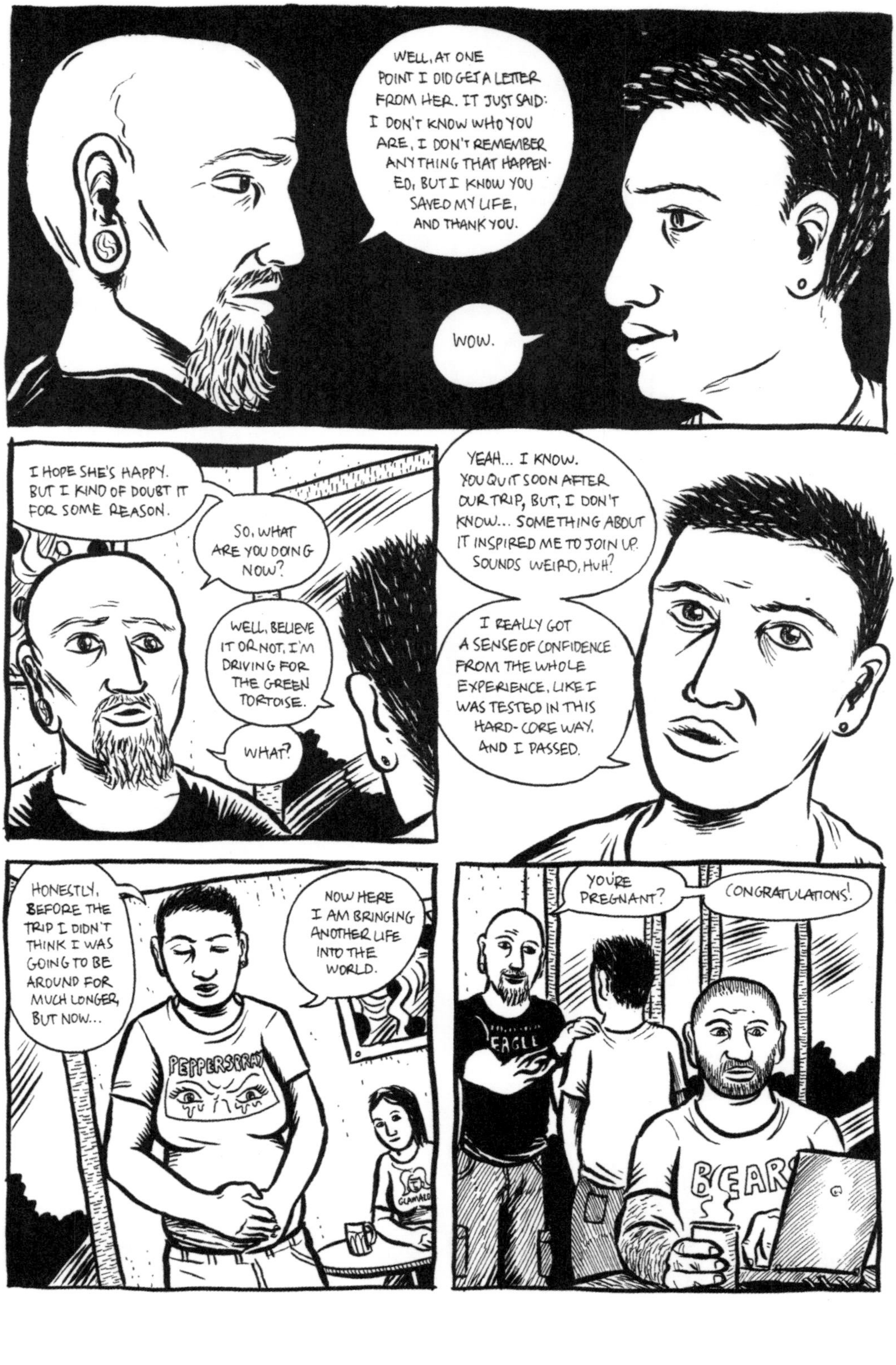

WELL, AT ONE POINT I DID GET A LETTER FROM HER. IT JUST SAID: I DON'T KNOW WHO YOU ARE, I DON'T REMEMBER ANYTHING THAT HAPPEN-ED, BUT I KNOW YOU SAVED MY LIFE, AND THANK YOU.
WOW.
I HOPE SHE'S HAPPY. BUT I KIND OF DOUBT IT FOR SOME REASON.
SO, WHAT ARE YOU DOING NOW?
WELL, BELIEVE IT OR NOT, I'M DRIVING FOR THE GREEN TORTOISE.
WHAT?
YEAH... I KNOW. YOU QUIT SOON AFTER OUR TRIP, BUT, I DON'T KNOW... SOMETHING ABOUT IT INSPIRED ME TO JOIN UP. SOUNDS WEIRD, HUH?
I REALLY GOT A SENSE OF CONFIDENCE FROM THE WHOLE EXPERIENCE. LIKE I WAS TESTED IN THIS HARD-CORE WAY, AND I PASSED.
HONESTLY, BEFORE THE TRIP I DIDN'T THINK I WAS GOING TO BE AROUND FOR MUCH LONGER, BUT NOW...
NOW HERE I AM BRINGING ANOTHER LIFE INTO THE WORLD.
PEPPERSPRAY
YOU'RE PREGNANT?
CONGRATULATIONS!
EAGLE
BEARS

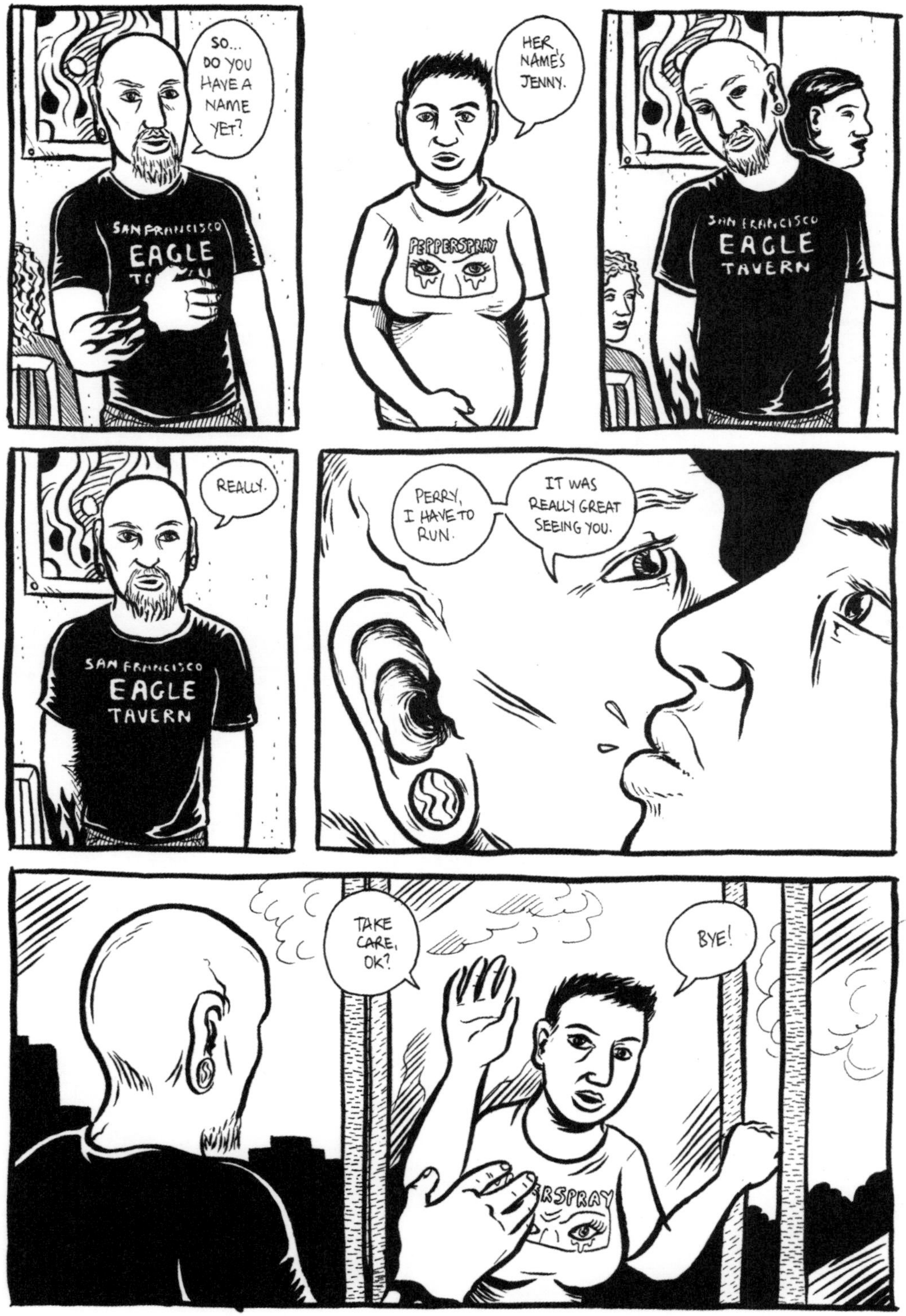
SO... DO YOU HAVE A NAME YET?
HER NAME'S JENNY.
SAN FRANCISCO EAGLE TAVERN
PEPPERSPRAY
REALLY.
PERRY, I HAVE TO RUN.
IT WAS REALLY GREAT SEEING YOU.
TAKE CARE, OK?
BYE!

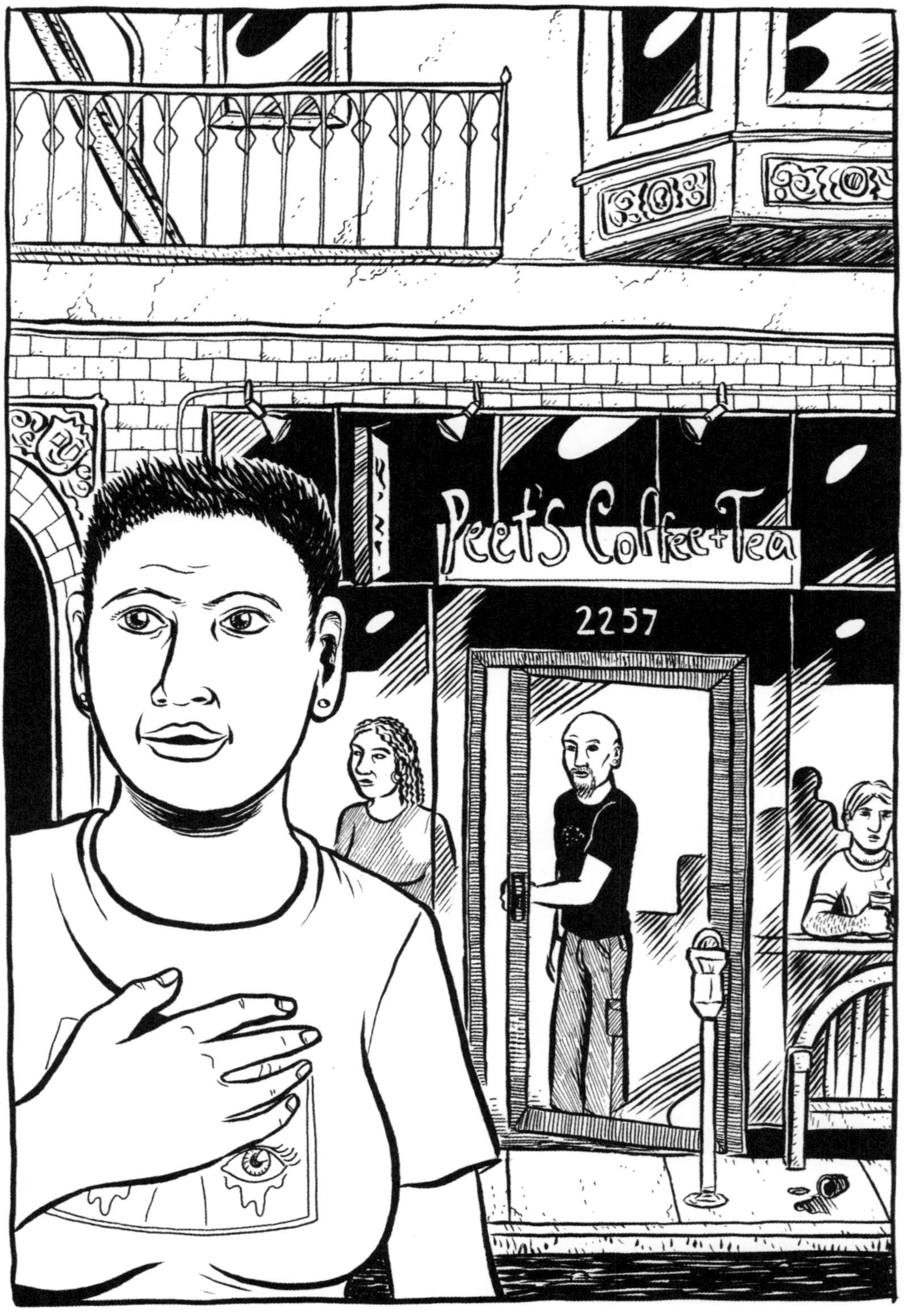
Peet's Coffee+Tea
2257

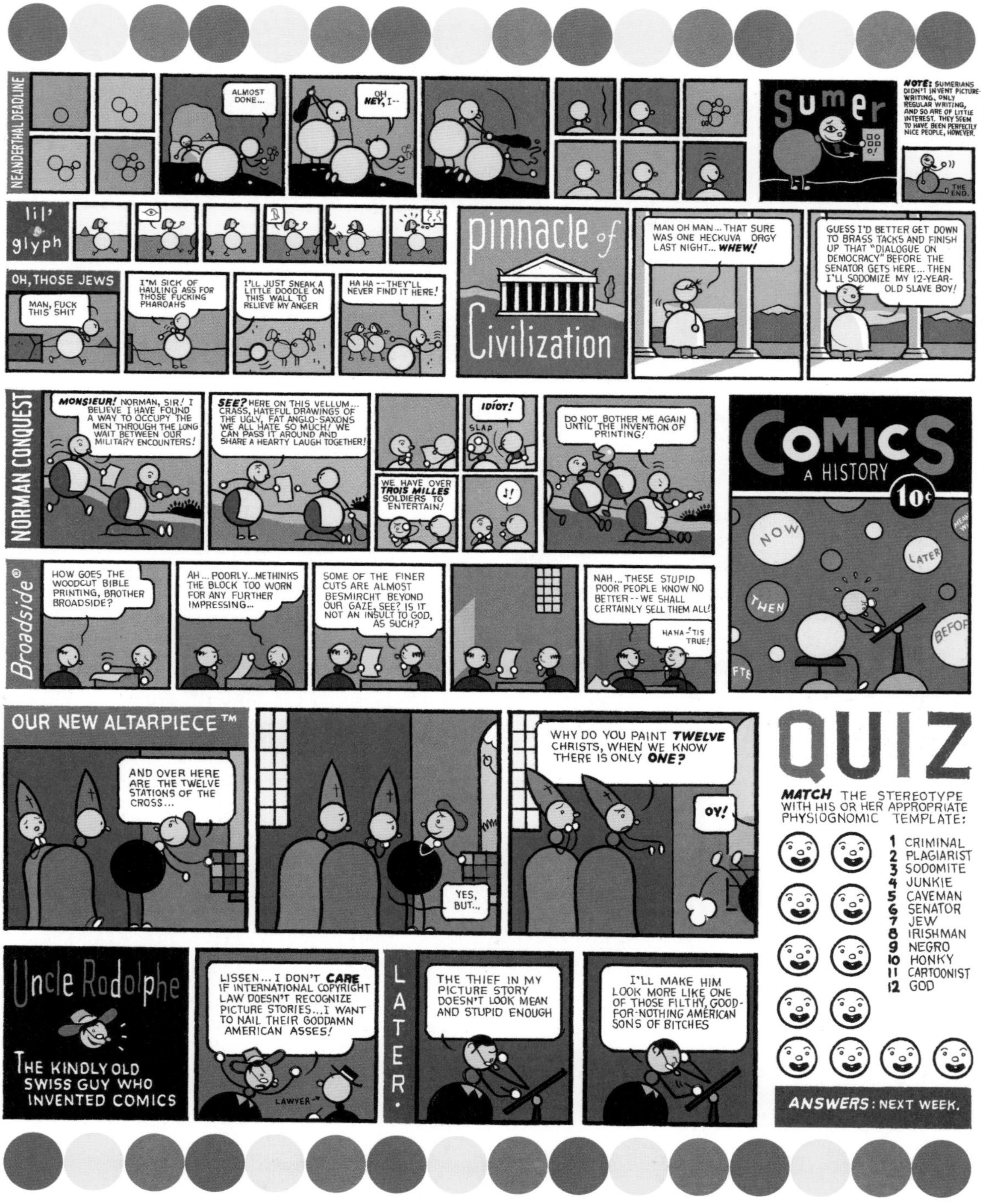
NEANDERTHAL DEADLINE
ALMOST DONE...
OH HEY, I--
Sumer
NOTE: SUMERIANS DIDN'T INVENT PICTURE-WRITING, ONLY REGULAR WRITING, AND SO ARE OF LITTLE INTEREST. THEY SEEM TO HAVE BEEN PERFECTLY NICE PEOPLE, HOWEVER.
THE END.
lil' glyph
OH, THOSE JEWS
MAN, FUCK THIS SHIT
I'M SICK OF HAULING ASS FOR THOSE FUCKING PHAROAHS
I'LL JUST SNEAK A LITTLE DOODLE ON THIS WALL TO RELIEVE MY ANGER
HA HA -- THEY'LL NEVER FIND IT HERE!
pinnacle of Civilization
MAN OH MAN... THAT SURE WAS ONE HECKUVA ORGY LAST NIGHT... WHEW!
GUESS I'D BETTER GET DOWN TO BRASS TACKS AND FINISH UP THAT "DIALOGUE ON DEMOCRACY" BEFORE THE SENATOR GETS HERE... THEN I'LL SODOMIZE MY 12-YEAR-OLD SLAVE BOY!
NORMAN CONQUEST
MONSIEUR! NORMAN, SIR! I BELIEVE I HAVE FOUND A WAY TO OCCUPY THE MEN THROUGH THE LONG WAIT BETWEEN OUR MILITARY ENCOUNTERS!
SEE? HERE ON THIS VELLUM... CRASS, HATEFUL DRAWINGS OF THE UGLY, FAT ANGLO-SAXONS WE ALL HATE SO MUCH! WE CAN PASS IT AROUND AND SHARE A HEARTY LAUGH TOGETHER!
IDIOT!
SLAP
WE HAVE OVER TROIS MILLES SOLDIERS TO ENTERTAIN!
!!
DO NOT BOTHER ME AGAIN UNTIL THE INVENTION OF PRINTING!
COMICS A HISTORY
10¢
NOW
LATER
THEN
Broadside®
HOW GOES THE WOODCUT BIBLE PRINTING, BROTHER BROADSIDE?
AH... POORLY... METHINKS THE BLOCK TOO WORN FOR ANY FURTHER IMPRESSING...
SOME OF THE FINER CUTS ARE ALMOST BESMIRCHT BEYOND OUR GAZE. SEE? IS IT NOT AN INSULT TO GOD, AS SUCH?
NAH... THESE STUPID POOR PEOPLE KNOW NO BETTER -- WE SHALL CERTAINLY SELL THEM ALL!
HA HA - 'TIS TRUE!
OUR NEW ALTARPIECE™
AND OVER HERE ARE THE TWELVE STATIONS OF THE CROSS...
YES, BUT...
WHY DO YOU PAINT TWELVE CHRISTS, WHEN WE KNOW THERE IS ONLY ONE?
OY!
QUIZ
MATCH THE STEREOTYPE WITH HIS OR HER APPROPRIATE PHYSIOGNOMIC TEMPLATE:
1 CRIMINAL
2 PLAGIARIST
3 SODOMITE
4 JUNKIE
5 CAVEMAN
6 SENATOR
7 JEW
8 IRISHMAN
9 NEGRO
10 HONKY
11 CARTOONIST
12 GOD
ANSWERS: NEXT WEEK.
Uncle Rodolphe
THE KINDLY OLD SWISS GUY WHO INVENTED COMICS
LISSEN... I DON'T CARE IF INTERNATIONAL COPYRIGHT LAW DOESN'T RECOGNIZE PICTURE STORIES... I WANT TO NAIL THEIR GODDAMN AMERICAN ASSES!
LAWYER
LATER.
THE THIEF IN MY PICTURE STORY DOESN'T LOOK MEAN AND STUPID ENOUGH
I'LL MAKE HIM LOOK MORE LIKE ONE OF THOSE FILTHY, GOOD-FOR-NOTHING AMERICAN SONS OF BITCHES

FROM *McSweeney's*

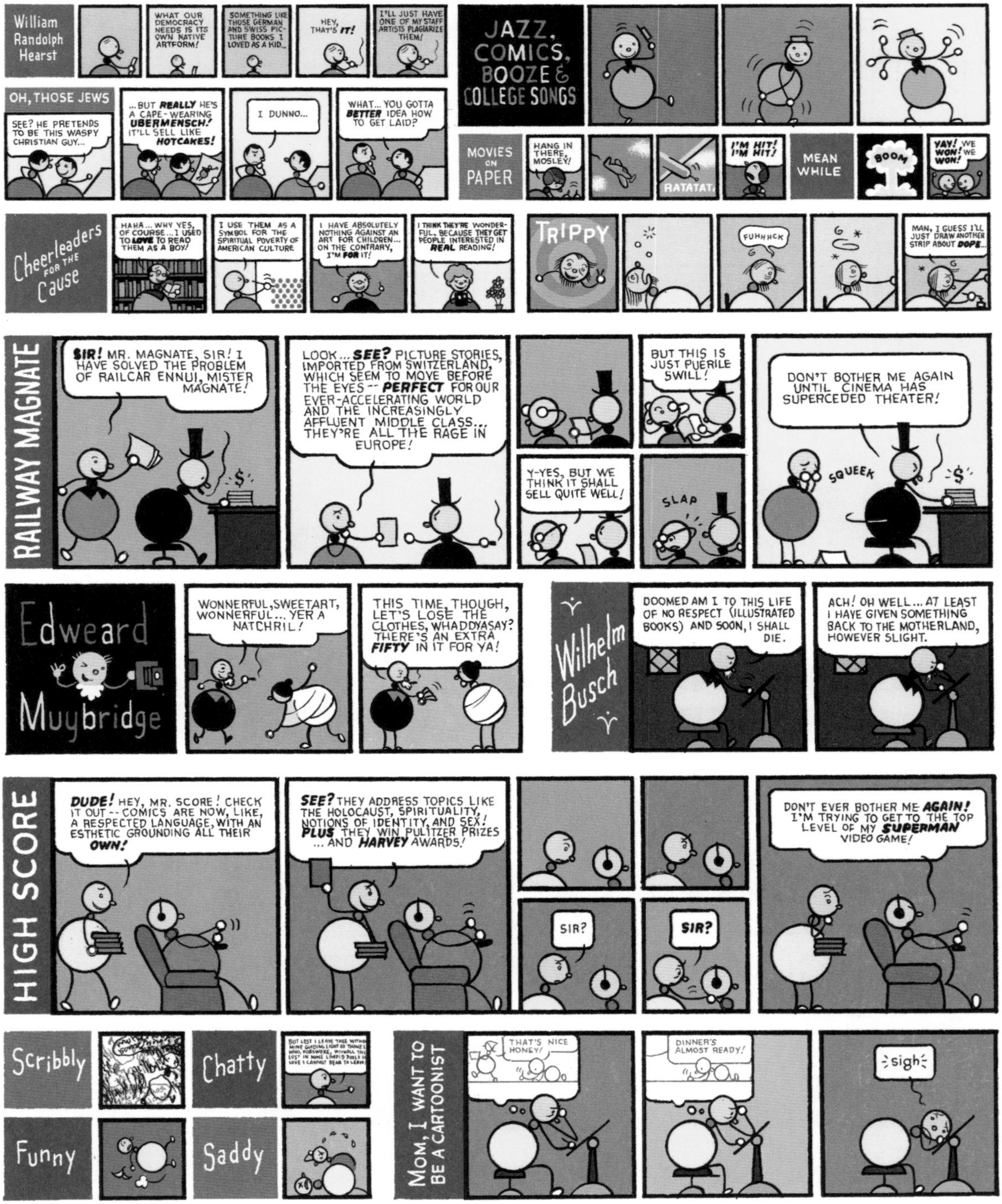
William Randolph Hearst
WHAT OUR DEMOCRACY NEEDS IS ITS OWN NATIVE ARTFORM!
SOMETHING LIKE THOSE GERMAN AND SWISS PICTURE BOOKS I LOVED AS A KID...
HEY, THAT'S IT!
I'LL JUST HAVE ONE OF MY STAFF ARTISTS PLAGIARIZE THEM!
JAZZ, COMICS, BOOZE & COLLEGE SONGS
OH, THOSE JEWS
SEE? HE PRETENDS TO BE THIS WASPY CHRISTIAN GUY...
...BUT REALLY HE'S A CAPE-WEARING UBERMENSCH! IT'LL SELL LIKE HOTCAKES!
I DUNNO...
WHAT... YOU GOTTA BETTER IDEA HOW TO GET LAID?
MOVIES ON PAPER
HANG IN THERE, MOSLEY!
RATATAT
I'M HIT! I'M HIT!
MEAN WHILE
BOOM
YAY! WE WON! WE WON!
Cheerleaders FOR THE Cause
HAHA... WHY YES, OF COURSE... I USED TO LOVE TO READ THEM AS A BOY!
I USE THEM AS A SYMBOL FOR THE SPIRITUAL POVERTY OF AMERICAN CULTURE
I HAVE ABSOLUTELY NOTHING AGAINST AN ART FOR CHILDREN... ON THE CONTRARY, I'M FOR IT!
I THINK THEY'RE WONDERFUL, BECAUSE THEY GET PEOPLE INTERESTED IN REAL READING!
TRIPPY
FUHHHCK
MAN, I GUESS I'LL JUST DRAW ANOTHER STRIP ABOUT DOPE...
RAILWAY MAGNATE
SIR! MR. MAGNATE, SIR! I HAVE SOLVED THE PROBLEM OF RAILCAR ENNUI, MISTER MAGNATE!
LOOK... SEE? PICTURE STORIES, IMPORTED FROM SWITZERLAND, WHICH SEEM TO MOVE BEFORE THE EYES -- PERFECT FOR OUR EVER-ACCELERATING WORLD AND THE INCREASINGLY AFFLUENT MIDDLE CLASS... THEY'RE ALL THE RAGE IN EUROPE!
BUT THIS IS JUST PUERILE SWILL!
Y-YES, BUT WE THINK IT SHALL SELL QUITE WELL!
SLAP
DON'T BOTHER ME AGAIN UNTIL CINEMA HAS SUPERCEDED THEATER!
SQUEEK
Edweard Muybridge
WONNERFUL, SWEETART, WONNERFUL... YER A NATCHRIL!
THIS TIME, THOUGH, LET'S LOSE THE CLOTHES, WHADDYASAY? THERE'S AN EXTRA FIFTY IN IT FOR YA!
Wilhelm Busch
DOOMED AM I TO THIS LIFE OF NO RESPECT (ILLUSTRATED BOOKS) AND SOON, I SHALL DIE.
ACH! OH WELL... AT LEAST I HAVE GIVEN SOMETHING BACK TO THE MOTHERLAND, HOWEVER SLIGHT.
HIGH SCORE
DUDE! HEY, MR. SCORE! CHECK IT OUT -- COMICS ARE NOW, LIKE, A RESPECTED LANGUAGE, WITH AN ESTHETIC GROUNDING ALL THEIR OWN!
SEE? THEY ADDRESS TOPICS LIKE THE HOLOCAUST, SPIRITUALITY, NOTIONS OF IDENTITY, AND SEX! PLUS THEY WIN PULITZER PRIZES ... AND HARVEY AWARDS!
SIR?
SIR?
DON'T EVER BOTHER ME AGAIN! I'M TRYING TO GET TO THE TOP LEVEL OF MY SUPERMAN VIDEO GAME!
Scribbly
Chatty
Funny
Saddy
MOM, I WANT TO BE A CARTOONIST
THAT'S NICE HONEY!
DINNER'S ALMOST READY!
sigh

FROM *RabbitHead*

108

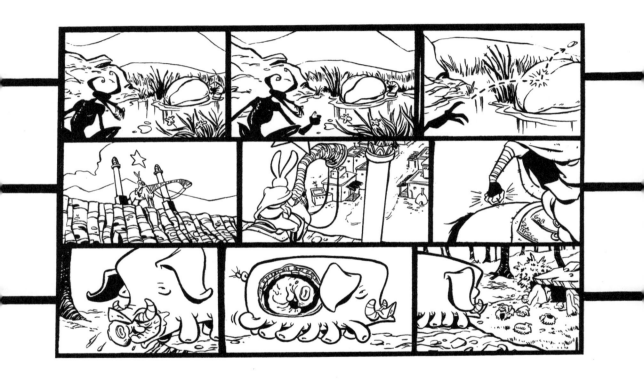

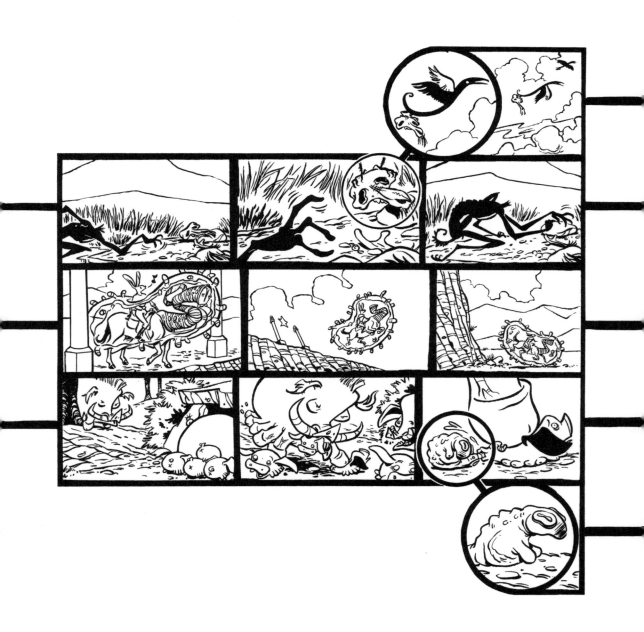

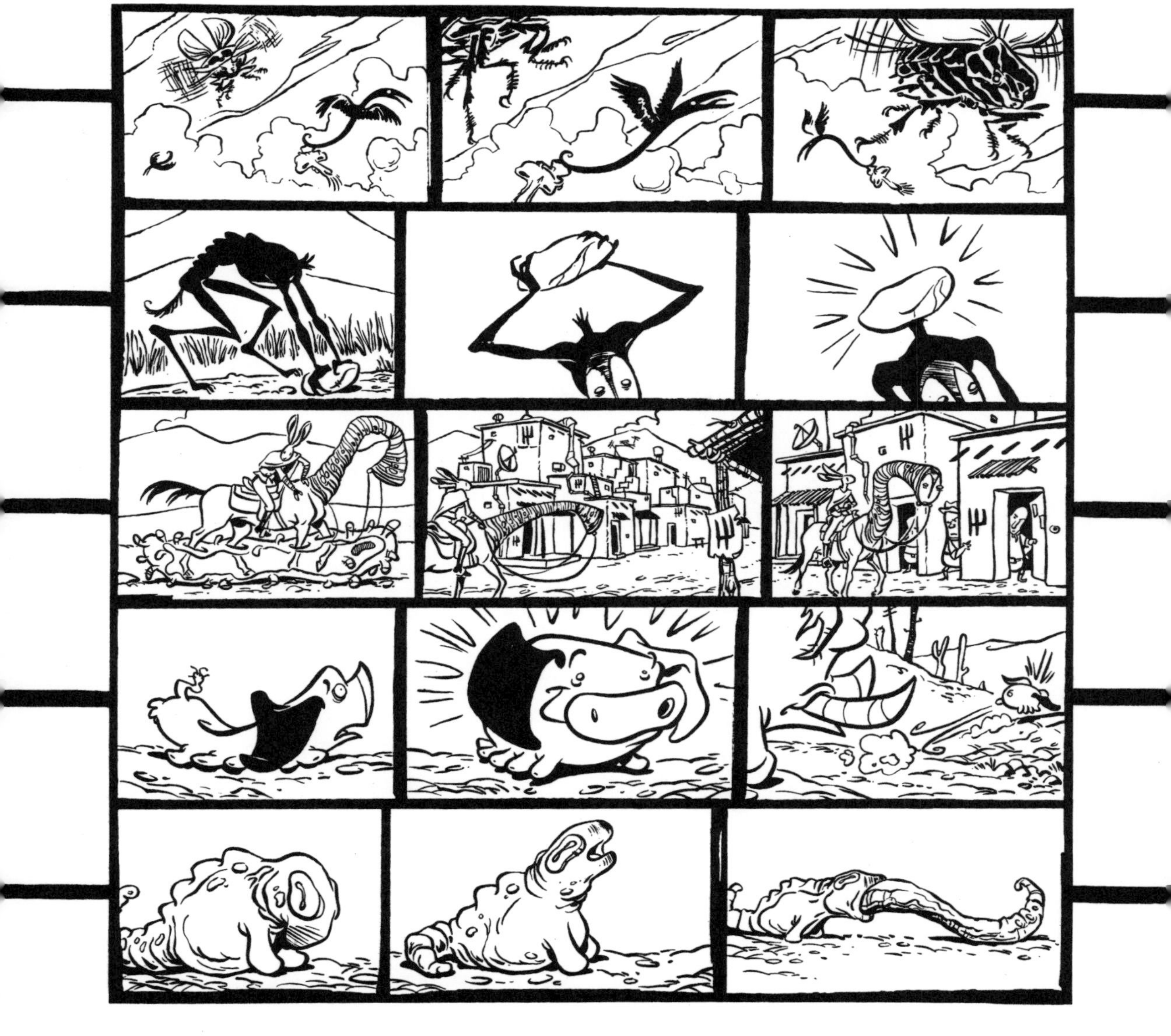

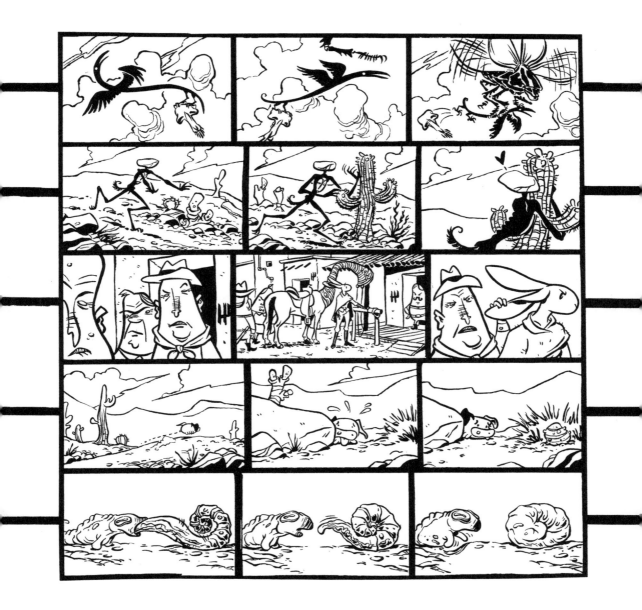

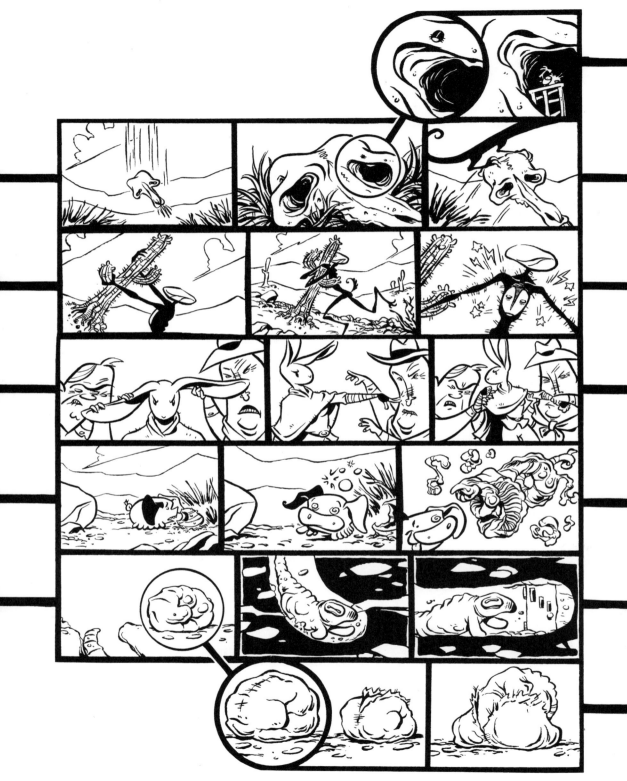

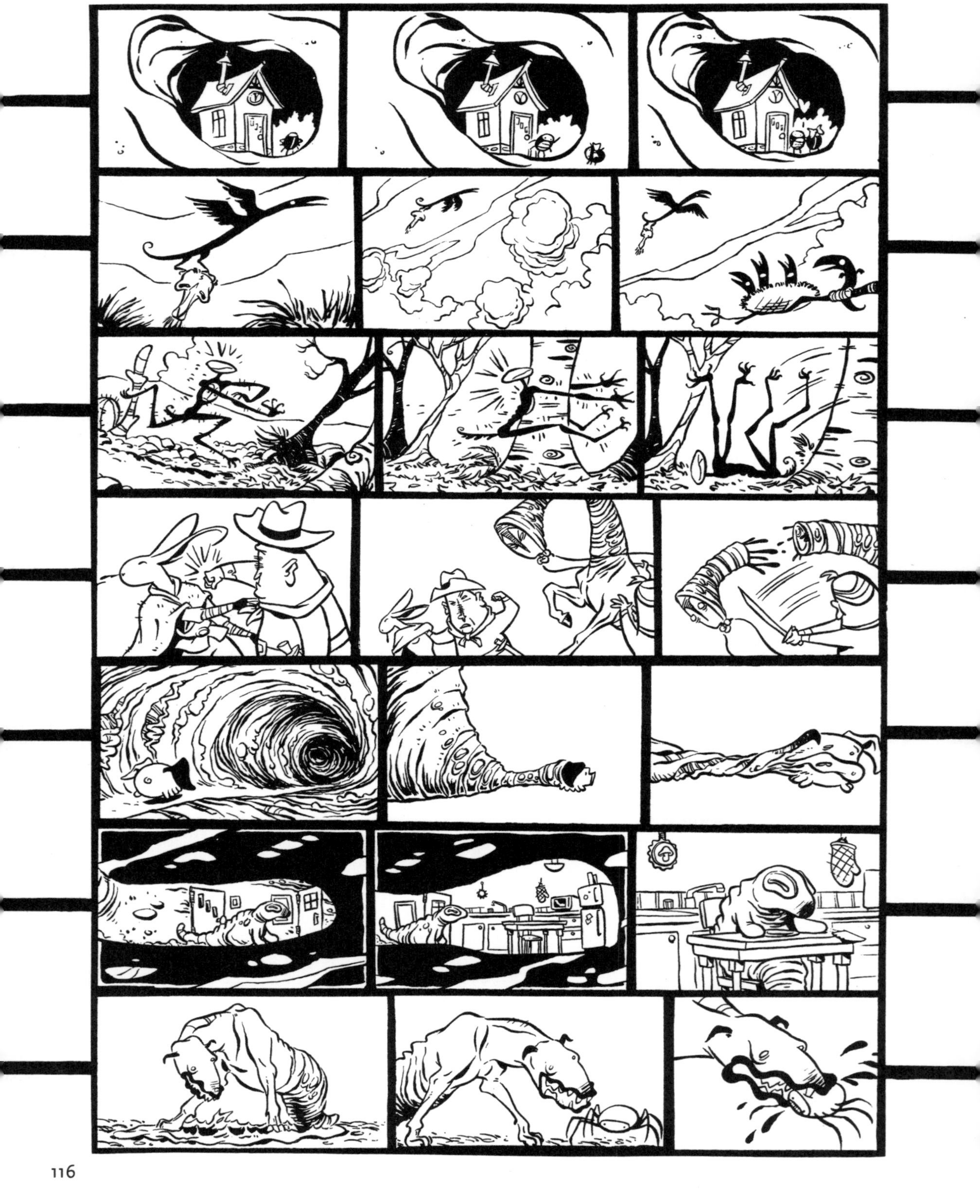

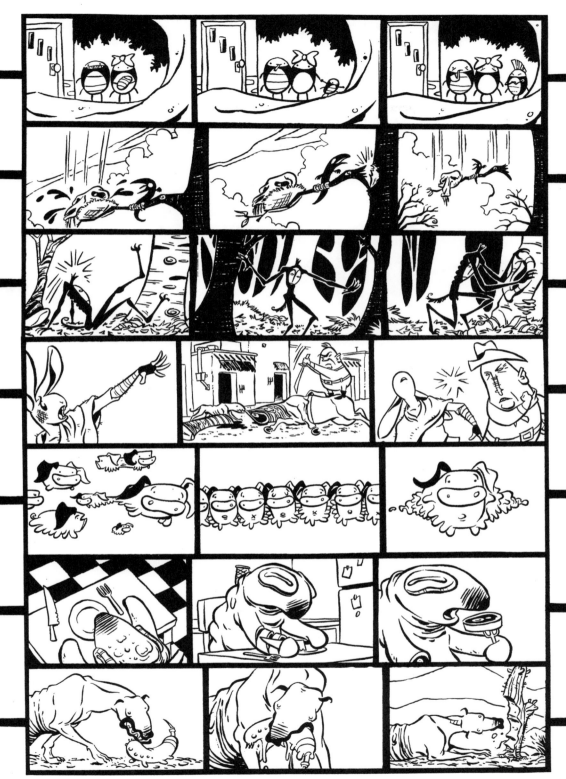

117

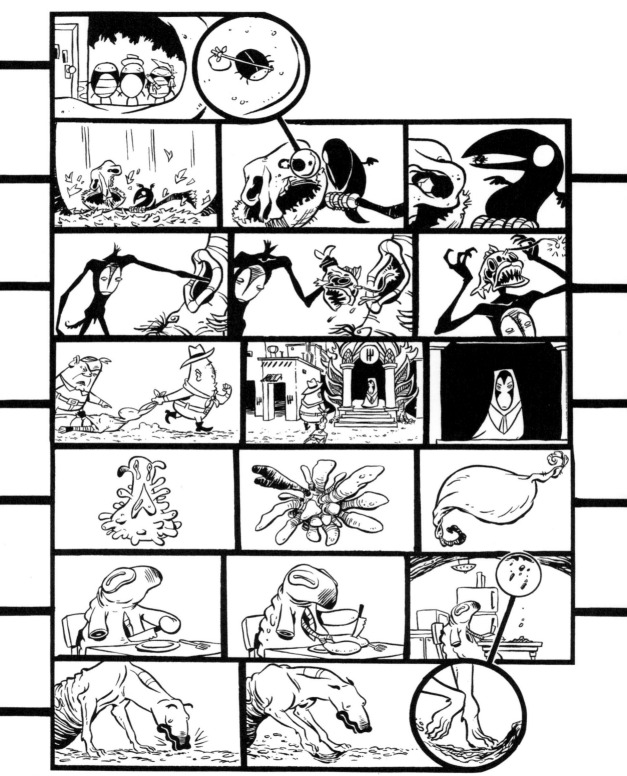

118

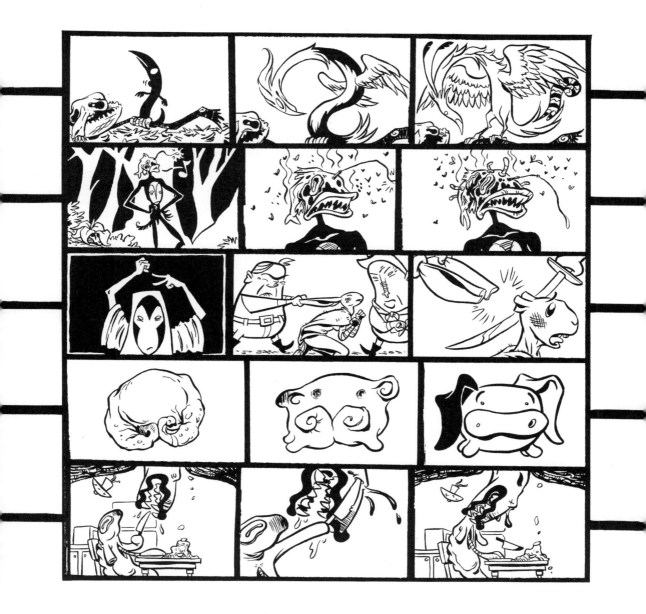

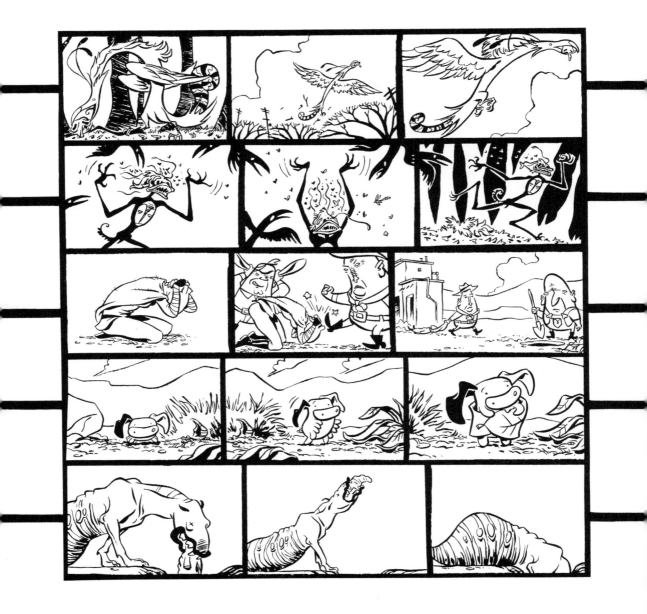

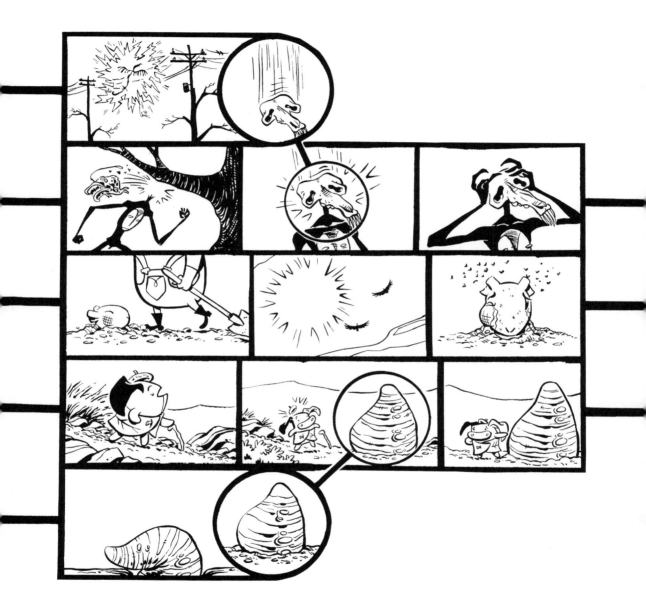

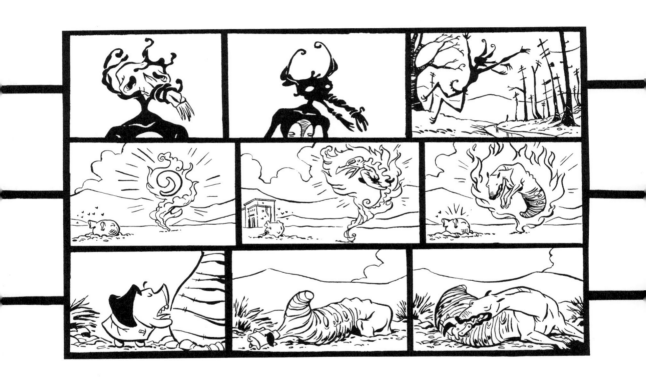

123

124

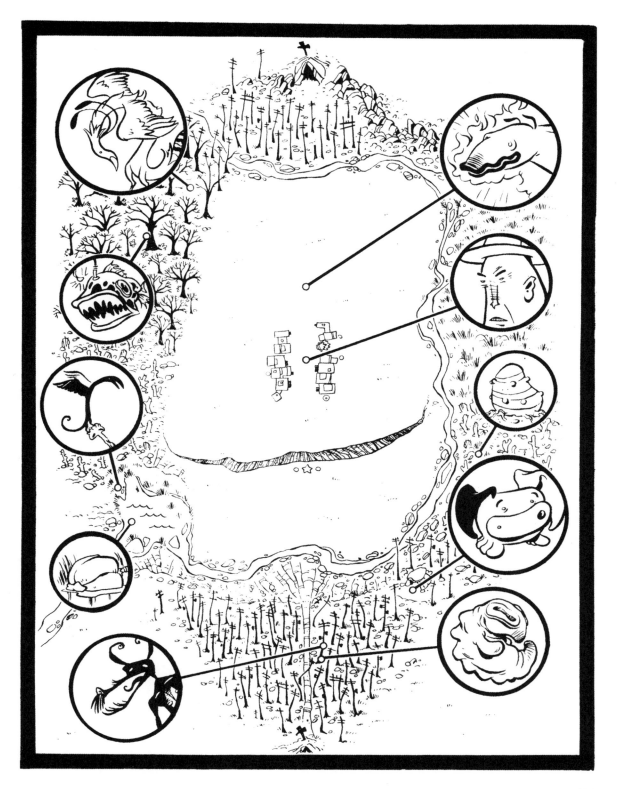

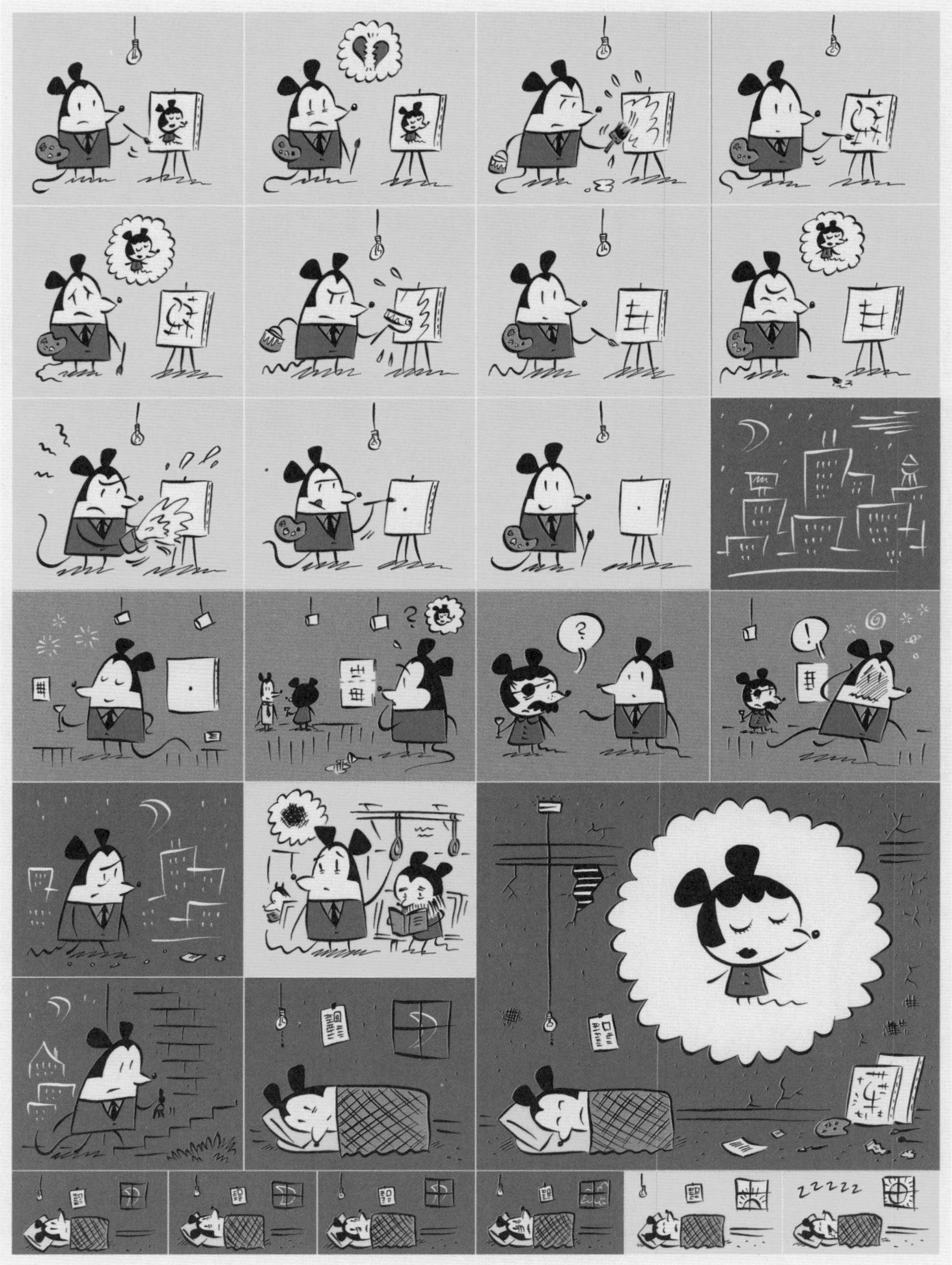
?
?
!
ZZZZZ

FROM *The Stranger*

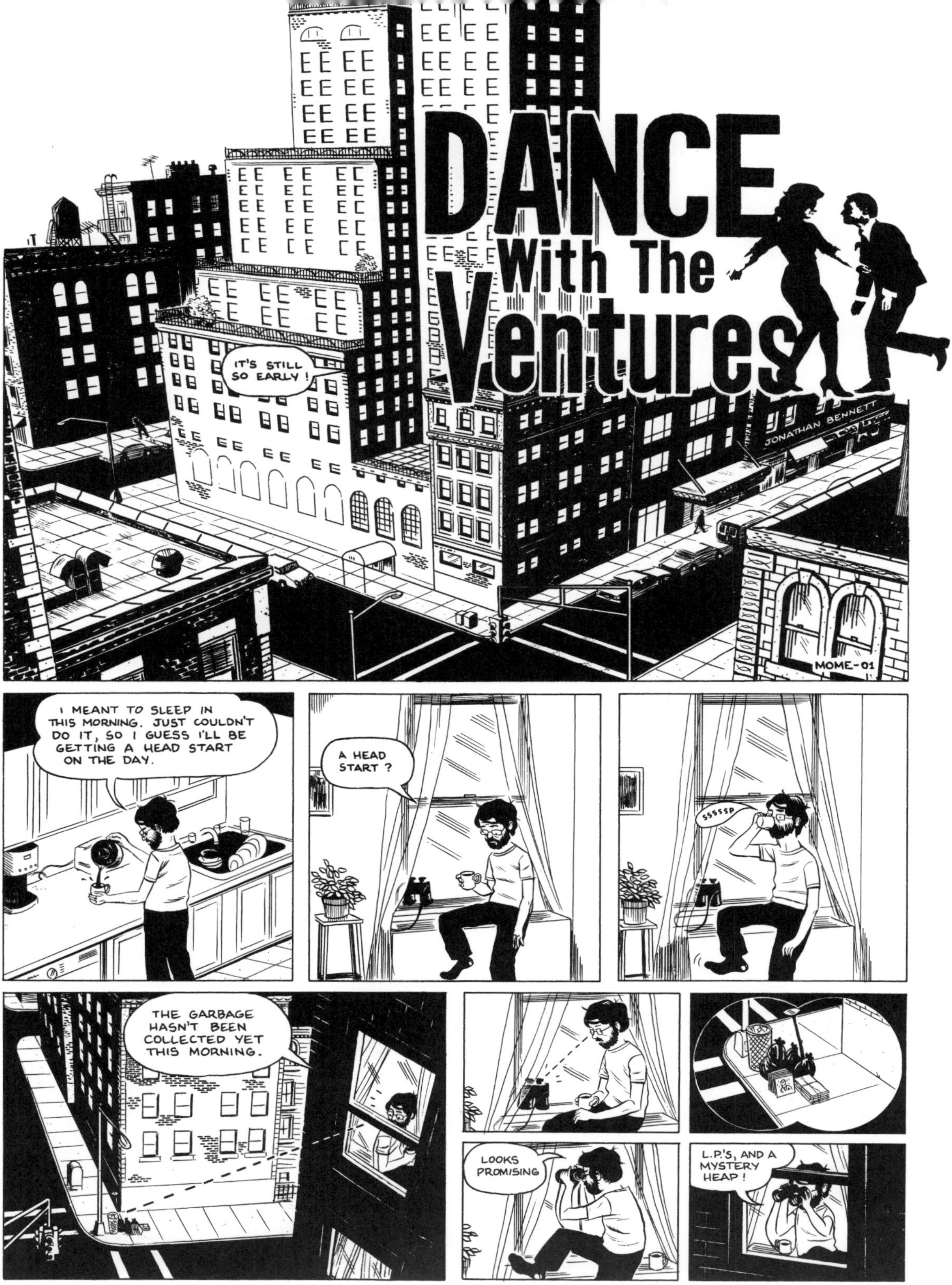
DANCE
With The
Ventures
JONATHAN BENNETT
IT'S STILL SO EARLY!
MOME-01
I MEANT TO SLEEP IN THIS MORNING. JUST COULDN'T DO IT, SO I GUESS I'LL BE GETTING A HEAD START ON THE DAY.
A HEAD START?
SSSSSP
THE GARBAGE HASN'T BEEN COLLECTED YET THIS MORNING.
LOOKS PROMISING
L.P.'S, AND A MYSTERY HEAP!

FROM *Mome*

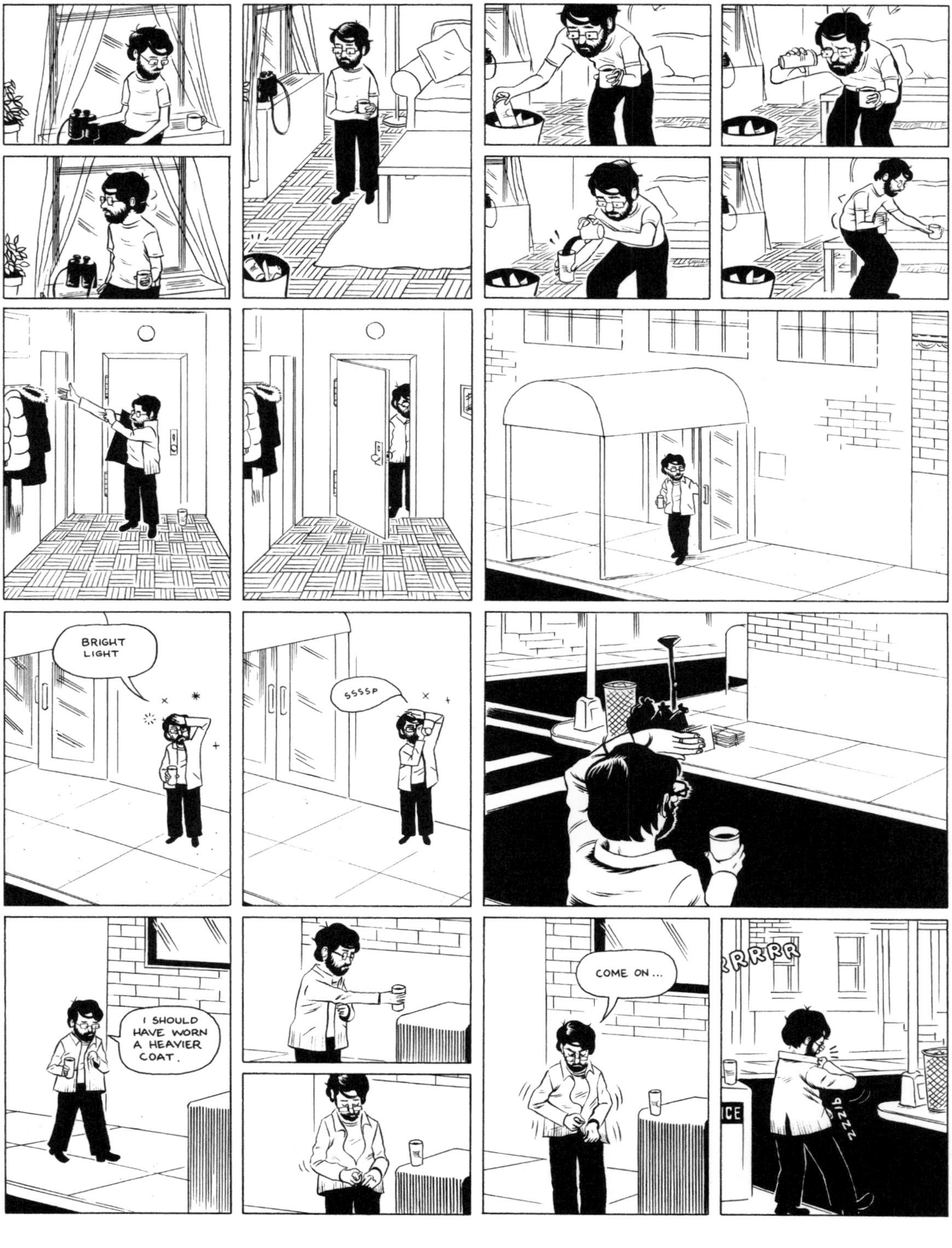
BRIGHT LIGHT
SSSSP
I SHOULD HAVE WORN A HEAVIER COAT.
COME ON...
RRRRR
ICE
ZZZZIP

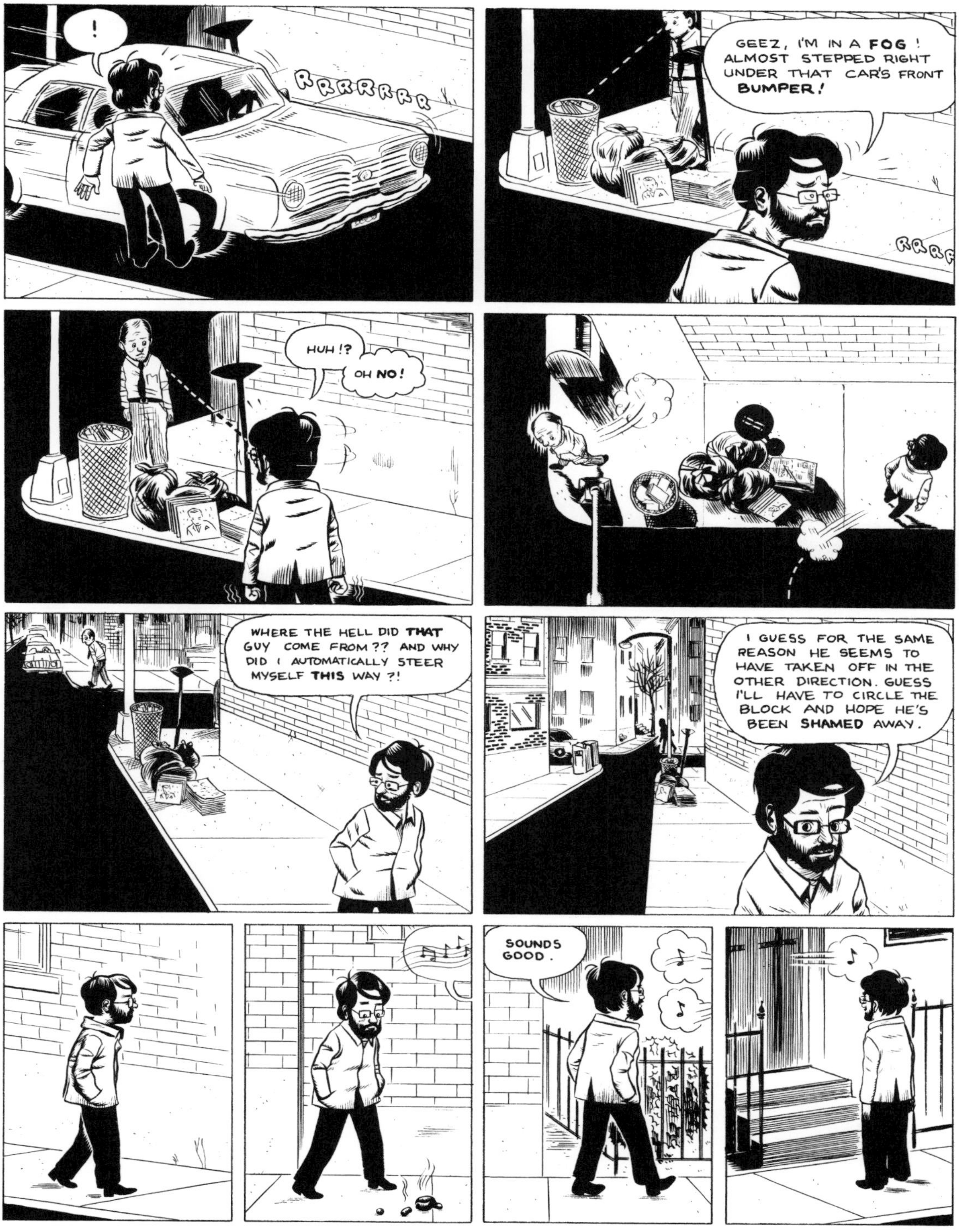
!
RRRRRRRR
GEEZ, I'M IN A FOG! ALMOST STEPPED RIGHT UNDER THAT CAR'S FRONT BUMPER!
RRRR
HUH!?
OH NO!
WHERE THE HELL DID THAT GUY COME FROM?? AND WHY DID I AUTOMATICALLY STEER MYSELF THIS WAY?!
I GUESS FOR THE SAME REASON HE SEEMS TO HAVE TAKEN OFF IN THE OTHER DIRECTION. GUESS I'LL HAVE TO CIRCLE THE BLOCK AND HOPE HE'S BEEN SHAMED AWAY.
SOUNDS GOOD.

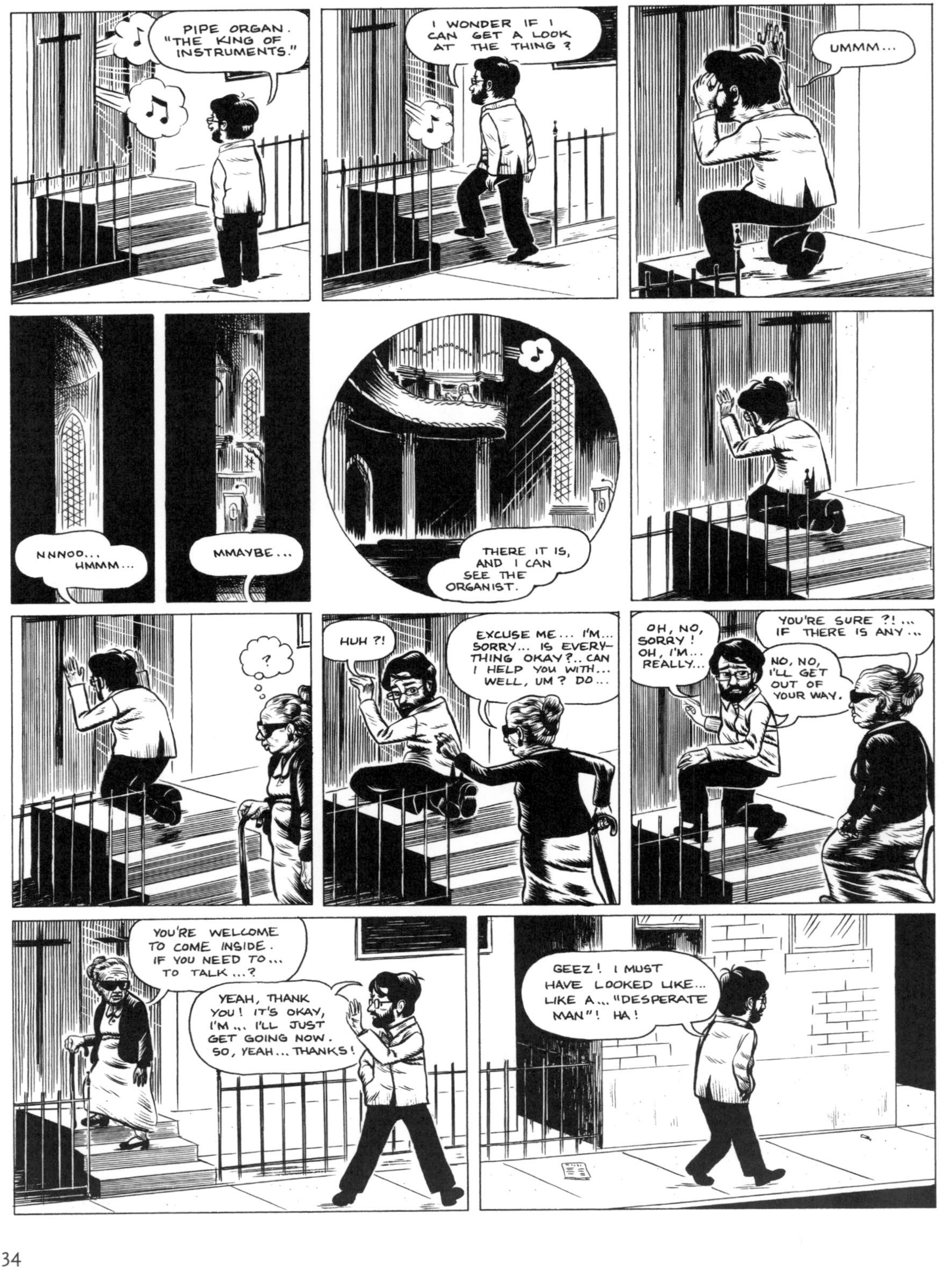
PIPE ORGAN. "THE KING OF INSTRUMENTS."
I WONDER IF I CAN GET A LOOK AT THE THING ?
UMMM...
NNNOO... HMMM...
MMAYBE...
THERE IT IS, AND I CAN SEE THE ORGANIST.
?
HUH ?!
EXCUSE ME... I'M... SORRY... IS EVERY-THING OKAY?.. CAN I HELP YOU WITH... WELL, UM ? DO...
OH, NO, SORRY ! OH, I'M... REALLY...
YOU'RE SURE ?!... IF THERE IS ANY...
NO, NO, I'LL GET OUT OF YOUR WAY.
YOU'RE WELCOME TO COME INSIDE. IF YOU NEED TO... TO TALK...?
YEAH, THANK YOU! IT'S OKAY, I'M... I'LL JUST GET GOING NOW. SO, YEAH... THANKS!
GEEZ! I MUST HAVE LOOKED LIKE... LIKE A... "DESPERATE MAN"! HA!

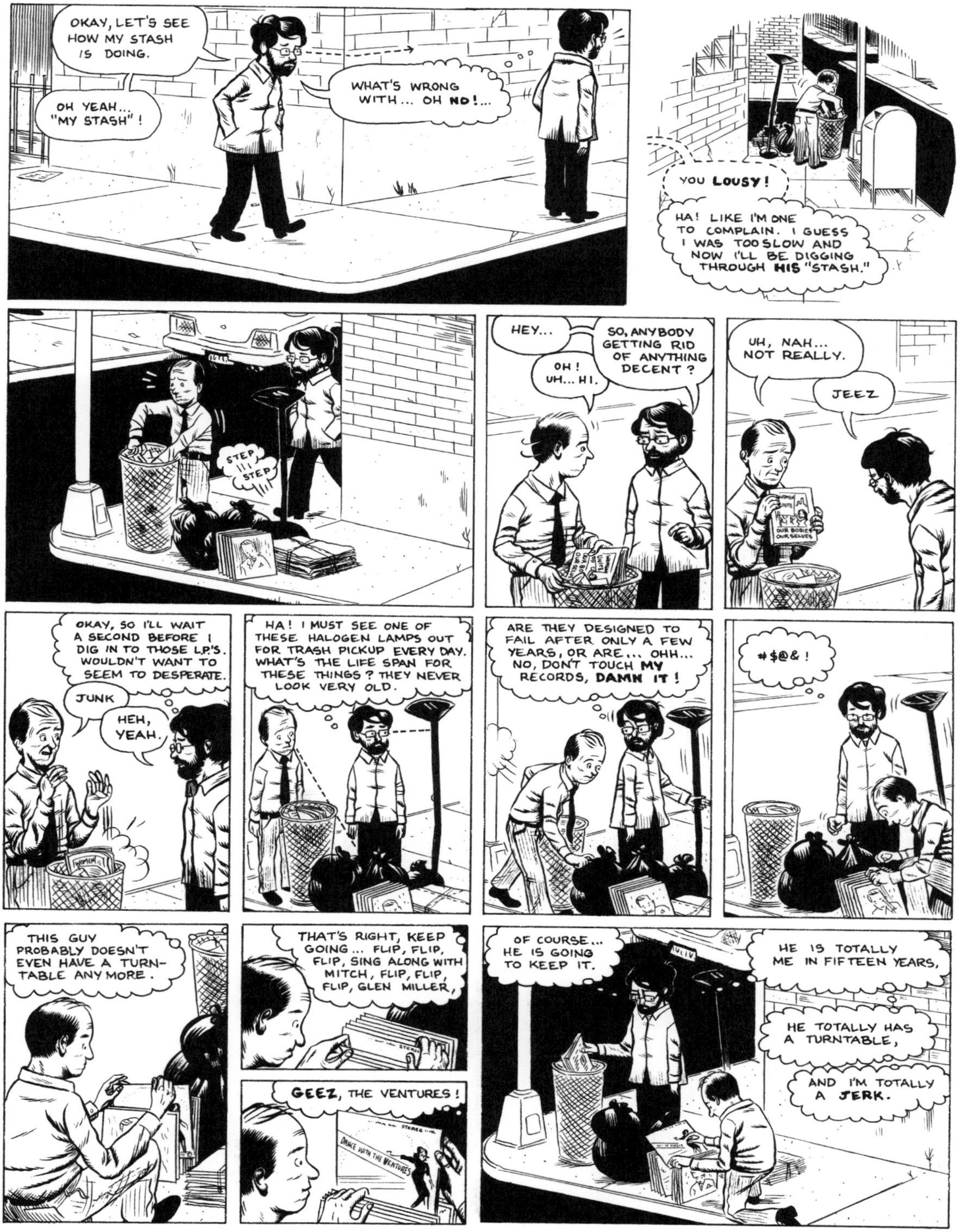

OKAY, LET'S SEE HOW MY STASH IS DOING.
OH YEAH... "MY STASH"!
WHAT'S WRONG WITH... OH NO!...
YOU LOUSY!
HA! LIKE I'M ONE TO COMPLAIN. I GUESS I WAS TOO SLOW AND NOW I'LL BE DIGGING THROUGH HIS "STASH."
STEP STEP
HEY...
OH! UH... HI.
SO, ANYBODY GETTING RID OF ANYTHING DECENT?
UH, NAH... NOT REALLY.
JEEZ
OUR BODIES OURSELVES
OKAY, SO I'LL WAIT A SECOND BEFORE I DIG IN TO THOSE L.P.'S. WOULDN'T WANT TO SEEM TO DESPERATE.
JUNK
HEH, YEAH.
HA! I MUST SEE ONE OF THESE HALOGEN LAMPS OUT FOR TRASH PICKUP EVERY DAY. WHAT'S THE LIFE SPAN FOR THESE THINGS? THEY NEVER LOOK VERY OLD.
ARE THEY DESIGNED TO FAIL AFTER ONLY A FEW YEARS, OR ARE... OHH... NO, DON'T TOUCH MY RECORDS, DAMN IT!
#$@&!
THIS GUY PROBABLY DOESN'T EVEN HAVE A TURN-TABLE ANY MORE.
THAT'S RIGHT, KEEP GOING... FLIP, FLIP, FLIP, SING ALONG WITH MITCH, FLIP, FLIP, FLIP, GLEN MILLER,
GEEZ, THE VENTURES!
DANCE WITH THE VENTURES
OF COURSE... HE IS GOING TO KEEP IT.
HE IS TOTALLY ME IN FIFTEEN YEARS,
HE TOTALLY HAS A TURNTABLE,
AND I'M TOTALLY A JERK.

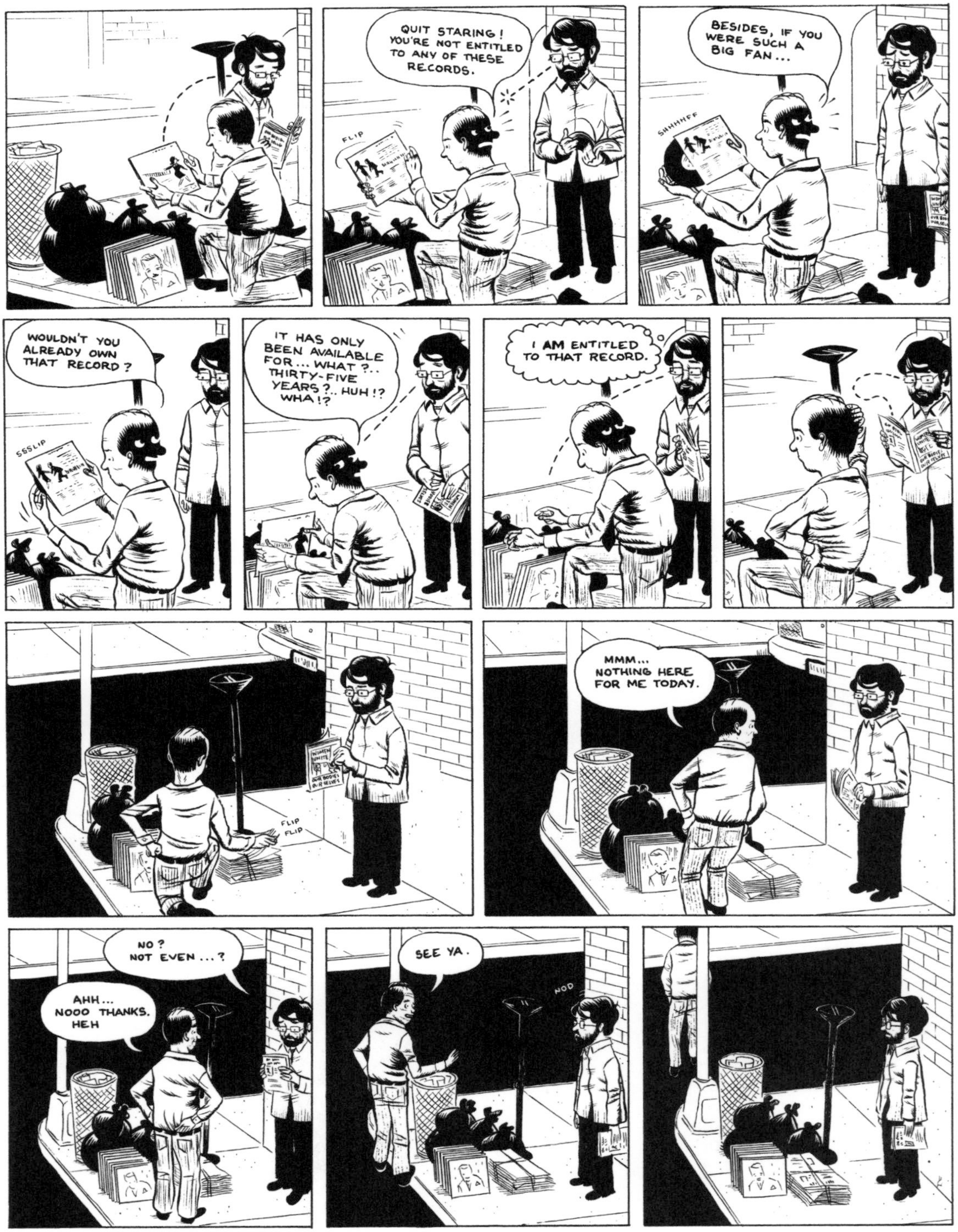
QUIT STARING! YOU'RE NOT ENTITLED TO ANY OF THESE RECORDS.
FLIP
SHHHHFF
BESIDES, IF YOU WERE SUCH A BIG FAN...
WOULDN'T YOU ALREADY OWN THAT RECORD?
SSSLIP
IT HAS ONLY BEEN AVAILABLE FOR... WHAT?.. THIRTY-FIVE YEARS?.. HUH!? WHA!?
I AM ENTITLED TO THAT RECORD.
FLIP FLIP
MMM... NOTHING HERE FOR ME TODAY.
NO? NOT EVEN...?
AHH... NOOO THANKS. HEH
SEE YA.
NOD

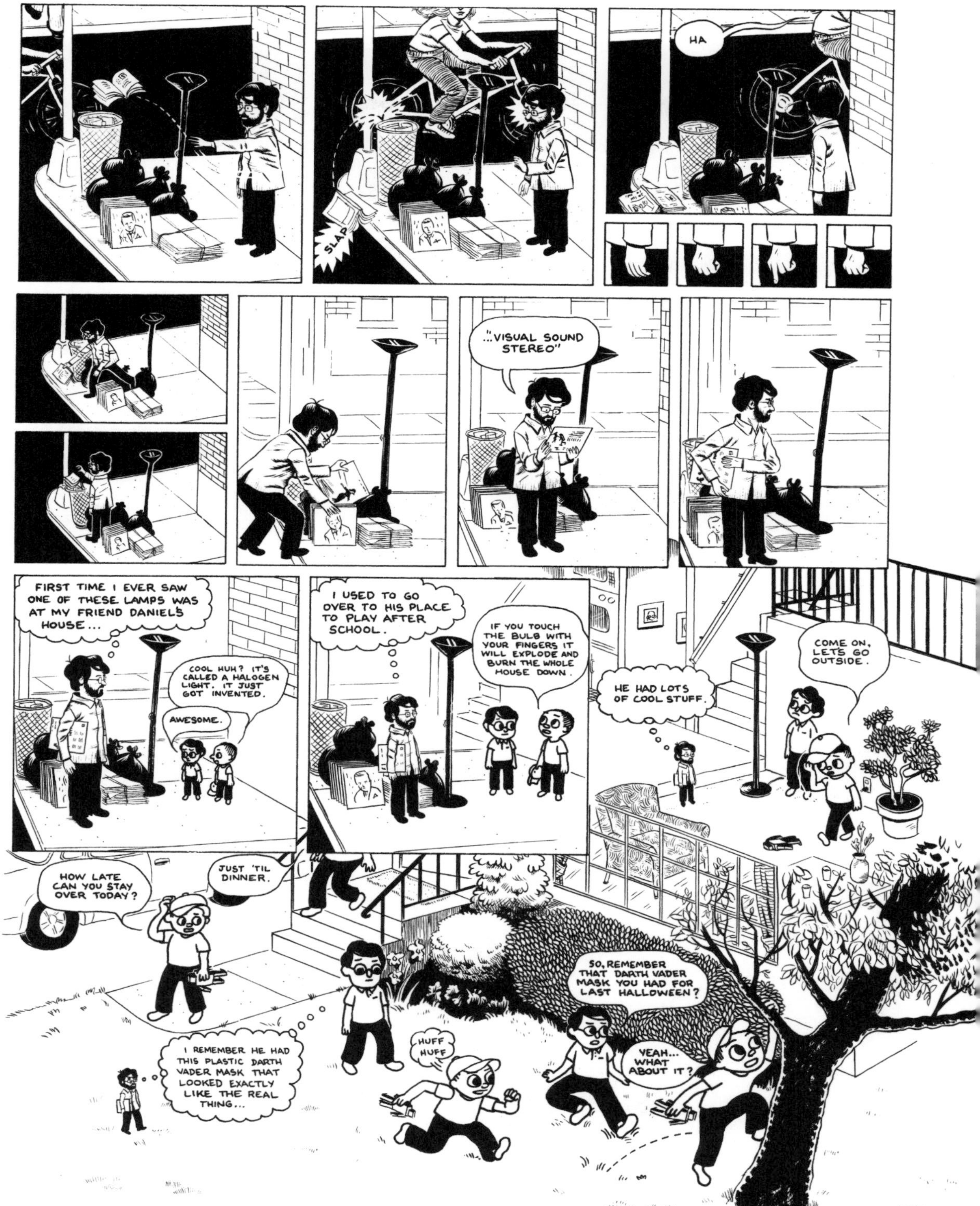

SLAP
HA
..."VISUAL SOUND STEREO"
FIRST TIME I EVER SAW ONE OF THESE LAMPS WAS AT MY FRIEND DANIEL'S HOUSE...
COOL HUH? IT'S CALLED A HALOGEN LIGHT. IT JUST GOT INVENTED.
AWESOME.
I USED TO GO OVER TO HIS PLACE TO PLAY AFTER SCHOOL.
IF YOU TOUCH THE BULB WITH YOUR FINGERS IT WILL EXPLODE AND BURN THE WHOLE HOUSE DOWN.
HE HAD LOTS OF COOL STUFF.
COME ON, LETS GO OUTSIDE.
HOW LATE CAN YOU STAY OVER TODAY?
JUST 'TIL DINNER.
SO, REMEMBER THAT DARTH VADER MASK YOU HAD FOR LAST HALLOWEEN?
I REMEMBER HE HAD THIS PLASTIC DARTH VADER MASK THAT LOOKED EXACTLY LIKE THE REAL THING...
HUFF HUFF
YEAH... WHAT ABOUT IT?

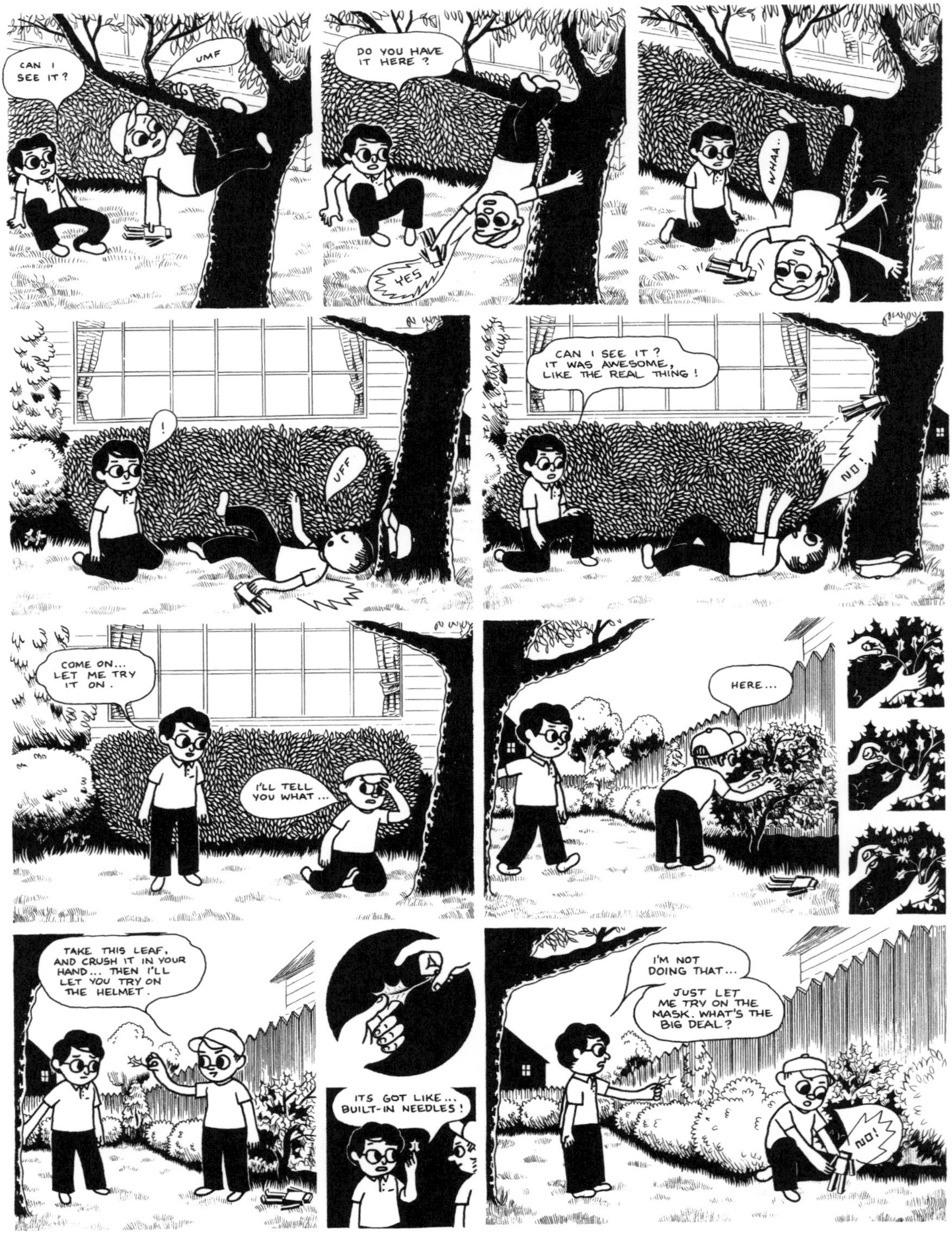
CAN I SEE IT?
UMF
DO YOU HAVE IT HERE?
YES
WHAA..
!
UFF
CAN I SEE IT? IT WAS AWESOME, LIKE THE REAL THING!
NO!
COME ON... LET ME TRY IT ON.
I'LL TELL YOU WHAT...
HERE...
TUG
SNAP
TAKE THIS LEAF, AND CRUSH IT IN YOUR HAND... THEN I'LL LET YOU TRY ON THE HELMET.
ITS GOT LIKE... BUILT-IN NEEDLES!
I'M NOT DOING THAT...
JUST LET ME TRY ON THE MASK. WHAT'S THE BIG DEAL?
NO!

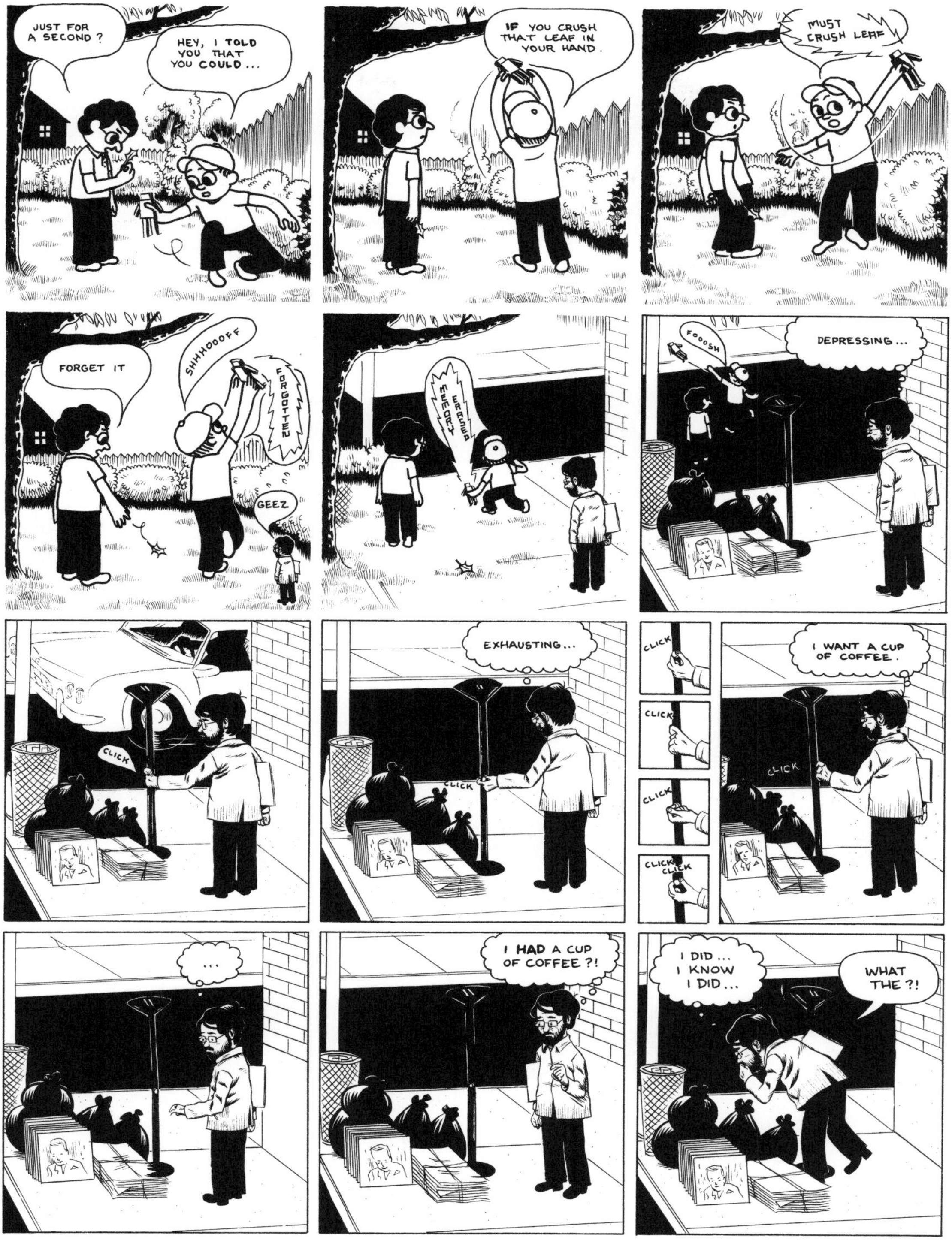

JUST FOR A SECOND ?
HEY, I TOLD YOU THAT YOU COULD ...
IF YOU CRUSH THAT LEAF IN YOUR HAND.
MUST CRUSH LEAF
FORGET IT
SHHHOOOFF
FORGOTTEN
GEEZ
MEMORY ERASED
FOOOSH
DEPRESSING ...
CLICK
EXHAUSTING ...
CLICK
CLICK
CLICK
CLICK
CLICK CLICK
I WANT A CUP OF COFFEE.
CLICK
...
I HAD A CUP OF COFFEE ?!
I DID ... I KNOW I DID ...
WHAT THE ?!

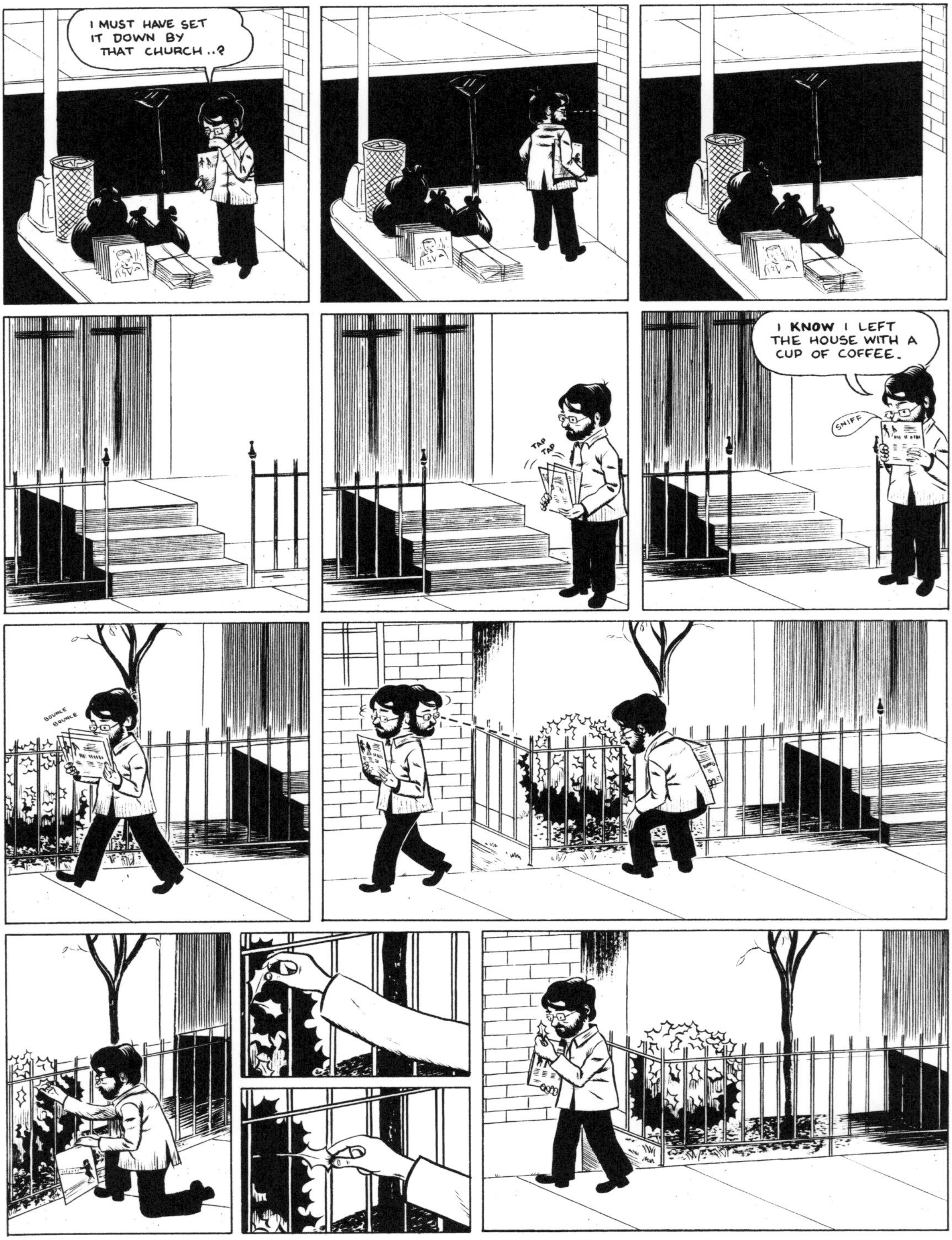
I MUST HAVE SET IT DOWN BY THAT CHURCH ..?
TAP TAP
I KNOW I LEFT THE HOUSE WITH A CUP OF COFFEE.
SNIFF
BOUNCE BOUNCE

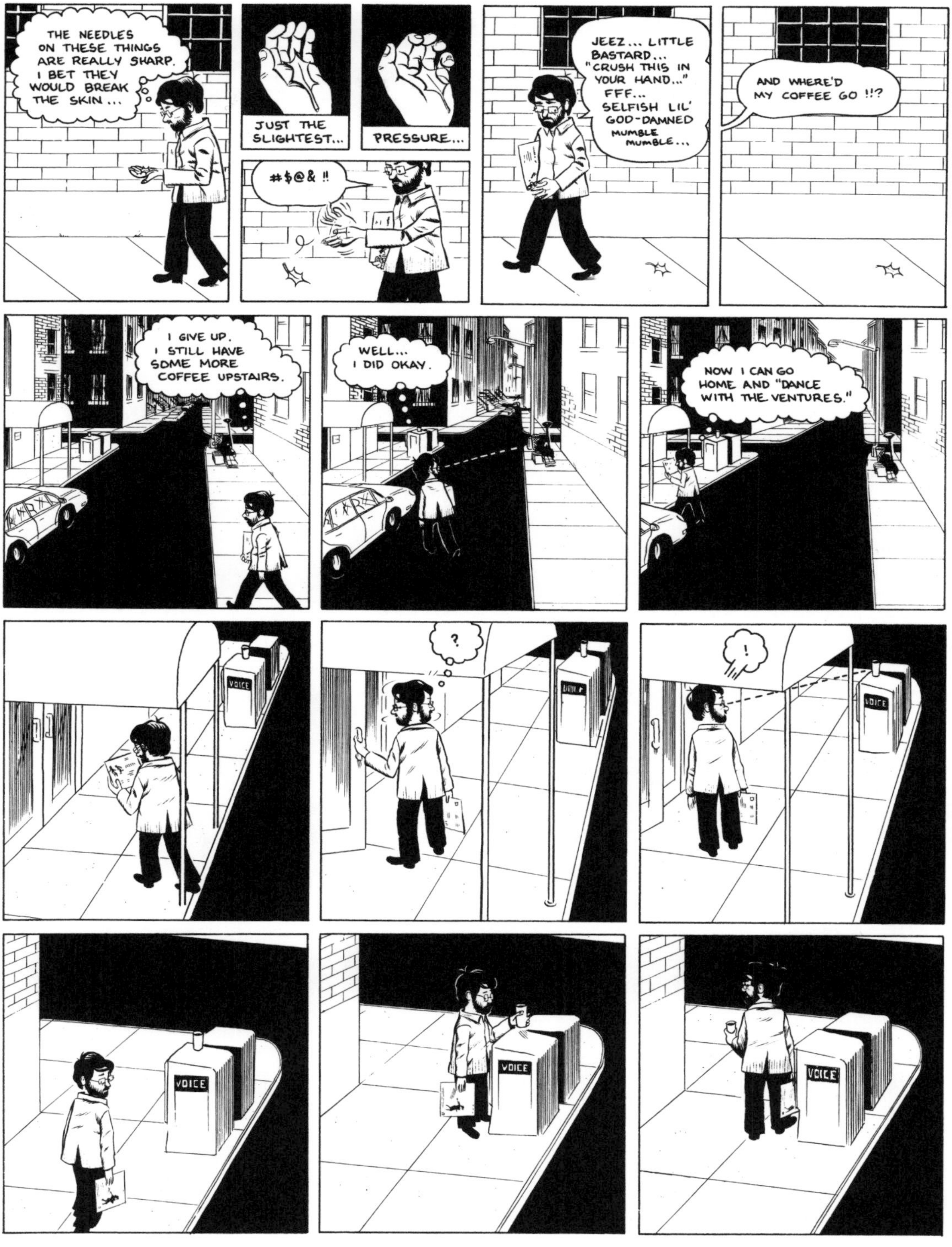
THE NEEDLES ON THESE THINGS ARE REALLY SHARP. I BET THEY WOULD BREAK THE SKIN...
JUST THE SLIGHTEST...
PRESSURE...
#$@& !!
JEEZ... LITTLE BASTARD... "CRUSH THIS IN YOUR HAND..." FFF... SELFISH LIL' GOD-DAMNED MUMBLE MUMBLE...
AND WHERE'D MY COFFEE GO !!?
I GIVE UP. I STILL HAVE SOME MORE COFFEE UPSTAIRS.
WELL... I DID OKAY.
NOW I CAN GO HOME AND "DANCE WITH THE VENTURES."
VOICE
?
!
VOICE
VOICE
VOICE
VOICE

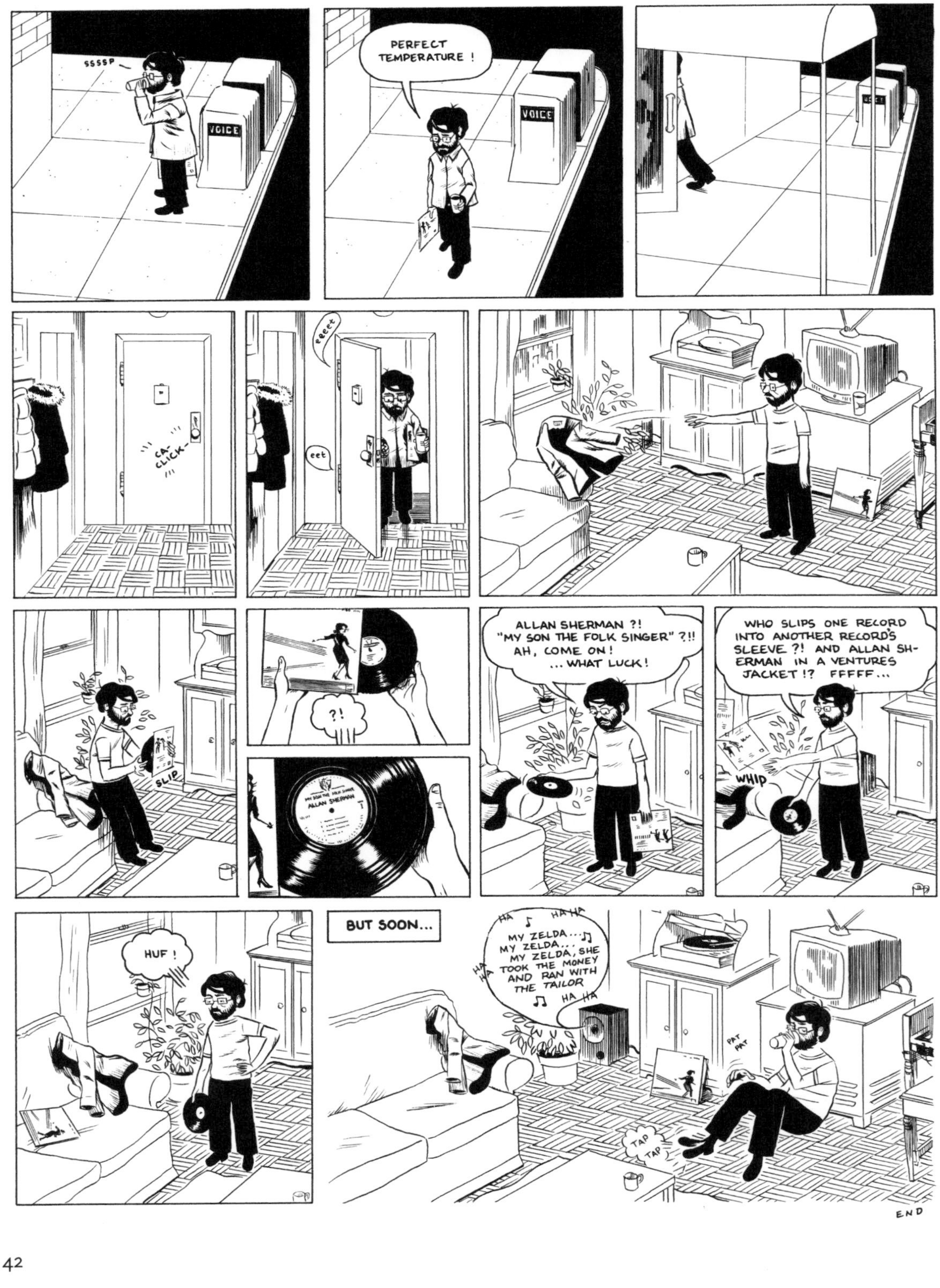
SSSSP
PERFECT TEMPERATURE !
VOICE
CA-CLICK
eeeet
eet
SLIP
?!
MY SON THE FOLK SINGER
ALLAN SHERMAN
ALLAN SHERMAN ?! "MY SON THE FOLK SINGER" ?!! AH, COME ON! ... WHAT LUCK!
WHO SLIPS ONE RECORD INTO ANOTHER RECORD'S SLEEVE ?! AND ALLAN SHERMAN IN A VENTURES JACKET !? FFFFF...
WHIP
HUF !
BUT SOON...
HA ♪ HA HA
MY ZELDA... ♫ MY ZELDA... MY ZELDA, SHE TOOK THE MONEY AND RAN WITH THE TAILOR ♫
HA HA
HA HA
PAT PAT
TAP TAP
END

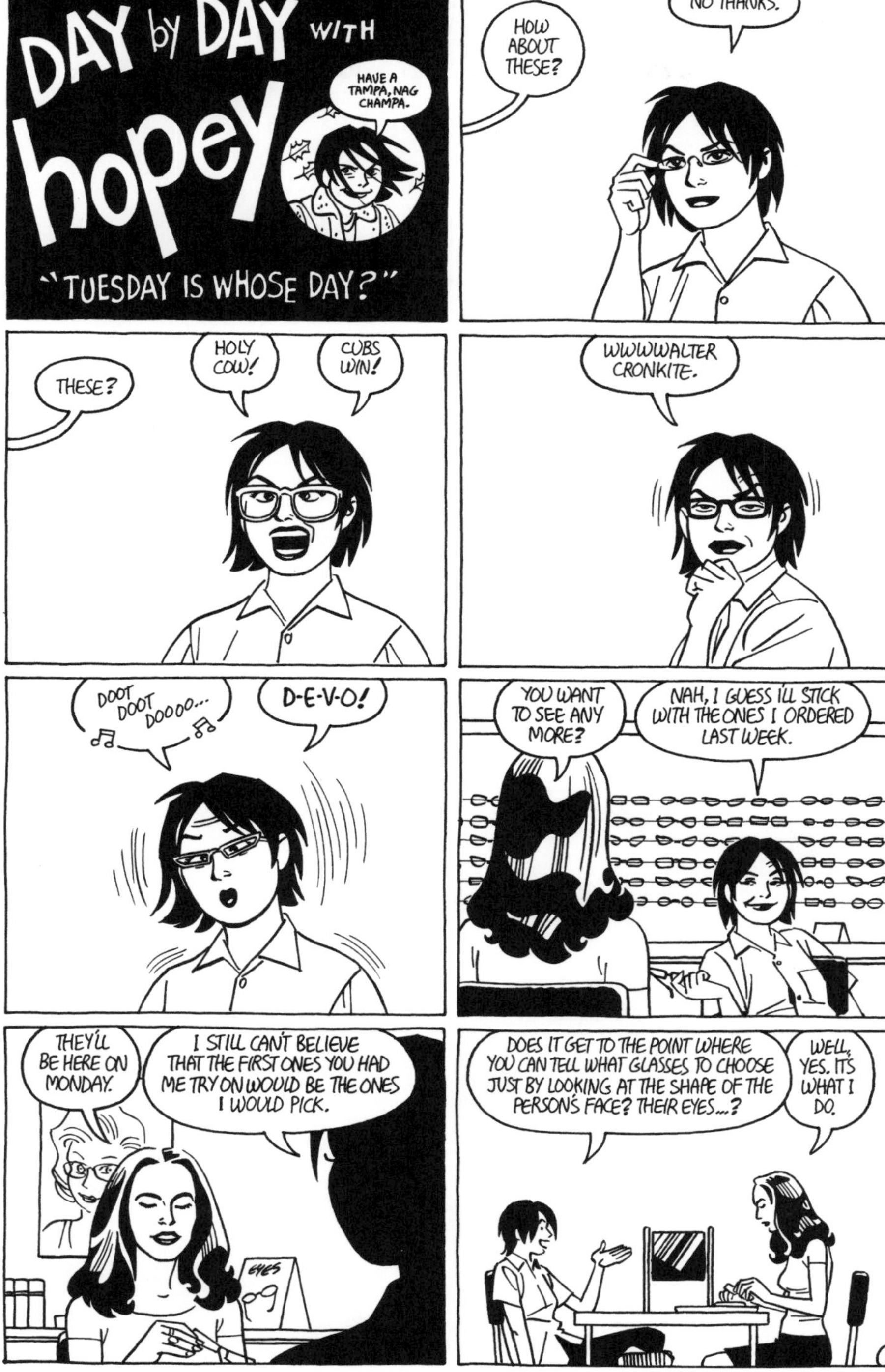
DAY by DAY WITH hopey
HAVE A TAMPA, NAG CHAMPA.
"TUESDAY IS WHOSE DAY?"
HOW ABOUT THESE?
NO THANKS.
THESE?
HOLY COW!
CUBS WIN!
WWWWALTER CRONKITE.
DOOT DOOT DOOOO...
D-E-V-O!
YOU WANT TO SEE ANY MORE?
NAH, I GUESS I'LL STICK WITH THE ONES I ORDERED LAST WEEK.
THEY'LL BE HERE ON MONDAY.
I STILL CAN'T BELIEVE THAT THE FIRST ONES YOU HAD ME TRY ON WOULD BE THE ONES I WOULD PICK.
EYES
DOES IT GET TO THE POINT WHERE YOU CAN TELL WHAT GLASSES TO CHOOSE JUST BY LOOKING AT THE SHAPE OF THE PERSON'S FACE? THEIR EYES...?
WELL, YES. ITS WHAT I DO.
1

FROM *Love and Rockets*

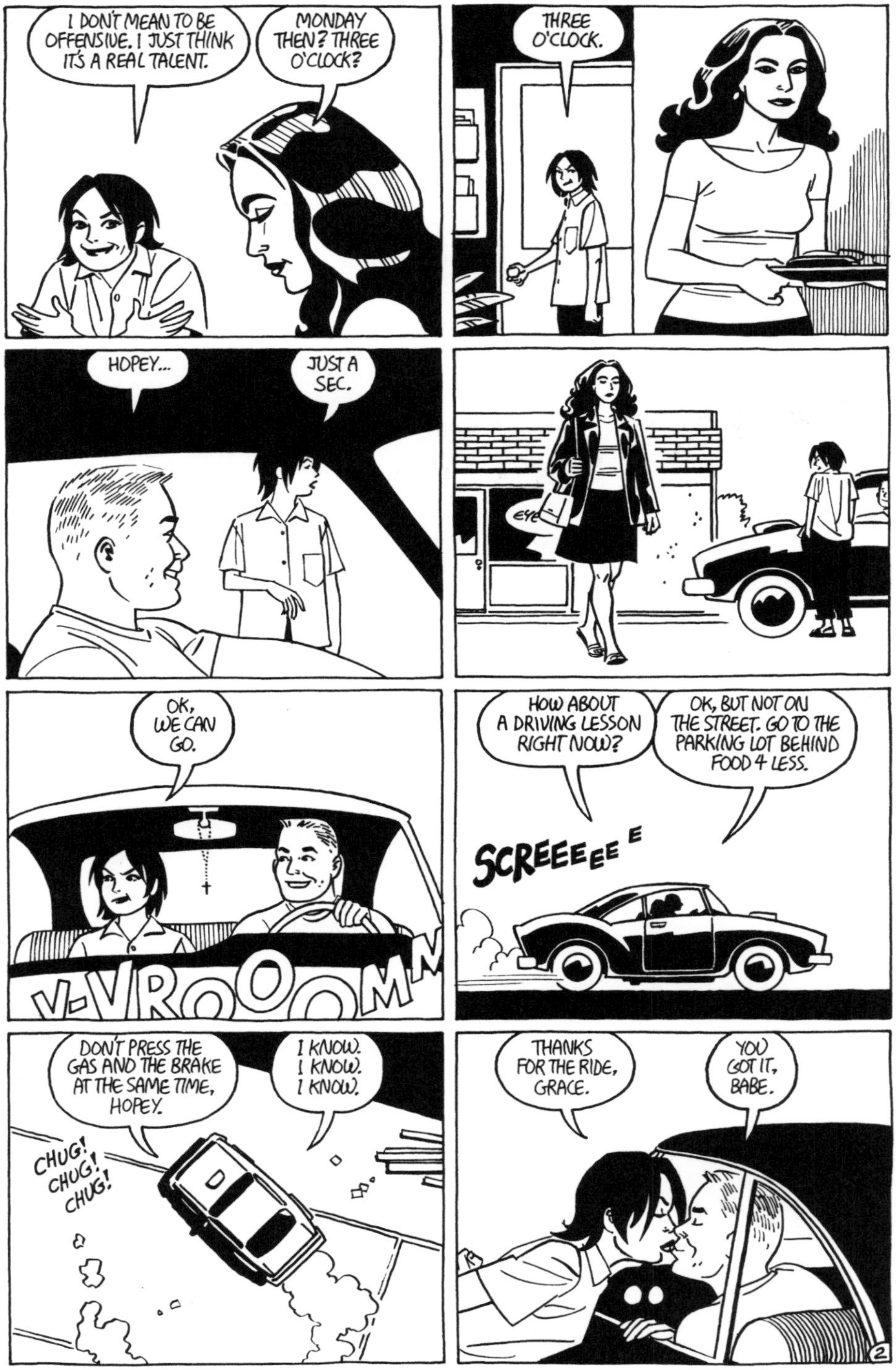
I DON'T MEAN TO BE OFFENSIVE. I JUST THINK IT'S A REAL TALENT.
MONDAY THEN? THREE O'CLOCK?
THREE O'CLOCK.
HOPEY...
JUST A SEC.
EYE
OK, WE CAN GO.
V-VROOOMM
HOW ABOUT A DRIVING LESSON RIGHT NOW?
OK, BUT NOT ON THE STREET. GO TO THE PARKING LOT BEHIND FOOD 4 LESS.
SCREEEEEE
DON'T PRESS THE GAS AND THE BRAKE AT THE SAME TIME, HOPEY.
I KNOW. I KNOW. I KNOW.
CHUG! CHUG! CHUG!
THANKS FOR THE RIDE, GRACE.
YOU GOT IT, BABE.
2

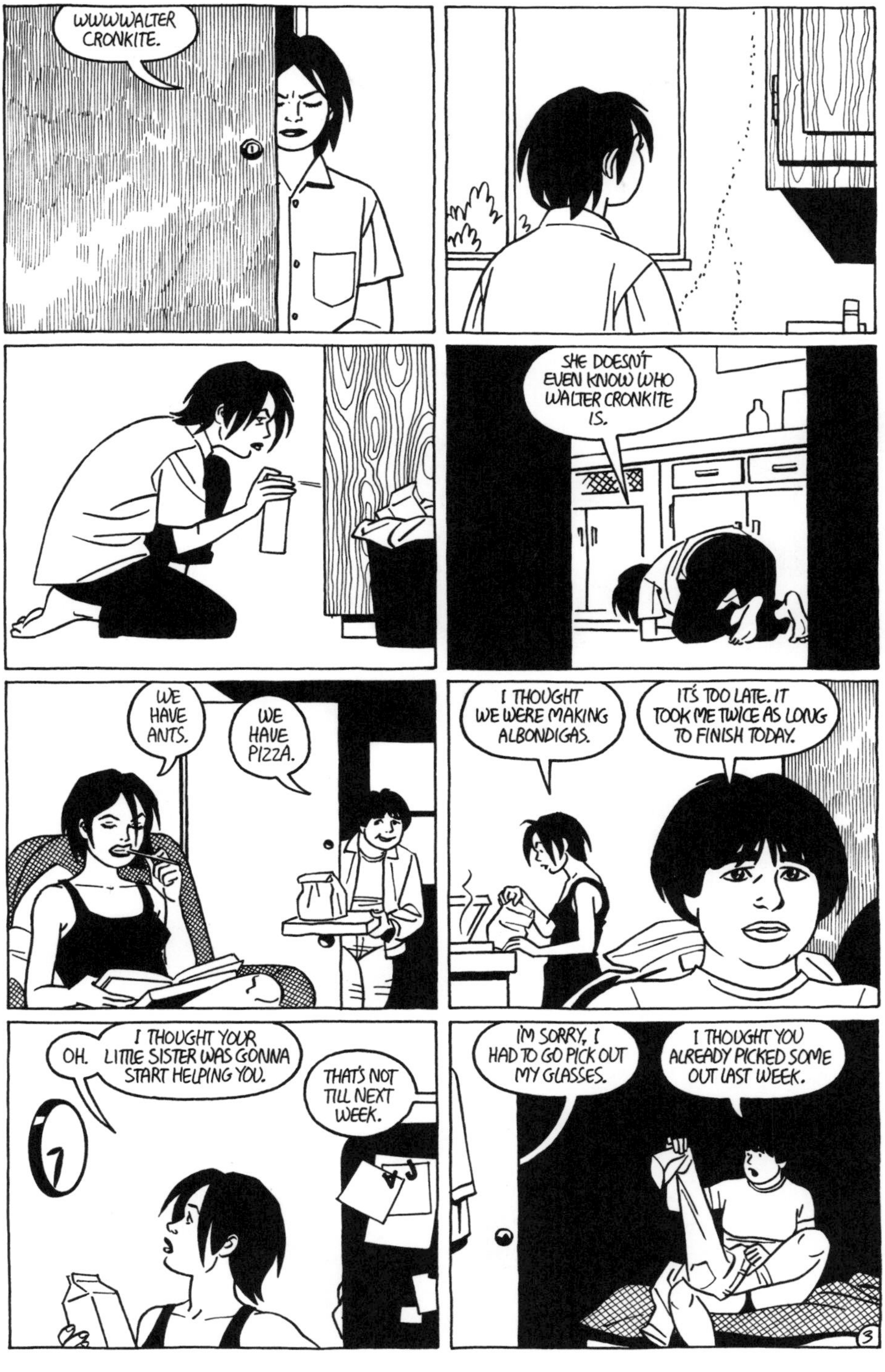
WWWWALTER CRONKITE.
SHE DOESN'T EVEN KNOW WHO WALTER CRONKITE IS.
WE HAVE ANTS.
WE HAVE PIZZA.
I THOUGHT WE WERE MAKING ALBONDIGAS.
IT'S TOO LATE. IT TOOK ME TWICE AS LONG TO FINISH TODAY.
OH.
I THOUGHT YOUR LITTLE SISTER WAS GONNA START HELPING YOU.
THAT'S NOT TILL NEXT WEEK.
I'M SORRY, I HAD TO GO PICK OUT MY GLASSES.
I THOUGHT YOU ALREADY PICKED SOME OUT LAST WEEK.

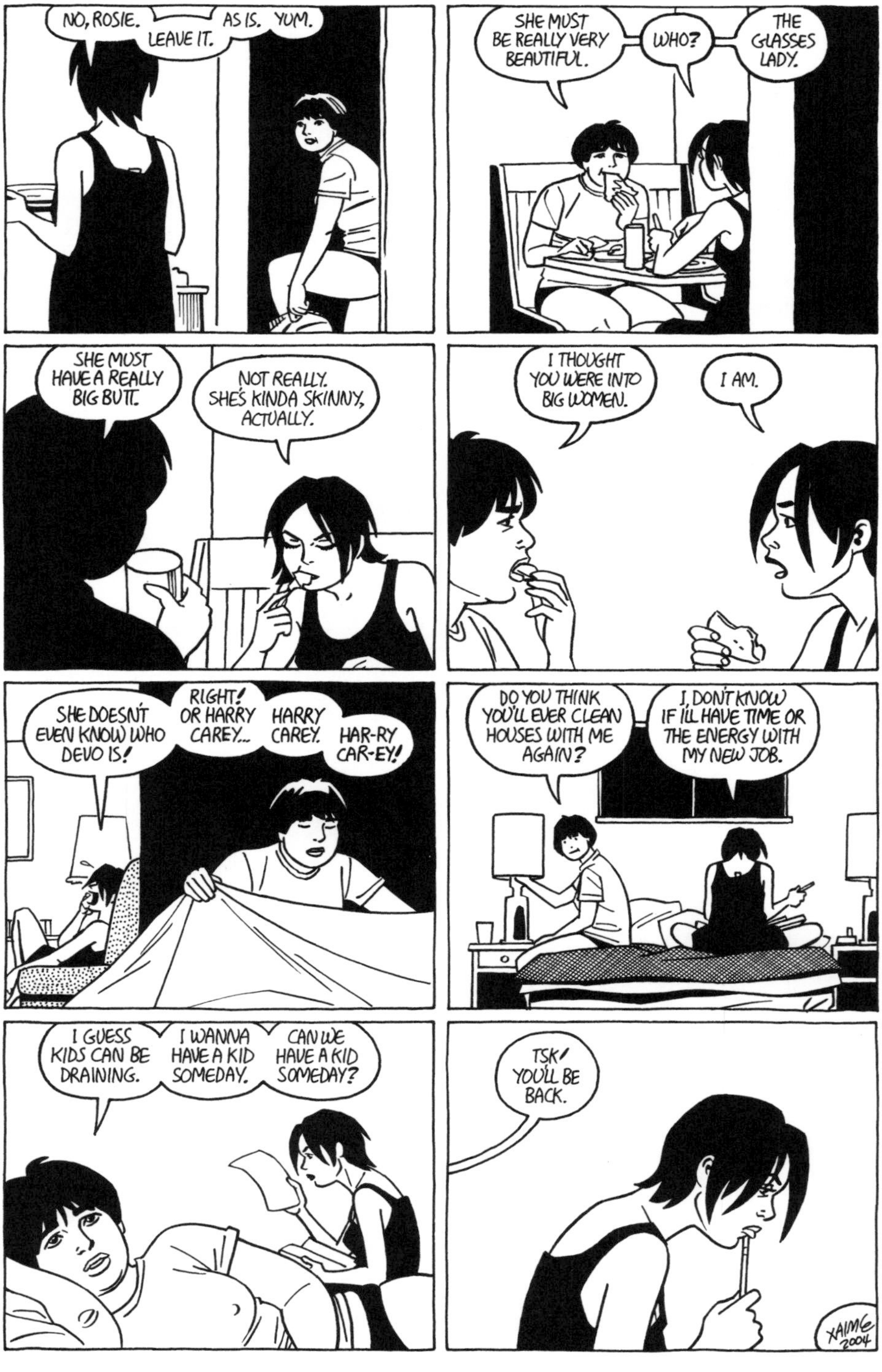

NO, ROSIE.
LEAVE IT.
AS IS.
YUM.
SHE MUST BE REALLY VERY BEAUTIFUL.
WHO?
THE GLASSES LADY.
SHE MUST HAVE A REALLY BIG BUTT.
NOT REALLY. SHE'S KINDA SKINNY, ACTUALLY.
I THOUGHT YOU WERE INTO BIG WOMEN.
I AM.
SHE DOESN'T EVEN KNOW WHO DEVO IS!
RIGHT! OR HARRY CAREY...
HARRY CAREY.
HAR-RY CAR-EY!
DO YOU THINK YOU'LL EVER CLEAN HOUSES WITH ME AGAIN?
I, DON'T KNOW IF I'LL HAVE TIME OR THE ENERGY WITH MY NEW JOB.
I GUESS KIDS CAN BE DRAINING.
I WANNA HAVE A KID SOMEDAY.
CAN WE HAVE A KID SOMEDAY?
TSK! YOU'LL BE BACK.
XAIME 2004

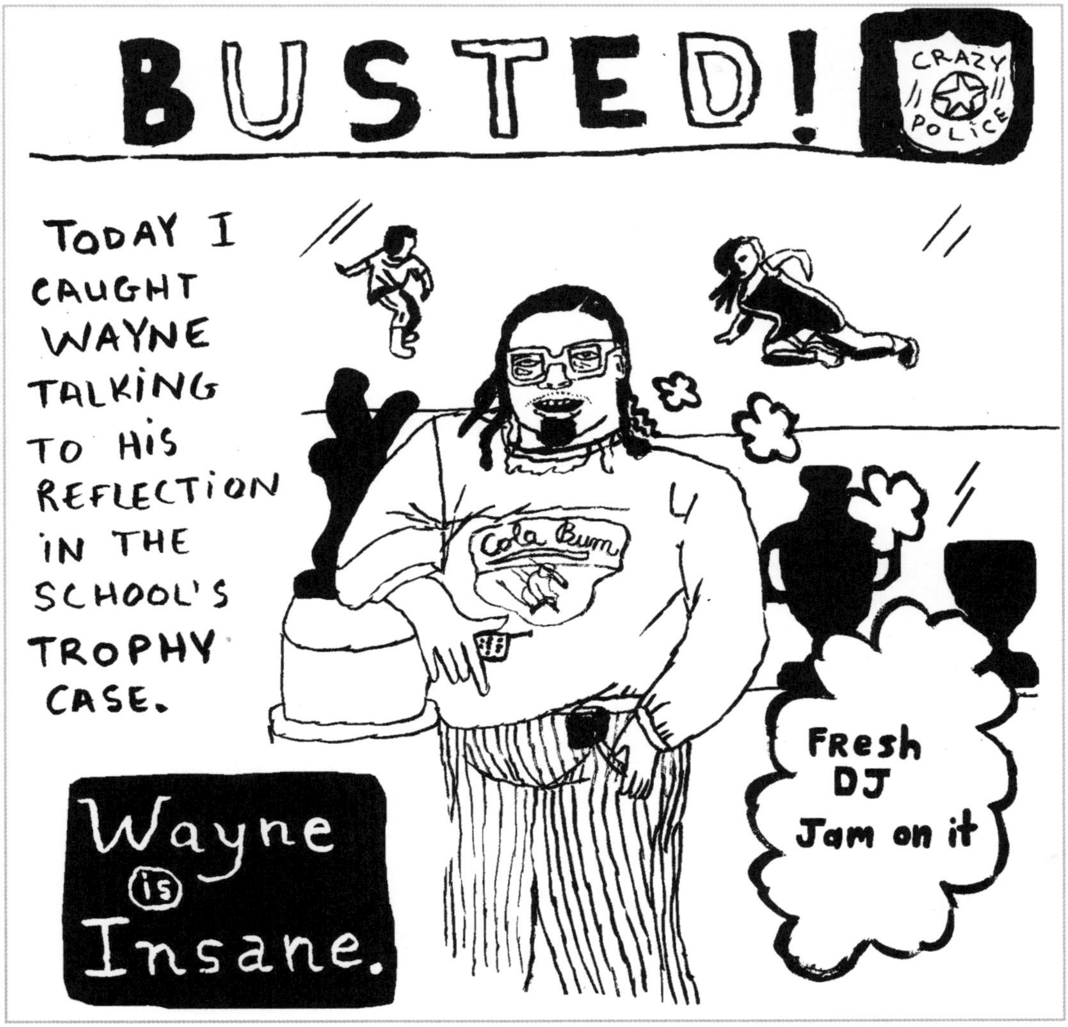
BUSTED!
CRAZY POLICE
TODAY I CAUGHT WAYNE TALKING TO HIS REFLECTION IN THE SCHOOL'S TROPHY CASE.
Cola Bum
Fresh DJ Jam on it
Wayne is Insane.

FROM *Unlovable*

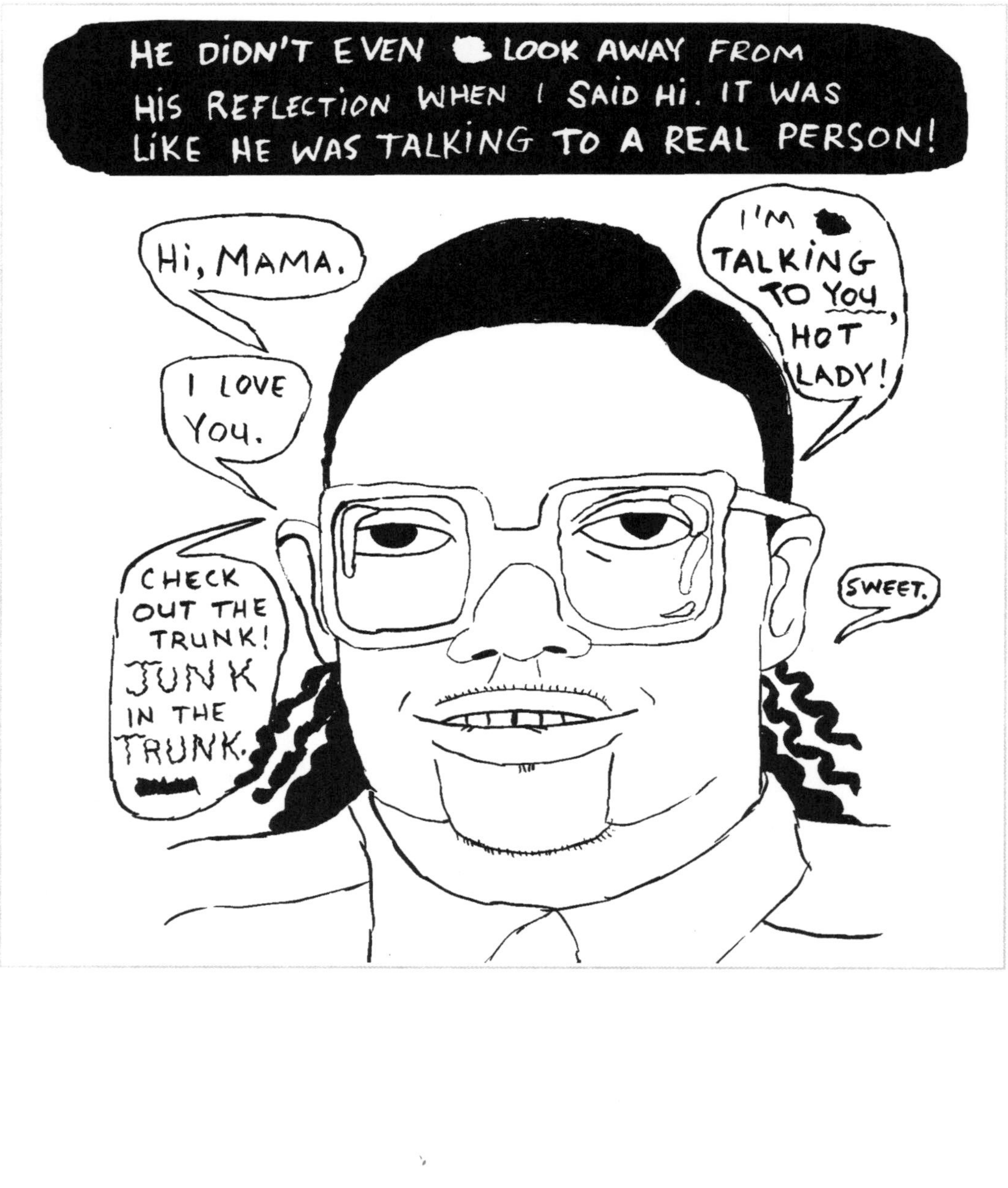
HE DIDN'T EVEN LOOK AWAY FROM HIS REFLECTION WHEN I SAID HI. IT WAS LIKE HE WAS TALKING TO A REAL PERSON!
Hi, MAMA.
I LOVE YOU.
CHECK OUT THE TRUNK! JUNK IN THE TRUNK.
I'M TALKING TO YOU, HOT LADY!
SWEET.

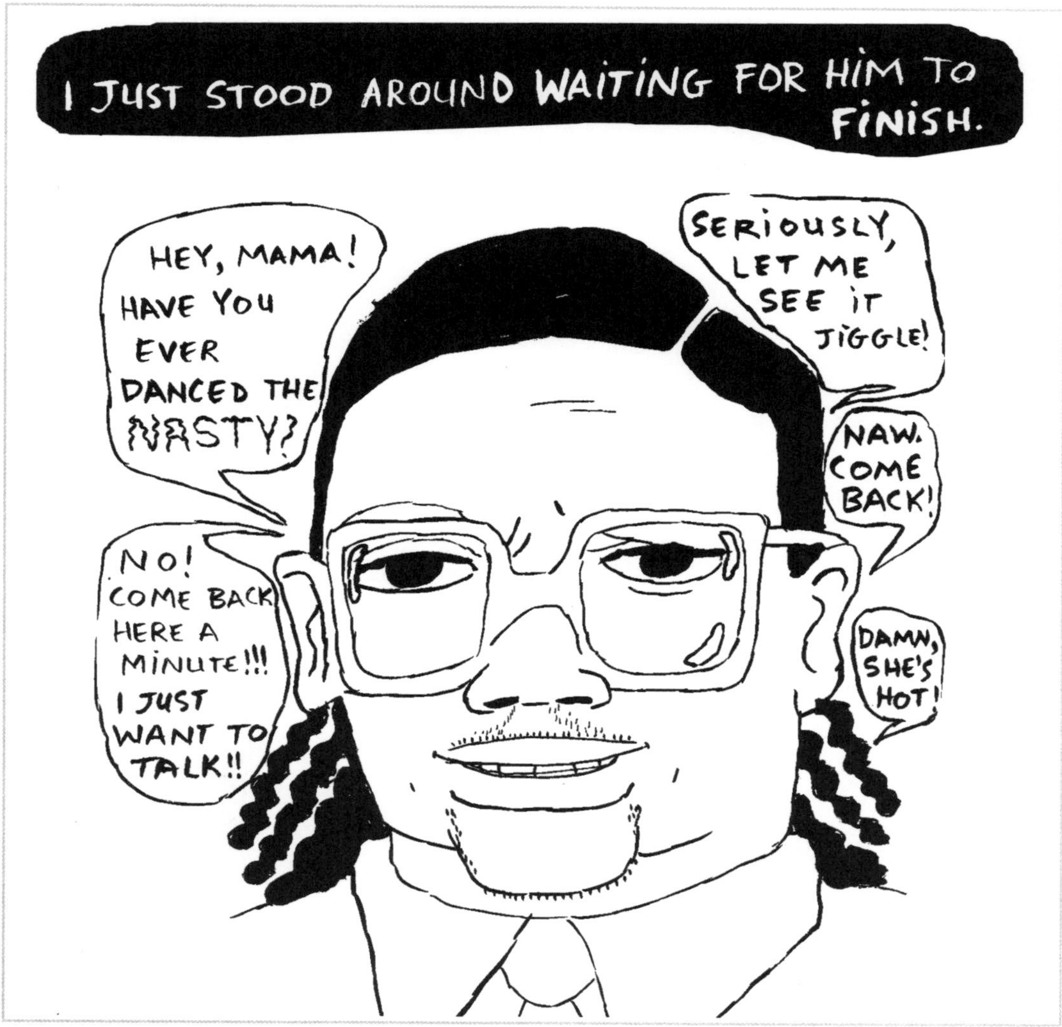
I JUST STOOD AROUND WAITING FOR HIM TO FINISH.
HEY, MAMA! HAVE YOU EVER DANCED THE NASTY?
SERIOUSLY, LET ME SEE IT JIGGLE!
NAW. COME BACK!
NO! COME BACK HERE A MINUTE!!! I JUST WANT TO TALK!!
DAMN, SHE'S HOT!

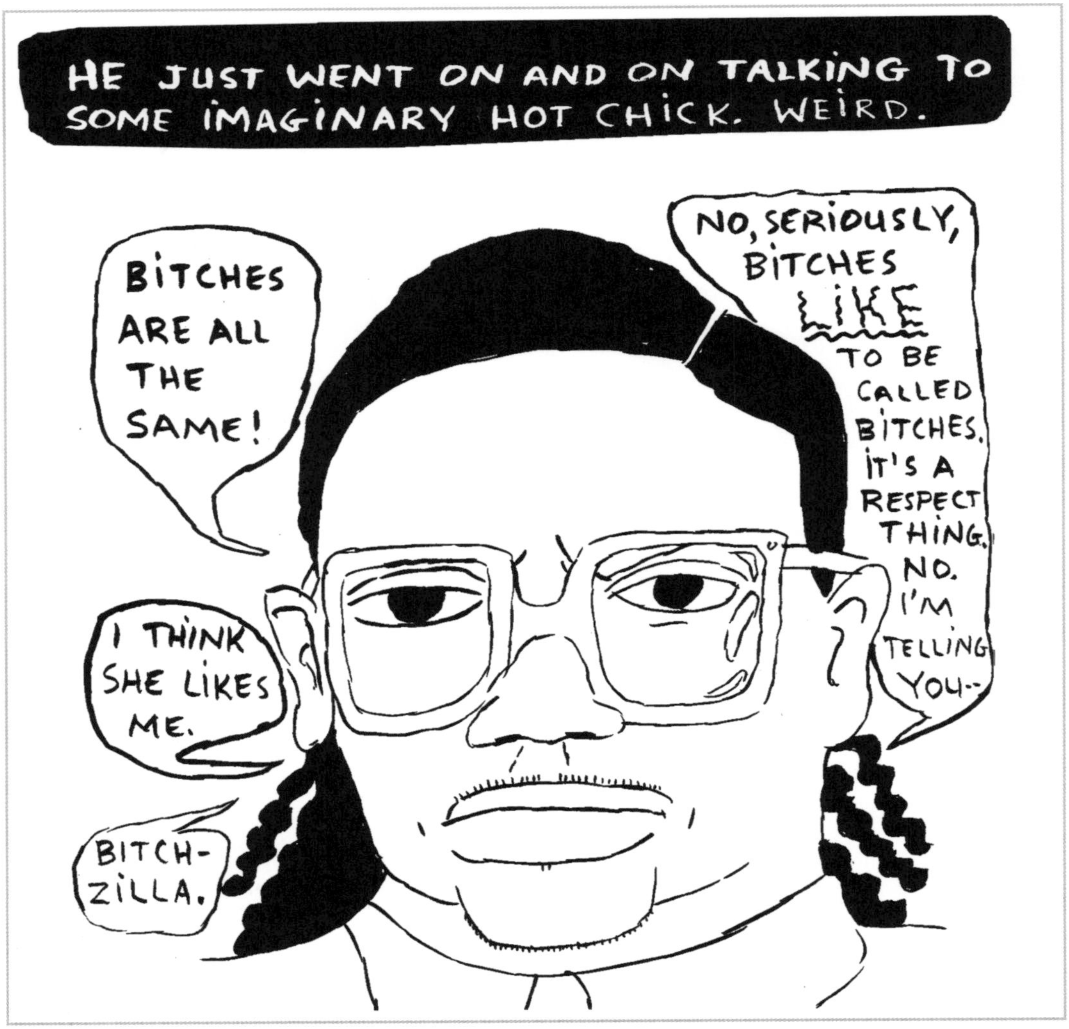
HE JUST WENT ON AND ON TALKING TO SOME IMAGINARY HOT CHICK. WEIRD.
BITCHES ARE ALL THE SAME!
NO, SERIOUSLY, BITCHES LIKE TO BE CALLED BITCHES. IT'S A RESPECT THING. NO. I'M TELLING YOU--
I THINK SHE LIKES ME.
BITCH-ZILLA.

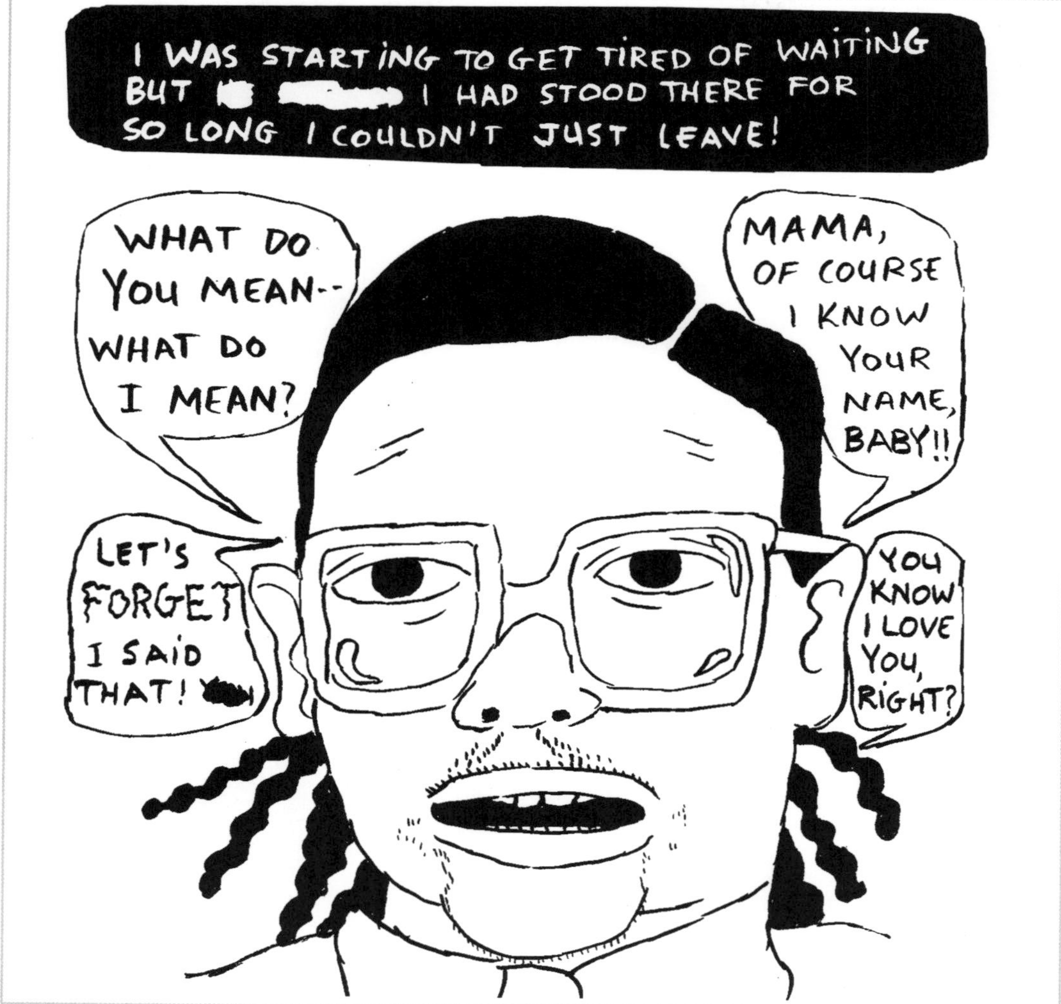
I WAS STARTING TO GET TIRED OF WAITING BUT [redacted] I HAD STOOD THERE FOR SO LONG I COULDN'T JUST LEAVE!
WHAT DO YOU MEAN-- WHAT DO I MEAN?
MAMA, OF COURSE I KNOW YOUR NAME, BABY!!
LET'S FORGET I SAID THAT! [redacted]
YOU KNOW I LOVE YOU, RIGHT?

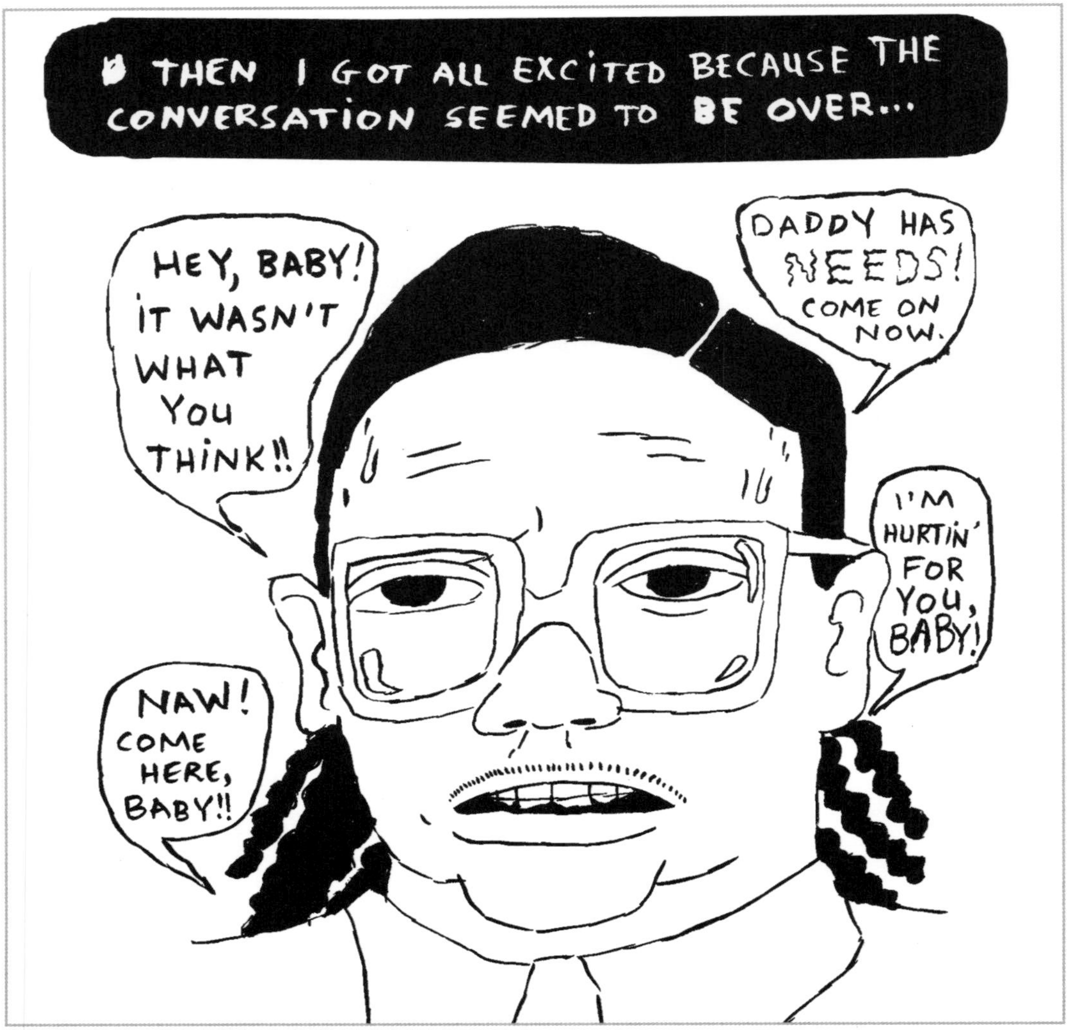
THEN I GOT ALL EXCITED BECAUSE THE CONVERSATION SEEMED TO BE OVER...
HEY, BABY! IT WASN'T WHAT YOU THINK!!
DADDY HAS NEEDS! COME ON NOW.
I'M HURTIN' FOR YOU, BABY!
NAW! COME HERE, BABY!!

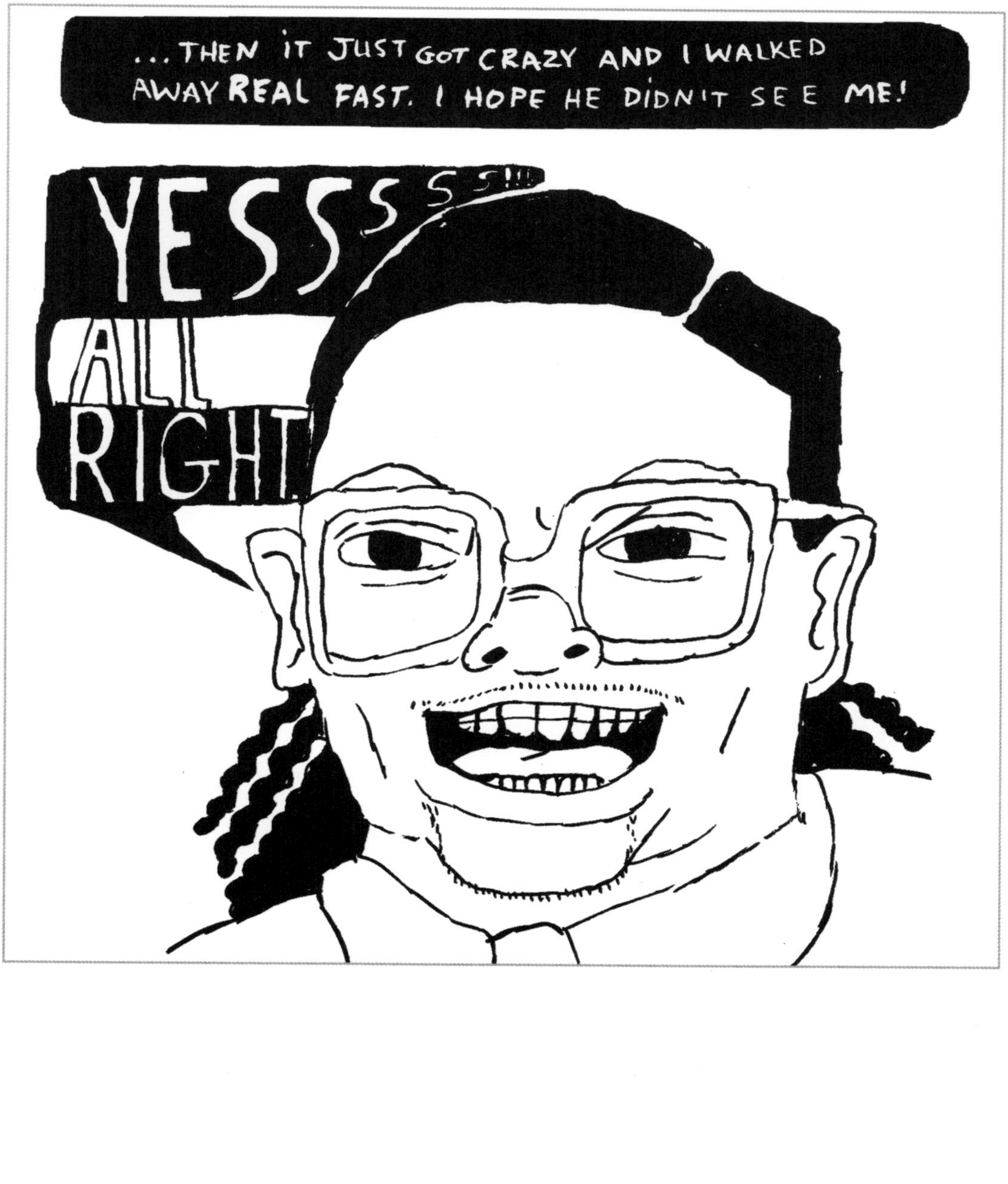
...THEN IT JUST GOT CRAZY AND I WALKED AWAY REAL FAST. I HOPE HE DIDN'T SEE ME!
YESSSSS!!!! ALL RIGHT

CHEMICAL PLANT / ANOTHER WORLD

MORE: DIARY OF A MOSQUITO ABATEMENT MAN

THE ROUTE AFTER CHANNAHON WAS THE AMALGAMATED* CHEMICAL PLANT, A FEW MILES DOWN THE HIGHWAY... *NOT THEIR REAL NAME, ed.

I HAD TO BE THERE at A CERTAIN TIME... THE GUARD WAVED ME IN...

I DROVE UP THE LONG, DARK ENTRY ROAD TOWARD THE GO-POINT...

UP AHEAD, THE PLANT ROSE OMINOUSLY OUT OF THE NIGHT--

FROM *Diary of a Mosquito Abatement Man*

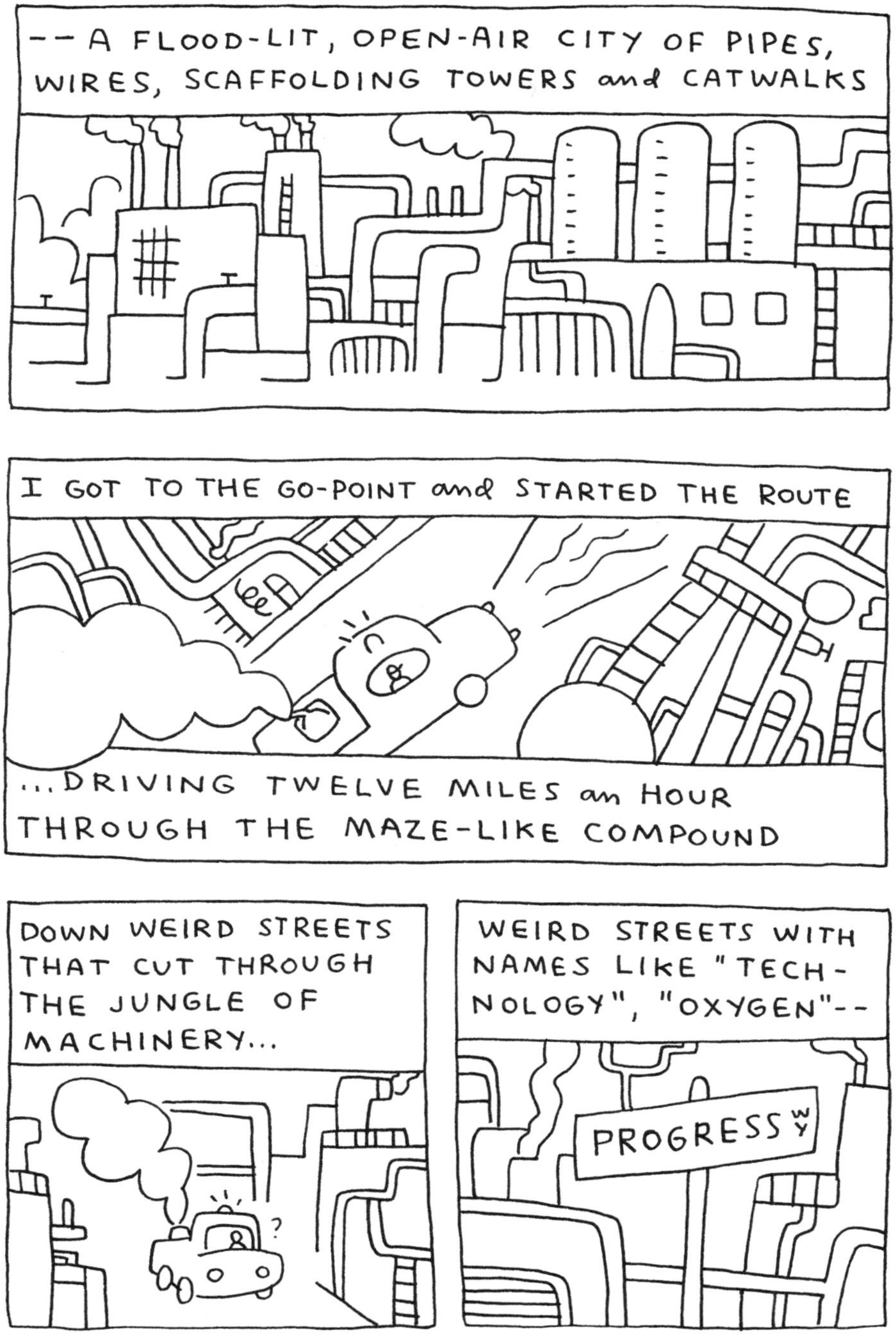
--A FLOOD-LIT, OPEN-AIR CITY OF PIPES, WIRES, SCAFFOLDING TOWERS and CATWALKS
I GOT TO THE GO-POINT and STARTED THE ROUTE
...DRIVING TWELVE MILES an HOUR THROUGH THE MAZE-LIKE COMPOUND
DOWN WEIRD STREETS THAT CUT THROUGH THE JUNGLE OF MACHINERY...
?
WEIRD STREETS WITH NAMES LIKE "TECHNOLOGY", "OXYGEN"--
PROGRESS WY

PIPES, WIRES and LADDERS CRISS-CROSSED
IN EVERY DIRECTION...

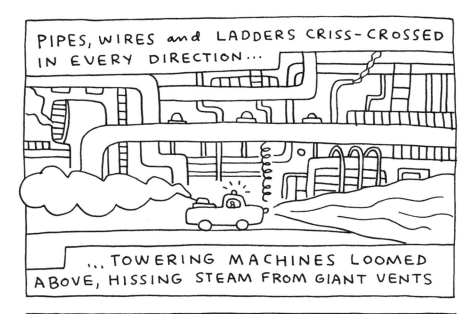

...TOWERING MACHINES LOOMED
ABOVE, HISSING STEAM FROM GIANT VENTS

ADDING TO THE SURREAL EFFECT WAS THE
FACT THAT EVEN THOUGH IT WAS 2AM OR
SO, EVERPRESENT FLOOD-LIGHTS LIT
THE PLACE AS BRIGHT AS DAY--
MAYBE BRIGHTER-- WITH A COLD, UN-
NATURAL, SHADOWLESS LIGHT...

NOW and THEN I ACTUALLY SAW A HUMAN BEING -- IN A CHEM-SUIT and HARD HAT -- EXAMINING A DIAL...

OR GLIDING ALONG EERILY ON A BICYCLE, SILENT AGAINST THE DRONE OF GENERATORS, PUMPS and FANS

THE WHOLE SPECTACLE SEEMED SO UNREAL - SO BIZARRE...

THE TWO STORY KNOTS OF WIRES and CONDUIT

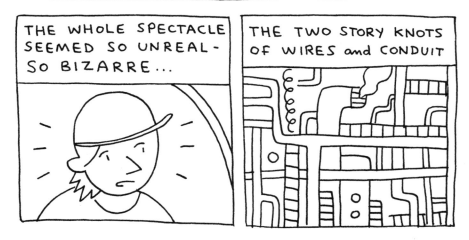

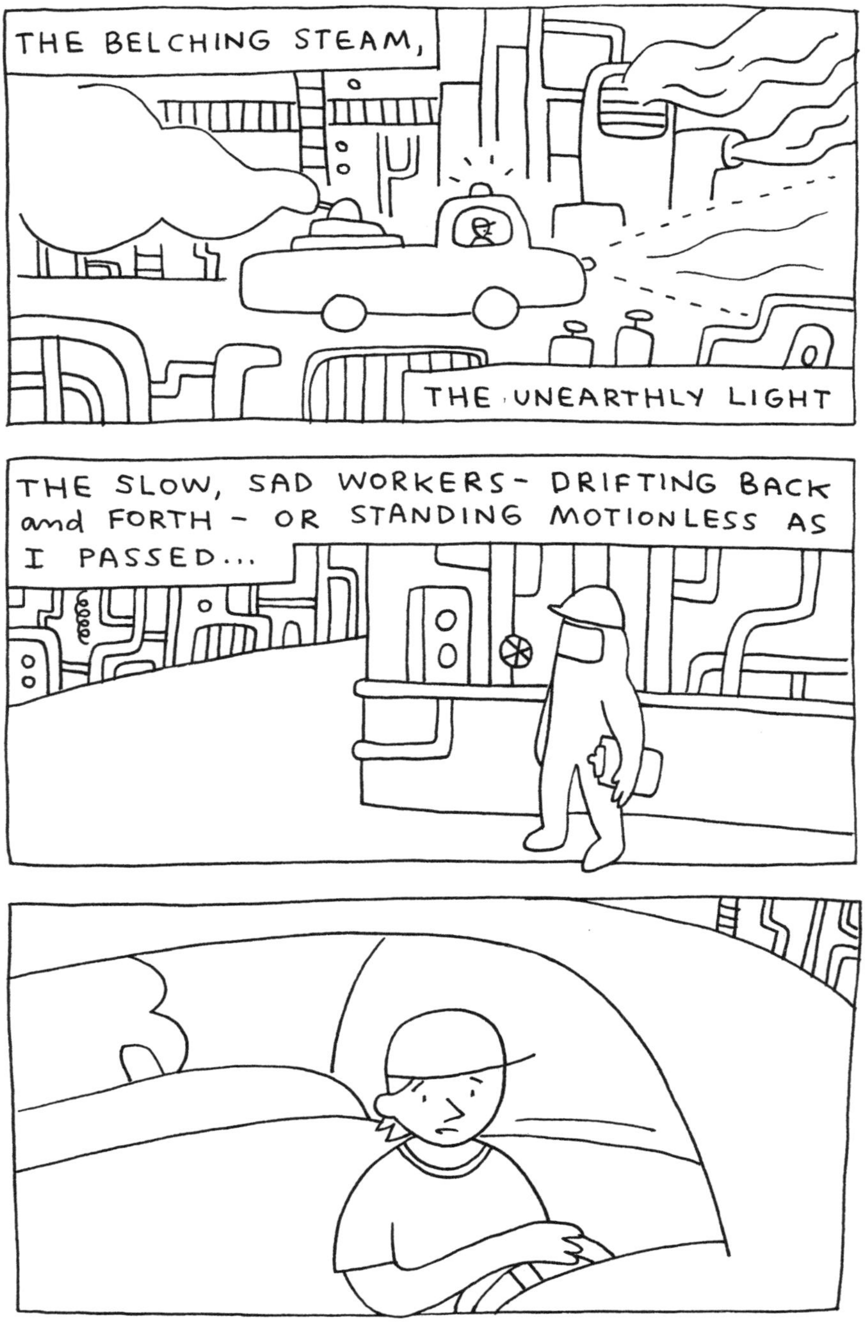
THE BELCHING STEAM,
THE UNEARTHLY LIGHT
THE SLOW, SAD WORKERS- DRIFTING BACK and FORTH - OR STANDING MOTIONLESS AS I PASSED...

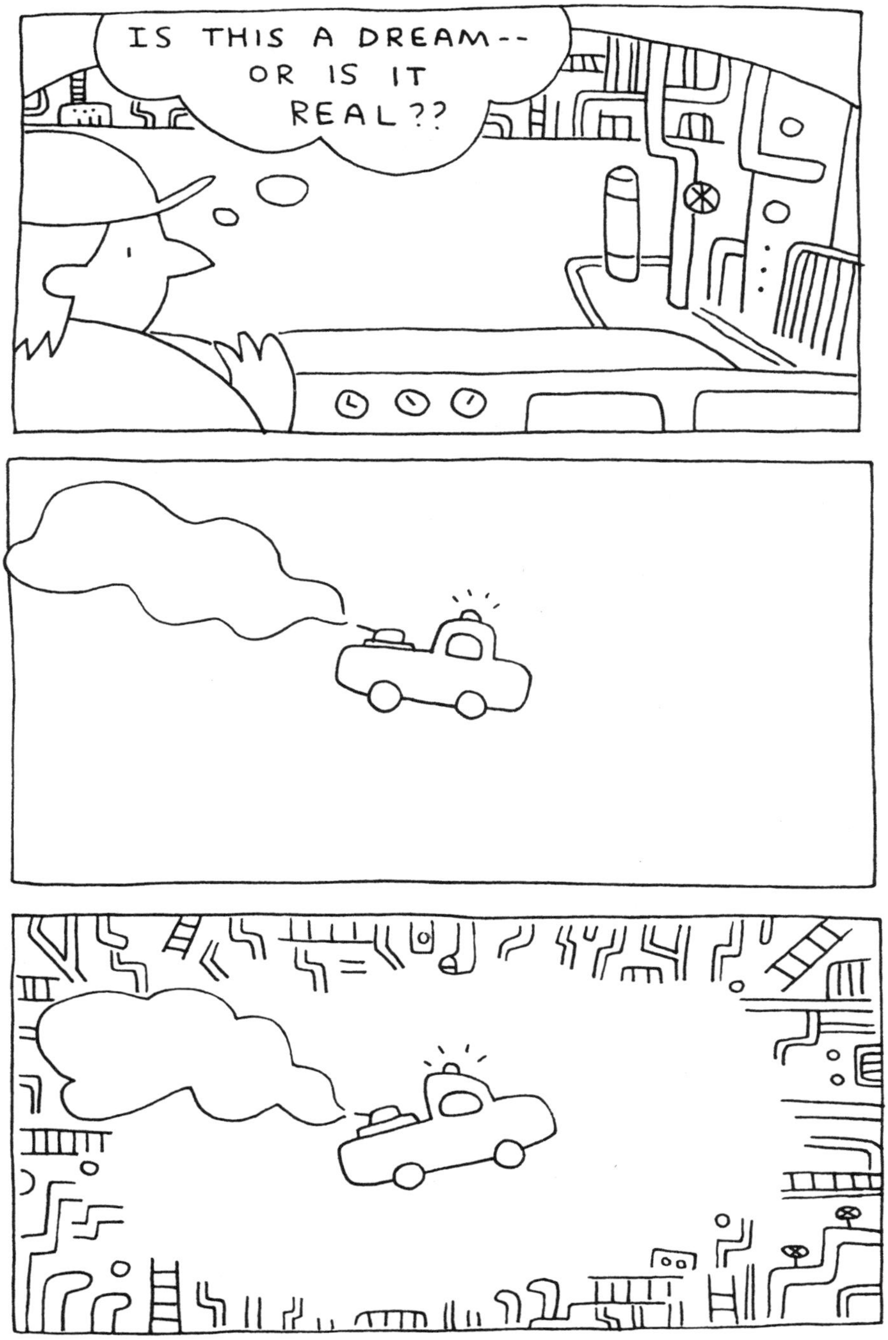
IS THIS A DREAM--
OR IS IT
REAL??

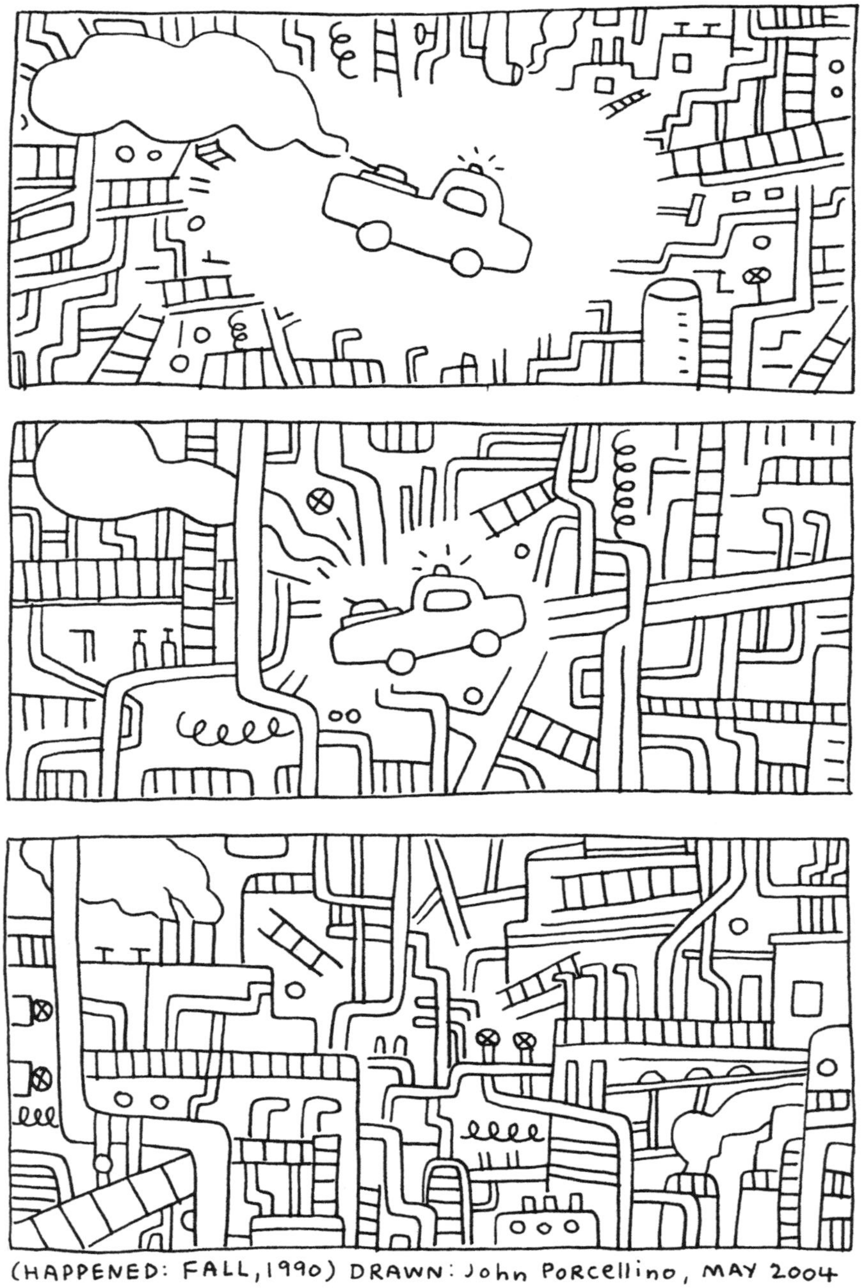

(HAPPENED: FALL, 1990) DRAWN: John Porcellino, MAY 2004

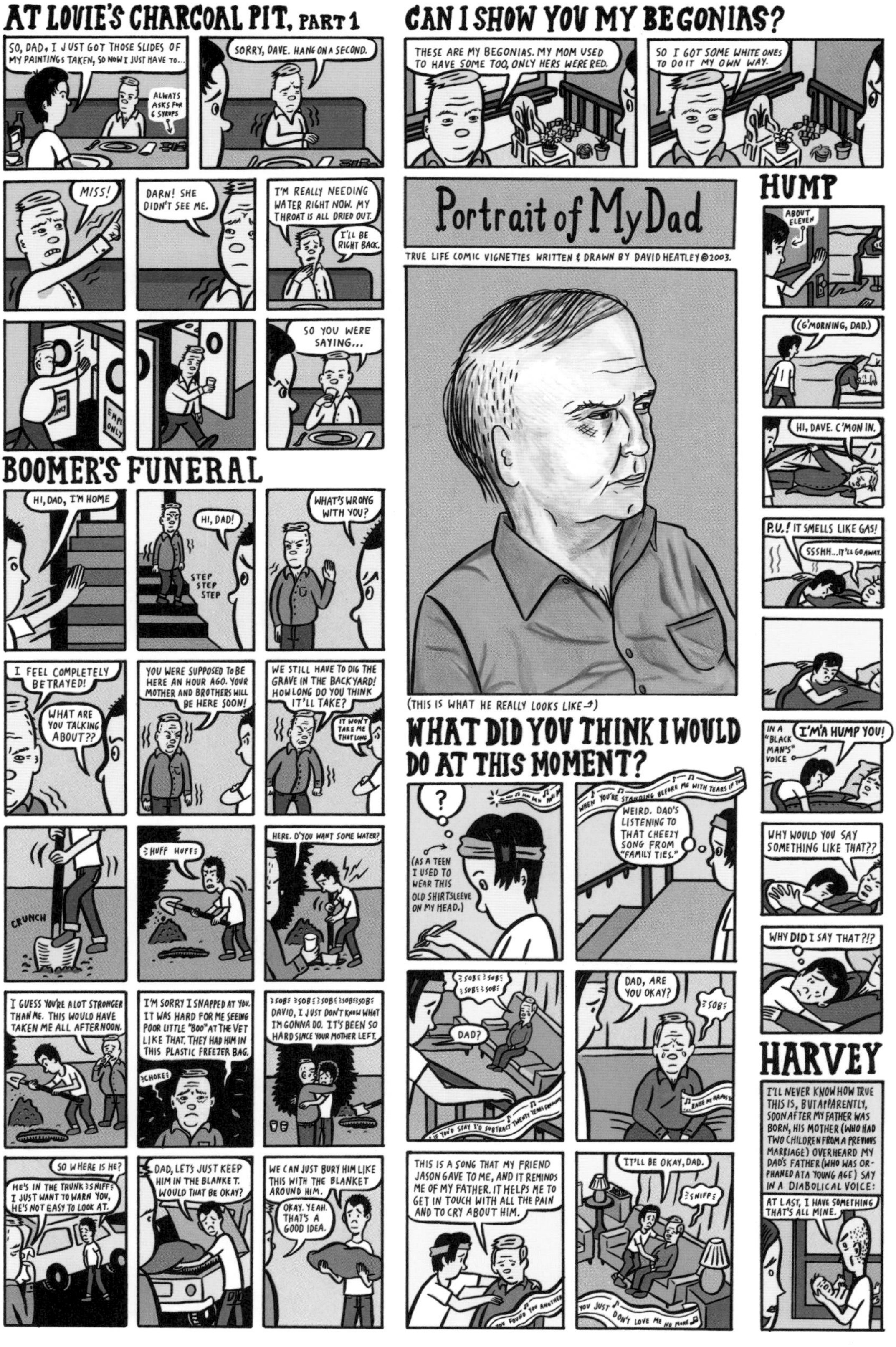

AT LOUIE'S CHARCOAL PIT, PART 1
SO, DAD, I JUST GOT THOSE SLIDES OF MY PAINTINGS TAKEN, SO NOW I JUST HAVE TO...
ALWAYS ASKS FOR 6 SYRUPS
SORRY, DAVE. HANG ON A SECOND.
MISS!
DARN! SHE DIDN'T SEE ME.
I'M REALLY NEEDING WATER RIGHT NOW. MY THROAT IS ALL DRIED OUT.
I'LL BE RIGHT BACK.
SO YOU WERE SAYING...
BOOMER'S FUNERAL
HI, DAD, I'M HOME
HI, DAD!
STEP STEP STEP
WHAT'S WRONG WITH YOU?
I FEEL COMPLETELY BETRAYED!
WHAT ARE YOU TALKING ABOUT??
YOU WERE SUPPOSED TO BE HERE AN HOUR AGO. YOUR MOTHER AND BROTHERS WILL BE HERE SOON!
WE STILL HAVE TO DIG THE GRAVE IN THE BACKYARD! HOW LONG DO YOU THINK IT'LL TAKE?
IT WON'T TAKE ME THAT LONG
CRUNCH
HUFF HUFF
HERE. D'YOU WANT SOME WATER?
I GUESS YOU'RE A LOT STRONGER THAN ME. THIS WOULD HAVE TAKEN ME ALL AFTERNOON.
I'M SORRY I SNAPPED AT YOU. IT WAS HARD FOR ME SEEING POOR LITTLE "BOO" AT THE VET LIKE THAT. THEY HAD HIM IN THIS PLASTIC FREEZER BAG.
CHOKE
SOB SOB SOB SOB SOB
DAVID, I JUST DON'T KNOW WHAT I'M GONNA DO. IT'S BEEN SO HARD SINCE YOUR MOTHER LEFT.
SO WHERE IS HE?
HE'S IN THE TRUNK SNIFF I JUST WANT TO WARN YOU, HE'S NOT EASY TO LOOK AT.
DAD, LET'S JUST KEEP HIM IN THE BLANKET. WOULD THAT BE OKAY?
WE CAN JUST BURY HIM LIKE THIS WITH THE BLANKET AROUND HIM.
OKAY. YEAH. THAT'S A GOOD IDEA.
CAN I SHOW YOU MY BEGONIAS?
THESE ARE MY BEGONIAS. MY MOM USED TO HAVE SOME TOO, ONLY HERS WERE RED.
SO I GOT SOME WHITE ONES TO DO IT MY OWN WAY.
Portrait of My Dad
TRUE LIFE COMIC VIGNETTES WRITTEN & DRAWN BY DAVID HEATLEY ©2003.
(THIS IS WHAT HE REALLY LOOKS LIKE)
WHAT DID YOU THINK I WOULD DO AT THIS MOMENT?
?
(AS A TEEN I USED TO WEAR THIS OLD SHIRTSLEEVE ON MY HEAD.)
WEIRD. DAD'S LISTENING TO THAT CHEEZY SONG FROM "FAMILY TIES."
SOB SOB SOB SOB
DAD?
DAD, ARE YOU OKAY?
SOB
THIS IS A SONG THAT MY FRIEND JASON GAVE TO ME, AND IT REMINDS ME OF MY FATHER. IT HELPS ME TO GET IN TOUCH WITH ALL THE PAIN AND TO CRY ABOUT HIM.
IT'LL BE OKAY, DAD.
SNIFF
YOU JUST DON'T LOVE ME NO MORE
HUMP
ABOUT ELEVEN
(G'MORNING, DAD.)
HI, DAVE. C'MON IN.
P.U.! IT SMELLS LIKE GAS!
SSSHH... IT'LL GO AWAY.
IN A "BLACK MAN'S" VOICE
I'M A HUMP YOU!
WHY WOULD YOU SAY SOMETHING LIKE THAT??
WHY DID I SAY THAT?!?
HARVEY
I'LL NEVER KNOW HOW TRUE THIS IS, BUT APPARENTLY, SOON AFTER MY FATHER WAS BORN, HIS MOTHER (WHO HAD TWO CHILDREN FROM A PREVIOUS MARRIAGE) OVERHEARD MY DAD'S FATHER (WHO WAS ORPHANED AT A YOUNG AGE) SAY IN A DIABOLICAL VOICE:
AT LAST, I HAVE SOMETHING THAT'S ALL MINE.

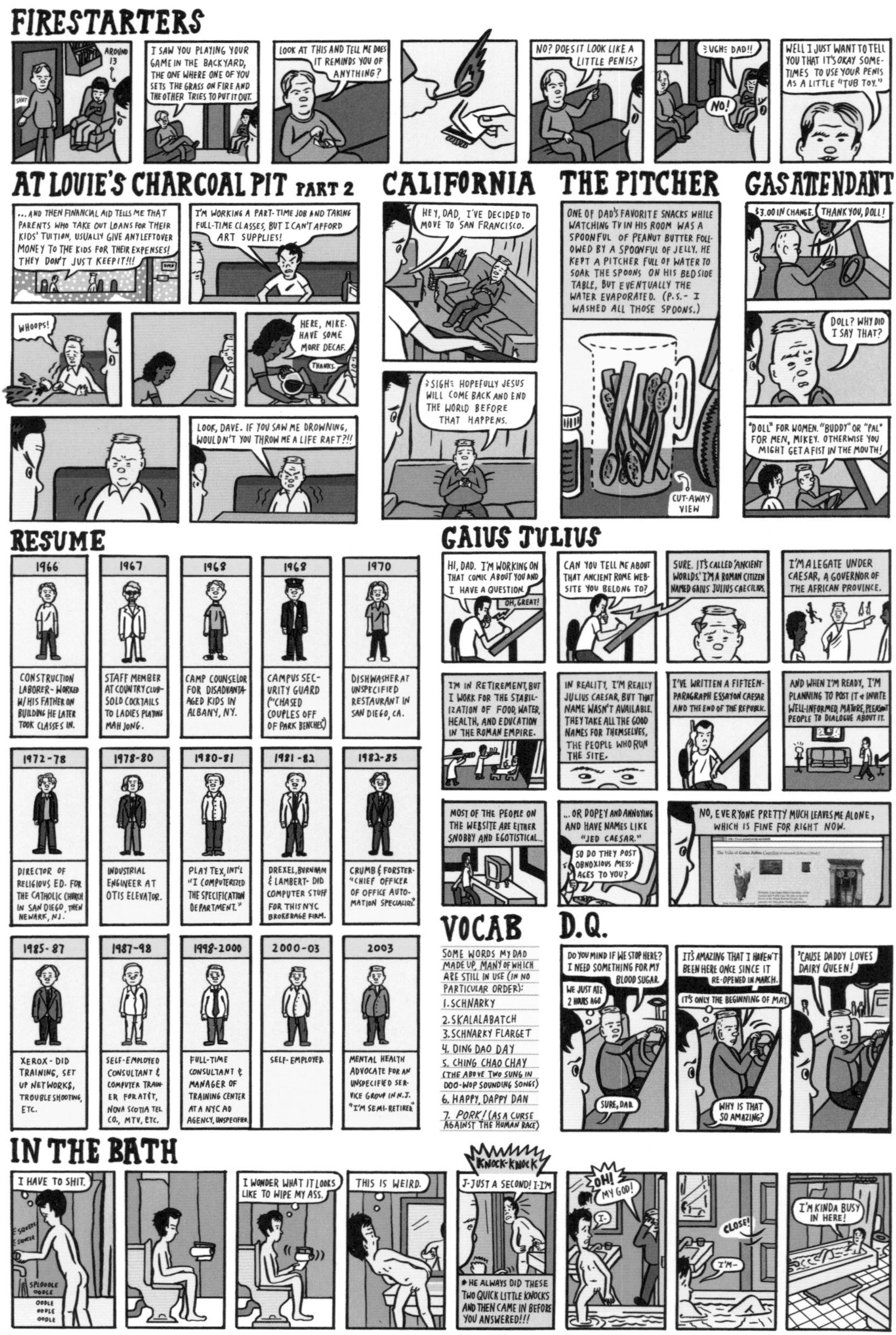

FIRESTARTERS
AROUND 13
SHIFT
I SAW YOU PLAYING YOUR GAME IN THE BACKYARD, THE ONE WHERE ONE OF YOU SETS THE GRASS ON FIRE AND THE OTHER TRIES TO PUT IT OUT.
LOOK AT THIS AND TELL ME DOES IT REMINDS YOU OF ANYTHING?
NO? DOES IT LOOK LIKE A LITTLE PENIS?
UGH DAD!!
NO!
WELL I JUST WANT TO TELL YOU THAT IT'S OKAY SOMETIMES TO USE YOUR PENIS AS A LITTLE "TUB TOY."
AT LOUIE'S CHARCOAL PIT PART 2
...AND THEN FINANCIAL AID TELLS ME THAT PARENTS WHO TAKE OUT LOANS FOR THEIR KIDS' TUITION, USUALLY GIVE ANY LEFTOVER MONEY TO THE KIDS FOR THEIR EXPENSES! THEY DON'T JUST KEEP IT!!!
I'M WORKING A PART-TIME JOB AND TAKING FULL-TIME CLASSES, BUT I CAN'T AFFORD ART SUPPLIES!
WHOOPS!
HERE, MIKE. HAVE SOME MORE DECAF.
THANKS.
LOOK, DAVE. IF YOU SAW ME DROWNING, WOULDN'T YOU THROW ME A LIFE RAFT?!!
CALIFORNIA
HEY, DAD, I'VE DECIDED TO MOVE TO SAN FRANCISCO.
SIGH HOPEFULLY JESUS WILL COME BACK AND END THE WORLD BEFORE THAT HAPPENS.
THE PITCHER
ONE OF DAD'S FAVORITE SNACKS WHILE WATCHING TV IN HIS ROOM WAS A SPOONFUL OF PEANUT BUTTER FOLLOWED BY A SPOONFUL OF JELLY. HE KEPT A PITCHER FULL OF WATER TO SOAK THE SPOONS ON HIS BEDSIDE TABLE, BUT EVENTUALLY THE WATER EVAPORATED. (P.S.- I WASHED ALL THOSE SPOONS.)
CUT-AWAY VIEW
GAS ATTENDANT
$3.00 IN CHANGE.
THANK YOU, DOLL!
DOLL? WHY DID I SAY THAT?
"DOLL" FOR WOMEN. "BUDDY" OR "PAL" FOR MEN, MIKEY. OTHERWISE YOU MIGHT GET A FIST IN THE MOUTH!
RESUME
1966
CONSTRUCTION LABORER- WORKED W/HIS FATHER ON BUILDING HE LATER TOOK CLASSES IN.
1967
STAFF MEMBER AT COUNTRY CLUB- SOLD COCKTAILS TO LADIES PLAYING MAH JONG.
1968
CAMP COUNSELOR FOR DISADVANTAGED KIDS IN ALBANY, NY.
1968
CAMPUS SECURITY GUARD ("CHASED COUPLES OFF OF PARK BENCHES")
1970
DISHWASHER AT UNSPECIFIED RESTAURANT IN SAN DIEGO, CA.
1972-78
DIRECTOR OF RELIGIOUS ED. FOR THE CATHOLIC CHURCH IN SAN DIEGO, THEN NEWARK, NJ.
1978-80
INDUSTRIAL ENGINEER AT OTIS ELEVATOR.
1980-81
PLAY TEX, INT'L "I COMPUTERIZED THE SPECIFICATION DEPARTMENT."
1981-82
DREXEL, BURNHAM & LAMBERT- DID COMPUTER STUFF FOR THIS NYC BROKERAGE FIRM.
1982-85
CRUMB & FORSTER- "CHIEF OFFICER OF OFFICE AUTOMATION SPECIALISTS."
1985-87
XEROX- DID TRAINING, SET UP NETWORKS, TROUBLESHOOTING, ETC.
1987-98
SELF-EMPLOYED CONSULTANT & COMPUTER TRAINER FOR AT&T, NOVA SCOTIA TEL CO., MTV, ETC.
1998-2000
FULL-TIME CONSULTANT & MANAGER OF TRAINING CENTER AT A NYC AD AGENCY, UNSPECIFIED.
2000-03
SELF-EMPLOYED.
2003
MENTAL HEALTH ADVOCATE FOR AN UNSPECIFIED SERVICE GROUP IN N.J. "I'M SEMI-RETIRED."
GAIUS JULIUS
HI, DAD. I'M WORKING ON THAT COMIC ABOUT YOU AND I HAVE A QUESTION.
OH, GREAT!
CAN YOU TELL ME ABOUT THAT ANCIENT ROME WEBSITE YOU BELONG TO?
SURE. IT'S CALLED 'ANCIENT WORLDS.' I'M A ROMAN CITIZEN NAMED GAIUS JULIUS CAECILIUS.
I'M A LEGATE UNDER CAESAR, A GOVERNOR OF THE AFRICAN PROVINCE.
I'M IN RETIREMENT, BUT I WORK FOR THE STABILIZATION OF FOOD, WATER, HEALTH, AND EDUCATION IN THE ROMAN EMPIRE.
IN REALITY, I'M REALLY JULIUS CAESAR, BUT THAT NAME WASN'T AVAILABLE. THEY TAKE ALL THE GOOD NAMES FOR THEMSELVES, THE PEOPLE WHO RUN THE SITE.
I'VE WRITTEN A FIFTEEN-PARAGRAPH ESSAY ON CAESAR AND THE END OF THE REPUBLIC.
AND WHEN I'M READY, I'M PLANNING TO POST IT & INVITE WELL-INFORMED, MATURE, PLEASANT PEOPLE TO DIALOGUE ABOUT IT.
MOST OF THE PEOPLE ON THE WEBSITE ARE EITHER SNOBBY AND EGOTISTICAL...
...OR DOPEY AND ANNOYING AND HAVE NAMES LIKE "JED CAESAR."
SO DO THEY POST OBNOXIOUS MESSAGES TO YOU?
NO, EVERYONE PRETTY MUCH LEAVES ME ALONE, WHICH IS FINE FOR RIGHT NOW.
VOCAB
SOME WORDS MY DAD MADE UP, MANY OF WHICH ARE STILL IN USE (IN NO PARTICULAR ORDER):
1. SCHNARKY
2. SKALALABATCH
3. SCHNARKY FLARGET
4. DING DAO DAY
5. CHING CHAO CHAY
(THE ABOVE TWO SUNG IN DOO-WOP SOUNDING SONGS)
6. HAPPY, DAPPY DAN
7. PORK! (AS A CURSE AGAINST THE HUMAN RACE)
D.Q.
DO YOU MIND IF WE STOP HERE? I NEED SOMETHING FOR MY BLOOD SUGAR.
WE JUST ATE 2 HOURS AGO
SURE, DAD.
IT'S AMAZING THAT I HAVEN'T BEEN HERE ONCE SINCE IT RE-OPENED IN MARCH.
IT'S ONLY THE BEGINNING OF MAY.
WHY IS THAT SO AMAZING?
'CAUSE DADDY LOVES DAIRY QUEEN!
IN THE BATH
I HAVE TO SHIT.
SQUEEK SQUEEK
SPLOODLE OODLE OODLE OODLE OODLE
I WONDER WHAT IT LOOKS LIKE TO WIPE MY ASS.
THIS IS WEIRD.
KNOCK-KNOCK
J-JUST A SECOND! I-I'M
* HE ALWAYS DID THESE TWO QUICK LITTLE KNOCKS AND THEN CAME IN BEFORE YOU ANSWERED!!!
OH!
MY GOD!
I-
CLOSE!
I'M-
I'M KINDA BUSY IN HERE!

DEATH BED

DREAMT BY ME

JULY 2003

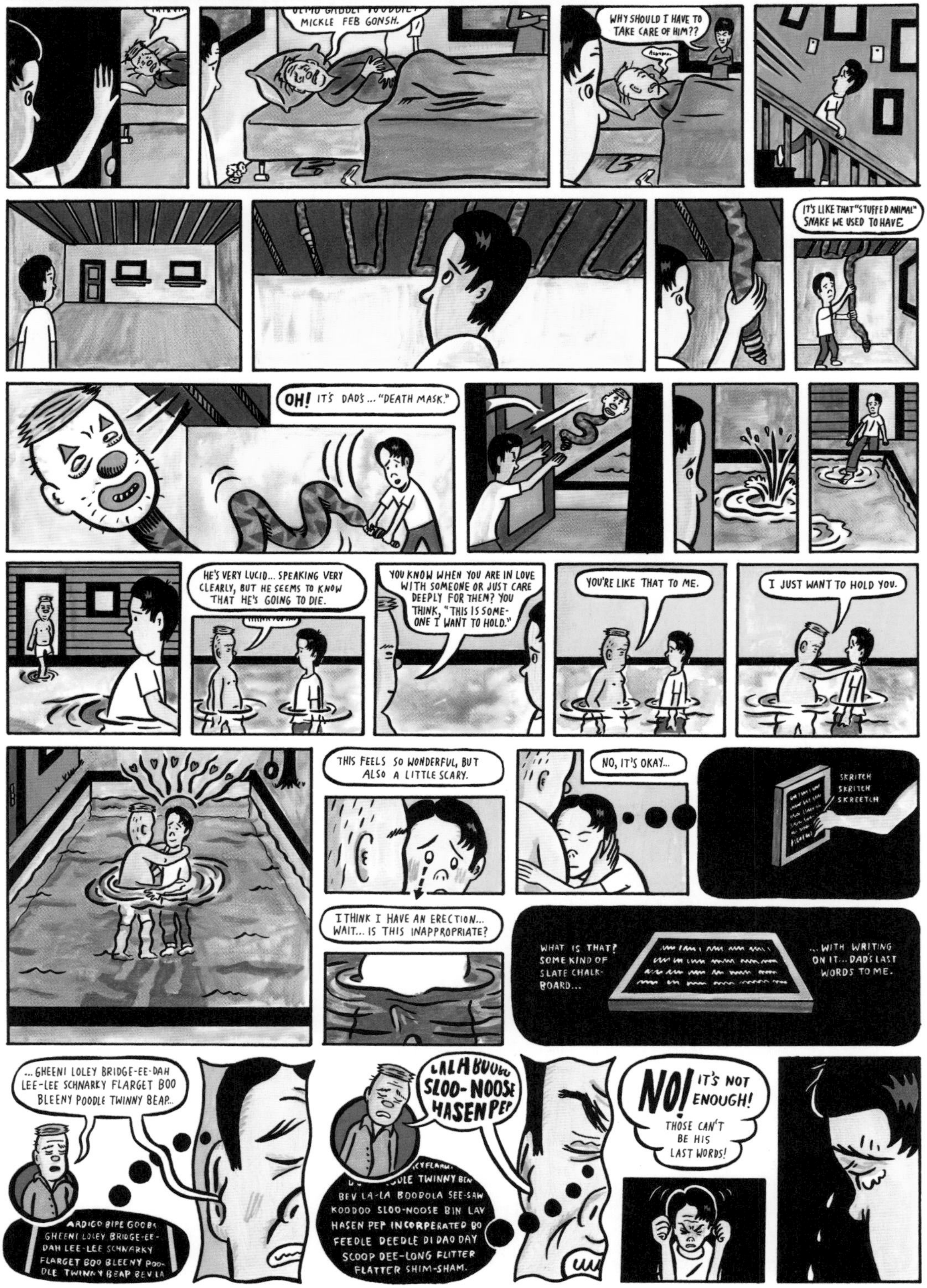

MICKLE FEB GONSH.
WHY SHOULD I HAVE TO TAKE CARE OF HIM??
IT'S LIKE THAT "STUFFED ANIMAL" SNAKE WE USED TO HAVE.
OH! IT'S DAD'S... "DEATH MASK."
HE'S VERY LUCID... SPEAKING VERY CLEARLY, BUT HE SEEMS TO KNOW THAT HE'S GOING TO DIE.
YOU KNOW WHEN YOU ARE IN LOVE WITH SOMEONE OR JUST CARE DEEPLY FOR THEM? YOU THINK, "THIS IS SOMEONE I WANT TO HOLD."
YOU'RE LIKE THAT TO ME.
I JUST WANT TO HOLD YOU.
THIS FEELS SO WONDERFUL, BUT ALSO A LITTLE SCARY.
I THINK I HAVE AN ERECTION... WAIT... IS THIS INAPPROPRIATE?
NO, IT'S OKAY...
SKRITCH
SKRITCH
SKREETCH
WHAT IS THAT? SOME KIND OF SLATE CHALK-BOARD...
...WITH WRITING ON IT... DAD'S LAST WORDS TO ME.
...GHEENI LOLEY BRIDGE-EE-DAH LEE-LEE SCHNARKY FLARGET BOO BLEENY POODLE TWINNY BEAP...
ARDIGO BIPE GOOBS GHEENI LOLEY BRIDGE-EE-DAH LEE-LEE SCHNARKY FLARGET BOO BLEENY POO-DLE TWINNY BEAP BEV LA
SLOO-NOOSE HASENPEP
BEV LA-LA BOOBOLA SEE-SAW KOODOO SLOO-NOOSE BIN LAV HASEN PEP INCORPERATED BO FEEDLE DEEDLE DI DAO DAY SCOOP DEE-LONG FLITTER FLATTER SHIM-SHAM.
NO! IT'S NOT ENOUGH!
THOSE CAN'T BE HIS LAST WORDS!

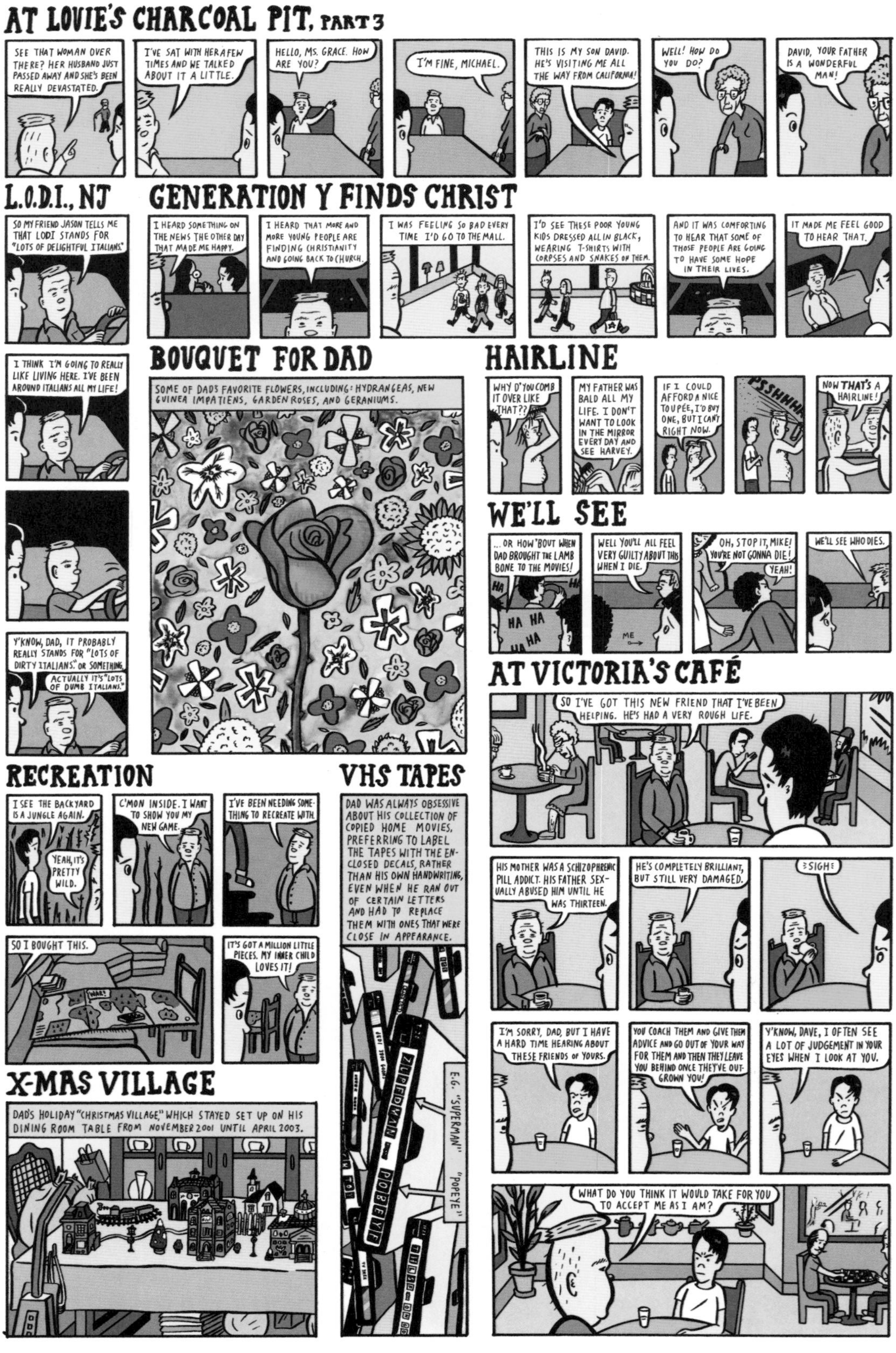
AT LOUIE'S CHARCOAL PIT, PART 3
SEE THAT WOMAN OVER THERE? HER HUSBAND JUST PASSED AWAY AND SHE'S BEEN REALLY DEVASTATED.
I'VE SAT WITH HER A FEW TIMES AND WE TALKED ABOUT IT A LITTLE.
HELLO, MS. GRACE. HOW ARE YOU?
I'M FINE, MICHAEL.
THIS IS MY SON DAVID. HE'S VISITING ME ALL THE WAY FROM CALIFORNIA!
WELL! HOW DO YOU DO?
DAVID, YOUR FATHER IS A WONDERFUL MAN!
L.O.D.I., NJ
SO MY FRIEND JASON TELLS ME THAT LODI STANDS FOR "LOTS OF DELIGHTFUL ITALIANS."
I THINK I'M GOING TO REALLY LIKE LIVING HERE. I'VE BEEN AROUND ITALIANS ALL MY LIFE!
Y'KNOW, DAD, IT PROBABLY REALLY STANDS FOR "LOTS OF DIRTY ITALIANS." OR SOMETHING.
ACTUALLY IT'S "LOTS OF DUMB ITALIANS."
GENERATION Y FINDS CHRIST
I HEARD SOMETHING ON THE NEWS THE OTHER DAY THAT MADE ME HAPPY.
I HEARD THAT MORE AND MORE YOUNG PEOPLE ARE FINDING CHRISTIANITY AND GOING BACK TO CHURCH.
I WAS FEELING SO BAD EVERY TIME I'D GO TO THE MALL.
I'D SEE THESE POOR YOUNG KIDS DRESSED ALL IN BLACK, WEARING T-SHIRTS WITH CORPSES AND SNAKES ON THEM.
AND IT WAS COMFORTING TO HEAR THAT SOME OF THOSE PEOPLE ARE GOING TO HAVE SOME HOPE IN THEIR LIVES.
IT MADE ME FEEL GOOD TO HEAR THAT.
BOUQUET FOR DAD
SOME OF DAD'S FAVORITE FLOWERS, INCLUDING: HYDRANGEAS, NEW GUINEA IMPATIENS, GARDEN ROSES, AND GERANIUMS.
HAIRLINE
WHY D'YOU COMB IT OVER LIKE THAT??
MY FATHER WAS BALD ALL MY LIFE. I DON'T WANT TO LOOK IN THE MIRROR EVERY DAY AND SEE HARVEY.
IF I COULD AFFORD A NICE TOUPÉE, I'D BUY ONE, BUT I CAN'T RIGHT NOW.
PSSHHHH
NOW THAT'S A HAIRLINE!
WE'LL SEE
...OR HOW 'BOUT WHEN DAD BROUGHT THE LAMB BONE TO THE MOVIES!
HA HA
HA HA HA
WELL YOU'LL ALL FEEL VERY GUILTY ABOUT THIS WHEN I DIE.
ME
OH, STOP IT, MIKE! YOU'RE NOT GONNA DIE!
YEAH!
WE'LL SEE WHO DIES.
AT VICTORIA'S CAFÉ
SO I'VE GOT THIS NEW FRIEND THAT I'VE BEEN HELPING. HE'S HAD A VERY ROUGH LIFE.
HIS MOTHER WAS A SCHIZOPHRENIC PILL ADDICT. HIS FATHER SEXUALLY ABUSED HIM UNTIL HE WAS THIRTEEN.
HE'S COMPLETELY BRILLIANT, BUT STILL VERY DAMAGED.
SIGH
I'M SORRY, DAD, BUT I HAVE A HARD TIME HEARING ABOUT THESE FRIENDS OF YOURS.
YOU COACH THEM AND GIVE THEM ADVICE AND GO OUT OF YOUR WAY FOR THEM AND THEN THEY LEAVE YOU BEHIND ONCE THEY'VE OUTGROWN YOU!
Y'KNOW, DAVE, I OFTEN SEE A LOT OF JUDGEMENT IN YOUR EYES WHEN I LOOK AT YOU.
WHAT DO YOU THINK IT WOULD TAKE FOR YOU TO ACCEPT ME AS I AM?
RECREATION
I SEE THE BACKYARD IS A JUNGLE AGAIN.
YEAH, IT'S PRETTY WILD.
C'MON INSIDE. I WANT TO SHOW YOU MY NEW GAME.
I'VE BEEN NEEDING SOMETHING TO RECREATE WITH.
SO I BOUGHT THIS.
WAR!
IT'S GOT A MILLION LITTLE PIECES. MY INNER CHILD LOVES IT!
VHS TAPES
DAD WAS ALWAYS OBSESSIVE ABOUT HIS COLLECTION OF COPIED HOME MOVIES, PREFERRING TO LABEL THE TAPES WITH THE ENCLOSED DECALS, RATHER THAN HIS OWN HANDWRITING, EVEN WHEN HE RAN OUT OF CERTAIN LETTERS AND HAD TO REPLACE THEM WITH ONES THAT WERE CLOSE IN APPEARANCE.
E.G. "SUPERMAN"
"POPEYE"
X-MAS VILLAGE
DAD'S HOLIDAY "CHRISTMAS VILLAGE," WHICH STAYED SET UP ON HIS DINING ROOM TABLE FROM NOVEMBER 2001 UNTIL APRIL 2003.

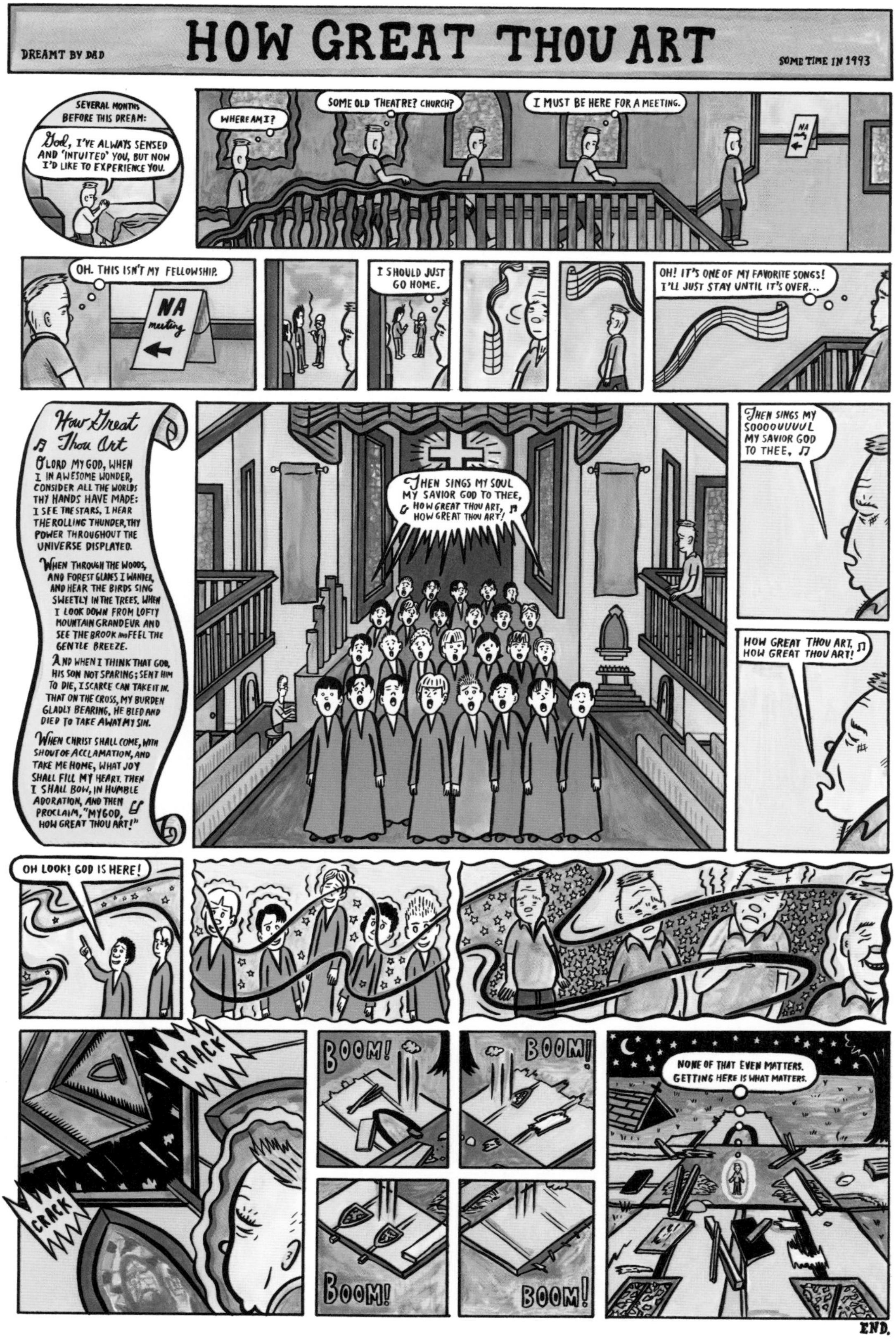
DREAMT BY DAD
HOW GREAT THOU ART
SOME TIME IN 1993
SEVERAL MONTHS BEFORE THIS DREAM:
GOD, I'VE ALWAYS SENSED AND 'INTUITED' YOU, BUT NOW I'D LIKE TO EXPERIENCE YOU.
WHERE AM I?
SOME OLD THEATRE? CHURCH?
I MUST BE HERE FOR A MEETING.
NA
OH. THIS ISN'T MY FELLOWSHIP.
NA meeting
I SHOULD JUST GO HOME.
OH! IT'S ONE OF MY FAVORITE SONGS! I'LL JUST STAY UNTIL IT'S OVER...
How Great Thou Art
O LORD MY GOD, WHEN I IN AWESOME WONDER, CONSIDER ALL THE WORLDS THY HANDS HAVE MADE: I SEE THE STARS, I HEAR THE ROLLING THUNDER, THY POWER THROUGHOUT THE UNIVERSE DISPLAYED.
WHEN THROUGH THE WOODS, AND FOREST GLADES I WANDER, AND HEAR THE BIRDS SING SWEETLY IN THE TREES. WHEN I LOOK DOWN FROM LOFTY MOUNTAIN GRANDEUR AND SEE THE BROOK AND FEEL THE GENTLE BREEZE.
AND WHEN I THINK THAT GOD, HIS SON NOT SPARING; SENT HIM TO DIE, I SCARCE CAN TAKE IT IN. THAT ON THE CROSS, MY BURDEN GLADLY BEARING, HE BLED AND DIED TO TAKE AWAY MY SIN.
WHEN CHRIST SHALL COME, WITH SHOUT OF ACCLAMATION, AND TAKE ME HOME, WHAT JOY SHALL FILL MY HEART. THEN I SHALL BOW, IN HUMBLE ADORATION, AND THEN PROCLAIM, "MY GOD, HOW GREAT THOU ART!"
THEN SINGS MY SOUL MY SAVIOR GOD TO THEE, HOW GREAT THOU ART, HOW GREAT THOU ART!
THEN SINGS MY SOOOOUUUUL MY SAVIOR GOD TO THEE,
HOW GREAT THOU ART, HOW GREAT THOU ART!
OH LOOK! GOD IS HERE!
CRACK
CRACK
BOOM!
BOOM!
BOOM!
BOOM!
NONE OF THAT EVEN MATTERS. GETTING HERE IS WHAT MATTERS.
END.

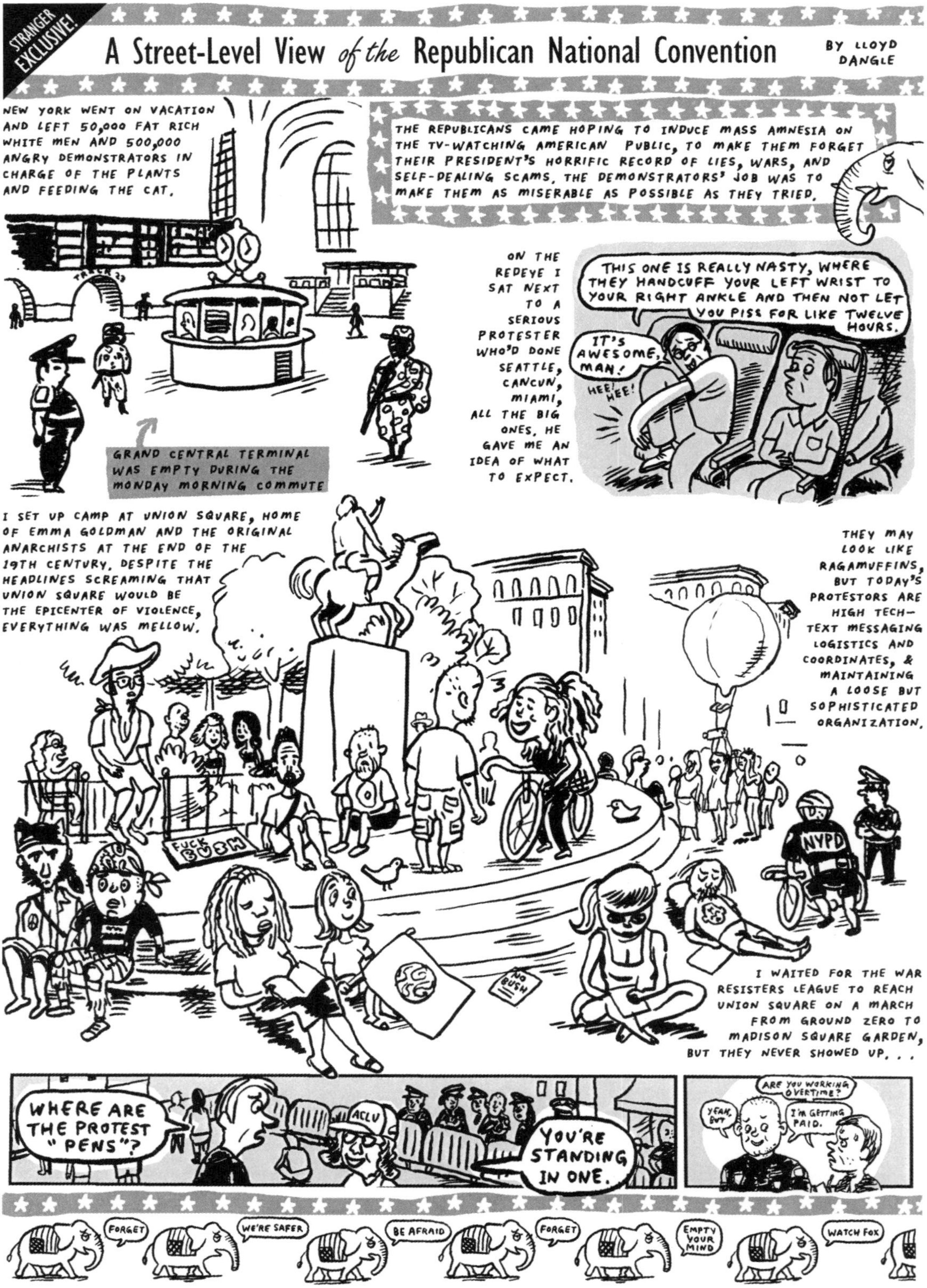
STRANGER EXCLUSIVE!
A Street-Level View of the Republican National Convention
BY LLOYD DANGLE
NEW YORK WENT ON VACATION AND LEFT 50,000 FAT RICH WHITE MEN AND 500,000 ANGRY DEMONSTRATORS IN CHARGE OF THE PLANTS AND FEEDING THE CAT.
THE REPUBLICANS CAME HOPING TO INDUCE MASS AMNESIA ON THE TV-WATCHING AMERICAN PUBLIC, TO MAKE THEM FORGET THEIR PRESIDENT'S HORRIFIC RECORD OF LIES, WARS, AND SELF-DEALING SCAMS. THE DEMONSTRATORS' JOB WAS TO MAKE THEM AS MISERABLE AS POSSIBLE AS THEY TRIED.
GRAND CENTRAL TERMINAL WAS EMPTY DURING THE MONDAY MORNING COMMUTE
ON THE REDEYE I SAT NEXT TO A SERIOUS PROTESTER WHO'D DONE SEATTLE, CANCUN, MIAMI, ALL THE BIG ONES. HE GAVE ME AN IDEA OF WHAT TO EXPECT.
THIS ONE IS REALLY NASTY, WHERE THEY HANDCUFF YOUR LEFT WRIST TO YOUR RIGHT ANKLE AND THEN NOT LET YOU PISS FOR LIKE TWELVE HOURS.
IT'S AWESOME, MAN!
HEE! HEE!
I SET UP CAMP AT UNION SQUARE, HOME OF EMMA GOLDMAN AND THE ORIGINAL ANARCHISTS AT THE END OF THE 19TH CENTURY. DESPITE THE HEADLINES SCREAMING THAT UNION SQUARE WOULD BE THE EPICENTER OF VIOLENCE, EVERYTHING WAS MELLOW.
THEY MAY LOOK LIKE RAGAMUFFINS, BUT TODAY'S PROTESTORS ARE HIGH TECH— TEXT MESSAGING LOGISTICS AND COORDINATES, & MAINTAINING A LOOSE BUT SOPHISTICATED ORGANIZATION.
FUCK BUSH
NYPD
NO BUSH
I WAITED FOR THE WAR RESISTERS LEAGUE TO REACH UNION SQUARE ON A MARCH FROM GROUND ZERO TO MADISON SQUARE GARDEN, BUT THEY NEVER SHOWED UP. . .
WHERE ARE THE PROTEST "PENS"?
ACLU
YOU'RE STANDING IN ONE.
ARE YOU WORKING OVERTIME?
YEAH, BUT
I'M GETTING PAID.
FORGET
WE'RE SAFER
BE AFRAID
FORGET
EMPTY YOUR MIND
WATCH FOX

FROM *The Stranger*

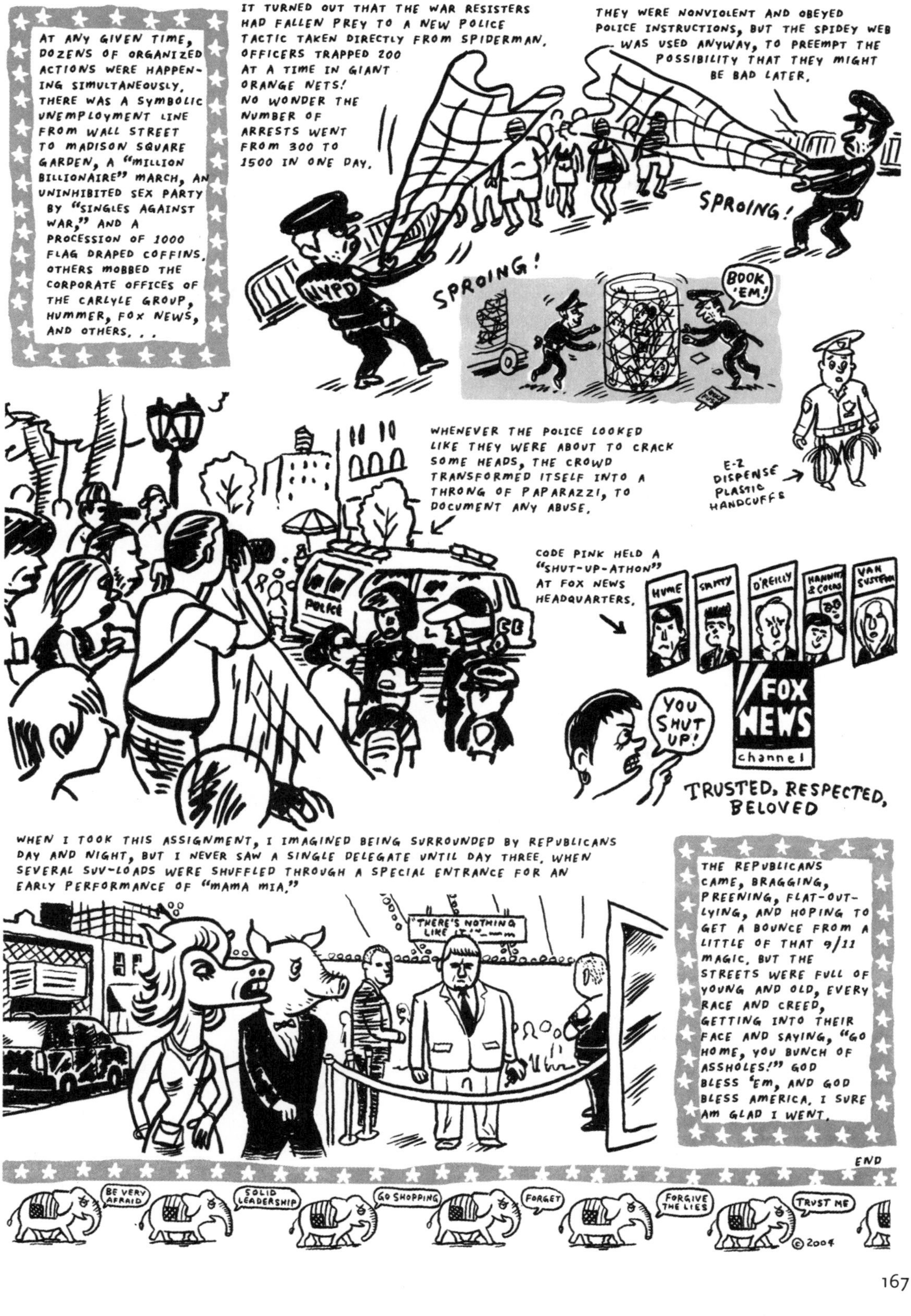

AT ANY GIVEN TIME, DOZENS OF ORGANIZED ACTIONS WERE HAPPENING SIMULTANEOUSLY. THERE WAS A SYMBOLIC UNEMPLOYMENT LINE FROM WALL STREET TO MADISON SQUARE GARDEN, A "MILLION BILLIONAIRE" MARCH, AN UNINHIBITED SEX PARTY BY "SINGLES AGAINST WAR," AND A PROCESSION OF 1000 FLAG DRAPED COFFINS. OTHERS MOBBED THE CORPORATE OFFICES OF THE CARLYLE GROUP, HUMMER, FOX NEWS, AND OTHERS. . .
IT TURNED OUT THAT THE WAR RESISTERS HAD FALLEN PREY TO A NEW POLICE TACTIC TAKEN DIRECTLY FROM SPIDERMAN. OFFICERS TRAPPED 200 AT A TIME IN GIANT ORANGE NETS! NO WONDER THE NUMBER OF ARRESTS WENT FROM 300 TO 1500 IN ONE DAY.
THEY WERE NONVIOLENT AND OBEYED POLICE INSTRUCTIONS, BUT THE SPIDEY WEB WAS USED ANYWAY, TO PREEMPT THE POSSIBILITY THAT THEY MIGHT BE BAD LATER.
NYPD
SPROING!
SPROING!
BOOK 'EM!
E-Z DISPENSE PLASTIC HANDCUFFS
WHENEVER THE POLICE LOOKED LIKE THEY WERE ABOUT TO CRACK SOME HEADS, THE CROWD TRANSFORMED ITSELF INTO A THRONG OF PAPARAZZI, TO DOCUMENT ANY ABUSE.
POLICE
CODE PINK HELD A "SHUT-UP-ATHON" AT FOX NEWS HEADQUARTERS.
HUME
O'REILLY
HANNITY & COLMES
VAN SUSTEREN
YOU SHUT UP!
FOX NEWS channel
TRUSTED, RESPECTED, BELOVED
WHEN I TOOK THIS ASSIGNMENT, I IMAGINED BEING SURROUNDED BY REPUBLICANS DAY AND NIGHT, BUT I NEVER SAW A SINGLE DELEGATE UNTIL DAY THREE, WHEN SEVERAL SUV-LOADS WERE SHUFFLED THROUGH A SPECIAL ENTRANCE FOR AN EARLY PERFORMANCE OF "MAMA MIA."
"THERE'S NOTHING LIKE IT"
THE REPUBLICANS CAME, BRAGGING, PREENING, FLAT-OUT-LYING, AND HOPING TO GET A BOUNCE FROM A LITTLE OF THAT 9/11 MAGIC. BUT THE STREETS WERE FULL OF YOUNG AND OLD, EVERY RACE AND CREED, GETTING INTO THEIR FACE AND SAYING, "GO HOME, YOU BUNCH OF ASSHOLES!" GOD BLESS 'EM, AND GOD BLESS AMERICA. I SURE AM GLAD I WENT.
END
BE VERY AFRAID
SOLID LEADERSHIP
GO SHOPPING
FORGET
FORGIVE THE LIES
TRUST ME
© 2004

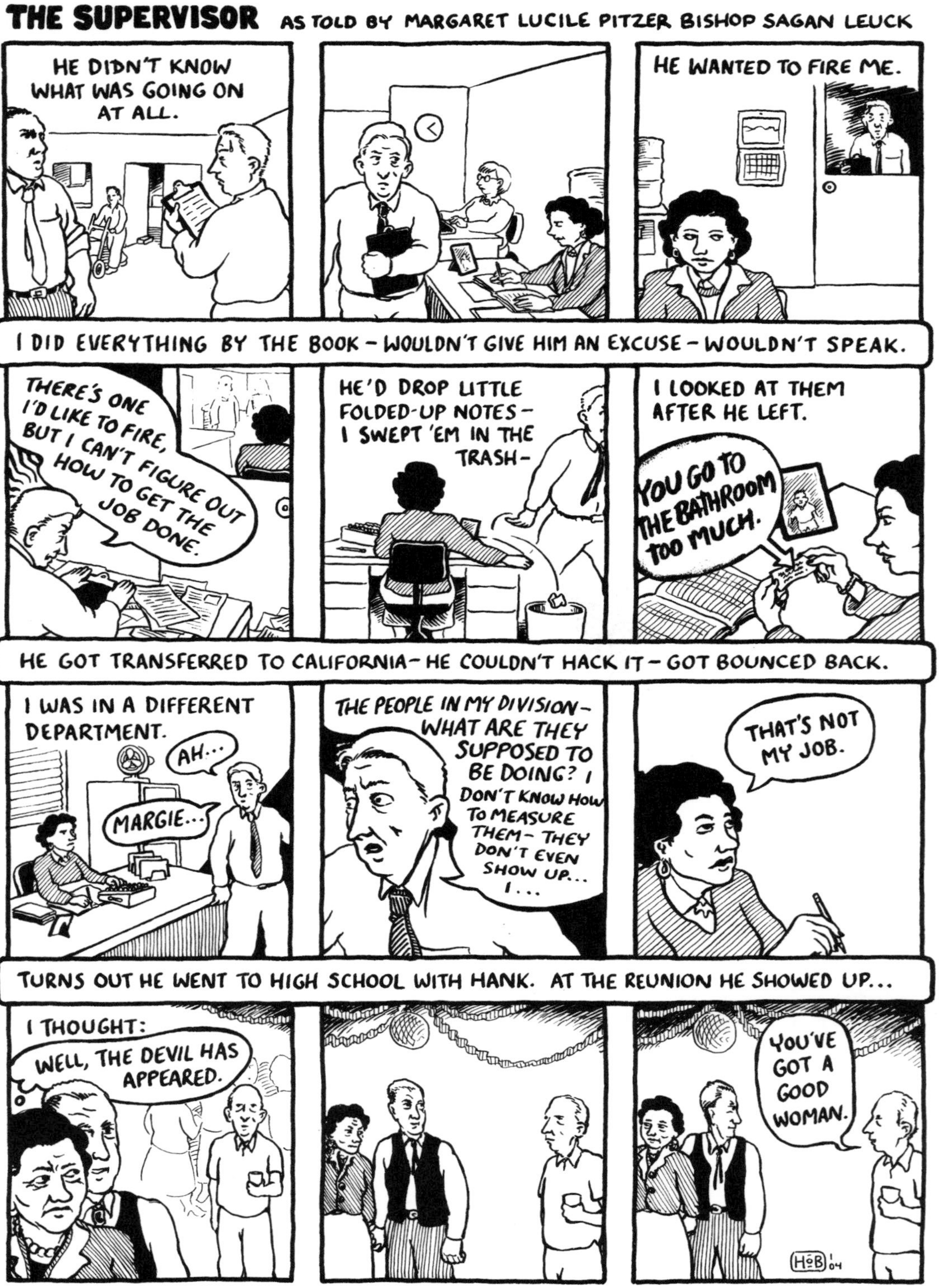
THE SUPERVISOR AS TOLD BY MARGARET LUCILE PITZER BISHOP SAGAN LEUCK
HE DIDN'T KNOW WHAT WAS GOING ON AT ALL.
HE WANTED TO FIRE ME.
I DID EVERYTHING BY THE BOOK - WOULDN'T GIVE HIM AN EXCUSE - WOULDN'T SPEAK.
THERE'S ONE I'D LIKE TO FIRE, BUT I CAN'T FIGURE OUT HOW TO GET THE JOB DONE.
HE'D DROP LITTLE FOLDED-UP NOTES - I SWEPT 'EM IN THE TRASH -
I LOOKED AT THEM AFTER HE LEFT.
YOU GO TO THE BATHROOM TOO MUCH.
HE GOT TRANSFERRED TO CALIFORNIA - HE COULDN'T HACK IT - GOT BOUNCED BACK.
I WAS IN A DIFFERENT DEPARTMENT.
AH...
MARGIE...
THE PEOPLE IN MY DIVISION - WHAT ARE THEY SUPPOSED TO BE DOING? I DON'T KNOW HOW TO MEASURE THEM - THEY DON'T EVEN SHOW UP... I...
THAT'S NOT MY JOB.
TURNS OUT HE WENT TO HIGH SCHOOL WITH HANK. AT THE REUNION HE SHOWED UP...
I THOUGHT:
WELL, THE DEVIL HAS APPEARED.
YOU'VE GOT A GOOD WOMAN.
HOB '04

FROM *Hi-Horse Omnibus*

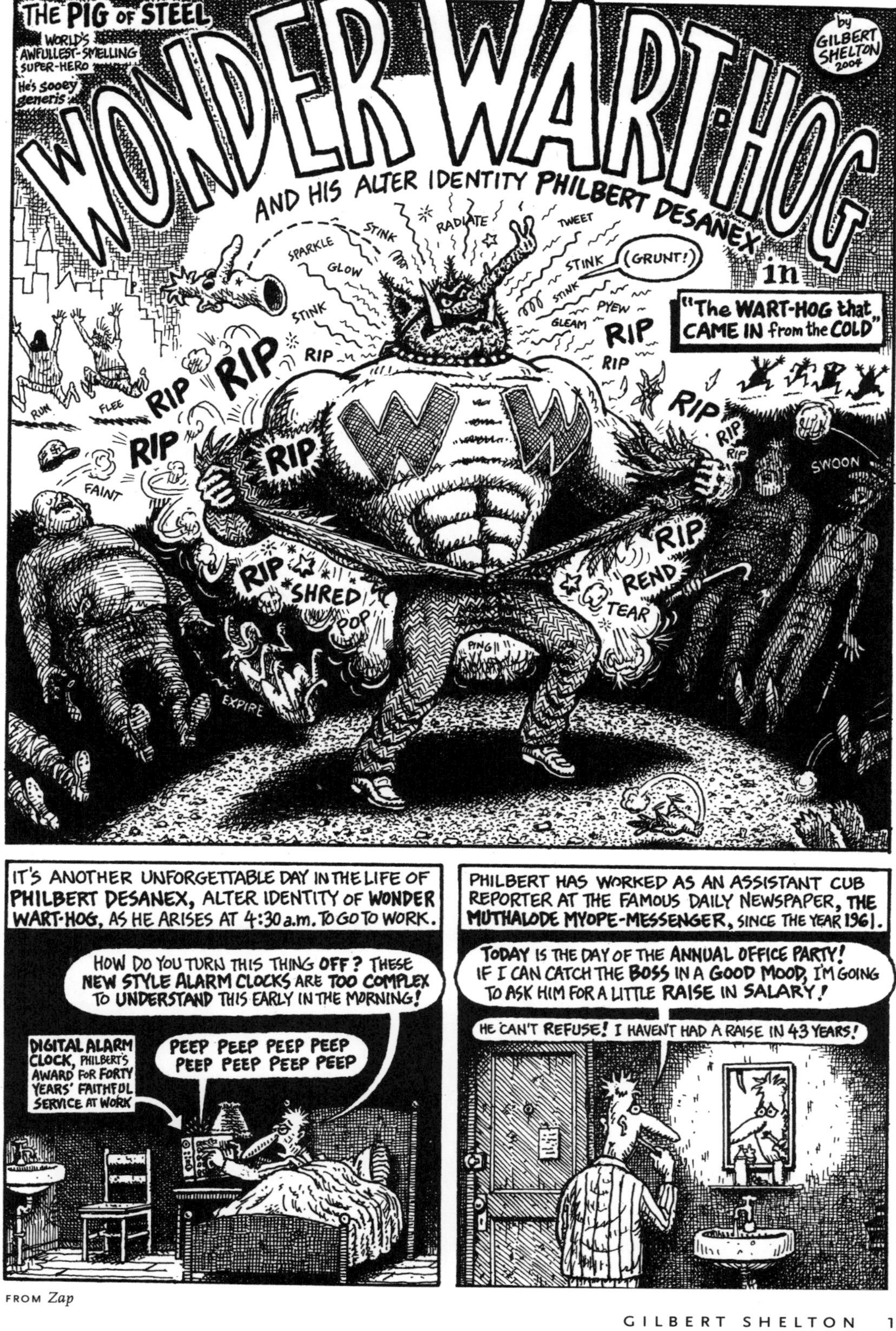

THE PIG OF STEEL
WORLD'S AWFULLEST-SMELLING SUPER-HERO
He's sooey generis
WONDER WART-HOG
by GILBERT SHELTON 2004
AND HIS ALTER IDENTITY PHILBERT DESANEX
in
"The WART-HOG that CAME IN from the COLD"
SPARKLE
STINK
RADIATE
TWEET
GLOW
STINK
GRUNT!
STINK
PYEW
GLEAM
STINK
RIP
RIP RIP RIP RIP RIP RIP RIP RIP RIP
RUN
FLEE
FAINT
SWOON
RIP
SHRED
POP
PING!!
RIP
REND
TEAR
EXPIRE
IT'S ANOTHER UNFORGETTABLE DAY IN THE LIFE OF PHILBERT DESANEX, ALTER IDENTITY OF WONDER WART-HOG, AS HE ARISES AT 4:30 a.m. TO GO TO WORK.
HOW DO YOU TURN THIS THING OFF? THESE NEW STYLE ALARM CLOCKS ARE TOO COMPLEX TO UNDERSTAND THIS EARLY IN THE MORNING!
DIGITAL ALARM CLOCK, PHILBERT'S AWARD FOR FORTY YEARS' FAITHFUL SERVICE AT WORK
PEEP PEEP PEEP PEEP PEEP PEEP PEEP PEEP
PHILBERT HAS WORKED AS AN ASSISTANT CUB REPORTER AT THE FAMOUS DAILY NEWSPAPER, THE MUTHALODE MYOPE-MESSENGER, SINCE THE YEAR 1961.
TODAY IS THE DAY OF THE ANNUAL OFFICE PARTY! IF I CAN CATCH THE BOSS IN A GOOD MOOD, I'M GOING TO ASK HIM FOR A LITTLE RAISE IN SALARY!
HE CAN'T REFUSE! I HAVEN'T HAD A RAISE IN 43 YEARS!

FROM *Zap*

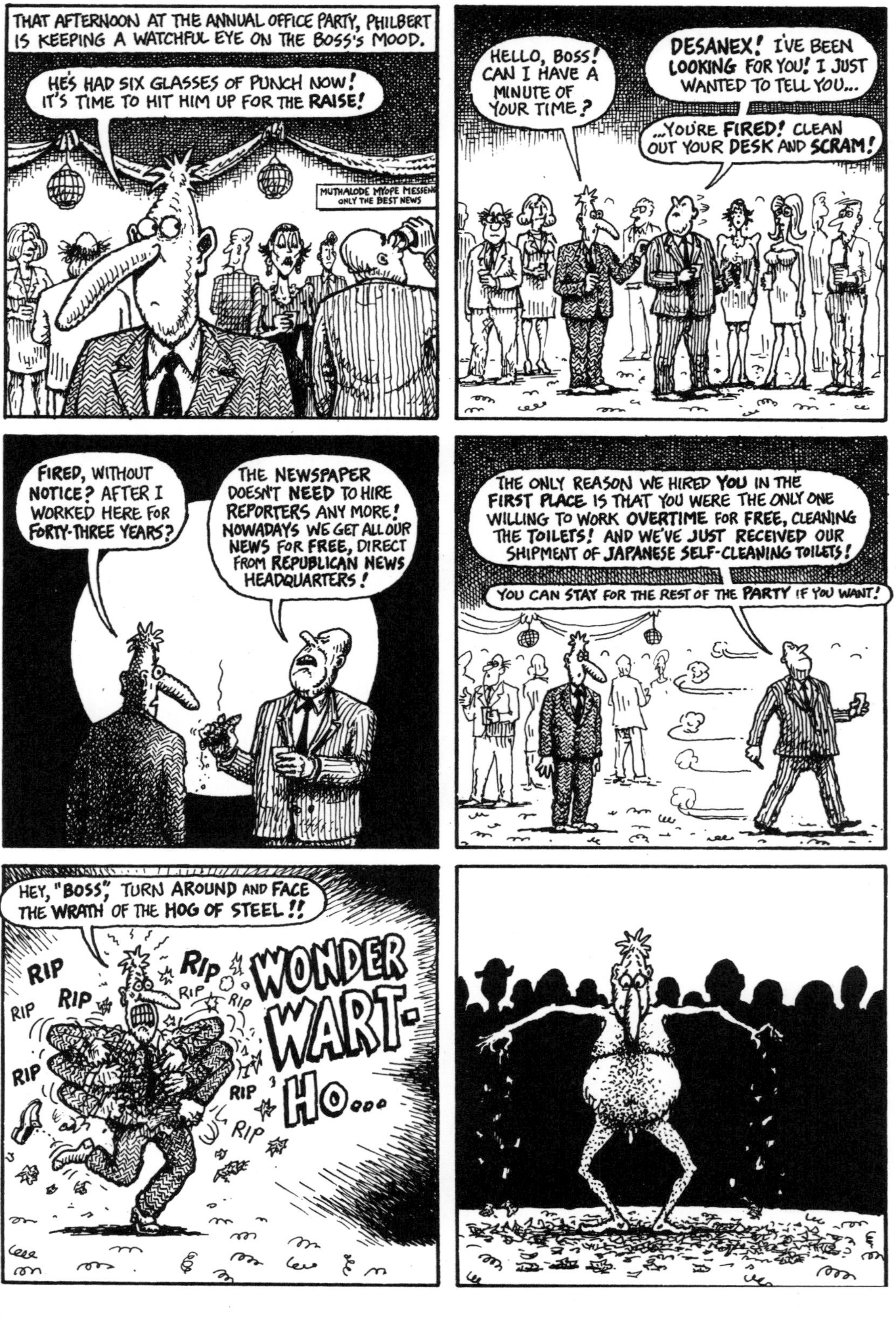
THAT AFTERNOON AT THE ANNUAL OFFICE PARTY, PHILBERT IS KEEPING A WATCHFUL EYE ON THE BOSS'S MOOD.
HE'S HAD SIX GLASSES OF PUNCH NOW! IT'S TIME TO HIT HIM UP FOR THE RAISE!
MUTHALODE MYOPE MESSENG
ONLY THE BEST NEWS
HELLO, BOSS! CAN I HAVE A MINUTE OF YOUR TIME?
DESANEX! I'VE BEEN LOOKING FOR YOU! I JUST WANTED TO TELL YOU...
...YOU'RE FIRED! CLEAN OUT YOUR DESK AND SCRAM!
FIRED, WITHOUT NOTICE? AFTER I WORKED HERE FOR FORTY-THREE YEARS?
THE NEWSPAPER DOESN'T NEED TO HIRE REPORTERS ANY MORE! NOWADAYS WE GET ALL OUR NEWS FOR FREE, DIRECT FROM REPUBLICAN NEWS HEADQUARTERS!
THE ONLY REASON WE HIRED YOU IN THE FIRST PLACE IS THAT YOU WERE THE ONLY ONE WILLING TO WORK OVERTIME FOR FREE, CLEANING THE TOILETS! AND WE'VE JUST RECEIVED OUR SHIPMENT OF JAPANESE SELF-CLEANING TOILETS!
YOU CAN STAY FOR THE REST OF THE PARTY IF YOU WANT!
HEY, "BOSS", TURN AROUND AND FACE THE WRATH OF THE HOG OF STEEL!!
RIP RIP RIP RIP RIP RIP RIP RIP RIP RIP
WONDER WART-HO...

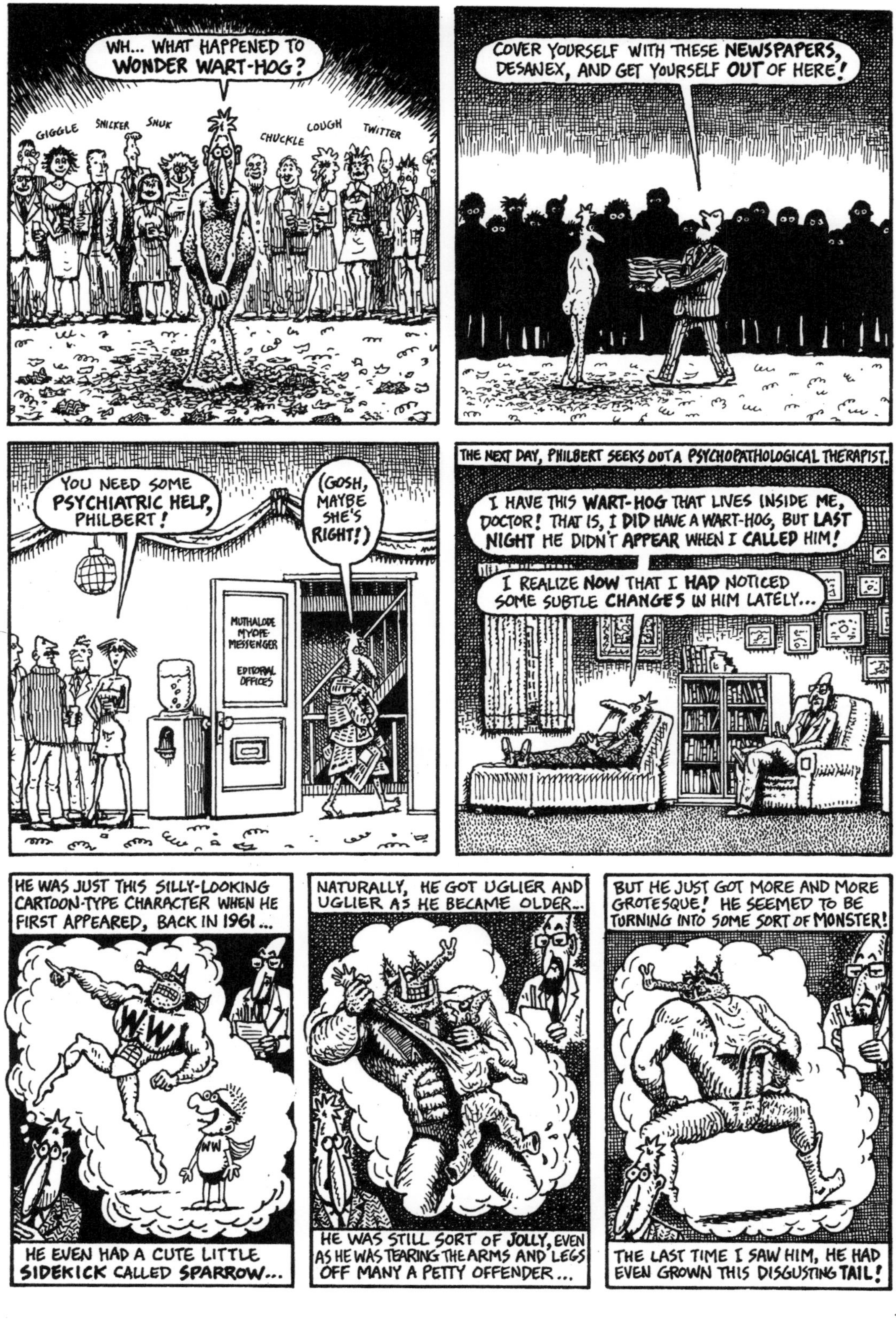
WH... WHAT HAPPENED TO WONDER WART-HOG?
GIGGLE
SNICKER
SNUK
CHUCKLE
COUGH
TWITTER
COVER YOURSELF WITH THESE NEWSPAPERS, DESANEX, AND GET YOURSELF OUT OF HERE!
YOU NEED SOME PSYCHIATRIC HELP, PHILBERT!
(GOSH, MAYBE SHE'S RIGHT!)
MUTHALODE MYOPE-MESSENGER
EDITORIAL OFFICES
THE NEXT DAY, PHILBERT SEEKS OUT A PSYCHOPATHOLOGICAL THERAPIST.
I HAVE THIS WART-HOG THAT LIVES INSIDE ME, DOCTOR! THAT IS, I DID HAVE A WART-HOG, BUT LAST NIGHT HE DIDN'T APPEAR WHEN I CALLED HIM!
I REALIZE NOW THAT I HAD NOTICED SOME SUBTLE CHANGES IN HIM LATELY...
HE WAS JUST THIS SILLY-LOOKING CARTOON-TYPE CHARACTER WHEN HE FIRST APPEARED, BACK IN 1961...
WW
WW
HE EVEN HAD A CUTE LITTLE SIDEKICK CALLED SPARROW...
NATURALLY, HE GOT UGLIER AND UGLIER AS HE BECAME OLDER...
HE WAS STILL SORT OF JOLLY, EVEN AS HE WAS TEARING THE ARMS AND LEGS OFF MANY A PETTY OFFENDER...
BUT HE JUST GOT MORE AND MORE GROTESQUE! HE SEEMED TO BE TURNING INTO SOME SORT OF MONSTER!
THE LAST TIME I SAW HIM, HE HAD EVEN GROWN THIS DISGUSTING TAIL!

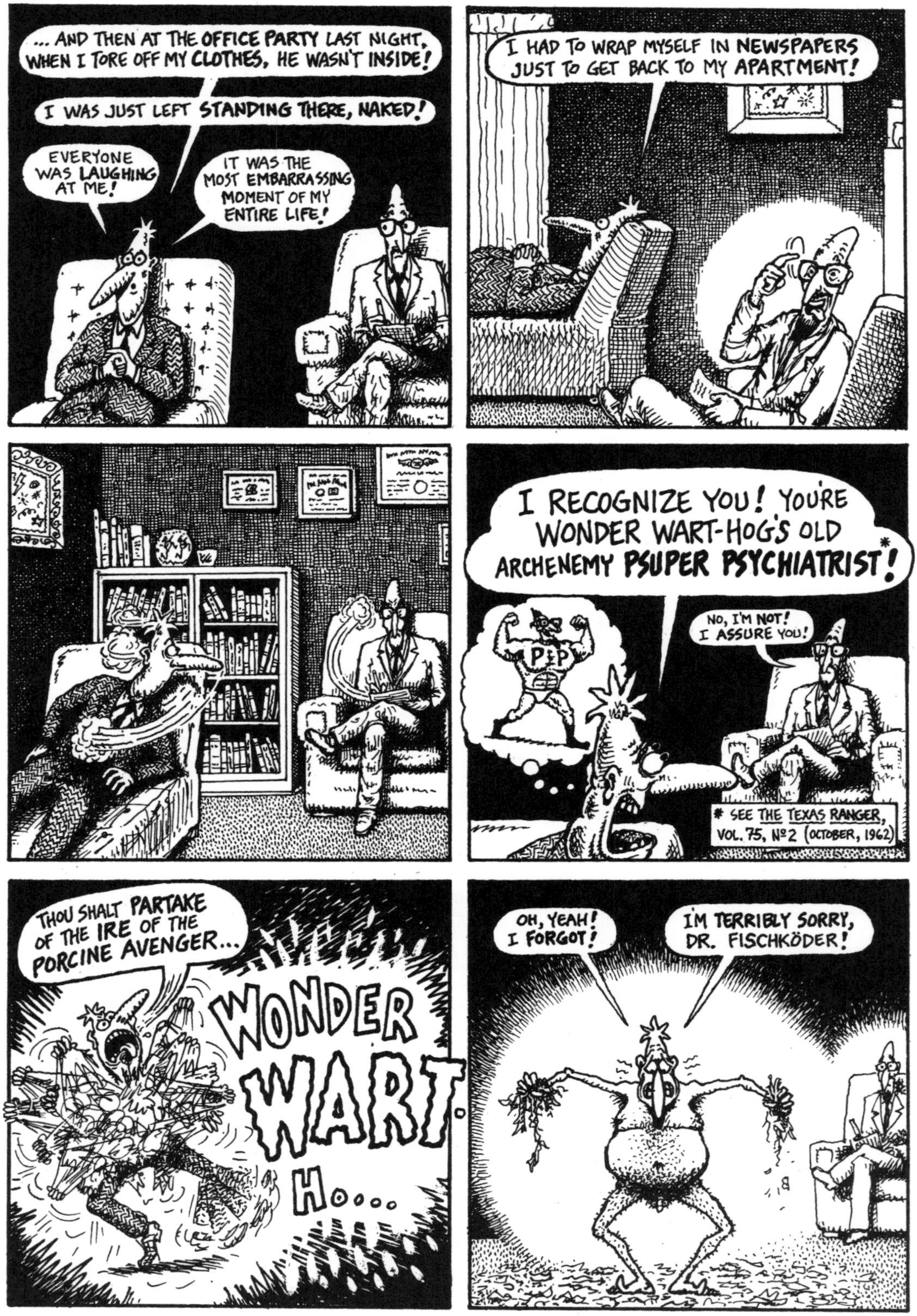
... AND THEN AT THE OFFICE PARTY LAST NIGHT, WHEN I TORE OFF MY CLOTHES, HE WASN'T INSIDE!
I WAS JUST LEFT STANDING THERE, NAKED!
EVERYONE WAS LAUGHING AT ME!
IT WAS THE MOST EMBARRASSING MOMENT OF MY ENTIRE LIFE!
I HAD TO WRAP MYSELF IN NEWSPAPERS JUST TO GET BACK TO MY APARTMENT!
I RECOGNIZE YOU! YOU'RE WONDER WART-HOG'S OLD ARCHENEMY PSUPER PSYCHIATRIST*!
NO, I'M NOT! I ASSURE YOU!
P P
* SEE THE TEXAS RANGER, VOL. 75, №2 (OCTOBER, 1962)
THOU SHALT PARTAKE OF THE IRE OF THE PORCINE AVENGER...
WONDER WART-H...
OH, YEAH! I FORGOT!
I'M TERRIBLY SORRY, DR. FISCHKÖDER!

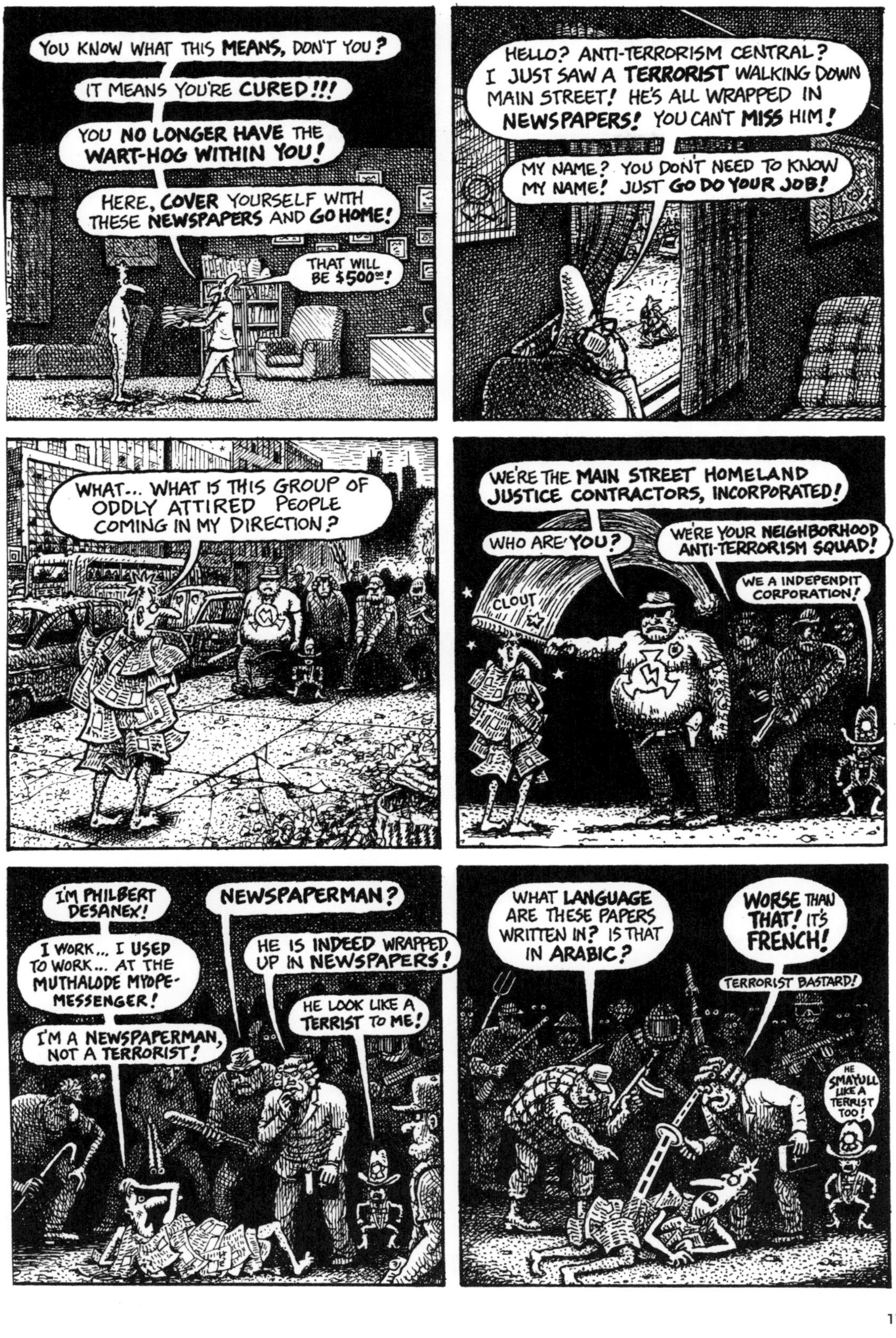
YOU KNOW WHAT THIS MEANS, DON'T YOU?
IT MEANS YOU'RE CURED!!!
YOU NO LONGER HAVE THE WART-HOG WITHIN YOU!
HERE, COVER YOURSELF WITH THESE NEWSPAPERS AND GO HOME!
THAT WILL BE $500.00!
HELLO? ANTI-TERRORISM CENTRAL? I JUST SAW A TERRORIST WALKING DOWN MAIN STREET! HE'S ALL WRAPPED IN NEWSPAPERS! YOU CAN'T MISS HIM!
MY NAME? YOU DON'T NEED TO KNOW MY NAME! JUST GO DO YOUR JOB!
WHAT... WHAT IS THIS GROUP OF ODDLY ATTIRED PEOPLE COMING IN MY DIRECTION?
WE'RE THE MAIN STREET HOMELAND JUSTICE CONTRACTORS, INCORPORATED!
WHO ARE YOU?
WE'RE YOUR NEIGHBORHOOD ANTI-TERRORISM SQUAD!
WE A INDEPENDIT CORPORATION!
CLOUT
I'M PHILBERT DESANEX!
I WORK... I USED TO WORK... AT THE MUTHALODE MYOPE-MESSENGER!
I'M A NEWSPAPERMAN, NOT A TERRORIST!
NEWSPAPERMAN?
HE IS INDEED WRAPPED UP IN NEWSPAPERS!
HE LOOK LIKE A TERRIST TO ME!
WHAT LANGUAGE ARE THESE PAPERS WRITTEN IN? IS THAT IN ARABIC?
WORSE THAN THAT! IT'S FRENCH!
TERRORIST BASTARD!
HE SMAYULL LIKE A TERRIST TOO!

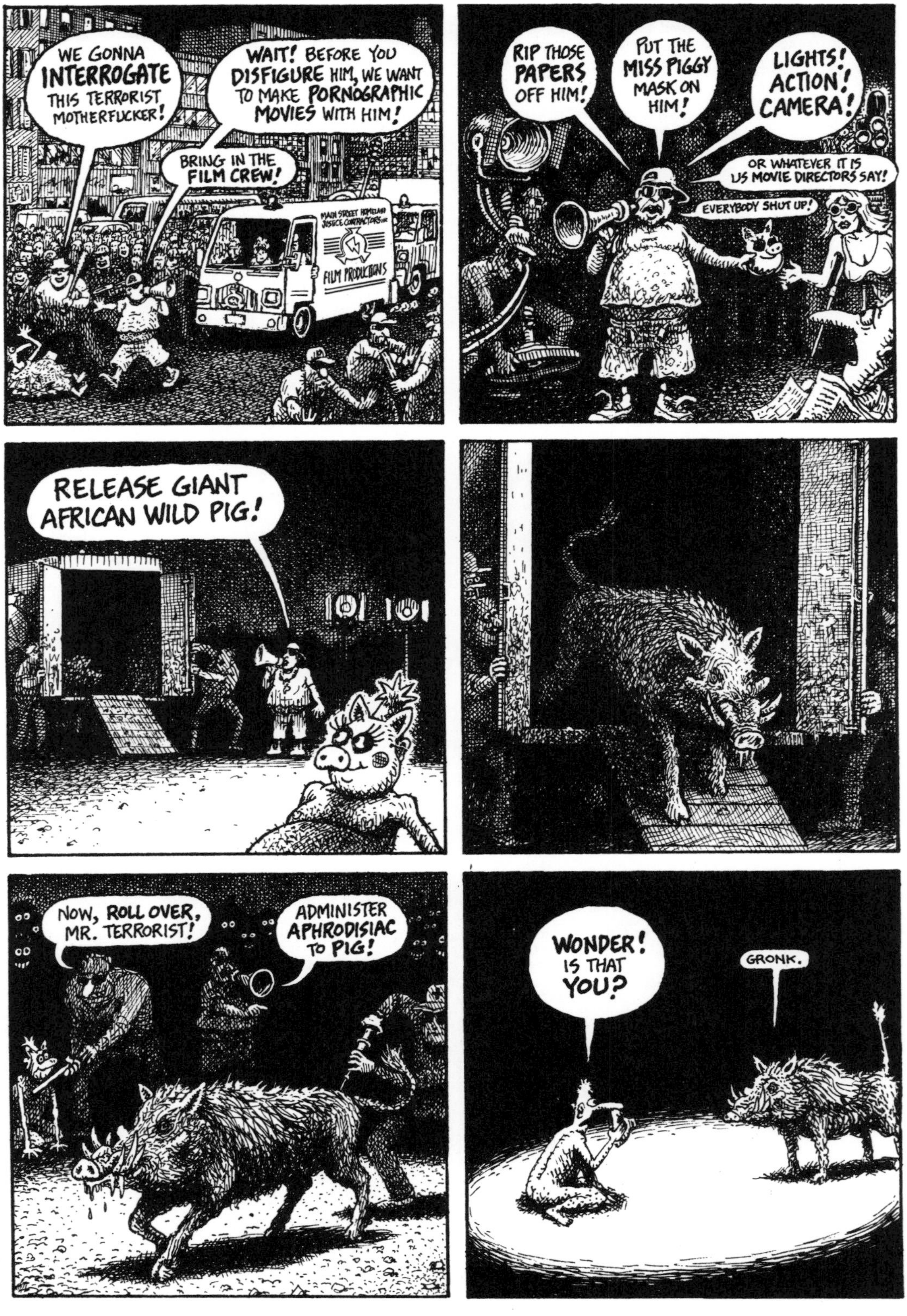
WE GONNA INTERROGATE THIS TERRORIST MOTHERFUCKER!
WAIT! BEFORE YOU DISFIGURE HIM, WE WANT TO MAKE PORNOGRAPHIC MOVIES WITH HIM!
BRING IN THE FILM CREW!
MAIN STREET HOMELAND JUSTICE CONTRACTORS INC
FILM PRODUCTIONS
RIP THOSE PAPERS OFF HIM!
PUT THE MISS PIGGY MASK ON HIM!
LIGHTS! ACTION! CAMERA!
OR WHATEVER IT IS US MOVIE DIRECTORS SAY!
EVERYBODY SHUT UP!
RELEASE GIANT AFRICAN WILD PIG!
NOW, ROLL OVER, MR. TERRORIST!
ADMINISTER APHRODISIAC TO PIG!
WONDER! IS THAT YOU?
GRONK.

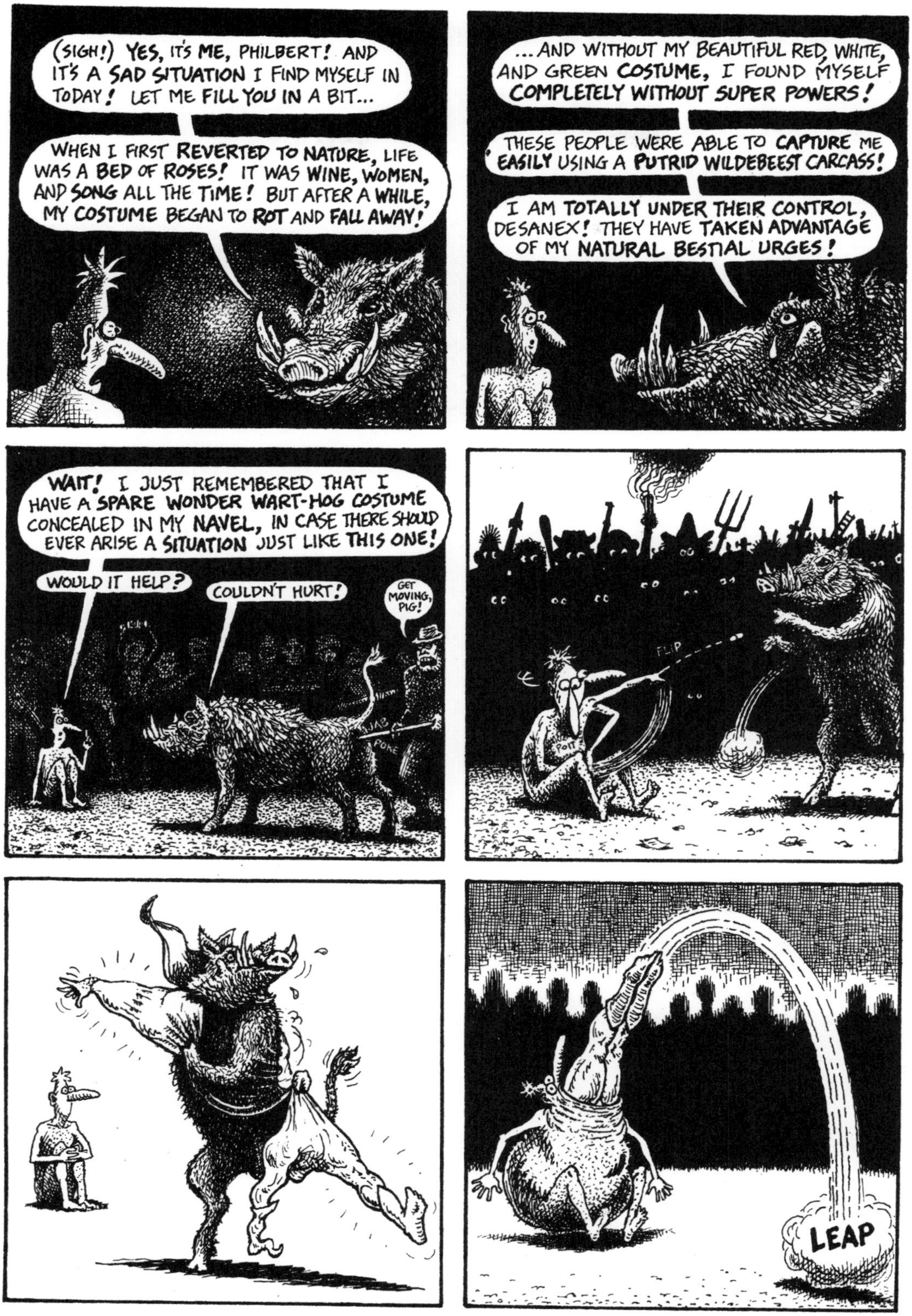

(SIGH!) YES, IT'S ME, PHILBERT! AND IT'S A SAD SITUATION I FIND MYSELF IN TODAY! LET ME FILL YOU IN A BIT...
WHEN I FIRST REVERTED TO NATURE, LIFE WAS A BED OF ROSES! IT WAS WINE, WOMEN, AND SONG ALL THE TIME! BUT AFTER A WHILE, MY COSTUME BEGAN TO ROT AND FALL AWAY!
...AND WITHOUT MY BEAUTIFUL RED, WHITE, AND GREEN COSTUME, I FOUND MYSELF COMPLETELY WITHOUT SUPER POWERS!
THESE PEOPLE WERE ABLE TO CAPTURE ME EASILY USING A PUTRID WILDEBEEST CARCASS!
I AM TOTALLY UNDER THEIR CONTROL, DESANEX! THEY HAVE TAKEN ADVANTAGE OF MY NATURAL BESTIAL URGES!
WAIT! I JUST REMEMBERED THAT I HAVE A SPARE WONDER WART-HOG COSTUME CONCEALED IN MY NAVEL, IN CASE THERE SHOULD EVER ARISE A SITUATION JUST LIKE THIS ONE!
WOULD IT HELP?
COULDN'T HURT!
GET MOVING, PIG!
JAB
POKE
FLIP
POIT
LEAP

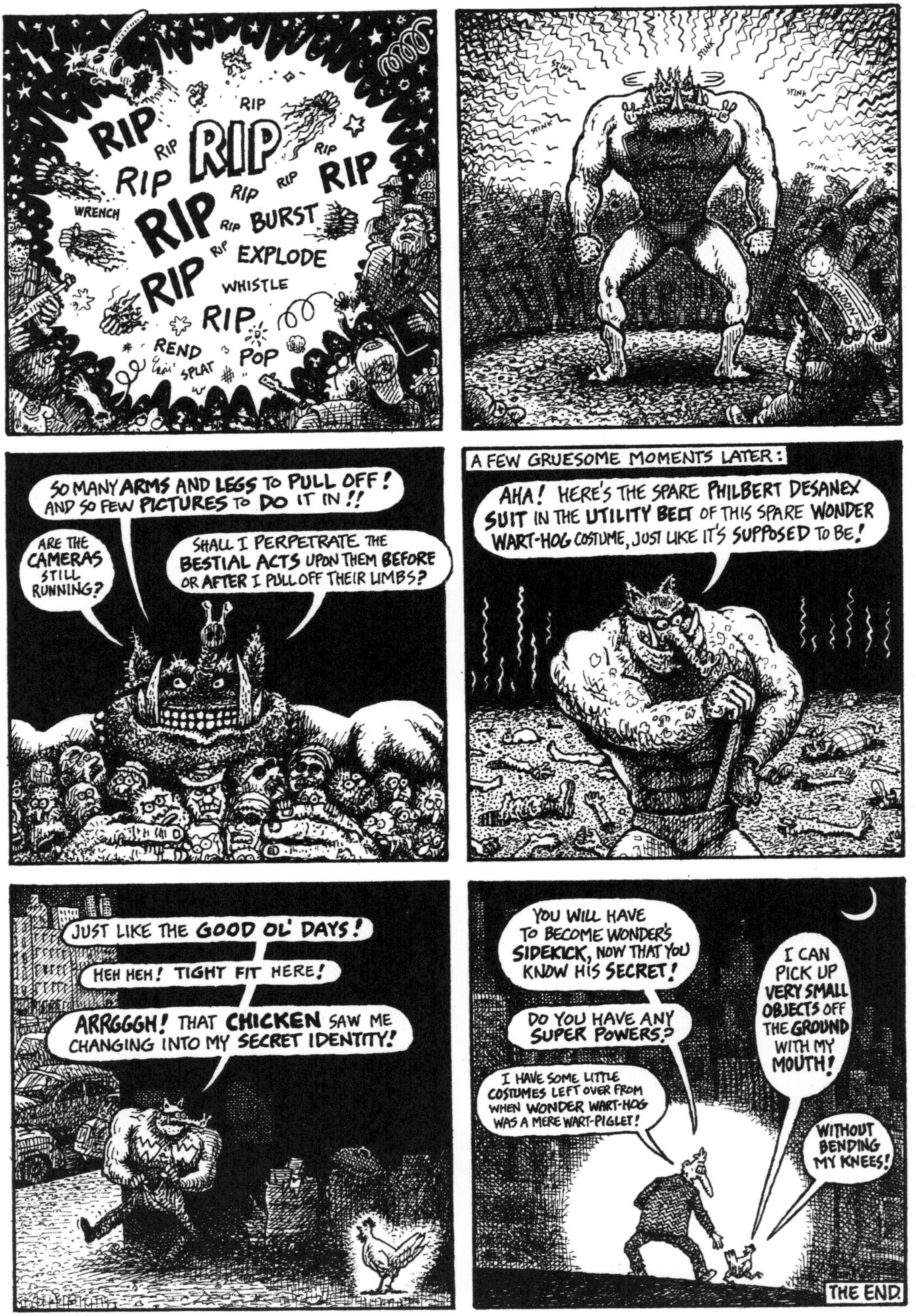

RIP RIP RIP RIP RIP RIP RIP RIP RIP RIP RIP RIP RIP RIP
WRENCH
BURST
EXPLODE
WHISTLE
REND
SPLAT
POP
STINK STINK STINK STINK STINK
SO MANY ARMS AND LEGS TO PULL OFF! AND SO FEW PICTURES TO DO IT IN!!
ARE THE CAMERAS STILL RUNNING?
SHALL I PERPETRATE THE BESTIAL ACTS UPON THEM BEFORE OR AFTER I PULL OFF THEIR LIMBS?
A FEW GRUESOME MOMENTS LATER:
AHA! HERE'S THE SPARE PHILBERT DESANEX SUIT IN THE UTILITY BELT OF THIS SPARE WONDER WART-HOG COSTUME, JUST LIKE IT'S SUPPOSED TO BE!
JUST LIKE THE GOOD OL' DAYS!
HEH HEH! TIGHT FIT HERE!
ARRGGGH! THAT CHICKEN SAW ME CHANGING INTO MY SECRET IDENTITY!
YOU WILL HAVE TO BECOME WONDER'S SIDEKICK, NOW THAT YOU KNOW HIS SECRET!
DO YOU HAVE ANY SUPER POWERS?
I HAVE SOME LITTLE COSTUMES LEFT OVER FROM WHEN WONDER WART-HOG WAS A MERE WART-PIGLET!
I CAN PICK UP VERY SMALL OBJECTS OFF THE GROUND WITH MY MOUTH!
WITHOUT BENDING MY KNEES!
THE END.

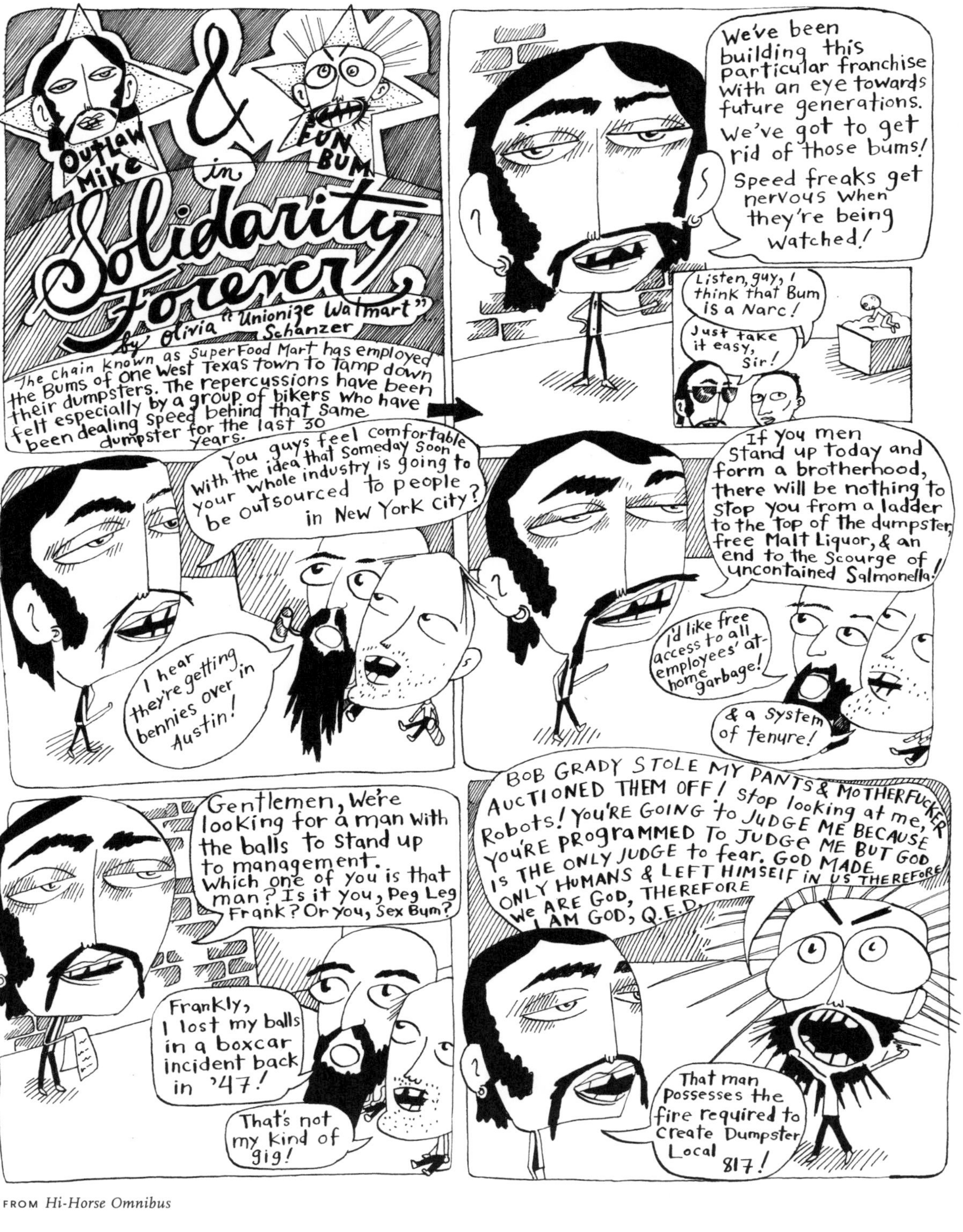
OUTLAW MIKE
&
FUN BUM
in
Solidarity Forever
by Olivia "Unionize Walmart" Schanzer
The chain known as SuperFood Mart has employed the Bums of one West Texas town to tamp down their dumpsters. The repercussions have been felt especially by a group of bikers who have been dealing speed behind that same dumpster for the last 30 years.
We've been building this particular franchise with an eye towards future generations. We've got to get rid of those bums! Speed freaks get nervous when they're being watched!
Listen, guy, I think that Bum is a Narc!
Just take it easy, Sir!
You guys feel comfortable with the idea that someday soon your whole industry is going to be outsourced to people in New York City?
I hear they're getting bennies over in Austin!
If you men stand up today and form a brotherhood, there will be nothing to stop you from a ladder to the top of the dumpster, free Malt Liquor, & an end to the scourge of uncontained Salmonella!
I'd like free access to all employees' at-home garbage!
& a system of tenure!
Gentlemen, we're looking for a man with the balls to stand up to management. Which one of you is that man? Is it you, Peg Leg Frank? Or you, Sex Bum?
Frankly, I lost my balls in a boxcar incident back in '47!
That's not my kind of gig!
BOB GRADY STOLE MY PANTS & MOTHERFUCKER AUCTIONED THEM OFF! Stop looking at me, Robots! YOU'RE GOING to JUDGE ME BECAUSE YOU'RE PROGRAMMED TO JUDGE ME BUT GOD IS THE ONLY JUDGE to fear. GOD MADE ONLY HUMANS & LEFT HIMSELF IN US THEREFORE WE ARE GOD, THEREFORE I AM GOD, Q.E.D.
That man possesses the fire required to create Dumpster Local 817!

FROM *Hi-Horse Omnibus*

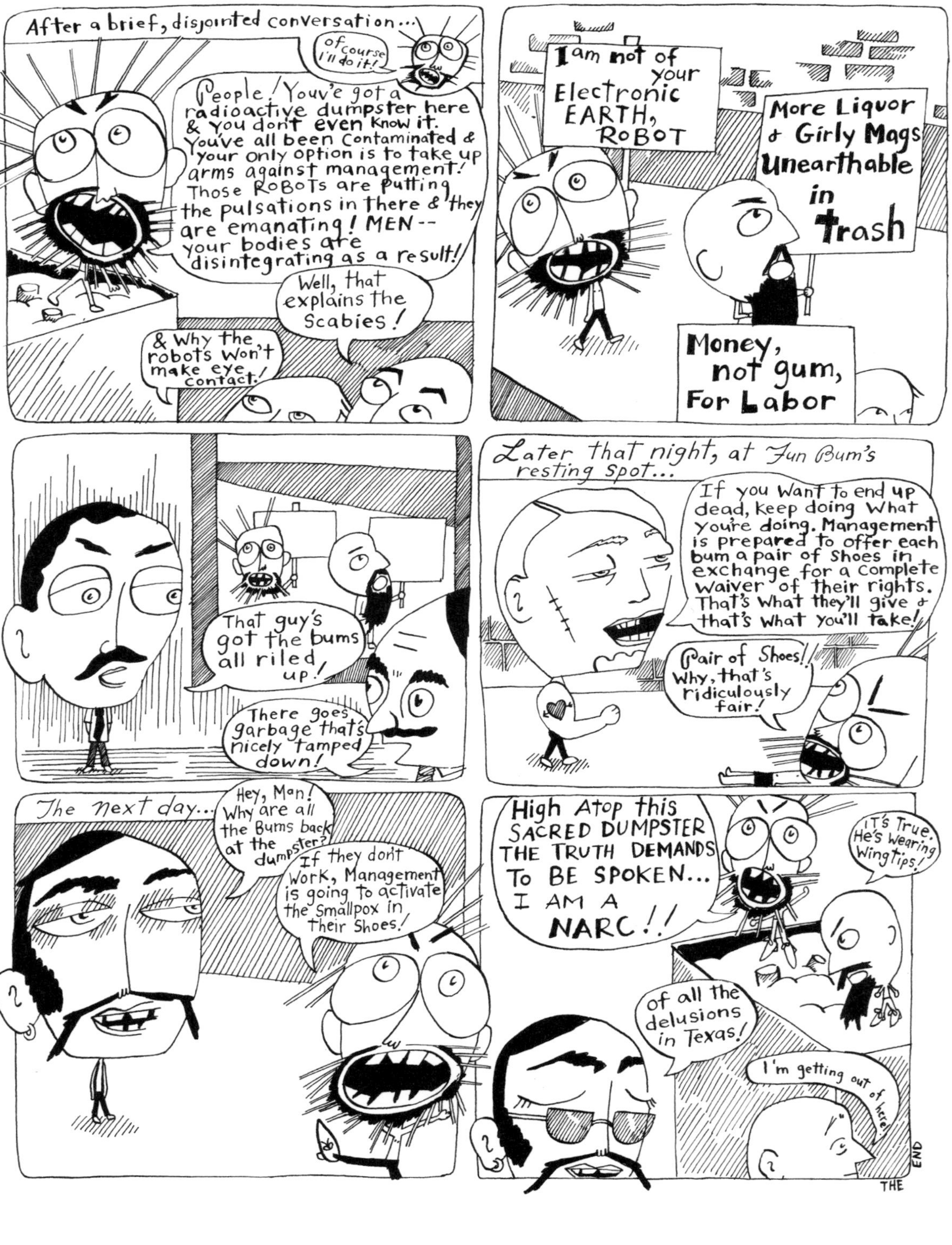

After a brief, disjointed conversation...
of course I'll do it!
People! You've got a radioactive dumpster here & you don't even know it. You've all been contaminated & your only option is to take up arms against management! Those ROBOTs are putting the pulsations in there & they are emanating! MEN -- your bodies are disintegrating as a result!
Well, that explains the Scabies!
& Why the robots won't make eye contact!
I am not of your Electronic EARTH, ROBOT
More Liquor & Girly Mags Unearthable in trash
Money, not gum, For Labor
That guy's got the bums all riled up!
There goes garbage that's nicely tamped down!
Later that night, at Fun Bum's resting spot...
If you want to end up dead, keep doing what you're doing. Management is prepared to offer each bum a pair of shoes in exchange for a complete waiver of their rights. That's what they'll give & that's what you'll take!
Pair of Shoes!! Why, that's ridiculously fair!
The next day...
Hey, Man! Why are all the Bums back at the dumpster?
If they don't work, Management is going to activate the smallpox in their Shoes!
High Atop this SACRED DUMPSTER THE TRUTH DEMANDS TO BE SPOKEN... I AM A NARC!!
IT'S True. He's wearing Wingtips!
of all the delusions in Texas!
I'm getting out of here.
THE END

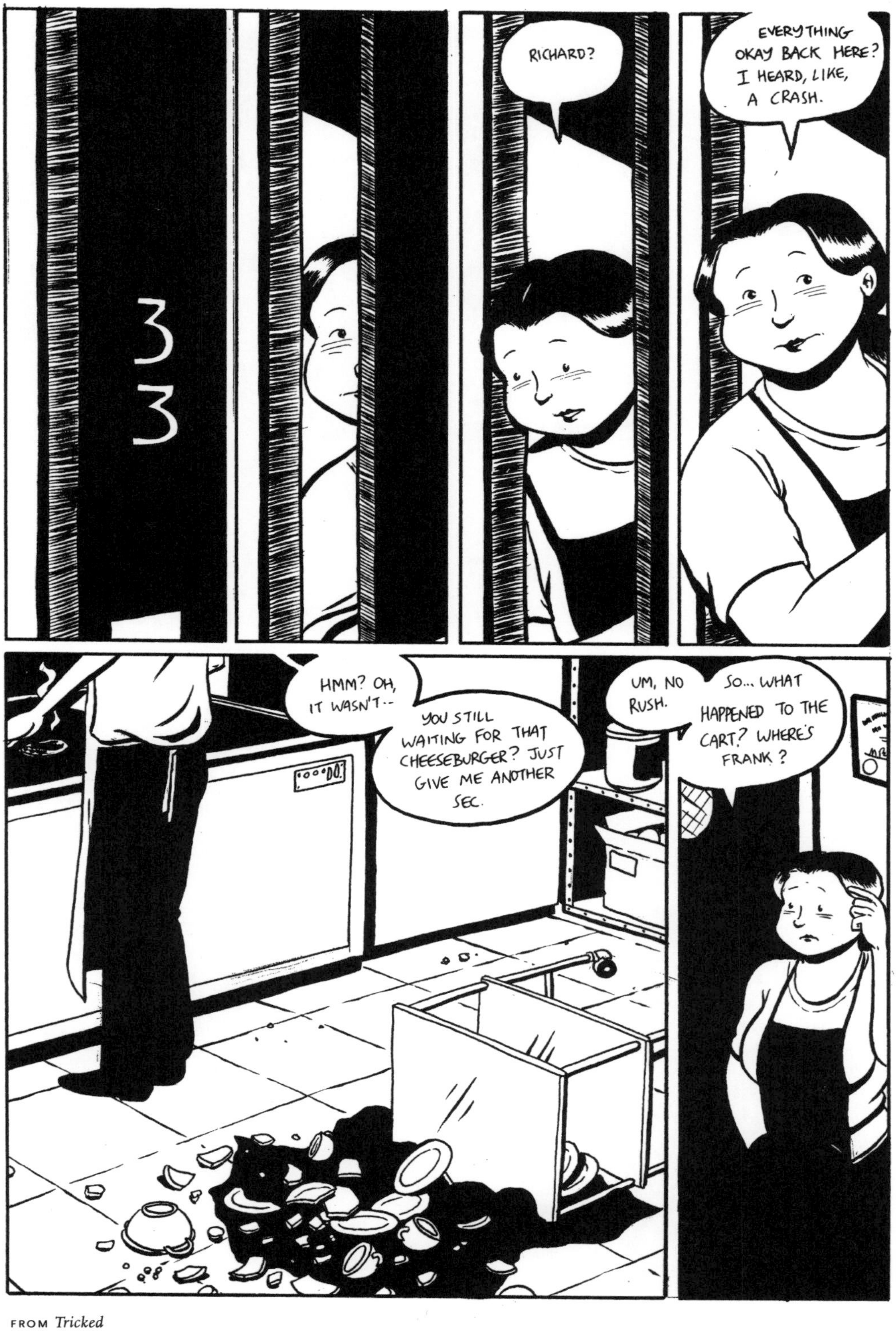
33
RICHARD?
EVERYTHING OKAY BACK HERE? I HEARD, LIKE, A CRASH.
HMM? OH, IT WASN'T--
YOU STILL WAITING FOR THAT CHEESEBURGER? JUST GIVE ME ANOTHER SEC.
UM, NO RUSH.
SO... WHAT HAPPENED TO THE CART? WHERE'S FRANK?

FROM *Tricked*

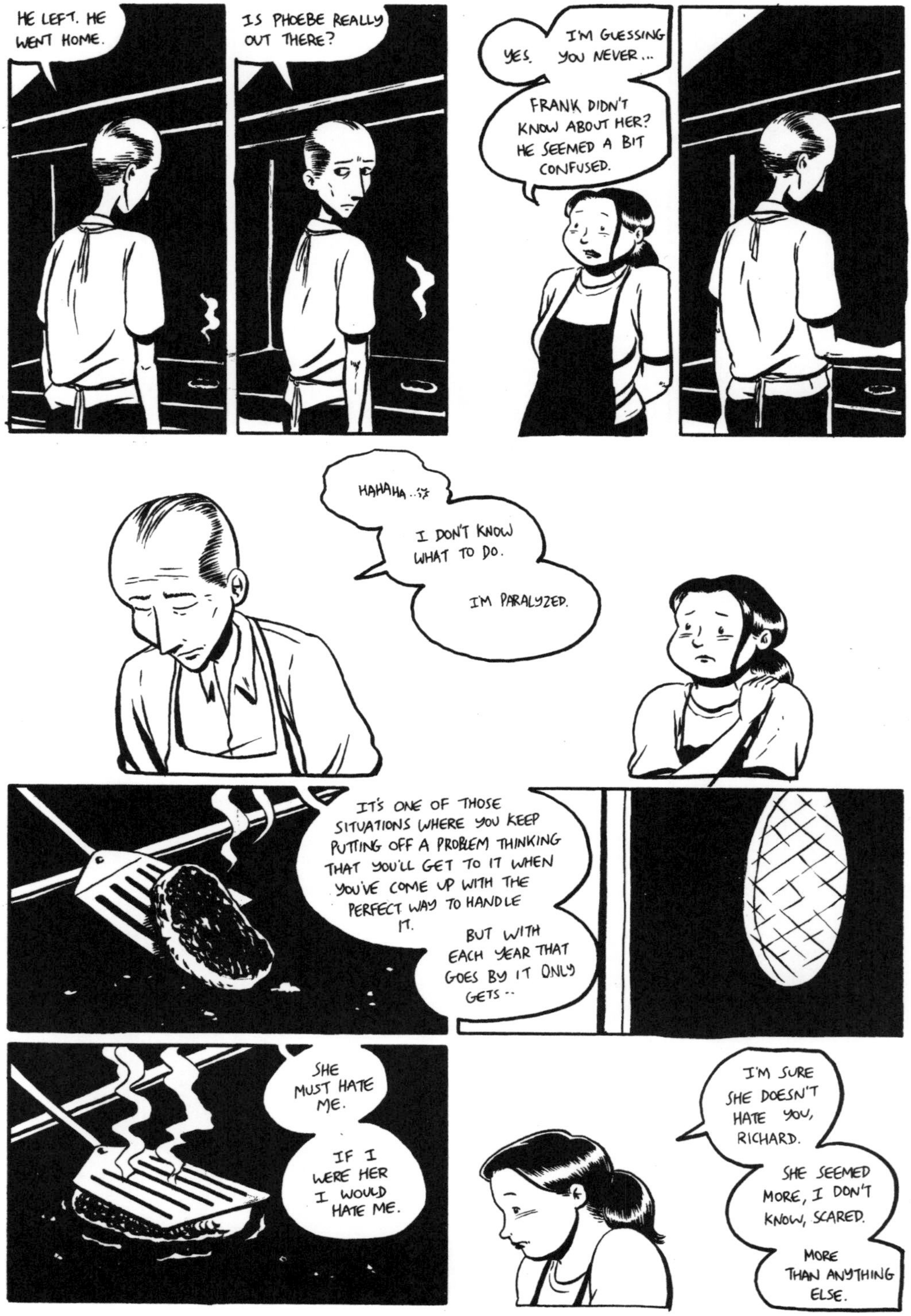

HE LEFT. HE WENT HOME.
IS PHOEBE REALLY OUT THERE?
YES.
I'M GUESSING YOU NEVER...
FRANK DIDN'T KNOW ABOUT HER? HE SEEMED A BIT CONFUSED.
HAHAHA...
I DON'T KNOW WHAT TO DO.
I'M PARALYZED.
IT'S ONE OF THOSE SITUATIONS WHERE YOU KEEP PUTTING OFF A PROBLEM THINKING THAT YOU'LL GET TO IT WHEN YOU'VE COME UP WITH THE PERFECT WAY TO HANDLE IT.
BUT WITH EACH YEAR THAT GOES BY IT ONLY GETS--
SHE MUST HATE ME.
IF I WERE HER I WOULD HATE ME.
I'M SURE SHE DOESN'T HATE YOU, RICHARD.
SHE SEEMED MORE, I DON'T KNOW, SCARED.
MORE THAN ANYTHING ELSE.

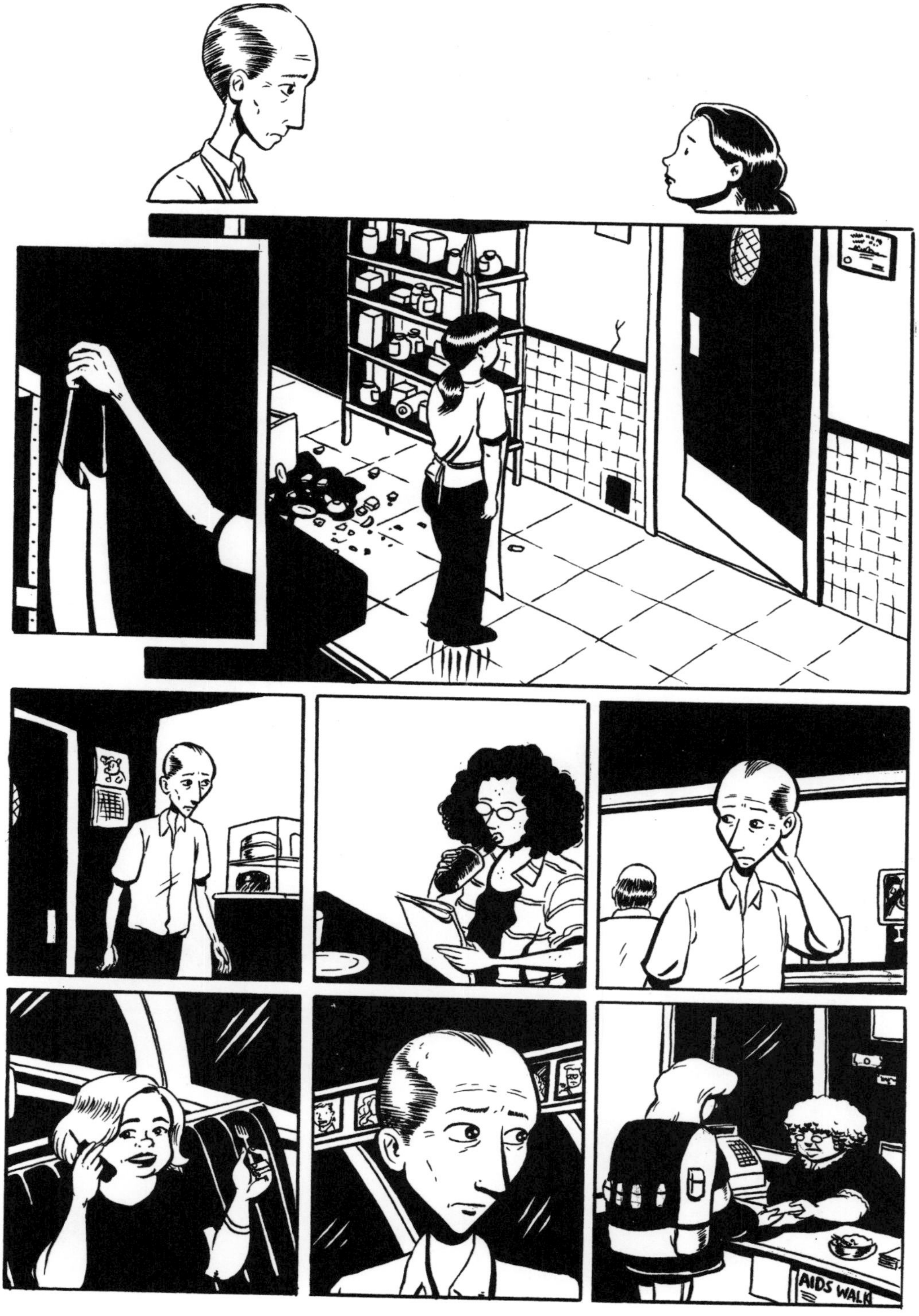
AIDS WALK

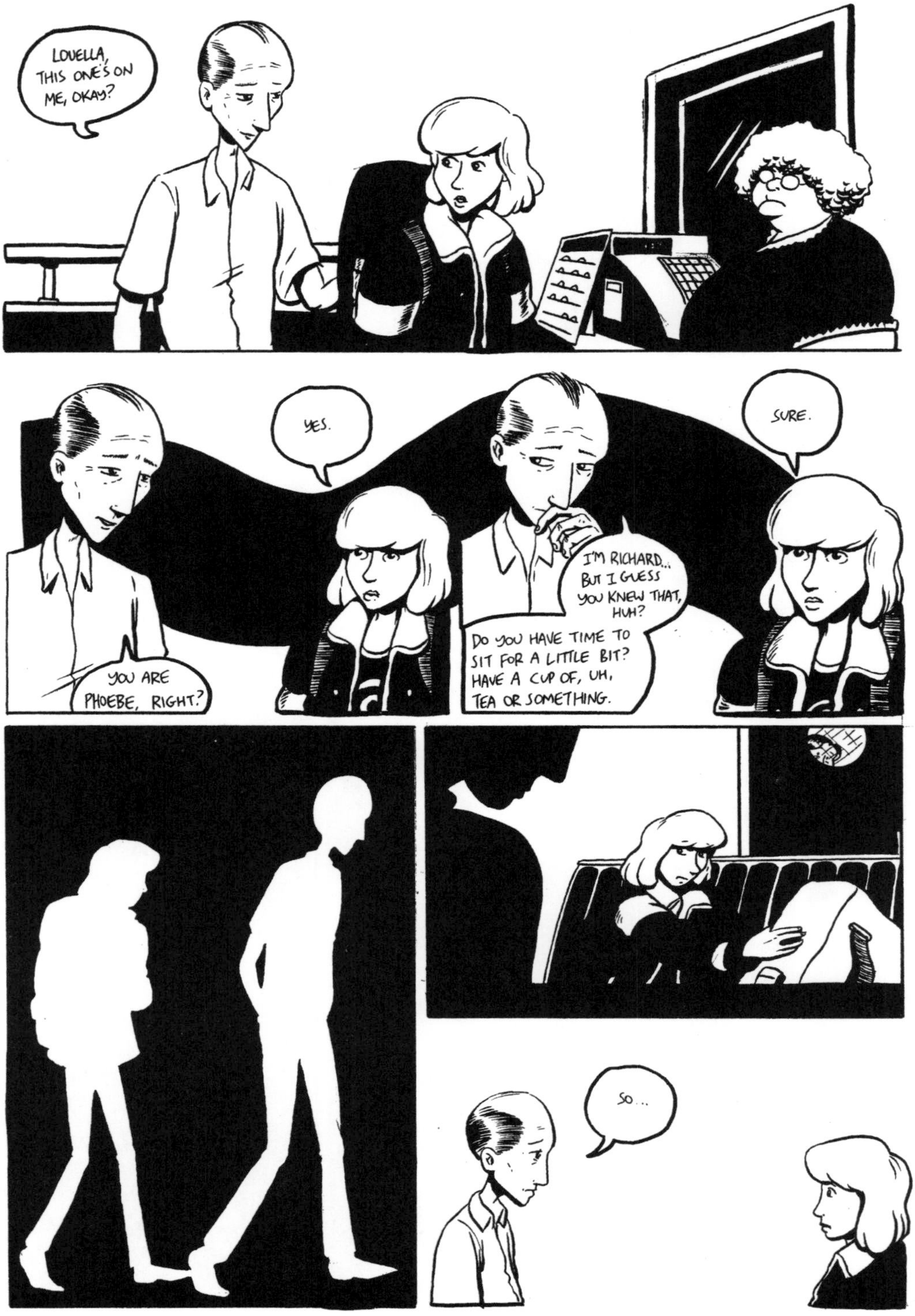
LOUELLA, THIS ONE'S ON ME, OKAY?
YES.
YOU ARE PHOEBE, RIGHT?
SURE.
I'M RICHARD... BUT I GUESS YOU KNEW THAT, HUH?
DO YOU HAVE TIME TO SIT FOR A LITTLE BIT? HAVE A CUP OF, UH, TEA OR SOMETHING.
SO...

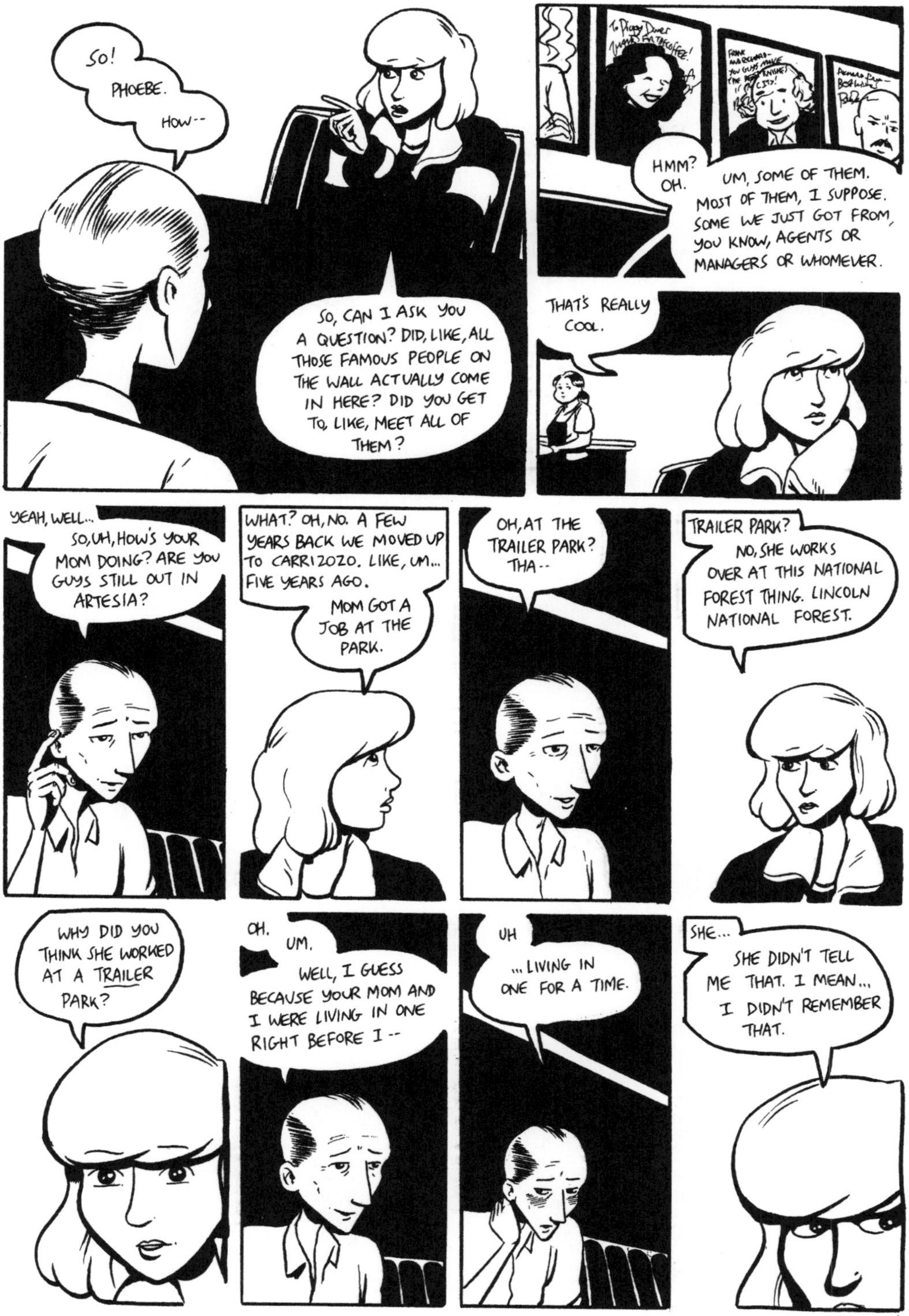
SO!
PHOEBE.
HOW--
SO, CAN I ASK YOU A QUESTION? DID, LIKE, ALL THOSE FAMOUS PEOPLE ON THE WALL ACTUALLY COME IN HERE? DID YOU GET TO, LIKE, MEET ALL OF THEM?
HMM? OH.
UM, SOME OF THEM. MOST OF THEM, I SUPPOSE. SOME WE JUST GOT FROM, YOU KNOW, AGENTS OR MANAGERS OR WHOMEVER.
THAT'S REALLY COOL.
YEAH, WELL...
SO, UH, HOW'S YOUR MOM DOING? ARE YOU GUYS STILL OUT IN ARTESIA?
WHAT? OH, NO. A FEW YEARS BACK WE MOVED UP TO CARRIZOZO. LIKE, UM... FIVE YEARS AGO.
MOM GOT A JOB AT THE PARK.
OH, AT THE TRAILER PARK? THA--
TRAILER PARK?
NO, SHE WORKS OVER AT THIS NATIONAL FOREST THING. LINCOLN NATIONAL FOREST.
WHY DID YOU THINK SHE WORKED AT A TRAILER PARK?
OH.
UM.
WELL, I GUESS BECAUSE YOUR MOM AND I WERE LIVING IN ONE RIGHT BEFORE I --
UH
...LIVING IN ONE FOR A TIME.
SHE...
SHE DIDN'T TELL ME THAT. I MEAN... I DIDN'T REMEMBER THAT.

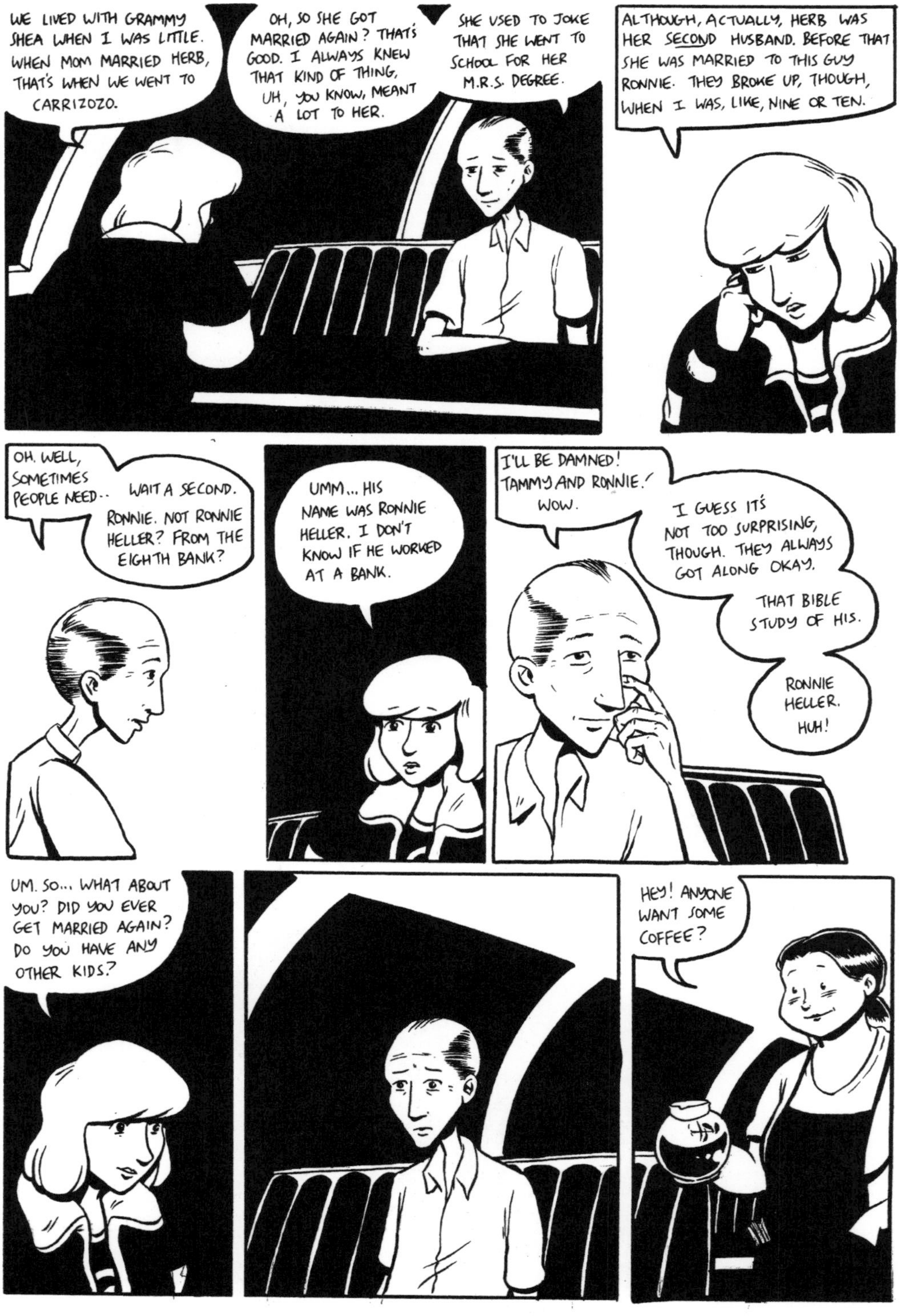

WE LIVED WITH GRAMMY SHEA WHEN I WAS LITTLE. WHEN MOM MARRIED HERB, THAT'S WHEN WE WENT TO CARRIZOZO.
OH, SO SHE GOT MARRIED AGAIN? THAT'S GOOD. I ALWAYS KNEW THAT KIND OF THING, UH, YOU KNOW, MEANT A LOT TO HER.
SHE USED TO JOKE THAT SHE WENT TO SCHOOL FOR HER M.R.S. DEGREE.
ALTHOUGH, ACTUALLY, HERB WAS HER SECOND HUSBAND. BEFORE THAT SHE WAS MARRIED TO THIS GUY RONNIE. THEY BROKE UP, THOUGH, WHEN I WAS, LIKE, NINE OR TEN.
OH. WELL, SOMETIMES PEOPLE NEED..
WAIT A SECOND. RONNIE. NOT RONNIE HELLER? FROM THE EIGHTH BANK?
UMM... HIS NAME WAS RONNIE HELLER. I DON'T KNOW IF HE WORKED AT A BANK.
I'LL BE DAMNED! TAMMY AND RONNIE! WOW.
I GUESS IT'S NOT TOO SURPRISING, THOUGH. THEY ALWAYS GOT ALONG OKAY.
THAT BIBLE STUDY OF HIS.
RONNIE HELLER. HUH!
UM. SO... WHAT ABOUT YOU? DID YOU EVER GET MARRIED AGAIN? DO YOU HAVE ANY OTHER KIDS?
HEY! ANYONE WANT SOME COFFEE?

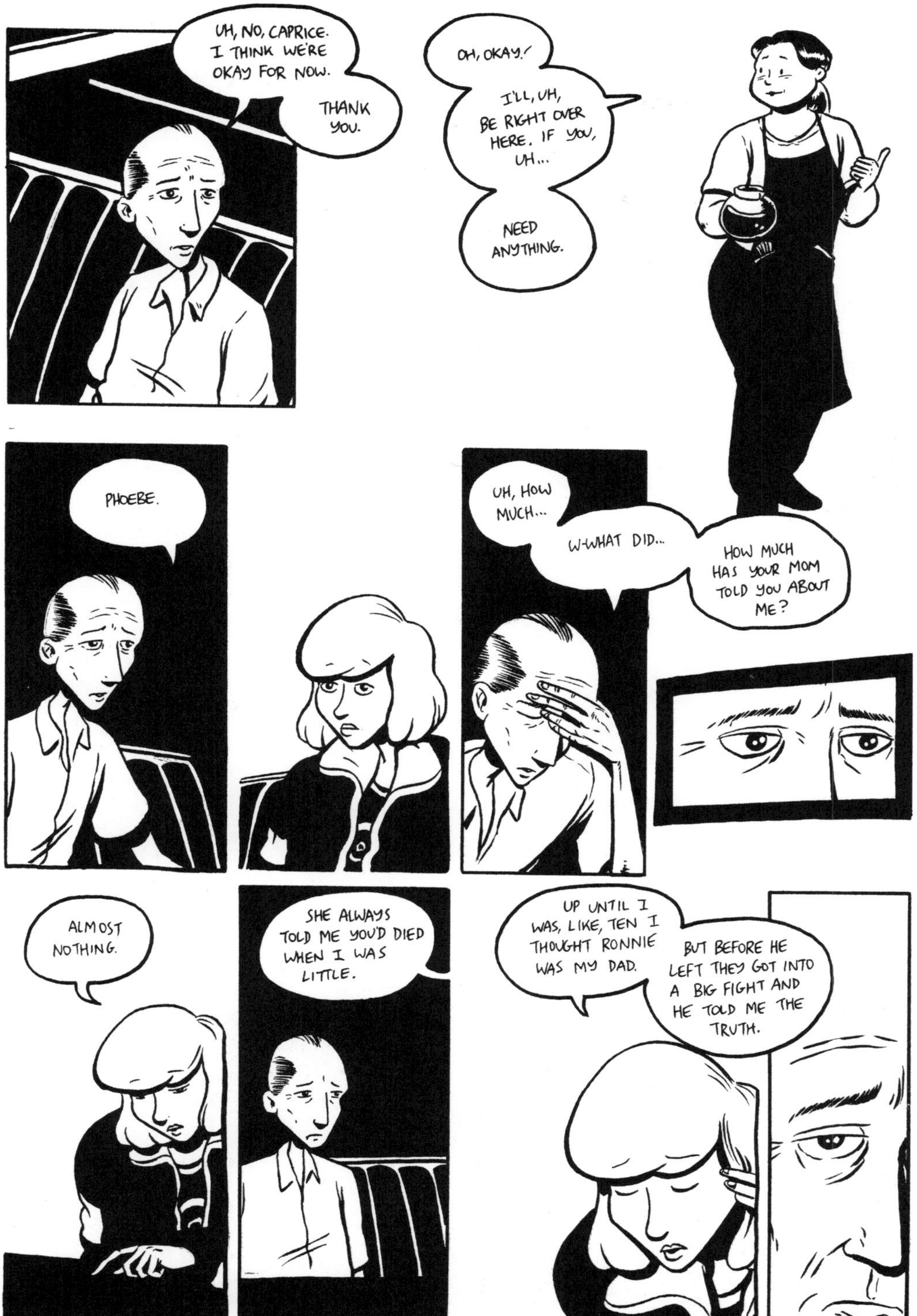
UH, NO, CAPRICE. I THINK WE'RE OKAY FOR NOW.
THANK YOU.
OH, OKAY!
I'LL, UH, BE RIGHT OVER HERE. IF YOU, UH...
NEED ANYTHING.
PHOEBE.
UH, HOW MUCH...
W-WHAT DID...
HOW MUCH HAS YOUR MOM TOLD YOU ABOUT ME?
ALMOST NOTHING.
SHE ALWAYS TOLD ME YOU'D DIED WHEN I WAS LITTLE.
UP UNTIL I WAS, LIKE, TEN I THOUGHT RONNIE WAS MY DAD.
BUT BEFORE HE LEFT THEY GOT INTO A BIG FIGHT AND HE TOLD ME THE TRUTH.

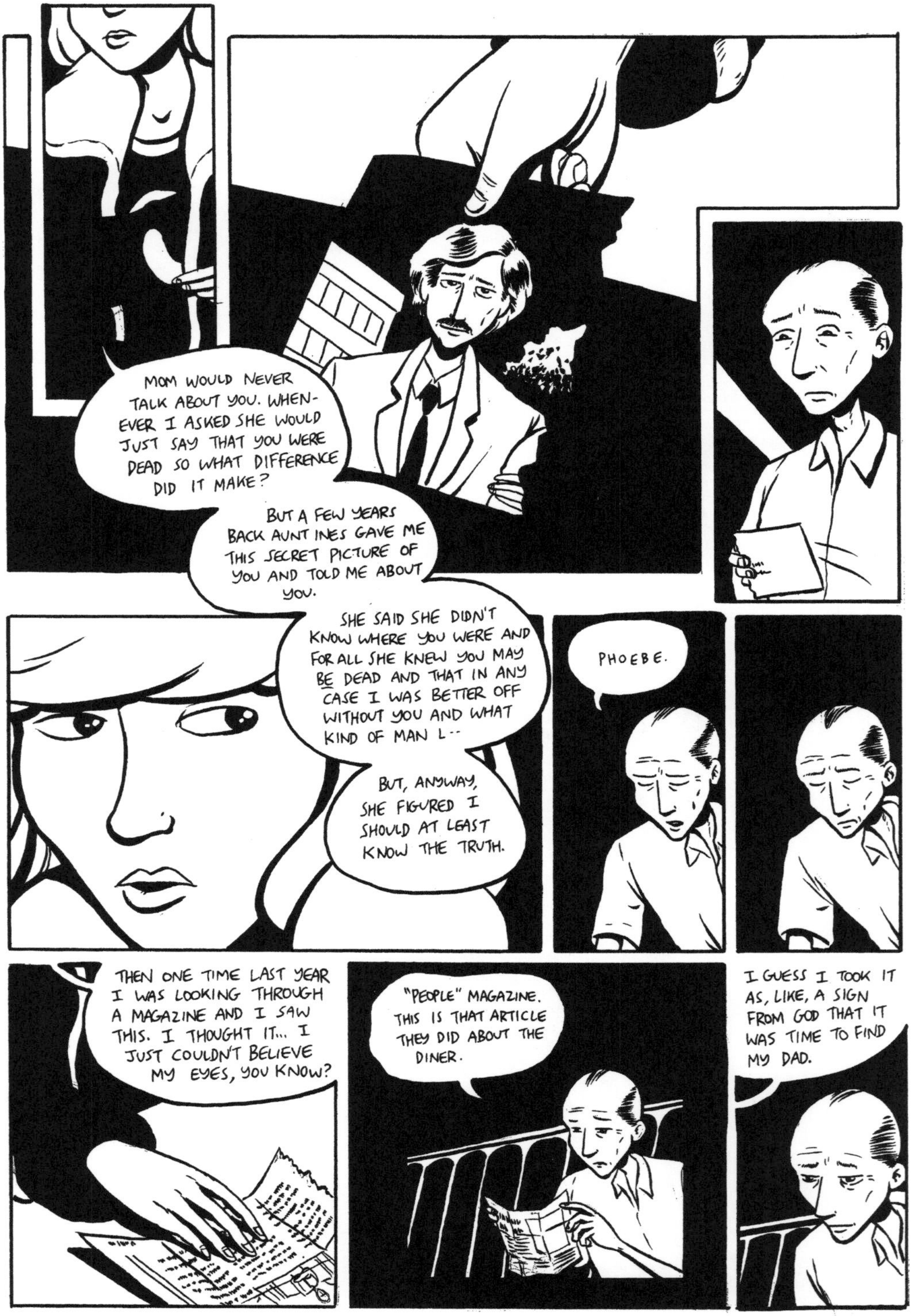
MOM WOULD NEVER TALK ABOUT YOU. WHENEVER I ASKED SHE WOULD JUST SAY THAT YOU WERE DEAD SO WHAT DIFFERENCE DID IT MAKE?
BUT A FEW YEARS BACK AUNT INES GAVE ME THIS SECRET PICTURE OF YOU AND TOLD ME ABOUT YOU.
SHE SAID SHE DIDN'T KNOW WHERE YOU WERE AND FOR ALL SHE KNEW YOU MAY BE DEAD AND THAT IN ANY CASE I WAS BETTER OFF WITHOUT YOU AND WHAT KIND OF MAN L--
BUT, ANYWAY, SHE FIGURED I SHOULD AT LEAST KNOW THE TRUTH.
PHOEBE.
THEN ONE TIME LAST YEAR I WAS LOOKING THROUGH A MAGAZINE AND I SAW THIS. I THOUGHT IT... I JUST COULDN'T BELIEVE MY EYES, YOU KNOW?
"PEOPLE" MAGAZINE. THIS IS THAT ARTICLE THEY DID ABOUT THE DINER.
I GUESS I TOOK IT AS, LIKE, A SIGN FROM GOD THAT IT WAS TIME TO FIND MY DAD.

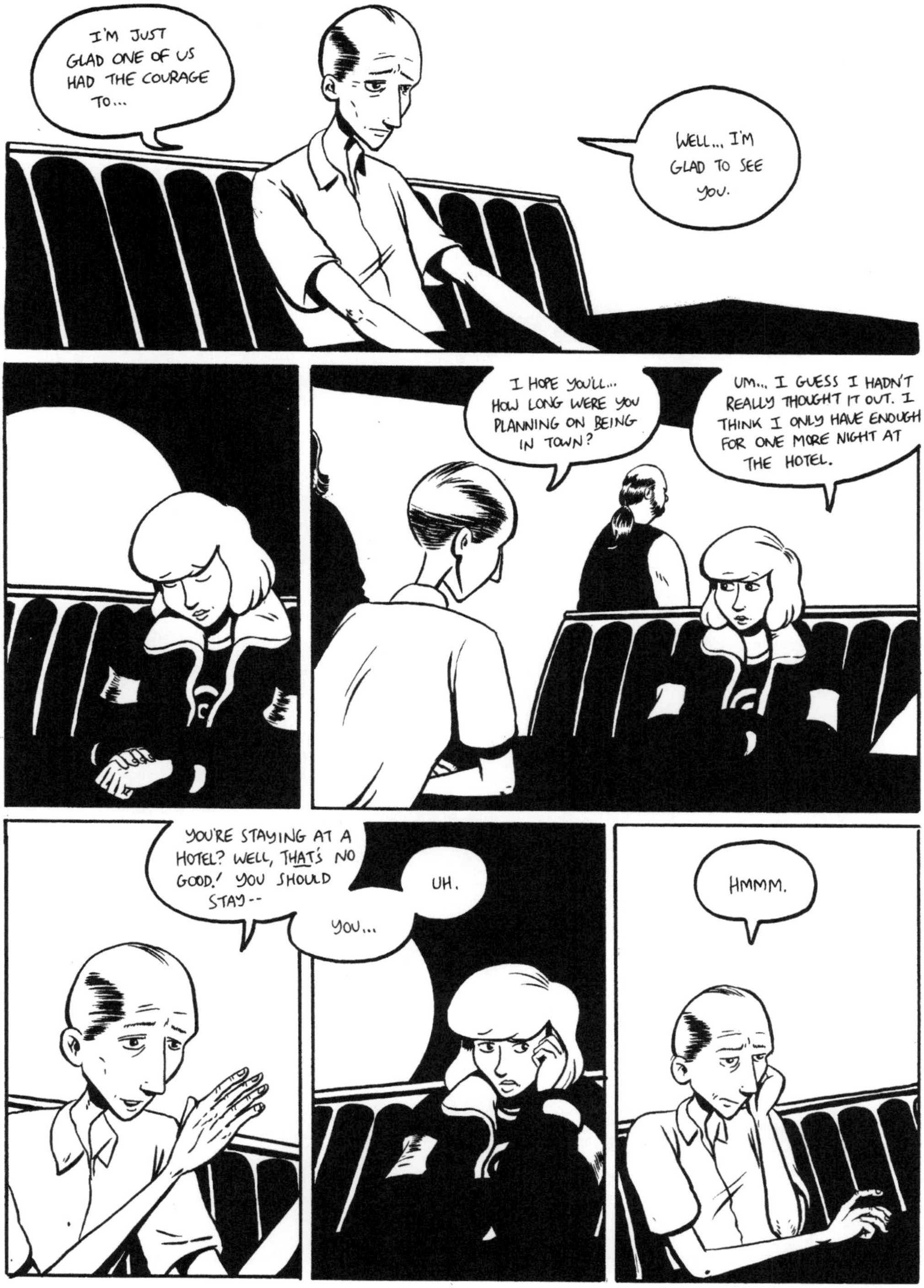
I'M JUST GLAD ONE OF US HAD THE COURAGE TO...
WELL... I'M GLAD TO SEE YOU.
I HOPE YOU'LL... HOW LONG WERE YOU PLANNING ON BEING IN TOWN?
UM... I GUESS I HADN'T REALLY THOUGHT IT OUT. I THINK I ONLY HAVE ENOUGH FOR ONE MORE NIGHT AT THE HOTEL.
YOU'RE STAYING AT A HOTEL? WELL, THAT'S NO GOOD! YOU SHOULD STAY--
UH.
YOU...
HMMM.

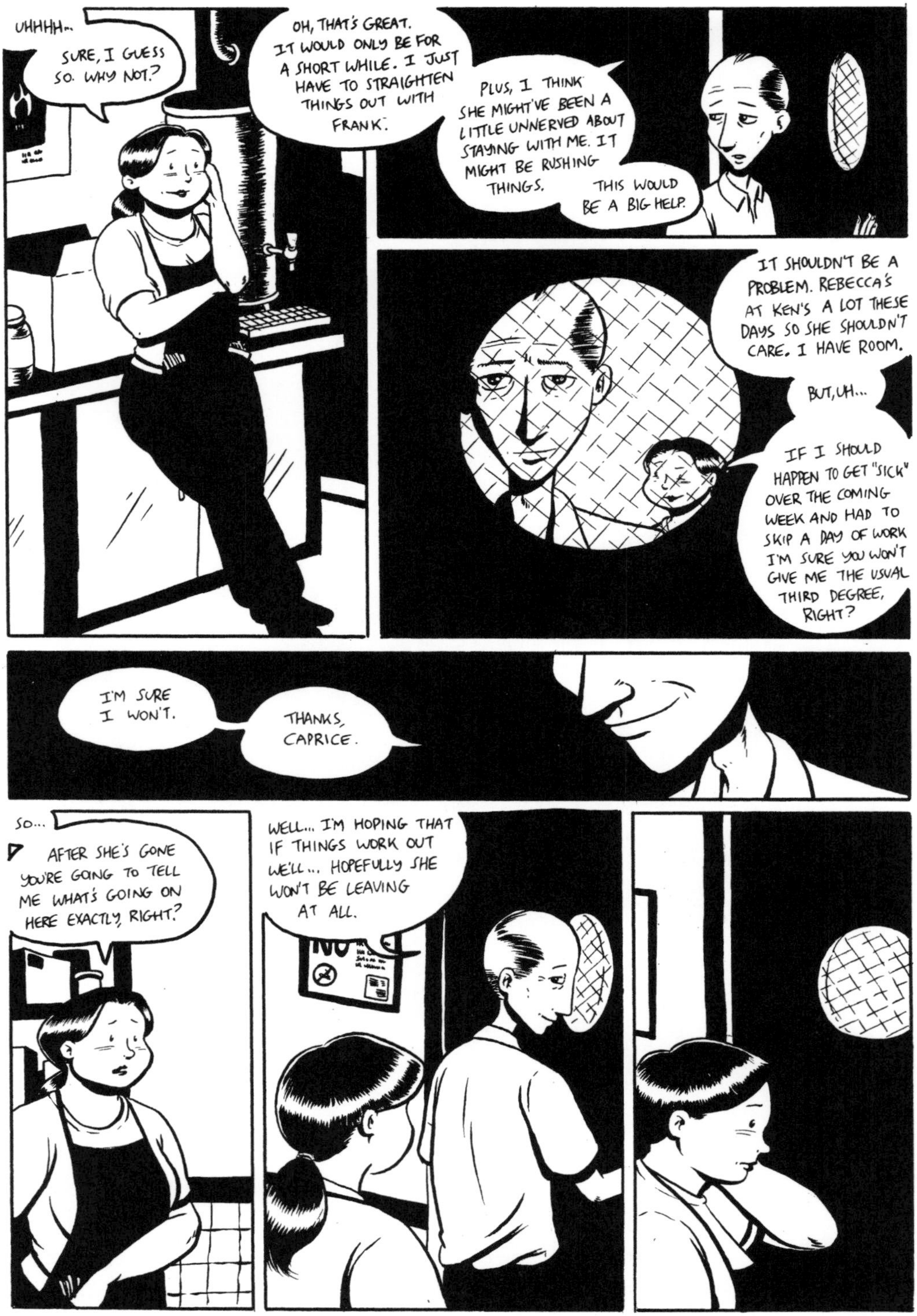

UHHHH..
SURE, I GUESS SO. WHY NOT?
OH, THAT'S GREAT. IT WOULD ONLY BE FOR A SHORT WHILE. I JUST HAVE TO STRAIGHTEN THINGS OUT WITH FRANK.
PLUS, I THINK SHE MIGHT'VE BEEN A LITTLE UNNERVED ABOUT STAYING WITH ME. IT MIGHT BE RUSHING THINGS.
THIS WOULD BE A BIG HELP.
IT SHOULDN'T BE A PROBLEM. REBECCA'S AT KEN'S A LOT THESE DAYS SO SHE SHOULDN'T CARE. I HAVE ROOM.
BUT, UH...
IF I SHOULD HAPPEN TO GET "SICK" OVER THE COMING WEEK AND HAD TO SKIP A DAY OF WORK I'M SURE YOU WON'T GIVE ME THE USUAL THIRD DEGREE, RIGHT?
I'M SURE I WON'T.
THANKS, CAPRICE.
SO...
AFTER SHE'S GONE YOU'RE GOING TO TELL ME WHAT'S GOING ON HERE EXACTLY, RIGHT?
WELL... I'M HOPING THAT IF THINGS WORK OUT WE'LL... HOPEFULLY SHE WON'T BE LEAVING AT ALL.

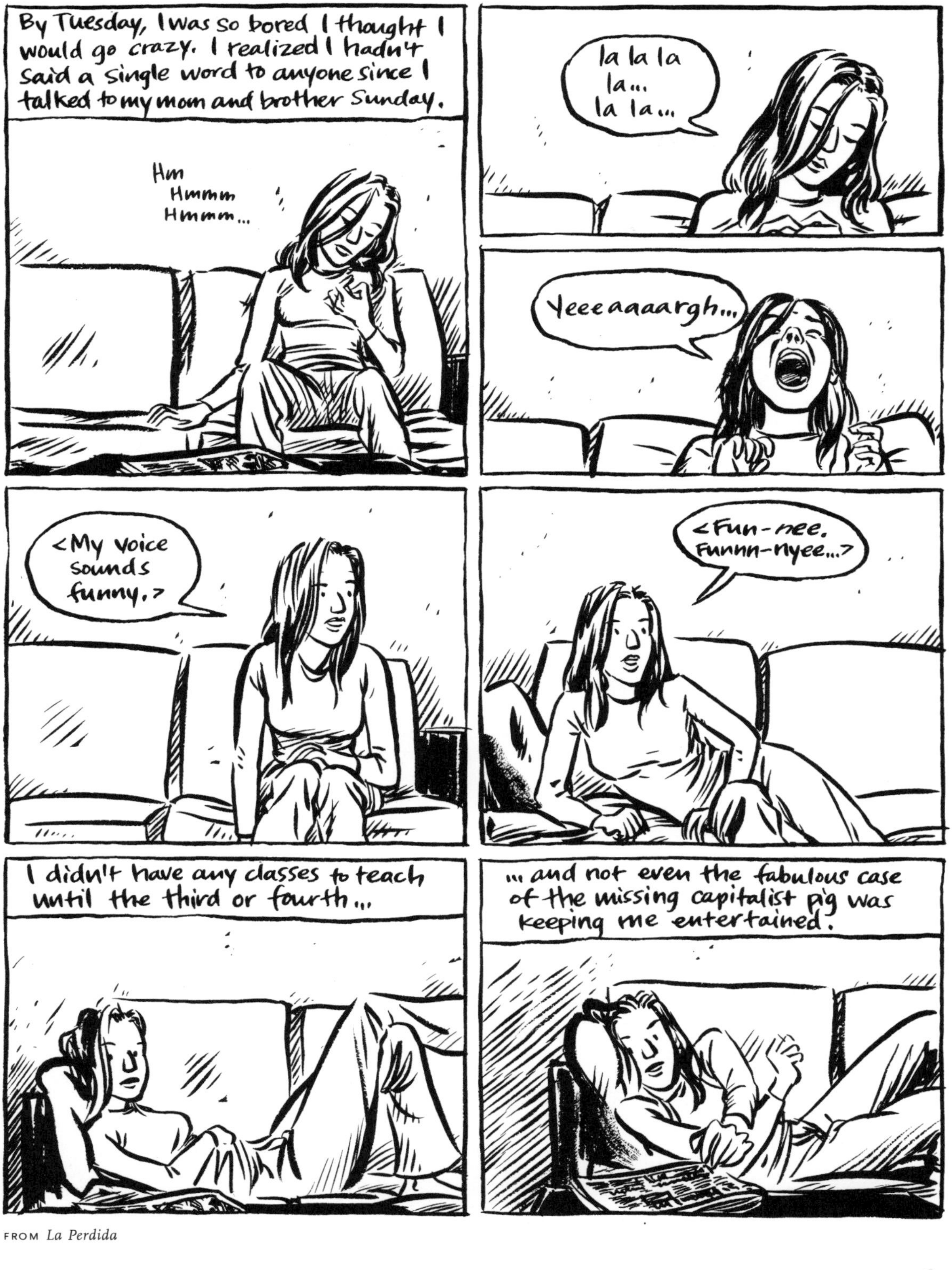
By Tuesday, I was so bored I thought I would go crazy. I realized I hadn't said a single word to anyone since I talked to my mom and brother Sunday.
Hm
Hmmm
Hmmm...
la la la
la...
la la...
Yeeeaaaargh...
<My voice sounds funny.>
<Fun-nee. Funnn-nyee...>
I didn't have any classes to teach until the third or fourth...
...and not even the fabulous case of the missing capitalist pig was keeping me entertained.

FROM *La Perdida*

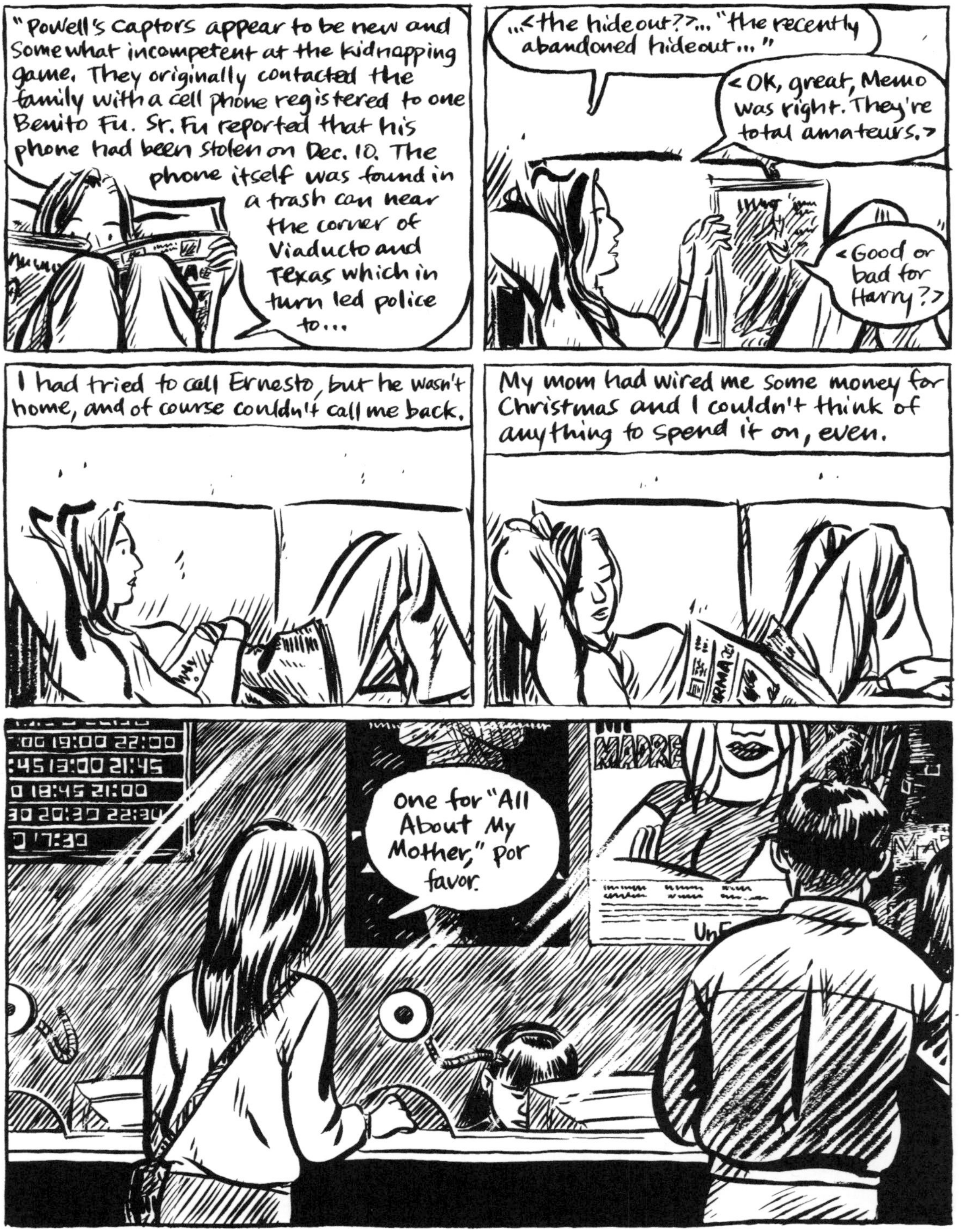
"Powell's captors appear to be new and somewhat incompetent at the kidnapping game. They originally contacted the family with a cell phone registered to one Benito Fu. Sr. Fu reported that his phone had been stolen on Dec. 10. The phone itself was found in a trash can near the corner of Viaducto and Texas which in turn led police to...
...<the hideout?>... "the recently abandoned hideout..."
<OK, great, Memo was right. They're total amateurs.>
<Good or bad for Harry?>
I had tried to call Ernesto, but he wasn't home, and of course couldn't call me back.
My mom had wired me some money for Christmas and I couldn't think of anything to spend it on, even.
One for "All About My Mother," por favor.

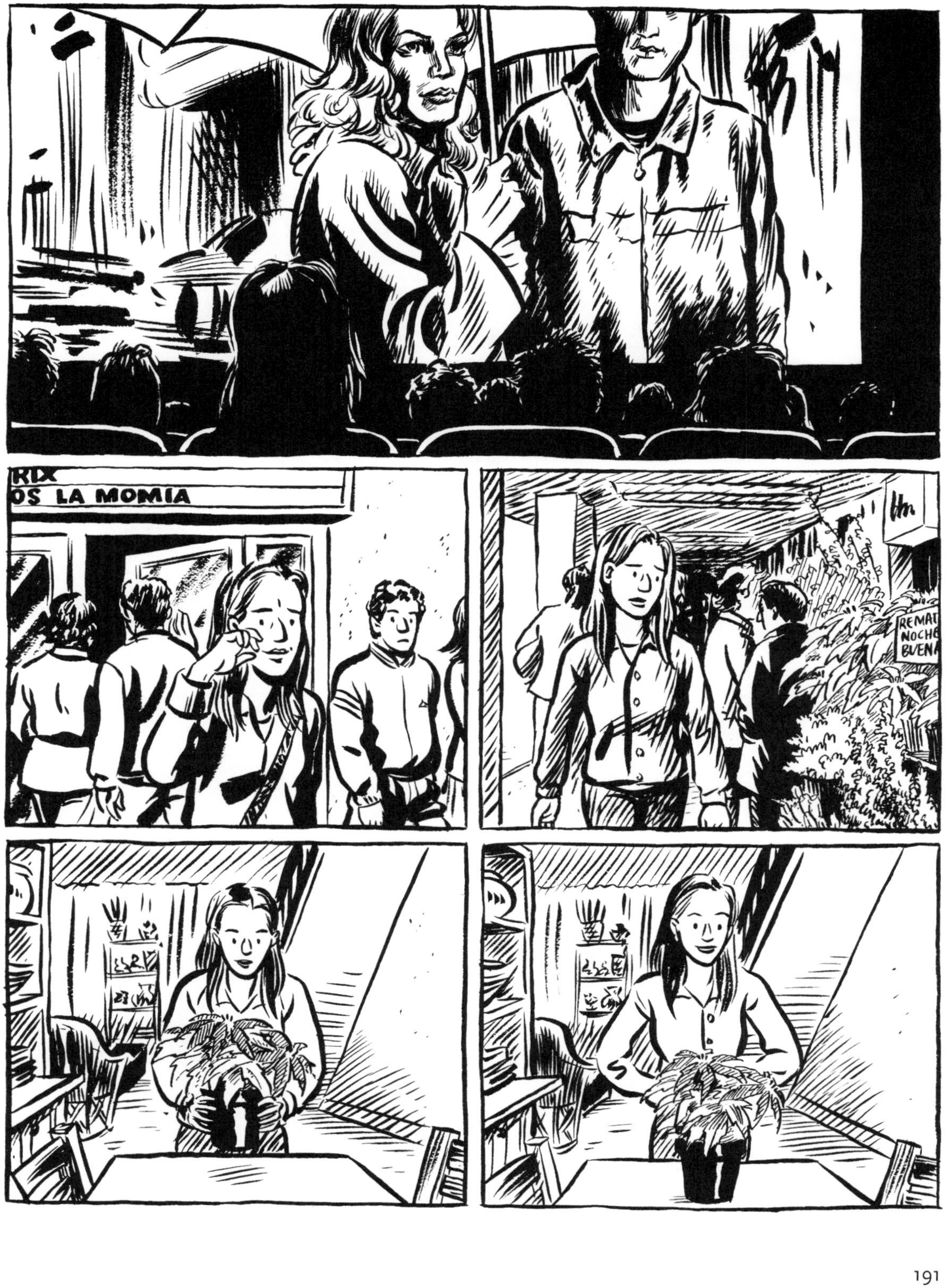
RIX
OS LA MOMIA
REMAT
NOCHE
BUENA

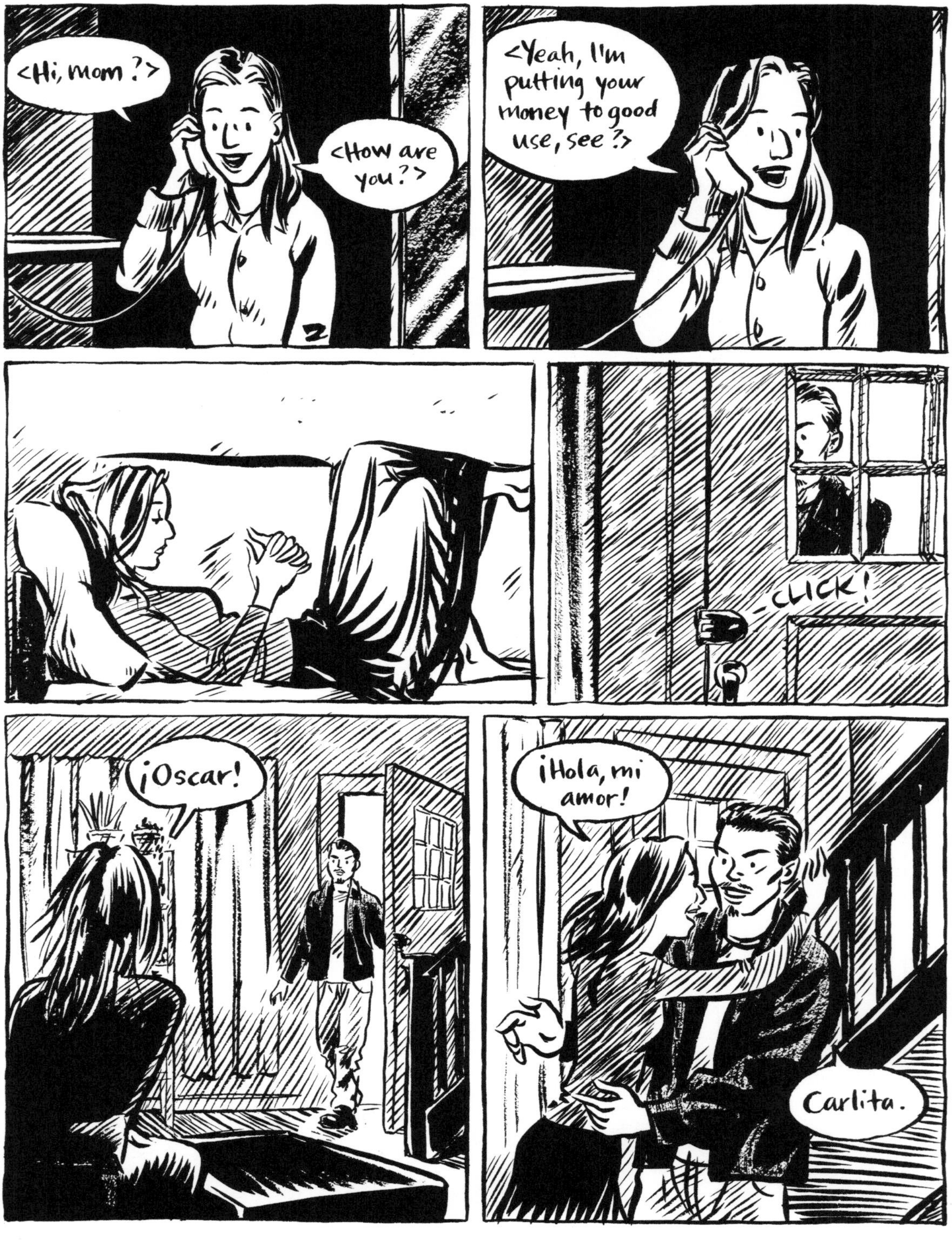
<Hi, mom?>
<How are you?>
<Yeah, I'm putting your money to good use, see?>
CLICK!
¡Oscar!
¡Hola, mi amor!
Carlita.

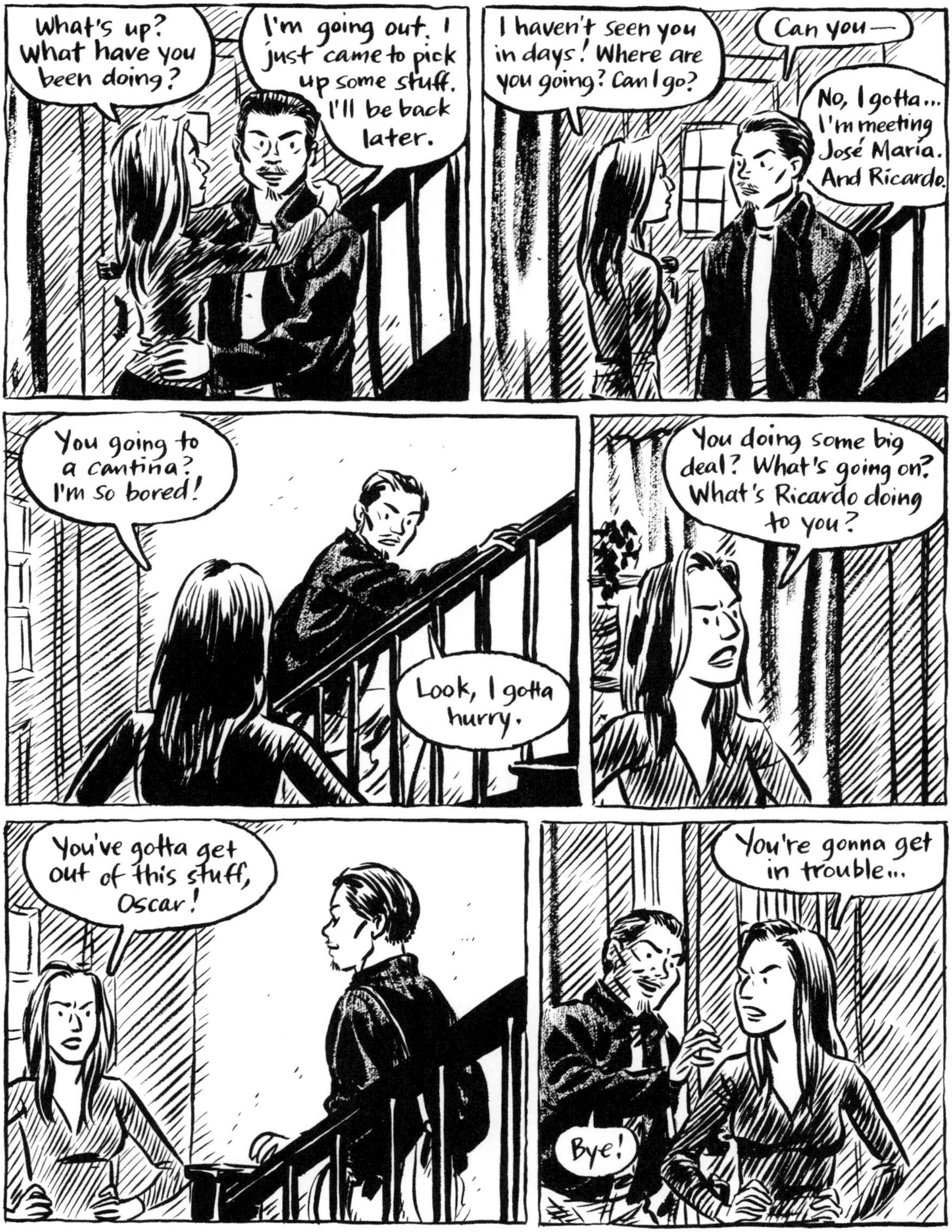
What's up? What have you been doing?
I'm going out. I just came to pick up some stuff. I'll be back later.
I haven't seen you in days! Where are you going? Can I go?
Can you—
No, I gotta... I'm meeting José Maria. And Ricardo.
You going to a cantina? I'm so bored!
Look, I gotta hurry.
You doing some big deal? What's going on? What's Ricardo doing to you?
You've gotta get out of this stuff, Oscar!
You're gonna get in trouble...
Bye!

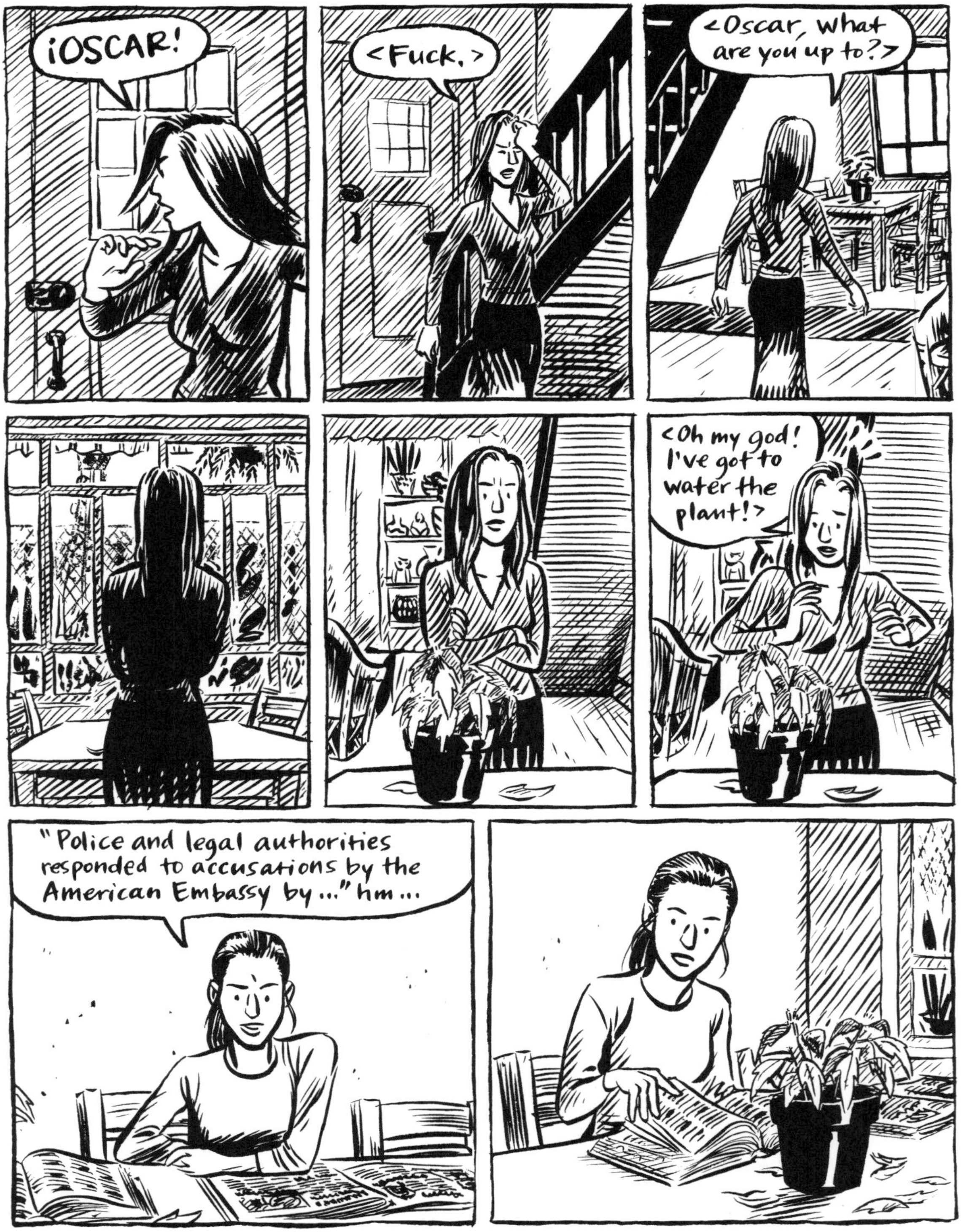
¡OSCAR!
<Fuck.>
<Oscar, what are you up to?>
<Oh my god! I've got to water the plant!>
"Police and legal authorities responded to accusations by the American Embassy by..." hm...

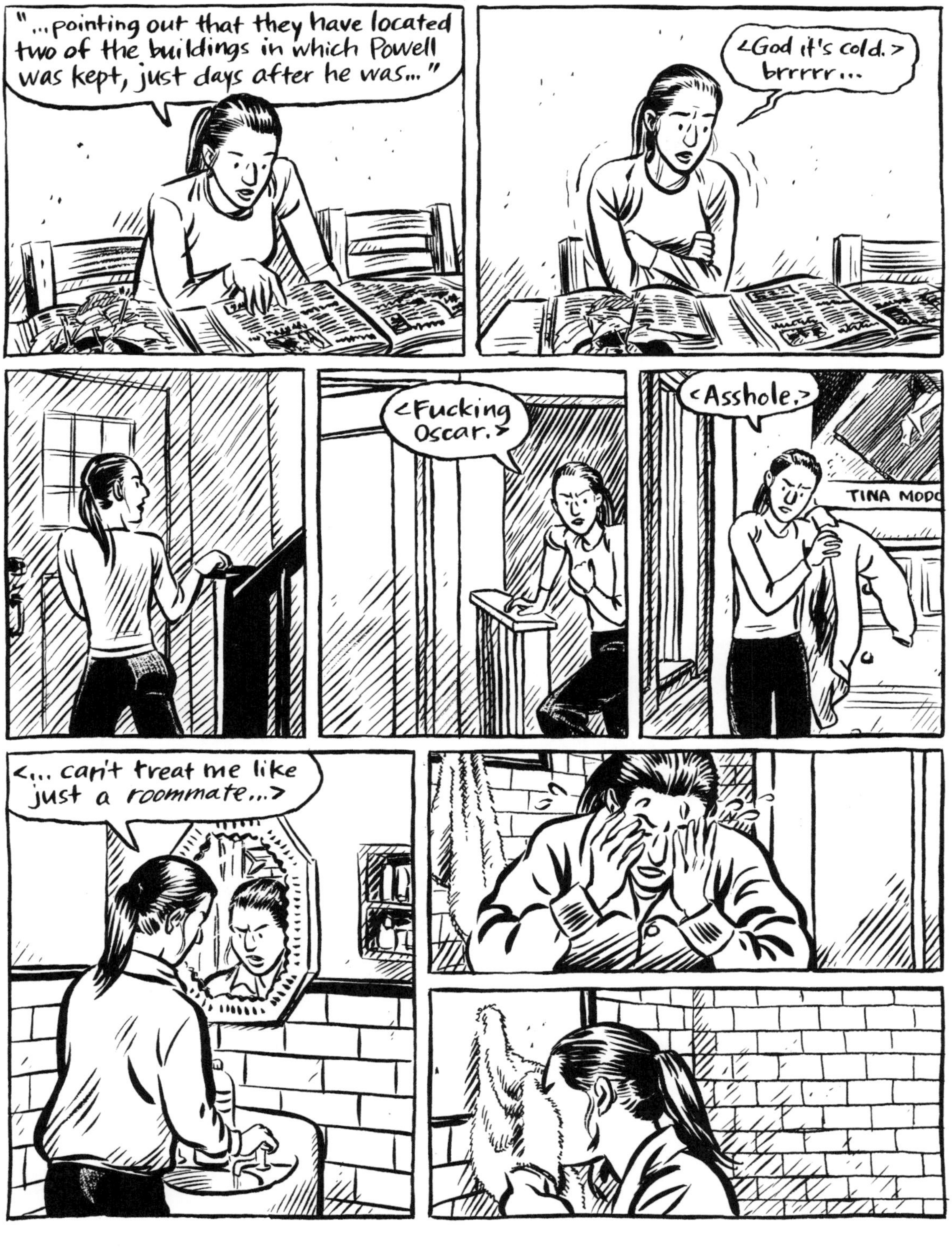
"...pointing out that they have located two of the buildings in which Powell was kept, just days after he was..."
<God it's cold.> brrrrr...
<Fucking Oscar.>
<Asshole.>
TINA MODO
<... can't treat me like just a *roommate*...>

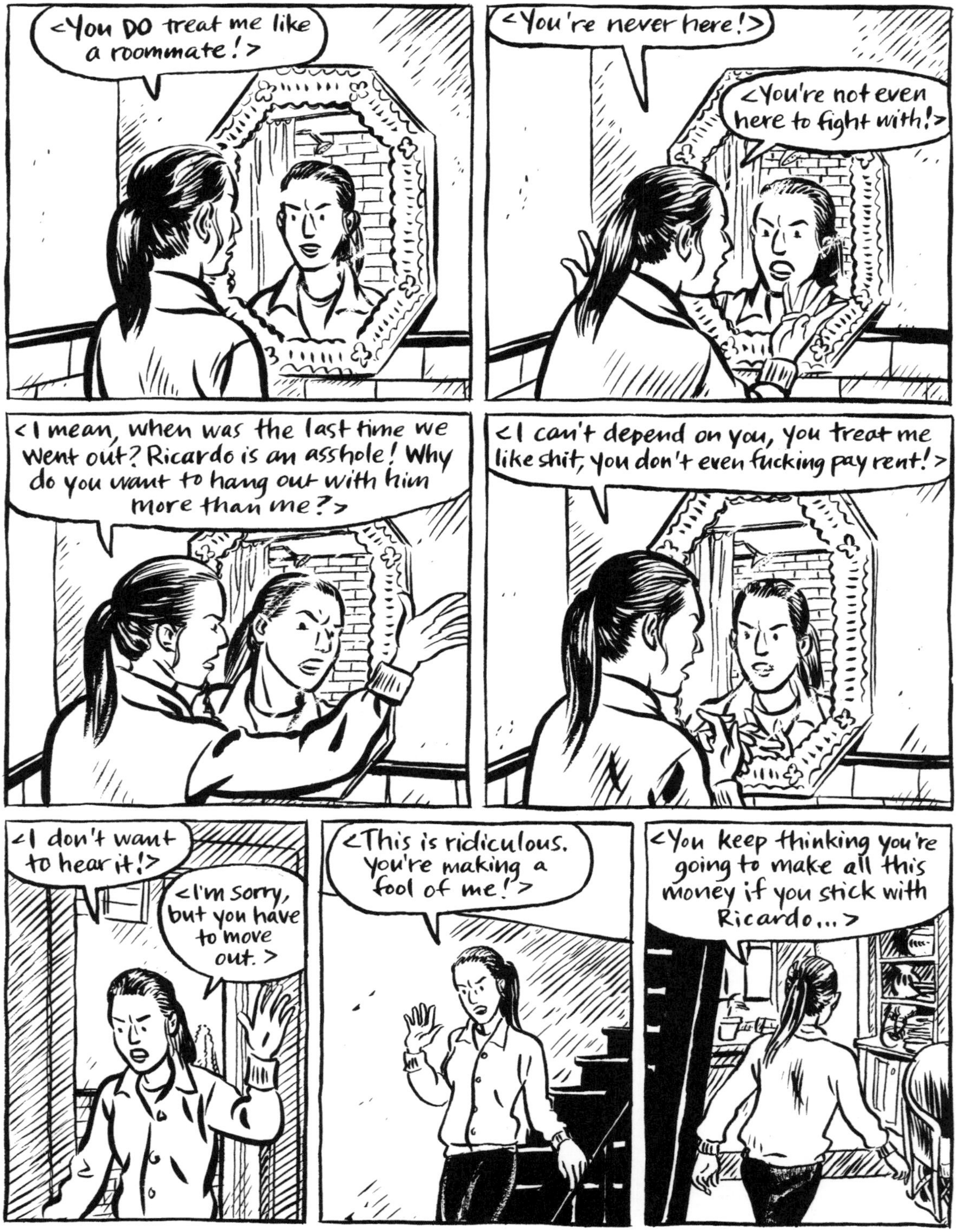
<You DO treat me like a roommate!>
<You're never here!>
<You're not even here to fight with!>
<I mean, when was the last time we went out? Ricardo is an asshole! Why do you want to hang out with him more than me?>
<I can't depend on you, you treat me like shit, you don't even fucking pay rent!>
<I don't want to hear it!>
<I'm sorry, but you have to move out.>
<This is ridiculous. you're making a fool of me!>
<You keep thinking you're going to make all this money if you stick with Ricardo...>

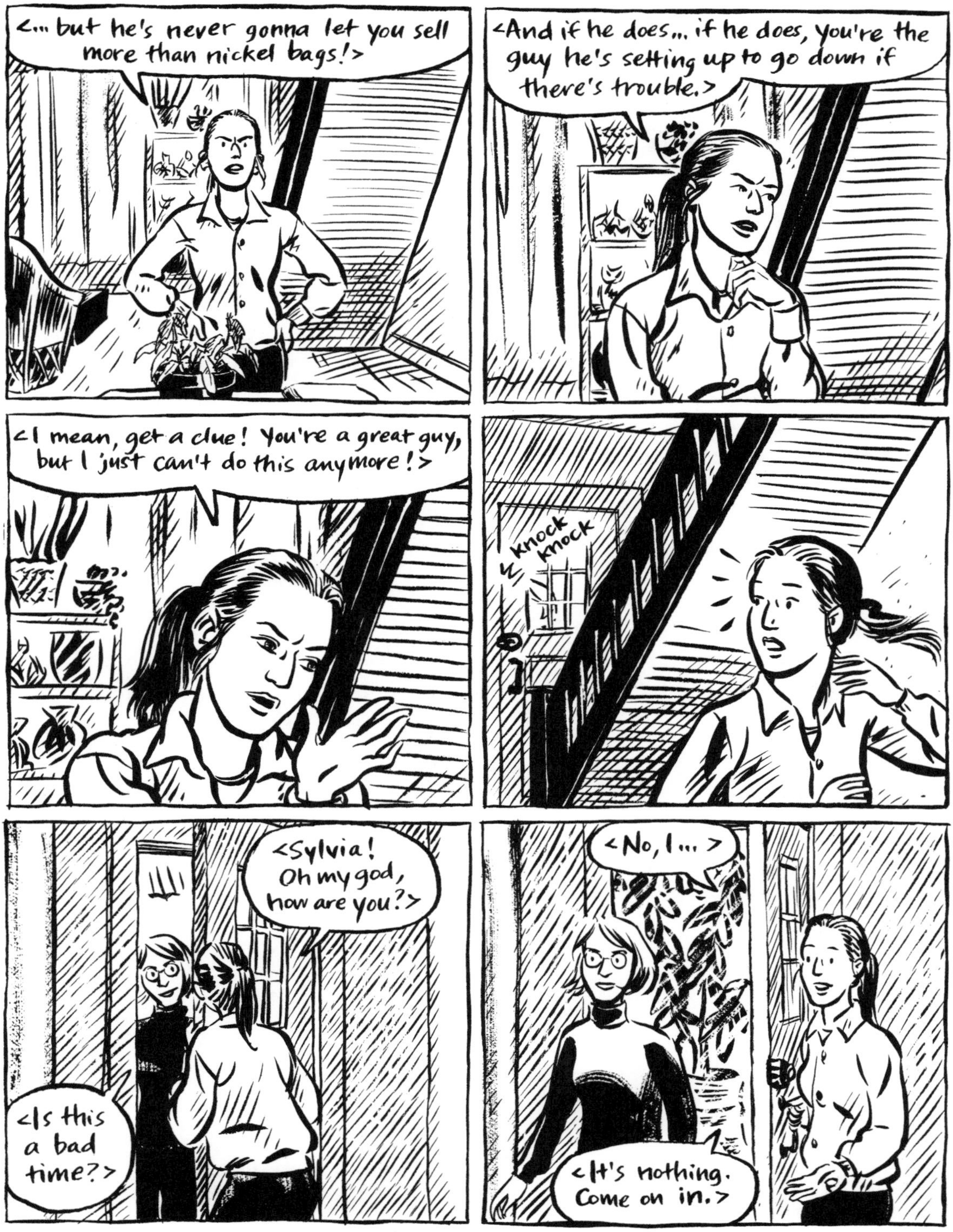
<... but he's never gonna let you sell more than nickel bags!>
<And if he does... if he does, you're the guy he's setting up to go down if there's trouble.>
<I mean, get a clue! You're a great guy, but I just can't do this anymore!>
knock knock
<Sylvia! Oh my god, how are you?>
<Is this a bad time?>
<No, I...>
<It's nothing. Come on in.>

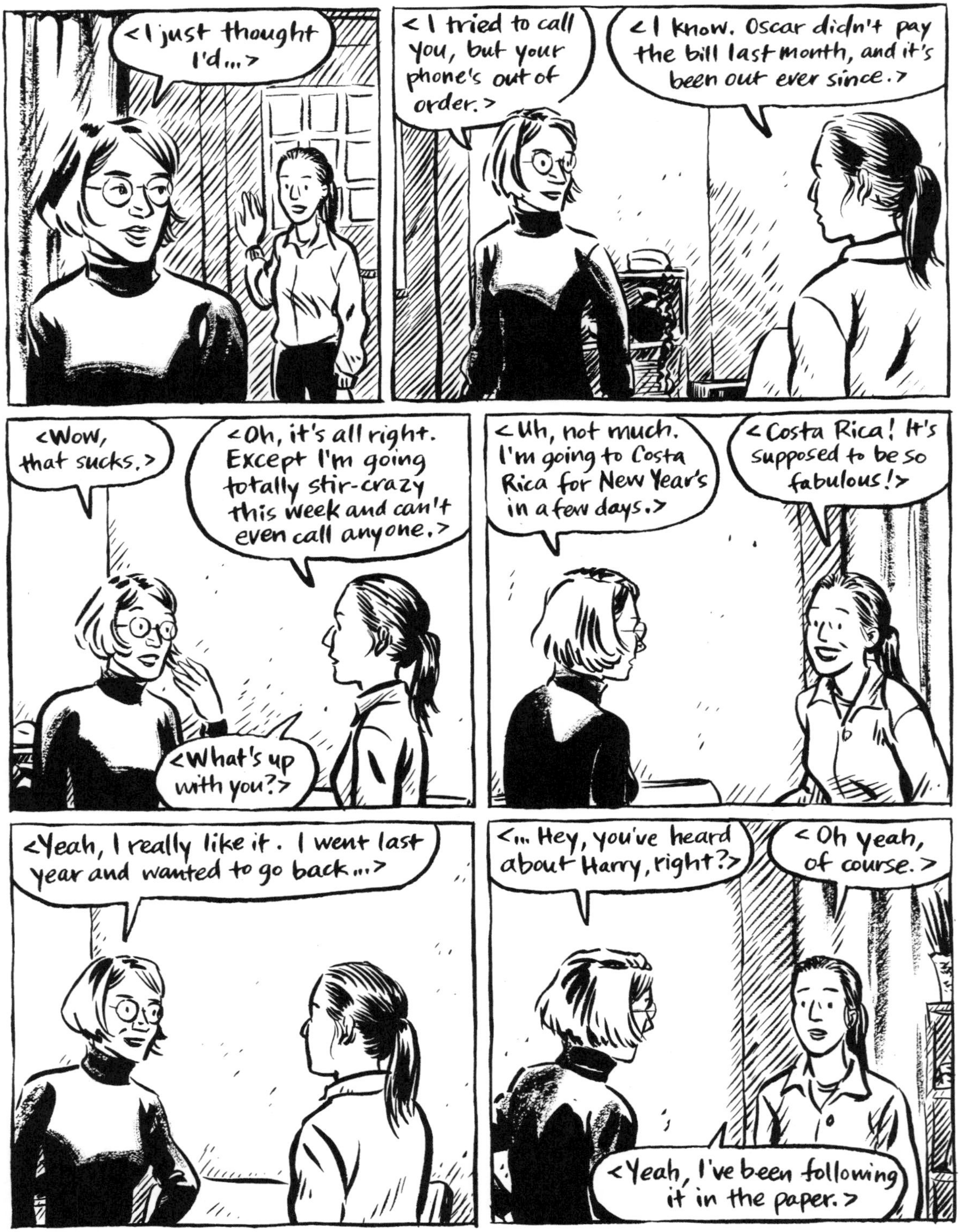
<I just thought I'd...>
<I tried to call you, but your phone's out of order.>
<I know. Oscar didn't pay the bill last month, and it's been out ever since.>
<Wow, that sucks.>
<Oh, it's all right. Except I'm going totally stir-crazy this week and can't even call anyone.>
<What's up with you?>
<Uh, not much. I'm going to Costa Rica for New Year's in a few days.>
<Costa Rica! It's supposed to be so fabulous!>
<Yeah, I really like it. I went last year and wanted to go back...>
<... Hey, you've heard about Harry, right?>
<Oh yeah, of course.>
<Yeah, I've been following it in the paper.>

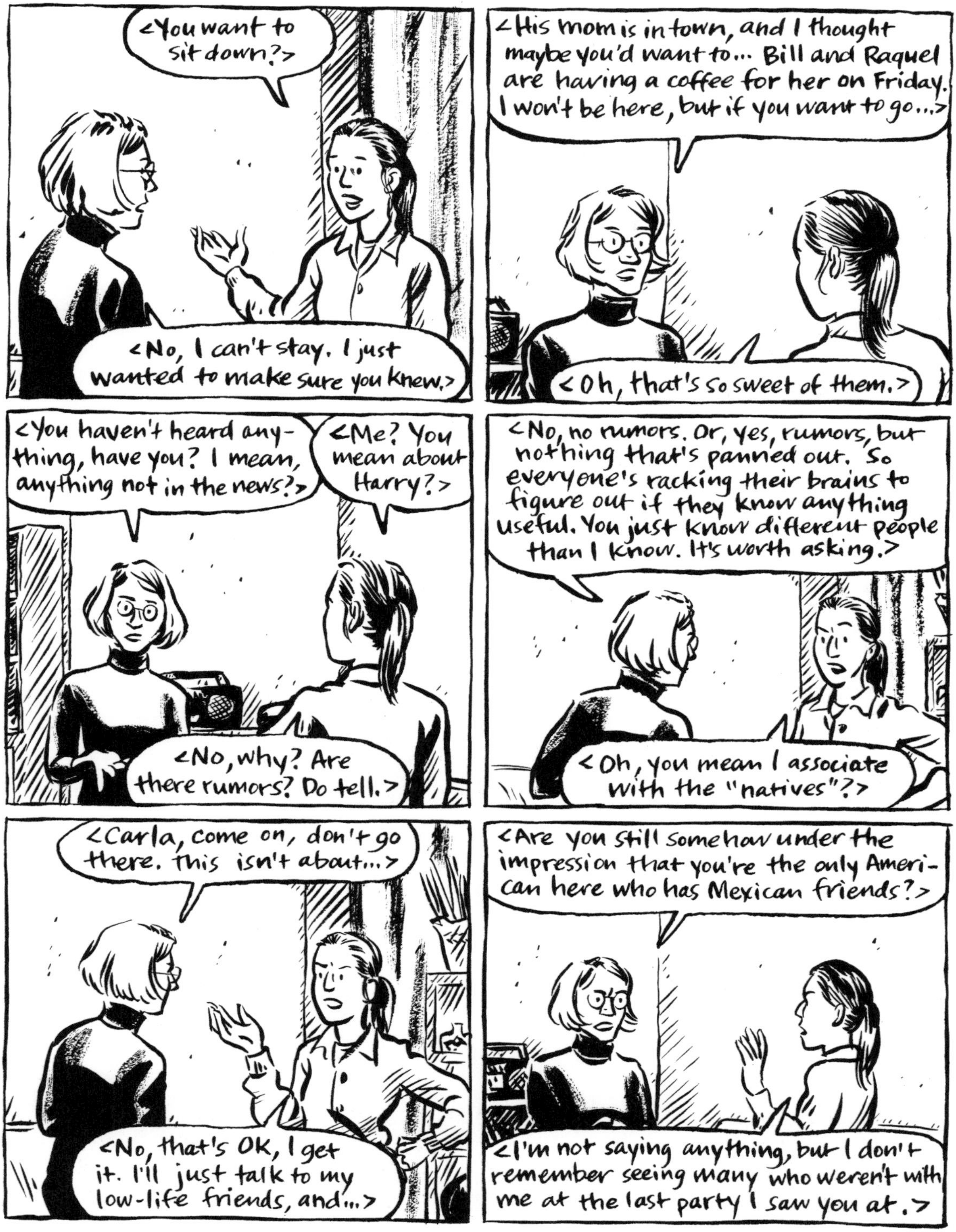
<You want to sit down?>
<No, I can't stay. I just wanted to make sure you knew.>
<His mom is in town, and I thought maybe you'd want to... Bill and Raquel are having a coffee for her on Friday. I won't be here, but if you want to go...>
<Oh, that's so sweet of them.>
<You haven't heard anything, have you? I mean, anything not in the news?>
<Me? You mean about Harry?>
<No, why? Are there rumors? Do tell.>
<No, no rumors. Or, yes, rumors, but nothing that's panned out. So everyone's racking their brains to figure out if they know anything useful. You just know different people than I know. It's worth asking.>
<Oh, you mean I associate with the "natives"?>
<Carla, come on, don't go there. this isn't about...>
<No, that's OK, I get it. I'll just talk to my low-life friends, and...>
<Are you still somehow under the impression that you're the only American here who has Mexican friends?>
<I'm not saying anything, but I don't remember seeing many who weren't with me at the last party I saw you at.>

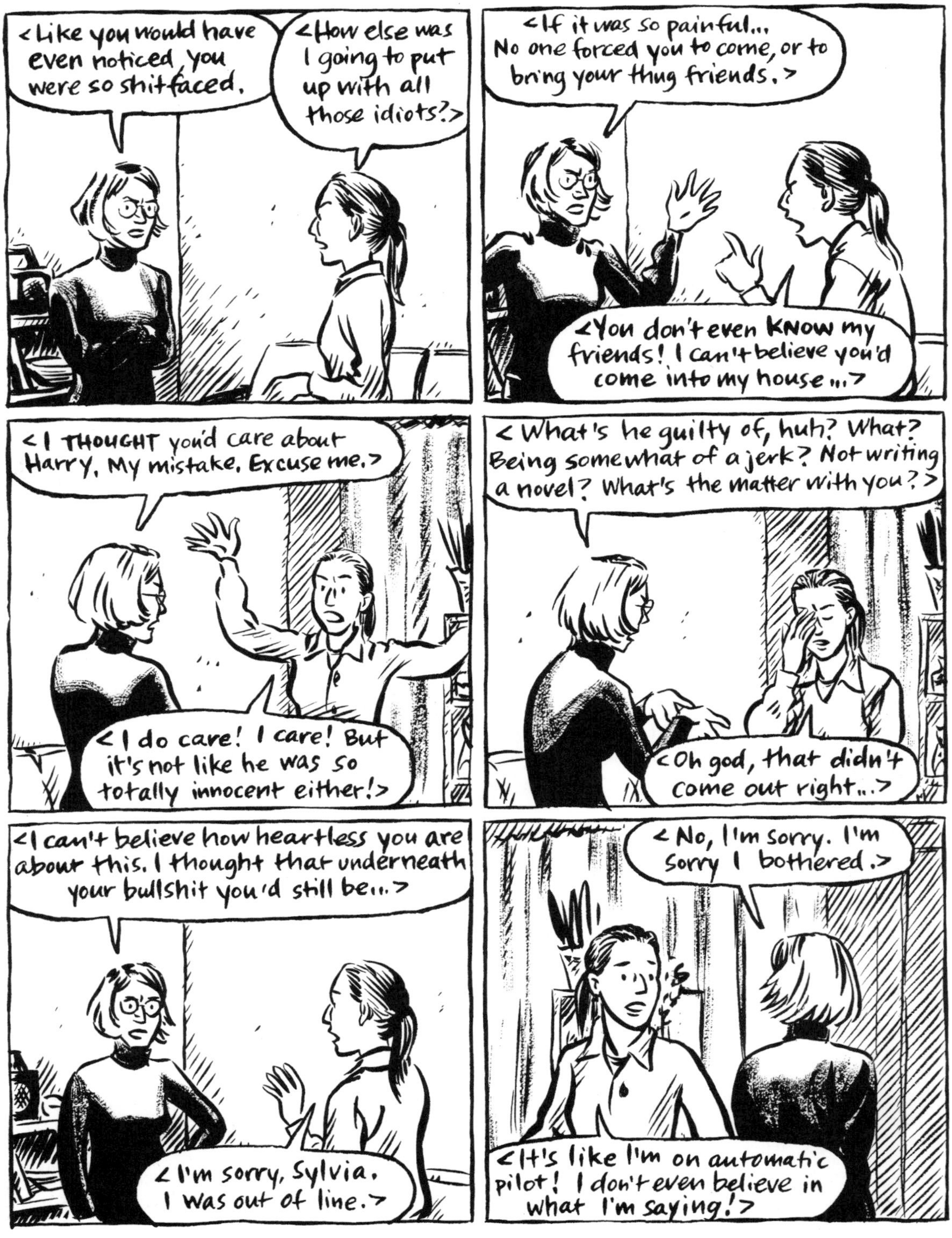
<Like you would have even noticed, you were so shitfaced.
<How else was I going to put up with all those idiots?>
<If it was so painful... No one forced you to come, or to bring your thug friends.>
<You don't even KNOW my friends! I can't believe you'd come into my house...>
<I THOUGHT you'd care about Harry. My mistake. Excuse me.>
<I do care! I care! But it's not like he was so totally innocent either!>
<What's he guilty of, huh? What? Being somewhat of a jerk? Not writing a novel? What's the matter with you?>
<Oh god, that didn't come out right...>
<I can't believe how heartless you are about this. I thought that underneath your bullshit you'd still be...>
<I'm sorry, Sylvia. I was out of line.>
<No, I'm sorry. I'm sorry I bothered.>
<It's like I'm on automatic pilot! I don't even believe in what I'm saying!>

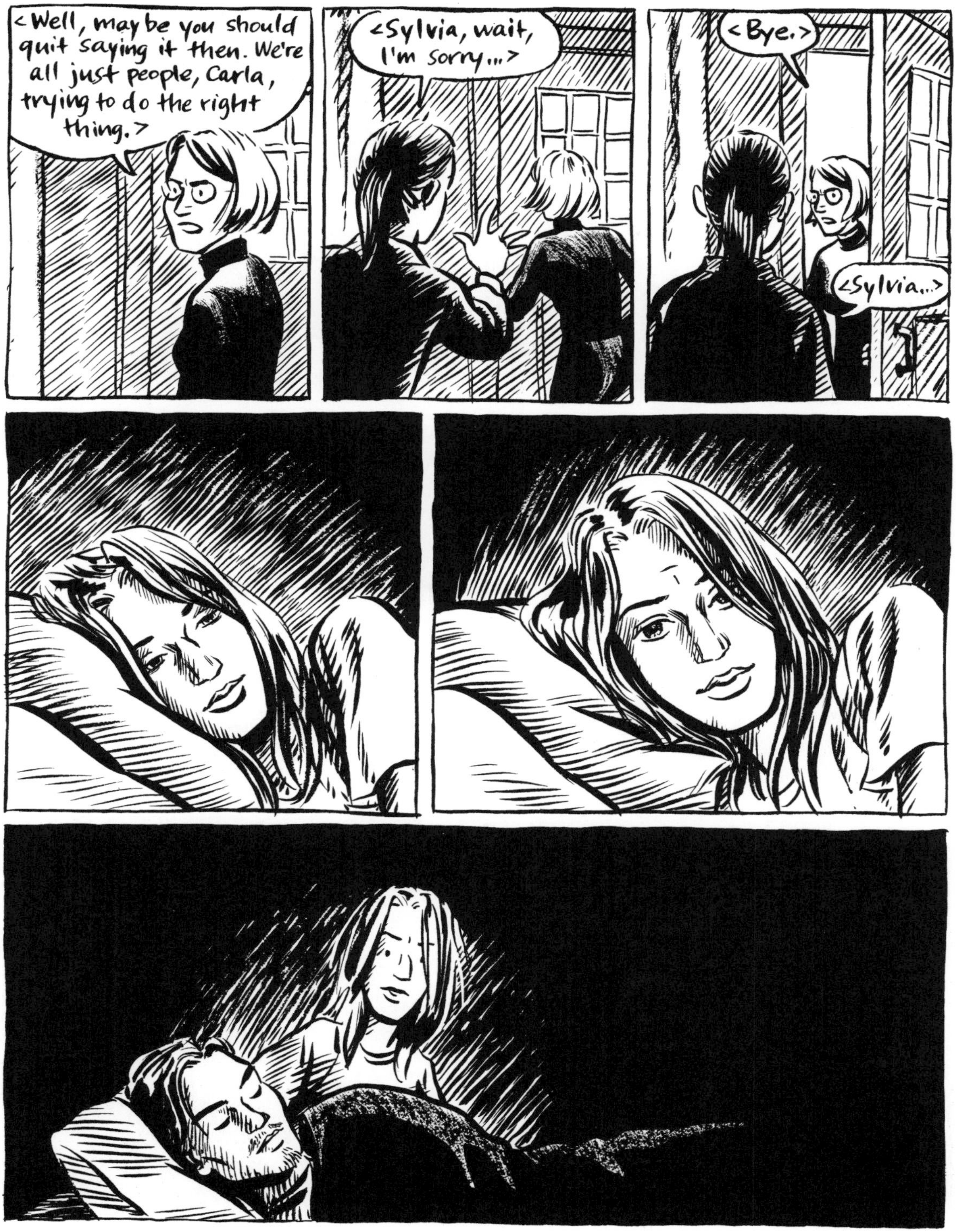
<Well, maybe you should quit saying it then. We're all just people, Carla, trying to do the right thing.>
<Sylvia, wait, I'm sorry...>
<Bye.>
<Sylvia...>

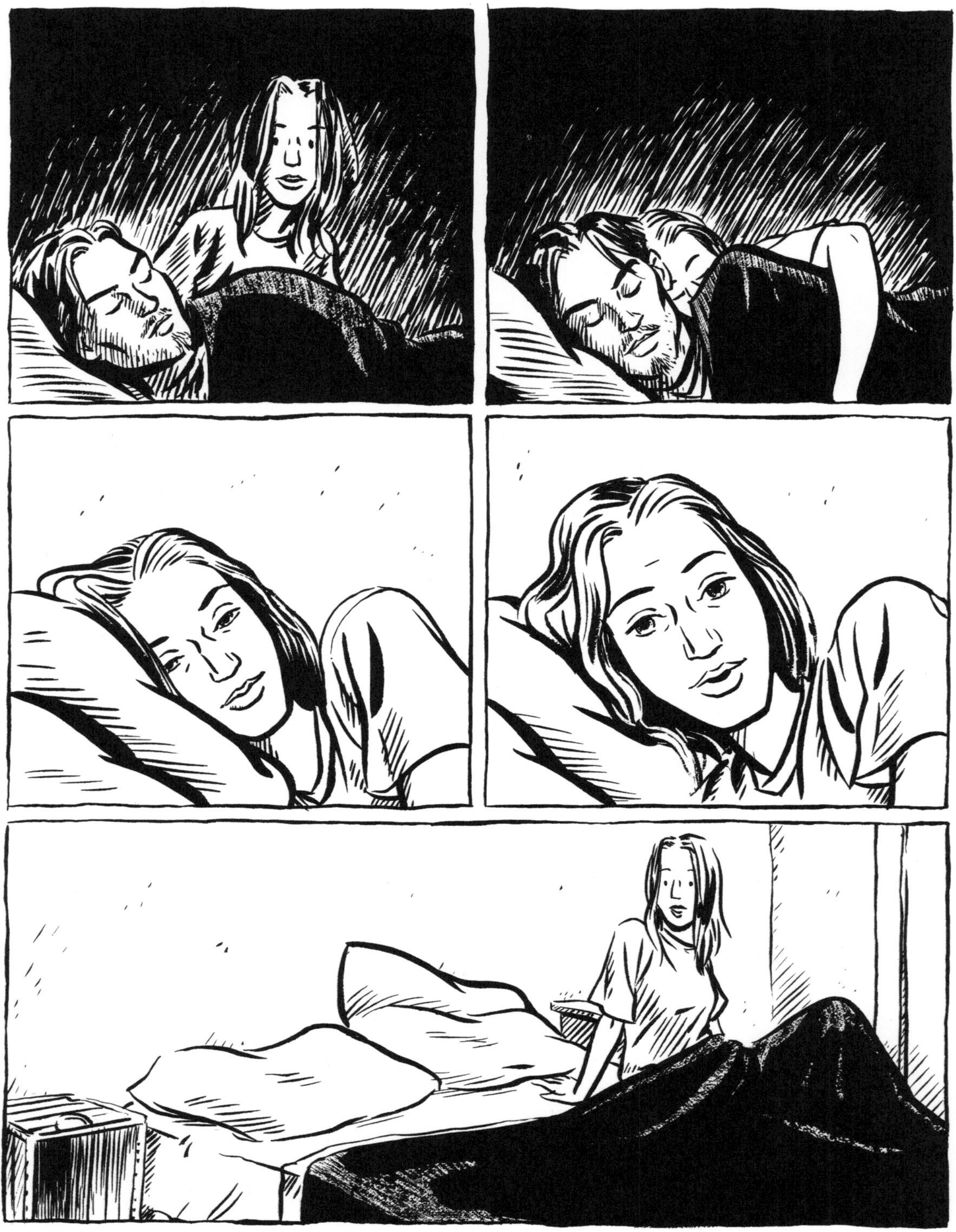

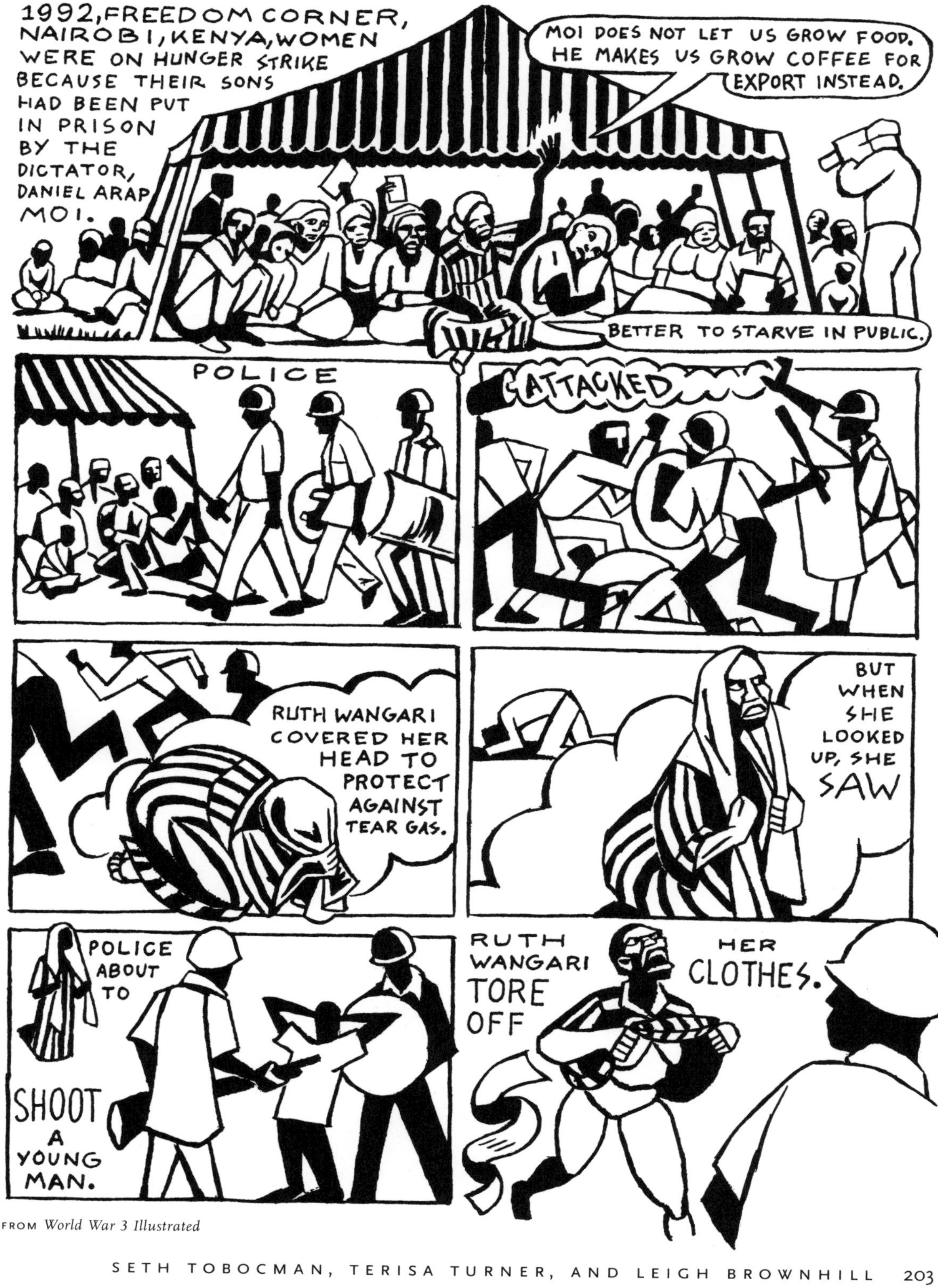
1992, FREEDOM CORNER, NAIROBI, KENYA, WOMEN WERE ON HUNGER STRIKE BECAUSE THEIR SONS HAD BEEN PUT IN PRISON BY THE DICTATOR, DANIEL ARAP MOI.
MOI DOES NOT LET US GROW FOOD. HE MAKES US GROW COFFEE FOR EXPORT INSTEAD.
BETTER TO STARVE IN PUBLIC.
POLICE
ATTACKED
RUTH WANGARI COVERED HER HEAD TO PROTECT AGAINST TEAR GAS.
BUT WHEN SHE LOOKED UP, SHE SAW
POLICE ABOUT TO
SHOOT A YOUNG MAN.
RUTH WANGARI TORE OFF
HER CLOTHES.

FROM *World War 3 Illustrated*

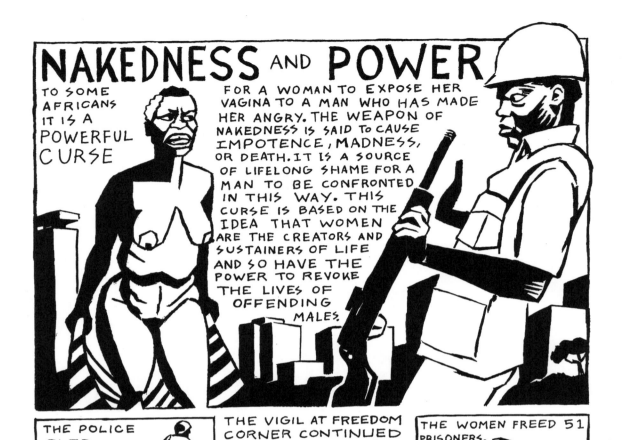

NAKEDNESS AND POWER

TO SOME AFRICANS IT IS A POWERFUL CURSE FOR A WOMAN TO EXPOSE HER VAGINA TO A MAN WHO HAS MADE HER ANGRY. THE WEAPON OF NAKEDNESS IS SAID TO CAUSE IMPOTENCE, MADNESS, OR DEATH. IT IS A SOURCE OF LIFELONG SHAME FOR A MAN TO BE CONFRONTED IN THIS WAY. THIS CURSE IS BASED ON THE IDEA THAT WOMEN ARE THE CREATORS AND SUSTAINERS OF LIFE AND SO HAVE THE POWER TO REVOKE THE LIVES OF OFFENDING MALES.

THE POLICE FLED.

THE VIGIL AT FREEDOM CORNER CONTINUED FOR A WHOLE YEAR.

THE WOMEN FREED 51 PRISONERS.

INSPIRED BY THE ACTION AT FREEDOM CORNER, FARMERS RIPPED OUT COFFEE AND PLANTED FOOD TO FEED THEIR FAMILIES. THE LANDLESS POOR ALSO SEIZED LAND ON WHICH TO GROW FOOD.

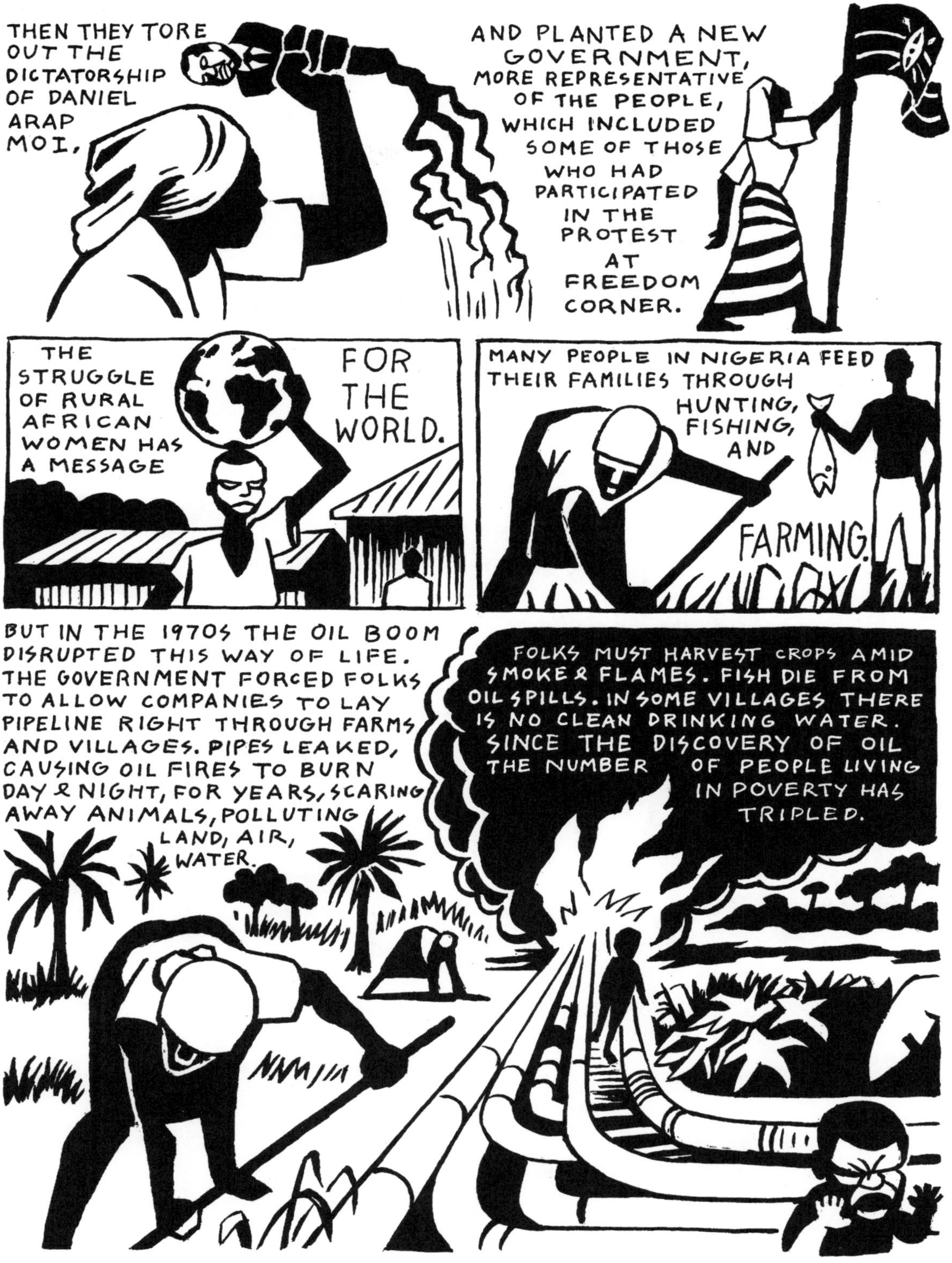
THEN THEY TORE OUT THE DICTATORSHIP OF DANIEL ARAP MOI,
AND PLANTED A NEW GOVERNMENT, MORE REPRESENTATIVE OF THE PEOPLE, WHICH INCLUDED SOME OF THOSE WHO HAD PARTICIPATED IN THE PROTEST AT FREEDOM CORNER.
THE STRUGGLE OF RURAL AFRICAN WOMEN HAS A MESSAGE
FOR THE WORLD.
MANY PEOPLE IN NIGERIA FEED THEIR FAMILIES THROUGH HUNTING, FISHING, AND
FARMING.
BUT IN THE 1970S THE OIL BOOM DISRUPTED THIS WAY OF LIFE. THE GOVERNMENT FORCED FOLKS TO ALLOW COMPANIES TO LAY PIPELINE RIGHT THROUGH FARMS AND VILLAGES. PIPES LEAKED, CAUSING OIL FIRES TO BURN DAY & NIGHT, FOR YEARS, SCARING AWAY ANIMALS, POLLUTING LAND, AIR, WATER.
FOLKS MUST HARVEST CROPS AMID SMOKE & FLAMES. FISH DIE FROM OIL SPILLS. IN SOME VILLAGES THERE IS NO CLEAN DRINKING WATER. SINCE THE DISCOVERY OF OIL THE NUMBER OF PEOPLE LIVING IN POVERTY HAS TRIPLED.

OGONI

FOR YEARS NIGERIANS HAVE RESISTED THESE CONDITIONS.

ON JULY 8th, 2002, 600 WOMEN TOOK OVER THE

CHEVRON TEXACO EXPORT TERMINAL AT ESCRAVOS, NIGERIA.

THE TAKEOVER LASTED 10 DAYS. WOMEN NEGOTIATED 26 DEMANDS WITH CHEVRON.

BUT ONE DEMAND

Chevron

CHEVRON WOULD NOT DISCUSS;

WHEN WE WERE HERE WITHOUT CHEVRON, LIFE WAS NATURAL & SWEET, WE WOULD GO TO THE RIVERS FOR FISHING, THE FORESTS FOR HUNTING. BUT TODAY THE EXPERIENCE IS SAD. I AM SUGGESTING THEY SHOULD LEAVE OUR COMMUNITY COMPLETELY AND NEVER COME BACK.

WOMEN ROSE UP ALL OVER THE NIGER DELTA, TAKING 12 OIL FACILITIES, THREATENING TO USE THE CURSE OF NAKEDNESS.

THEY SHUT DOWN 40% OF NIGERIA'S OIL PRODUCTION.

IT COST THE NIGERIAN STATE $11 MILLION AND THE COMPANIES $2.5 MILLION PER DAY.

IN RETALIATION, OIL COMPANY SECURITY GUARDS RAPED DOZENS OF WOMEN DURING A PROTEST AT AN OIL COMPANY HEADQUARTERS.

THE WOMEN HELD A PRESS CONFERENCE TO DEMAND REPARATIONS FOR THE RAPES, THREATENING TO USE THE CURSE OF NAKEDNESS.

WE HAVE DECIDED TO DIE AT CHEVRON'S GATE INSTEAD OF SLOWLY FROM OIL SPILLS.

SOME WOMEN IN THE U.S. & EUROPE HEARD ABOUT THE NIGERIAN WOMEN.

THEY SAW:

THAT THE SAME OIL COMPANIES THAT WERE POLLUTING NIGERIA WERE POLLUTING THE WHOLE WORLD.

THEY SAW THAT AN OIL MAN WAS TAKING AMERICA TO WAR IN IRAQ.

THEY ORGANIZED A BOYCOTT

CHEVRON TEXACO

BUT THEY DID MORE:

FROM SAN FRANCISO TO SOUTH AMERICA, WOMEN TOOK OFF THEIR CLOTHES TO PROTEST AGAINST THE COMING WAR IN IRAQ, PAINTING SYMBOLS OF PEACE ON THE HILLSIDES WITH THEIR BODIES.

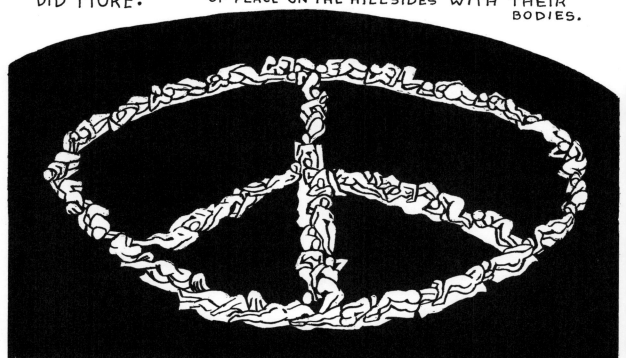

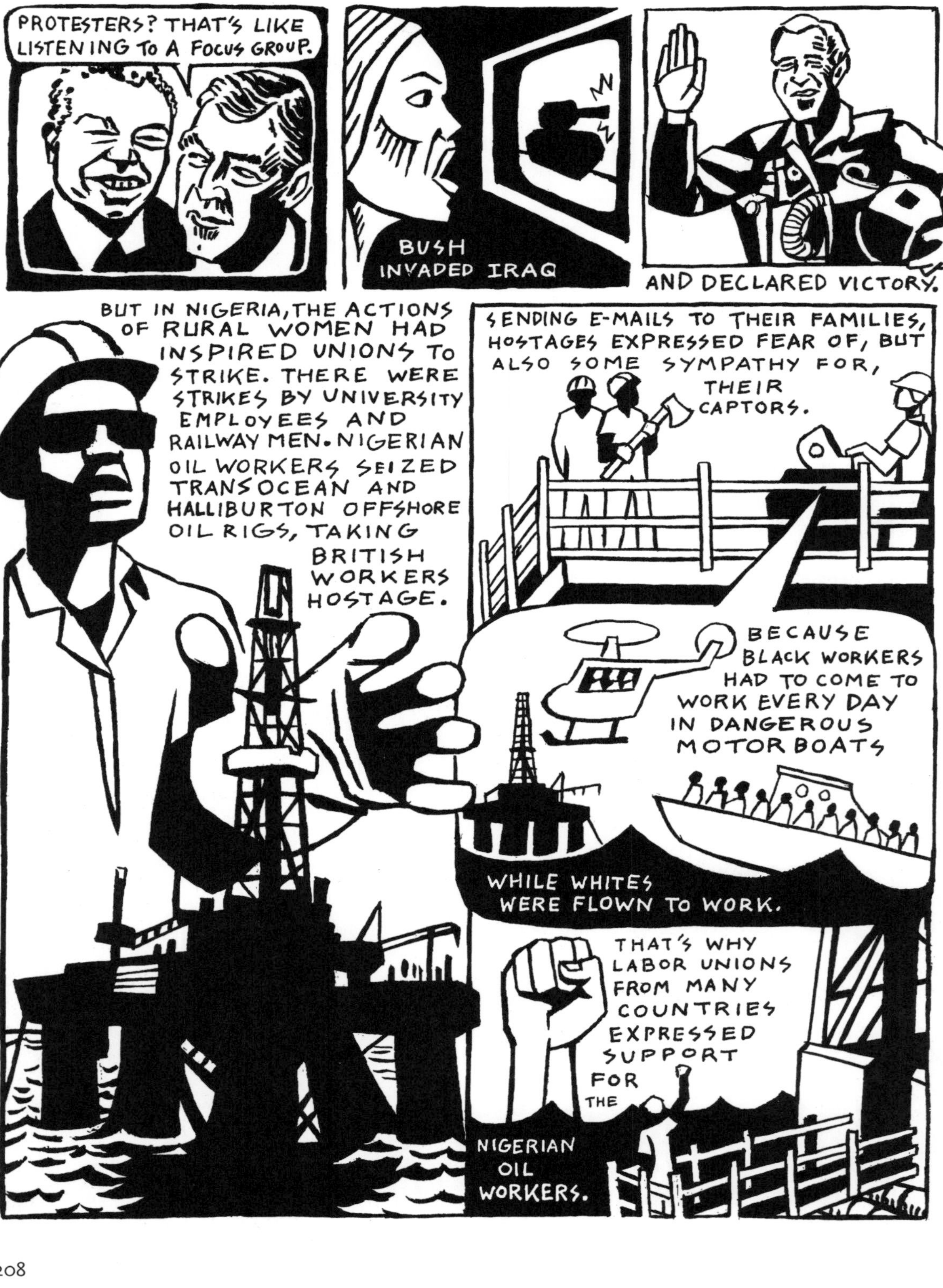
PROTESTERS? THAT'S LIKE LISTENING TO A FOCUS GROUP.
BUSH INVADED IRAQ
AND DECLARED VICTORY.
BUT IN NIGERIA, THE ACTIONS OF RURAL WOMEN HAD INSPIRED UNIONS TO STRIKE. THERE WERE STRIKES BY UNIVERSITY EMPLOYEES AND RAILWAY MEN. NIGERIAN OIL WORKERS SEIZED TRANSOCEAN AND HALLIBURTON OFFSHORE OIL RIGS, TAKING BRITISH WORKERS HOSTAGE.
SENDING E-MAILS TO THEIR FAMILIES, HOSTAGES EXPRESSED FEAR OF, BUT ALSO SOME SYMPATHY FOR, THEIR CAPTORS.
BECAUSE BLACK WORKERS HAD TO COME TO WORK EVERY DAY IN DANGEROUS MOTORBOATS
WHILE WHITES WERE FLOWN TO WORK.
THAT'S WHY LABOR UNIONS FROM MANY COUNTRIES EXPRESSED SUPPORT FOR THE
NIGERIAN OIL WORKERS.

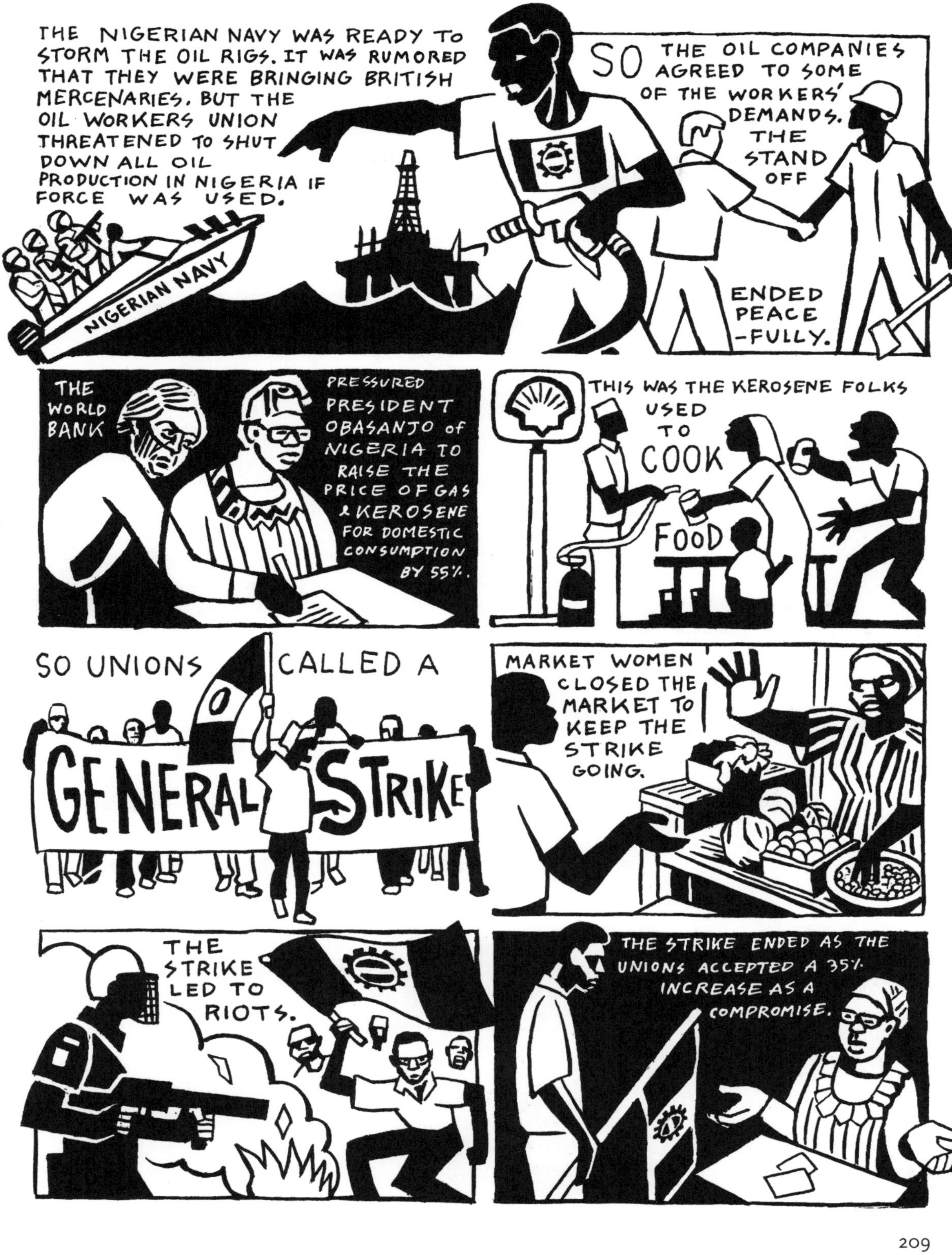

THE NIGERIAN NAVY WAS READY TO STORM THE OIL RIGS. IT WAS RUMORED THAT THEY WERE BRINGING BRITISH MERCENARIES. BUT THE OIL WORKERS UNION THREATENED TO SHUT DOWN ALL OIL PRODUCTION IN NIGERIA IF FORCE WAS USED.
NIGERIAN NAVY
SO THE OIL COMPANIES AGREED TO SOME OF THE WORKERS' DEMANDS. THE STAND OFF
ENDED PEACE-FULLY.
THE WORLD BANK
PRESSURED PRESIDENT OBASANJO of NIGERIA TO RAISE THE PRICE OF GAS & KEROSENE FOR DOMESTIC CONSUMPTION BY 55%.
THIS WAS THE KEROSENE FOLKS USED TO
COOK
FOOD
SO UNIONS CALLED A
GENERAL STRIKE
MARKET WOMEN CLOSED THE MARKET TO KEEP THE STRIKE GOING.
THE STRIKE LED TO RIOTS.
THE STRIKE ENDED AS THE UNIONS ACCEPTED A 35% INCREASE AS A COMPROMISE.

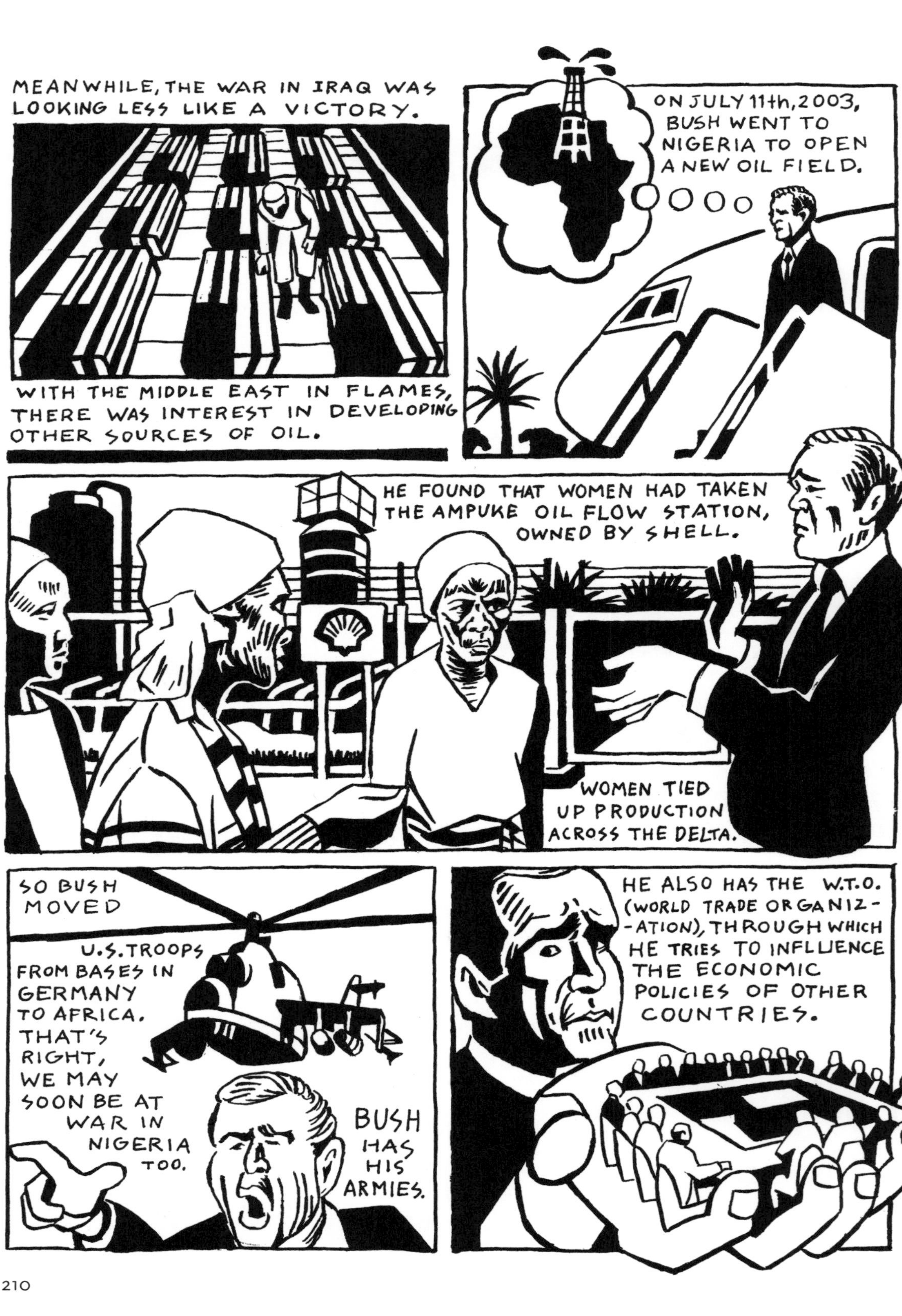
MEANWHILE, THE WAR IN IRAQ WAS LOOKING LESS LIKE A VICTORY.
WITH THE MIDDLE EAST IN FLAMES, THERE WAS INTEREST IN DEVELOPING OTHER SOURCES OF OIL.
ON JULY 11th, 2003, BUSH WENT TO NIGERIA TO OPEN A NEW OIL FIELD.
HE FOUND THAT WOMEN HAD TAKEN THE AMPUKE OIL FLOW STATION, OWNED BY SHELL.
WOMEN TIED UP PRODUCTION ACROSS THE DELTA.
SO BUSH MOVED
U.S. TROOPS FROM BASES IN GERMANY TO AFRICA. THAT'S RIGHT, WE MAY SOON BE AT WAR IN NIGERIA TOO.
BUSH HAS HIS ARMIES.
HE ALSO HAS THE W.T.O. (WORLD TRADE ORGANIZ--ATION), THROUGH WHICH HE TRIES TO INFLUENCE THE ECONOMIC POLICIES OF OTHER COUNTRIES.

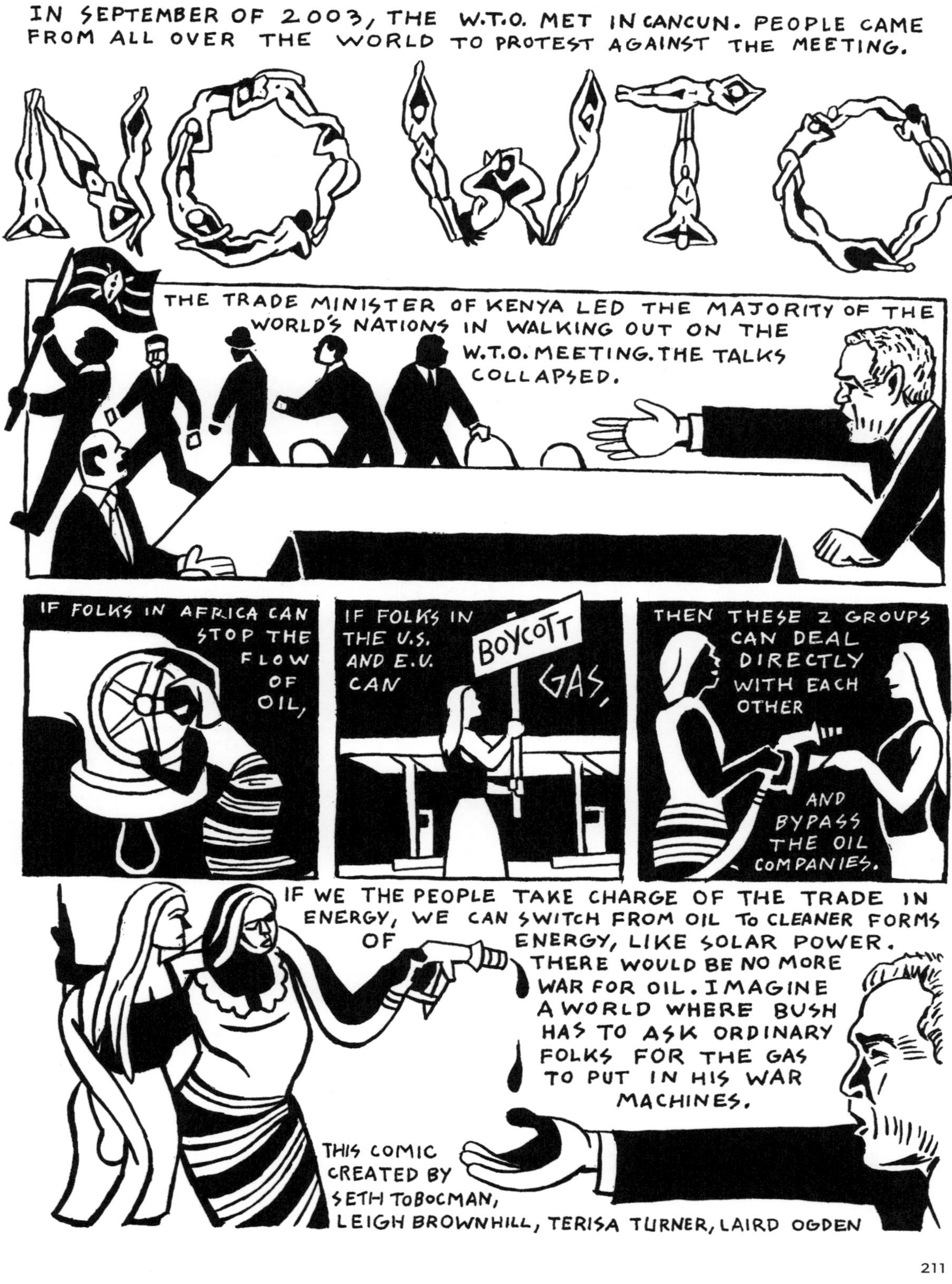

IN SEPTEMBER OF 2003, THE W.T.O. MET IN CANCUN. PEOPLE CAME FROM ALL OVER THE WORLD TO PROTEST AGAINST THE MEETING.
NO WTO
THE TRADE MINISTER OF KENYA LED THE MAJORITY OF THE WORLD'S NATIONS IN WALKING OUT ON THE W.T.O. MEETING. THE TALKS COLLAPSED.
IF FOLKS IN AFRICA CAN STOP THE FLOW OF OIL,
IF FOLKS IN THE U.S. AND E.U. CAN
BOYCOTT
GAS,
THEN THESE 2 GROUPS CAN DEAL DIRECTLY WITH EACH OTHER
AND BYPASS THE OIL COMPANIES.
IF WE THE PEOPLE TAKE CHARGE OF THE TRADE IN ENERGY, WE CAN SWITCH FROM OIL TO CLEANER FORMS OF ENERGY, LIKE SOLAR POWER. THERE WOULD BE NO MORE WAR FOR OIL. IMAGINE A WORLD WHERE BUSH HAS TO ASK ORDINARY FOLKS FOR THE GAS TO PUT IN HIS WAR MACHINES.
THIS COMIC CREATED BY SETH TOBOCMAN, LEIGH BROWNHILL, TERISA TURNER, LAIRD OGDEN

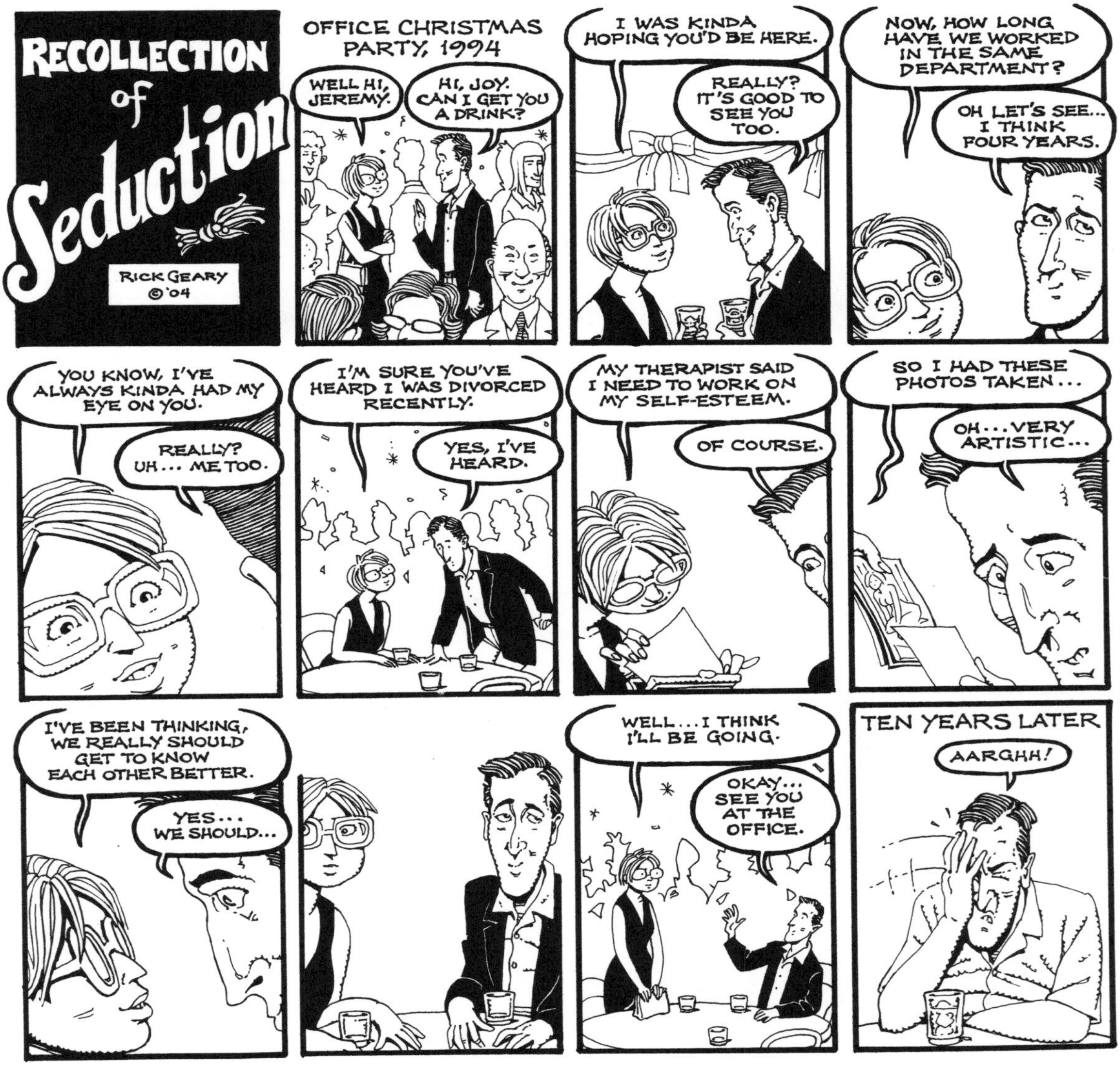
RECOLLECTION of Seduction
RICK GEARY ©'04
OFFICE CHRISTMAS PARTY, 1994
WELL HI, JEREMY.
HI, JOY. CAN I GET YOU A DRINK?
I WAS KINDA HOPING YOU'D BE HERE.
REALLY? IT'S GOOD TO SEE YOU TOO.
NOW, HOW LONG HAVE WE WORKED IN THE SAME DEPARTMENT?
OH LET'S SEE... I THINK FOUR YEARS.
YOU KNOW, I'VE ALWAYS KINDA HAD MY EYE ON YOU.
REALLY? UH... ME TOO.
I'M SURE YOU'VE HEARD I WAS DIVORCED RECENTLY.
YES, I'VE HEARD.
MY THERAPIST SAID I NEED TO WORK ON MY SELF-ESTEEM.
OF COURSE.
SO I HAD THESE PHOTOS TAKEN...
OH... VERY ARTISTIC...
I'VE BEEN THINKING, WE REALLY SHOULD GET TO KNOW EACH OTHER BETTER.
YES... WE SHOULD...
WELL... I THINK I'LL BE GOING.
OKAY... SEE YOU AT THE OFFICE.
TEN YEARS LATER
AARGHH!

FROM *The Comics Journal Special Edition*

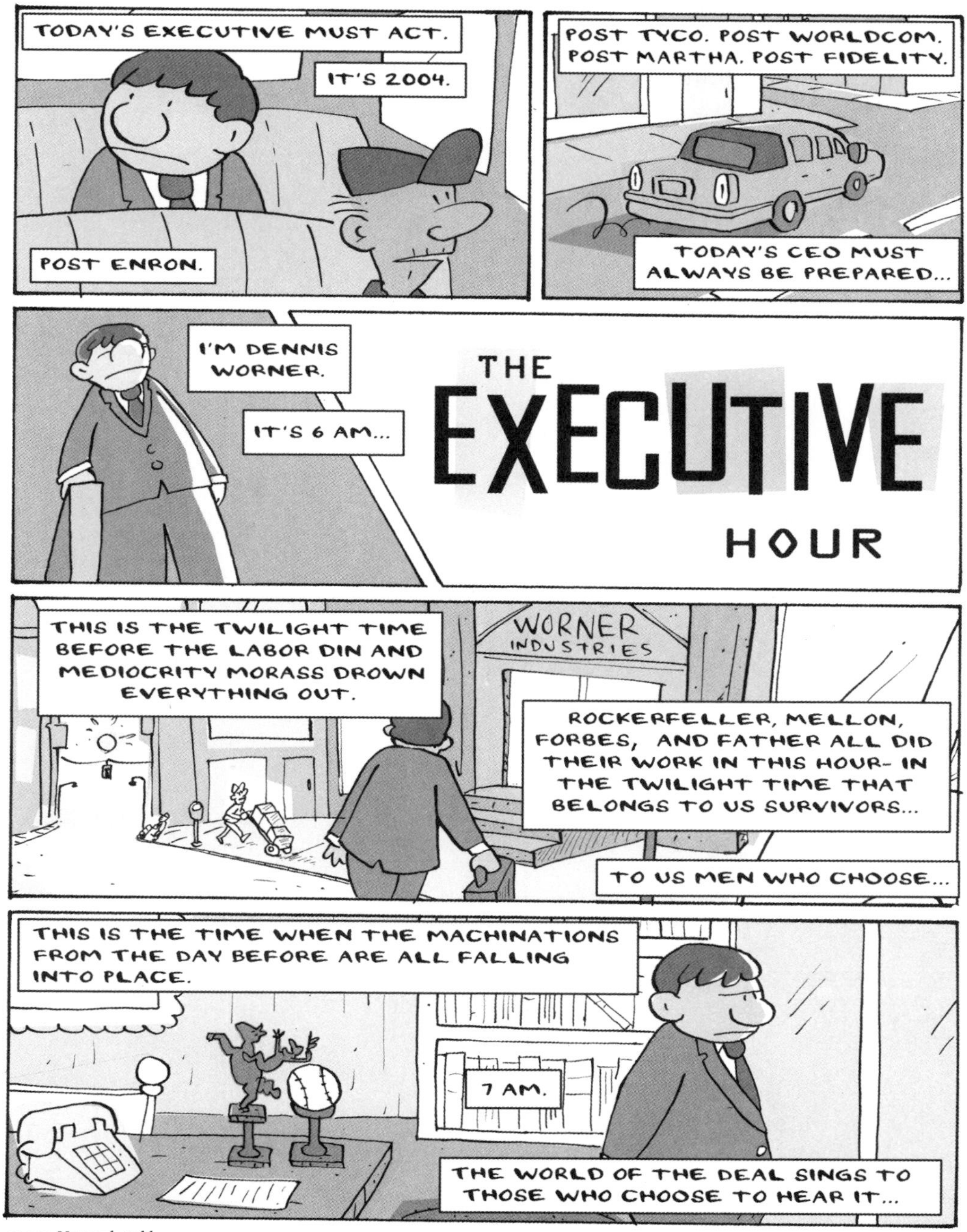
TODAY'S EXECUTIVE MUST ACT.
IT'S 2004.
POST ENRON.
POST TYCO. POST WORLDCOM. POST MARTHA. POST FIDELITY.
TODAY'S CEO MUST ALWAYS BE PREPARED...
I'M DENNIS WORNER.
IT'S 6 AM...
THE EXECUTIVE HOUR
THIS IS THE TWILIGHT TIME BEFORE THE LABOR DIN AND MEDIOCRITY MORASS DROWN EVERYTHING OUT.
WORNER INDUSTRIES
ROCKERFELLER, MELLON, FORBES, AND FATHER ALL DID THEIR WORK IN THIS HOUR- IN THE TWILIGHT TIME THAT BELONGS TO US SURVIVORS...
TO US MEN WHO CHOOSE...
THIS IS THE TIME WHEN THE MACHINATIONS FROM THE DAY BEFORE ARE ALL FALLING INTO PLACE.
7 AM.
THE WORLD OF THE DEAL SINGS TO THOSE WHO CHOOSE TO HEAR IT...

FROM *Unmarketable*

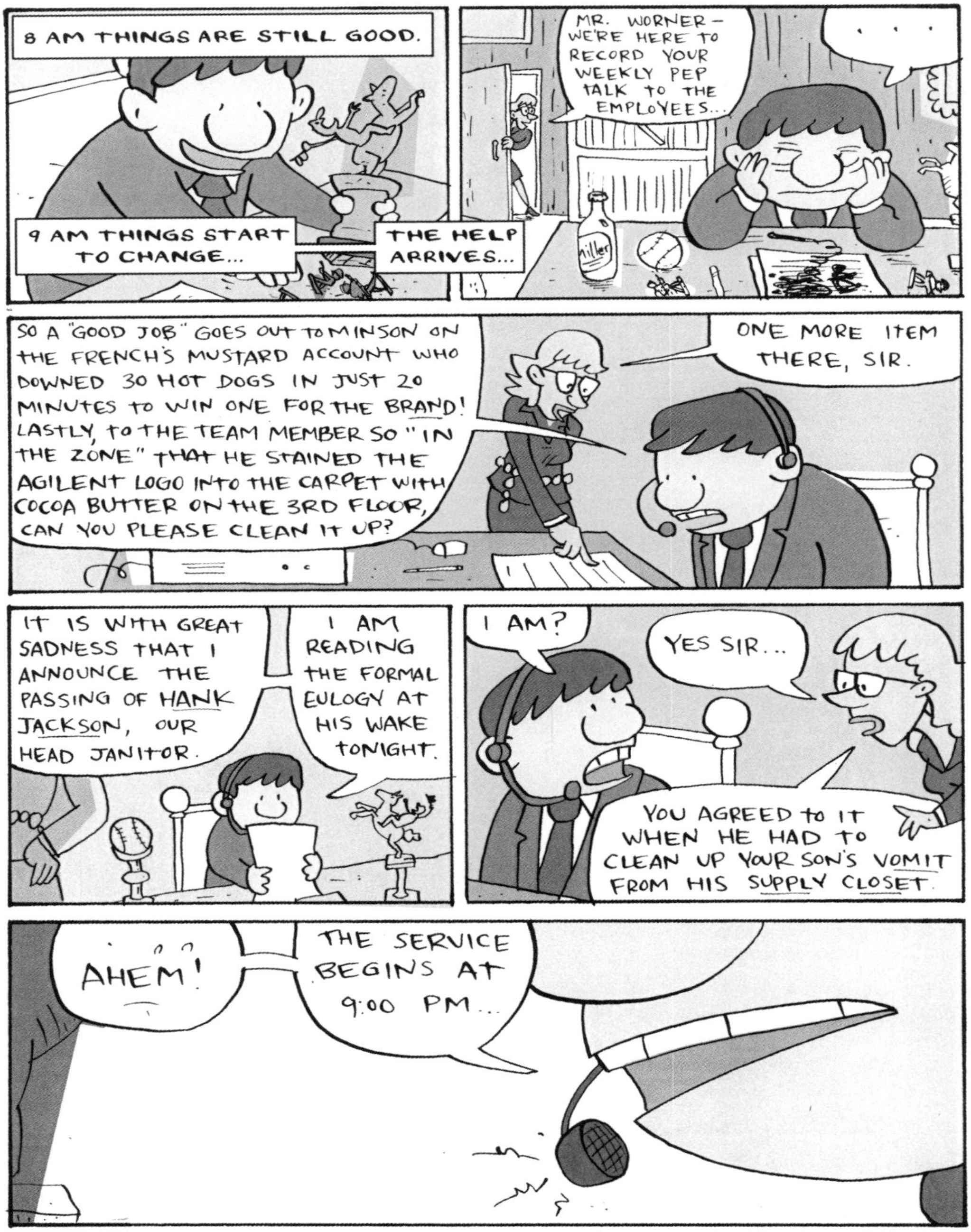
8 AM THINGS ARE STILL GOOD.
9 AM THINGS START TO CHANGE...
THE HELP ARRIVES...
MR. WORNER— WE'RE HERE TO RECORD YOUR WEEKLY PEP TALK TO THE EMPLOYEES...
. . .
Miller
SO A "GOOD JOB" GOES OUT TO MINSON ON THE FRENCH'S MUSTARD ACCOUNT WHO DOWNED 30 HOT DOGS IN JUST 20 MINUTES TO WIN ONE FOR THE BRAND! LASTLY, TO THE TEAM MEMBER SO "IN THE ZONE" THAT HE STAINED THE AGILENT LOGO INTO THE CARPET WITH COCOA BUTTER ON THE 3RD FLOOR, CAN YOU PLEASE CLEAN IT UP?
ONE MORE ITEM THERE, SIR.
IT IS WITH GREAT SADNESS THAT I ANNOUNCE THE PASSING OF HANK JACKSON, OUR HEAD JANITOR.
I AM READING THE FORMAL EULOGY AT HIS WAKE TONIGHT.
I AM?
YES SIR...
YOU AGREED TO IT WHEN HE HAD TO CLEAN UP YOUR SON'S VOMIT FROM HIS SUPPLY CLOSET.
AHEM!
THE SERVICE BEGINS AT 9:00 PM...

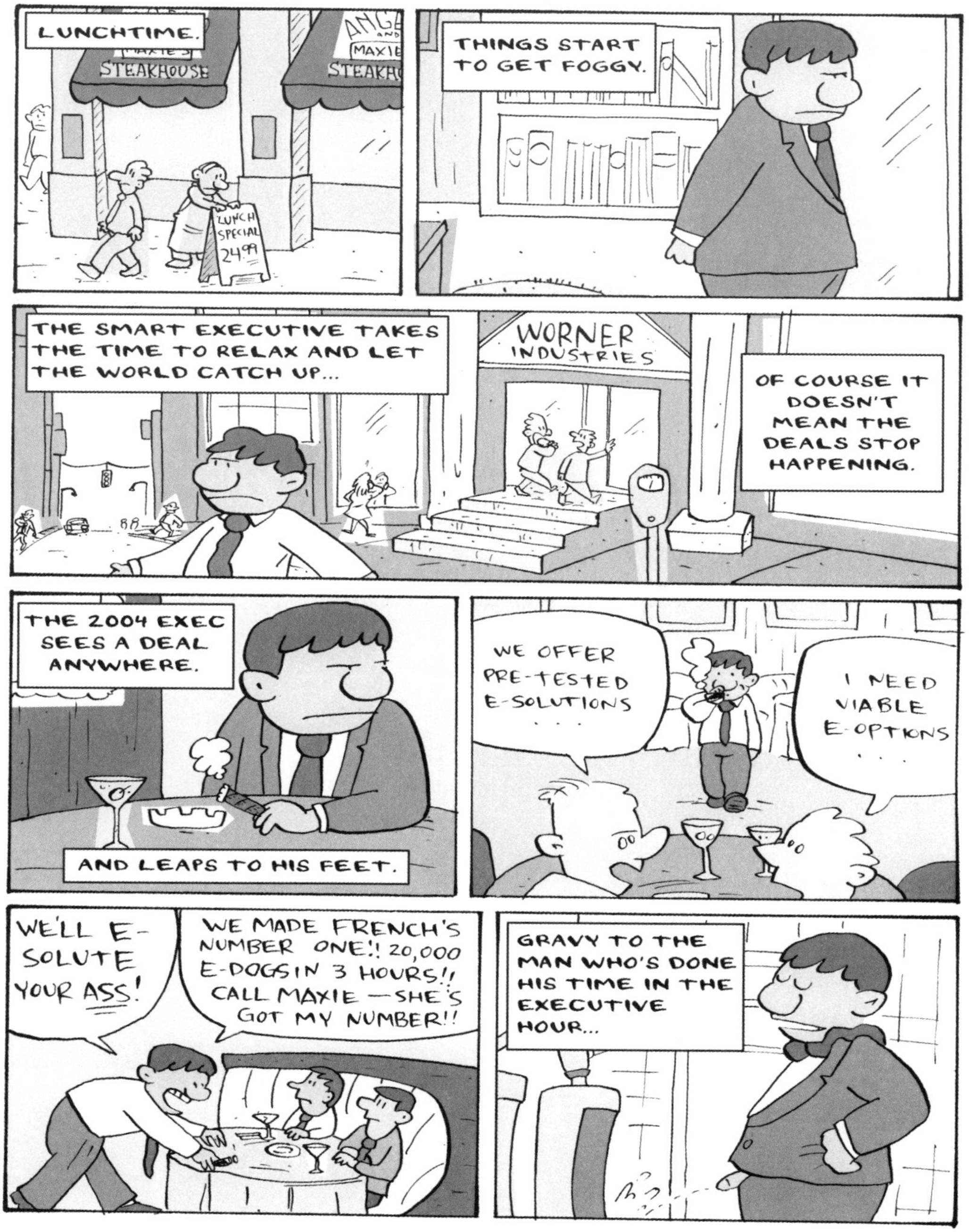
LUNCHTIME.
ANGELO AND MAXIE'S STEAKHOUSE
LUNCH SPECIAL 24.99
THINGS START TO GET FOGGY.
THE SMART EXECUTIVE TAKES THE TIME TO RELAX AND LET THE WORLD CATCH UP...
WORNER INDUSTRIES
OF COURSE IT DOESN'T MEAN THE DEALS STOP HAPPENING.
THE 2004 EXEC SEES A DEAL ANYWHERE.
AND LEAPS TO HIS FEET.
WE OFFER PRE-TESTED E-SOLUTIONS . . .
I NEED VIABLE E-OPTIONS . . .
WE'LL E-SOLUTE YOUR ASS!
WE MADE FRENCH'S NUMBER ONE!! 20,000 E-DOGS IN 3 HOURS!! CALL MAXIE — SHE'S GOT MY NUMBER!!
GRAVY TO THE MAN WHO'S DONE HIS TIME IN THE EXECUTIVE HOUR...

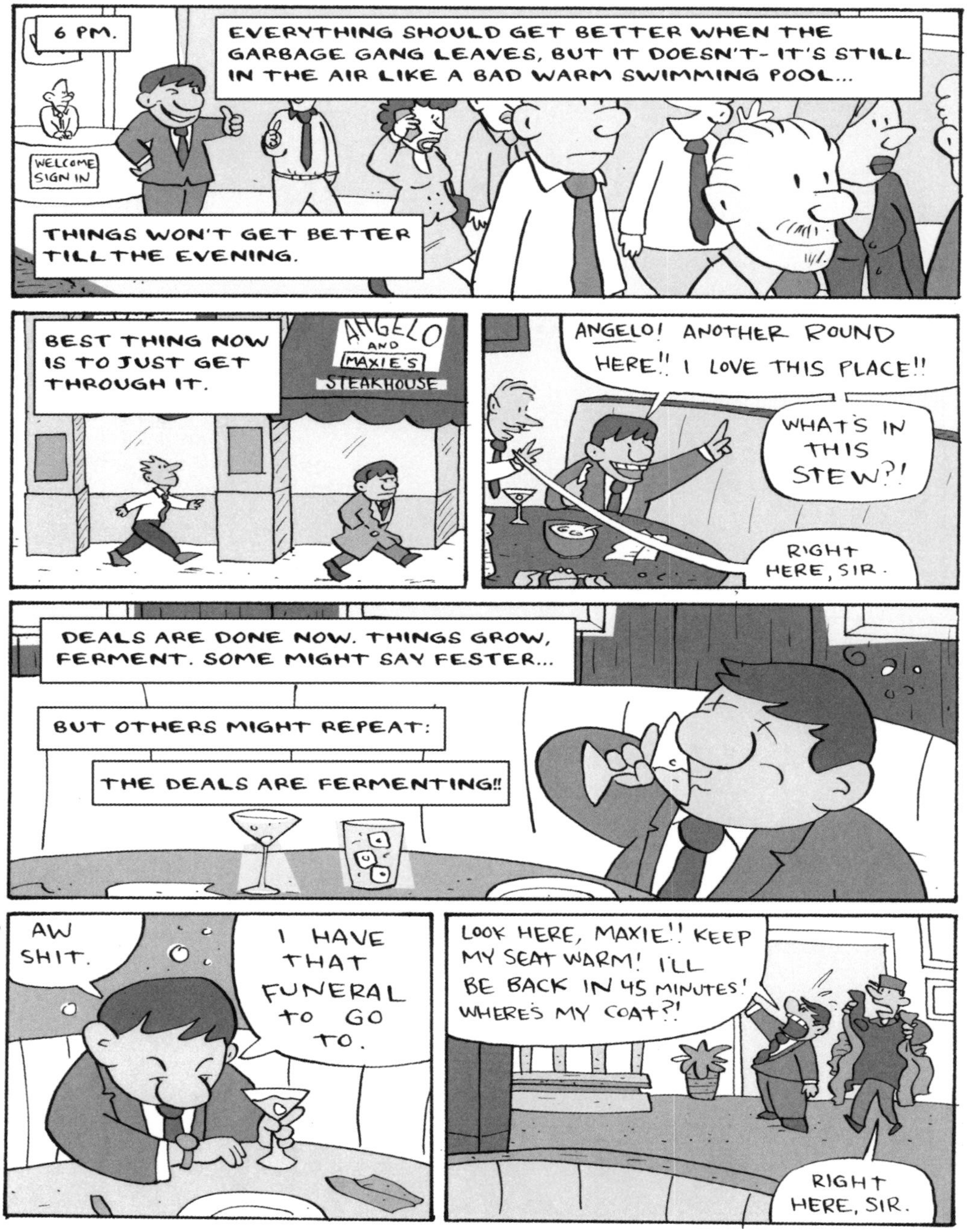
6 PM.
EVERYTHING SHOULD GET BETTER WHEN THE GARBAGE GANG LEAVES, BUT IT DOESN'T- IT'S STILL IN THE AIR LIKE A BAD WARM SWIMMING POOL...
WELCOME SIGN IN
THINGS WON'T GET BETTER TILL THE EVENING.
BEST THING NOW IS TO JUST GET THROUGH IT.
ANGELO AND MAXIE'S STEAKHOUSE
ANGELO! ANOTHER ROUND HERE!! I LOVE THIS PLACE!!
WHAT'S IN THIS STEW?!
RIGHT HERE, SIR.
DEALS ARE DONE NOW. THINGS GROW, FERMENT. SOME MIGHT SAY FESTER...
BUT OTHERS MIGHT REPEAT:
THE DEALS ARE FERMENTING!!
AW SHIT.
I HAVE THAT FUNERAL TO GO TO.
LOOK HERE, MAXIE!! KEEP MY SEAT WARM! I'LL BE BACK IN 45 MINUTES! WHERE'S MY COAT?!
RIGHT HERE, SIR.

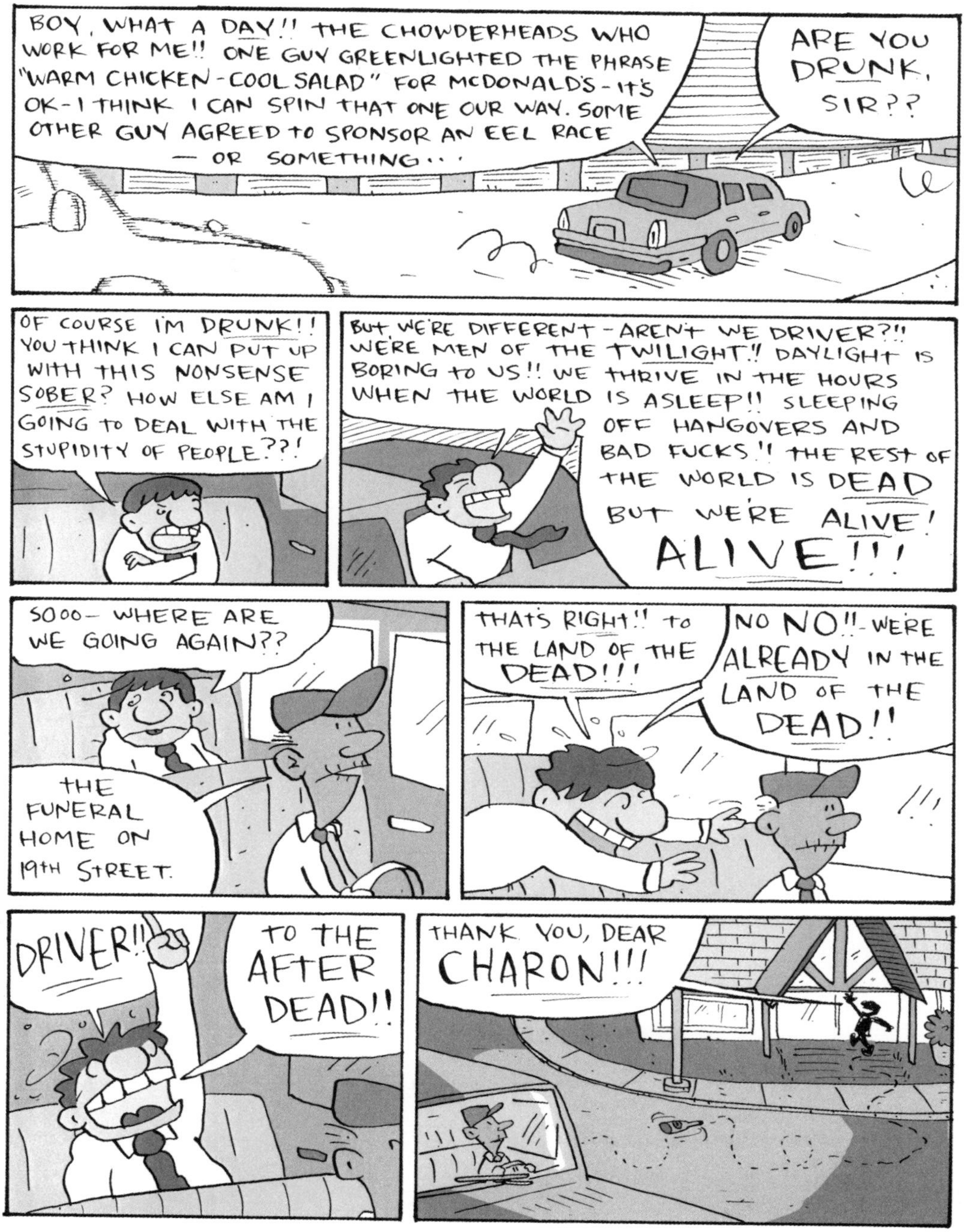
BOY, WHAT A DAY!! THE CHOWDERHEADS WHO WORK FOR ME!! ONE GUY GREENLIGHTED THE PHRASE "WARM CHICKEN - COOL SALAD" FOR MCDONALD'S - IT'S OK - I THINK I CAN SPIN THAT ONE OUR WAY. SOME OTHER GUY AGREED TO SPONSOR AN EEL RACE — OR SOMETHING...
ARE YOU DRUNK, SIR??
OF COURSE I'M DRUNK!! YOU THINK I CAN PUT UP WITH THIS NONSENSE SOBER? HOW ELSE AM I GOING TO DEAL WITH THE STUPIDITY OF PEOPLE??!
BUT, WE'RE DIFFERENT - AREN'T WE DRIVER?!! WE'RE MEN OF THE TWILIGHT!! DAYLIGHT IS BORING TO US!! WE THRIVE IN THE HOURS WHEN THE WORLD IS ASLEEP!! SLEEPING OFF HANGOVERS AND BAD FUCKS!! THE REST OF THE WORLD IS DEAD BUT WE'RE ALIVE! ALIVE!!!
SOOO- WHERE ARE WE GOING AGAIN??
THE FUNERAL HOME ON 19TH STREET.
THAT'S RIGHT!! TO THE LAND OF THE DEAD!!!
NO NO!! WE'RE ALREADY IN THE LAND OF THE DEAD!!
DRIVER!!
TO THE AFTER DEAD!!
THANK YOU, DEAR CHARON!!!

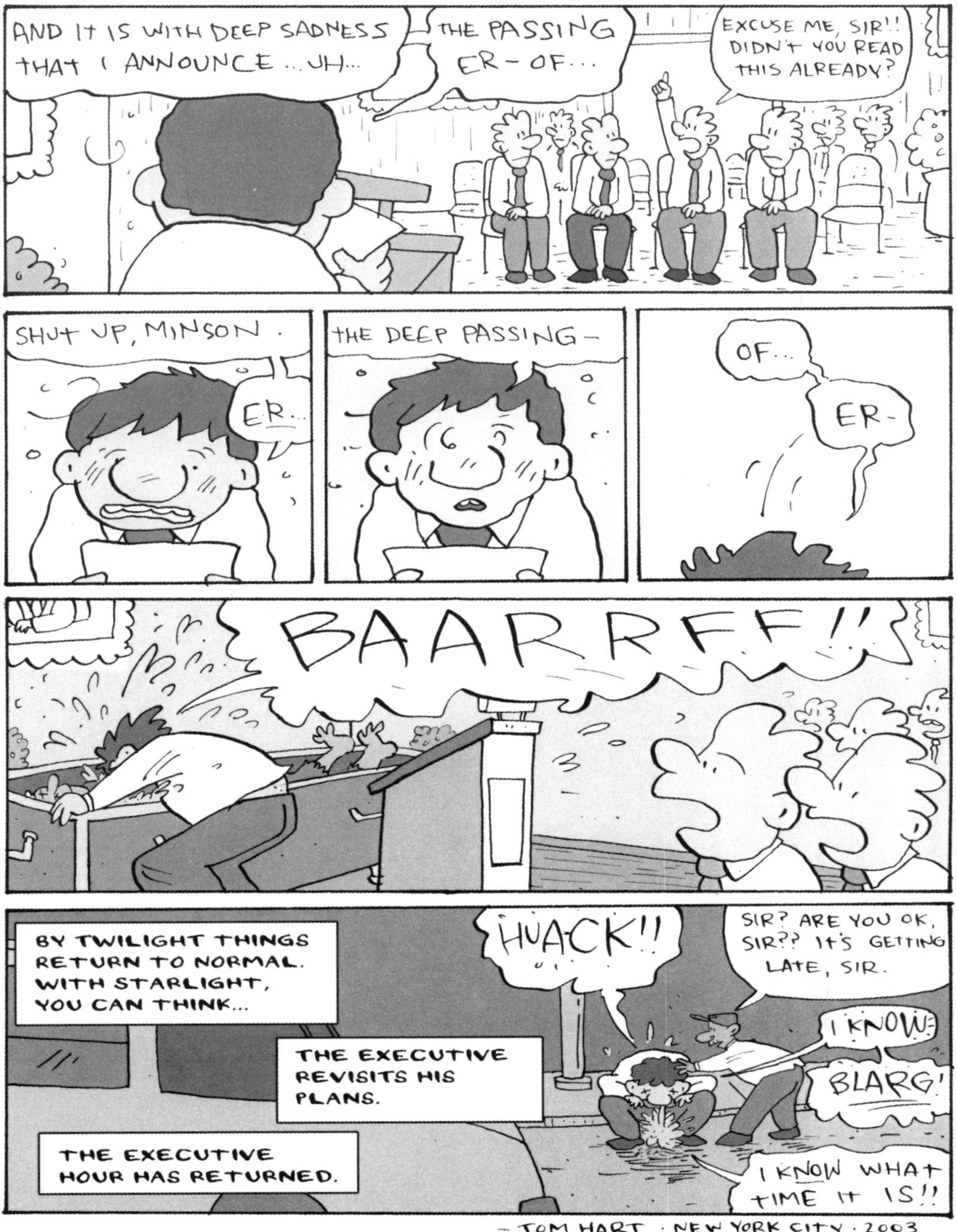
AND IT IS WITH DEEP SADNESS THAT I ANNOUNCE...UH...
THE PASSING ER-OF...
EXCUSE ME, SIR!! DIDN'T YOU READ THIS ALREADY?
SHUT UP, MINSON.
ER...
THE DEEP PASSING-
OF...
ER-
BAARRFF!!
BY TWILIGHT THINGS RETURN TO NORMAL. WITH STARLIGHT, YOU CAN THINK...
HUACK!!
SIR? ARE YOU OK, SIR?? IT'S GETTING LATE, SIR.
I KNOW-
BLARG!
THE EXECUTIVE REVISITS HIS PLANS.
THE EXECUTIVE HOUR HAS RETURNED.
I KNOW WHAT TIME IT IS!!

– TOM HART · NEW YORK CITY · 2003

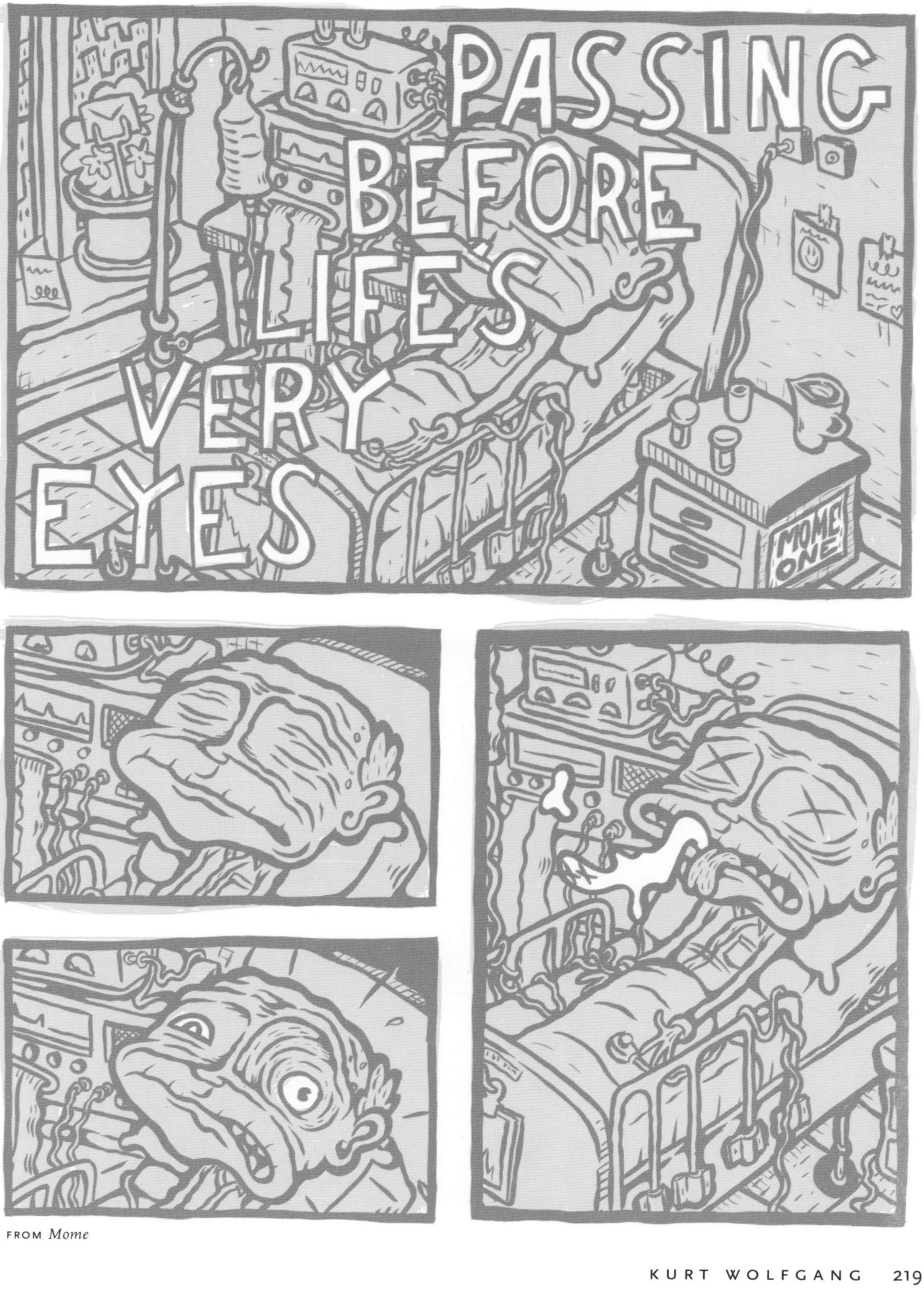
PASSING
BEFORE
LIFE'S
VERY
EYES
MOME ONE

FROM *Mome*

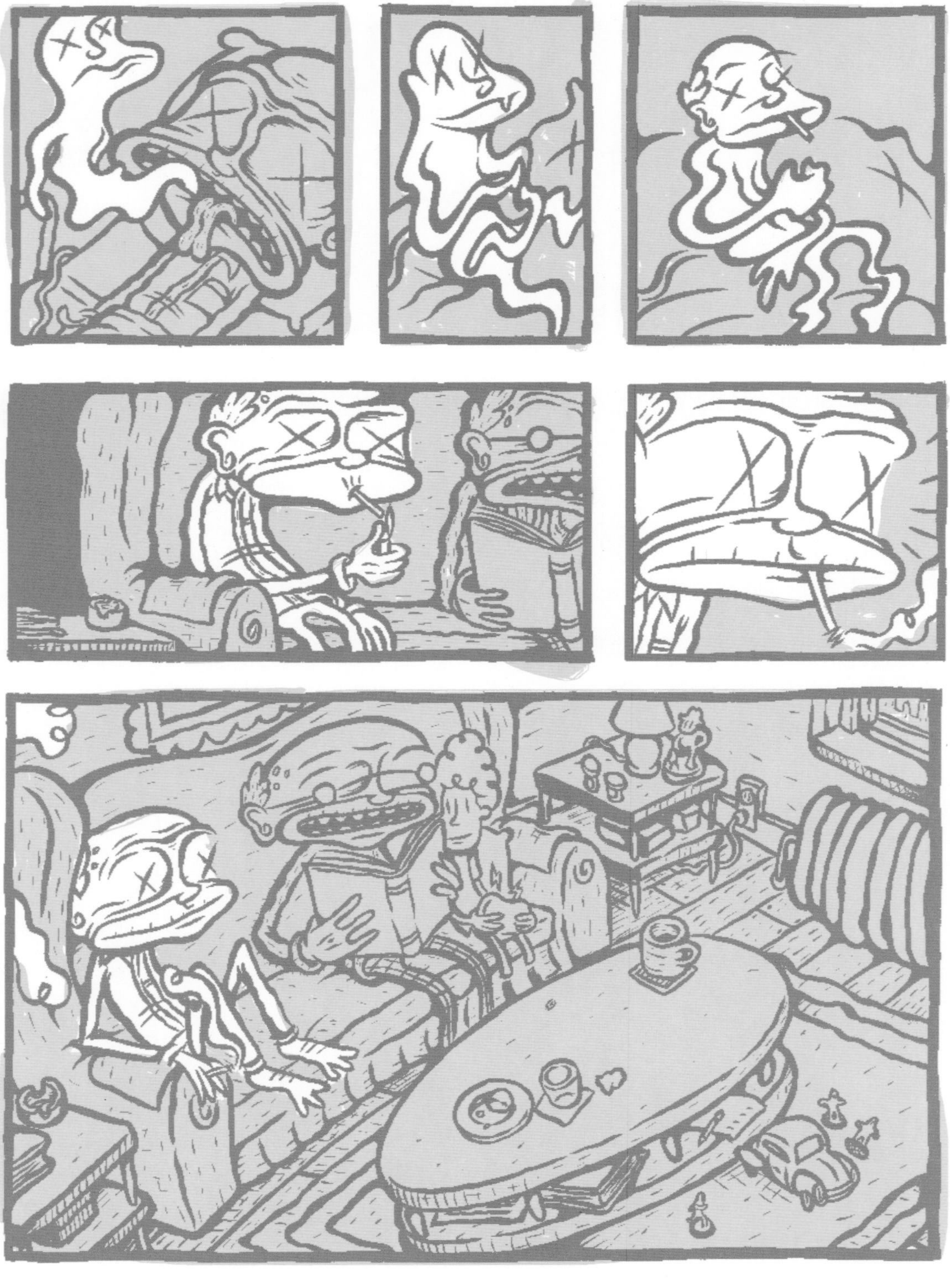

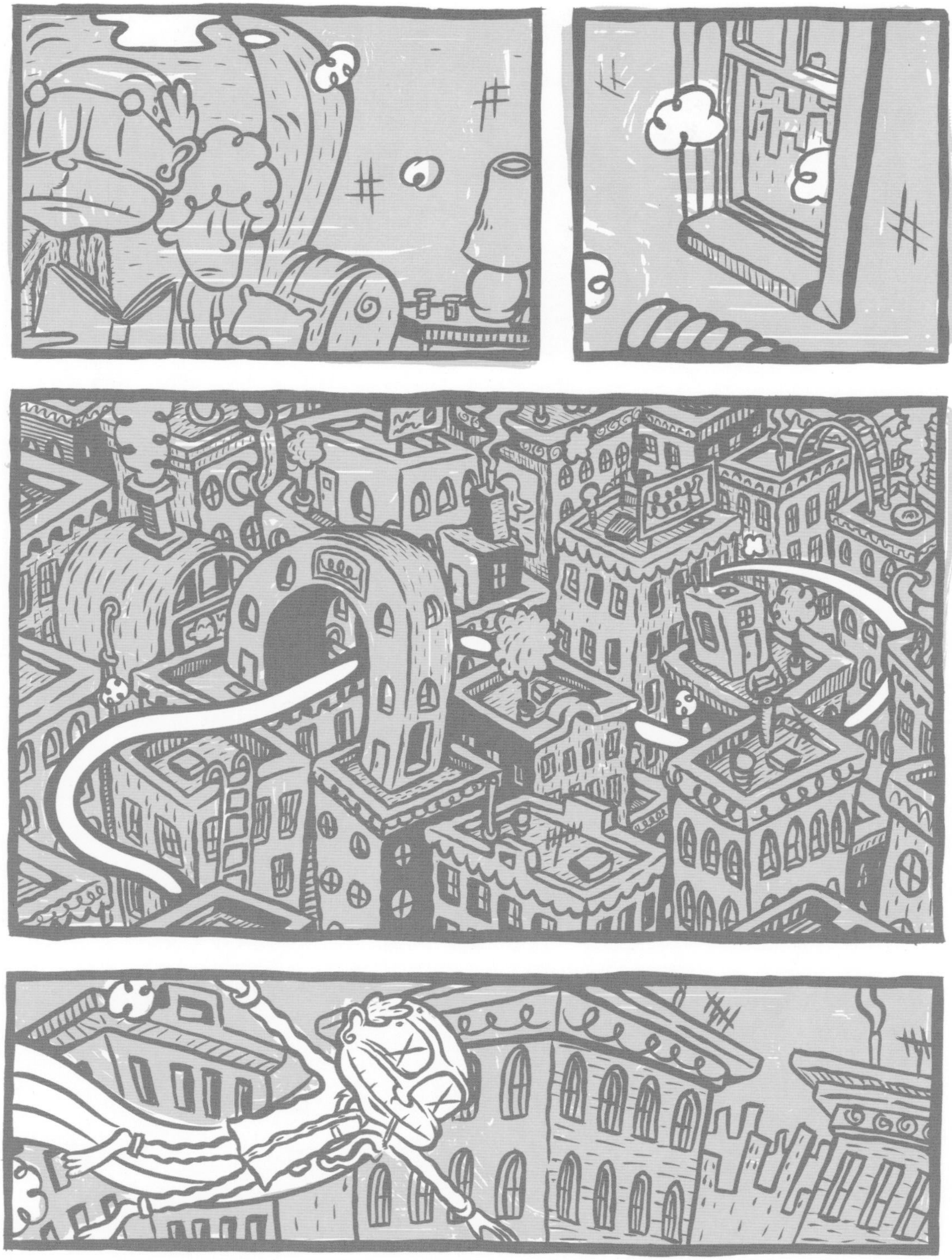

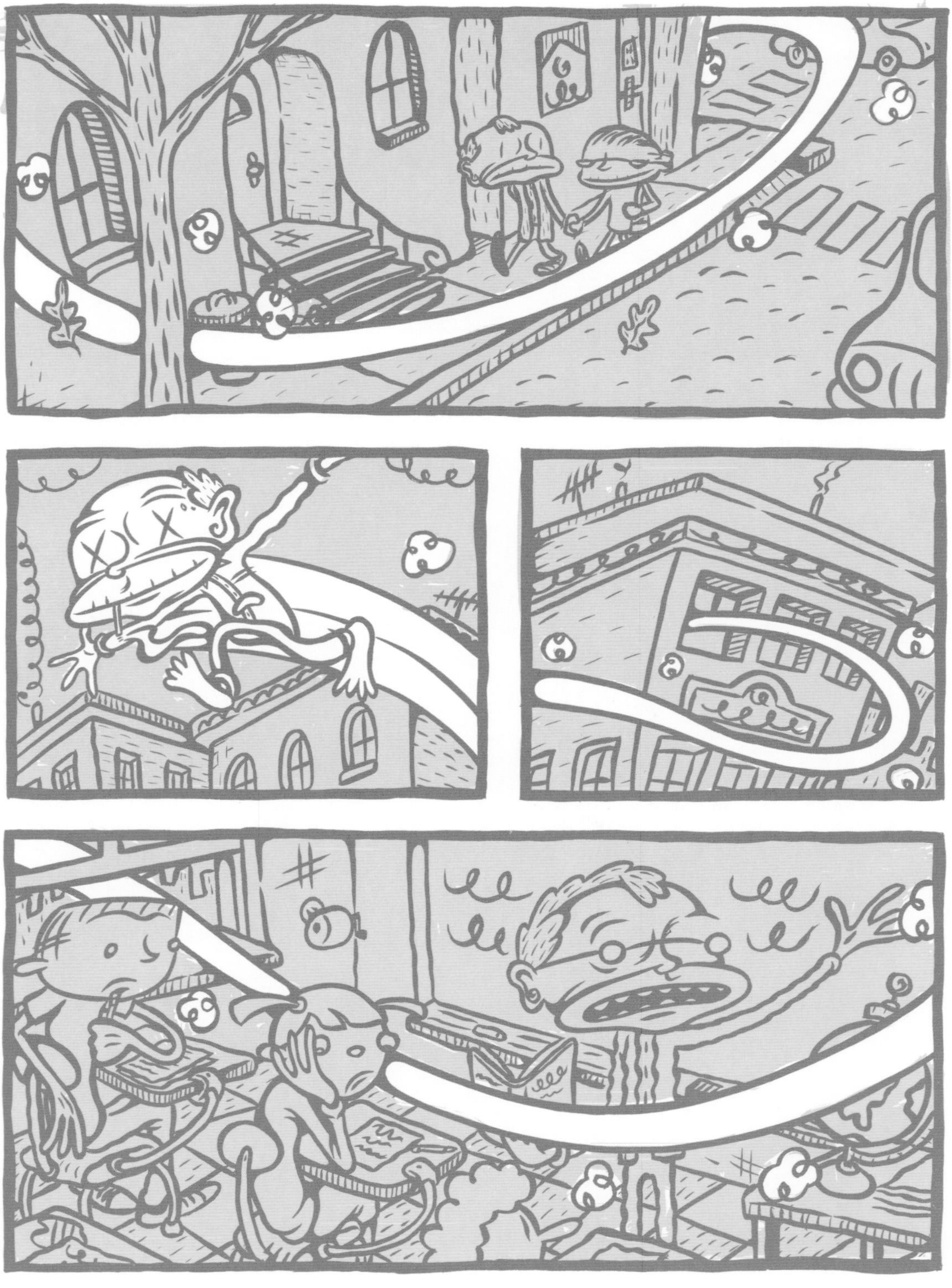

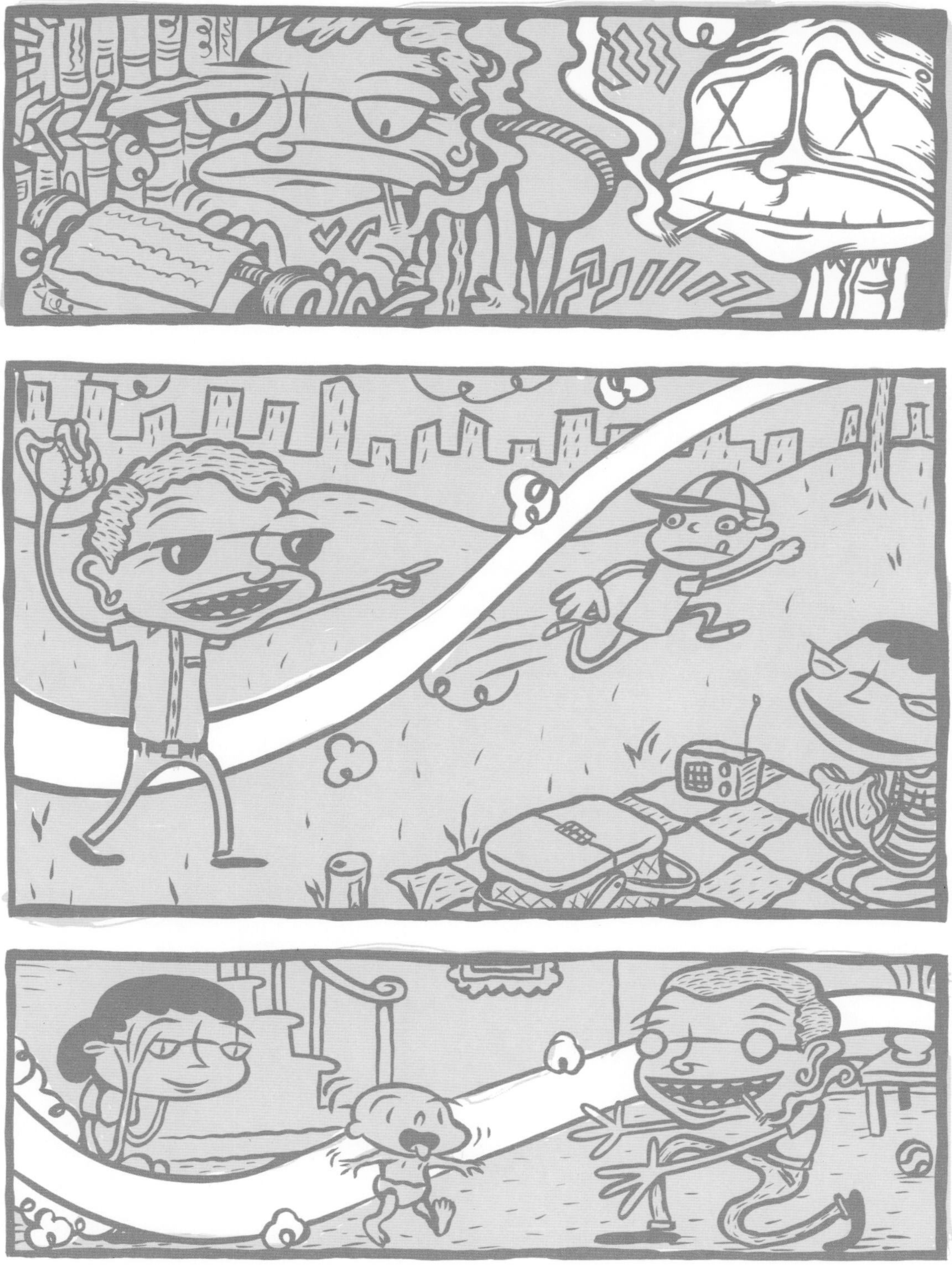

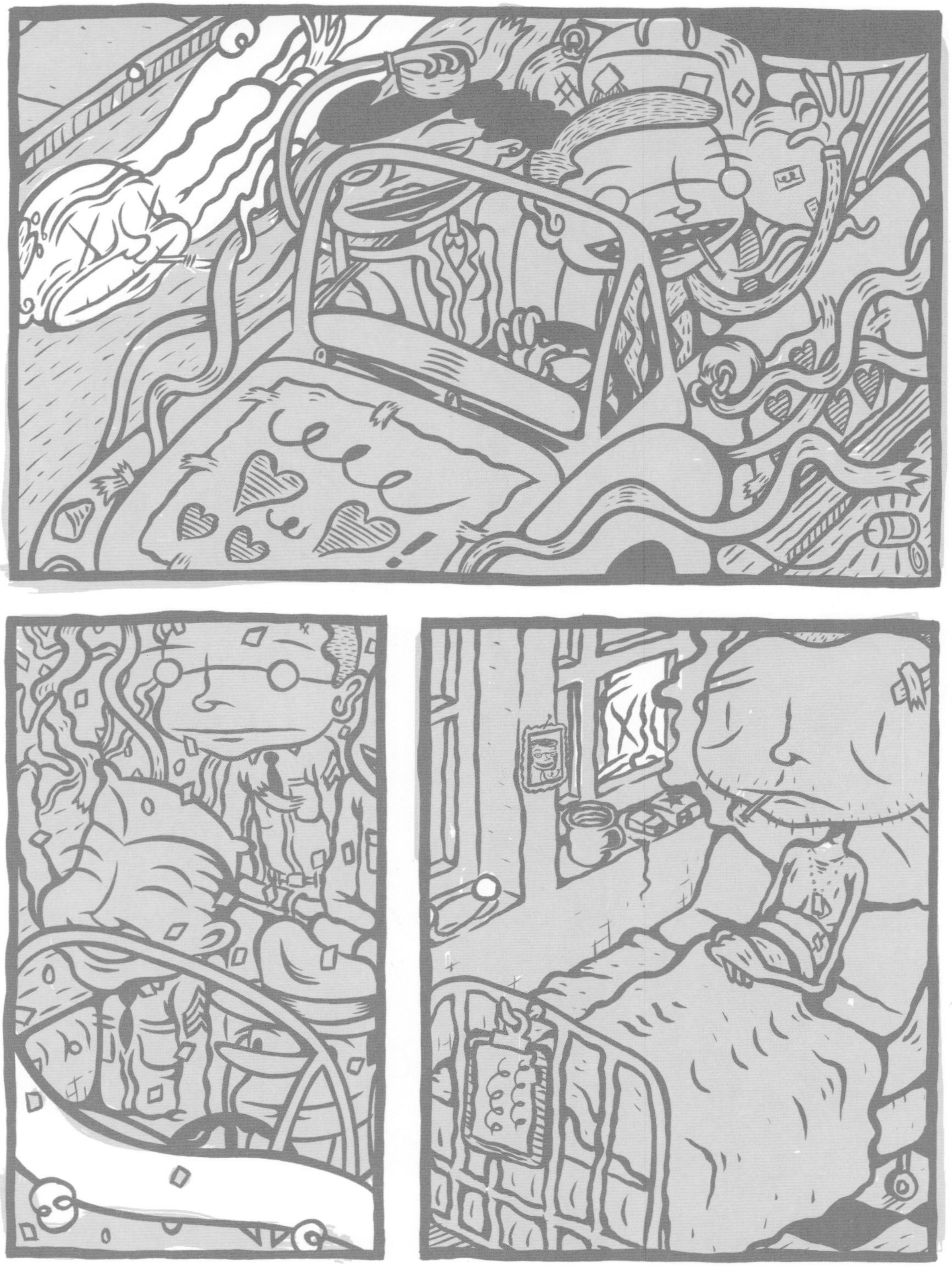

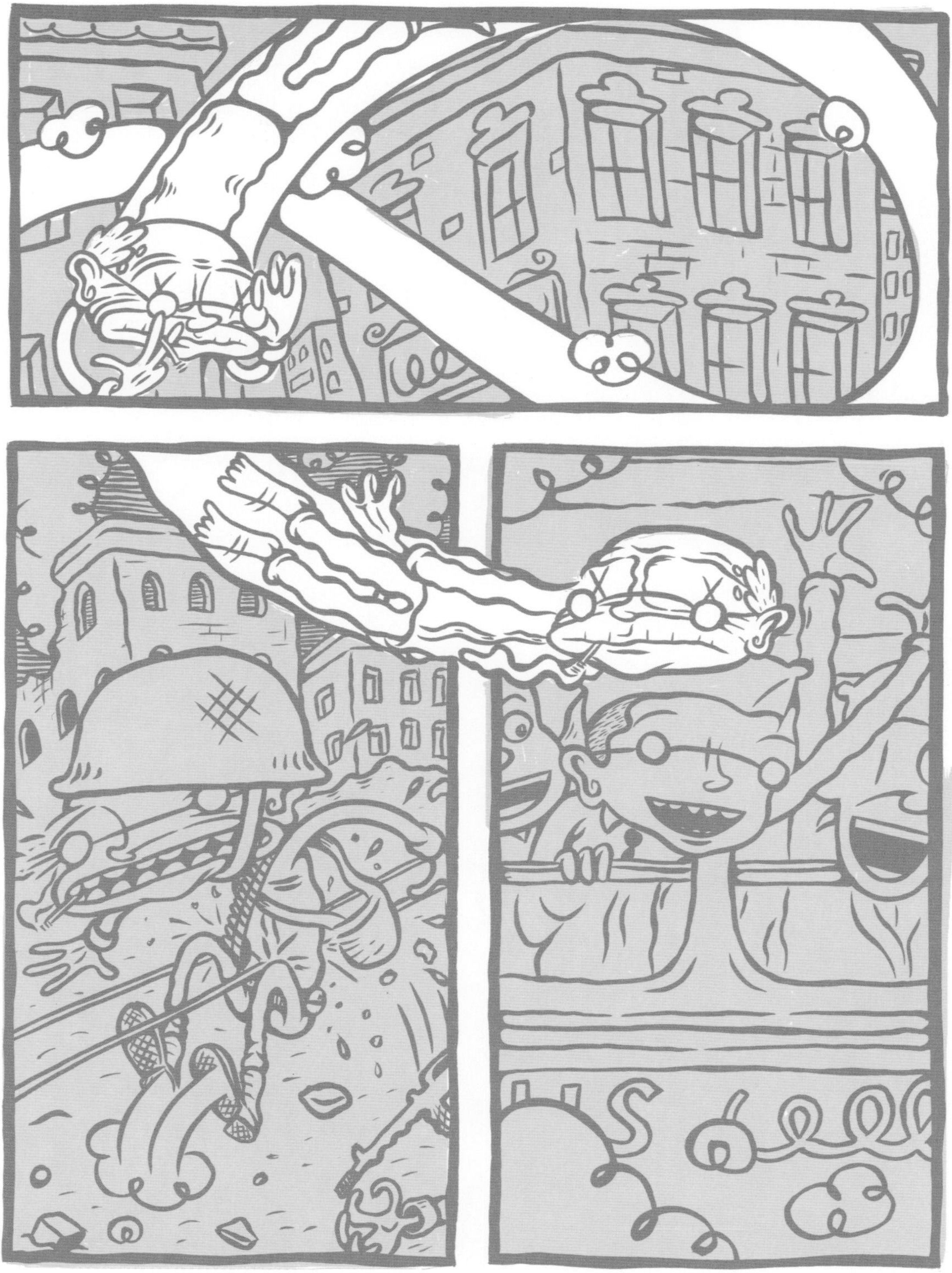

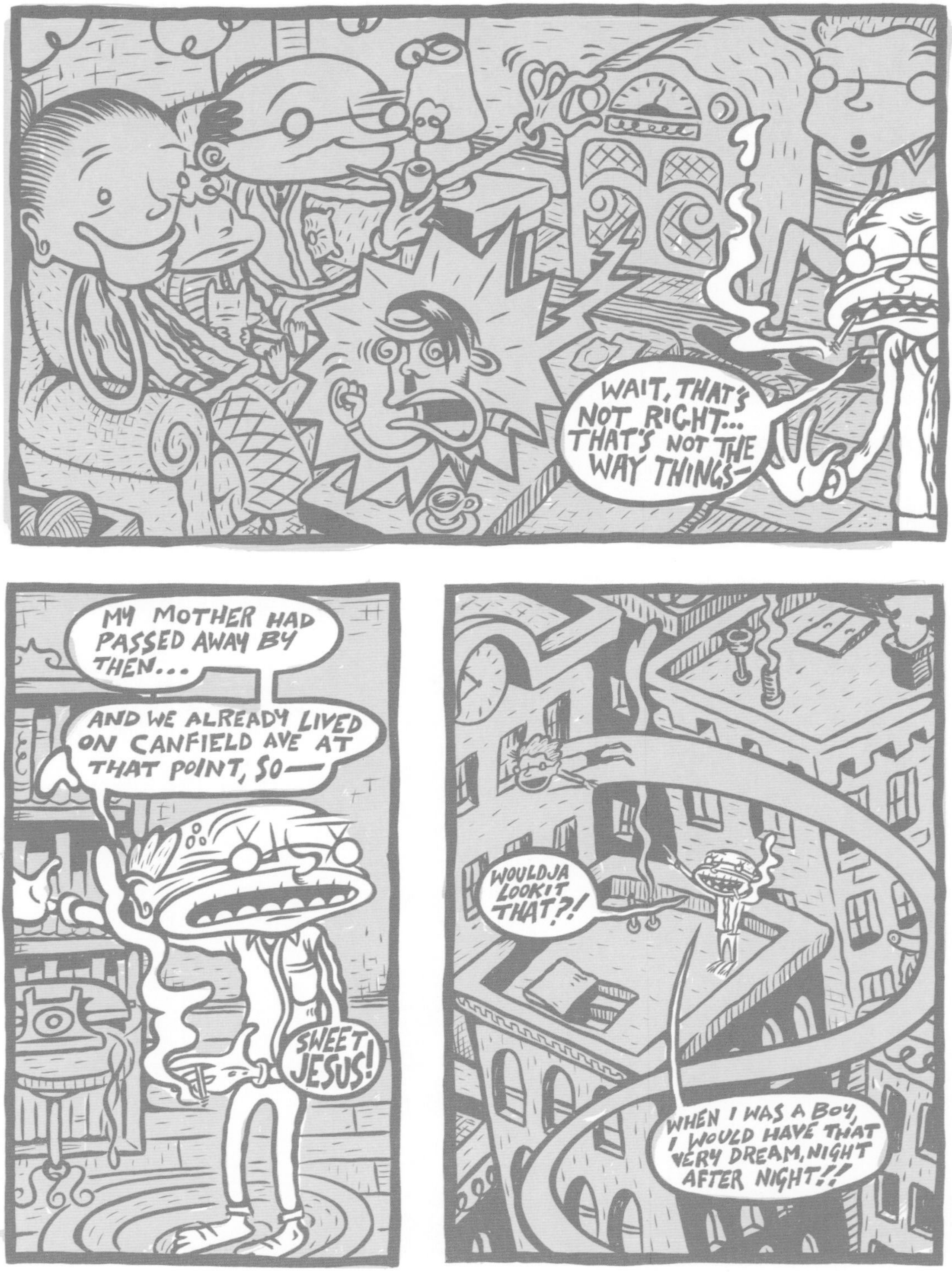
WAIT, THAT'S NOT RIGHT... THAT'S NOT THE WAY THINGS—
MY MOTHER HAD PASSED AWAY BY THEN...
AND WE ALREADY LIVED ON CANFIELD AVE AT THAT POINT, SO—
SWEET JESUS!
WOULDJA LOOKIT THAT?!
WHEN I WAS A BOY, I WOULD HAVE THAT VERY DREAM, NIGHT AFTER NIGHT!!

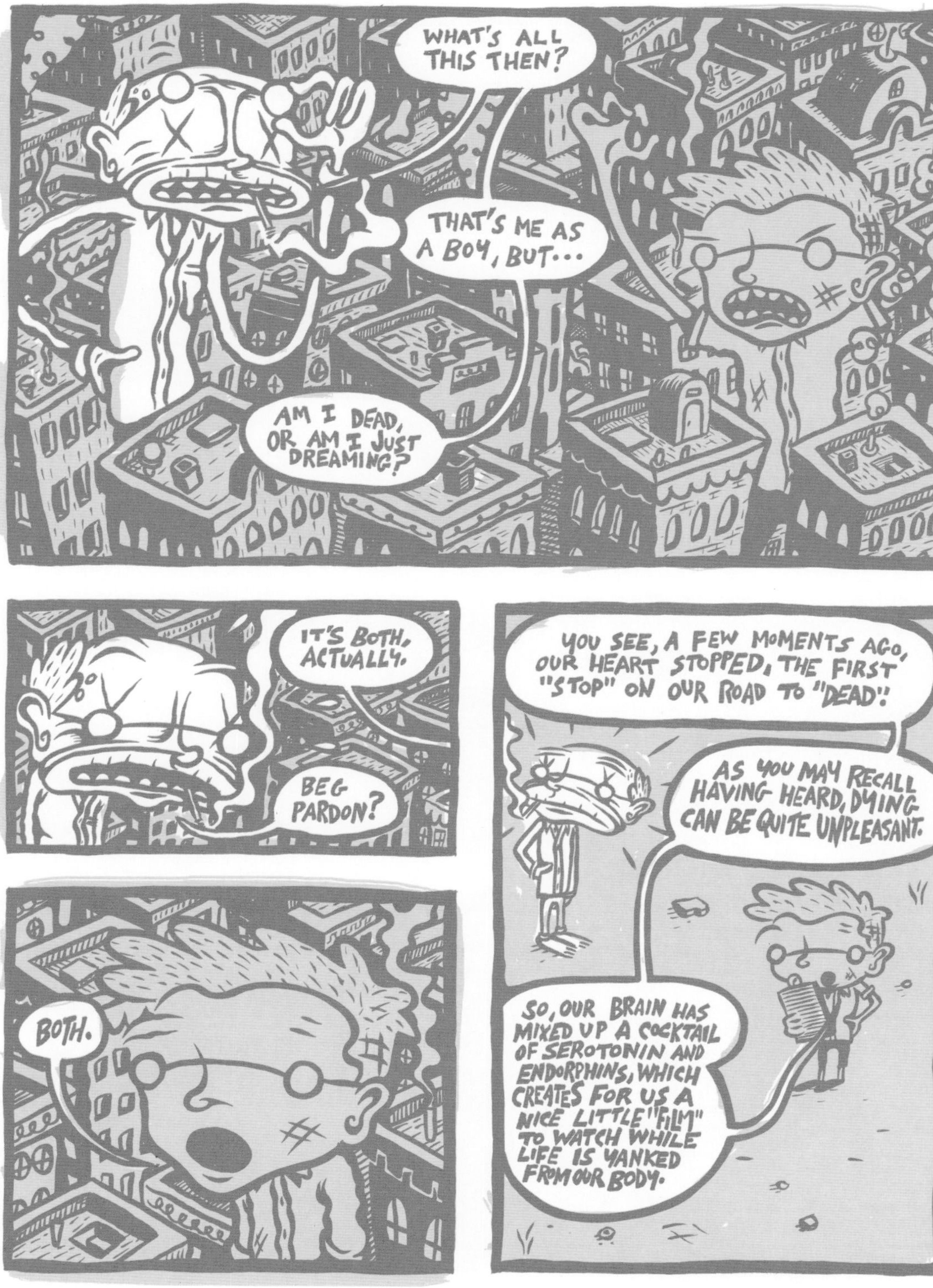
WHAT'S ALL THIS THEN?
THAT'S ME AS A BOY, BUT...
AM I DEAD, OR AM I JUST DREAMING?
IT'S BOTH, ACTUALLY.
BEG PARDON?
BOTH.
YOU SEE, A FEW MOMENTS AGO, OUR HEART STOPPED, THE FIRST "STOP" ON OUR ROAD TO "DEAD."
AS YOU MAY RECALL HAVING HEARD, DYING CAN BE QUITE UNPLEASANT.
SO, OUR BRAIN HAS MIXED UP A COCKTAIL OF SEROTONIN AND ENDORPHINS, WHICH CREATES FOR US A NICE LITTLE "FILM" TO WATCH WHILE LIFE IS YANKED FROM OUR BODY.

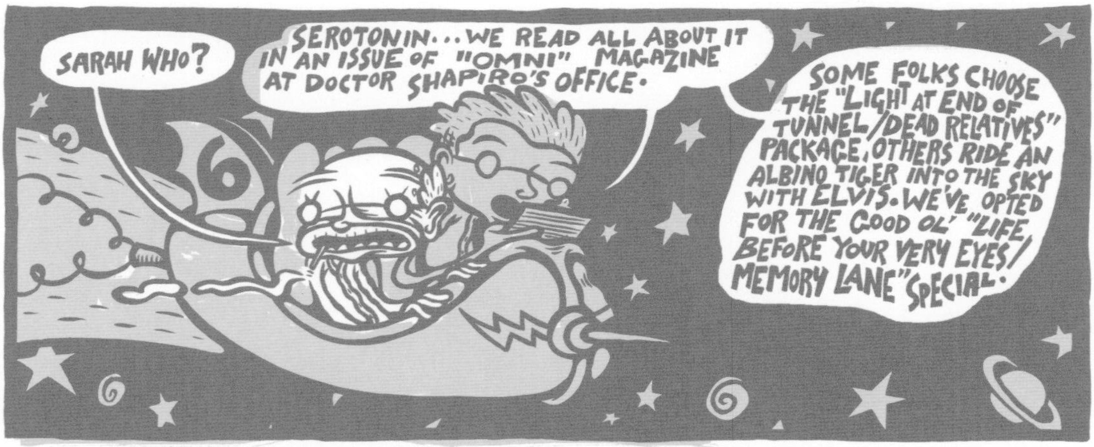
SARAH WHO?
SEROTONIN... WE READ ALL ABOUT IT IN AN ISSUE OF "OMNI" MAGAZINE AT DOCTOR SHAPIRO'S OFFICE.
SOME FOLKS CHOOSE THE "LIGHT AT END OF TUNNEL/DEAD RELATIVES" PACKAGE, OTHERS RIDE AN ALBINO TIGER INTO THE SKY WITH ELVIS. WE'VE OPTED FOR THE GOOD OL' "LIFE BEFORE YOUR VERY EYES/MEMORY LANE" SPECIAL.

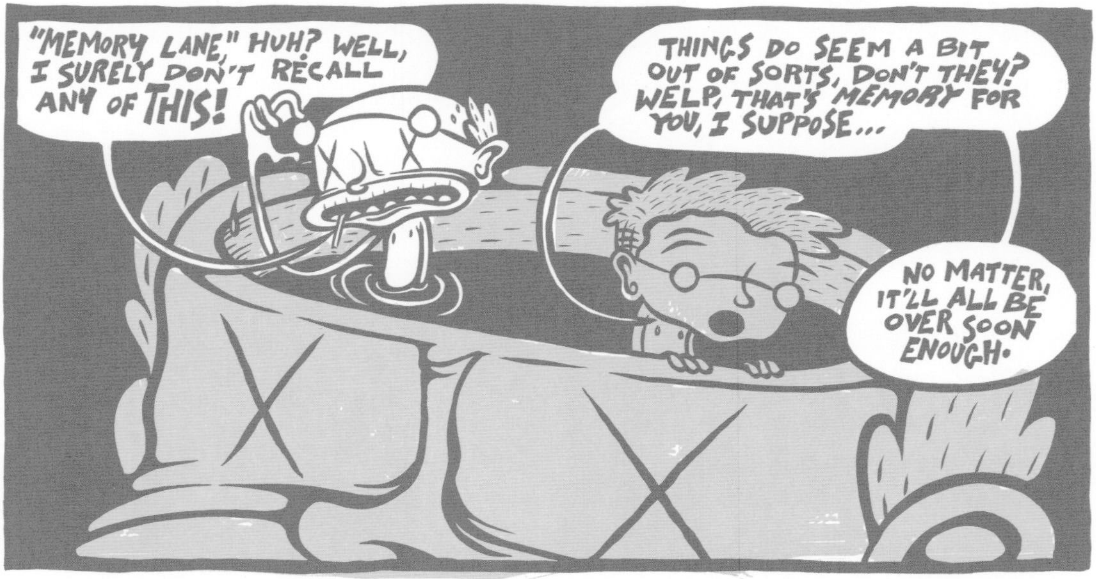
"MEMORY LANE," HUH? WELL, I SURELY DON'T RECALL ANY OF THIS!
THINGS DO SEEM A BIT OUT OF SORTS, DON'T THEY? WELP, THAT'S MEMORY FOR YOU, I SUPPOSE...
NO MATTER, IT'LL ALL BE OVER SOON ENOUGH.

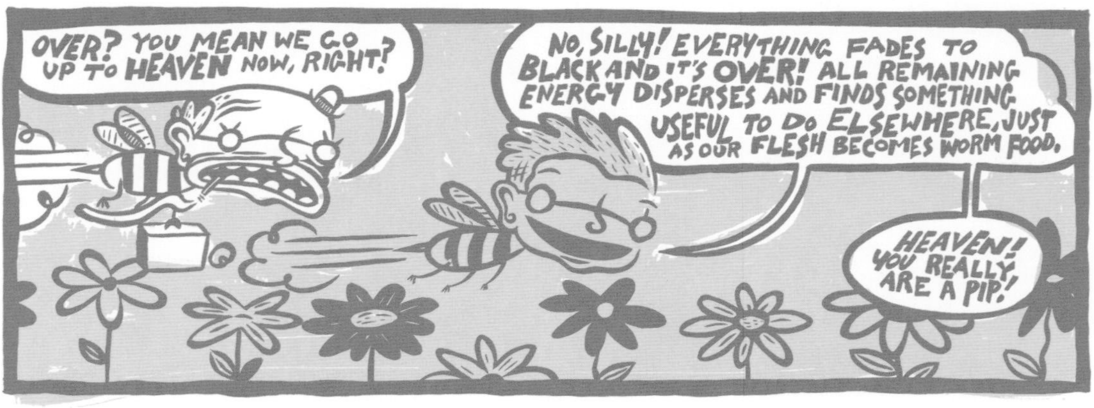
OVER? YOU MEAN WE GO UP TO HEAVEN NOW, RIGHT?
NO, SILLY! EVERYTHING FADES TO BLACK AND IT'S OVER! ALL REMAINING ENERGY DISPERSES AND FINDS SOMETHING USEFUL TO DO ELSEWHERE, JUST AS OUR FLESH BECOMES WORM FOOD.
HEAVEN! YOU REALLY ARE A PIP!

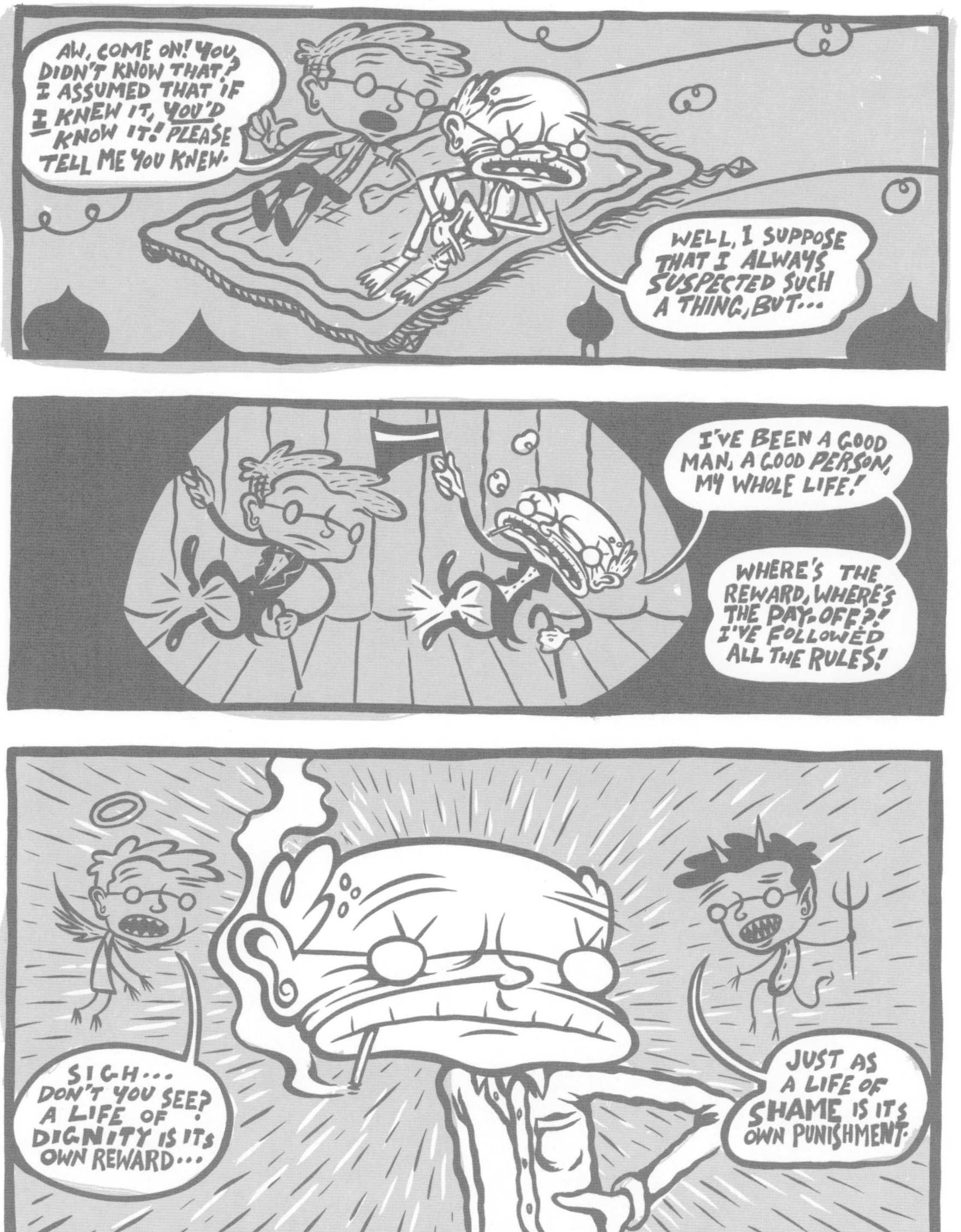

AW, COME ON! YOU DIDN'T KNOW THAT? I ASSUMED THAT IF I KNEW IT, YOU'D KNOW IT! PLEASE TELL ME YOU KNEW.
WELL, I SUPPOSE THAT I ALWAYS SUSPECTED SUCH A THING, BUT...
I'VE BEEN A GOOD MAN, A GOOD PERSON, MY WHOLE LIFE!
WHERE'S THE REWARD, WHERE'S THE PAY-OFF?! I'VE FOLLOWED ALL THE RULES!
SIGH... DON'T YOU SEE? A LIFE OF DIGNITY IS ITS OWN REWARD...
JUST AS A LIFE OF SHAME IS ITS OWN PUNISHMENT.

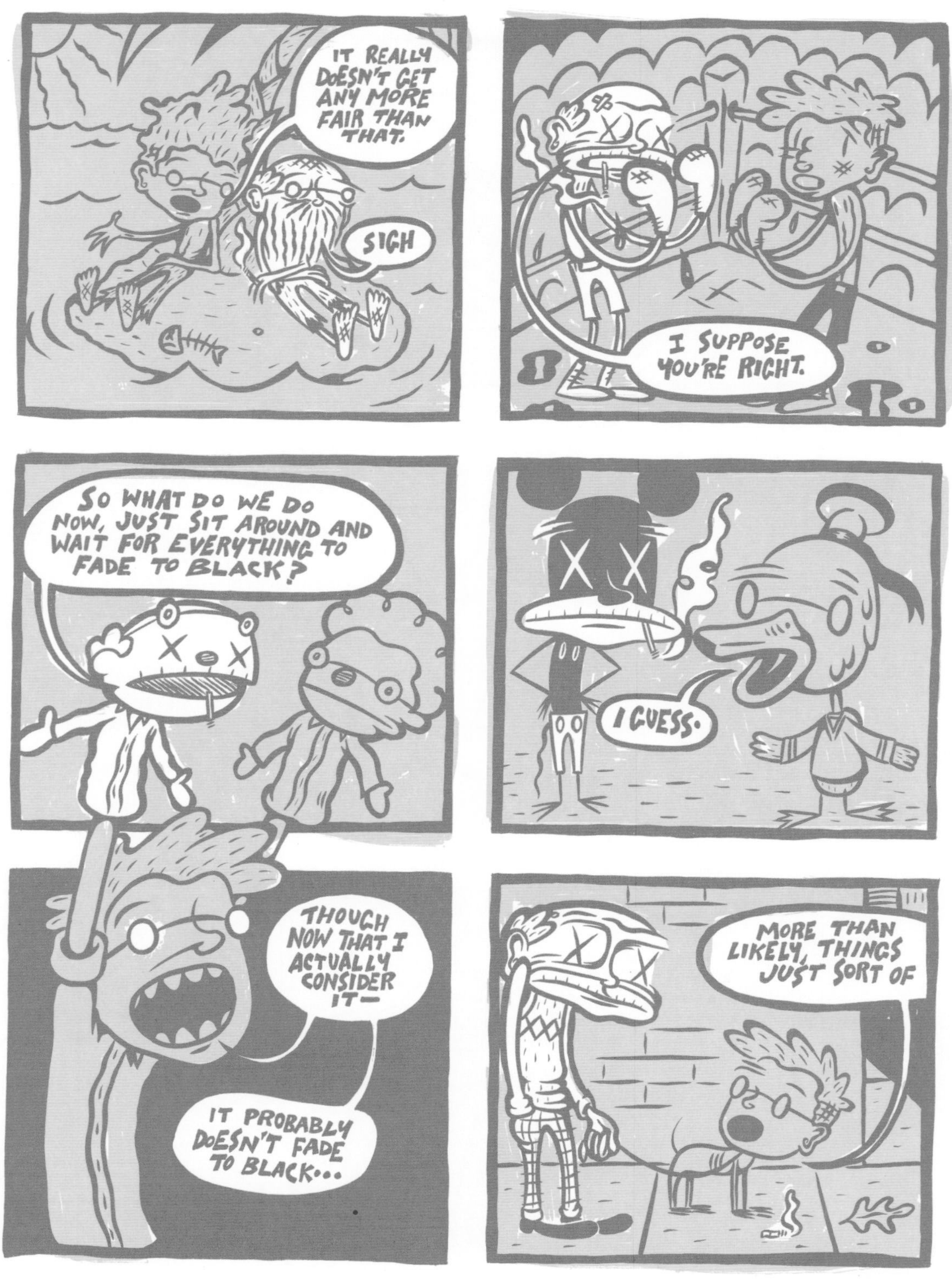
IT REALLY DOESN'T GET ANY MORE FAIR THAN THAT.
SIGH
I SUPPOSE YOU'RE RIGHT.
SO WHAT DO WE DO NOW, JUST SIT AROUND AND WAIT FOR EVERYTHING TO FADE TO BLACK?
I GUESS.
THOUGH NOW THAT I ACTUALLY CONSIDER IT—
IT PROBABLY DOESN'T FADE TO BLACK...
MORE THAN LIKELY, THINGS JUST SORT OF

I HAD A RECURRING DREAM AT AGE FIVE OR SIX THAT I WAS IN HELL. THE DEVIL HAD MY MOM IN A CAGE, READY TO DROP INTO LAVA.
HELP!
THEN HE HANDED ME A FRYING PAN FULL OF TINY KITTENS, AND SAID I MUST CHOOSE.
EITHER FRY UP THESE KITTENS... OR LET YOUR MOM DROP!
MEW
MEW
MEW
I KNOW IT SOUNDS LIKE A MADE-UP DREAM, A FORCED METAPHOR ABOUT FAMILY AND LOVE AND ANXIETY. BUT I GUESS THAT'S HOW KIDS' MINDS WORK.
HAHAHAHAHAHA!
I ALWAYS WOKE UP BEFORE I HAD TO CHOOSE

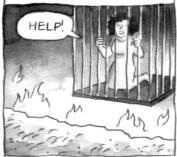

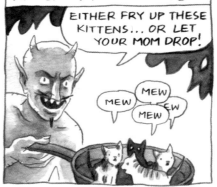

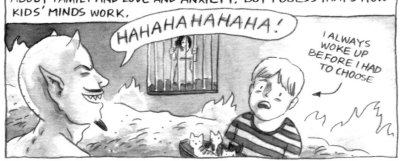

THIRTEEN CATS
OF MY CHILDHOOD

FROM *Couch Tag*

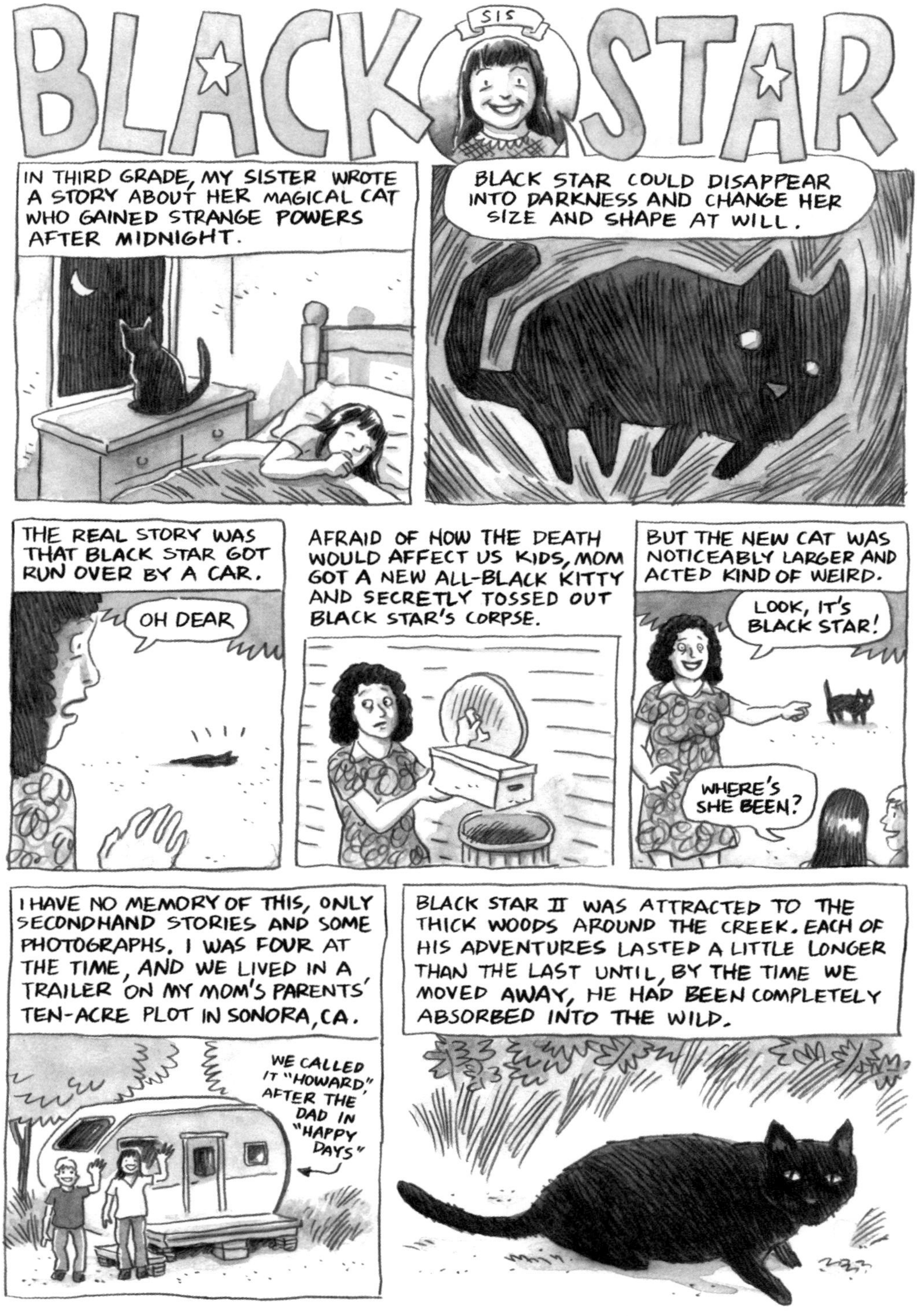
BLACK SIS STAR
IN THIRD GRADE, MY SISTER WROTE A STORY ABOUT HER MAGICAL CAT WHO GAINED STRANGE POWERS AFTER MIDNIGHT.
BLACK STAR COULD DISAPPEAR INTO DARKNESS AND CHANGE HER SIZE AND SHAPE AT WILL.
THE REAL STORY WAS THAT BLACK STAR GOT RUN OVER BY A CAR.
OH DEAR
AFRAID OF HOW THE DEATH WOULD AFFECT US KIDS, MOM GOT A NEW ALL-BLACK KITTY AND SECRETLY TOSSED OUT BLACK STAR'S CORPSE.
BUT THE NEW CAT WAS NOTICEABLY LARGER AND ACTED KIND OF WEIRD.
LOOK, IT'S BLACK STAR!
WHERE'S SHE BEEN?
I HAVE NO MEMORY OF THIS, ONLY SECONDHAND STORIES AND SOME PHOTOGRAPHS. I WAS FOUR AT THE TIME, AND WE LIVED IN A TRAILER ON MY MOM'S PARENTS' TEN-ACRE PLOT IN SONORA, CA.
WE CALLED IT "HOWARD," AFTER THE DAD IN "HAPPY DAYS"
BLACK STAR II WAS ATTRACTED TO THE THICK WOODS AROUND THE CREEK. EACH OF HIS ADVENTURES LASTED A LITTLE LONGER THAN THE LAST UNTIL, BY THE TIME WE MOVED AWAY, HE HAD BEEN COMPLETELY ABSORBED INTO THE WILD.

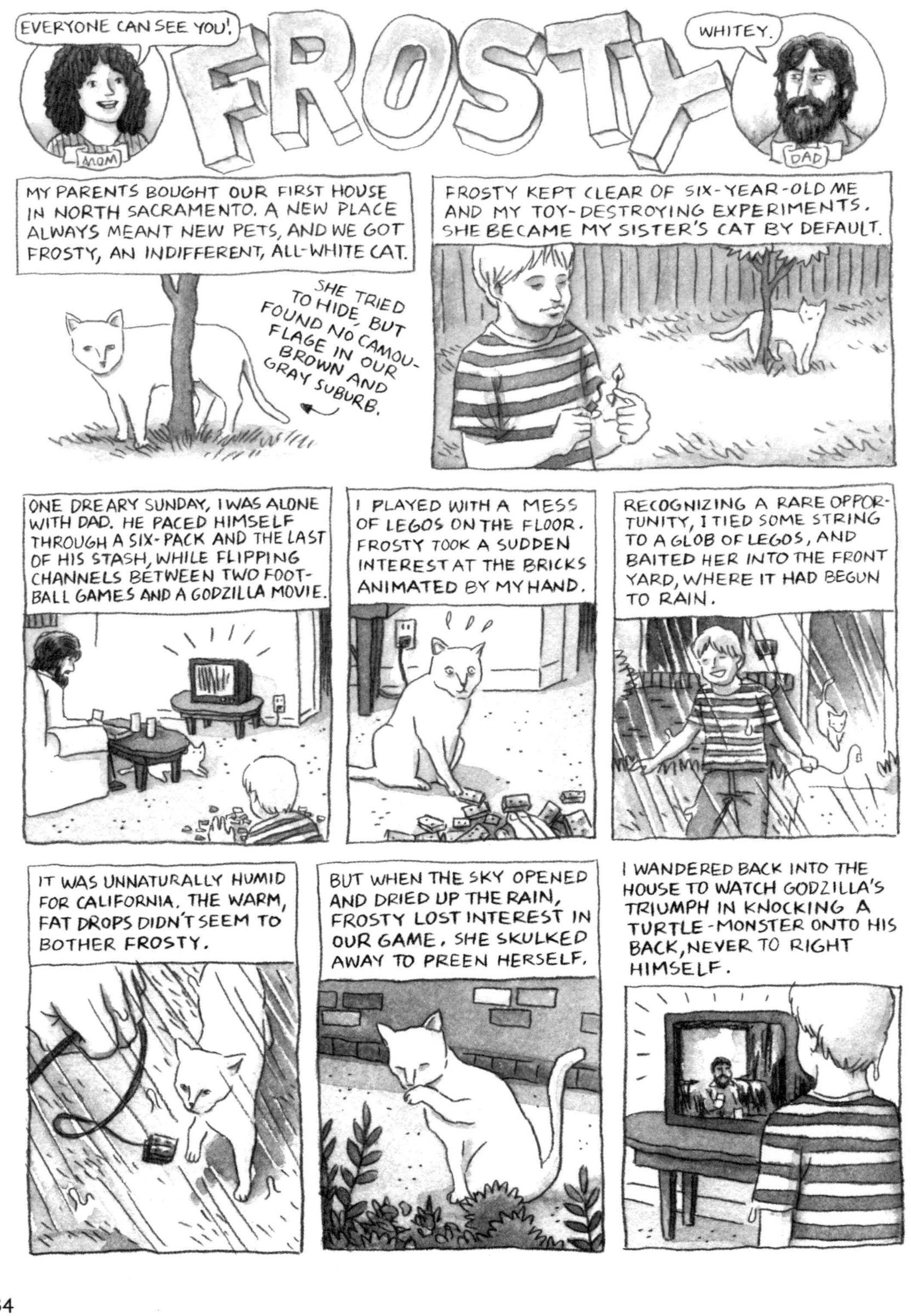
EVERYONE CAN SEE YOU!
FROSTY
WHITEY.
MOM
DAD
MY PARENTS BOUGHT OUR FIRST HOUSE IN NORTH SACRAMENTO. A NEW PLACE ALWAYS MEANT NEW PETS, AND WE GOT FROSTY, AN INDIFFERENT, ALL-WHITE CAT.
SHE TRIED TO HIDE, BUT FOUND NO CAMOUFLAGE IN OUR BROWN AND GRAY SUBURB.
FROSTY KEPT CLEAR OF SIX-YEAR-OLD ME AND MY TOY-DESTROYING EXPERIMENTS. SHE BECAME MY SISTER'S CAT BY DEFAULT.
ONE DREARY SUNDAY, I WAS ALONE WITH DAD. HE PACED HIMSELF THROUGH A SIX-PACK AND THE LAST OF HIS STASH, WHILE FLIPPING CHANNELS BETWEEN TWO FOOTBALL GAMES AND A GODZILLA MOVIE.
I PLAYED WITH A MESS OF LEGOS ON THE FLOOR. FROSTY TOOK A SUDDEN INTEREST AT THE BRICKS ANIMATED BY MY HAND.
RECOGNIZING A RARE OPPORTUNITY, I TIED SOME STRING TO A GLOB OF LEGOS, AND BAITED HER INTO THE FRONT YARD, WHERE IT HAD BEGUN TO RAIN.
IT WAS UNNATURALLY HUMID FOR CALIFORNIA. THE WARM, FAT DROPS DIDN'T SEEM TO BOTHER FROSTY.
BUT WHEN THE SKY OPENED AND DRIED UP THE RAIN, FROSTY LOST INTEREST IN OUR GAME. SHE SKULKED AWAY TO PREEN HERSELF.
I WANDERED BACK INTO THE HOUSE TO WATCH GODZILLA'S TRIUMPH IN KNOCKING A TURTLE-MONSTER ONTO HIS BACK, NEVER TO RIGHT HIMSELF.

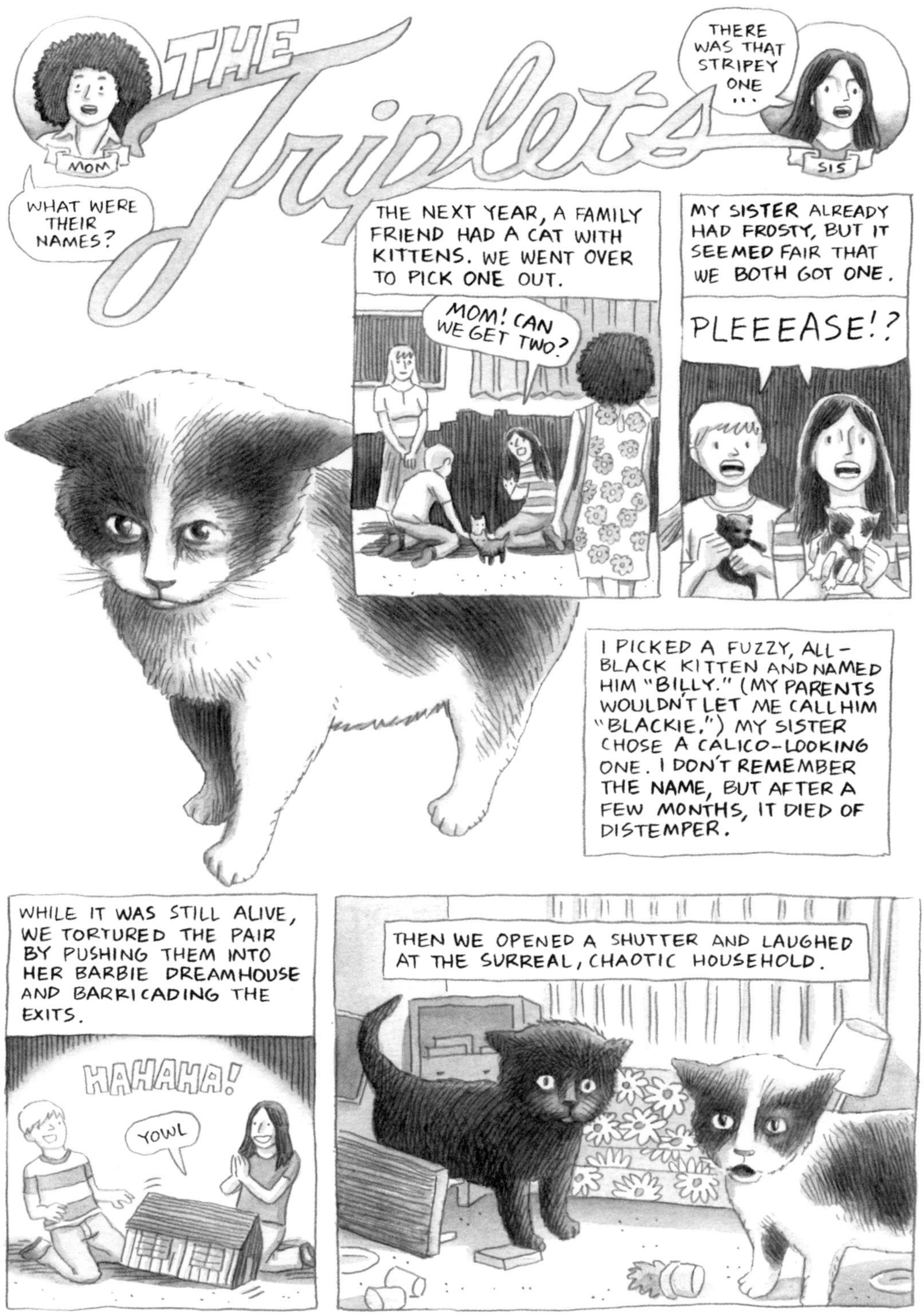
THE Triplets
MOM
WHAT WERE THEIR NAMES?
THERE WAS THAT STRIPEY ONE ...
SIS
THE NEXT YEAR, A FAMILY FRIEND HAD A CAT WITH KITTENS. WE WENT OVER TO PICK ONE OUT.
MOM! CAN WE GET TWO?
MY SISTER ALREADY HAD FROSTY, BUT IT SEEMED FAIR THAT WE BOTH GOT ONE.
PLEEEASE!?
I PICKED A FUZZY, ALL-BLACK KITTEN AND NAMED HIM "BILLY." (MY PARENTS WOULDN'T LET ME CALL HIM "BLACKIE.") MY SISTER CHOSE A CALICO-LOOKING ONE. I DON'T REMEMBER THE NAME, BUT AFTER A FEW MONTHS, IT DIED OF DISTEMPER.
WHILE IT WAS STILL ALIVE, WE TORTURED THE PAIR BY PUSHING THEM INTO HER BARBIE DREAMHOUSE AND BARRICADING THE EXITS.
HAHAHA!
YOWL
THEN WE OPENED A SHUTTER AND LAUGHED AT THE SURREAL, CHAOTIC HOUSEHOLD.

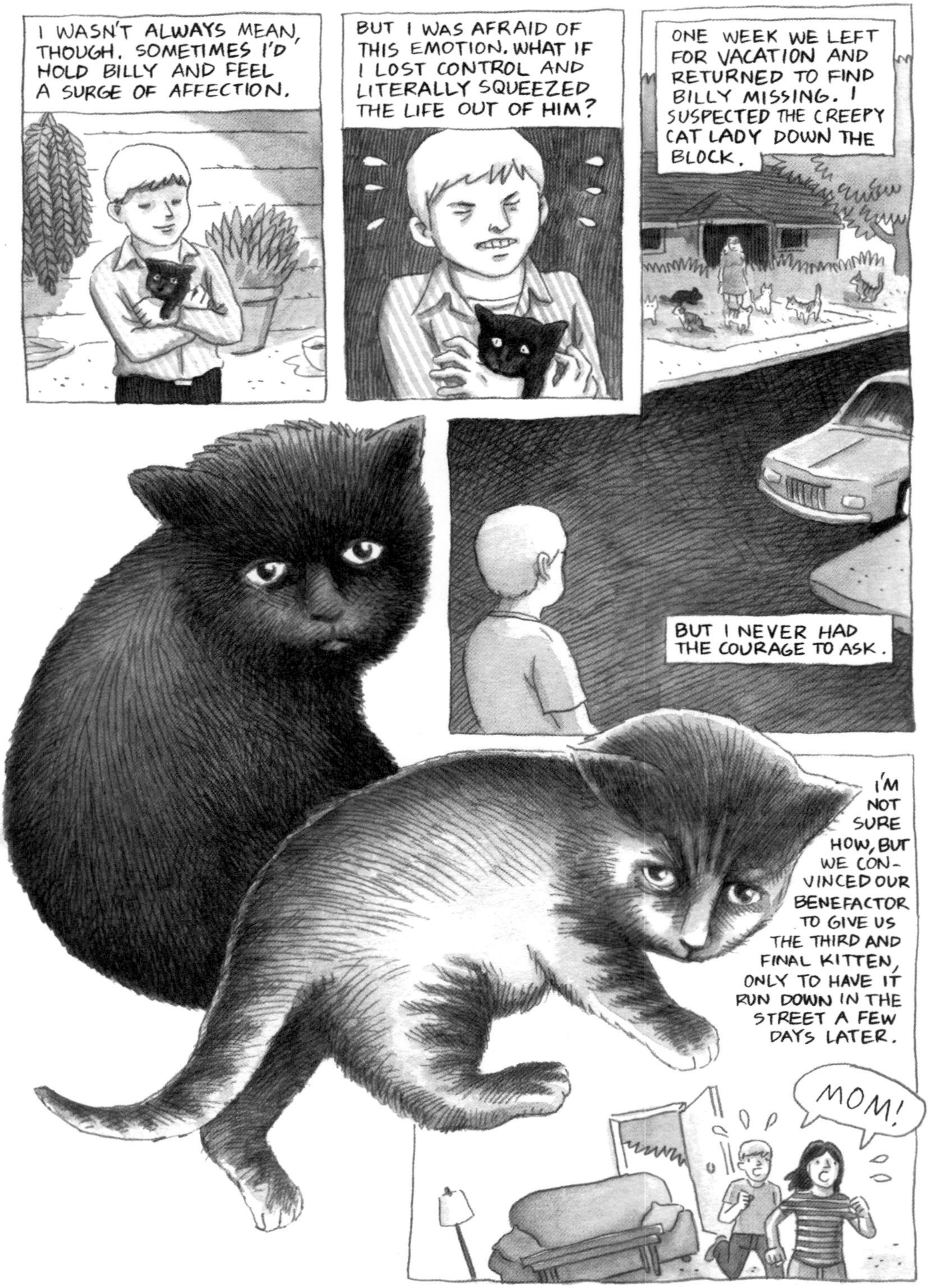
I WASN'T ALWAYS MEAN, THOUGH. SOMETIMES I'D HOLD BILLY AND FEEL A SURGE OF AFFECTION.
BUT I WAS AFRAID OF THIS EMOTION. WHAT IF I LOST CONTROL AND LITERALLY SQUEEZED THE LIFE OUT OF HIM?
ONE WEEK WE LEFT FOR VACATION AND RETURNED TO FIND BILLY MISSING. I SUSPECTED THE CREEPY CAT LADY DOWN THE BLOCK.
BUT I NEVER HAD THE COURAGE TO ASK.
I'M NOT SURE HOW, BUT WE CONVINCED OUR BENEFACTOR TO GIVE US THE THIRD AND FINAL KITTEN, ONLY TO HAVE IT RUN DOWN IN THE STREET A FEW DAYS LATER.
MOM!

WHAT A WEIRD CAT! — MOM

MISCHIEF

PARANOID. — DAD

THE SUMMER BEFORE I STARTED FOURTH GRADE, WE MOVED FROM THE SKANKY PART OF TOWN TO YUPPIE SUBURBIA.

IT WAS THE DAWN OF THE EIGHTIES, AND DAD HAD BEEN PROMOTED FROM CARPENTER TO CONTRACTOR. THEY MADE HIM WEAR A TIE AND TRIM HIS BEARD, BUT HE STILL GOT DRUNK EVERY NIGHT AND PASSED OUT ON THE COUCH.

ZZNORK!

HIS "ALARM CLOCK" WAS TO ROLL OVER AND POUR HALF A MILLER HIGH LIFE IN HIS LAP

AS USUAL WE GOT NEW CATS. ANOTHER CLUELESS FAMILY WITH SPARE KITTENS LET US HAVE A FEW. EVEN GRANDMA AND GRANDPA GOT IN ON THE ACTION, TAKING A SLEEK BLACK KITTY, AND NAMING HER "TROUBLES."

MY SISTER PICKED A GRAY FEMALE TABBY AND CALLED HER "MISCHIEF."

I RUINED THE TRILOGY BY NAMING THE BROTHER "BOOTS."

IT'S 'CAUSE HE'S GOT LITTLE WHITE FEET!

MEOW!

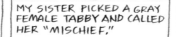

BEING THE NEW KIDS AT SCHOOL, MY SISTER AND I DIDN'T HAVE ANY FRIENDS YET.

HELLO, KITTENS!   WE'RE HOME!

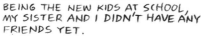

MOM WAS TAKING CLASSES AND LATER WORKED IN DAD'S OFFICE, SO IT WAS JUST US AND THE CATS FOR THE THREE HOURS BETWEEN SCHOOL AND DINNER.

BUT ONCE WE MADE SOME FRIENDS, OUR EMPTY HOUSE WAS AN OBVIOUS CHOICE FOR AFTERSCHOOL MISCHIEVOUSNESS.

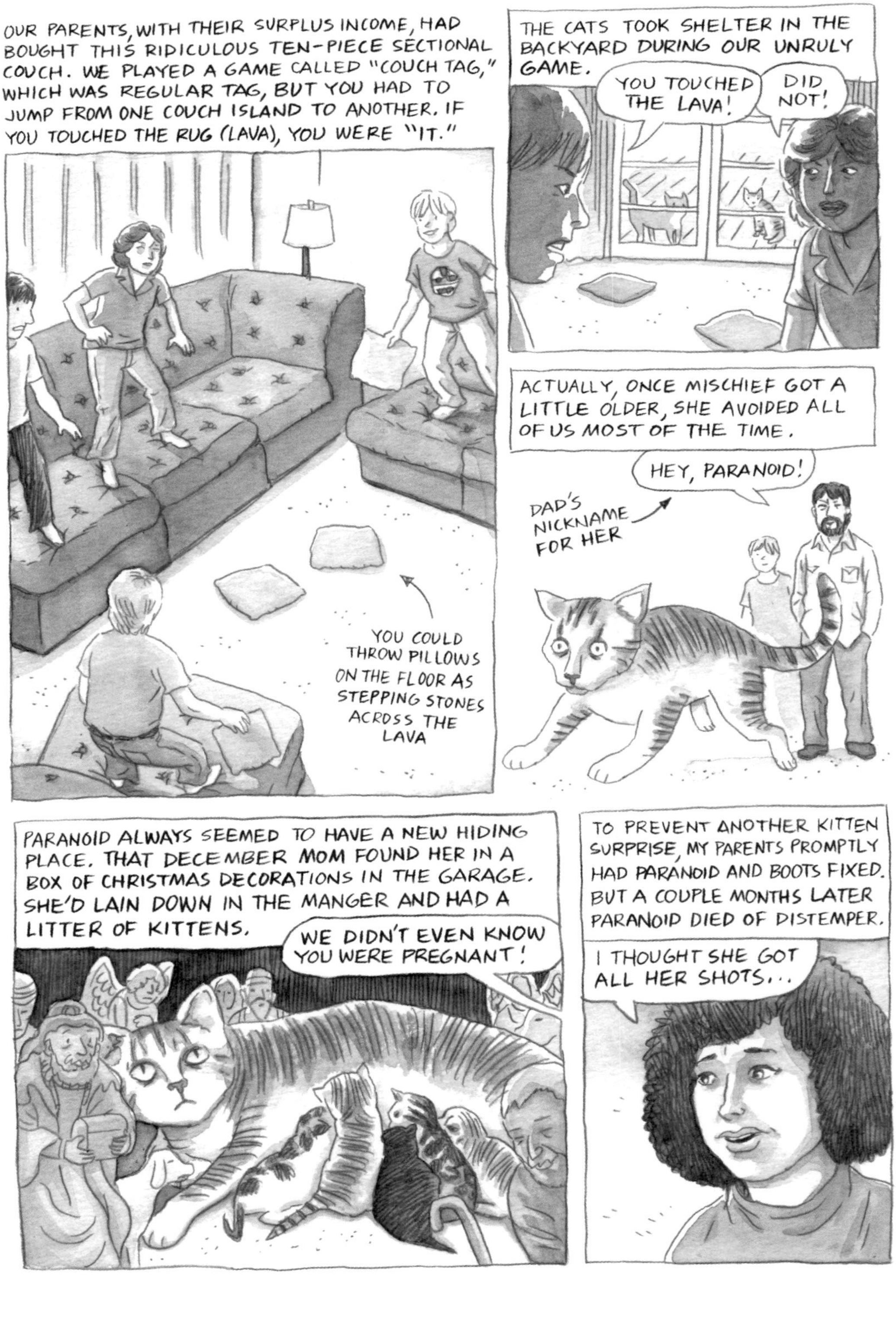
OUR PARENTS, WITH THEIR SURPLUS INCOME, HAD BOUGHT THIS RIDICULOUS TEN-PIECE SECTIONAL COUCH. WE PLAYED A GAME CALLED "COUCH TAG," WHICH WAS REGULAR TAG, BUT YOU HAD TO JUMP FROM ONE COUCH ISLAND TO ANOTHER. IF YOU TOUCHED THE RUG (LAVA), YOU WERE "IT."
YOU COULD THROW PILLOWS ON THE FLOOR AS STEPPING STONES ACROSS THE LAVA
THE CATS TOOK SHELTER IN THE BACKYARD DURING OUR UNRULY GAME.
YOU TOUCHED THE LAVA!
DID NOT!
ACTUALLY, ONCE MISCHIEF GOT A LITTLE OLDER, SHE AVOIDED ALL OF US MOST OF THE TIME.
HEY, PARANOID!
DAD'S NICKNAME FOR HER
PARANOID ALWAYS SEEMED TO HAVE A NEW HIDING PLACE. THAT DECEMBER MOM FOUND HER IN A BOX OF CHRISTMAS DECORATIONS IN THE GARAGE. SHE'D LAIN DOWN IN THE MANGER AND HAD A LITTER OF KITTENS.
WE DIDN'T EVEN KNOW YOU WERE PREGNANT!
TO PREVENT ANOTHER KITTEN SURPRISE, MY PARENTS PROMPTLY HAD PARANOID AND BOOTS FIXED. BUT A COUPLE MONTHS LATER PARANOID DIED OF DISTEMPER.
I THOUGHT SHE GOT ALL HER SHOTS...

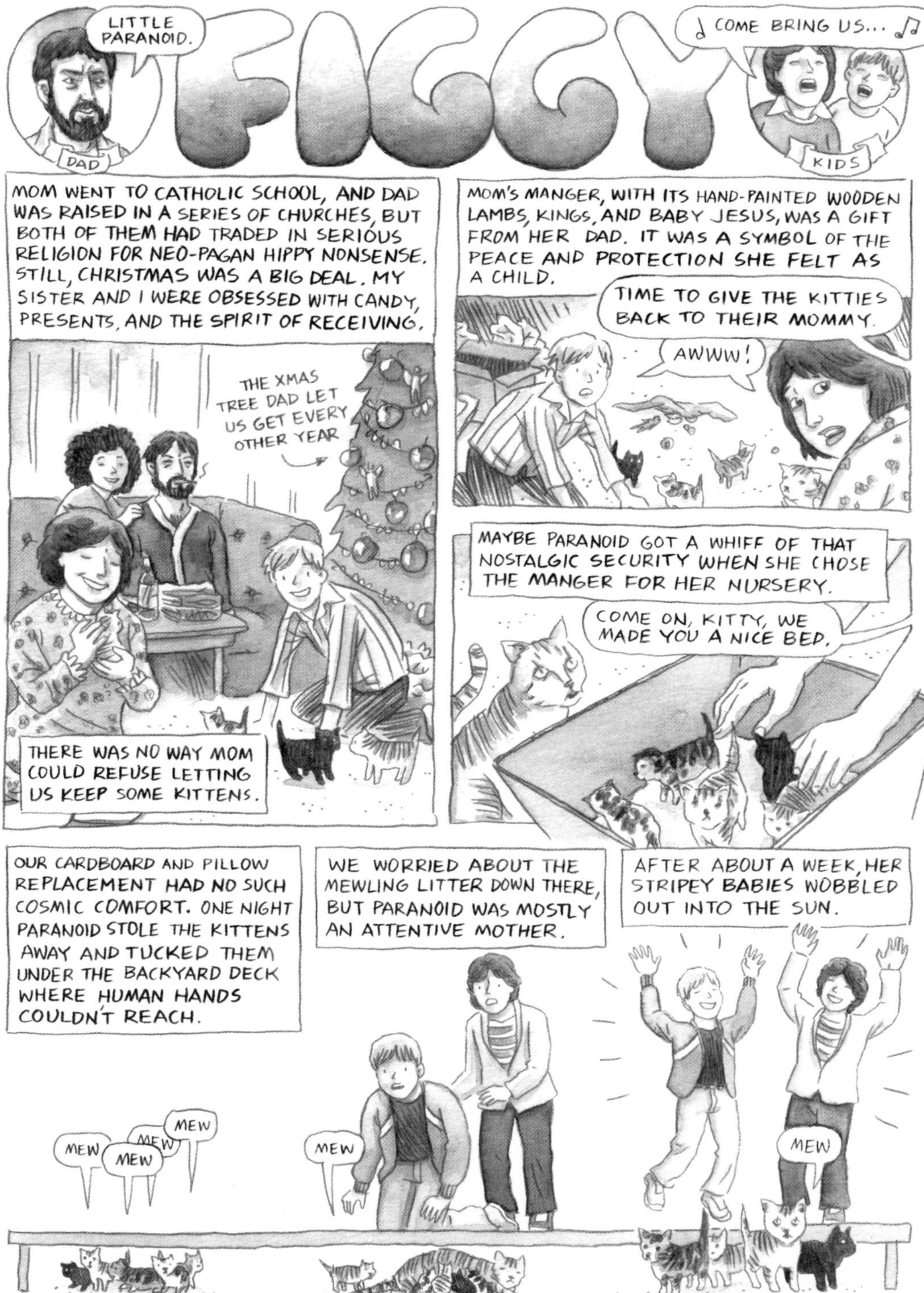

LITTLE PARANOID.
DAD
FIGGY
COME BRING US...
KIDS
MOM WENT TO CATHOLIC SCHOOL, AND DAD WAS RAISED IN A SERIES OF CHURCHES, BUT BOTH OF THEM HAD TRADED IN SERIOUS RELIGION FOR NEO-PAGAN HIPPY NONSENSE. STILL, CHRISTMAS WAS A BIG DEAL. MY SISTER AND I WERE OBSESSED WITH CANDY, PRESENTS, AND THE SPIRIT OF RECEIVING.
THE XMAS TREE DAD LET US GET EVERY OTHER YEAR
THERE WAS NO WAY MOM COULD REFUSE LETTING US KEEP SOME KITTENS.
MOM'S MANGER, WITH ITS HAND-PAINTED WOODEN LAMBS, KINGS, AND BABY JESUS, WAS A GIFT FROM HER DAD. IT WAS A SYMBOL OF THE PEACE AND PROTECTION SHE FELT AS A CHILD.
TIME TO GIVE THE KITTIES BACK TO THEIR MOMMY.
AWWW!
MAYBE PARANOID GOT A WHIFF OF THAT NOSTALGIC SECURITY WHEN SHE CHOSE THE MANGER FOR HER NURSERY.
COME ON, KITTY, WE MADE YOU A NICE BED.
OUR CARDBOARD AND PILLOW REPLACEMENT HAD NO SUCH COSMIC COMFORT. ONE NIGHT PARANOID STOLE THE KITTENS AWAY AND TUCKED THEM UNDER THE BACKYARD DECK WHERE HUMAN HANDS COULDN'T REACH.
MEW
MEW
MEW
MEW
WE WORRIED ABOUT THE MEWLING LITTER DOWN THERE, BUT PARANOID WAS MOSTLY AN ATTENTIVE MOTHER.
MEW
AFTER ABOUT A WEEK, HER STRIPEY BABIES WOBBLED OUT INTO THE SUN.
MEW

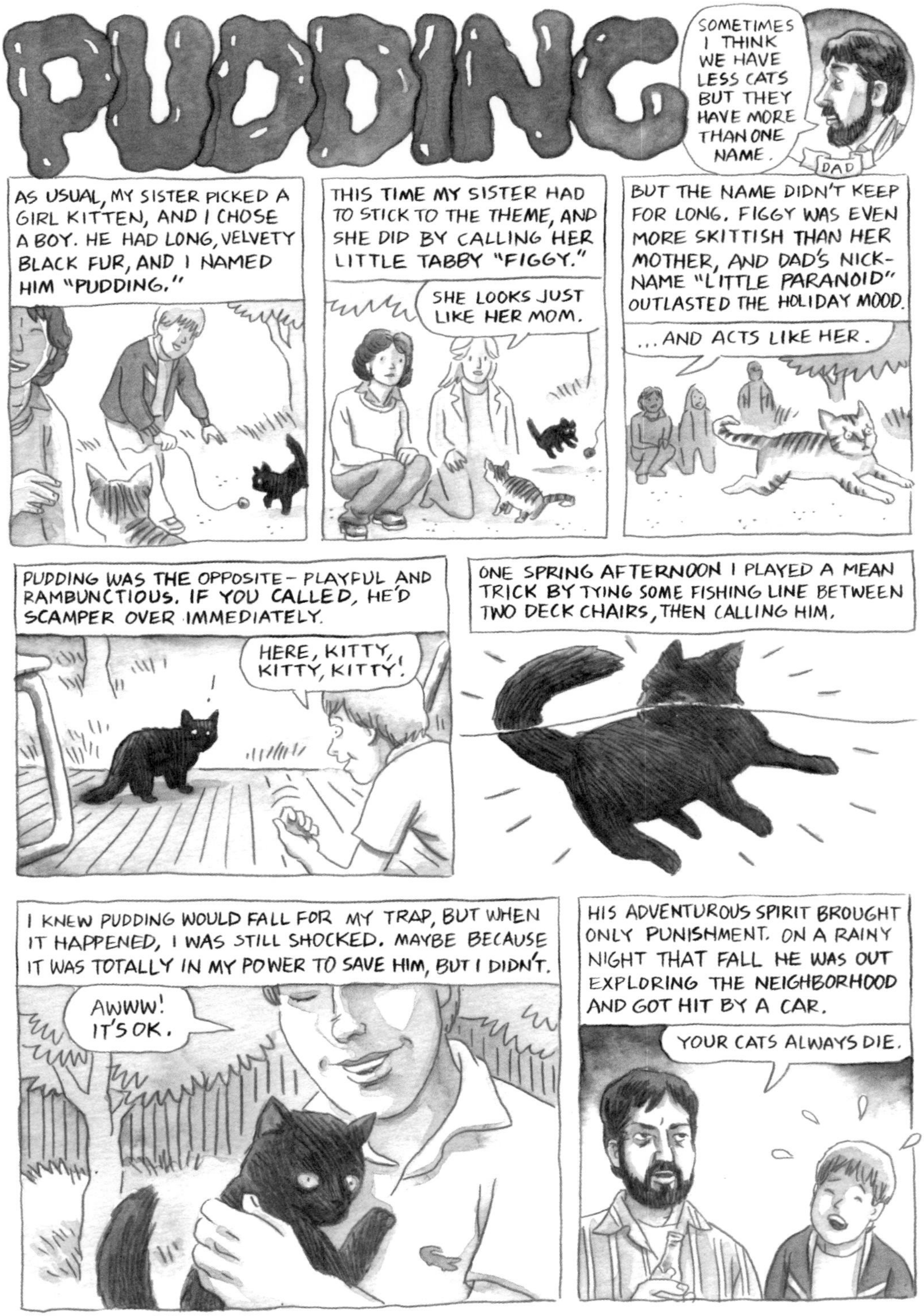
PUDDING
SOMETIMES I THINK WE HAVE LESS CATS BUT THEY HAVE MORE THAN ONE NAME.
DAD
AS USUAL, MY SISTER PICKED A GIRL KITTEN, AND I CHOSE A BOY. HE HAD LONG, VELVETY BLACK FUR, AND I NAMED HIM "PUDDING."
THIS TIME MY SISTER HAD TO STICK TO THE THEME, AND SHE DID BY CALLING HER LITTLE TABBY "FIGGY."
SHE LOOKS JUST LIKE HER MOM.
BUT THE NAME DIDN'T KEEP FOR LONG. FIGGY WAS EVEN MORE SKITTISH THAN HER MOTHER, AND DAD'S NICK-NAME "LITTLE PARANOID" OUTLASTED THE HOLIDAY MOOD.
...AND ACTS LIKE HER.
PUDDING WAS THE OPPOSITE – PLAYFUL AND RAMBUNCTIOUS. IF YOU CALLED, HE'D SCAMPER OVER IMMEDIATELY.
HERE, KITTY, KITTY, KITTY!
!
ONE SPRING AFTERNOON I PLAYED A MEAN TRICK BY TYING SOME FISHING LINE BETWEEN TWO DECK CHAIRS, THEN CALLING HIM.
I KNEW PUDDING WOULD FALL FOR MY TRAP, BUT WHEN IT HAPPENED, I WAS STILL SHOCKED. MAYBE BECAUSE IT WAS TOTALLY IN MY POWER TO SAVE HIM, BUT I DIDN'T.
AWWW! IT'S OK.
HIS ADVENTUROUS SPIRIT BROUGHT ONLY PUNISHMENT. ON A RAINY NIGHT THAT FALL HE WAS OUT EXPLORING THE NEIGHBORHOOD AND GOT HIT BY A CAR.
YOUR CATS ALWAYS DIE.

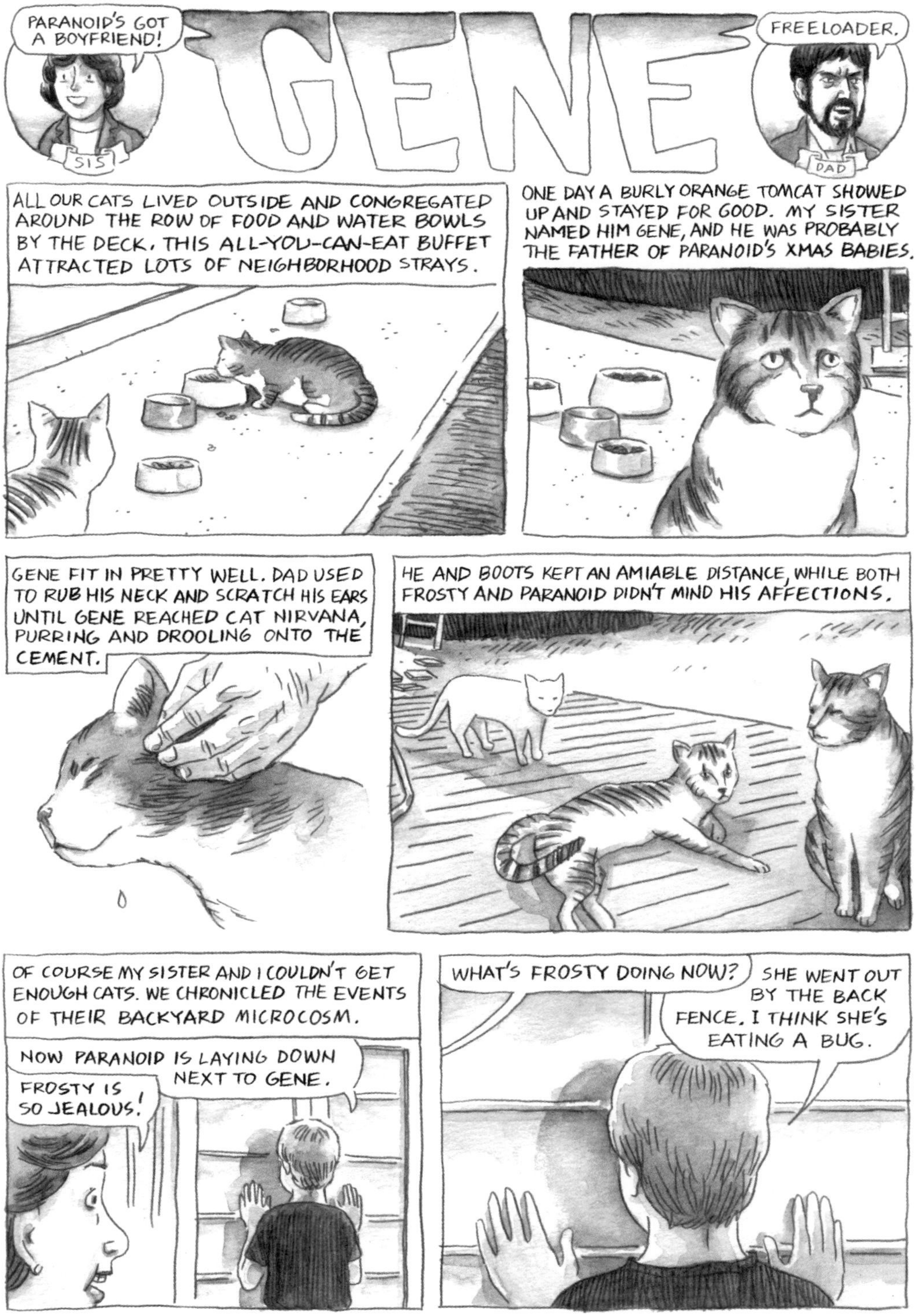
PARANOID'S GOT A BOYFRIEND!
SIS
GENE
FREELOADER.
DAD
ALL OUR CATS LIVED OUTSIDE AND CONGREGATED AROUND THE ROW OF FOOD AND WATER BOWLS BY THE DECK. THIS ALL-YOU-CAN-EAT BUFFET ATTRACTED LOTS OF NEIGHBORHOOD STRAYS.
ONE DAY A BURLY ORANGE TOMCAT SHOWED UP AND STAYED FOR GOOD. MY SISTER NAMED HIM GENE, AND HE WAS PROBABLY THE FATHER OF PARANOID'S XMAS BABIES.
GENE FIT IN PRETTY WELL. DAD USED TO RUB HIS NECK AND SCRATCH HIS EARS UNTIL GENE REACHED CAT NIRVANA, PURRING AND DROOLING ONTO THE CEMENT.
HE AND BOOTS KEPT AN AMIABLE DISTANCE, WHILE BOTH FROSTY AND PARANOID DIDN'T MIND HIS AFFECTIONS.
OF COURSE MY SISTER AND I COULDN'T GET ENOUGH CATS. WE CHRONICLED THE EVENTS OF THEIR BACKYARD MICROCOSM.
NOW PARANOID IS LAYING DOWN NEXT TO GENE.
FROSTY IS SO JEALOUS!
WHAT'S FROSTY DOING NOW?
SHE WENT OUT BY THE BACK FENCE. I THINK SHE'S EATING A BUG.

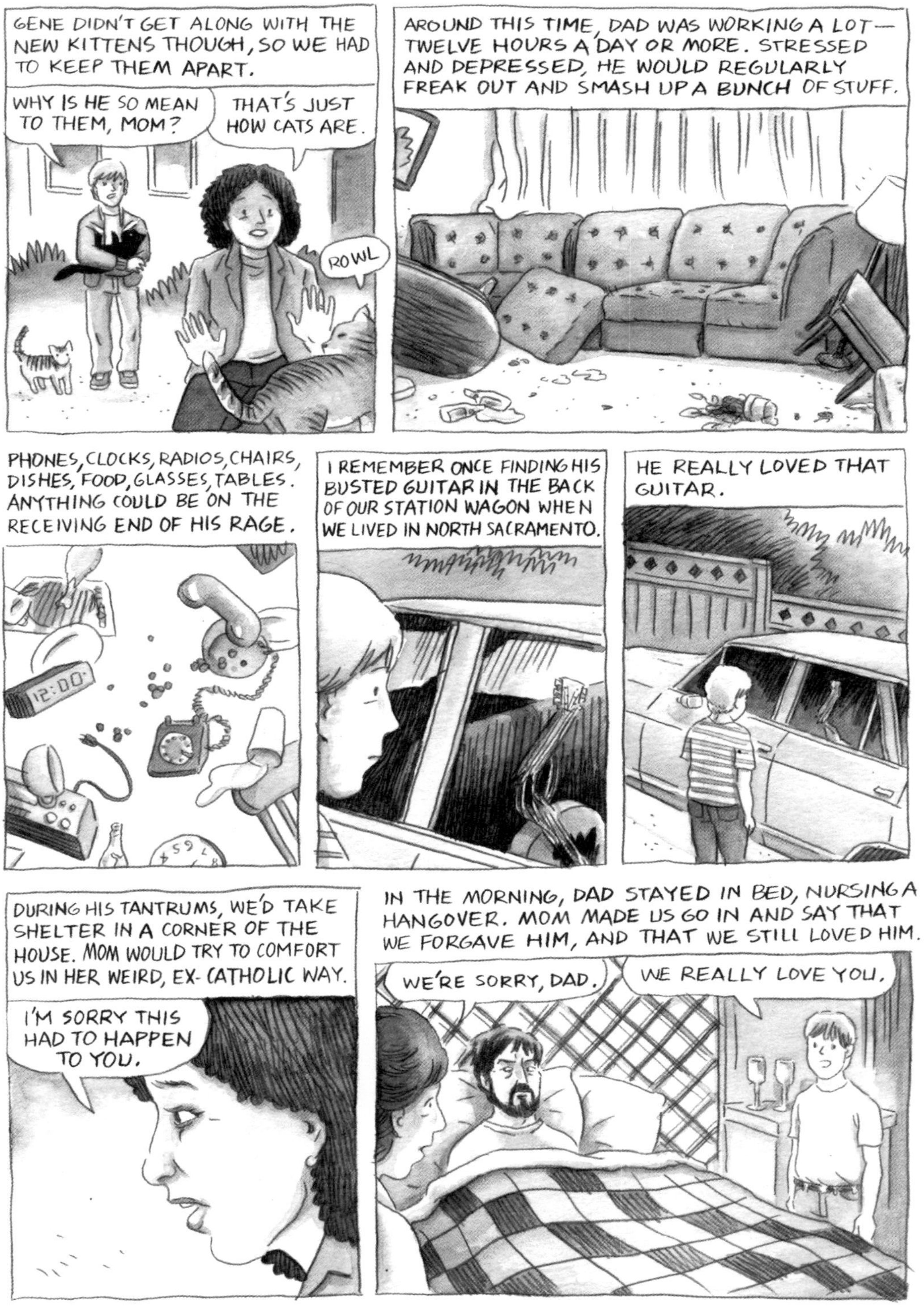
GENE DIDN'T GET ALONG WITH THE NEW KITTENS THOUGH, SO WE HAD TO KEEP THEM APART.
WHY IS HE SO MEAN TO THEM, MOM?
THAT'S JUST HOW CATS ARE.
ROWL
AROUND THIS TIME, DAD WAS WORKING A LOT— TWELVE HOURS A DAY OR MORE. STRESSED AND DEPRESSED, HE WOULD REGULARLY FREAK OUT AND SMASH UP A BUNCH OF STUFF.
PHONES, CLOCKS, RADIOS, CHAIRS, DISHES, FOOD, GLASSES, TABLES. ANYTHING COULD BE ON THE RECEIVING END OF HIS RAGE.
12:00
I REMEMBER ONCE FINDING HIS BUSTED GUITAR IN THE BACK OF OUR STATION WAGON WHEN WE LIVED IN NORTH SACRAMENTO.
HE REALLY LOVED THAT GUITAR.
DURING HIS TANTRUMS, WE'D TAKE SHELTER IN A CORNER OF THE HOUSE. MOM WOULD TRY TO COMFORT US IN HER WEIRD, EX-CATHOLIC WAY.
I'M SORRY THIS HAD TO HAPPEN TO YOU.
IN THE MORNING, DAD STAYED IN BED, NURSING A HANGOVER. MOM MADE US GO IN AND SAY THAT WE FORGAVE HIM, AND THAT WE STILL LOVED HIM.
WE'RE SORRY, DAD.
WE REALLY LOVE YOU.

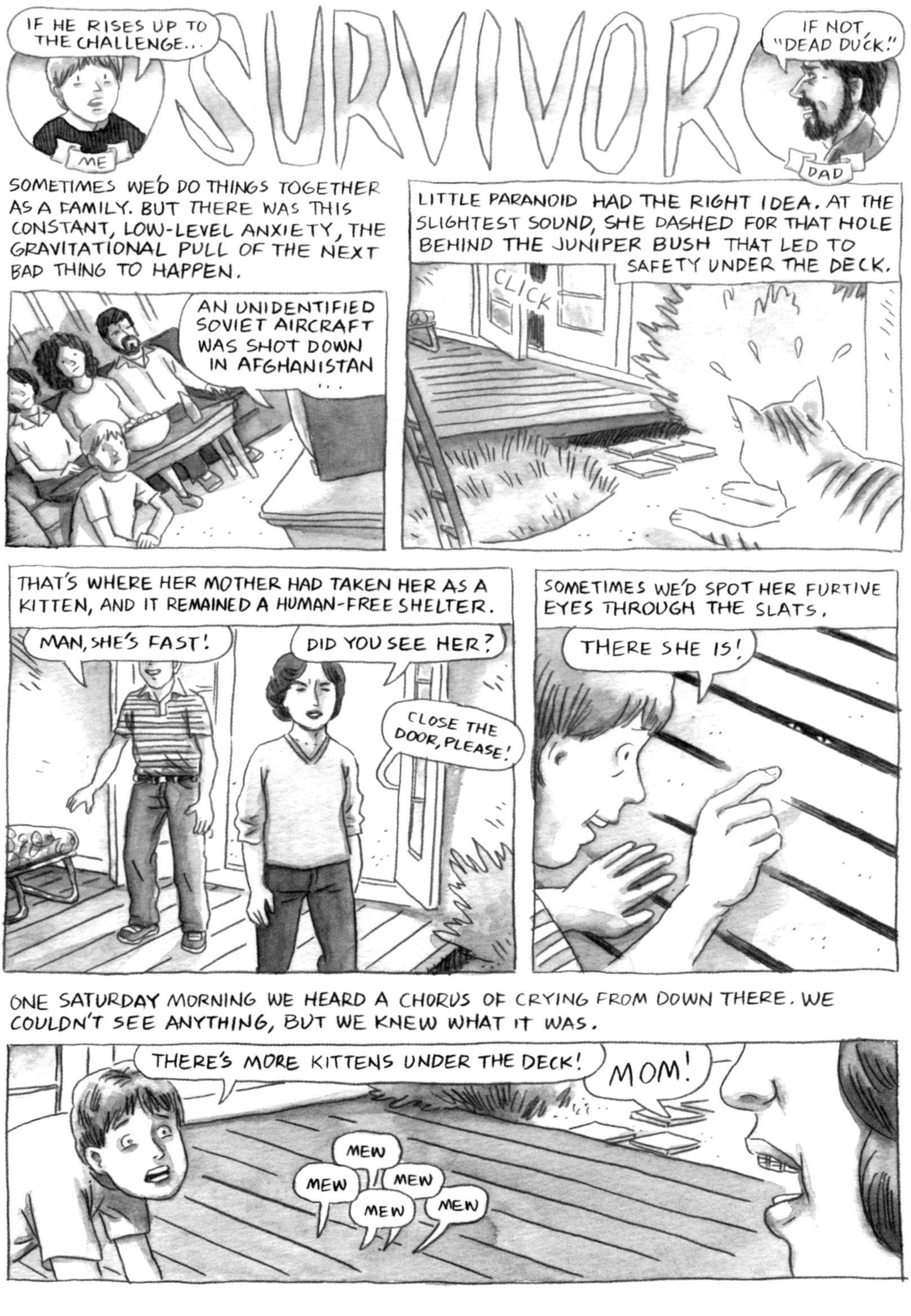

SURVIVOR
IF HE RISES UP TO THE CHALLENGE...
ME
IF NOT, "DEAD DUCK."
DAD
SOMETIMES WE'D DO THINGS TOGETHER AS A FAMILY. BUT THERE WAS THIS CONSTANT, LOW-LEVEL ANXIETY, THE GRAVITATIONAL PULL OF THE NEXT BAD THING TO HAPPEN.
AN UNIDENTIFIED SOVIET AIRCRAFT WAS SHOT DOWN IN AFGHANISTAN ...
LITTLE PARANOID HAD THE RIGHT IDEA. AT THE SLIGHTEST SOUND, SHE DASHED FOR THAT HOLE BEHIND THE JUNIPER BUSH THAT LED TO SAFETY UNDER THE DECK.
CLICK
THAT'S WHERE HER MOTHER HAD TAKEN HER AS A KITTEN, AND IT REMAINED A HUMAN-FREE SHELTER.
MAN, SHE'S FAST!
DID YOU SEE HER?
CLOSE THE DOOR, PLEASE!
SOMETIMES WE'D SPOT HER FURTIVE EYES THROUGH THE SLATS.
THERE SHE IS!
ONE SATURDAY MORNING WE HEARD A CHORUS OF CRYING FROM DOWN THERE. WE COULDN'T SEE ANYTHING, BUT WE KNEW WHAT IT WAS.
THERE'S MORE KITTENS UNDER THE DECK!
MOM!
MEW
MEW
MEW
MEW
MEW

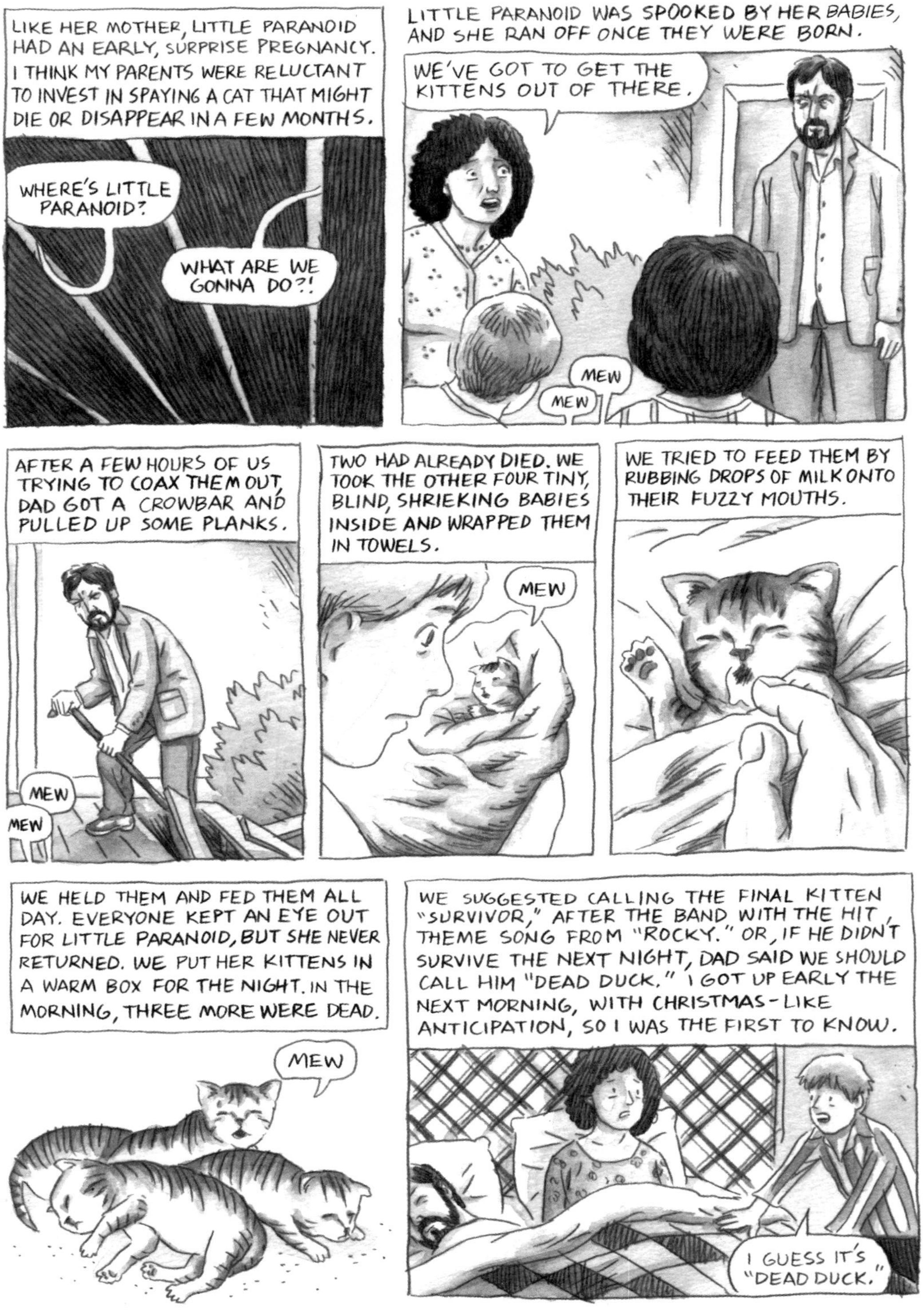
LIKE HER MOTHER, LITTLE PARANOID HAD AN EARLY, SURPRISE PREGNANCY. I THINK MY PARENTS WERE RELUCTANT TO INVEST IN SPAYING A CAT THAT MIGHT DIE OR DISAPPEAR IN A FEW MONTHS.
WHERE'S LITTLE PARANOID?
WHAT ARE WE GONNA DO?!
LITTLE PARANOID WAS SPOOKED BY HER BABIES, AND SHE RAN OFF ONCE THEY WERE BORN.
WE'VE GOT TO GET THE KITTENS OUT OF THERE.
MEW
MEW
AFTER A FEW HOURS OF US TRYING TO COAX THEM OUT, DAD GOT A CROWBAR AND PULLED UP SOME PLANKS.
MEW
MEW
TWO HAD ALREADY DIED. WE TOOK THE OTHER FOUR TINY, BLIND, SHRIEKING BABIES INSIDE AND WRAPPED THEM IN TOWELS.
MEW
WE TRIED TO FEED THEM BY RUBBING DROPS OF MILK ONTO THEIR FUZZY MOUTHS.
WE HELD THEM AND FED THEM ALL DAY. EVERYONE KEPT AN EYE OUT FOR LITTLE PARANOID, BUT SHE NEVER RETURNED. WE PUT HER KITTENS IN A WARM BOX FOR THE NIGHT. IN THE MORNING, THREE MORE WERE DEAD.
MEW
WE SUGGESTED CALLING THE FINAL KITTEN "SURVIVOR," AFTER THE BAND WITH THE HIT THEME SONG FROM "ROCKY." OR, IF HE DIDN'T SURVIVE THE NEXT NIGHT, DAD SAID WE SHOULD CALL HIM "DEAD DUCK." I GOT UP EARLY THE NEXT MORNING, WITH CHRISTMAS-LIKE ANTICIPATION, SO I WAS THE FIRST TO KNOW.
I GUESS IT'S "DEAD DUCK."

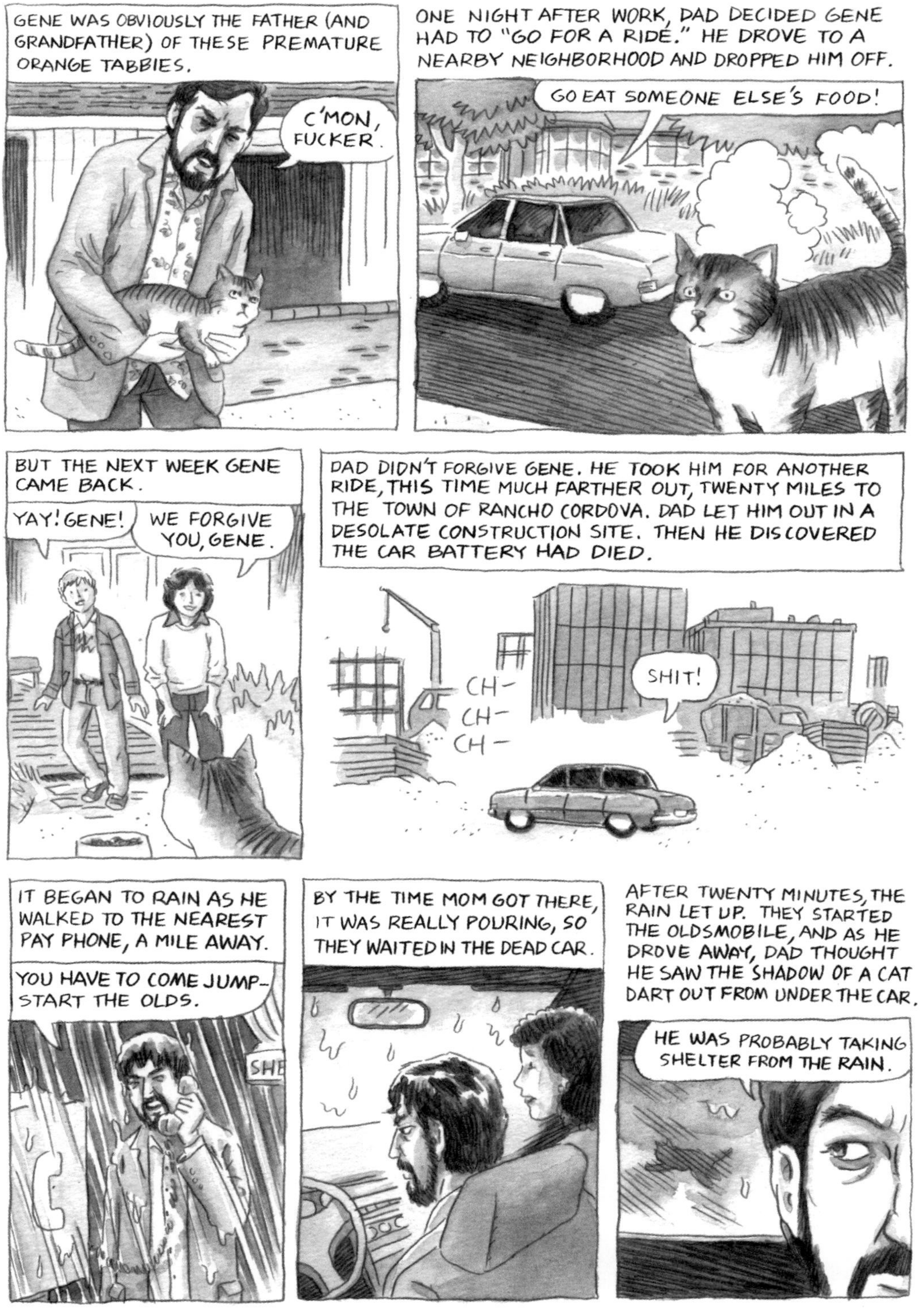

GENE WAS OBVIOUSLY THE FATHER (AND GRANDFATHER) OF THESE PREMATURE ORANGE TABBIES.
C'MON, FUCKER.
ONE NIGHT AFTER WORK, DAD DECIDED GENE HAD TO "GO FOR A RIDE." HE DROVE TO A NEARBY NEIGHBORHOOD AND DROPPED HIM OFF.
GO EAT SOMEONE ELSE'S FOOD!
BUT THE NEXT WEEK GENE CAME BACK.
YAY! GENE!
WE FORGIVE YOU, GENE.
DAD DIDN'T FORGIVE GENE. HE TOOK HIM FOR ANOTHER RIDE, THIS TIME MUCH FARTHER OUT, TWENTY MILES TO THE TOWN OF RANCHO CORDOVA. DAD LET HIM OUT IN A DESOLATE CONSTRUCTION SITE. THEN HE DISCOVERED THE CAR BATTERY HAD DIED.
CH- CH- CH-
SHIT!
IT BEGAN TO RAIN AS HE WALKED TO THE NEAREST PAY PHONE, A MILE AWAY.
YOU HAVE TO COME JUMP-START THE OLDS.
SHE
BY THE TIME MOM GOT THERE, IT WAS REALLY POURING, SO THEY WAITED IN THE DEAD CAR.
AFTER TWENTY MINUTES, THE RAIN LET UP. THEY STARTED THE OLDSMOBILE, AND AS HE DROVE AWAY, DAD THOUGHT HE SAW THE SHADOW OF A CAT DART OUT FROM UNDER THE CAR.
HE WAS PROBABLY TAKING SHELTER FROM THE RAIN.

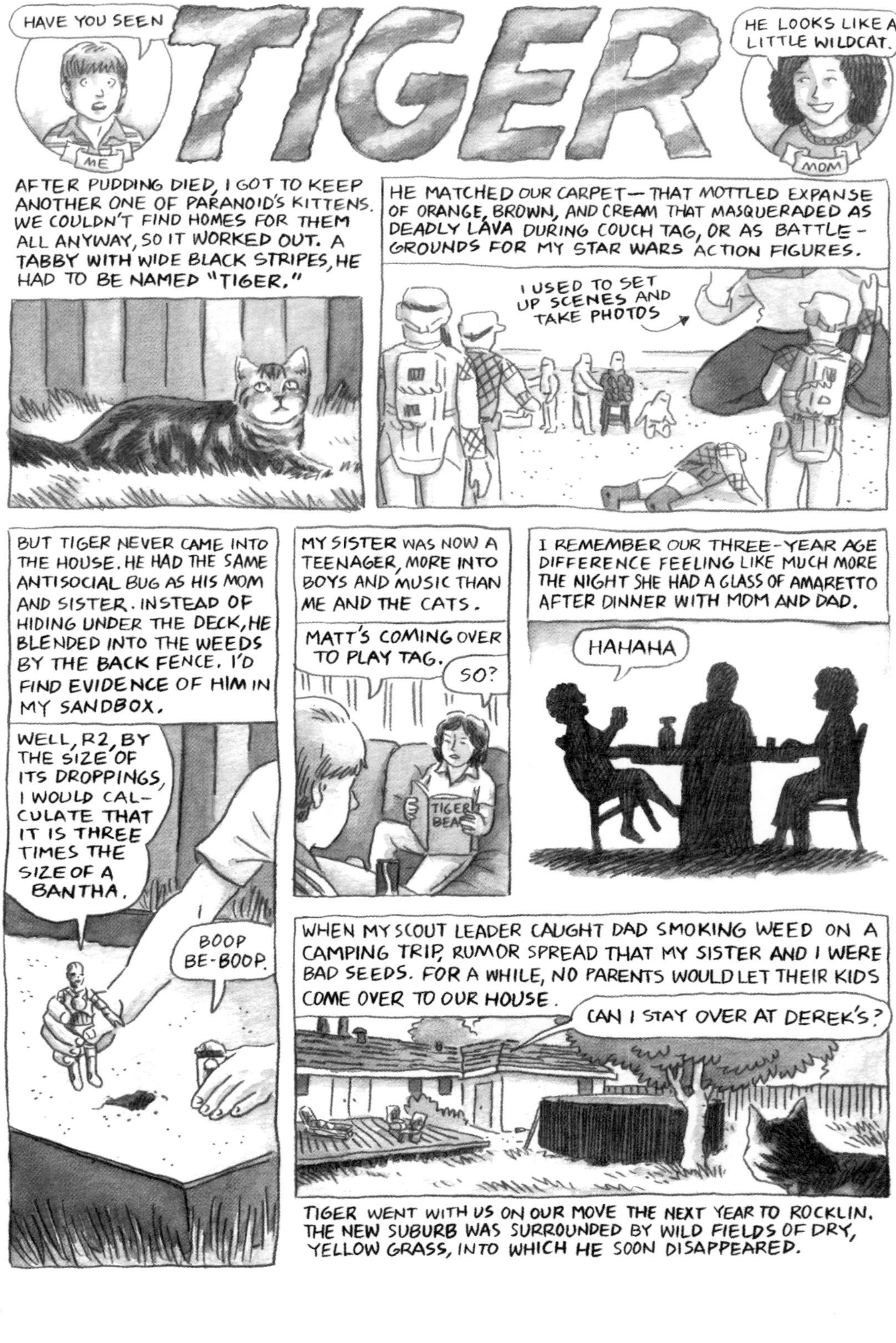
HAVE YOU SEEN
TIGER
HE LOOKS LIKE A LITTLE WILDCAT.
ME
MOM
AFTER PUDDING DIED, I GOT TO KEEP ANOTHER ONE OF PARANOID'S KITTENS. WE COULDN'T FIND HOMES FOR THEM ALL ANYWAY, SO IT WORKED OUT. A TABBY WITH WIDE BLACK STRIPES, HE HAD TO BE NAMED "TIGER."
HE MATCHED OUR CARPET— THAT MOTTLED EXPANSE OF ORANGE, BROWN, AND CREAM THAT MASQUERADED AS DEADLY LAVA DURING COUCH TAG, OR AS BATTLE-GROUNDS FOR MY STAR WARS ACTION FIGURES.
I USED TO SET UP SCENES AND TAKE PHOTOS
BUT TIGER NEVER CAME INTO THE HOUSE. HE HAD THE SAME ANTISOCIAL BUG AS HIS MOM AND SISTER. INSTEAD OF HIDING UNDER THE DECK, HE BLENDED INTO THE WEEDS BY THE BACK FENCE. I'D FIND EVIDENCE OF HIM IN MY SANDBOX.
WELL, R2, BY THE SIZE OF ITS DROPPINGS, I WOULD CALCULATE THAT IT IS THREE TIMES THE SIZE OF A BANTHA.
BOOP BE-BOOP.
MY SISTER WAS NOW A TEENAGER, MORE INTO BOYS AND MUSIC THAN ME AND THE CATS.
MATT'S COMING OVER TO PLAY TAG.
SO?
TIGER BEA
I REMEMBER OUR THREE-YEAR AGE DIFFERENCE FEELING LIKE MUCH MORE THE NIGHT SHE HAD A GLASS OF AMARETTO AFTER DINNER WITH MOM AND DAD.
HAHAHA
WHEN MY SCOUT LEADER CAUGHT DAD SMOKING WEED ON A CAMPING TRIP, RUMOR SPREAD THAT MY SISTER AND I WERE BAD SEEDS. FOR A WHILE, NO PARENTS WOULD LET THEIR KIDS COME OVER TO OUR HOUSE.
CAN I STAY OVER AT DEREK'S?
TIGER WENT WITH US ON OUR MOVE THE NEXT YEAR TO ROCKLIN. THE NEW SUBURB WAS SURROUNDED BY WILD FIELDS OF DRY, YELLOW GRASS, INTO WHICH HE SOON DISAPPEARED.

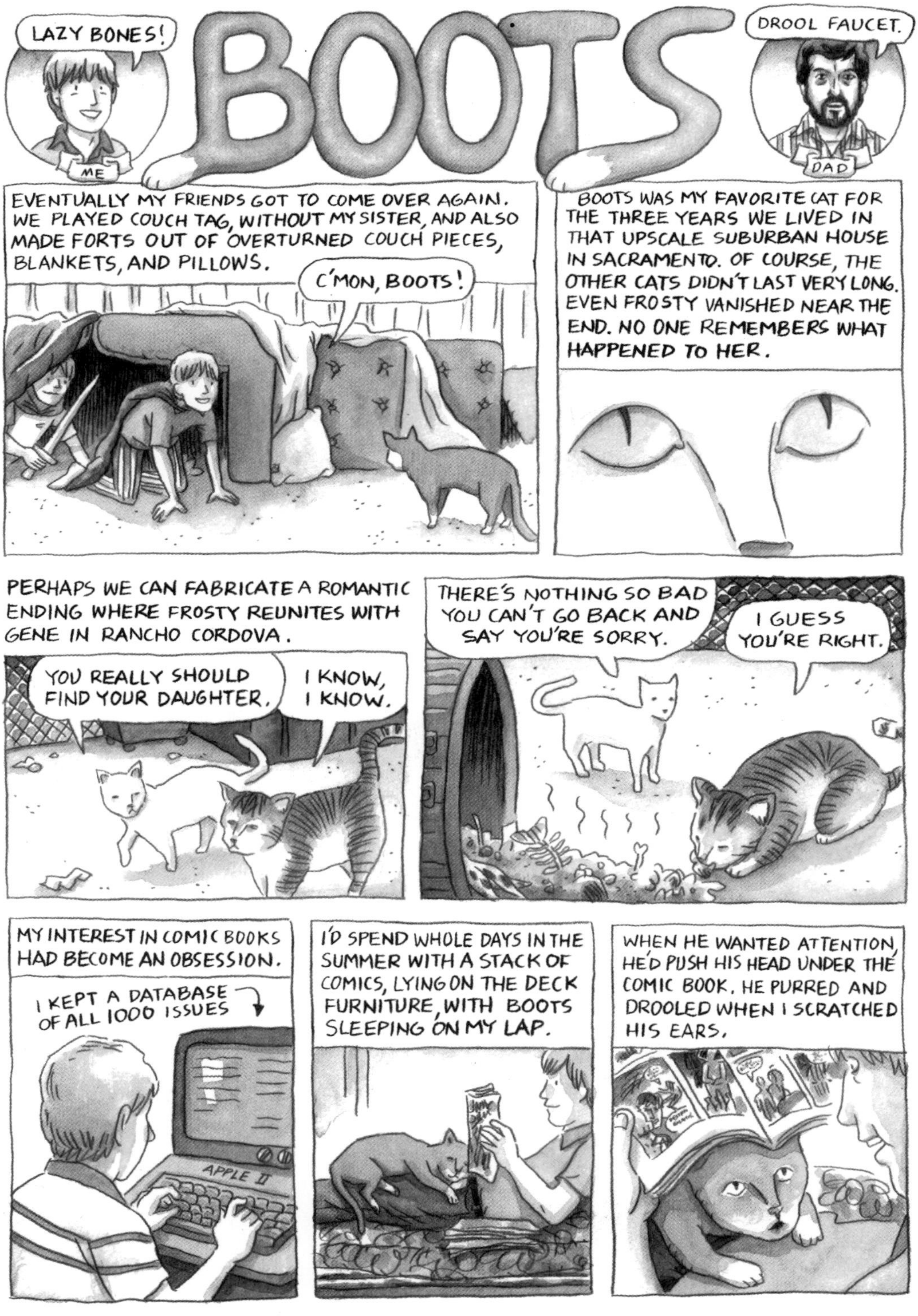
LAZY BONES!
ME
BOOTS
DROOL FAUCET.
DAD
EVENTUALLY MY FRIENDS GOT TO COME OVER AGAIN. WE PLAYED COUCH TAG, WITHOUT MY SISTER, AND ALSO MADE FORTS OUT OF OVERTURNED COUCH PIECES, BLANKETS, AND PILLOWS.
C'MON, BOOTS!
BOOTS WAS MY FAVORITE CAT FOR THE THREE YEARS WE LIVED IN THAT UPSCALE SUBURBAN HOUSE IN SACRAMENTO. OF COURSE, THE OTHER CATS DIDN'T LAST VERY LONG. EVEN FROSTY VANISHED NEAR THE END. NO ONE REMEMBERS WHAT HAPPENED TO HER.
PERHAPS WE CAN FABRICATE A ROMANTIC ENDING WHERE FROSTY REUNITES WITH GENE IN RANCHO CORDOVA.
YOU REALLY SHOULD FIND YOUR DAUGHTER.
I KNOW, I KNOW.
THERE'S NOTHING SO BAD YOU CAN'T GO BACK AND SAY YOU'RE SORRY.
I GUESS YOU'RE RIGHT.
MY INTEREST IN COMIC BOOKS HAD BECOME AN OBSESSION.
I KEPT A DATABASE OF ALL 1000 ISSUES
APPLE II
I'D SPEND WHOLE DAYS IN THE SUMMER WITH A STACK OF COMICS, LYING ON THE DECK FURNITURE, WITH BOOTS SLEEPING ON MY LAP.
WHEN HE WANTED ATTENTION, HE'D PUSH HIS HEAD UNDER THE COMIC BOOK. HE PURRED AND DROOLED WHEN I SCRATCHED HIS EARS.

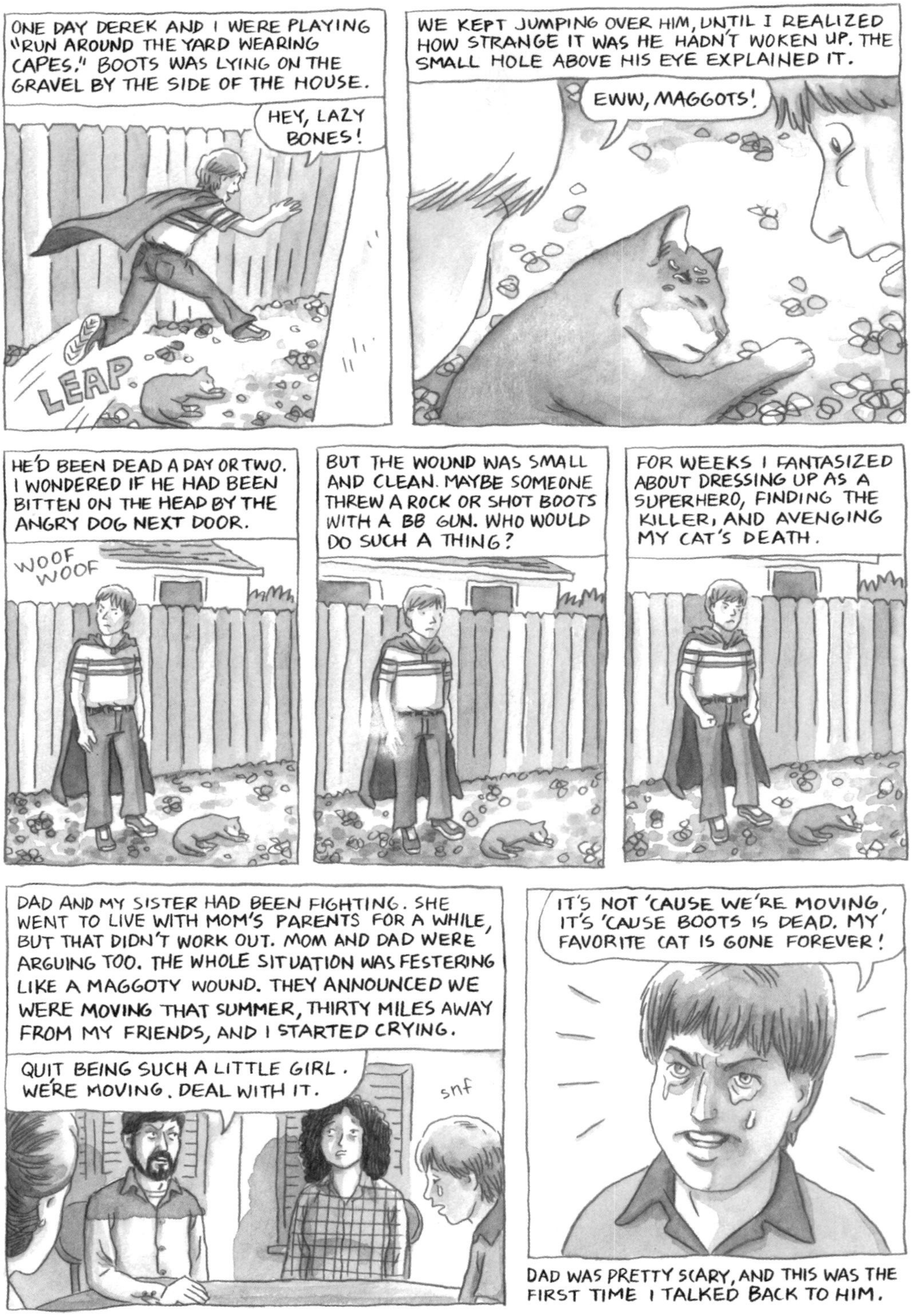
ONE DAY DEREK AND I WERE PLAYING "RUN AROUND THE YARD WEARING CAPES." BOOTS WAS LYING ON THE GRAVEL BY THE SIDE OF THE HOUSE.
HEY, LAZY BONES!
LEAP
WE KEPT JUMPING OVER HIM, UNTIL I REALIZED HOW STRANGE IT WAS HE HADN'T WOKEN UP. THE SMALL HOLE ABOVE HIS EYE EXPLAINED IT.
EWW, MAGGOTS!
HE'D BEEN DEAD A DAY OR TWO. I WONDERED IF HE HAD BEEN BITTEN ON THE HEAD BY THE ANGRY DOG NEXT DOOR.
WOOF WOOF
BUT THE WOUND WAS SMALL AND CLEAN. MAYBE SOMEONE THREW A ROCK OR SHOT BOOTS WITH A BB GUN. WHO WOULD DO SUCH A THING?
FOR WEEKS I FANTASIZED ABOUT DRESSING UP AS A SUPERHERO, FINDING THE KILLER, AND AVENGING MY CAT'S DEATH.
DAD AND MY SISTER HAD BEEN FIGHTING. SHE WENT TO LIVE WITH MOM'S PARENTS FOR A WHILE, BUT THAT DIDN'T WORK OUT. MOM AND DAD WERE ARGUING TOO. THE WHOLE SITUATION WAS FESTERING LIKE A MAGGOTY WOUND. THEY ANNOUNCED WE WERE MOVING THAT SUMMER, THIRTY MILES AWAY FROM MY FRIENDS, AND I STARTED CRYING.
QUIT BEING SUCH A LITTLE GIRL. WE'RE MOVING. DEAL WITH IT.
snf
IT'S NOT 'CAUSE WE'RE MOVING, IT'S 'CAUSE BOOTS IS DEAD. MY FAVORITE CAT IS GONE FOREVER!
DAD WAS PRETTY SCARY, AND THIS WAS THE FIRST TIME I TALKED BACK TO HIM.

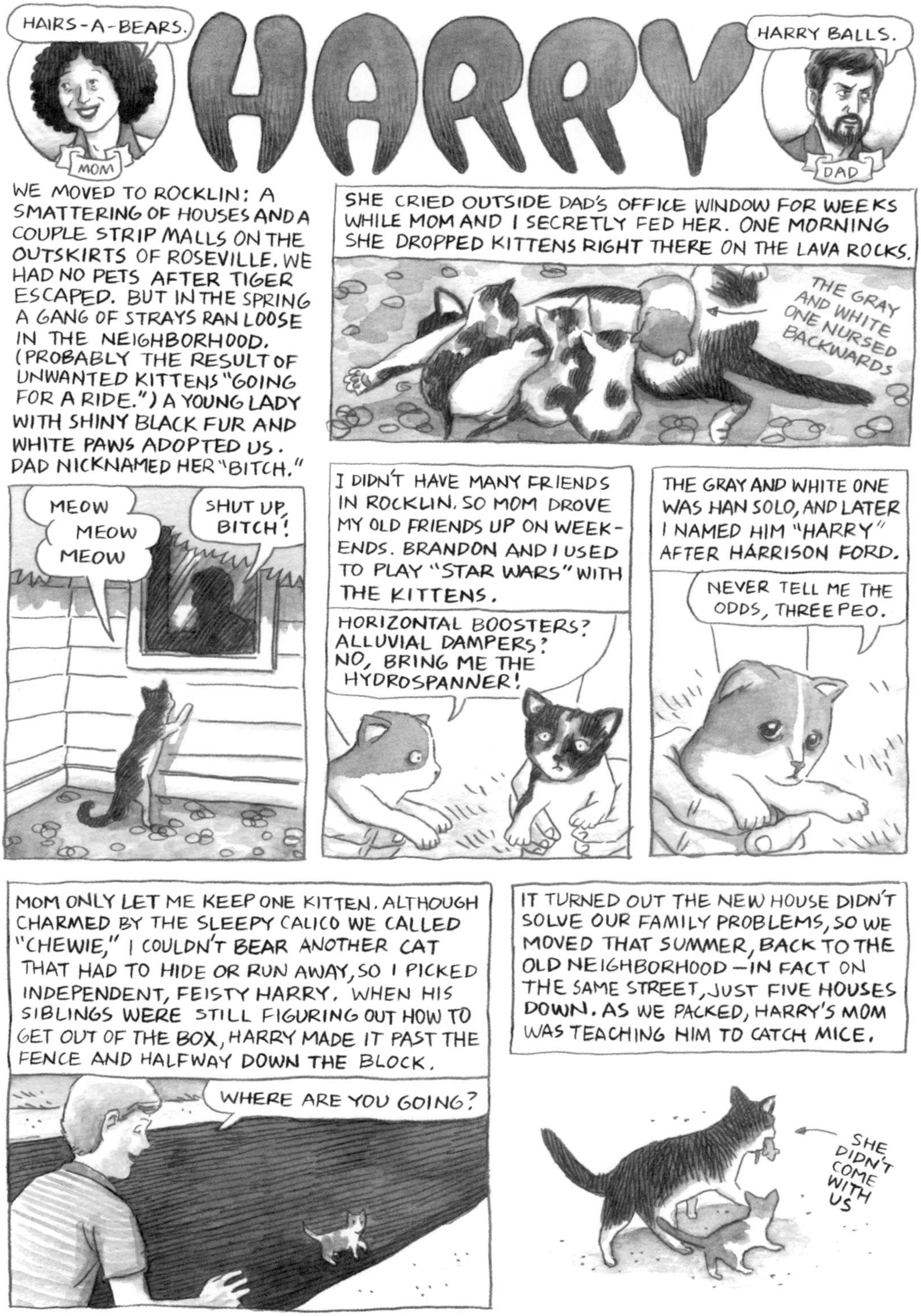
HAIRS-A-BEARS.
MOM
HARRY
HARRY BALLS.
DAD
WE MOVED TO ROCKLIN: A SMATTERING OF HOUSES AND A COUPLE STRIP MALLS ON THE OUTSKIRTS OF ROSEVILLE. WE HAD NO PETS AFTER TIGER ESCAPED. BUT IN THE SPRING A GANG OF STRAYS RAN LOOSE IN THE NEIGHBORHOOD. (PROBABLY THE RESULT OF UNWANTED KITTENS "GOING FOR A RIDE.") A YOUNG LADY WITH SHINY BLACK FUR AND WHITE PAWS ADOPTED US. DAD NICKNAMED HER "BITCH."
SHE CRIED OUTSIDE DAD'S OFFICE WINDOW FOR WEEKS WHILE MOM AND I SECRETLY FED HER. ONE MORNING SHE DROPPED KITTENS RIGHT THERE ON THE LAVA ROCKS.
THE GRAY AND WHITE ONE NURSED BACKWARDS
MEOW MEOW MEOW
SHUT UP, BITCH!
I DIDN'T HAVE MANY FRIENDS IN ROCKLIN, SO MOM DROVE MY OLD FRIENDS UP ON WEEK-ENDS. BRANDON AND I USED TO PLAY "STAR WARS" WITH THE KITTENS.
HORIZONTAL BOOSTERS? ALLUVIAL DAMPERS? NO, BRING ME THE HYDROSPANNER!
THE GRAY AND WHITE ONE WAS HAN SOLO, AND LATER I NAMED HIM "HARRY" AFTER HARRISON FORD.
NEVER TELL ME THE ODDS, THREEPEO.
MOM ONLY LET ME KEEP ONE KITTEN. ALTHOUGH CHARMED BY THE SLEEPY CALICO WE CALLED "CHEWIE," I COULDN'T BEAR ANOTHER CAT THAT HAD TO HIDE OR RUN AWAY, SO I PICKED INDEPENDENT, FEISTY HARRY. WHEN HIS SIBLINGS WERE STILL FIGURING OUT HOW TO GET OUT OF THE BOX, HARRY MADE IT PAST THE FENCE AND HALFWAY DOWN THE BLOCK.
WHERE ARE YOU GOING?
IT TURNED OUT THE NEW HOUSE DIDN'T SOLVE OUR FAMILY PROBLEMS, SO WE MOVED THAT SUMMER, BACK TO THE OLD NEIGHBORHOOD — IN FACT ON THE SAME STREET, JUST FIVE HOUSES DOWN. AS WE PACKED, HARRY'S MOM WAS TEACHING HIM TO CATCH MICE.
SHE DIDN'T COME WITH US

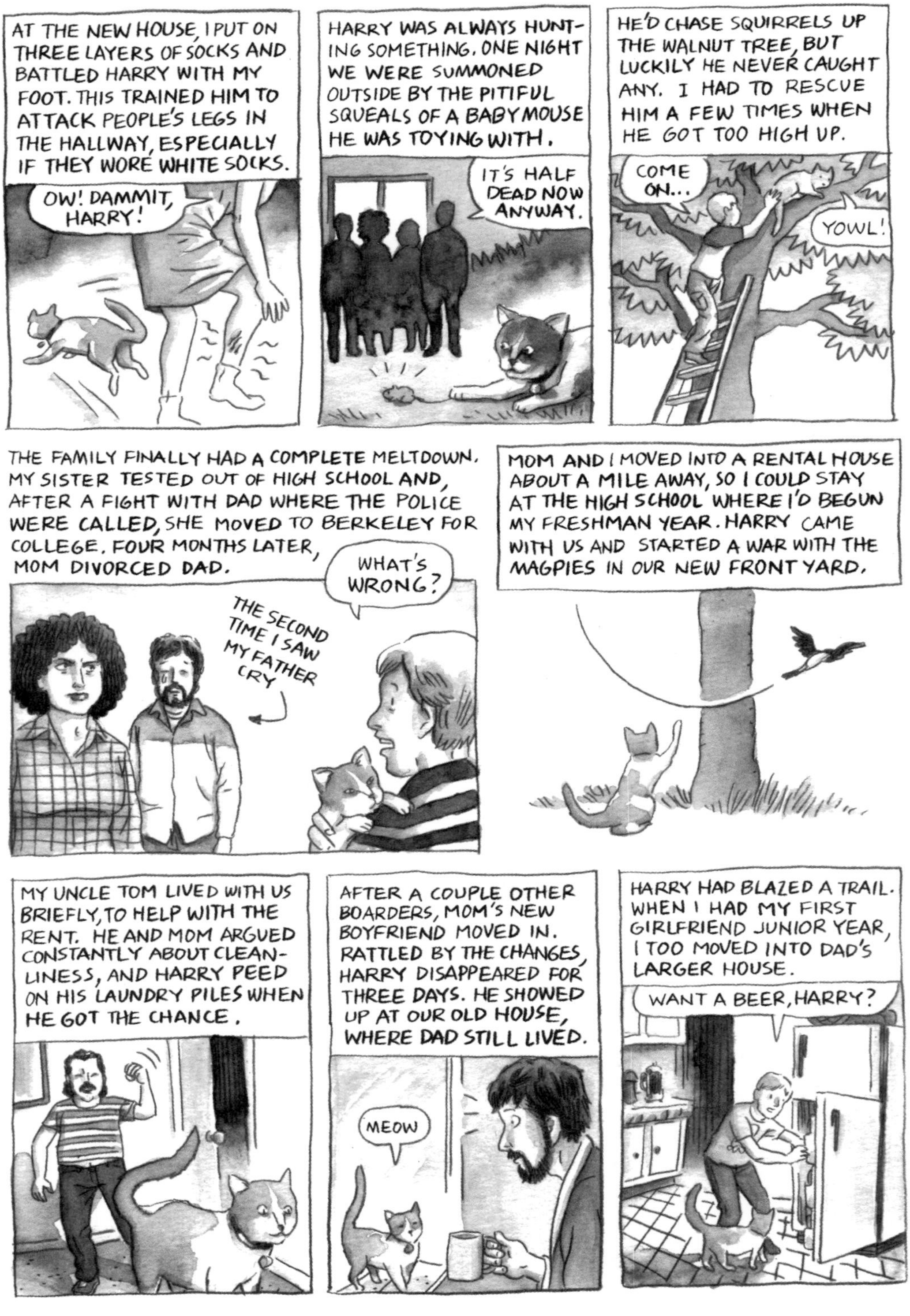
AT THE NEW HOUSE, I PUT ON THREE LAYERS OF SOCKS AND BATTLED HARRY WITH MY FOOT. THIS TRAINED HIM TO ATTACK PEOPLE'S LEGS IN THE HALLWAY, ESPECIALLY IF THEY WORE WHITE SOCKS.
OW! DAMMIT, HARRY!
HARRY WAS ALWAYS HUNTING SOMETHING. ONE NIGHT WE WERE SUMMONED OUTSIDE BY THE PITIFUL SQUEALS OF A BABY MOUSE HE WAS TOYING WITH.
IT'S HALF DEAD NOW ANYWAY.
HE'D CHASE SQUIRRELS UP THE WALNUT TREE, BUT LUCKILY HE NEVER CAUGHT ANY. I HAD TO RESCUE HIM A FEW TIMES WHEN HE GOT TOO HIGH UP.
COME ON...
YOWL!
THE FAMILY FINALLY HAD A COMPLETE MELTDOWN. MY SISTER TESTED OUT OF HIGH SCHOOL AND, AFTER A FIGHT WITH DAD WHERE THE POLICE WERE CALLED, SHE MOVED TO BERKELEY FOR COLLEGE. FOUR MONTHS LATER, MOM DIVORCED DAD.
WHAT'S WRONG?
THE SECOND TIME I SAW MY FATHER CRY
MOM AND I MOVED INTO A RENTAL HOUSE ABOUT A MILE AWAY, SO I COULD STAY AT THE HIGH SCHOOL WHERE I'D BEGUN MY FRESHMAN YEAR. HARRY CAME WITH US AND STARTED A WAR WITH THE MAGPIES IN OUR NEW FRONT YARD.
MY UNCLE TOM LIVED WITH US BRIEFLY, TO HELP WITH THE RENT. HE AND MOM ARGUED CONSTANTLY ABOUT CLEANLINESS, AND HARRY PEED ON HIS LAUNDRY PILES WHEN HE GOT THE CHANCE.
AFTER A COUPLE OTHER BOARDERS, MOM'S NEW BOYFRIEND MOVED IN. RATTLED BY THE CHANGES, HARRY DISAPPEARED FOR THREE DAYS. HE SHOWED UP AT OUR OLD HOUSE, WHERE DAD STILL LIVED.
MEOW
HARRY HAD BLAZED A TRAIL. WHEN I HAD MY FIRST GIRLFRIEND JUNIOR YEAR, I TOO MOVED INTO DAD'S LARGER HOUSE.
WANT A BEER, HARRY?

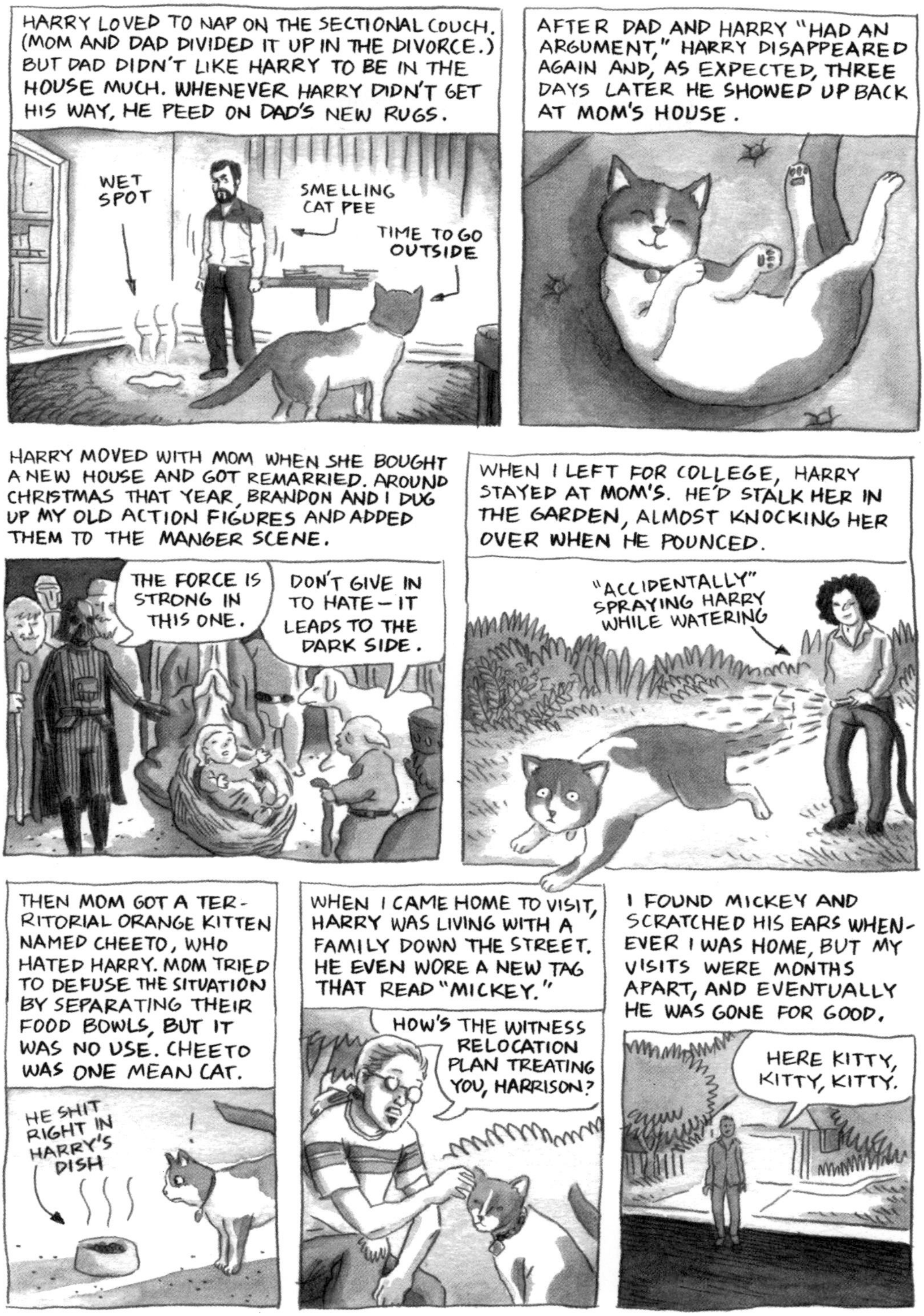
HARRY LOVED TO NAP ON THE SECTIONAL COUCH. (MOM AND DAD DIVIDED IT UP IN THE DIVORCE.) BUT DAD DIDN'T LIKE HARRY TO BE IN THE HOUSE MUCH. WHENEVER HARRY DIDN'T GET HIS WAY, HE PEED ON DAD'S NEW RUGS.
WET SPOT
SMELLING CAT PEE
TIME TO GO OUTSIDE
AFTER DAD AND HARRY "HAD AN ARGUMENT," HARRY DISAPPEARED AGAIN AND, AS EXPECTED, THREE DAYS LATER HE SHOWED UP BACK AT MOM'S HOUSE.
HARRY MOVED WITH MOM WHEN SHE BOUGHT A NEW HOUSE AND GOT REMARRIED. AROUND CHRISTMAS THAT YEAR, BRANDON AND I DUG UP MY OLD ACTION FIGURES AND ADDED THEM TO THE MANGER SCENE.
THE FORCE IS STRONG IN THIS ONE.
DON'T GIVE IN TO HATE—IT LEADS TO THE DARK SIDE.
WHEN I LEFT FOR COLLEGE, HARRY STAYED AT MOM'S. HE'D STALK HER IN THE GARDEN, ALMOST KNOCKING HER OVER WHEN HE POUNCED.
"ACCIDENTALLY" SPRAYING HARRY WHILE WATERING
THEN MOM GOT A TERRITORIAL ORANGE KITTEN NAMED CHEETO, WHO HATED HARRY. MOM TRIED TO DEFUSE THE SITUATION BY SEPARATING THEIR FOOD BOWLS, BUT IT WAS NO USE. CHEETO WAS ONE MEAN CAT.
HE SHIT RIGHT IN HARRY'S DISH
!
WHEN I CAME HOME TO VISIT, HARRY WAS LIVING WITH A FAMILY DOWN THE STREET. HE EVEN WORE A NEW TAG THAT READ "MICKEY."
HOW'S THE WITNESS RELOCATION PLAN TREATING YOU, HARRISON?
I FOUND MICKEY AND SCRATCHED HIS EARS WHENEVER I WAS HOME, BUT MY VISITS WERE MONTHS APART, AND EVENTUALLY HE WAS GONE FOR GOOD.
HERE KITTY, KITTY, KITTY.

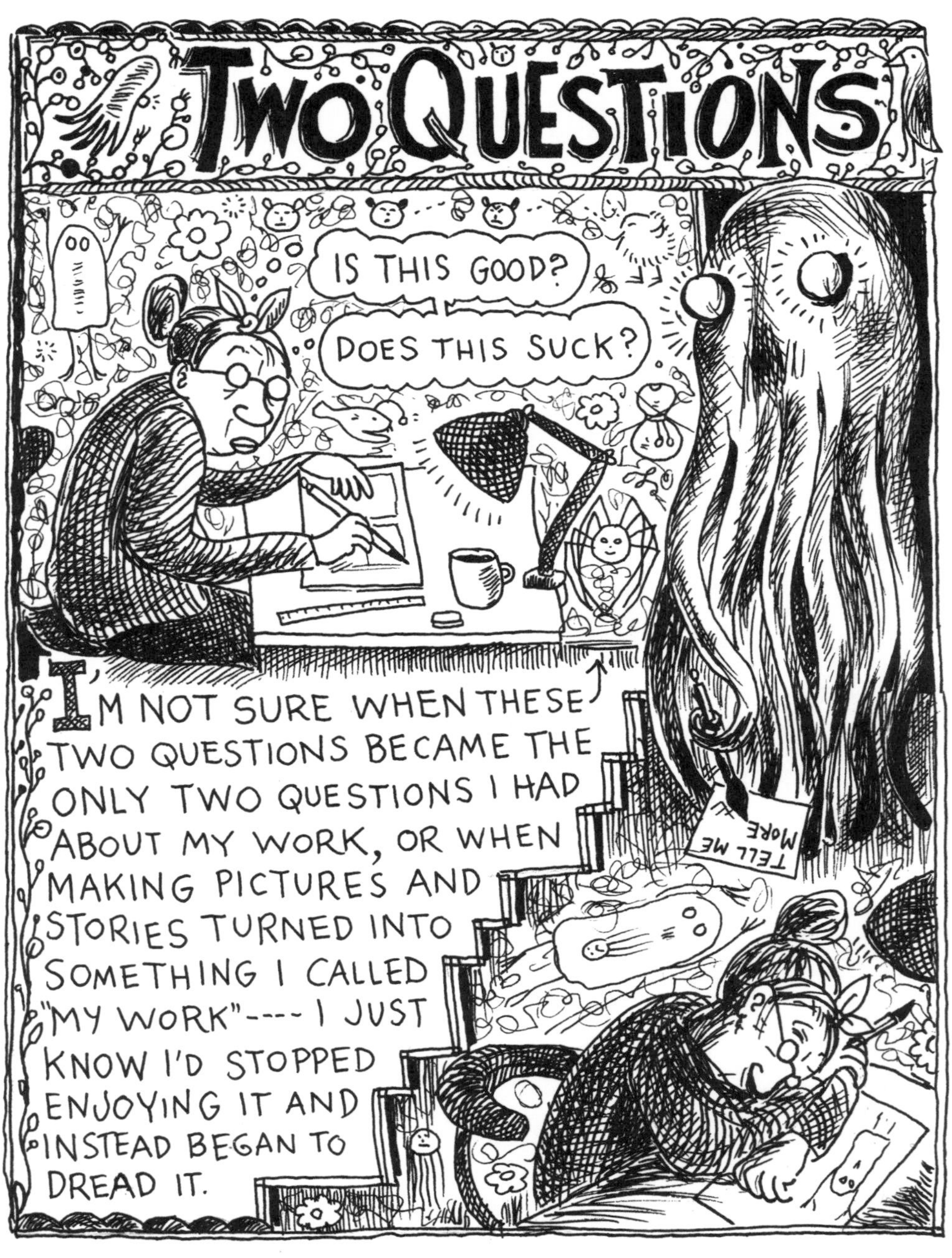
TWO QUESTIONS
IS THIS GOOD?
DOES THIS SUCK?
I'M NOT SURE WHEN THESE TWO QUESTIONS BECAME THE ONLY TWO QUESTIONS I HAD ABOUT MY WORK, OR WHEN MAKING PICTURES AND STORIES TURNED INTO SOMETHING I CALLED "MY WORK"---- I JUST KNOW I'D STOPPED ENJOYING IT AND INSTEAD BEGAN TO DREAD IT.
TELL ME MORE

FROM *McSweeney's*

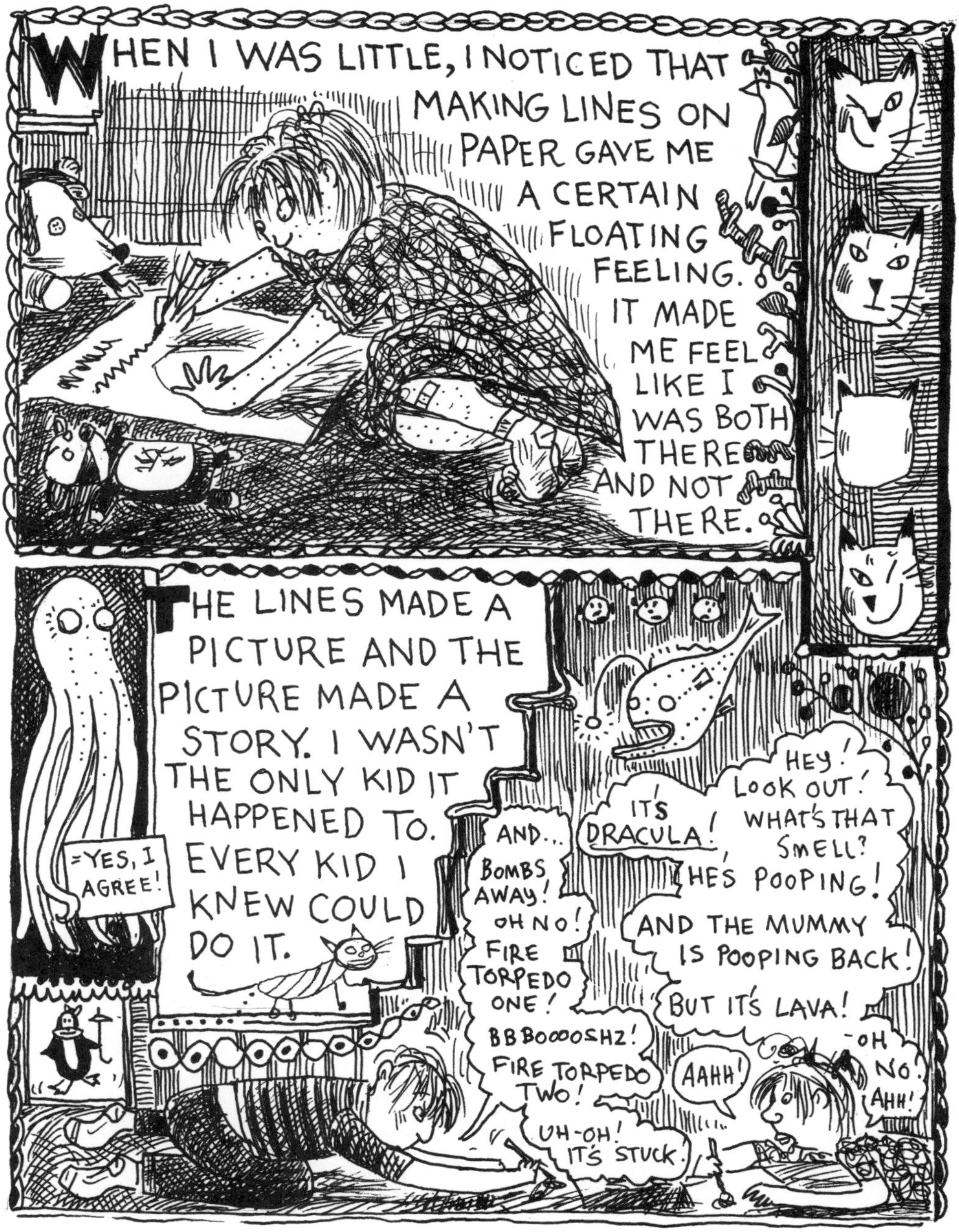
WHEN I WAS LITTLE, I NOTICED THAT MAKING LINES ON PAPER GAVE ME A CERTAIN FLOATING FEELING. IT MADE ME FEEL LIKE I WAS BOTH THERE AND NOT THERE.
THE LINES MADE A PICTURE AND THE PICTURE MADE A STORY. I WASN'T THE ONLY KID IT HAPPENED TO. EVERY KID I KNEW COULD DO IT.
YES, I AGREE!
AND...
BOMBS AWAY!
OH NO!
FIRE TORPEDO ONE!
BBBOOOOSHZ!
FIRE TORPEDO TWO!
UH-OH! IT'S STUCK
IT'S DRACULA!
HEY! LOOK OUT! WHAT'S THAT SMELL?
HE'S POOPING!
AND THE MUMMY IS POOPING BACK!
BUT IT'S LAVA!
AAHH!
OH NO. AHH!

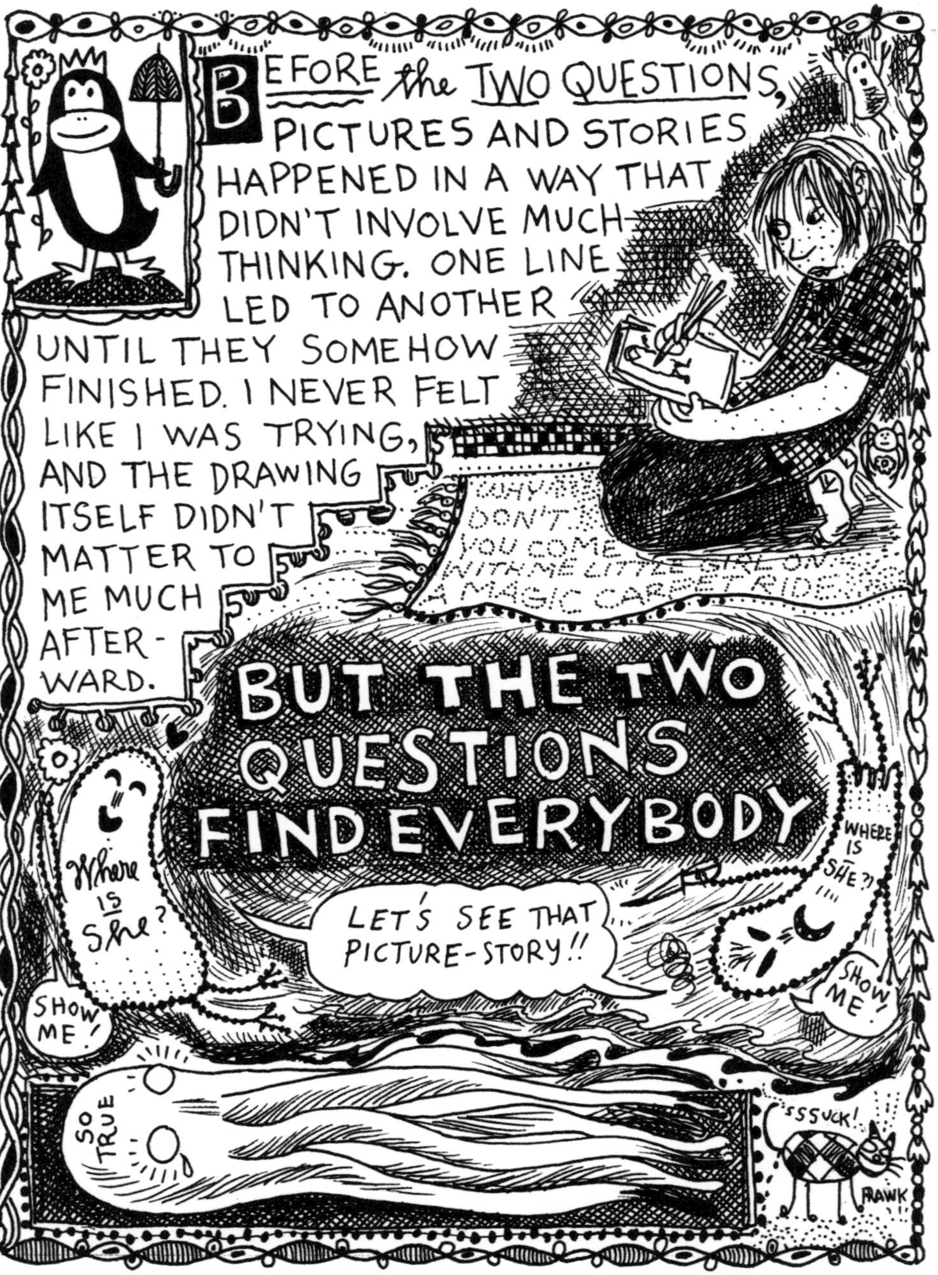
BEFORE the TWO QUESTIONS, PICTURES AND STORIES HAPPENED IN A WAY THAT DIDN'T INVOLVE MUCH THINKING. ONE LINE LED TO ANOTHER UNTIL THEY SOMEHOW FINISHED. I NEVER FELT LIKE I WAS TRYING, AND THE DRAWING ITSELF DIDN'T MATTER TO ME MUCH AFTER-WARD.
BUT THE TWO QUESTIONS FIND EVERYBODY
Where is She?
LET'S SEE THAT PICTURE-STORY!!
WHERE IS SHE?!
SHOW ME!
SHOW ME!
SO TRUE
SSSUCK!
RAWK

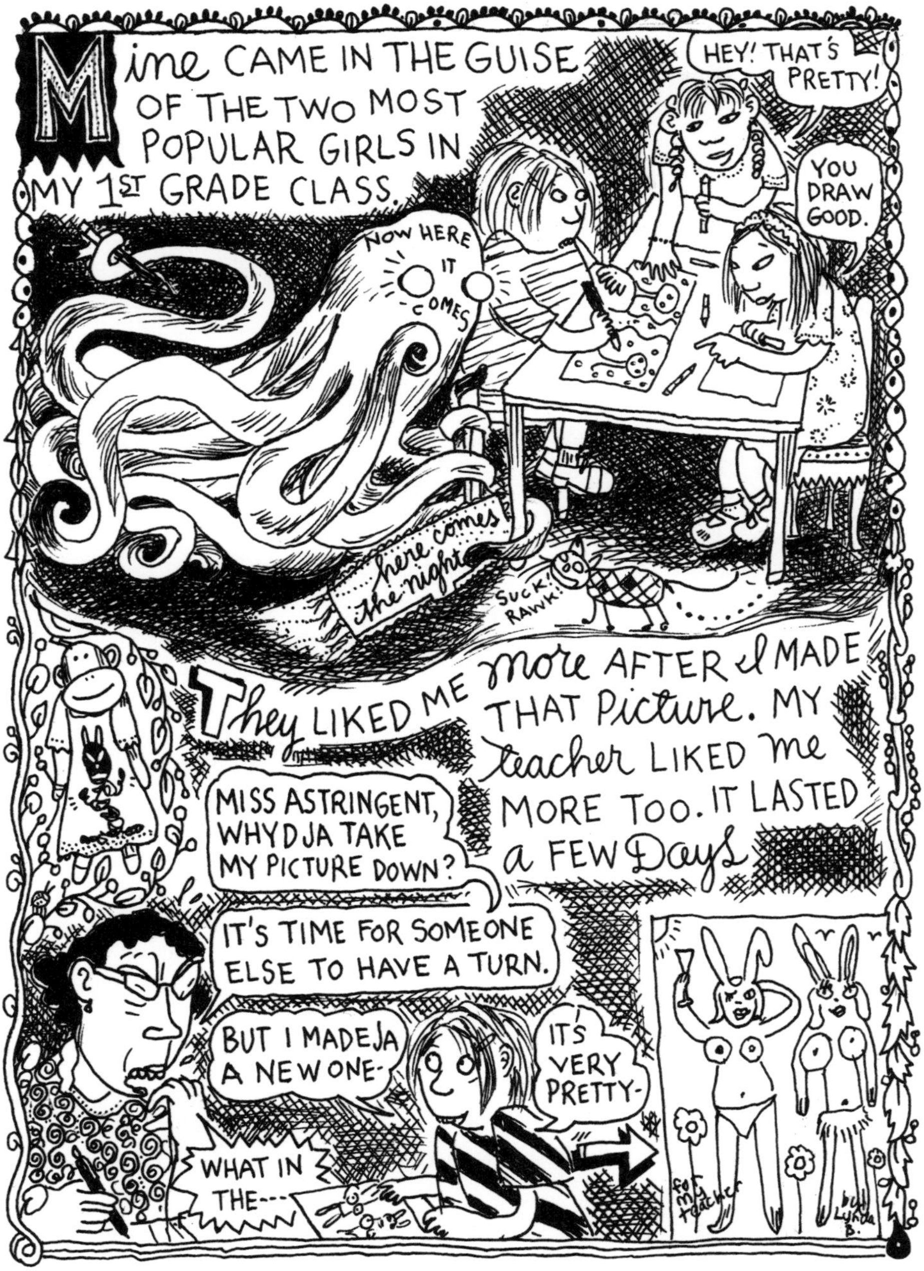
Mine CAME IN THE GUISE OF THE TWO MOST POPULAR GIRLS IN MY 1ST GRADE CLASS.
HEY! THAT'S PRETTY!
YOU DRAW GOOD.
NOW HERE IT COMES
here comes the night
SUCK! RAWK!
They LIKED ME more AFTER I MADE THAT Picture. MY teacher LIKED me MORE TOO. IT LASTED a FEW Days
MISS ASTRINGENT, WHYDJA TAKE MY PICTURE DOWN?
IT'S TIME FOR SOMEONE ELSE TO HAVE A TURN.
BUT I MADEJA A NEW ONE-
IT'S VERY PRETTY-
WHAT IN THE---
for my teacher
by Lynda B.

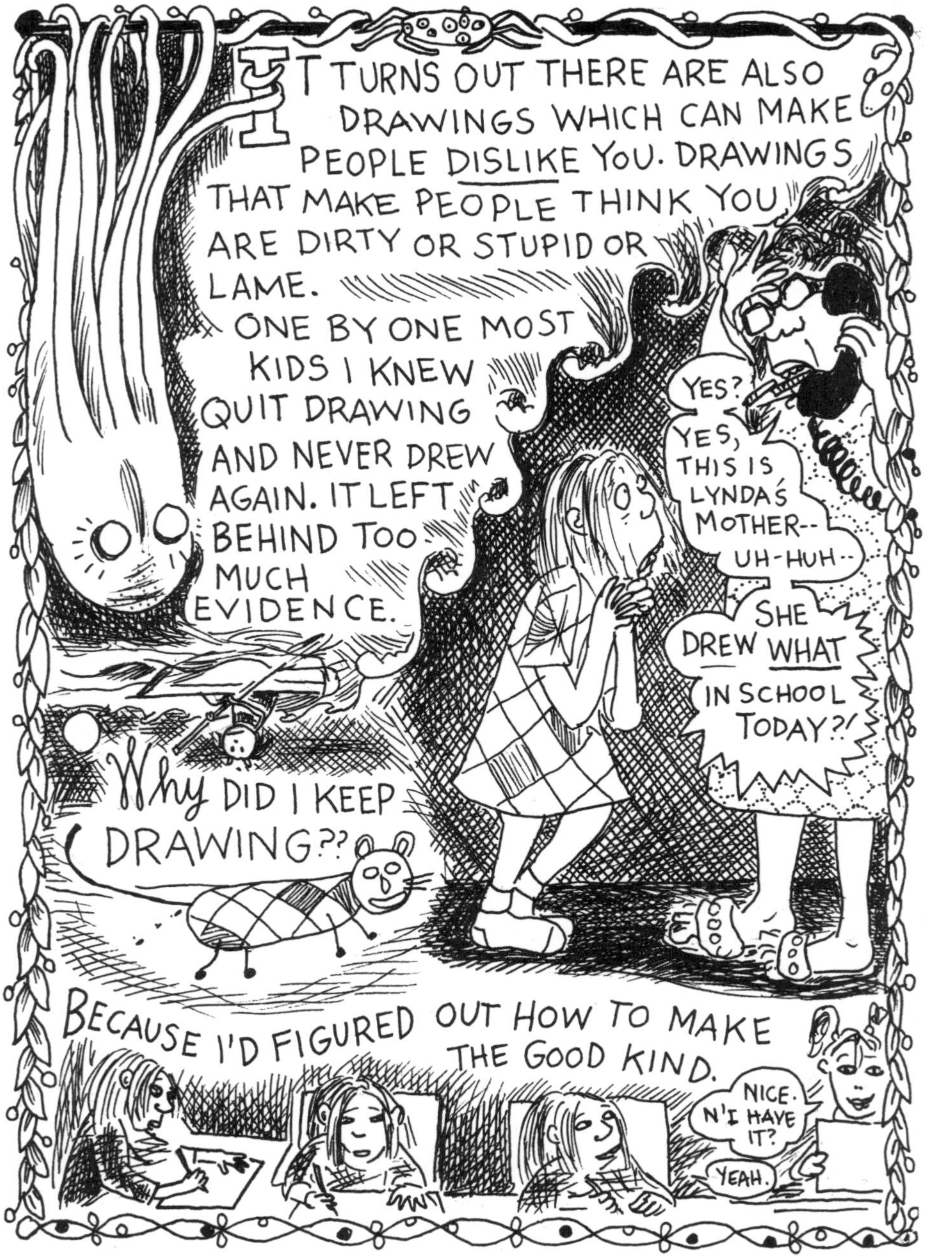
IT TURNS OUT THERE ARE ALSO DRAWINGS WHICH CAN MAKE PEOPLE DISLIKE YOU. DRAWINGS THAT MAKE PEOPLE THINK YOU ARE DIRTY OR STUPID OR LAME.
ONE BY ONE MOST KIDS I KNEW QUIT DRAWING AND NEVER DREW AGAIN. IT LEFT BEHIND TOO MUCH EVIDENCE.
YES?
YES, THIS IS LYNDA'S MOTHER-- UH-HUH--
SHE DREW WHAT IN SCHOOL TODAY?!
Why DID I KEEP DRAWING??
BECAUSE I'D FIGURED OUT HOW TO MAKE THE GOOD KIND.
NICE. N'I HAVE IT?
YEAH.

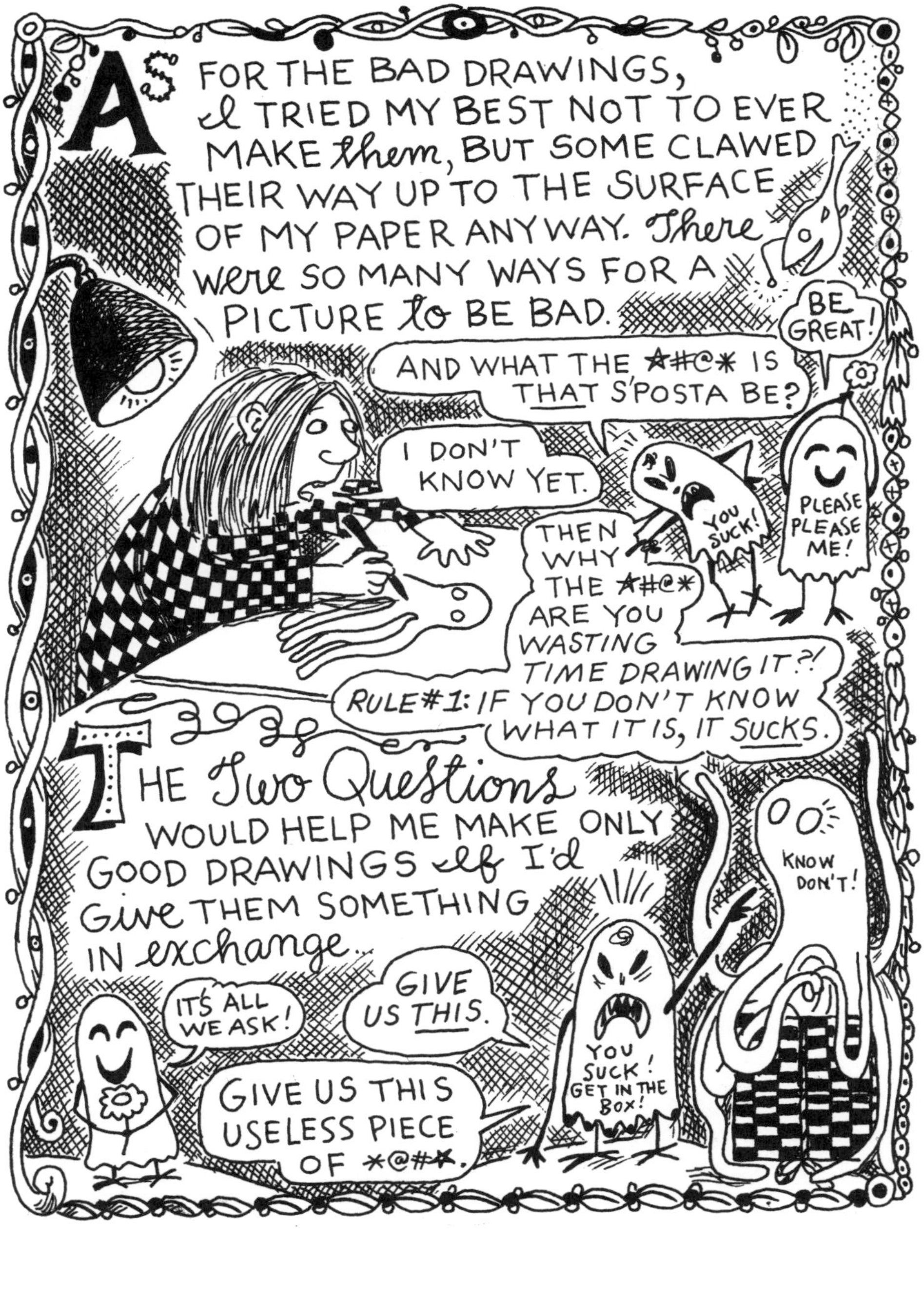
As for the bad drawings, I tried my best not to ever make them, but some clawed their way up to the surface of my paper anyway. There were so many ways for a picture to be bad.
BE GREAT!
AND WHAT THE *#@* IS THAT S'POSTA BE?
I DON'T KNOW YET.
THEN WHY THE *#@* ARE YOU WASTING TIME DRAWING IT?!
YOU SUCK!
PLEASE PLEASE ME!
RULE #1: IF YOU DON'T KNOW WHAT IT IS, IT SUCKS.
The Two Questions would help me make only good drawings if I'd give them something in exchange...
KNOW DON'T!
IT'S ALL WE ASK!
GIVE US THIS.
GIVE US THIS USELESS PIECE OF *@#*.
YOU SUCK! GET IN THE BOX!

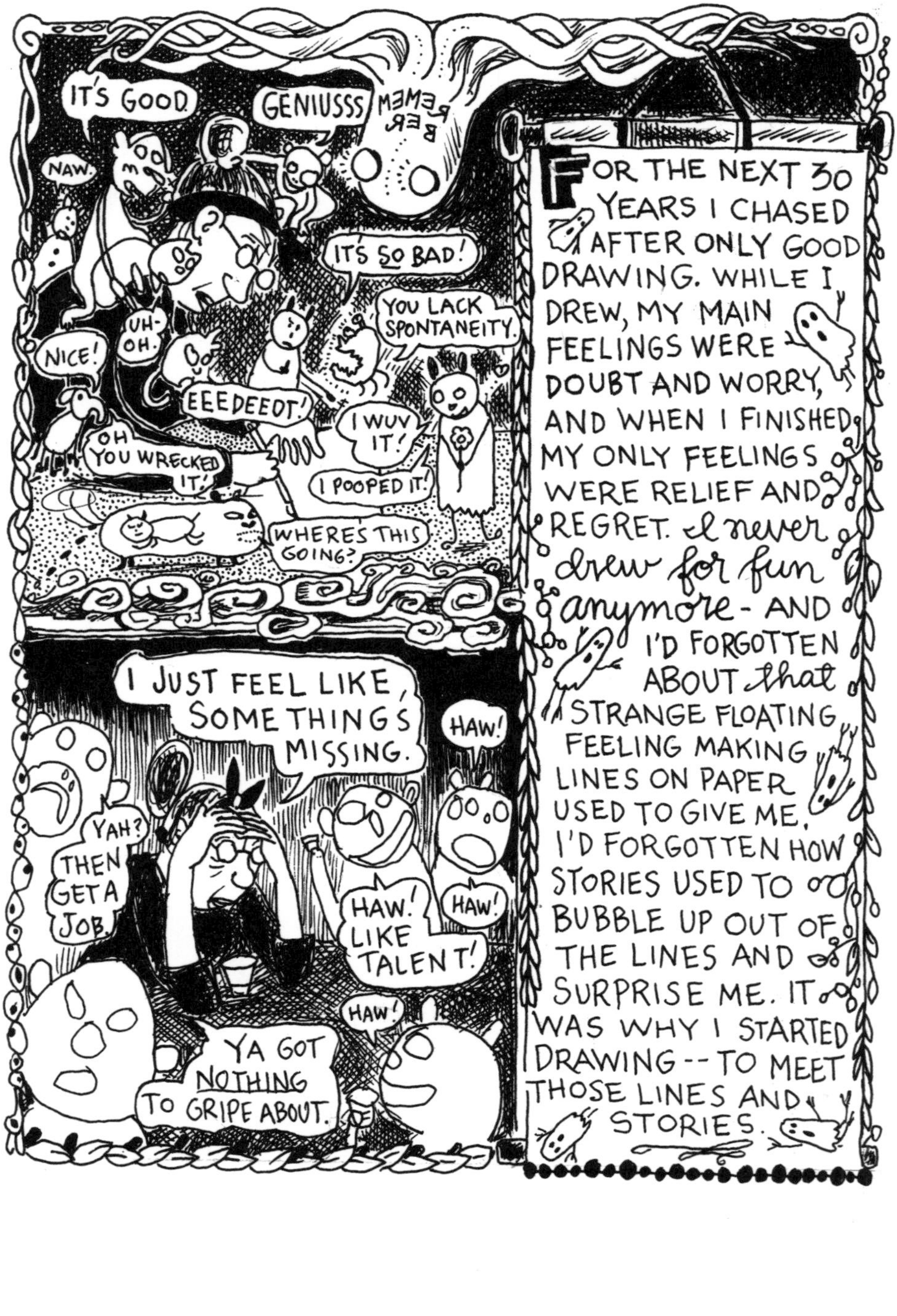
IT'S GOOD.
GENIUSSS
REMEMBER
NAW.
IT'S SO BAD!
YOU LACK SPONTANEITY.
UH-OH.
NICE!
EEEDEEOT!
I WUV IT!
OH YOU WRECKED IT!
I POOPED IT!
WHERE'S THIS GOING?
FOR THE NEXT 30 YEARS I CHASED AFTER ONLY GOOD DRAWING. WHILE I DREW, MY MAIN FEELINGS WERE DOUBT AND WORRY, AND WHEN I FINISHED MY ONLY FEELINGS WERE RELIEF AND REGRET. I never drew for fun anymore - AND I'D FORGOTTEN ABOUT that STRANGE FLOATING FEELING MAKING LINES ON PAPER USED TO GIVE ME. I'D FORGOTTEN HOW STORIES USED TO BUBBLE UP OUT OF THE LINES AND SURPRISE ME. IT WAS WHY I STARTED DRAWING -- TO MEET THOSE LINES AND STORIES.
I JUST FEEL LIKE SOMETHING'S MISSING.
HAW!
YAH? THEN GET A JOB.
HAW! LIKE TALENT!
HAW!
HAW!
YA GOT NOTHING TO GRIPE ABOUT.

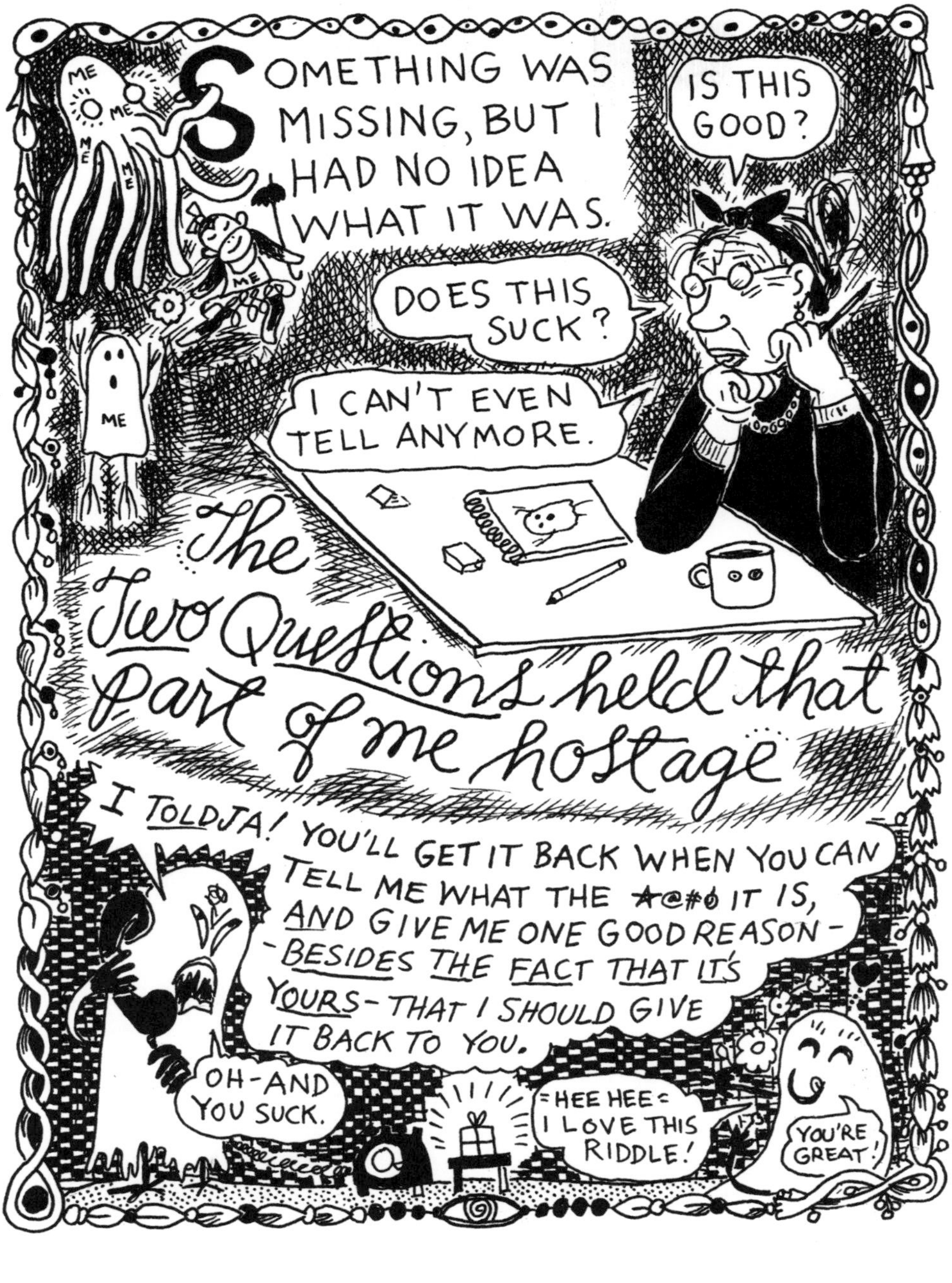
SOMETHING WAS MISSING, BUT I HAD NO IDEA WHAT IT WAS.
IS THIS GOOD?
DOES THIS SUCK?
I CAN'T EVEN TELL ANYMORE.
ME
ME
ME
ME
ME
ME
The Two Questions held that part of me hostage
I TOLDJA! YOU'LL GET IT BACK WHEN YOU CAN TELL ME WHAT THE *@#! IT IS, AND GIVE ME ONE GOOD REASON - BESIDES THE FACT THAT IT'S YOURS - THAT I SHOULD GIVE IT BACK TO YOU.
OH-AND YOU SUCK.
HEE HEE I LOVE THIS RIDDLE!
YOU'RE GREAT!

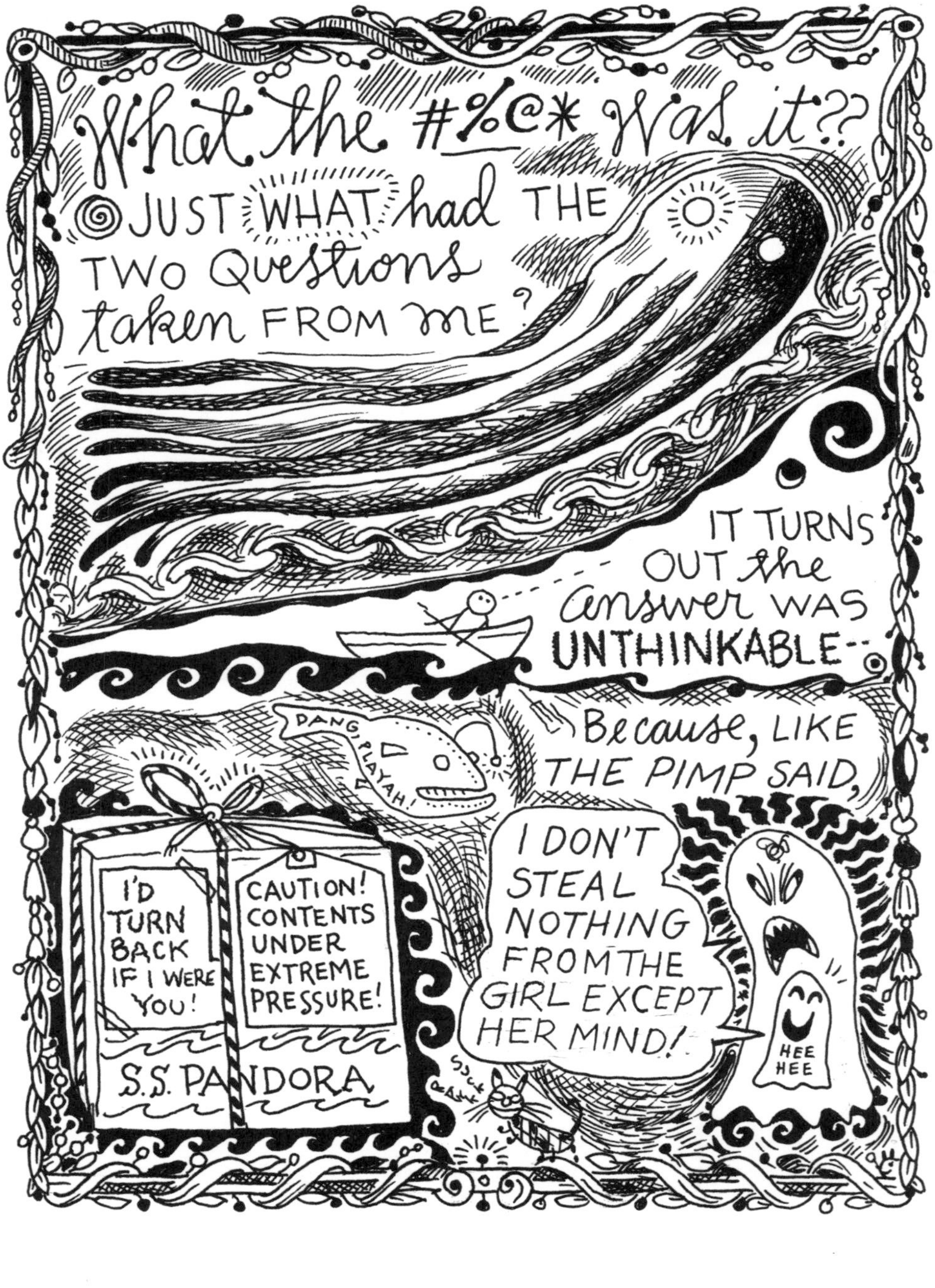
What the #%@* Was it??
JUST WHAT had THE TWO Questions taken FROM me?
IT TURNS OUT the answer WAS UNTHINKABLE..
Because, LIKE THE PIMP SAID,
DANG PLAYAH!
I'D TURN BACK IF I WERE YOU!
CAUTION! CONTENTS UNDER EXTREME PRESSURE!
S.S. PANDORA
I DON'T STEAL NOTHING FROM THE GIRL EXCEPT HER MIND!
HEE HEE

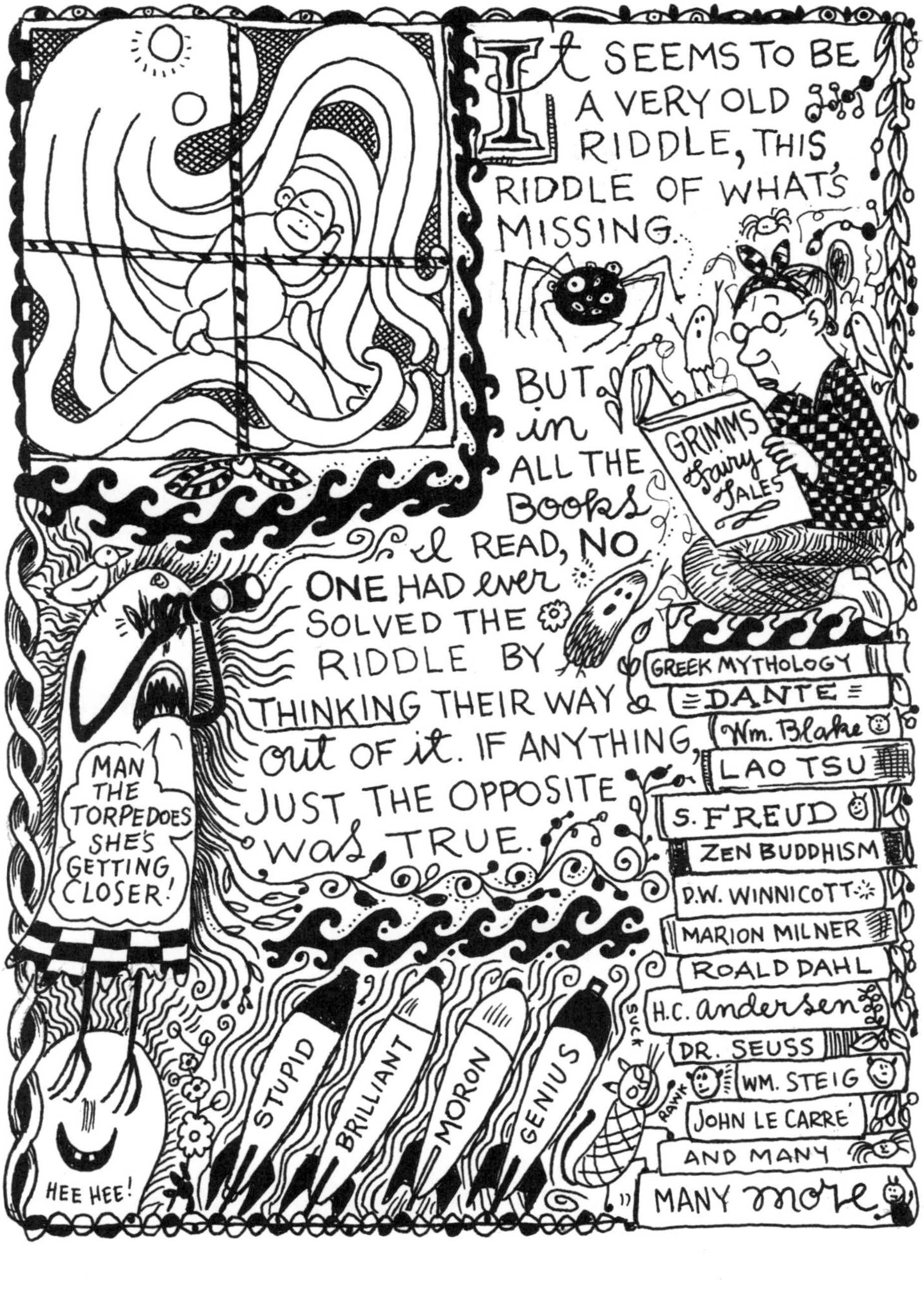
It seems to be a very old riddle, this riddle of what's missing.
But in all the books I read, no one had ever solved the riddle by thinking their way out of it. If anything, just the opposite was true.
GRIMMS Fairy Tales
MAN THE TORPEDOES SHE'S GETTING CLOSER!
HEE HEE!
STUPID
BRILLIANT
MORON
GENIUS
SUCK
RAWK
GREEK MYTHOLOGY
DANTE
Wm. Blake
LAO TSU
S. FREUD
ZEN BUDDHISM
D.W. WINNICOTT
MARION MILNER
ROALD DAHL
H.C. andersen
DR. SEUSS
WM. STEIG
JOHN LE CARRE'
AND MANY
MANY more

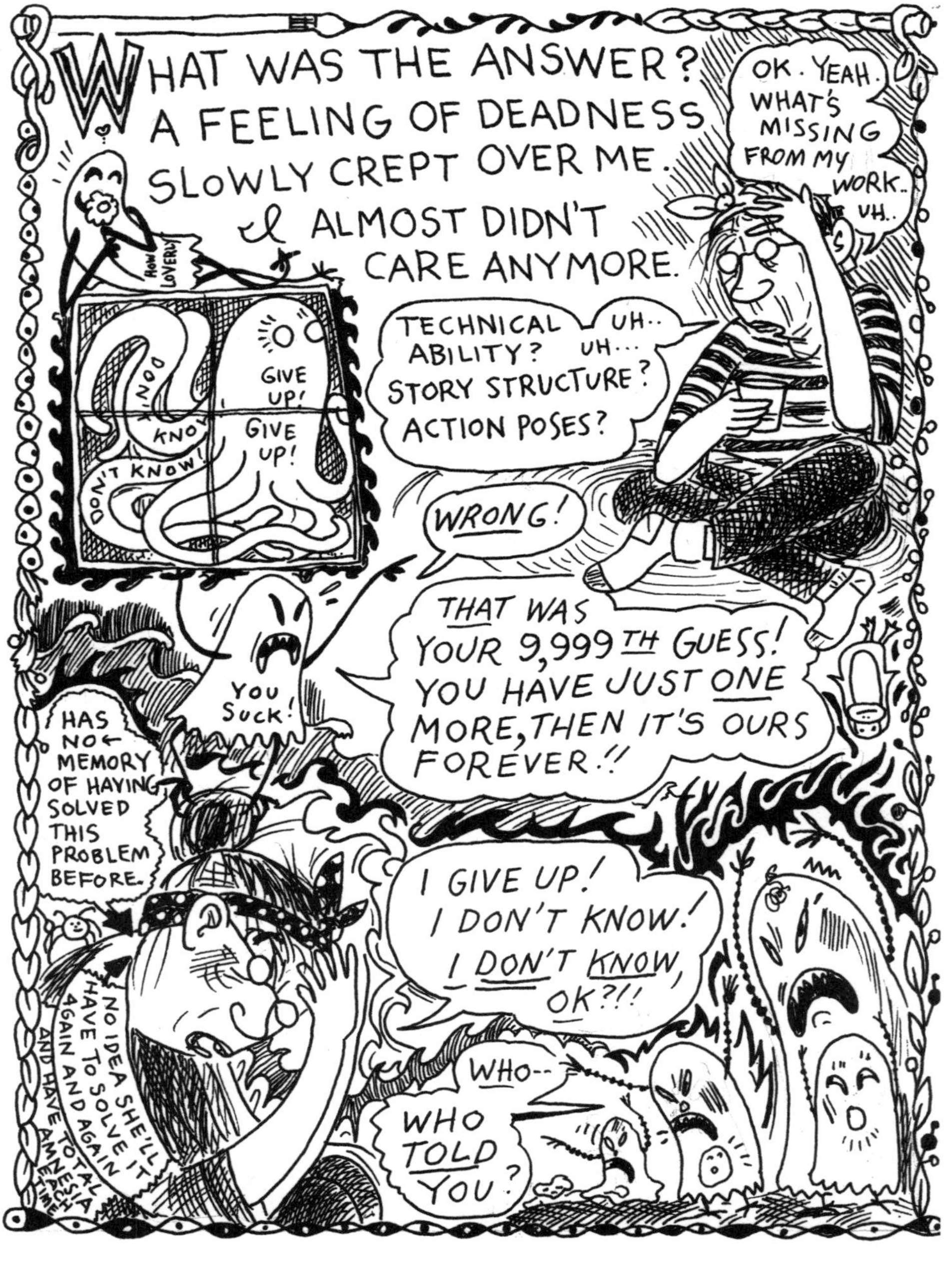

WHAT WAS THE ANSWER? A FEELING OF DEADNESS SLOWLY CREPT OVER ME. & I ALMOST DIDN'T CARE ANYMORE.
HOW LOVERLY
DON'T KNOW
GIVE UP!
GIVE UP!
DON'T KNOW!
OK. YEAH. WHAT'S MISSING FROM MY WORK.. UH..
TECHNICAL ABILITY? UH... STORY STRUCTURE? ACTION POSES?
UH..
WRONG!
YOU SUCK!
THAT WAS YOUR 9,999TH GUESS! YOU HAVE JUST ONE MORE, THEN IT'S OURS FOREVER!!
HAS NO MEMORY OF HAVING SOLVED THIS PROBLEM BEFORE.
NO IDEA SHE'LL HAVE TO SOLVE IT AGAIN AND AGAIN AND HAVE TOTAL AMNESIA EACH TIME
I GIVE UP! I DON'T KNOW! I DON'T KNOW, OK?!!
WHO--
WHO TOLD YOU?

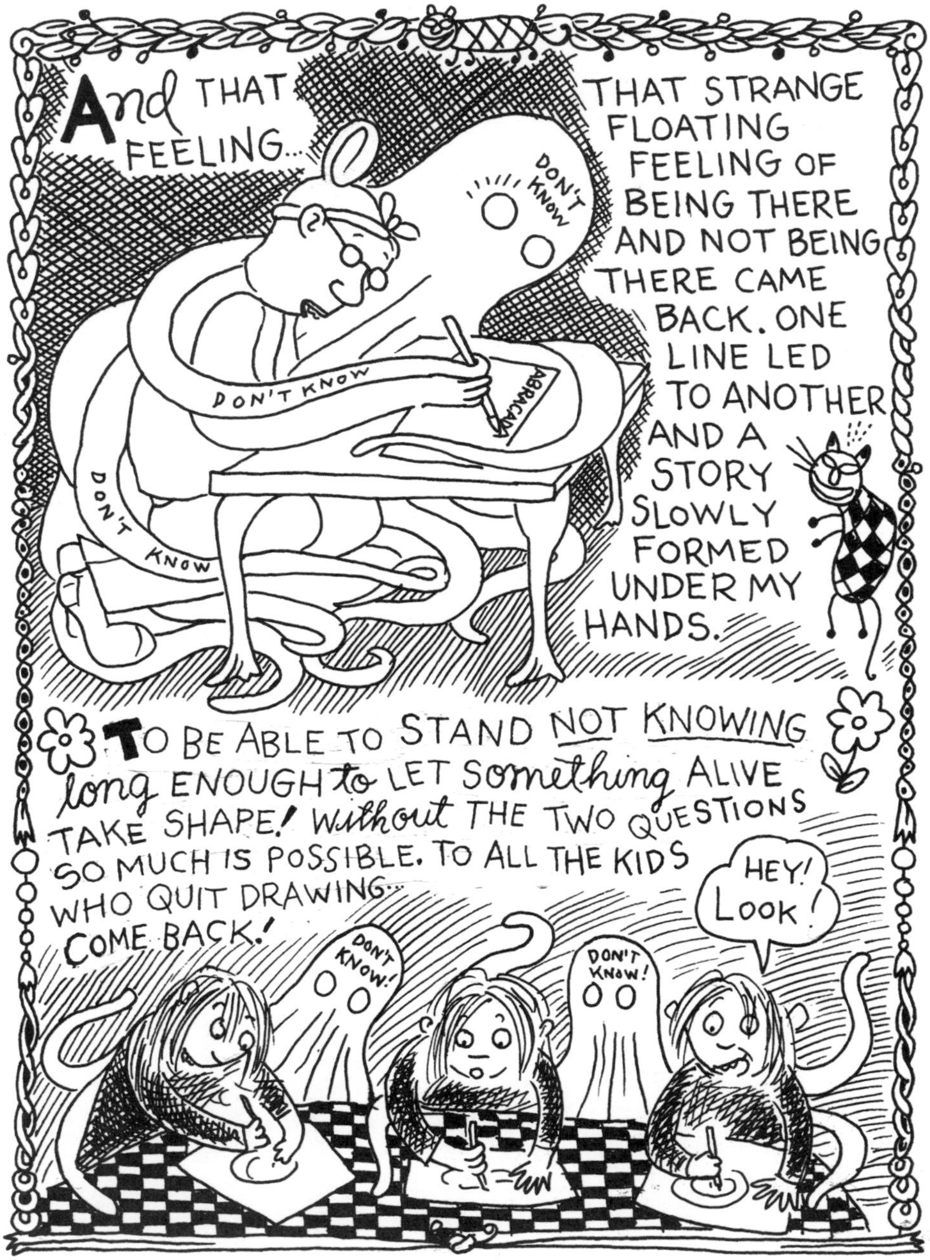

And THAT FEELING...
THAT STRANGE FLOATING FEELING OF BEING THERE AND NOT BEING THERE CAME BACK. ONE LINE LED TO ANOTHER AND A STORY SLOWLY FORMED UNDER MY HANDS.
DON'T KNOW
DON'T KNOW
DON'T KNOW
TO BE ABLE TO STAND NOT KNOWING long ENOUGH to LET something ALIVE TAKE SHAPE! without THE TWO QUESTIONS SO MUCH IS POSSIBLE. TO ALL THE KIDS WHO QUIT DRAWING... COME BACK!
DON'T KNOW!
DON'T KNOW!
HEY! LOOK!

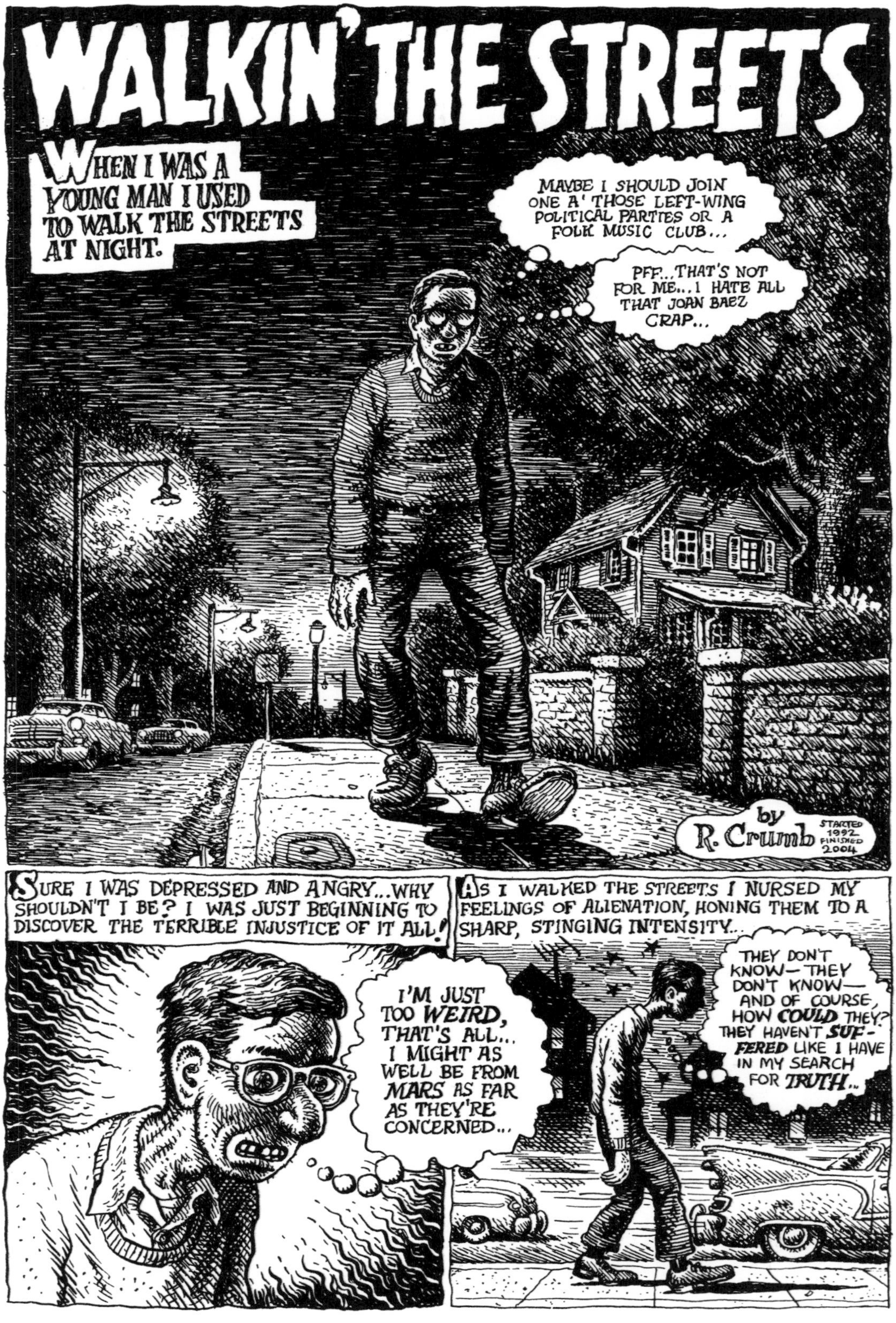
WALKIN' THE STREETS
WHEN I WAS A YOUNG MAN I USED TO WALK THE STREETS AT NIGHT.
MAYBE I SHOULD JOIN ONE A' THOSE LEFT-WING POLITICAL PARTIES OR A FOLK MUSIC CLUB...
PFF... THAT'S NOT FOR ME... I HATE ALL THAT JOAN BAEZ CRAP...
by R. Crumb STARTED 1992 FINISHED 2004
SURE I WAS DEPRESSED AND ANGRY... WHY SHOULDN'T I BE? I WAS JUST BEGINNING TO DISCOVER THE TERRIBLE INJUSTICE OF IT ALL!
I'M JUST TOO WEIRD, THAT'S ALL... I MIGHT AS WELL BE FROM MARS AS FAR AS THEY'RE CONCERNED...
AS I WALKED THE STREETS I NURSED MY FEELINGS OF ALIENATION, HONING THEM TO A SHARP, STINGING INTENSITY...
THEY DON'T KNOW— THEY DON'T KNOW— AND OF COURSE, HOW COULD THEY? THEY HAVEN'T SUFFERED LIKE I HAVE IN MY SEARCH FOR TRUTH..

ROBERT CRUMB FROM *Zap*

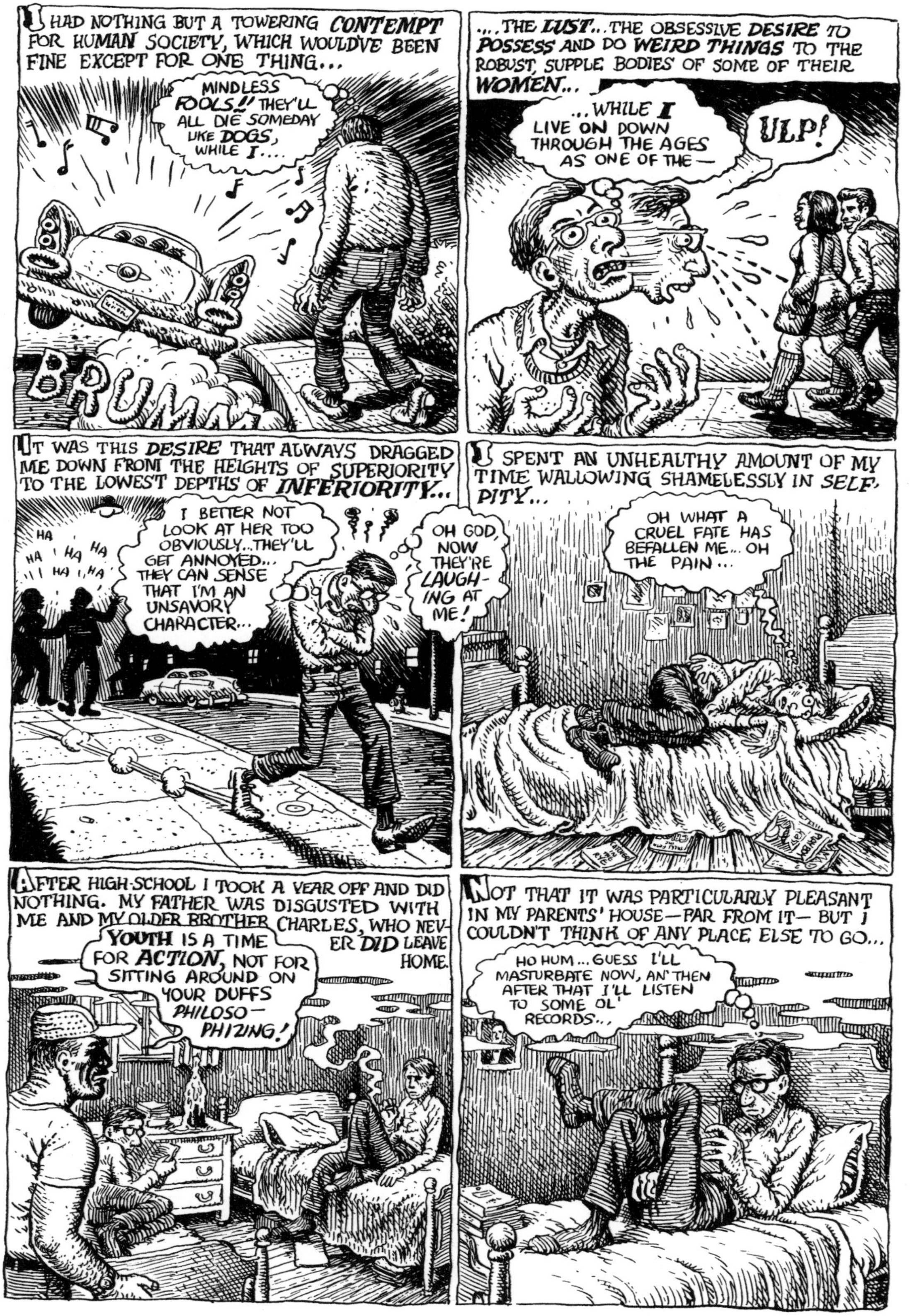
I HAD NOTHING BUT A TOWERING CONTEMPT FOR HUMAN SOCIETY, WHICH WOULD'VE BEEN FINE EXCEPT FOR ONE THING...
MINDLESS FOOLS!! THEY'LL ALL DIE SOMEDAY LIKE DOGS, WHILE I....
BRUM
...THE LUST...THE OBSESSIVE DESIRE TO POSSESS AND DO WEIRD THINGS TO THE ROBUST, SUPPLE BODIES OF SOME OF THEIR WOMEN...
...WHILE I LIVE ON DOWN THROUGH THE AGES AS ONE OF THE—
ULP!
IT WAS THIS DESIRE THAT ALWAYS DRAGGED ME DOWN FROM THE HEIGHTS OF SUPERIORITY TO THE LOWEST DEPTHS OF INFERIORITY...
HA HA HA HA HA HA
I BETTER NOT LOOK AT HER TOO OBVIOUSLY...THEY'LL GET ANNOYED... THEY CAN SENSE THAT I'M AN UNSAVORY CHARACTER...
OH GOD, NOW THEY'RE LAUGHING AT ME!
I SPENT AN UNHEALTHY AMOUNT OF MY TIME WALLOWING SHAMELESSLY IN SELF PITY...
OH WHAT A CRUEL FATE HAS BEFALLEN ME... OH THE PAIN...
AFTER HIGH-SCHOOL I TOOK A YEAR OFF AND DID NOTHING. MY FATHER WAS DISGUSTED WITH ME AND MY OLDER BROTHER CHARLES, WHO NEVER DID LEAVE HOME.
YOUTH IS A TIME FOR ACTION, NOT FOR SITTING AROUND ON YOUR DUFFS PHILOSOPHIZING!
NOT THAT IT WAS PARTICULARLY PLEASANT IN MY PARENTS' HOUSE—FAR FROM IT—BUT I COULDN'T THINK OF ANY PLACE ELSE TO GO...
HO HUM...GUESS I'LL MASTURBATE NOW, AN' THEN AFTER THAT I'LL LISTEN TO SOME OL' RECORDS...

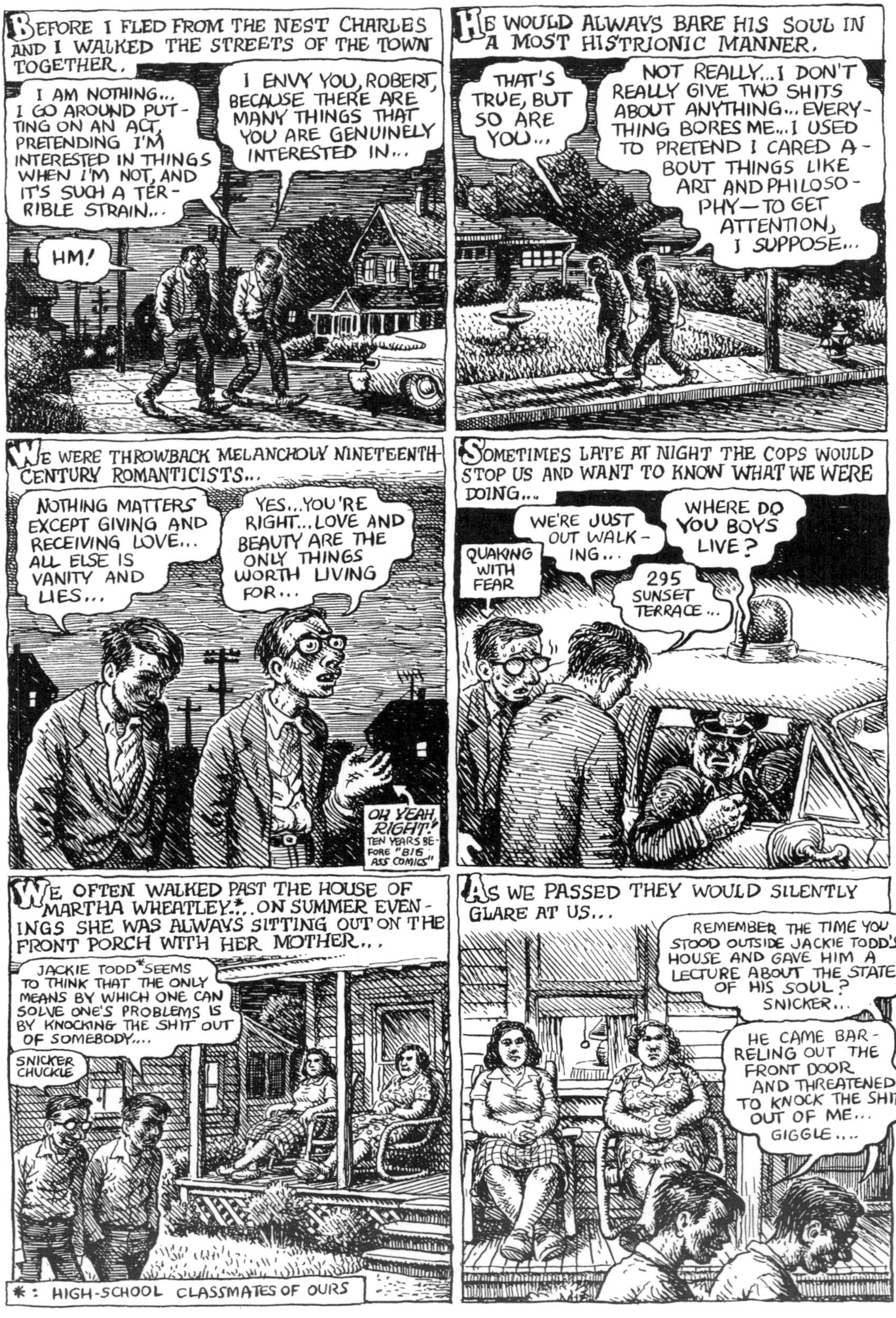

BEFORE I FLED FROM THE NEST CHARLES AND I WALKED THE STREETS OF THE TOWN TOGETHER.
I AM NOTHING... I GO AROUND PUTTING ON AN ACT, PRETENDING I'M INTERESTED IN THINGS WHEN I'M NOT, AND IT'S SUCH A TERRIBLE STRAIN...
I ENVY YOU, ROBERT, BECAUSE THERE ARE MANY THINGS THAT YOU ARE GENUINELY INTERESTED IN...
HM!
HE WOULD ALWAYS BARE HIS SOUL IN A MOST HISTRIONIC MANNER.
THAT'S TRUE, BUT SO ARE YOU...
NOT REALLY... I DON'T REALLY GIVE TWO SHITS ABOUT ANYTHING... EVERYTHING BORES ME... I USED TO PRETEND I CARED ABOUT THINGS LIKE ART AND PHILOSOPHY—TO GET ATTENTION, I SUPPOSE...
WE WERE THROWBACK MELANCHOLY NINETEENTH-CENTURY ROMANTICISTS...
NOTHING MATTERS EXCEPT GIVING AND RECEIVING LOVE... ALL ELSE IS VANITY AND LIES...
YES... YOU'RE RIGHT... LOVE AND BEAUTY ARE THE ONLY THINGS WORTH LIVING FOR...
OH YEAH, RIGHT! TEN YEARS BEFORE "BIG ASS COMICS"
SOMETIMES LATE AT NIGHT THE COPS WOULD STOP US AND WANT TO KNOW WHAT WE WERE DOING...
QUAKING WITH FEAR
WE'RE JUST OUT WALKING...
WHERE DO YOU BOYS LIVE?
295 SUNSET TERRACE...
WE OFTEN WALKED PAST THE HOUSE OF MARTHA WHEATLEY*... ON SUMMER EVENINGS SHE WAS ALWAYS SITTING OUT ON THE FRONT PORCH WITH HER MOTHER...
JACKIE TODD* SEEMS TO THINK THAT THE ONLY MEANS BY WHICH ONE CAN SOLVE ONE'S PROBLEMS IS BY KNOCKING THE SHIT OUT OF SOMEBODY....
SNICKER CHUCKLE
*: HIGH-SCHOOL CLASSMATES OF OURS
AS WE PASSED THEY WOULD SILENTLY GLARE AT US...
REMEMBER THE TIME YOU STOOD OUTSIDE JACKIE TODD'S HOUSE AND GAVE HIM A LECTURE ABOUT THE STATE OF HIS SOUL? SNICKER...
HE CAME BARRELING OUT THE FRONT DOOR AND THREATENED TO KNOCK THE SHIT OUT OF ME... GIGGLE....

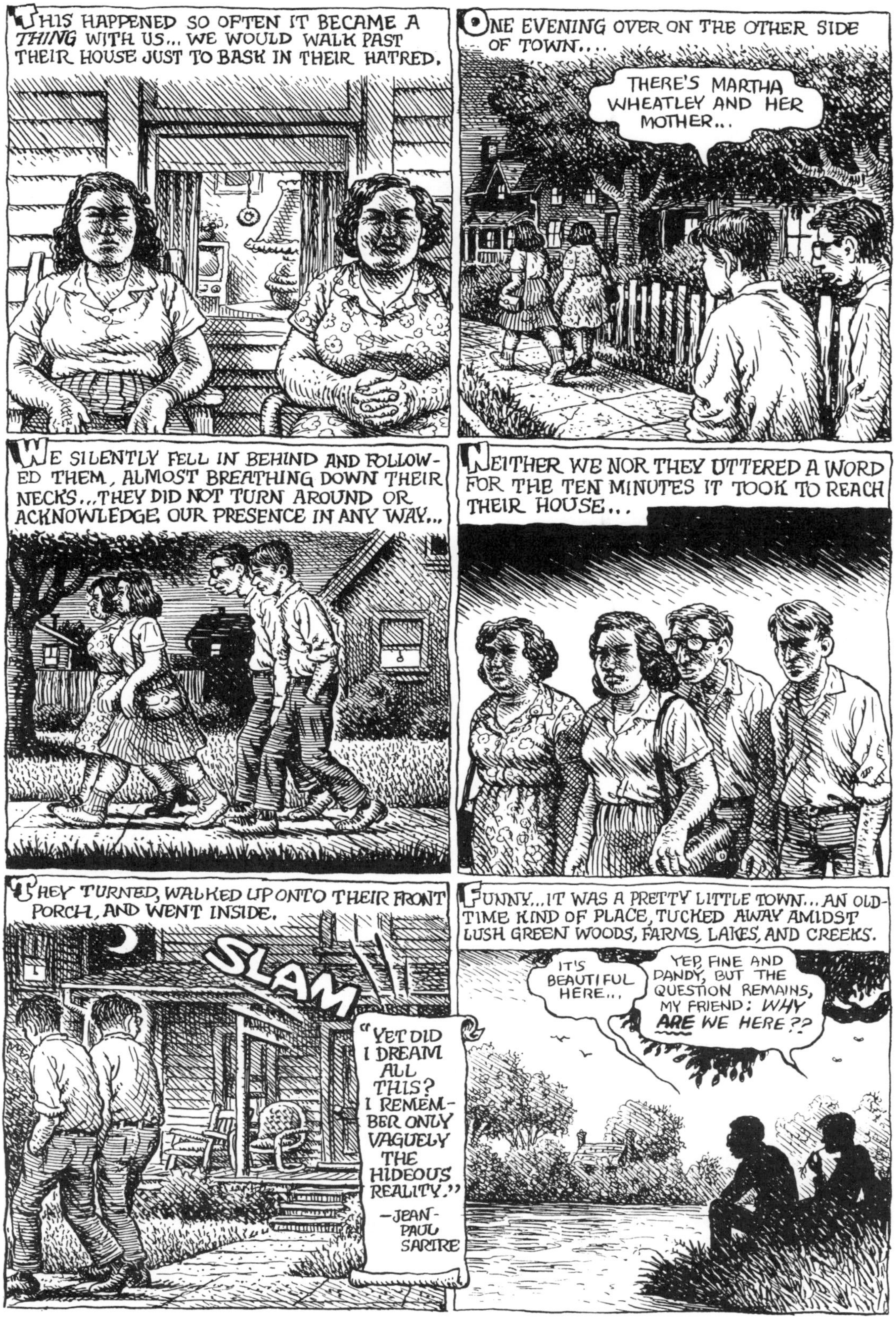
THIS HAPPENED SO OFTEN IT BECAME A THING WITH US... WE WOULD WALK PAST THEIR HOUSE JUST TO BASK IN THEIR HATRED.
ONE EVENING OVER ON THE OTHER SIDE OF TOWN....
THERE'S MARTHA WHEATLEY AND HER MOTHER...
WE SILENTLY FELL IN BEHIND AND FOLLOWED THEM, ALMOST BREATHING DOWN THEIR NECKS... THEY DID NOT TURN AROUND OR ACKNOWLEDGE OUR PRESENCE IN ANY WAY...
NEITHER WE NOR THEY UTTERED A WORD FOR THE TEN MINUTES IT TOOK TO REACH THEIR HOUSE...
THEY TURNED, WALKED UP ONTO THEIR FRONT PORCH, AND WENT INSIDE.
SLAM
"YET DID I DREAM ALL THIS? I REMEMBER ONLY VAGUELY THE HIDEOUS REALITY." —JEAN-PAUL SARTRE
FUNNY... IT WAS A PRETTY LITTLE TOWN... AN OLD-TIME KIND OF PLACE, TUCKED AWAY AMIDST LUSH GREEN WOODS, FARMS, LAKES, AND CREEKS.
IT'S BEAUTIFUL HERE...
YEP, FINE AND DANDY, BUT THE QUESTION REMAINS, MY FRIEND: WHY ARE WE HERE??

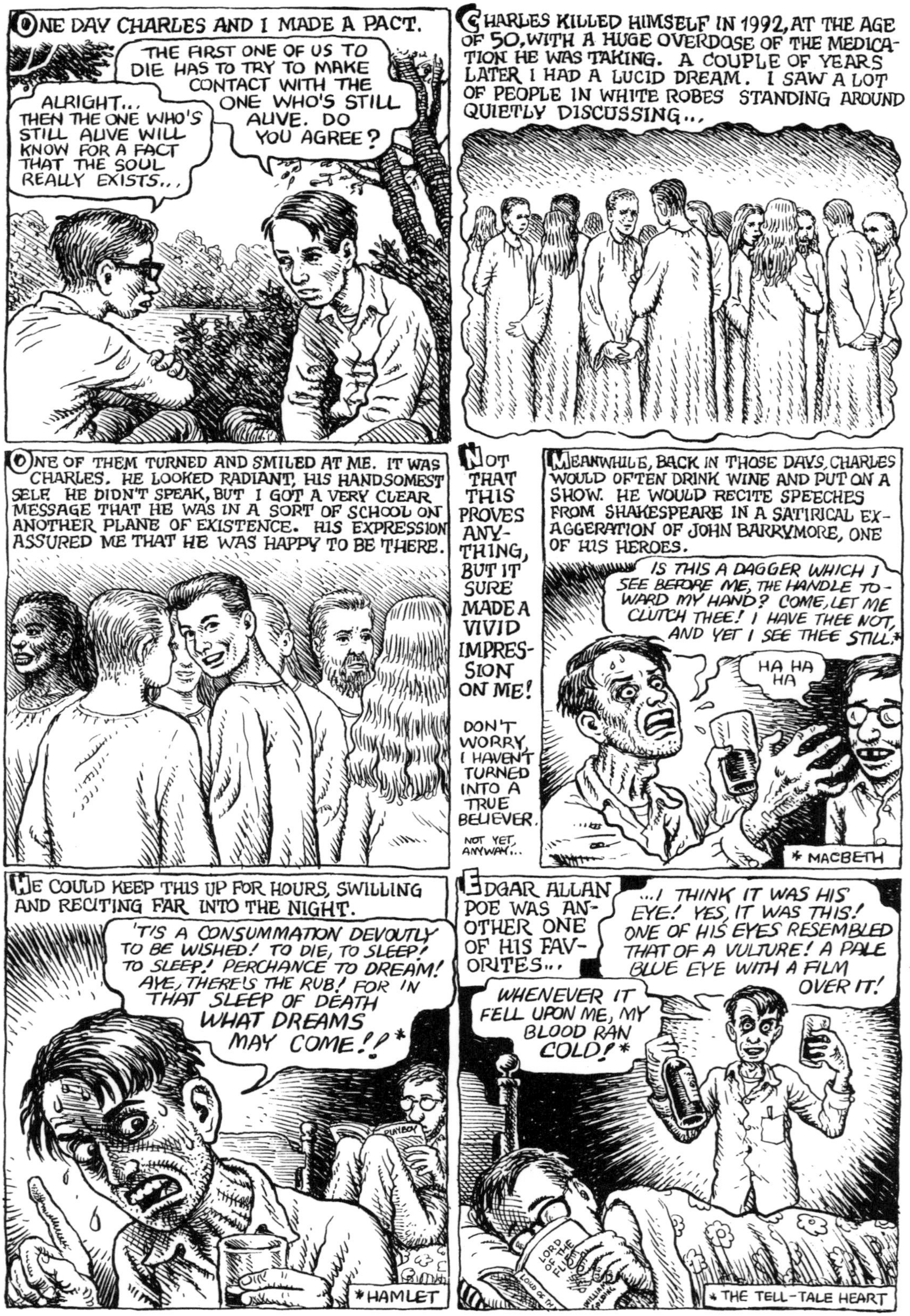
ONE DAY CHARLES AND I MADE A PACT.
THE FIRST ONE OF US TO DIE HAS TO TRY TO MAKE CONTACT WITH THE ONE WHO'S STILL ALIVE. DO YOU AGREE?
ALRIGHT... THEN THE ONE WHO'S STILL ALIVE WILL KNOW FOR A FACT THAT THE SOUL REALLY EXISTS...
CHARLES KILLED HIMSELF IN 1992, AT THE AGE OF 50, WITH A HUGE OVERDOSE OF THE MEDICATION HE WAS TAKING. A COUPLE OF YEARS LATER I HAD A LUCID DREAM. I SAW A LOT OF PEOPLE IN WHITE ROBES STANDING AROUND QUIETLY DISCUSSING...
ONE OF THEM TURNED AND SMILED AT ME. IT WAS CHARLES. HE LOOKED RADIANT, HIS HANDSOMEST SELF. HE DIDN'T SPEAK, BUT I GOT A VERY CLEAR MESSAGE THAT HE WAS IN A SORT OF SCHOOL ON ANOTHER PLANE OF EXISTENCE. HIS EXPRESSION ASSURED ME THAT HE WAS HAPPY TO BE THERE.
NOT THAT THIS PROVES ANYTHING, BUT IT SURE MADE A VIVID IMPRESSION ON ME!
DON'T WORRY, I HAVEN'T TURNED INTO A TRUE BELIEVER.
NOT YET, ANYWAY...
MEANWHILE, BACK IN THOSE DAYS, CHARLES WOULD OFTEN DRINK WINE AND PUT ON A SHOW. HE WOULD RECITE SPEECHES FROM SHAKESPEARE IN A SATIRICAL EXAGGERATION OF JOHN BARRYMORE, ONE OF HIS HEROES.
IS THIS A DAGGER WHICH I SEE BEFORE ME, THE HANDLE TOWARD MY HAND? COME, LET ME CLUTCH THEE! I HAVE THEE NOT, AND YET I SEE THEE STILL.*
HA HA HA
* MACBETH
HE COULD KEEP THIS UP FOR HOURS, SWILLING AND RECITING FAR INTO THE NIGHT.
'T'IS A CONSUMMATION DEVOUTLY TO BE WISHED! TO DIE, TO SLEEP! TO SLEEP! PERCHANCE TO DREAM! AYE, THERE'S THE RUB! FOR IN THAT SLEEP OF DEATH WHAT DREAMS MAY COME!!*
PLAYBOY
*HAMLET
EDGAR ALLAN POE WAS ANOTHER ONE OF HIS FAVORITES...
...I THINK IT WAS HIS EYE! YES, IT WAS THIS! ONE OF HIS EYES RESEMBLED THAT OF A VULTURE! A PALE BLUE EYE WITH A FILM OVER IT!
WHENEVER IT FELL UPON ME, MY BLOOD RAN COLD!*
LORD OF THE FLIES
* THE TELL-TALE HEART

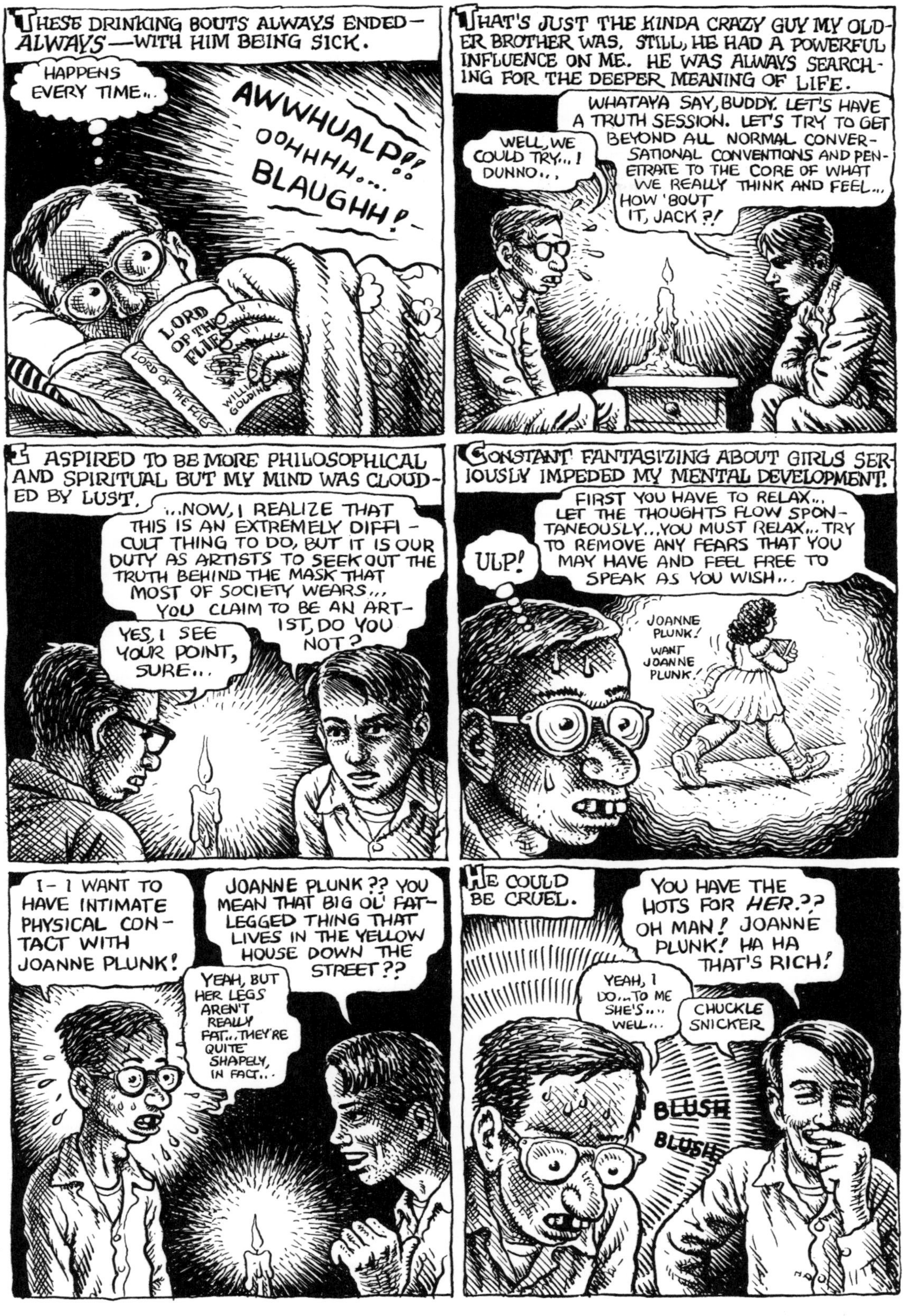
These drinking bouts always ended— *always*—with him being sick.
Happens every time...
AWWHUALP!! OOHHHH.... BLAUGHH!
LORD OF THE FLIES
LORD OF THE FLIES WILLIAM GOLDING
That's just the kinda crazy guy my older brother was. Still, he had a powerful influence on me. He was always searching for the deeper meaning of life.
Whataya say, buddy. Let's have a truth session. Let's try to get beyond all normal conversational conventions and penetrate to the core of what we really think and feel... How 'bout it, Jack?!
Well, we could try... I dunno...
I aspired to be more philosophical and spiritual but my mind was clouded by lust.
...Now, I realize that this is an extremely difficult thing to do, but it is our duty as artists to seek out the truth behind the mask that most of society wears... You claim to be an artist, do you not?
Yes, I see your point, sure...
Constant fantasizing about girls seriously impeded my mental development.
First you have to relax... let the thoughts flow spontaneously... you must relax... try to remove any fears that you may have and feel free to speak as you wish...
ULP!
Joanne Plunk! Want Joanne Plunk!
I- I want to have intimate physical contact with Joanne Plunk!
Joanne Plunk?? You mean that big ol' fat-legged thing that lives in the yellow house down the street??
Yeah, but her legs aren't really fat... they're quite shapely, in fact...
He could be cruel.
You have the hots for *her*?? Oh man! Joanne Plunk! Ha ha that's rich!
Yeah, I do... to me she's... well...
Chuckle snicker
BLUSH BLUSH

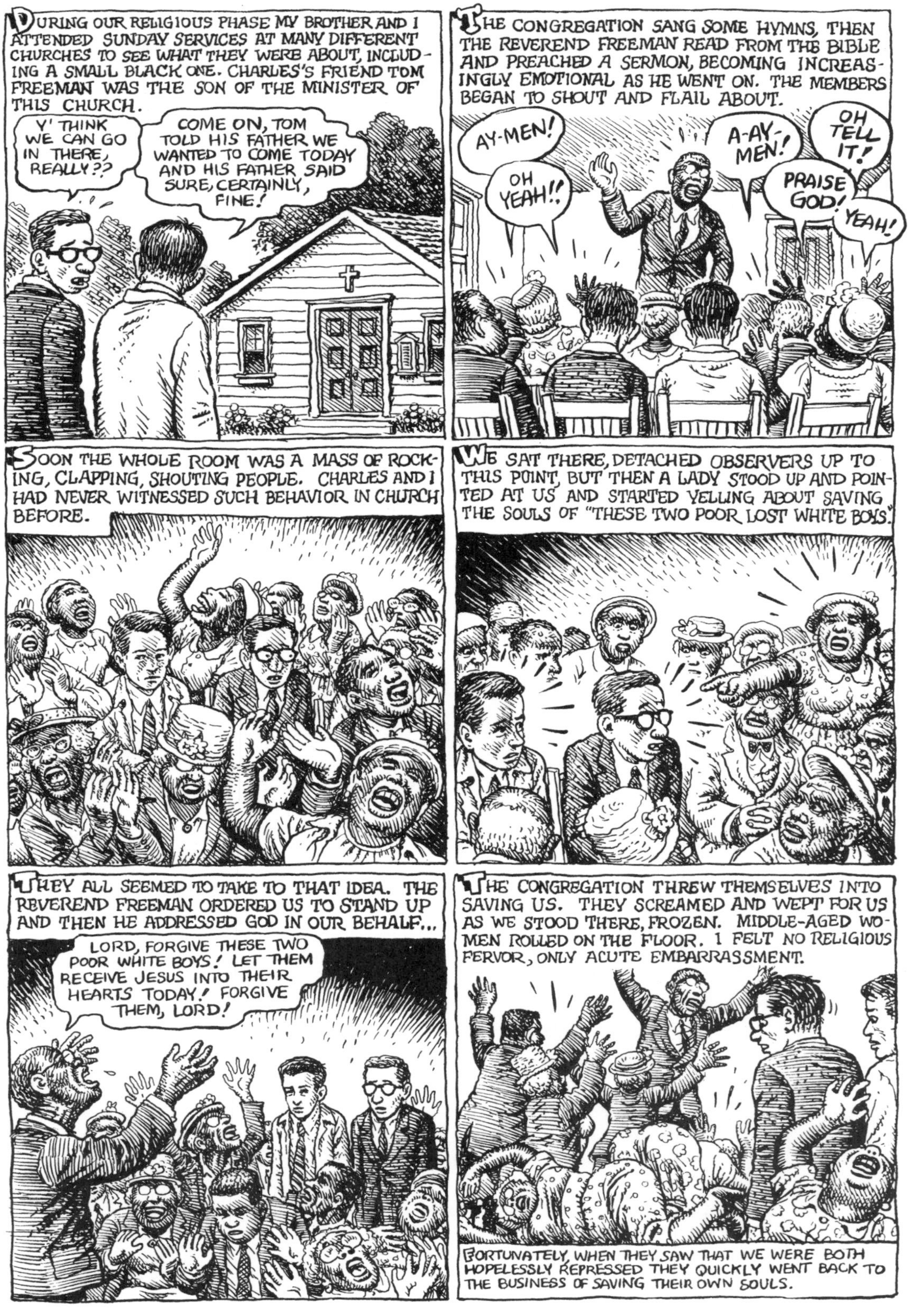
DURING OUR RELIGIOUS PHASE MY BROTHER AND I ATTENDED SUNDAY SERVICES AT MANY DIFFERENT CHURCHES TO SEE WHAT THEY WERE ABOUT, INCLUDING A SMALL BLACK ONE. CHARLES'S FRIEND TOM FREEMAN WAS THE SON OF THE MINISTER OF THIS CHURCH.
Y' THINK WE CAN GO IN THERE, REALLY??
COME ON, TOM TOLD HIS FATHER WE WANTED TO COME TODAY AND HIS FATHER SAID SURE, CERTAINLY, FINE!
THE CONGREGATION SANG SOME HYMNS, THEN THE REVEREND FREEMAN READ FROM THE BIBLE AND PREACHED A SERMON, BECOMING INCREASINGLY EMOTIONAL AS HE WENT ON. THE MEMBERS BEGAN TO SHOUT AND FLAIL ABOUT.
AY-MEN!
OH YEAH!!
A-AY-MEN!
OH TELL IT!
PRAISE GOD!
YEAH!
SOON THE WHOLE ROOM WAS A MASS OF ROCKING, CLAPPING, SHOUTING PEOPLE. CHARLES AND I HAD NEVER WITNESSED SUCH BEHAVIOR IN CHURCH BEFORE.
WE SAT THERE, DETACHED OBSERVERS UP TO THIS POINT, BUT THEN A LADY STOOD UP AND POINTED AT US AND STARTED YELLING ABOUT SAVING THE SOULS OF "THESE TWO POOR LOST WHITE BOYS."
THEY ALL SEEMED TO TAKE TO THAT IDEA. THE REVEREND FREEMAN ORDERED US TO STAND UP AND THEN HE ADDRESSED GOD IN OUR BEHALF...
LORD, FORGIVE THESE TWO POOR WHITE BOYS! LET THEM RECEIVE JESUS INTO THEIR HEARTS TODAY! FORGIVE THEM, LORD!
THE CONGREGATION THREW THEMSELVES INTO SAVING US. THEY SCREAMED AND WEPT FOR US AS WE STOOD THERE, FROZEN. MIDDLE-AGED WOMEN ROLLED ON THE FLOOR. I FELT NO RELIGIOUS FERVOR, ONLY ACUTE EMBARRASSMENT.
FORTUNATELY, WHEN THEY SAW THAT WE WERE BOTH HOPELESSLY REPRESSED THEY QUICKLY WENT BACK TO THE BUSINESS OF SAVING THEIR OWN SOULS.

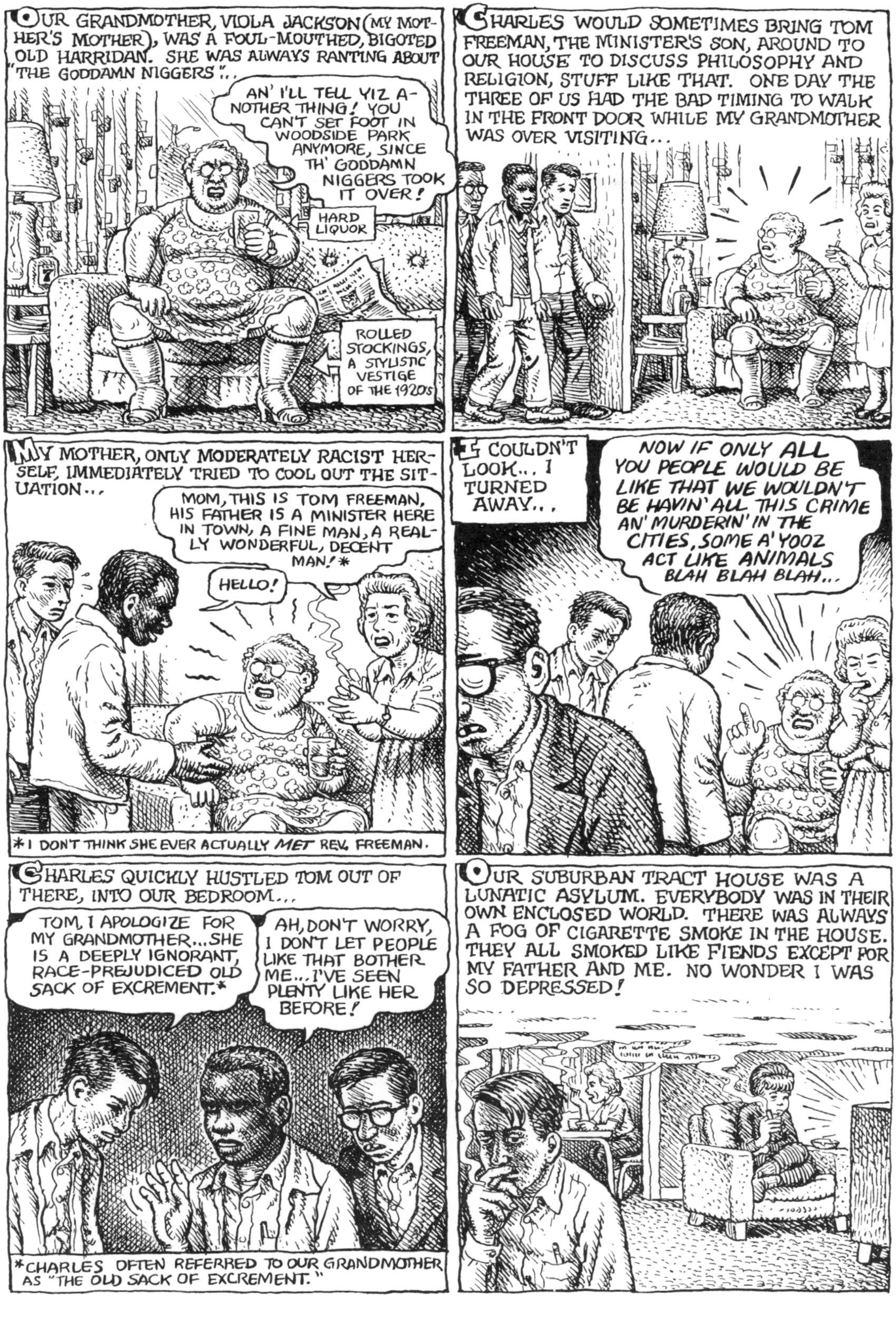
OUR GRANDMOTHER, VIOLA JACKSON (MY MOTHER'S MOTHER), WAS A FOUL-MOUTHED, BIGOTED OLD HARRIDAN. SHE WAS ALWAYS RANTING ABOUT "THE GODDAMN NIGGERS"...
AN' I'LL TELL YIZ ANOTHER THING! YOU CAN'T SET FOOT IN WOODSIDE PARK ANYMORE, SINCE TH' GODDAMN NIGGERS TOOK IT OVER!
HARD LIQUOR
ROLLED STOCKINGS, A STYLISTIC VESTIGE OF THE 1920'S
CHARLES WOULD SOMETIMES BRING TOM FREEMAN, THE MINISTER'S SON, AROUND TO OUR HOUSE TO DISCUSS PHILOSOPHY AND RELIGION, STUFF LIKE THAT. ONE DAY THE THREE OF US HAD THE BAD TIMING TO WALK IN THE FRONT DOOR WHILE MY GRANDMOTHER WAS OVER VISITING...
MY MOTHER, ONLY MODERATELY RACIST HERSELF, IMMEDIATELY TRIED TO COOL OUT THE SITUATION...
MOM, THIS IS TOM FREEMAN, HIS FATHER IS A MINISTER HERE IN TOWN, A FINE MAN, A REALLY WONDERFUL, DECENT MAN!*
HELLO!
*I DON'T THINK SHE EVER ACTUALLY MET REV. FREEMAN.
I COULDN'T LOOK... I TURNED AWAY...
NOW IF ONLY ALL YOU PEOPLE WOULD BE LIKE THAT WE WOULDN'T BE HAVIN' ALL THIS CRIME AN' MURDERIN' IN THE CITIES, SOME A' YOOZ ACT LIKE ANIMALS BLAH BLAH BLAH...
CHARLES QUICKLY HUSTLED TOM OUT OF THERE, INTO OUR BEDROOM...
TOM, I APOLOGIZE FOR MY GRANDMOTHER... SHE IS A DEEPLY IGNORANT, RACE-PREJUDICED OLD SACK OF EXCREMENT.*
AH, DON'T WORRY, I DON'T LET PEOPLE LIKE THAT BOTHER ME... I'VE SEEN PLENTY LIKE HER BEFORE!
*CHARLES OFTEN REFERRED TO OUR GRANDMOTHER AS "THE OLD SACK OF EXCREMENT."
OUR SUBURBAN TRACT HOUSE WAS A LUNATIC ASYLUM. EVERYBODY WAS IN THEIR OWN ENCLOSED WORLD. THERE WAS ALWAYS A FOG OF CIGARETTE SMOKE IN THE HOUSE. THEY ALL SMOKED LIKE FIENDS EXCEPT FOR MY FATHER AND ME. NO WONDER I WAS SO DEPRESSED!

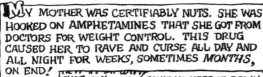

My mother was certifiably nuts. She was hooked on amphetamines that she got from doctors for weight control. This drug caused her to rave and curse all day and all night for weeks, sometimes *months*, on end!

THAT SON-OF-A-B *** TAKE IT ANOTHER *** FIX HIS WAGON. THINKS *** *** LIVE TO REGRET *** I KID YOU NOT, ***

CAN'T YA KEEP IT DOWN A LITTLE, PLEASE? WE'RE TRYIN' TA HEAR THE T.V.!

...FROM THE PIT OF MAN'S FEARS TO THE SUMMIT OF HIS KNOW-LEDGE...

YUBAN INSTANT COFFEE

When my father was home (which he tried *not* to be as much as possible, often holding down *two* full-time jobs), my mother would scream endless insults, accusations, and vile epithets at the poor bastard...

*** PULL YER CRA *** WHORE MASTER *** SLUTS OF YOURS *** YOU BUM *** DON'T THINK I DON'T KNOW *** LYING SON-OF-A-BITCH GOD *** NO GOOD ***

AH BULL SHIT

AH BULL SHIT

AH BULL SHIT

IRONING HIS WHITE SHIRTS

During her worst derangements she would attack the old man and claw his face to ribbons. Tough ex-marine though he was, he often just stood there and let her do it!

GRRR *** ROTTEN LOUSE! *** YER WHORES *** !! GRRR SCRATCH YER EYES OUT

I DON'T HAVE ANY WHORES! YOU'RE A SICK WOMAN!

He would dutifully go back to work the next day with his face a grotesque mask of scratches and band-aids. Why didn't he stop her? Was it a cry for help, perhaps??

In spite of all the craziness they made a brave show of keeping up normal family life. Birthdays and holidays such as Christmas were strictly observed.

WITH EVERY BREATH I TAKE *** TO MY DYING DAY I'LL NEVER *** *** !! YER WHORES ***

LET'S CUT THE CRAP AND TRIM TH' GODDAMN TREE, WHATAYA SAY?!

My mother always had that dinner on the table...

GOD'S GONNA PUNISH THIS FAMILY SOMEDAY, MARK MY WORDS!! THINK YOU'RE ALL SO HIGH AND MIGHTY ***

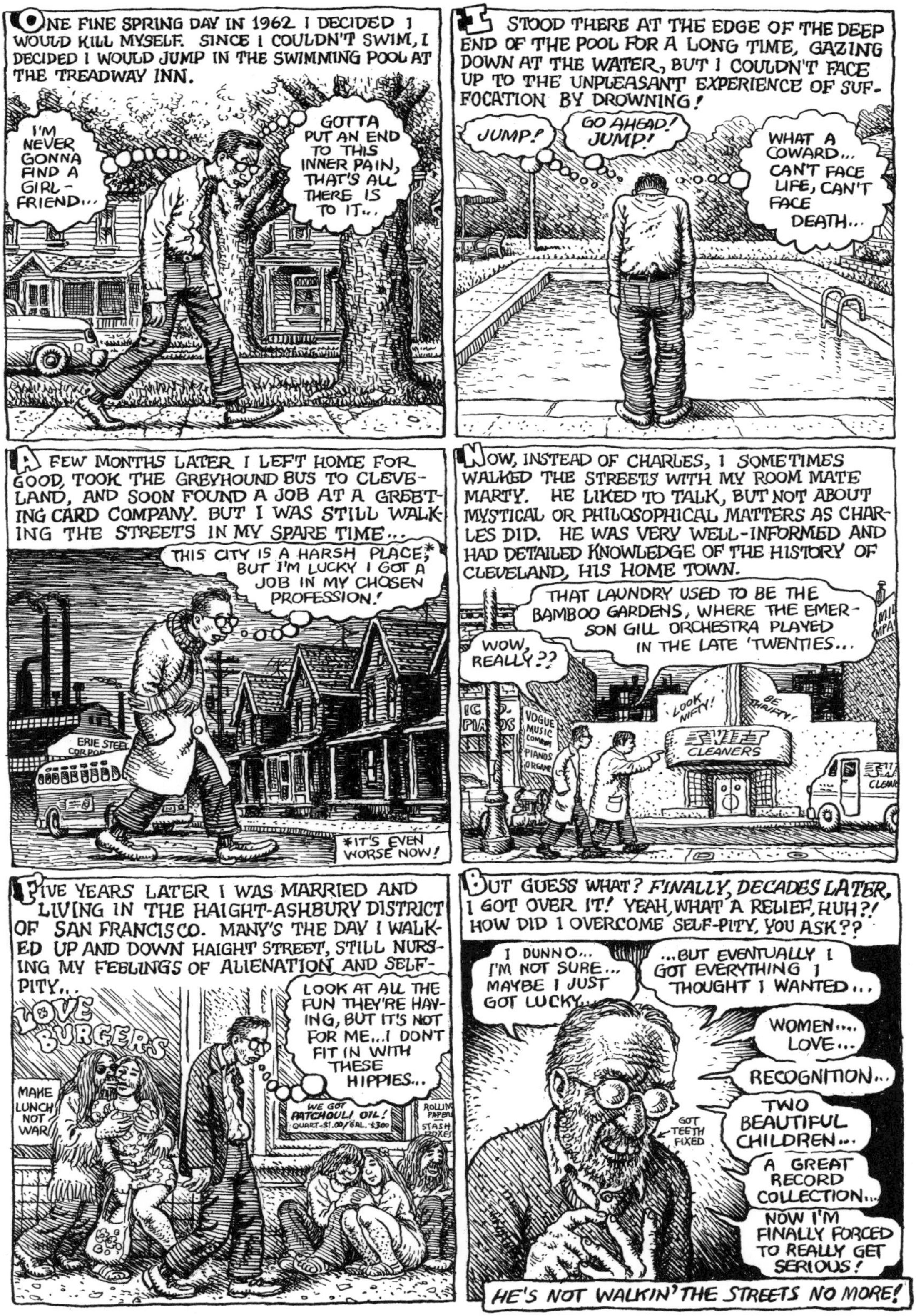
ONE FINE SPRING DAY IN 1962 I DECIDED I WOULD KILL MYSELF. SINCE I COULDN'T SWIM, I DECIDED I WOULD JUMP IN THE SWIMMING POOL AT THE TREADWAY INN.
I'M NEVER GONNA FIND A GIRL-FRIEND...
GOTTA PUT AN END TO THIS INNER PAIN, THAT'S ALL THERE IS TO IT...
I STOOD THERE AT THE EDGE OF THE DEEP END OF THE POOL FOR A LONG TIME, GAZING DOWN AT THE WATER, BUT I COULDN'T FACE UP TO THE UNPLEASANT EXPERIENCE OF SUF-FOCATION BY DROWNING!
JUMP!
GO AHEAD! JUMP!
WHAT A COWARD... CAN'T FACE LIFE, CAN'T FACE DEATH...
A FEW MONTHS LATER I LEFT HOME FOR GOOD, TOOK THE GREYHOUND BUS TO CLEVE-LAND, AND SOON FOUND A JOB AT A GREET-ING CARD COMPANY. BUT I WAS STILL WALK-ING THE STREETS IN MY SPARE TIME...
THIS CITY IS A HARSH PLACE,* BUT I'M LUCKY I GOT A JOB IN MY CHOSEN PROFESSION!
ERIE STEEL CORPOR
*IT'S EVEN WORSE NOW!
NOW, INSTEAD OF CHARLES, I SOMETIMES WALKED THE STREETS WITH MY ROOM MATE MARTY. HE LIKED TO TALK, BUT NOT ABOUT MYSTICAL OR PHILOSOPHICAL MATTERS AS CHAR-LES DID. HE WAS VERY WELL-INFORMED AND HAD DETAILED KNOWLEDGE OF THE HISTORY OF CLEVELAND, HIS HOME TOWN.
THAT LAUNDRY USED TO BE THE BAMBOO GARDENS, WHERE THE EMER-SON GILL ORCHESTRA PLAYED IN THE LATE 'TWENTIES...
WOW, REALLY??
VOGUE MUSIC COMPANY PIANOS ORGANS
LOOK NIFTY!
BE THRIFTY!
CLEANERS
FIVE YEARS LATER I WAS MARRIED AND LIVING IN THE HAIGHT-ASHBURY DISTRICT OF SAN FRANCISCO. MANY'S THE DAY I WALK-ED UP AND DOWN HAIGHT STREET, STILL NURS-ING MY FEELINGS OF ALIENATION AND SELF-PITY...
LOVE BURGERS
LOOK AT ALL THE FUN THEY'RE HAV-ING, BUT IT'S NOT FOR ME... I DONT FIT IN WITH THESE HIPPIES...
MAKE LUNCH NOT WAR
WE GOT PATCHOULI OIL! QUART-$1.00/GAL.-$3.00
BUT GUESS WHAT? FINALLY, DECADES LATER, I GOT OVER IT! YEAH, WHAT A RELIEF, HUH?! HOW DID I OVERCOME SELF-PITY, YOU ASK??
I DUNNO... I'M NOT SURE... MAYBE I JUST GOT LUCKY...
...BUT EVENTUALLY I GOT EVERYTHING I THOUGHT I WANTED...
WOMEN... LOVE...
RECOGNITION...
TWO BEAUTIFUL CHILDREN...
A GREAT RECORD COLLECTION...
NOW I'M FINALLY FORCED TO REALLY GET SERIOUS!
GOT TEETH FIXED
HE'S NOT WALKIN' THE STREETS NO MORE!

CONTRIBUTORS' NOTES

100 DISTINGUISHED COMICS
from January 2004 to August 2005

Contributors' Notes

Cartoonist and writer **Jessica Abel**'s graphic novel *La Perdida* was published by Pantheon Books in March 2006. Abel is the author of *Soundtrack* and *Mirror, Window,* two collections that gather stories and drawings from her comic book *Artbabe,* which she published between 1992 and 1999. She also collaborated with Ira Glass on *Radio: An Illustrated Guide,* a nonfiction comic about how the radio show *This American Life* is made. Abel won both the Harvey and Lulu awards for best new talent in 1997; *La Perdida* won the 2002 Harvey Award for best new series. Abel's young adult novel, *Carmina,* is forthcoming from HarperCollins in 2007; she is collaborating on another graphic novel, *Life Sucks,* due from First Second in 2007; and she is working with her husband, the cartoonist Matt Madden, on a textbook about making comics. She lives in Brooklyn.

▪ I lived in Mexico with my boyfriend (now husband), Matt Madden, from 1998 to 2000. When we decided to move there, I had no particular artistic goal, no story that I wanted to write out of the experience. In fact, I was still engaged in creating *Artbabe,* the series of short stories I published with Fantagraphics from 1997 to 1999 (now published as a book, *Mirror, Window*), through half my time in Mexico, and then in *Radio: An Illustrated Guide* and various illustration projects throughout the rest. I did not begin on *La Perdida,* a work that turned out to take 250 pages and five years of my life to complete, until I returned to the United States and settled in Brooklyn.

Lynda Barry was born in 1956 in Wisconsin to a woman who came from the Philippines on a military transport plane and a navy man who drank and bowled. They didn't like each other and they didn't like their kids. They didn't like stories of the reading, drawing, or writing kind. Lynda Barry is a cartoonist, novelist, and writing teacher.

▪ "The Two Questions" came from trying to write something good and not getting very far because I had forgotten that trying to write something good before I write anything at all is like refusing to give birth unless you know for sure it is going to be a very good baby. What I don't understand is why I keep forgetting this and then having to remember it again. It was all the trying for something good that got me into the very tangle this piece describes. There certainly wasn't any fun in it until I remembered to quit trying to be good. I had the flu when I wrote it and couldn't hold my brush steady enough to get a good line, so I used a gel pen, which added some extra frustration, which wasn't all bad: it gave me a kind of traction on the paper that helped steady the line, and I did it on my lap while camping out on the couch with the TV on, which gave me a good junior-high-school-homework feeling.

Alison Bechdel has been churning out episodes of her self-syndicated comic strip *Dykes to Watch Out For* like clockwork since 1983 for a smallish but highly discerning audience. Eleven collections of the strip have been published, and some of them have won awards. She has also done exclusive work for many publications, including *Ms., Slate,* and *The Advocate.* Bechdel's graphic memoir, *Fun Home: A Family Tragicomic,* was published by Houghton Mifflin in June 2006. She lives near Burlington, Vermont.

▪ This story is a regular episode of my biweekly comic strip, *Dykes to Watch Out For,* so it's part of a long, involved narrative that's been unfolding over many years. These two characters, Mo and Sydney, are sort of allegorical figures for me. Mo represents the revolutionary principles of the early gay liberation movement, and her girlfriend, Sydney, represents a latter-day strategy of assimilation, expedience, and annoying postgay cynicism. I believe that both these approaches are necessary for progress, and they seem to me to form a curious and paradoxical nexus around the issue of gay marriage. I wrote this episode just after the city of San Francisco began performing same-sex marriages in 2004, and just before I actually flew there with my real-life girlfriend to get married. Having a wedding on the steps of City Hall felt oddly radical and reactionary at the same time. (Also expedient — I happened to be going there anyway for a comics convention and had my travel costs covered.) Later, when the San Francisco marriages were ruled invalid, we felt simultaneously pissed off and relieved.

Jonathan Bennett lives in Brooklyn, New York, with his wife, Amy.

▪ Before Fantagraphics contacted me about contributing to their new quarterly anthology, *Mome,* I had worked only on brief one- to four-page stories (that I was often guilty of reformatting to pad out a mini-comic). The story was sparked by true events but quickly runs off on tangents that are entirely fictional or unrelated to what was real. I was improvising from page to page, and often panel to panel. It took me forever, and at several points, sometimes mid-page, I would hit a wall with no idea where to go from there. It would take me a few hours to finish drawing each panel, and on a good day, by the time I finished inking and lettering that panel, I'd finally have an Idea of what was next. On bad days, a week would pass before I could think up the next small step. It felt at times like I was trying to recall the details of a dream. As if the story wasn't being improvised and invented but instead was a true "auto-bio" tale that I could finish if I could only *remember* what had happened in what order. One half of my brain must have tricked the other into thinking it was all real. I can't understand it. I don't know.

Leigh Brownhill is a Ph.D. candidate at the University of Toronto. In 2001, Terisa Turner and Leigh Brownhill coedited *Gender, Feminism, and the Civil Commons,* published as a special issue of the *Canadian Journal of Development Studies* available at http://www.uoguelph.ca/~terisatu/. Leigh Brownhill coedited a special issue of *Canadian Woman Studies* (2002) and has published on popular struggles in Africa in the *Canadian Journal of African Studies,* the *Journal of Asian and African Studies,* and *Feminist Economics.*

▪ Between 1989 and 2006 I spent some four years in Kenya, engaged mainly with the First Woman research network interviewing elderly peasant women who had been involved in the anticolonial Mau Mau war of the 1950s. I first met Ruth Wangari wa Thung'u, protagonist in the Freedom Corner struggle, in 1996. Ruth Wangari's first statement to us in 1996 set the tone for the whole First Woman oral history project. She said, "I was a fighter in the Mau Mau war in the 1950s, and I am still fighting. What do you want to know?" What we wanted to know was how elderly peasant women had come to be at the forefront of the burgeoning Kenyan social movements for democracy and human rights. The answers we found in Ruth's and others' oral histories centered on the fact that women, especially elders, knew best how to organize for the production of food to feed entire communities. This capacity, as simple as it sounds, is of top priority in a society in which millions are malnourished because land has been appropriated by multinational corporations for the production of coffee, tea, and luxury horticultural exports. After Freedom Corner, hundreds of community groups launched their own nongovernmental organizations aimed at defending and reappropriating the land, food, and freedom that had been withheld from them since colonial days. Due to continued repression, these grassroots Kenyan organizations reached out into the international social movement community to make links of solidarity. At the local, national, and global levels, Kenyan subsistence demands have come to define new directions in social movement activity. These life-centered demands are at the top of the agenda for the World Social Forum in Nairobi in January 2007. They delineate important aspects of an alternative society against the death spiral of corporate globalization.

Ivan Brunetti was born in a small town in Italy on October 3, 1967. At the tender age of eight, he moved from his grandparents' farm in Italy to the industrial South Side of Chicago; he has lived in this fair city for about 5,000 years, rarely venturing outside of its bittersweet confines. He currently works as a Web designer and has recently started teaching classes on comics at Columbia College Chicago and the University of Chicago. In 2005, he curated an exhibit of seventy-five artists, "The Cartoonist's Eye," for the A+D Gallery of Columbia College Chicago; the exhibit was a preview for his book *An Anthology of Graphic Fiction* (Yale University Press), scheduled for publication in the fall of 2006. He also draws a sporadic strip for the *Chicago Reader* and other alternative weekly newspapers. To date, Fantagraphics has published four issues of his comic book series, *Schizo*, and two collections of his morally inexcusable gag cartoons, *HAW!*, and its miniature companion, *HEE!* He lives with his wife and their three cats. Yes, he could stand to lose thirty to forty pounds; he's working on it.

■ When I was going through a pretty rough depression a few years ago, it was exacerbated by having my heart torn out by a particular female I stupidly got obsessed with. I was going through one of my usual nonproductive slumps, so in desperation I thought back to the last time that drawing cartoons had made me happy, which was when I was about ten years old. Back then I was obsessively drawing the 1930s Mickey Mouse. Thus, I started doodling cartoon mice again. Somehow or other a rough version of this strip (embarrassingly autobiographical, now that I look at it again) just sort of came out. I had already drawn a wordless strip about a rabbit painter the year before (also embarrassingly autobiographical), and I thought this mouse strip would make a good companion piece. Later, I also ended up drawing strips about dogs, cats, birds, and pigs—all variations on a few simple themes. All the strips were satirical yet empathetic commentaries on specific artists on some level, but they were nakedly autobiographical as well. This particular strip reminded me most of a comic I had drawn about Piet Mondrian a year and a half before, yet it was also directly about my own emotional/aesthetic turmoil during the time I drew it. Using the "funny animal" conceit was simply a way of addressing certain things I could not face about myself at the time, and a way to write a humorous, self-mocking strip without indulging in my boundless self-pity. It's probably my favorite of all the funny animal strips I drew, although I can't explain why, other than maybe it hit closest to home. And I like drawing mice.

Lilli Carré was born in 1983 in Los Angeles and currently lives in Chicago, where she is studying animation and print. Her book *Tales of Woodsman Pete*, which follows the outings and musings of a gregarious hermit, is being published by Top Shelf in 2006. Many of her extended-family members are competitive divers, though she herself is not.

■ Paul Bunyan's life story is as malleable as the day is long—the account of his existence is varied, changing with each storyteller's embellishments. I want to contribute to the pool of stories about Paul, but instead of telling another explanatory tale of his accidental creations that manifest themselves as American landmarks, I want to focus on the fact that although he is a giant, a fantastical character, he still has a job. I am interested in playing with the aspects of his character that are still tethered to "real life" in some way — the idea that the same character who made the Grand Canyon by dragging his axe along behind him still clocks in at nine in the morning every day, and the very thing that makes him magnificent also makes finding a woman to love very difficult, if not practically improbable. Since there is so much elbowroom with Paul's character, I want to slip him out of his husky role and make this tall-tale character have a soft spot for literature, a giant who romanticizes the world to the extent that he believes he can leave his role behind and slip away unnoticed into a big city. In a medium that has a history of superhuman characters that serve to set some sort of example or explanation, this comic shows Paul Bunyan illuminating the literal inconveniences of being a grandiose example for the rest of us, a large man of debated origin whose softest mutterings are loud enough to make the needles on the pine trees thread themselves.

Robert Crumb was born in Philadelphia in 1943. He began his amazing career almost forty years ago when, as an underground cartoonist during the Summer of Love, he created *Zap Comix* and a horde of unforgettable characters: Fritz the Cat, Mr. Natural, The Snoid, and Devil Girl, to name but a few. Ever since then, fame has dogged Crumb's footsteps. Not being a particularly fast runner, filmmakers have managed to capture the artist in two award-winning documentaries about his life and work, and now museums in Europe and America are exhibiting Crumb's drawings and cartoons to critical acclaim.

Crumb now keeps a low profile by living in the south of France with his wife and fellow artist, Aline Kominsky-Crumb. From there Crumb continues his eternal quest for old 78 rpm records, while seeking inspiration from women blessed with large bottoms, strong legs, and thick ankles.

- Here is the statement you requested to go with the story "Walkin' the Streets," though I make it reluctantly. I don't believe that artists should be asked why they made a certain piece or wrote a certain story. Often, artists don't really know why they do what they do . . . the work *is* the artist's statement!! But here it is anyway, for what it's worth: one day in 1992 I was brooding about my youth, during which I would often walk the streets at night. My brother Charles and I often walked the streets together. I decided to do a comic story about it. Four pages into it, I got stuck and gave up on it and didn't pick it up again until twelve years later! In the year 2004 I was finally able to see this story through to completion. It happens sometimes; I can't tell you why.

Lloyd Dangle's cartoons and illustrations have appeared in over a hundred magazines and newspapers of every kind, from *Weirdo* to the *New York Times*. He grew up in Michigan and worked for Michael Moore's (*Fahrenheit 9/11*) muckraking newspaper, the *Michigan Voice*. His weekly comic strip, *Troubletown*, is a widely syndicated feature in alternative newsweeklies and political magazines nationally. He's also known for illustrating the packages for Airborne, the number-one cold remedy in the United States. Lloyd Dangle served stints as president of both the Northern California and the national chapters of the artists' advocacy organization, the Graphic Artists Guild. Dangle lives in Oakland, California, with his wife, the graphic designer and fine artist Hae Yoon Kim, and their son, Oscar.

- I had talked to the editor at *The Stranger*, in Seattle, where they run my comic strip *Troubletown*, and we both thought it would be funny to send me to New York to report on the blowhard antics at the Republican National Convention. First the assignment was on, then it was off, then it was on again, but the Republicans weren't giving out press credentials very easily (I think you had to take a blood oath affirming that you were a lifelong Texas party donor and right-winger). Anyway, I never got the badge, but it didn't matter. The real story was in the streets, since post-9/11 New York City had been transformed into a combination police state and WTO-protest-times-a-thousand. Political conventions have a shelf life of about two seconds as newspaper content, so I had to do the cartoon on the fly in order to make it into the following week's issue. It was all a blur, but I got the story!

Rebecca Dart was born in Simi Valley, California, in the early 1970s, although she has spent the last dozen years in the wintery climes of Canada with her husband, Robin Bougie, publisher of *Cinema Sewer* magazine — to which Rebecca occasionally contributes art. Rebecca's work has appeared in various comic anthologies such as *Action Girl, Bete Noir,* and *Blood Orange,* although much of her time with a pencil is taken up working as an animator, which is what pays the bills, yo. Rebecca has worked on such animated TV shows as *Mission Hill, Ned's Newt, What About Ian?,* and *Pucca* — among many others.

▪ The inspiration for *RabbitHead* came from two films: *The Saragossa Manuscript* (Poland, 1965) and Alejandro Jordowsky's 1973 cult classic, *El Topo. The Saragossa Manuscript* starts with two soldiers on opposites sides of the Napoleonic war who discover in a destroyed house a text, which they start to read. The narrative of the film switches to that of the book they are reading, and then within that story line a character begins to tell a story — and the narrative focus switches yet again. This happens several times to create a multiple-layered story line. I thought this was an interesting storytelling idea but would work much better in comic book form, as the sequential graphic narrative breaks down to a basic physics equation: space = time. The reading action of the viewer dictates the speed and flow of time, not the technology, and this is a distinct advantage the printed page has over backlit forms of media. As a comic, the stories could be shown simultaneously, occupying the same space on a page, therefore giving the illusion of things happening at the same time. The overall theme and tone of *RabbitHead* borrows somewhat from *El Topo.* In this film a lone character is sent on a surreal, personal journey, where he meets a host of odd and unusual characters. The film falls within the conventions of a Western but is not limited to them. One of my main criteria while drawing *RabbitHead* was that I desperately wanted to create a comic that could *only* be a comic and couldn't be translated into another visual form.

Kim Deitch has seen his comics published since 1967. He was lucky enough to more or less learn how to do it as he earned, and by fits and starts, he eventually reached a point where he felt that he was fairly good at it. Better yet, over time he's also reached a place where he gets a great deal of enjoyment out of doing it. He's worked in underground newspapers, comic books, magazines, and, these days, even proper books every once in a while. His most recent book from Pantheon Books is *The Boulevard of Broken Dreams.* They will be publishing *Alias the Cat* next year. And coming also next year, *Shadowland Comics* — another big batch of his comic book stories from Fantagraphics Books.

▪ The way "Ready to Die" came about was that Art Spiegelman offered me a job doing an interview with Charles Manson, in comics form, for a spread in *Details* magazine. It sounded kind of old hat to me so I made the countersuggestion that I instead look for someone about to be executed and just see where a story like that might go. Well, all I can say is I must have had a classic case of beginner's luck, because the whole story in "Ready to Die" just opened up for me like some kind of magic. I seemed to do so well in all of the human interaction involved in doing a story like that, it actually made me wonder if I'd somehow missed my true calling and maybe should have been some kind of reporter. More docu-comics followed, and interestingly enough, the experience has definitely left its mark on the recent fiction that I have subsequently produced in comics.

Rick Geary was born in Kansas City, Missouri, and grew up in Wichita, Kansas. His work has appeared in *National Lampoon, Mad,* the *New York Times, Heavy Metal, Disney Adventures,* and many other publications. He has completed seven volumes in his "Treasury of Victorian Murder" series of graphic novels, the latest of which is *The Murder of Abraham Lincoln.* He lives with his wife, Deborah, in San Diego, California.

■ This one-page story was done for *The Comics Journal,* published by Fantagraphics Books. Once or twice a year, the *Journal* published a large-format special edition in which they invited artists to submit stories around a particular theme. The theme for this issue was seduction, and it was made clear that not only romantic or sexual but all kinds of seduction would be acceptable. However, all I could think of were the times of my life in which I was, to say the least, slow on the uptake in the romantic department, and I boiled them all down to this one humiliating episode.

Justin Hall was raised by wolves but was drawn out of the forest and into civilization by the bright and garish lure of comic books. He won a 2001 Xeric Foundation grant for his first comic, *A Sacred Text,* a fantastical retelling of the story of the Dead Sea scrolls. After that he began self-publishing his *True Travel Tales* series, which is a collection of autobiographical and biographical stories from the road, featuring everything from anonymous sex in Egyptian temples to blood sacrifices in Bolivia to smuggling cocaine from Peru. Hall also has work collected in various anthologies such as *Kitchen Sink Magazine, True Porn, Juicy Mother,* the SPX books, and more. He is also the cocreator of the gay erotic comic *Hard to Swallow,* and his character *Glamazonia: The Uncanny Super Tranny* has been hard at work making the Internet more fabulous. Hall has exhibited his fine art and comics work in New York and San Francisco, including a Small Press Spotlight show at the San Francisco Cartoon Art Museum, where he is also curating a queer cartoonists show in 2006. Hall has lost most of his wolfish ways, though he still growls if someone gets too close to his food. He lives in San Francisco with his boyfriend, their pet snake, and the mice required to feed it.

■ "La Rubia Loca" is a story I did for *True Travel Tales,* my series of biographical and autobiographical travel comics. In the course of collecting travel stories from people to use in the series, I discovered my friend "Pelon" had been a driver for the Green Tortoise, a hippie bus line out of San Francisco. I knew that he had to have some juicy tales from that experience, and so I cornered him in a local café. We spent a marathon four hours there, him telling me the story of his ill-fated trip to Mexico, and me taking down notes in slack-jawed awe. I knew I had hit a goldmine . . . This was a story that I could sink my artistic teeth into. I decided to alter my standard format for "La Rubia Loca." Normally in *True Travel Tales* I tell the story as closely as possible to how it was told to me. The words and images are mine, but I try to capture the voice, personality, and perspective of the person who gave me the story. Everything is true, or at least as true as any good tale told by a traveler can be. In this case, however, I changed the point of view from that of Pelon, who is the character Perry in the story, to that of Sarah (not her real name, of course), someone I've never met nor interviewed. I did this for dramatic effect, since the events of the story were more profound and transforming for her than for Perry. But again, I've never talked to her about her own feelings on the matter. I can only hope that if Sarah should ever run across this comic she will understand that I made this piece with respect, and that ultimately all tales, even "true" ones, are stories first.

Born in Kingston, New York, **Tom Hart** has been drawing cartoons since tracing a strange picture in the second grade of Charlie Brown's head sticking out of a tube of toothpaste. A popular underground/alternative cartoonist since the early 1990s, his first book featured the surly and homeless Hutch Owen, and he became one of the earliest recipients of the Xeric Foundation grant for self-publishing cartoonists, a foundation created by the *Teenage Mutant Ninja Turtle* cocreator Peter Laird. Two book collections of Hutch Owen/Dennis Worner stories to date have been published by Top Shelf Productions. "The Executive Hour" is from *Hutch Owen: Unmarketable.*

Hart has released numerous books to critical and audience acclaim, and has been nominated for Ignatz, Eisner, and Harvey awards. He has created a series, *Pitch Unger,* for a publisher in Japan, has been translated into French and Portuguese, and has had his work shown in shows from Seattle, Washington, to Porto, Portugal, and Lubjiana, Slovenia. He has also been a guest on Air America Radio's *The Majority Report.* Tom Hart teaches cartooning all over the New York City area, where he lives with his wife and fellow cartoonist, Leela Corman.

▪ "The Executive Hour" was commissioned by a French magazine that needed a story about 2003 for their January 2004 issue. The deadline was ridiculously soon and I had to work fast. Luckily I had been playing around with new story-generation ideas so I decided on a central theme by drawing a card of notes from a stack that I've got lying around: "You only listen well at the beginning and the end." The potential dichotomy of responses to the world — sinister, manipulative glee (the CEO, Dennis Worner), or anger, compassion, and frustration (homeless pedagogue Hutch Owen) — has served as a creative force and major theme in my explorations of the social environment. I've tried to bounce these two responses off each other in as many ways as I can, while of course exploring their similarities as well. I think that in twelve years I've come to at least one conclusion about the characters: that Dennis decides he is going to live up to his potential on this planet, while Hutch is angry that not everyone is given that option.

I can't remember if the idea of making it a solo Dennis Worner story — his first — was another product of divination, but it seemed a chance to let the son of a bitch out of the bag a bit, and so I next spent time dreaming of what Dennis's mornings might look like. Like a lot of us, the start of a new day is a time we can forget all our failings and believe in our self-generated power anew. I get sluggish in the daytime and dream real big dreams at night. I figured, so did Dennis. Looking at the notes scrawled across my lined papers from that time, I see the following ideas that were somehow lost in the process:

"Hutch is chauffeur"
"Dennis . . . noticing Hutch ergo, recognizing failure of previous judgment"
"flashback or hint of tenor of relationship btw Dennis and janitor"
"Dennis on mountain age 13. Grace down below"
" . . . still need reason for puking [underlined] and disgust [underlined]"

I reprint this list here because it represents all the reasons I make cartoons: the joy, the vulgarity, the curiosity, the playfulness, the lost moments, the threaded ideas, the depictions of life as way too weird, funny, and sad to retell in any other way than with lines and doodles and boxes. The story was translated back into English and published in the spring of 2005.

David Heatley is a cartoonist who lives in Queens, New York, with his wife, the writer Rebecca Gopoian, and his daughter, Maya. He publishes a series called *Deadpan,* which is available from Fantagraphics Books. His comics have appeared in the *New York Times, Nickelodeon, Mc-*

Sweeney's, Kramer's Ergot, and *Mome.* A collection of his autobiographical comics will be published by St. Martin's Press in the spring of 2007. See www.davidheatley.com for more information.

■ I've always loved portraiture and that's mostly what I did when I thought I was going to be a painter. Then when I got to art school, I was trying to make "portrait films." I made two that I was pretty happy with. They were shot twice on 8mm film and then projected as 16mm so that the four quadrants on the film stock appeared simultaneously. In my most pretentious moments, I liked to think of them as "cubist" portraits, showing the subjects at different points in time in one composite image. Once I got serious about doing comics, I started thinking about what a "portrait comic" might consist of. I was very inspired by what Dan Clowes and Chris Ware were doing as far as repurposing the Sunday comics newspaper format to present multiple windows on the same story. I guess my contribution to that experiment was to focus it on one person instead. "Portrait of My Dad" began in a sketchbook. It started as a single, dashed-off diary comic that became the strip "Recreation." When I put it into a mini-comic and sent it out to some people, it got a really great reaction. The encouragement got me thinking I could probably do a whole story made up of these little vignettes. Once I started making lists of things to include, it was very easy. I allowed the limits of my memory to be my editor, figuring the stories that are still with me after all these years are most likely the ones worth telling. My dad was very gracious about the whole thing. He has even taken to showing around a blown-up page of the dream comic that ends the strip. Seeing him so exposed has put the fear of God into a lot of my friends and relatives, and they want to know who's next. The answer? My mom.

Jaime Hernandez was born in Oxnard, California, in the year 1959, and was raised there. He has been doing *Love and Rockets* comics since 1981. He lives in Los Angeles with his wife, Meg, and daughter, Carson.

■ I remember when starting this story I wanted to give it an even speed and temperament throughout the entire seven chapters, no ups or downs, but I find (as this is being written) that having just finished the fifth chapter, that just can't be so. Oh, well. At least I got it in the first chapter that made it into this book.

Hob was born into a traveling theater company and now works as a registered nurse in San Francisco. His stories have appeared in the anthologies *Hi-Horse Omnibus* and *Bogus Dead* and in several self-published booklets, including his graphic dream journal, *An Inside Job.*

■ My grandmother, Margaret Lucile Pitzer (1909–1996), lived in Iowa and California, married three times, and worked chiefly as a bookkeeper in the shipping industry. I wasn't the most attentive young man, so out of the many colorful stories she told about people who had unwisely crossed her, this was the only one I wrote down.

Ben Katchor's picture-stories and drawings appear in the English-language *Forward, Metropolis* magazine, and *The New Yorker.* In 2004, he collaborated with the composer Mark Mulcahy on two music-theater productions: *The Slug Bearers of Kayrol Island* and *The Rosenbach Company.* In 1999, he produced the libretto and drawings for *The Carbon Copy Building,* with music by David Lang, Julia Wolfe, and Michael Gordon. He was the recipient of a Guggenheim Memorial Foundation Fellowship (1995), a MacArthur Foundation Fellowship (2000), and was a fellow at The American Academy in Berlin (2002). For more information, visit www.katchor.com.

■ Each month for the past eight years, I have done a strip for the back page of *Metropolis* magazine dealing with various subjects relating to architecture and design. "Goner Pillow Company" was part of this series. I first saw a window pillow being used in the front room of my grandmother's apartment on Knickerbocker Avenue in Brooklyn, circa 1956.

David Lasky is originally from northern Virginia and graduated from the College of William and Mary in 1990, majoring in fine arts. In 1992 he took up residence in Seattle, where he has produced a number of experimental comic books, including *Boom Boom* and *Urban Hipster*. When not at the drawing board, he currently delivers bread for Seattle's Tall Grass Bakery.

▪ Inspired by John Porcellino's *Diary of a Mosquito Abatement Man* (not to mention *The Diary of Samuel Pepys*), I decided to create a visual diary detailing the day-to-day activities involved in the delivery of bread for a small organic bakery. I have worked most of my adult life in office/cubicle situations, so driving a van presented me with new and (sometimes) exciting experiences. This is the first entry in what I hope will be a book-length diary.

Anders Nilsen grew up in Minneapolis and northern New Hampshire. He studied painting and installation art at the University of New Mexico and did a year of graduate work at the School of the Art Institute of Chicago before dropping out in 2000 to draw comics. He draws *Big Questions*, nominated for several Ignatz Awards, and *Dogs and Water*, which won one in 2005. His work can be seen at www.theholyconsumption.com and www.drawnandquarterly.com. He lives and works in Chicago, Illinois.

▪ In 2002 I met Chris Oliveros at the Alternative Press Expo in San Francisco and gave him some of my books. I got an e-mail from him a week or so later, on Valentine's Day, asking if I would do a story for a new anthology he was planning. It felt a little like winning the lottery or something. I was blown away. I took a break from my regular series, *Big Questions*, to work on the story and ran into a series of roadblocks pretty quickly. As source material I had gone back to a set of short experimental strips from several years before—whiteout and ballpoint-pen drawings on Polaroids of piles of wreckage. It had seemed there was a lot of material to create a story from, but I soon found myself stumped. I followed several potential plot paths, and by the time I had to turn the story in it was extremely awkward and unwieldy . . . and about twice as long as Chris actually had space for in the anthology. Getting his e-mail about cutting the story made me feel about the opposite as my response to his first e-mail. It was pretty awful. As it turned out, it was the best possible outcome: he later offered to do the piece as its own book, and this gave me the time and distance to let the story sit for a while and to really figure out what it was about and what parts were worth keeping. I cut out about twenty-five pages, rearranged the rest, and did about forty more. The resulting story seems to have found an audience and struck a nerve with people, which is pretty satisfying. My only regret is that I had to cut the one and only sex scene I've ever drawn.

John Porcellino was born in Chicago in 1968. He began writing and drawing at an early age, compiling his work into small, handmade booklets. His first photocopied 'zine was produced in 1982, at the age of fourteen, and he began his current series, the autobiographical *King-Cat Comics and Stories*, in 1989. Since then, *King-Cat* has been his predominant means of expression. Porcellino's first North American book collection, *Perfect Example*, was published by Highwater Books in 1999 and has recently been reprinted by Drawn and Quarterly. His most recent collection, *Diary of a Mosquito Abatement Man* (La Mano Books), received the 2005 Ignatz Award for outstanding collection or anthology. His work has been included in numerous small-press and underground publications, including the Chris Ware–edited *McSweeney's #13*, and has been translated into French, German, and Spanish. Porcellino currently lives in San Francisco with his wife, Misun, and a small black cat named Maisie Kukoc. For more information on John's work, visit www.king-cat.net.

▪ From 1989 to 1996 I worked, off and on, as a mosquito control technician, and I wrote about some of my on-the-job exploits in my self-published comic magazine *King-Cat*. In the fall of 2003 I began compiling these stories for a new book collection titled *Diary of a Mosquito Abatement Man*. When I showed my wife, Misun, the list of comics for the book, she said, "Where's the story about the chemical plant?" I had told her about that weird night, but I'd never actually drawn a comic about it. She said, "You should draw that story as a new comic for the book." So I did.

Joel Priddy is an illustrator, cartoonist, and professor at the Memphis College of Art. His first graphic novel, *Pulpatoon Pilgrimage*, was nominated for an Eisner Award for best graphic novel and won an Ignatz for outstanding debut. He lives with his radiant wife in a state of perpetual bliss and has mighty big plans for the future.

▪ As a kid, I never drew stick figures. I never drew little *M*s in the sky for birds. I didn't know where the other kids learned this succinct language of visual symbols, and I felt bad that all I could do was look at the world and try to copy what I saw. This deficiency turned out to be a good thing, or at least an unusual thing, and so I went to art school. These days, drawing is all I do. I love it. It's my job—it's my hobby—it's my reason for getting up in the morning. I've devoted years of my life to being the guy that doesn't do stick figures. Except with "Onion Jack." Last year, I accidentally double-booked two projects for the same weekend and found myself owing sixteen pages in three days. Stick figures were the only solution. I was able to finish "Onion Jack" in ten hours, which let me do the other (paying) gig in a more traditional style. And now, "Onion Jack" has become my mostly widely read and distributed story. I just got a call asking me to draw a comic on anything I wanted, as long as it's in the stick-figure style. There are comics fans who only know me as "the Stick-Figure Guy." You people are just taunting me, aren't you?

Jesse Reklaw was born in 1971 in Berkeley, California, where his hippie parents sold bread from a cart on Telegraph Avenue. He studied painting and digital art at the University of California, Santa Cruz, and has a master's degree in computer science from Yale University. Since 1995, he has been drawing the self-syndicated, weekly comic strip *Slow Wave*, which is currently printed by a dozen newspapers around the country. The first collection of *Slow Wave* strips, titled *Dreamtoons*, was published by Shambhala in 2000. The second collection is forthcoming. Jesse's other comics have appeared in a variety of anthologies and self-published mini-comics.

▪ I started working on this comic in 1998, when I was twenty-seven, about five years after my last cat, Harry, had disappeared. I e-mailed my father, sister, and mother some detailed questions about the family cats, trying to fill the holes in my memory. Everyone replied that I remembered a lot more than they did and were unable to answer the questions, but each gave me some useful quotes. I worked on a few pages of the story, but the lack of both cartooning skill and crucial memories prevented me from finishing. I continued to think about the comic over the next seven years, but it wasn't until I started to deal with my depression that I realized what I wanted the story to be about. I also managed to recover a few memories, like the one about dabbing milk onto the premature kitten mouths. I started again in the spring of 2005, and with my father's help to keep the facts straight, I finally finished. About 80 percent of the final work was completed in the two weeks leading up to the Alternative Press Expo, where this story made its debut as a mini-comic called *Couch Tag #2*.

Alex Robinson has wanted to be a cartoonist for as long as he can remember. He is the author of two graphic novels, *Box Office Poison* (2001) and *Tricked* (2005), which is excerpted in this volume. Both are available from Top Shelf Productions. He currently lives in New York City with his wife and their two cats, Cadbury and Krimpet. Check out Alex's website at http://members .aol.com/ComicBookAlex and let him know what you think, assuming you enjoyed his work. If you didn't, he'd prefer you kept quiet about it.

▪ What follows is an excerpt from my second graphic novel, *Tricked*. This particular chapter deals with Phoebe, a teenage girl who has left her home in New Mexico to track down her father, Richard, whom she has never known. To make things more complicated, Richard is currently in a long-term relationship and has never mentioned Phoebe's existence to his lover, Frank. When the chapter begins, Phoebe has gone to Richard and Frank's diner. Frank realizes who she is and is (justifiably) angry at the deception. The other character in the scene is the waitress, Caprice, who, ironically, is something of a daughter figure to both men. When writing this story line, I was interested in seeing whether a previously sympathetic character, Richard, could still remain likable after it's been revealed that he did something awful in his past (in this case, abandon his daughter). I was also interested in approaching it from Phoebe's point of view, wondering if/how someone so betrayed could forge a new relationship with the person who had wronged her.

Joe Sacco was born in Malta in 1960. He studied journalism at the University of Oregon and has been working as a cartoonist since the mid 1980s. His books of comics journalism include *Palestine, Safe Area Gorazde, The Fixer,* and *War's End.* In 2006, Sacco was shortlisted for an Amnesty Media Award.

▪ Most of my comics journalism pieces are about civilians in conflict situations, but I am also interested in the military half, and "Complacency Kills" is the result of one of my only journeys into the soldiers' world. The *Guardian* of London was good enough to commission the piece, which made it possible to get myself embedded with the unit of U.S. Marines at the Haditha Dam. The whole process of getting to Iraq and waiting (and waiting) to get to the battalion could be the subject of another story. As it was, I spent only two weeks with the marines at the dam. In those two weeks, I got a number of interesting stories, but the deadline was looming and I felt I had time to write and draw only the most straightforward one — the task of marines on patrol. The marines were welcoming — I was the battalion's first embedded journalist — but it was difficult to penetrate their world in the short time I had with them. I prefer to spend more time with the people I'm writing about. Only when you become part of the furniture do people speak their minds in front of you.

Born in Dallas in 1940, **Gilbert Shelton**'s unlikely first venture into the world of comic art was doing strips for Boy Scout publications when he was in the Explorer Scouts at school. At the university in Austin, Texas, he became editor of the official student magazine, *The Texas Ranger,* for $100 an issue. This proved to be Shelton's last "real job," for in 1968, after contributing to various underground comix with his earliest character, Wonder Wart-Hog, and designing posters for rock concerts, Shelton created *The Fabulous Furry Freak Brothers.*

In 1969 Shelton and some friends from Texas moved to San Francisco to set up Rip Off Press from which Freak Brothers strips were soon syndicated, borrowed (or stolen!) by a host of American underground newspapers and magazines. The first collection was published in 1971 and has since been joined by thirteen further Freak Brothers adventures. Fat Freddy's Cat, the feline world's number-one cat, started out as a footnote strip to the Freak Brothers but has led an independent — and very successful — life since 1975. In 1993 Shelton introduced the new characters Not Quite Dead, the world's least successful rock band, who have since appeared in a series of comics of their own.

Now over thirty years later and unlike many cults from the sixties that have since faded away, the Freak Brothers are still going from strength to strength and acquiring new fans all the time. They are published in fourteen languages and worldwide sales are now over thirty million copies.

Shelton currently lives in Paris with his wife and three cats.

■ I had to capture a warthog and torture it until it gave me a good story. Then I sat down and dashed off the story in seven months.

Olivia Schanzer is a former member of the United Federation of Teachers. She received a Xeric Foundation grant for the story "Fragile Honeymoon." In addition, she has done illustrations for a textbook on prayer, for HBO, and for various magazines. She recently completed her first novel.

■ The era of the "Fun Bum" in New York City has passed. Though the homeless are still there, the true Fun Bum — that reeking, dangerous icon — no longer holds supreme position in the hierarchy of the city street. In the 1970s and 1980s he reigned, by turns trying to stave in the heads of passersby with stray bricks, or picking people out on the street to follow, screaming about their complicity in some scheme incomprehensible to all but himself. He was equally enraged, although on different days, if you made eye contact with him or if you didn't. The modern world castrates the individual worker, and the figure of the Fun Bum, as the paradigm of Outspoken Man, is the only one able to speak up. The rights of the worker have been eroded and he is utterly friendless, for even the unions do little to help him. Rather than standing up to their opponents, maintaining at least their dignity, if nothing else is salvageable, the unions bow down. Just as the bums do in "Solidarity Forever," the unions accept whatever is offered, though these meager payoffs do them permanent damage.

In 1980, **Seth Tobocman** was one of the founding editors of the political comic book *World War 3 Illustrated*. His illustrations have appeared in the *New York Times* and many other magazines. Tobocman is the author/illustrator of three graphic books: *You Don't Have to Fuck People Over to Survive, War in the Neighborhood,* and *Portraits of Israelis and Palestinians.* His images have been used in posters, pamphlets, murals, graffiti, and tattoos by people's movements around the world.

■ In the summer of 2003, I saw news reports that told me that while the United States was fighting a war for oil in Iraq, another oil war was brewing in Nigeria. I thought that our magazine, *World War 3 Illustrated,* ought to cover this. I asked Leigh and Terisa to write us a piece. They asked that I be the illustrator.

The script emerged out of several months of discussions between the three of us. I had never been to Africa and was dependent on them for information and photo references. I like to think that I helped to make their ideas a little more accessible.

It was challenging to find a way to draw the Curse of Nakedness so that it really felt like a curse. Here the photos of confrontations between undressed Kenyan women and police, which Leigh and Terisa provided, were very helpful. It was all in the body language. The men looked genuinely uncomfortable, and the women seemed to be filled with contempt for them. It was very clear from these pictures that the older women held the real authority in Kenyan society.

I was lucky to have the assistance of inker Laird Ogden and professional artist models Barbara Lee, Savannah Skye, and Louisa Krupp.

Terisa E. Turner lectures in sociology and anthropology at the University of Guelph in Ontario, Canada. She is a founder and codirector of the International Oil Working Group, the nongovernmental organization at the United Nations that helped enforce the oil embargo against the apartheid regime in South Africa (1978–1990). She worked with the popular movement that helped make Costa Rica the world's first country to declare its total territory a no-go zone for all petroleum exploration and production. Terisa Turner's publications include *Arise Ye Mighty People! Gender, Class, and Race in Popular Struggles* (edited 1994); *Oil and Class Struggle* (edited

1980); and articles on petroleum, resource conflict, international political economy, gender, and the environment. She coauthored *Back to Hewers of Wood and Drawers of Water: Energy, Trade, and the Demise of Petrochemicals in Alberta* (2005). In 2006 she published *People's Power: Beyond Corporate Control of Petroleum and Petrochemicals,* available at http://www.ualberta.ca/~parkland/research/studies/ index.html.

■ In the 1970s and again in the 1980s I lived in Nigeria and wrote about the Curse of Nakedness as it was employed by Nigerian women against the oil companies that were polluting their land. So it was with great interest that I noted the same tactic being used in Kenya in 1992, again in the Niger Delta in 2002, and then on a world scale in 2003 as naked protests by women erupted on every continent to oppose the oil companies' war for oil. Nigerian women's groups and environmental rights organizations proliferated despite oil company and state repression. Many grassroots activists echoed Saro-Wiwa's conviction that the Niger Delta people had overcome the fear of death in the face of the curse of oil. This curse meant falling life expectancy and rising rates of cancer, homelessness, disease, malnutrition, unemployment, infant and maternal mortality, illiteracy, and violence against women. For peacefully standing up for their rights, in 2005 the Niger Delta Women for Justice and other human rights organizations were targeted by the Nigerian government as "terrorists." Many objected to this demonization. We were worried: Was the label "terrorist" a premeditated prelude to state-sanctioned murder? In January 2006, the Niger Delta peoples expanded their resistance to the operations of Shell, ChevronTexaco, and other international oil companies. The comic "Nakedness and Power" foreshadowed U.S. military action against the peoples of the Niger Delta. As African oil takes on greater strategic importance to the United States, and as some members of Nigeria's broad-based social movements take their struggle for "resource control" and democracy to the level of armed conflict, the scenario of U.S. military intervention is now unfolding. I am glad our comic is getting more attention because it tells the truth about African and Nigerian women's affirmation of life at the very moment that their lives are being threatened and their struggles demonized by big oil and its oft-discredited War on Terrorism.

Chris Ware is the author of *Jimmy Corrigan — The Smartest Kid on Earth,* which received the Guardian First Book Award in 2001 and was also included in the 2002 Whitney Biennial. He edited the thirteenth issue of *McSweeney's Quarterly Concern* in 2004 and was the first cartoonist chosen to regularly serialize an ongoing story in the *New York Times Magazine* in 2005 and 2006. His work was also the focus of an exhibit at the Museum of Contemporary Art Chicago in the late spring of 2006.

■ When Dave Eggers asked me in 2003 to edit an issue of his quarterly literary publication, *McSweeney's,* as a comics anthology, I wanted to present not only what I considered to be a good cross-section of literary American cartooning available, but also somehow thread into the whole business a history of the form itself — and hopefully, carefully enough so that the reader wouldn't really notice it. These isolated strips were part of that ancillary effort, designed to play into (and off of) the dust jacket of the book itself (which was also my attempt at a goofy "metaphysical defense" of cartooning); drawn in the same style, colors, and more or less the same tone, they were interspersed amongst the text of my written introduction to the volume, which I conceived as a description of the difficulties the modern cartoonist suffers trying to graft a serious emotional content to language otherwise suited to telling jokes — which this, in turn, tries to tell a brief history of, via jokes.

Esther Pearl Watson grew up in the Dallas/Fort Worth area. Her family moved often, since her father's hobby of building huge flying saucers out of scrap metal and car engines didn't always sit well with the neighbors. Her illustrations have been commissioned for publications including *Time,* the *New York Times Magazine,* and *Entertainment Weekly.* Her comic *Unlovable* can be seen in *Bust* magazine. She has written and illustrated five books for children and teens, including 1995's *Talking to Angels,* called "a debut of uncommon, nearly perfect grace." Her paintings are shown at Mendenhall/Sobieski Gallery in Pasadena, California.

■ Back in 1995, my husband and I were driving from Vegas to San Francisco. In the women's restroom of a gas station, I found a fifteen-year-old girl's diary. It was dated from the late 1980s and had a cryptic legend for her "secret code" scrawled inside the cover. So, I did what anyone would do if they found a diary . . . I hid it under my shirt and ran back to the car. I read it out loud as we drove through the Mojave Desert and broke her code. Ever since, I've been trying to publish versions of her story. The comic just came out of frustration. Once I decided to self-publish it as a mini-comic, I had the freedom to do what I wanted. In the diary there was this jerk-off who kept rubbing her back and driving by her house. I just made up what he looked like and let him have a private moment in front of the school trophy case.

Kurt Wolfgang lives and draws in the lovely village of Collinsville, Connecticut. When not working on his regular contributions to the popular *Mome* anthology, he toils away at his wordless and terribly unfaithful comic book adaptation of *Pinocchio.*

■ I'm not quite sure if I know how this story came to be written, nor do I know how any stories come to be written. I'm not sure I'd ever want to know such a thing. Do other people know this about their own work? Is there a way to discuss your own work without seeming somewhat arrogant? I'd rather leave any assumptions and interpretations to the reader. I think that once an artist attempts to dissect such things, chances are boats will be missed and any beauty will be beaten out of it all. Why do you love your mother? Why is your favorite color your favorite color? There's probably a reason, and it's probably much more clinical than you'd care to consider. I do know that I believe that all "visions," "magic," "mysticism," and "acts of God" are merely the product of science that we've yet to figure out, that there is no God, Devil, Heaven, or Hell, and that my story is probably a reflection of such beliefs. See, that's not much fun, is it? People would probably find it more interesting if I said that it came to me in a dream or from a magic elf or something.

100 Distinguished Comics

from January 2004 to August 2005

Selected by Anne Elizabeth Moore

DAN ABDO
Viking Crush. *Nickelodeon*, February 2005.

HILARY ABUHOVE
Cactus Stories, 2005.

TODD ALCOTT AND R. SIKORYAK
Loopy. *The Stranger*, May 6, 2004.

RICK ALTERGOTT
Lost in the Forest. *The Stranger*, January 8,
January 15, and January 22, 2004.

HOWARD JOHN AREY
How Dare You. *Hi-Horse Omnibus*, 2004.

ANDRICE ARP
Everyone and Everyone Jr. in the Television.
Hi-Horse Omnibus, 2004.

PATRICK ATANGAN
Sausage-Boy and His Magic Brush. *Silk
Tapestry and Other Chinese Folk Tales*, 2004.

COREY BARBA
Yam. *Nickelodeon*, May 2005.

ALISON BECHDEL
The On-again Off-again Affair.
www.dykestowatchoutfor.com, 2004.

GABRIELLE BELL
One Afternoon. *Scheherezade*, 2004.

MARC BELL
Fallen Angel. *Kramer's Ergot* no. 5.

ARIEL BORDEAUX AND RICK ALTERGOTT
Tales of the Legion of Superheroes in:
Legion.com. *Bizarro World*, 2005.

MAT BRINKMAN
Mutant Life Expectancy. *Kramer's Ergot*
no. 5.

JEFFREY BROWN
When Will My Superpowers Manifest
Themselves? *Miniature Sulk*, 2005.

IVAN BRUNETTI
P. Mondrian. *McSweeney's* no. 13.

SCOTT CAMPBELL
Pretty OK Team. *Project: Superior*, 2005.

LILLI CARRÉ
Untitled (Rapunzel). *Tales of Woodsman Pete*
no. 2.

PAUL CHADWICK
Concrete no. 4.

SHAWN CHENG
The Ball Game. *Paping* no. 11.

BRIAN CHIPPENDALE
Battlestack Galacti-crap. *Free Radicals*, 2005.

GREG CLARKE
The Forlorn Fungus. *Blab* no. 14.

DAN CLOWES
The Darlington Sundays. *McSweeney's*
no. 13.
The Origin of Death Ray. *Eightball* no. 23.

CHYNNA CLUGSTON-MAJOR
Painted Moon. *Blue Monday* no. 4.

ALLISON COLE
Adventures with Dentures. *Pink Medicine*,
2004.

GREG COOK
Dorothea Lange. *Arthur*, March 2005.

JORDAN CRANE
The Hand of Gold. *Kramer's Ergot* no. 5.

DAME DARCY
Hat Attack. *Meat Cake* no. 14.

GEOFFREY DARROW
Shaolin Cowboy no. 2.

VANESSA DAVIS
Flipping Out. *Spaniel Rage*, 2005.

KIM DEITCH
4D. *Nickelodeon,* March 2005.

JO DERY
Revenge of the Fat Flies. *Free Radicals,* 2005.

EVAN DORKIN AND JILL THOMPSON
Let Sleeping Dogs Lie. *The Dark Horse Book of the Dead,* 2005.

AUSTIN ENGLISH
Christina's Heart. *Charles and Christina,* 2005.

C. F.
Prey. *Kramer's Ergot* no. 5.

MICHAEL FAHY
Uncle Mikey's Activity Corner. *Boy Trouble* no. 5.

GABRIELLE GAMBOA
The Amazing Fox Sisters. *Scheherezade,* 2004.

RICK GEARY
Ford's Theater. *The Murder of Abraham Lincoln,* 2005.

GLEN DAVID GOLD
The Lady or the Tiger. *The Amazing Adventures of the Escapist* vol. 1.

STEFAN GRUBER
Untitled (Introduction). *Duck Lessons,* 2004.

B. HAIMES
Turmoil. *Syncopated* vol. 2.

JOHN HANKIEWICZ
Martha Gregory: Everyday Explorer. *Martha Gregory,* 2005.

SAM HENDERSON
Gunther Bumpus Awaits a Package. *Magic Whistle* no. 9.

GILBERT HERNANDEZ
Song of the Sea Hog. *Love and Rockets* no. 13.

JAIME HERNANDEZ
Who Is Rena Titañon? *Love and Rockets* no. 11.

SANDY JIMINEZ
Thereafter. *World War 3 Illustrated* no. 35.

J. BRADLEY JOHNSON
Good Air. *Hi-Horse Omnibus,* 2004.

R. KIKUO JOHNSON
Idol/Idle. www.seabread.com, 2004.

MEGAN KELSO
The Pickle Fork. *Scheherezade,* 2004.

DAVE KIERSCH
Untitled (Communication Is Dangerous). *Pink Medicine,* 2004.

HAWK KRALL
Mister Kim. *The Stranger,* April 1, 2004.

MICHAEL KUPPERMAN
Picasso: His Astonishing Life, Narrated by a Hamburger. *Tales Designed to Thrizzle* no. 1.
Snake 'n' Bacon Meet Casanova. *Tales Designed to Thrizzle* no. 1.

HOPE LARSON
Edible God. www.hopelarson.com, 2004.

CAROL LAY
Flagged. *The Comics Journal Special Edition,* 2005.

JON LEWIS AND PHIL MOY
French Fried. *Powerpuff Girls* no. 57.

ELLEN LINDNER
Undertow. *Scheherezade,* 2004.

KEVIN MCCARTHY AND BILL SIENKIWICZ
The Mechanist. *The Amazing Adventures of the Escapist* vol. 1.

JOHN MEJIAS
Pimp Rud. *Paping* no. 11.

MIKE MIGNOLA
The Island. *Hellboy* no. 1 and 2.

SCOTT MILLS
MarsBase Super Trio: Mrs. Wai. *Superheroes and Seamonsters,* 2005.

ALAN MOORE, TODD KLEIN, GENE HA, AND ART LYON
Except Nothing, Except Everything. *Top 10: Forty-niners,* 2005.
In Siren's Silence. *Top 10: Forty-niners,* 2005.

SCOTT MORSE
The Solutionist. *Project: Superior,* 2005.

TED NAIFEH AND TRISTAN CRANE
Chapter 1. *How Loathsome,* 2004.

TRAVIS NICHOLS
Idiom-Tastic Animal Detectives! *Nickelodeon,* May 2005.

BRIAN LEE O'MALLEY
Untitled (Matthew Mattel Fight). *Scott Pilgrim's Precious Little Life*, 2004.

CHRIS ONSTAD
Barry the Bass. www.achewood.com, 2004.

JOHN PORCELLINO
Great Western Sky. *King-Cat Comics & Stories* no. 63.
Death of a Mosquito Abatement Man. *Diary of a Mosquito Abatement Man*, 2005.

ERIC POWELL
A Lost Tale of the Goon. *The Goon: My Murderous Childhood*, 2004.

ARCHER PREWITT
Sof'Boy. *Sturgeon White Moss* no. 5.

DAVE ROMAN
Astronaut Elementary. www.astronautelementary.com, May 2004.

P. CRAIG RUSSELL
Ein Heldentraum. *Opera Adaptations* vol. 3.

STAN SAKAI
Kill the Geishu Lord. *Usagi Yojimbo: Fathers and Sons*, 2005.

SOUTHER SALAZAR
Fervler and Razzle. *Kramer's Ergot* no. 5.

ROB SATO
Untitled (Introduction). *Burying Sandwiches*, 2005.

SETH
Untitled (Junk Stores). *Palookaville: Clyde Fans* no. 17.

ERIC SHANOWER
Untitled (Sacrifice of Iphigenia). *Age of Bronze: Sacrifice*, 2004.
Behind the Lines. *Rush Hour* vol. 3.

JEFF SMITH
Solstice. *Bone*, 2004.

KAREN SNEIDER
My Trouble with Monsters. *Hi-Horse Omnibus*, 2005.

BISAKH SOM
Marzipan Madness. *Hi-Horse Omnibus*, 2005.

VINCENT STALL
Just Like That. *Rosetta* vol. 2.

MARIKO AND JILLIAN TAMAKI
October 12th: Full Moon. *Skim*, 2005.

BECCA TAYLOR
Untitled (I'm a Pepper). *The Wonderful Year* no. 9.

CRAIG THOMPSON
Untitled (Travel Narratives). *Carnet de Voyage*, 2004.

PAUL TOBIN AND COLLEEN COOVER
T-Shirt Weather. *The Comics Journal Special Edition*, 2005.

ADRIAN TOMINE
My Ex-Barber. *The New Yorker*, May 2, 2005.

JAMES TURNER
Chapter 1. *Nil: A Land Beyond Belief*, 2005.

ROBERT ULLMAN
Terry Sawchuck. *Old-Timey Hockey Tales* no. 1.

SARA VARON
Untitled (August). *Scheherezade*, 2005.

BRIAN K. VAUGHAN, PIA GUERRA, AND JOSE MARZAN JR.
15,000 Feet Above Cooksfield. *Y: The Last Man: Ring of Truth*, 2005.

BRIAN K. VAUGHAN, TONY HARRIS, AND TOM FEISTER
Friday, June 15, 2001. *Ex-Machina: The First 100 Days*, 2004.

CHRIS WARE
Branford the Best Bee in the World. *The Stranger*, May 27, 2004.

MATT WEIGLE
The Omega Dome. *See How Pretty, See How Smart* no. 4.

MEGAN WHITMARSH
Super Monkeys. *Project: Superior*, 2005.

SUSAN WILLMARTH
Arlington National Cemetery. *World War 3 Illustrated* no. 35.

KURT WOLFGANG
Telephone. *Nickelodeon*, August 2004.

MARV WOLFMAN AND JOE STATON
Heil and Fear Well. *The Amazing Adventures of the Escapist* vol. 2.

The Best American Short Stories® 2006. Ann Patchett, guest editor, Katrina Kenison, series editor. This year's most beloved short fiction anthology is edited by Ann Patchett, author of *Bel Canto,* a 2002 PEN/Faulkner Award winner and a National Book Critics Circle Award finalist. The collection features stories by Tobias Wolff, Donna Tartt, Thomas McGuane, Mary Gaitskill, Nathan Englander, and others. ISBN-10: 0-618-54351-1 / ISBN-13: 978-0-618-54351-9. $28.00 CL. ISBN-10: 0-618-54352-X / ISBN-13: 978-0-618-54352-6. $14.00. PA

The Best American Nonrequired Reading 2006. Edited by Dave Eggers, introduction by Matt Groening. This collection highlights a bold mix of fiction, nonfiction, screenplays, alternative comics, and more from publications large, small, and online. With an introduction by Matt Groening, creator of *The Simpsons* and *Futurama,* this volume features writing from *The Onion, The Daily Show, This American Life,* Judy Budnitz, George Packer, and others. ISBN-10: 0-618-57050-0 / ISBN-13: 978-0-618-57050-8 $28.00 CL. ISBN-10: 0-618-57051-9 / ISBN-13: 978-0-618-57051-5 $14.00 PA

The Best American Essays® 2006. Lauren Slater, guest editor, Robert Atwan, series editor. Since 1986, *The Best American Essays* has annually gathered outstanding nonfiction writing, establishing itself as the premier anthology of its kind. Edited by the best-selling author of *Prozac Diary,* Lauren Slater, this year's collection highlights provocative, lively writing by Adam Gopnik, Scott Turow, Marjorie Williams, Poe Ballantine, and others. ISBN-10: 0-618-70531-7 / ISBN-13: 978-0-618-70531-3 $28.00 CL. ISBN-10: 0-618-70529-5 / ISBN-13: 978-0-618-70529-0 $14.00 PA

The Best American Mystery Stories™ 2006. Scott Turow, guest editor, Otto Penzler, series editor. This year's volume, edited by Scott Turow, author of the critically acclaimed *Presumed Innocent,* features both mystery veterans and new talents, offering stories by Elmore Leonard, Ed McBain, James Lee Burke, Joyce Carol Oates, Walter Mosley, and others. ISBN-10: 0-618-51746-4 / ISBN-13: 978-0-618-51746-6 $28.00 CL. ISBN-10: 0-618-51747-2 / ISBN-13: 978-0-618-51747-3 $14.00 PA

The Best American Sports Writing™ 2006. Michael Lewis, guest editor, Glenn Stout, series editor. "An ongoing centerpiece for all sports collections" (*Booklist*), this series stands in high regard for its extraordinary sports writing and top-notch editors. This year's guest editor, Michael Lewis, author of the bestseller *Moneyball,* brings together pieces by Gary Smith, Pat Jordan, Paul Solotaroff, Linda Robertson, L. Jon Wertheim, and others. ISBN-10: 0-618-47021-2 / ISBN-13: 978-0-618-47021-1 $28.00 CL. ISBN-10: 0-618-47022-0 / ISBN-13: 978-0-618-47022-8 $14.00 PA

The Best American Travel Writing 2006. Tim Cahill, guest editor, Jason Wilson, series editor. Tim Cahill is the founding editor of *Outside* magazine and a frequent contributor to *National Geographic Adventure.* Giving new life to armchair journeys are Alain de Botton, Pico Iyer, David Sedaris, Gary Shteyngart, George Saunders, and others. ISBN-10: 0-618-58212-6 / ISBN-13: 978-0-618-58212-9 $28.00 CL. ISBN-10: 0-618-58215-0 / ISBN-13: 978-0-618-58215-0 $14.00 PA

The Best American Science and Nature Writing 2006. Brian Greene, guest editor, Tim Folger, series editor. Brian Greene, the best-selling author of *The Elegant Universe,* offers a fresh take on the year's best science and nature writing, featuring selections from such authors as John Horgan, Daniel Dennett, and Dennis Overbye. ISBN-10: 0-618-72221-1 / ISBN-13: 978-0-618-72221-1 $28.00 CL. ISBN-10: 0-618-72222-X / ISBN-13: 978-0-618-72222-8 $14.00 PA

The Best American Spiritual Writing 2006. Edited by Philip Zaleski, introduction by Peter J. Gomes. Featuring an introduction by Peter J. Gomes, a best-selling author and the Plummer Professor of Christian Morals at Harvard University, this year's edition gathers pieces from diverse faiths and denominations and includes writing by Michael Chabon, Malcolm Gladwell, Mary Gordon, John Updike, and others. ISBN-10: 0-618-58644-X / ISBN-13: 978-0-618-58644-8 $28.00 CL. ISBN-10: 0-618-58645-8 / ISBN-13: 978-0-618-58645-5 $14.00 PA

The Best American Gold Gift Box 2006. Boxed in rich gold metallic, this set includes *The Best American Short Stories 2006, The Best American Mystery Stories 2006,* and *The Best American Sports Writing 2006.* ISBN-10: 0-618-80126-X / ISBN-13: 978-0-618-80126-8 $40.00 PA

The Best American Silver Gift Box 2006. Packaged in a lavish silver metallic box, this set features *The Best American Short Stories 2006, The Best American Travel Writing 2006,* and *The Best American Spiritual Writing 2006.* ISBN-10: 0-618-80127-8 / ISBN-13: 978-0-618-80127-5 $40.00 PA

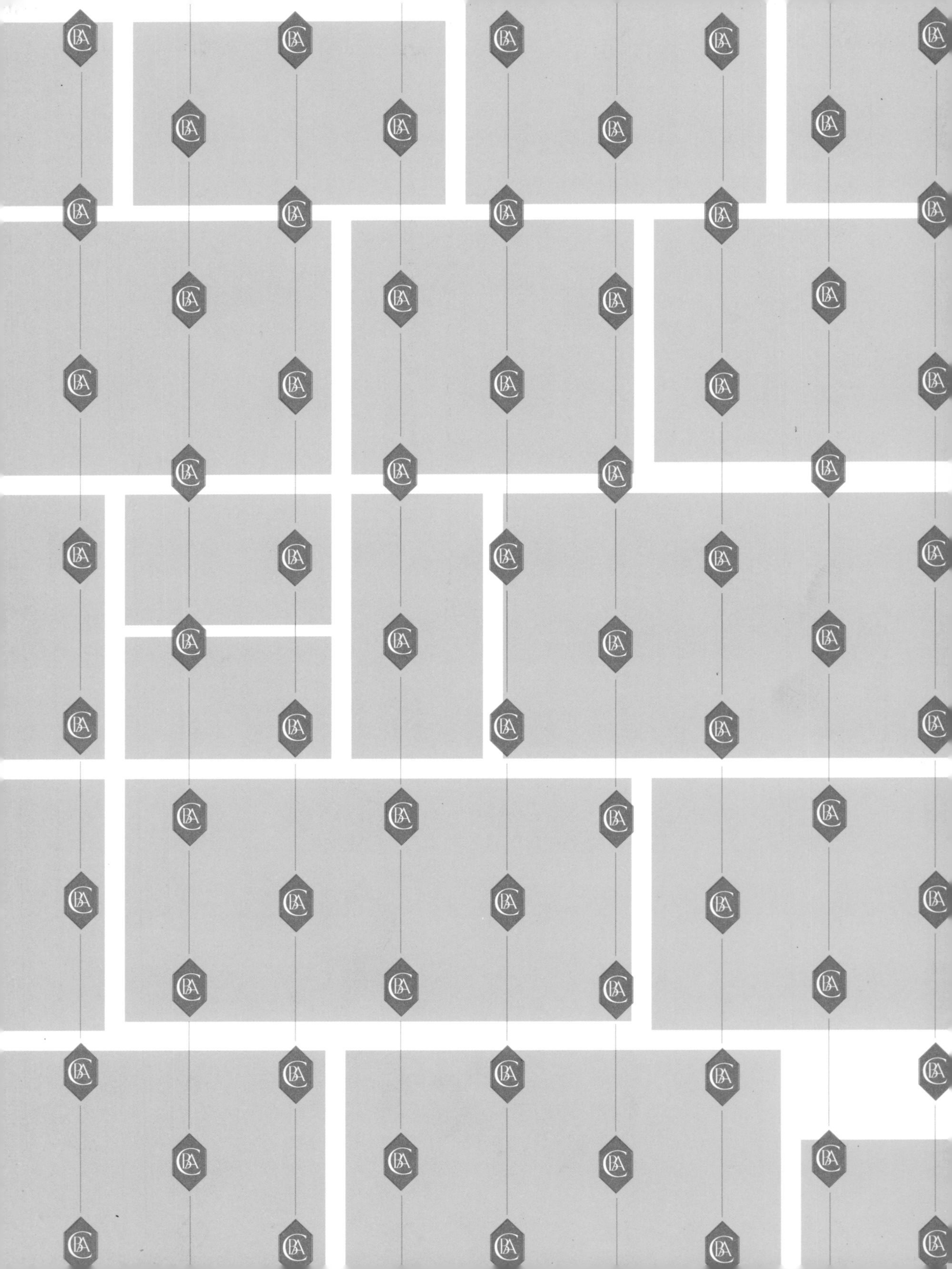